ADVANCED PRAISE FOR
INQUIRY, ARGUMENT & CHANGE

"This book has several significant strengths. First, I am most impressed by the opening emphasis on writer, instead of on audience. I find Chapters 1 and 2 to both be particularly effective in introducing lots of examples of writing as a means of exploring where one already stands on a position and why, exploring gaps in one's knowledge, and exploring possibilities for filling the gaps. These chapters provide students with a veritable arsenal of exploratory writing techniques. I was also very impressed with Chapter 3 and its detailed examination of quoting, paraphrasing, and summary. Of all the texts I have seen (which is quite a few), this text does the best job of examining the intricacies of and providing multiple helpful examples for students. That chapter is an invaluable resource. Another feature I really like, which is quite different from the approach in other argument texts, is the introduction to the four general types of argumentative inquiry and then the application of the 4 questions in each of the subsequent essay assignment chapters. Students have the option to freely choose an approach for addressing the subject matter at hand. I think students will appreciate that level of freedom. On the other hand, for instructors who wish to exert a little more control, obviously one of the methods of inquiry could be selected."

KATHLEEN HICKS
Arizona State University

"I am most impressed by the coherent vision of this text: the way section builds on section. The authors also do a wonderful job of explaining and illustrating some of the nitty-gritty aspects of writing (logic, syntax, style, etc.). They also provide . . . an acute awareness of the need both to listen carefully to others and to think about where others are so that we may shape our writing into a more digestible and comprehensible form."

ṬHOMAS STONE
Technology

"The coverage of the Toulmin model is one of the cle̤ xplanations I've seen and doesn't overcomplicate or oversimplify r and more accessible than in the current argument rhetorics we ̣ ̣ English 101. I also like the discussion of logic that precedes the Toulmin discussion since students really have to understand basic logic in order for Toulmin's model to make sense."

MARY JO REIFF
University of Tennessee—Knoxville

"*Inquiry, Argument & Change* is terrific in vital ways. It's unusually good, especially in encouraging the mind-building process. Encouraging accuracy in thinking and personal sensitivity to the world are the clear goals. I've previewed many rhetoric/readers over the last more than thirty years, and I can't think of one that accomplishes this within such a cogently argued framework that's fully integrated with the readings, step by step."

ELLEN LANZANO
Hellenic College

"This book takes an innovative and novel approach. The collaborative, interactive focus is unique and creative . . . and a welcomed addition to the textbook market. It is very exciting to see such a book."

LISA HOGAN
Pennsylvania State University

"I like this book's writing style. The authors maintain a professional voice, communicate academic ideas, and yet manage to remain casual/conversational enough to appeal to a typical first-year student."

SUSAN STALLINGS
University of North Carolina—Charlotte

"The book's greatest strength is the readings. Fresh and original (so long abortion and gun control). . . . I think that this book is a step forward for standard composition texts, mainly because of the readings the authors chose but also because of the book's overall clarity."

ROBERT PELTIER
Trinity College—CT

"The structure and organization of the book set a layering approach. We dip a little into rhetoric, try some essays with it, and then dip into the next draft concept, basically going in the order the writing of an essay would. The sequence is sensible and as engaging as one might expect in such a text. I'd still have to do most of the engaging myself, but the book would be a good adjunct."

TIM ADELL
Victor Valley Community College

"The book includes a wonderful style manual, an addition teachers could use for any type of student, from the student who needs a boost with sentence pattern variation to the student who is relatively advanced and wants to improve his or her sense of style/flair."

LINDA TOONEN
University of Wisconsin—Green Bay

INQUIRY, ARGUMENT & CHANGE

A RHETORIC
WITH READINGS

BRIEF EDITION

Barbara Jo Krieger
State University of New York at Potsdam

Paul G. Saint-Amand
State University of New York at Potsdam

Warren A. Neal
Oklahoma City Community College

Alan L. Steinberg
State University of New York at Potsdam

 **FENTON BOOKS**

GLOUCESTER, MASSACHUSETTS

A FENTON BOOKS FIRST EDITION

Copyright © 2013 by Barbara Jo Krieger and Paul G. Saint-Amand

All rights reserved. No part of this publication may be reproduced, stored in a retrieval system, or transmitted, in any form or by any means, electronic, mechanical, photocopying, recording, or otherwise, without the prior written permission of the copyright owner.

Cover art © 2009 by Lance Hidy

Printing and Binding: J. S. McCarthy Printers

Manufactured in the United States of America

For information, write:
Fenton Books
127 Eastern Avenue PMB
Gloucester, MA 01930
or call 855.210.3536

Special Edition: 13: 978-0-9850244-1-3
                 10:      0-9850244-1-0

         ISBN 13: 978-0-9850244-0-6
               10:      0-9850244-0-2

Credits
Text and illustration credits appear on pages 531–532 at the back of the book and constitute a continuation of the copyright page. Thanks are due to all copyright holders for permission to use copyrighted material.

For Herman Krieger (1921–2008)
—*a life dedicated to living the questions
and transforming wisdom to action*

Philosophy

When we drafted this brief version of *Inquiry, Argument, & Change*, we labored to produce a smaller, more streamlined book that maintained the sense and the spirit of the Full. As with the Full, the scope and content of this book stem from a conversation we began in the early 1990s about learning to write—what it means and how it can happen. We immediately recognized that we shared the conviction that learning to write is integral to the larger process of individual and intellectual development and that understanding this process is essential to shaping an effective writing course. We also recognized that our students often came to us sensing an incongruity between what they learn in school about the world and what they learn elsewhere about themselves and their everyday lives. We soon concluded that their academic learning depended largely on accepting the authority of teachers and texts, while what they learned outside of school proceeded largely by experiment and active inquiry. We became convinced that students must integrate these two modes of learning, if they are to become fully engaged adults, and that college writing courses can be important to this integration. Consequently, our conversation and our courses have increasingly stressed three main themes:

- **Students' introduction to academic writing must build on their prior knowledge and personal experiences.**

- **The rhetorical choices that students make must be based on a coherent and workable understanding of the ways audiences—readers in particular—come to accept or reject complex, debatable information.**

- **Argument, properly taught, will help students begin to achieve autonomy as learners, thinkers, and communicators in an increasingly complex and diverse world.**

Our teaching is driven by a student-centered pedagogy that incorporates debates and discussions of topics central to our students' lives. We are also aware of the need to provide structured "moments of decision," or enabling interventions, to insure that our students do not retreat from the challenge of engaging these topics in their writing. Central to this focus is our belief that students are more satisfied with their work and are generally more successful when they have a stake in what they are confronting.

To that end, the chapters of this book initially engage students in extensive journal work that focuses on their own experiences and attitudes. Very quickly, however, the book encourages students to develop a deeper, more informed understanding of issues, through a variety of readings and through class discussions. The texts we present to the student include a variety of perspectives, styles, and formats. They encourage further exploration of issues and themes students first encountered in their journal activities. Writing assignments similarly work directly from and with the readings. Rather than serve merely as models of writing, such texts prompt students to test, extend, and refine their thinking.

A controlling factor throughout this book is our approach to argument. We believe that effective argument involves more than a mastery of conventions. It must be integral to the ways in which students learn about the world; that is, it should be a primary process of inquiry through which students seek, find, and test answers to questions they or their society consider significant. Thus, we believe that meaningful argument must begin with as open and honest an inquiry into a subject as time allows—an inquiry which takes into account each student's own past experiences with and attitudes towards the subject. We are convinced that if this is done well, the student will come to see her or himself not only as the arguer/writer, but also as the first audience/reader. In offering an argument to a wider audience, the student will, in effect, be saying: "Here are the information and logical and rhetorical processes that shaped my understanding of the topic, and I now offer it for your consideration." By constantly stressing that the choices one makes as one posits a position must directly relate both to what one knows about a topic and what one believes one's audience already knows, we hope to avoid a dangerous consequence of many college writing courses—that academic argument means arbitrarily or cynically selecting a rhetorical approach in order to manipulate an audience into accepting something they really don't want to embrace.

In many ways, "change" is the most important word in our title. Because of the exponential growth of knowledge in recent times and the intensely dynamic but conflicted world we face, change itself has become a constant in our lives. We must, more than ever, give our students the cognitive and rhetorical skills to make sense out of all the information hurtling at them. By focusing on the methods people use to embrace or reject new information, we want to make college writing courses much more than an introduction to academic discourse. They ought to encourage a student's conversation with the world. How the world responds depends largely on how effectively and gracefully books such as this one do their jobs.

We address this book to instructors who share similar notions about the role and objectives of composition courses. We offer them an approach to invention and argument that is process-oriented, as well as being based on stasis theory. It synthesizes five essential elements:

- an engaging and supportive reading program to help students become aware of the various ways communication takes place: cognitively, emotionally, logically, visually, and so forth.

- writing instruction that helps students to contend with conventional rules and expectations without making them feel like "outsiders" who must learn specific rites and rituals before contributing anything of their own.

- an extensive and balanced treatment which stresses argument, first, as a means of discovering, developing, and testing ideas and, then, as a means of effectively communicating those ideas
- heavy emphasis on critical thinking throughout.
- affirmation of students' past achievements and experiences as a basis for their introduction to the expectations they will confront in their college courses.

Structure

The book falls into four parts that taken together provide a comprehensive, process-oriented treatment of argument strongly supported by principles of critical reading and thinking. We present argument primarily as a means of inquiry and make its role in the process of change explicit.

The general structure models the evolution of a full writing project:

- clarifying and refining the initial questions that motivate inquiry.
- careful reading and reflection to deepen one's understanding of the facts and of the feelings and experiences relevant to the questions.
- generating and refining the argument.
- preparing the public draft.

Early in Chapter 1, we introduce four types of questions (a modern version of the classical stases) meant to help students direct their explorations.

- Questions about the nature of things.
- Questions about the causes and effects of things.
- Questions about the value of things.
- Questions about what sort of action we should take.

Such inquiries help students to generate issues as they consider different subjects. The approach established here is largely meant to show how students can use their exploration of material to examine their own knowledge and beliefs so that they can have confidence in the quality and accuracy of what they understand before they engage others.

We believe that such activity will lead the student to an appreciation of the dynamic nature of the rhetorical process. They will learn that the more complete and accurate grasp a writer has of the reader and subject, the more intense and productive the writing will be. To that end, we show how the goal or intent of an argument is as important as the nature of the argument. The lines of inquiry and the types of claims (Definition, Causality, Evaluation, Proposal) are undoubtedly important, but we show how any consideration of these elements is incomplete without setting these factors in the rhetorical context—that is, taking into account what one wants the argument to accomplish.

Subsequent chapters present students with tools for analyzing and improving the structure of their arguments. We introduce concepts from traditional and modern logic that students can use to make their arguments sound enough to justify the claims they posit. We also urge students to consider how the content, structure, and appearance of their argument contribute to its effectiveness. For example, we show how a graph, chart, or picture is not only a visual element, but can also be a way of deepening an understanding of the subject.

Format

Within each chapter, subsections fall into one of three categories, based on their primary function:

- **Instruction:**
  Here we introduce and elaborate on the principles and practices of good writing that are relevant to the part of the book in which the subsections occur.

- **Demonstration:**
  Modeling is an important way of learning, as well as a means of building confidence. These sections offer annotated examples of student work in which aspects of the rhetorical process are highlighted and explained. They also give students the opportunity of encountering the voices of their peers.

- **Activity:**
  In these sections, students are asked to write. While there is a wide variety in the types of activities that we offer, they almost always require a written result.

  - **Collaborations**
    In keeping with the philosophy underlying this book, collaborative activities are encouraged. While many of the ones we suggest take on the flavor of class or small-group discussions, each has a goal achieved by producing a document.

  - **Exercises**
    Normally, exercises require short responses to specific questions. In some cases, they ask for written evaluation of the student's own work in the form of responses to a checklist, a set of guidelines, or a list of criteria for successful completion of an assignment.

  - **Journals**
    Informal journal assignments are the heart of the book. Students use them throughout to generate, explore, and respond to ideas. They are the basis of every major writing assignment and are usually paired with collaborative exercises.

- **Short Essays**

  Students normally like journals because journals allow them to explore ideas outside the constraints of the formal essay. One problem, especially with beginning writers, is helping them make the transition from the journal into the kind of assignment that requires more intellectual rigor and an acceptance of academic conventions. Short essay assignments can create the needed bridge. Though they are not quite as challenging as a major essay assignment, such assignments still ask for clarity of thought and structure. The assignments we suggest generally produce two- to four-page essays that are focused on a specific goal or topic.

- **Major Essays**

  There is one major essay assignment associated with each section of the book. These assignments center on a general topic, phenomenon, or issue and tend to be more open-ended than the short essays. While they are designed to produce longer, more fully developed papers, each is constructed so that individual instructors can establish the criteria for length, scope, development, types of support, etc.

Research

We sometimes forget that the word "research" simply means a thorough and thoughtful inquiry or investigation. In practice, this task usually involves undertaking library or Internet research but often, in college writing courses, research is treated as either a mechanical activity ("consult at least three 'outside' sources"), or as something to be done only when writing a formal "research paper." In this text, however, we have decided to treat research as part of every serious attempt at understanding. Consequently, we have made research a central part of each chapter and activity, rather than reserving it for "extended" writing activities.

We are convinced that every time students think, read and write about a complex issue, they are doing research. When they write about a memorable experience, they are doing research—this time in their memory banks. When they interview one of their professors or a community official, they are doing research. When they read an essay or book and then seek out reviews or responses to that essay or book, they are doing research. When they seek out the latest "facts and figures" or undertake a survey, they are doing research. All these efforts are aimed at one goal—to make them more informed, more knowledgeable about a subject. As they gather and evaluate information they are developing the confidence to address an audience.

Right from the beginning, we ask students to consider issues that seriously impact their lives; then, we ask them to consider their attitudes towards those issues; then, we present them with a selection of readings reflecting a variety of perspectives on those issues; and, finally, we ask them to engage in "research" activities to deepen their understanding of how such issues might be resolved. Within this general framework, we present a full treatment of two basic kinds of research: library and field research. In Chapter 5, though we briefly introduce library research, we emphasize field research—hoping to encourage students to be active gatherers rather than passive compilers of knowledge. The approaches we cover include the interview, first-hand investigation, and the survey/questionnaire. In Chapter 9, we place the emphasis on library research, encouraging students to make use of search engines as tools to use to develop key terms and categories and as aids in the construction of a working bibliography.

Believing that many instructors may find it distracting to face a full treatment of research in the early chapters of a book, we placed this material later in the text. On the other hand, this placement in no way deters instructors from making assignments that expose students to some research methodology earlier.

Readings

As with the Full Edition, we have integrated a challenging set of thematic readings into all parts of the text (See TOC). We recognize that this choice has risks: some instructors may feel constrained by the topics and/or the selections. Some may feel that the main function of a writing text's readings should be to model the rhetorical techniques presented. While we are aware of these concerns, we strongly believe that a text must be true to its own principles. Hence, from the beginning to the end, we emphasize that good writing results from committed and careful inquiry into subjects that have real and immediate meaning and consequence for both the writer and reader. Seldom do we instruct students to practice specific strategies in isolation before putting them to work on a meaningful assignment. Rather, students practice such strategies in response to arguments they need to understand and evaluate before constructing their own work. Within each set of readings, instructors will find a variety of opinions, genres, and formats, including the highly visual. Instructors can and should mix and match to suit their individual goals.

Though we have been careful to present a balanced approach, in terms of concepts and styles, we believe that the readings must do more than model rhetorical techniques. They should model the serious consideration that is to be given to the complex issues that students might encounter both in, and outside, the university. We hope that the student will, as a result, be prepared not only for the kind of writing college requires, but also for being a more thoughtful citizen.

The Stases as Heuristic Tools for Effective Argument

The book provides a systematic unfolding of how the stases (questions about the nature of things, causality, value, and action) serve as the heart of a dynamic and coherent critical thinking and writing pedagogy. We maintain that the stases—properly understood as a way of thinking about the world and then communicating one's insights to others—lie at the center of any sustained inquiry.

To that end, we continuously reinforce that the stases are themselves not static and separate rhetorical categories. In trying to understand the nature of something, students also have to know something about its causes and effects, its harms and benefits, and if it requires any actions on their part. To enhance this point, students learn how an application of the stases helps to raise serious questions about class material. Similarly, students learn to engage the stases in several different essay assignments.

USING THE STASES TO GUIDE CLAIMS, ASSERTIONS, AND SUPPORT

The book's structure is based on the premise that focusing assignments on one type of stasis, for example "Writing a Causal Argument," has an adverse effect on student writing, requiring students to bend their perceptions around a pre-conceived formal or rhetorical goal and more or less precluding any meaningful response that evolves naturally out of the students' experience and the reality of a situation. We submit that the only rhetorical element that is absolutely necessary, no matter what students argue or to whom, is the one establishing their way of understanding the subject or issue—their way of describing or defining it. No intelligent, reasoned discussion can proceed if students and their readers do not share a basic understanding of the issue at hand: what it is and what it is not.

Beyond establishing the "nature of" their subject, we maintain that all other rhetorical choices are a matter of emphasis—a matter of students deciding what they want to focus on, given the various limits placed on them. These decisions will depend on what they know about the subject; what they wish their audience to know; and how much time and space they have for making their argument. Do they know enough to discuss the causal aspects of their subject—why it is what it is and what results from it? Do they wish to evaluate it—judge what it is or its effects? Do they have a plan for promoting its desirable and inhibiting its undesirable aspects? Is their audience in a position to take action? Or is it enough that they ask their audience to consider their way of thinking about the subject? Do they have enough time, given their writing task, to take the issue all the way through to a plan of action? Is there enough information available? Too much? We maintain that it is the students' answers to these and similar questions that should determine what they argue and how they shape that argument. Their choices must reflect the limits of their knowledge, their goals in relation to their audience, and any practical constraints.

Acknowledgements

This book is testimony to the axiom that no writer works alone, for it represents the collective spirit of many people from whom we have learned and to whom we are indebted. While we have learned from many works in the field of composition, we gratefully acknowledge, in particular, the pioneering work of Young, Becker and Pike's *Rhetoric: Discovery and Change* in connecting rhetoric with cognition, and Fahnestock and Secor's *A Rhetoric of Argument* (2nd ed) in modernizing and enriching the connection between composition and classical stasis theory. We also owe a debt of gratitude to Professor Robert W. Emery of Boston University, coauthor on an earlier project and a major influence on the content and pedagogical apparatus of *Inquiry, Argument, & Change.*

Our very special thanks goes to SUNY-Potsdam English Professor Anthony J. Boyle, who wrote our Appendix. Tony also worked closely with the project for the last year, contributing his expertise to discussions throughout the book. We are particularly indebted to Tony for his extremely astute copyediting. In many instances, Tony saw what we could not, mining the very gems in the book that we had inadvertently buried. Tony's contribution, both as a colleague and a friend, was indispensable.

We also thank Professor Jim O'Brien of the University of Massachusetts—Boston for his insightful comments and editorial suggestions. Similarly, Professors Jon Chatlos of SUNY-Plattsburgh and Michael Basseches of Suffolk University contributed immeasurably and sustained us with their insights and comments. Much thanks also to Carrie Bates for writing our documentation chapter. And special thanks to Professor Lance Hidy of Northern Essex Community College for designing a book cover that brilliantly conveys the book's central theme.

We gratefully acknowledge those students whose writing appears throughout the book. From SUNY-Potsdam we thank Lee Adams, Doug Booth, Matt Burkhardt, Mark Camp, Victoria Charles, Scott Davies, David Dewhirst, Sarah Elkhayat, Adriana Hemans, Tierney Jayne, Sarah Lynne, and Melissa Manchester. From Bentley College we thank Stephan Demers and Keith Mantia. We also owe a debt of gratitude to student assistants at Potsdam College: Sheryl Adkins, Bridget Baker, Jill Towers, and Heather Valyou, and to Brian Jasiak at Bentley College, whose diligent research helped strengthen the Social Trends Indexes in Chapters 1 and 2.

In addition, we thank Content Connections™ for identifying reviewers whose perceptive responses to evolving manuscripts pushed us headlong into revising with purpose and new understanding: Tim Adell, Victor Valley Community College; Jake Agatucci, Central Oregon Community College; Kamala Balasubramanian, Grossmont College; Paul Carbonaro, Sinclair Community College; Gina Claywell, Murray State University; Robert Cummings, Columbus State University; Julie Foust, Utah State University; Lisa Gring-Pemble, George Mason University; Kathleen Hicks, Arizona State University; Lisa Hogan, Pennsylvania State University; Peggy Jolly, University of Alabama—Birmingham; David Kaloustian, Bowie State University; Carol Lowe, McClennan Community College; Alan Marks, University of Maine—Orono; Robert Peltier, Trinity College—CT; Mary Jo Reiff, University of Tennessee—Knoxville; Susan Stallings, University of North Carolina—Charlotte; Thomas Stone, Rochester Institute of Technology; and Linda Toonen, University of Wisconsin—Green Bay.

Special thanks must also go to Technologies 'N Typography, whose team worked diligently and unrelentingly to meet many formatting challenges. Tireless and knowledgeable, TNT treated the project with all the care any writer can hope for. We also thank Reverend Gail Seavey and Graphic Artists Ellen Hopkins and Susan Stehfest for their insight and immeasurable support. Much thanks also to Lisa Clark, LKC Design, who produced engaging publicity materials, and to Julie Carey for her skillful attention to sections of the manuscript. And a particular debt of gratitude is owed to Executive Editor Lisa Moore at McGraw Hill and Development Editor Julie McBurney for their guidance in the formative stages of the project (2001-2002).

Finally, a special note of thanks must go to Herman and Lorraine Krieger for their unflagging encouragement throughout the project.

Barbara Jo Krieger
Paul G. Saint-Amand
Warren A. Neal
Alan L. Steinberg

Please consider the following claims.

- This course is among the important college experiences you will have. Now, if you value restraint, you're wondering why we can be so assertive.
- It is essential that you learn to write well. If you are skeptical, you're wondering why.
- This book will teach you the elements of effective writing. If you are curious, you're wondering how.

If our claims raise such issues, you have the tool you will need to succeed in this course, a critical intelligence. And, faced with such a reader, how can we not support our claims?

First, let us clarify some of the questions we will answer in this section and throughout the book.

- What is the nature of the writing we want you to do? Since there are many types of writing, serving diverse purposes and audiences, which type do we have in mind, and what are its characteristics?
- What are the *causes and effects* of this type? That is, why do people undertake such writing tasks, and what effects do their efforts have on others?
- What is the *value* of this writing? What good is it? More to the point, why should you spend your time and energy learning to create it?
- Finally, once we k`now the nature, cause, and value of such writing, what do we do about it? What *action* do we take on the basis of our knowledge?

The kind of writing we'll address throughout this book is *argument.* Of course, as with many important terms, its meaning depends on specific contexts. We take "argument" to mean an assertion that is established by the weight of credible evidence. More importantly, we envision argument as embodying the intellectual process that leads one to an assertion in the first place. In other words, argument is a *way* to think as well as a statement of what and why you think as you do. All three are essential; you can't have a genuine argument without them. We'll explore these points more fully in the chapters that follow.

Why do people write arguments? Easy. They write because they want something. They might need to meet the requirements for a college degree, they might want a job or a raise, or they might be evaluating the work of those they supervise. They construct arguments, then, because they want someone to agree with or at least seriously consider their point of view. But, most importantly, they often write arguments to satisfy their own curiosity. They particularly enjoy the process of inquiry, of asking questions and creating answers, that constructing arguments involves.

What good is it? This seems a no-brainer. If you write because you want something, you stand a much better chance of obtaining it if you write well. Effective writing can help you get a degree, a job, a promotion. As you set your career goals, consider what is and will be in demand in the workplace. What do you have that an employer might want? If this were the 20th century and you were destined for a job on an assembly line or even on a farm, you might offer a strong back and nimble fingers. However, as automation and the export of manufacturing jobs have intensified, manufacturing jobs have disappeared as have the small farms that once employed so many Americans. The market now demands those who can think, those who are able to handle *ideas*. What can you do to enhance your ability to come up with new ideas? The processes of inquiry and argument are essential to this effort, and, like many tools, they get better the more they're used. The nice thing about intellectual tools is they don't wear out.

Of course argument is valuable on other levels as well. Some would say these other levels are more important than professional success. As a citizen, you will need responses for the important questions facing our society and for a host of issues yet to emerge. Simply put, the intellectual processes involved in the construction of argument leads to good answers. Good answers will help you to anticipate and determine a response to the transformations that will mark your life.

Now, what do you do about developing or refining your skills in constructing arguments? What action can you take? Perhaps we can best answer that by letting you know what you'll find in this book and how you can use it.

The book has four main parts, each dealing with a stage of the writing process. The book's overall structure corresponds to the steps in a full writing project:

- clarifying and refining initial questions about a topic to discover the aspects that most interest you and to determine possible approaches to a project you would undertake.
- invention activities to help you to raise relevant questions and a group of focused readings to deepen your understanding of facts, of other people's points of view, and of your individual feelings and experiences connected to your initial questions.
- generating a first draft of your argument—getting ideas down in a structured format that makes sense to you and that helps your reader to see the relationships among your ideas.
- fine tuning the argument you developed in a first draft, as well as addressing the feedback you received from your peers and your instructor.
- preparing the public draft by refining the draft's language to insure that what you've written is what you mean.

Within all the chapters in the book, you'll find three types of material. To make your experience more rewarding, you should recognize the kind of material being presented and adjust your response accordingly.

- **Instruction:**

  These are the "how-to" and "why should you" sections of the chapters. They include principles and practices of effective writing that will help you to define and achieve your goals for various writing projects. You should treat these sections as you would most other material on which you might be tested. Read each section carefully, more than once. Make notes. Ask questions when you do not understand the material.

- **Demonstration:**

  Reading and understanding fundamental principles is important, but, often as not, you'll learn more if you see how other people have approached the projects you face. These sections offer annotated examples of student work in which important aspects of the writing process are highlighted and explained. They present the experiences of other students and, in some cases, allow you "to hear their voices" as they moved toward the completion of their projects. Your encounters with these sections will be more useful if you're careful to make connections between the principles and practices presented in the Instruction sections and the experiences of others—their successes and errors—presented in the Demonstration sections.

- **Activity:**

  In these sections, we ask you to put words on the page. While you will find a range of activities, what they have in common is that they'll almost always ask you to write. The tasks include short answers to specific exercises, response statements generated by your participation in group discussions, informal journals that will record your subjective responses to what you encounter in the course, and major essay assignments. The more vigorously you participate in these projects, the more helpful they'll be in leading you to a more compelling writing style.

In general, all sections of this book are relatively brief. Our goal is to make it as interactive as possible. You'll get small chunks of instruction and examples and then immediately have something to do or produce.

Each part of the book focuses on a central theme about contemporary life. Our objective is for you to explore what you think about different aspects of the themes and to expand your thinking by engaging with the ideas of other writers. To accomplish this goal, you will read a number of texts connected to each theme. Such activity will help to establish you as an intelligent and informed observer of issues that affect your life. Then, you will undertake some writing activities. Finally, you will bring your skills in inquiry and argument to different writing assignments, including major essays.

A WORD ON THINKING CRITICALLY

Most of the issues you will encounter in college are complex, and to understand them fully you will need to explore them from diverse viewpoints. As you add to your knowledge, it is likely that your positions will change or evolve. In the chapters ahead, you will be asked to continue consolidating and reviewing your positions in reaction to other, often opposing voices.

In his essay "Critical Thinking: Fundamental to Education for a Free Society," Richard W. Paul, a leading figure in the Critical Thinking Movement, explores the implications of this reasoning process. Paul notes that research and writing within different fields and disciplines are driven by questions about reality that generate multiple and often contradictory answers. Genuine problems are, in Paul's words, "logically messy," and as you grapple with them, you will become increasingly suspicious of simple, tidy, or absolute answers. You will learn to avoid the trap of adopting a single, fixed point of view that supersedes any inquiry and predetermines the answers you will find. You will learn to avoid what Paul calls "monological [one-sided] reasoning." You will discover that important issues require open discussion and dialogue—what Paul refers to as *dialogical reasoning*—that is, "thinking critically and reciprocally within opposing points of view."

If you are to arrive at realistic and useful answers to significant questions, dialogical reasoning is a talent that you must work to develop. The more importance you attach to certain issues, and the more established your personality becomes, the more likely you are to feel emotionally committed to a single perspective. You may find it difficult to suspend, even temporarily, your long-held and cherished notions about issues. Yet, you must. Monologic reasoning inhibits your ability to learn from others and to contribute to society. You must consider different and often opposing points of view in order to come up with new ideas and solutions. This process, introduced in the late eighteenth century by the philosopher Hegel, was the basis for "the dialectic," where one weighs a thesis against its opposite (antithesis) to produce a higher truth (synthesis). Creation is in large part synthesis; if you never bring competing ideas together, no synthesis can occur.

On a more personal level, dialogical reasoning is a tool for achieving intellectual growth and maturity. As Paul puts it, "the capacity and willingness to listen to and empathize with all contending perspectives on an issue, even to empathize with the strongest case that can be made against our own conclusion" is the "ultimate attribute of a free and open mind" and the "master-principal of all rational experience and human emancipation."

Questions

1. In speaking of genuine problems, what do you think Paul means by "logically messy"? Can you give an example of a problem where the issues involved are logically messy?

2. Using your previous example, how might someone use monological reasoning to arrive at a position? How would this process differ from reasoning dialogically? Why does Paul prefer one kind of reasoning over the other?

Before you started college, you had already spent a number of years within an educational system that often expects and rewards the "right" answer. Paul's view on critical thinking takes you beyond this linear search for a single answer and allows you to expand your field of vision to include many possibilities. His perspective will serve as a vital resource for the writing and reading activities you will encounter throughout this book and in the years to come.

BRIEF CONTENTS

▶ **PART THREE**   TESTING ANSWERS: REFINING THE ARGUMENT

Chapters 10, 11, and 12 introduce concepts from traditional and modern logic that you should keep in mind when developing and revising your arguments. The concepts are also essential when confronting the arguments of others, since they can help you to identify shoddy or even abusive thought. Chapter 11 will acquaint you with a very practical system to use in your writing and reading, the Toulmin model for argument.

Theme: *Analyzing the Role of Media in American Democracy*

The readings in this section aim to spark your reaction to the information industries, to the various media that, by definition, inform and conceivably empower citizens to engage as active and valued members of a community. The readings ask you to consider, discuss, and debate the media's capacity for shaping what counts as fact, the influence wielded by those to whom the media grants power and status, and, especially, the repeal of long-established regulations meant to encourage a diverse and democratic media landscape.

READINGS

Ben Bagdikian   THE ACTORS IN THE MEDIA UNIVERSE

Bill Moyers   ADDRESSES TO THE NATIONAL CONFERENCES ON MEDIA REFORM

Ben Compaine   DOMINATION FANTASIES

Melissa Manchester (*STUDENT*)   POVERTY SLIGHTED BY THE MEDIA

▶ **PART FOUR**   PRESENTING CONCLUSIONS: WRITING A PUBLIC DRAFT

Chapters 13, 14, and 15 are designed to assist you in polishing the language of your draft so that it more readily engages your readers. While no one will expect that you will always write with eloquence, there are steps that you can use to insure that your work is free of cumbersome phrasing. Thus, in these chapters, you will learn how to diagnose and repair language problems that can confuse your readers. In addition, because the papers that you will write for college courses will often require extensive documentation of the materials you have used to create them, Chapter 15 presents the system used by the Modern Language Association for citing and naming sources in the humanities. Throughout your college career and during your professional life, you will be required to reveal what you have used to create your oral and written presentations.

Theme: *Calling for Community Action and Social Change*

The readings focus your attention on the nature and the results of citizen involvement in a variety of social issues – from local poverty to the threat of nuclear war. The essays were also chosen to ask you to identify and react to the factors that make some people commit themselves to a life of social involvement and others to turn away from it.

READINGS

Benjamin R. Barber   THE CONCEPT OF CITIZENSHIP

Paul Rogat Loeb   EXCERPT FROM *SOUL OF A CITIZEN*

Silja Talvi   THE NEW FACE OF PHILANTHROPY

CONTENTS

PART ONE

Exploring Questions: Invention, Reading and Writing

Part One (Chapters 1 through 5) addresses the general stages of the writing process. First, in Chapter 1, you will learn how to determine the context within which academic writing happens. Next, you will find instruction that will help you use the readings in the book. The instruction focuses on how you can take control of texts and become actively and critically involved in the process. Then, you will find techniques for clarifying the scope, audience, and purpose of your writing. The chapter also offers four categories of questions that will assist you in shaping your inquiries and arguments.

Chapter 1 closes by leading you through the construction of a first essay. The essay is based on the chapter's readings, as well as on an array of facts and statistics that reflect contemporary life in America. One of your goals is to deploy the four categories of questions in the exploration of this material.

Chapter 2 provides specific invention techniques that will aid you in making explicit your underlying attitudes toward your topic. They will also assist both in recognizing what you already know about it and what you need to discover. The chapter also provides guidance on the kind of reading and thinking expected throughout the book. We stress the importance of active and critical reading at every stage of the writing process.

Chapter 3 shows how to bring what you've learned from your reading into your writing. You will learn how direct quotation, paraphrase, and summary can help your readers to understand how you arrived at your point of view, thus lending credibility to your thinking. You will also learn how to synthesize what you have gathered from your sources so that you are not just piling one piece of support for your position on another.

Later chapters in this part of the book will give you the opportunity to put these principles to work through journal exercises and short essays that are based on the unit's readings and, finally, in a major assignment.

1   *Joining the Conversation*

Your college experience will help you understand and appreciate the remarkable things human beings achieve and the many ways we transcend and extend ourselves. We raise children and build families and communities. We create books, paintings, and symphonies. Common to all our greatest achievements is communication; indeed, human society might be thought of as the great conversation. This book brings you into that conversation. You are invited to join student and professional writers to share experiences and to offer your ideas and insights. As you engage each assignment, you will see that the act of writing goes beyond submitting a finished product. It is an ongoing process of extension and growth. The writers you meet here are creating themselves as they write, as you will, as we all do.

Talking and Listening: A Community of Voices

Voices fill your life. They reflect where you have been, what you have done, read, and heard. Even in solitary moments, you can rarely shut out the sounds of your experience. Voices whisper and shout, wheedle and whine, praise and complain. Many of these voices demand attention when you write and, like all writers, you must decide which you will listen to and with which voice you will speak.

College writing challenges you to engage a diverse and growing community of other voices. The more you write for this community, the more it will influence how you express the voice that is uniquely yours. While it must not drown you out, neither can you ignore it. Learn to hear and name those voices and to identify their interests, values, and traditions. By internalizing these voices and finding ways to use what they say, you can become a more vital part of that community.

Reviewing a Classroom Discussion

Consider the following classroom discussion about family values, the subject of this chapter's reading and writing assignments. By observing how the students exchange thoughts and feelings, you should see how you could begin to explore a subject on your own and in dialogue with others.

Rebecca: Why do I have this little sick, sinking feeling in my stomach?

Kent: What? You don't like this topic?

Rebecca: No, I do not. Some of this reading is beginning to sound like sociology class, which I really hate.

Kent: And why is that?

Rebecca: Oh, they just can't leave anything alone for two seconds. It's always pick at this, dig into that, screw around with something else. It's a lot of high-sounding nonsense that doesn't have anything to do with anything real.

Liz: I don't know. I'd say families are real enough.

Rebecca: Exactly. Families *are* real. It's real people in real relationships doing what they do that means something. All this dithering around about them means precisely zip. And "family values"? Give me a break…

Jeff: I agree. Very lame. Politicians get a lot of mileage out of it, but I think most people are really sick of the empty rhetoric. Does the family values crowd really think we can solve all our problems by putting everybody in the same pew?

Kent: Well, I agree the term is a problem, but I think it's got to mean *something*. And we'd better figure out what it is, because we've got some real problems.

Rebecca: What problems?

Liz: Don't you read the newspapers? School shootings and meth labs on every corner and the most troubled new generation in history . . . And you can trace all that right back to the decay of the family.

Rebecca: I'm not buying that for a minute. It's just too easy an answer, and who says the family is decaying, anyway?

Kent: Only about every other person you read. You don't see a problem with an incredibly high divorce rate and half the kids in the country being raised by single parents?

Rebecca: No, I don't. There's nothing wrong with single parent families. My mother raised my brother and me since I was four, and it wasn't easy. But we're just fine, thank you.

Liz: That's the point. It's not easy. And maybe you, and your mother, and your brother are strong enough to make it, but I don't think that's usually the case. That good old nuclear family—mom, dad, kids, dog, cat, and picket fence—that's still the best way to raise children.

Jeff: What do you want? The Brady Bunch? That's a fantasy and always has been . . . an invention of television and wishful thinking.

Kent: No, I don't think that's true. Things really have changed in the past few decades. There are a lot more busted up families and single parents than there ever have been.

Rebecca: Even if that's true, it's just a change, not a disaster. Change is not a problem unless we make it one. That nuclear family nonsense is a really narrow view of what a family is or can be.

Liz: And so you think those other kinds of so-called families meet people's needs as well as the traditional family?

Rebecca: Absolutely. At least I think they can if we'll give them a chance. We have to realize that a traditional family complete with stay-at-home-mom is not the only way to do things.

Kent: And you think kids can be raised as well by day care centers as their mothers?

Rebecca: I think it's possible if we'll pay more attention to day care centers and put some money into them for a change.

Jeff: And even if day care centers are crummy, who has a choice? Sometimes Mom has to work.

Kent: You're just making my point for me. The only real solution is to stop the breakdown of the nuclear family.

Jeff: And how do you suggest we do that? Make divorce illegal?

Kent: I don't think anyone has suggested that, but I do think we need to do *something* about it. Maybe if we gave some thought to why things are falling apart this way…

Rebecca: But I don't think they *are* falling apart. They're just changing.

Kent: Okay, okay. Have it your way. But these changes are creating some problems, and we still need to figure out exactly what's changing and why.

Liz: I think it's obvious that the old way of doing things was not meeting people's needs…. especially women's.

Kent: I don't remember reading anything to suggest that a majority of women in the first part of this century felt horribly oppressed. What did they do? Just spontaneously grow all these new needs about fifty years ago?

Rebecca: You need to expand your reading. The needs were always there; they just didn't have any opportunity to meet them.

Jeff: And how did they suddenly get these opportunities?

Rebecca: Well, the pill for one thing. Women weren't forced to be baby machines any more.

Liz: And World War II. With all the men gone, the women had to take jobs. They found out they could do something besides make beds.

Kent: I think there's more to making a home and caring for children than that. And I think there's more to this whole family values issue than what we're saying.

Rebecca: For once, I absolutely agree with you.

Liz: Me too. On one hand we have the family values crowd that wants to dump us all in a time machine and send us back to 1926. On the other, we have people who want to call anything a family. It's all just more complicated than that.

Jeff: Isn't everything?

Clearly, these students are having trouble making progress with some difficult issues. While they seem to realize that their existing notions are too simplistic and the issues are, as Liz notes, "just more complicated than that," they seem to have little luck unraveling the complications. What's the problem? One problem may be that they haven't kept in mind the important distinction between *fact* and *judgment*.

Perhaps a quick exercise will help illustrate this point.

Read their discussion again. You will see that the students make a great many claims. In your notebook:

- List three claims offered by the students that you would regard as *fact*.
- List three that you would regard as *judgments* or *opinions*.

(Note: We've used *judgment* and *opinion* synonymously here because people often think of them that way. However, that's not entirely accurate, and from now on we'll use the term *judgment* exclusively.)

Did you find the second list easier to make? You should have, because the students above are wading in a swamp of judgments with little, if any, factual support.

One important requirement of good reasoning is that we ultimately base our *judgments* on *facts*. However, as you may have found in the preceding exercise, the distinction is not always as clear as we might like.

We tend to regard *facts* as true claims about the nature of reality, and we tend to regard *judgments* as *subjective* results of human emotion and reason. If we follow this view, facts are verifiable, *objective* descriptions of reality and, once verified, are not usually suitable subjects for argument. For example, why argue about whether or not all the men were gone to war during WWII, as Liz claims in the dialogue, when you can check the accuracy of such assertions in history books or, better, military records?

Judgments, on the other hand, because of their subjectivity, are often questioned and sometimes lead to interesting and productive arguments. For example, Liz's claim that taking the jobs of men during WWII led women to a greater sense of their own worth is not a simple fact. It is a judgment and, as such, it provides a worthwhile topic for further inquiry.

Conveniently, this is exactly what we, as writers, want to see—good topics for further inquiry. And the students in the dialogue certainly need to explore some important questions before they can begin to penetrate that issue-filled swamp of which they are at present only dimly aware.

For example, they will need to ask and answer some basic questions about the nature of the unit we call a family. A general definition would not be a bad place to start. Do we define "family" by the quality and utility of human relationships within it, or do we define it in terms of a structure imposed by tradition?

The students are also realizing the need to consider what causes change in the nature of the family and the results that may be produced. Are current variations in family structure just part of a natural evolution? Or are those changes a dangerous mutation and a potential dead end? In their discussion, they've hinted at economic, historical, political, and emotional factors that might be at play. They'll need to add other questions to their list and explore them more fully through reading, writing, and further discussion.

Obviously, there is work to complete before any of the students can settle on a line of inquiry and follow it through to a viable position on the subject. But, as Jeff noted, they have to start somewhere.

Collaboration

The students who were discussing the family have benefited from interacting with their peers. By listening and being heard, they were testing and refining their own perspectives. Moreover, they were gaining insight into the kinds of questions and responses others would have to their insights.

Similar activity can help you with your writing and reading. As you encounter new writing situations, your peers and instructors will bring their own perspectives to your projects, perspectives that will challenge you to develop your thoughts and express them clearly. Active engagement with others will assist you in becoming a better writer and a better student.

The discussion above also shows how intellectual growth occurs when we integrate new and sometimes conflicting ideas into what we already feel and believe. As you engage others, speak your mind, of course, but remain open to alternative views. It is not always clear where collaboration will lead, but the exchange will sharpen your thinking.

To explore some of the themes that mark contemporary American life, first read through the following array of statistics. They should raise your curiosity and encourage you to begin discussion with your peers and instructors.

Social Trends Index

[1]Percentage of college freshmen who say "being well off financially" is important:
In 1970: 40%; In 2006: 72%

[2]Who say "developing a philosophy of life" is important: In 1970: 70%; In 2006: 42%

[3]Percentage of parents who rated "thinking for oneself" as the most important trait a child could learn: 99%
Percentage who ranked "obedience" as the most important trait: 23%

[4]United States households headed by married couples in 1950: 78.2%
In 1980: 61%; In 1998: 53%; In 2005: 49.7%

[5]Percentage of traditional households with an employed husband, a wife keeping house, and children attending school
In 1972: 60%; In 1998: 27%; In 2006: 7%

[6]Percentage of married couples who say they are "happier in general with their lives": 40%
Percentage of never-married persons who say this: 23%

[7]Percentage of married couples who say that they share childcare equally in 1985: 25%
In 1998: 49%; In 2006: 49%

[8]Number of hours each day the average child between two and eighteen spends alone watching television,
at a computer, playing video games, on the Internet, or reading: In 2000: 5 1/2; In 2005: 6 1/2

[9]Percentage increase of U.S. children living in a household maintained by a grandparent between 1970–2005: 105%

[10]Proportion of one's life that he or she will spend unmarried: more than 1/2

[11]Life span of the usual marriage in the United States in 2005: 6–7 years.

[12]Percentage of all married men who will eventually commit adultery: 22% Of married women: 14%

[13]Percentage increase since 1990 of families headed by single mothers: 35%

[14]Chances that a child living in a single mother household will be living below the poverty line:
In 1996: 47%; In 2005: 54%

[15]Proportion of U.S. men aged 25–34 holding full-time jobs who earn too little to lift a family of four
above the poverty line: 1 in 3

[16]Proportion of money an American family borrows compared to what it saves: 18 to 1

[17]Percentage of children living with a single parent who will have to repeat a grade in school: 30%

[18]Percentage of children living with both parents who will fail a grade: 10%

[19]Odds that one will have some sort of serious mental disorder in his or her lifetime: 1 in 5

[20]Odds that a child will become an alcoholic in his or her lifetime: 1 in 18

[21]The most common drug involved in hospital emergency rooms: alcohol

Sources: [1]Harper's Index, 1990-2001); *Journal of College and Character* Volume IX, No. 1, September 2007
[2]Harper's Index, 1990-2001); *Journal of College and Character* Volume IX, No. 1, September 2007
[3]*Harper's Index*, (1990-2001).
[4]Roberts, Sam. "To be Married Means to be Outnumbered," *NY Times,* October 15, 2006;
2006 The Seattle Times Company
[5]*Statistical Handbook on the American Family,* 2ed., Ed: Bruce A. Chadwick and Tim B. Heaton, 1999–2000.
U.S. Census Bureau: Women by the Numbers 2006
[6]< http://pewresearch.org/pubs/?ChartID=17>

[7]<http://www.census.gov/population/www/socdemo/child/ppl-177>; Coontz, Stephanie. "The Family Revolution," *Greater Good Magazine,* Fall, 2007.

[8]Eitzen, Stanley D. "The Fragmentation of Social Life," *Vital Speeches,* July 1, 2000.; U.S. Census Bureau, 2005.

[9]NYSOFA, "Exploring Aging," Project 2015 <http://www.aging.state.ny.us/explore/project 2015/artgrandparents.htm>; U.S. Census Bureau, 2005.

[10]Laudan, Larry. *Danger Ahead,* NY: John Wiley & Sons, 1997.

[11]U.S. Census Bureau, 2005.

[12]2007 MSNBC

[13]2007 MSNBC

[14]<http://www.census.gov/population/www/socdemo/child/ppl-177>

[15]Committee on General Welfare in NYC (Sept. 2006).

[16]See Laudan, Larry.

[17]<http://www.futureofchildren.org/information2827/information_show.htm>

[18]Ibid.

[19]Mental Health: A Report of the Surgeon General, 2006.

[20]<http://www.gdcada.org/statistics/alcohol.htm>

[21]See Laudan, Larry.

At this point, you might find it interesting to compare the list of statistical claims you have just read with the claims in the student discussion you read earlier. The differences may be clearer if you repeat the exercise that followed that discussion.

In your notebook:

- List three claims listed in the Social Trends Index that you would regard as *facts*.
- List three that you would regard as *judgments*.

This time you should have been able to identify facts more easily. Most of the claims in the Social Trends Index involve statistics, and statistical data are often recognized as facts. Indeed, it may have seemed more difficult this time to identify judgments. Actually, there are plenty of judgments in the Social Trends Index; but since they are expressed in "statistical" language, you may have been tempted to see them as factual. The way that statistical claims are presented can be deceptive, and you should be careful when evaluating these sorts of claims.

For example, consider the following claim from the Index.

United States households headed by married couples in 1950: 78.2%

This is apparently statistical data from 1950, perhaps from a government survey. It is clearly intended as fact.

Now consider another claim from the Index.

Percentage of children living with both parents who will fail a grade: 10%

At first, the two claims seem alike; however, notice the verb tenses. The second is not a claim that something *is* the case (present tense) or *has* happened (past tense); rather, it is a claim that something *will* happen (future tense). Because it makes a *prediction*, we must regard the assertion as a *judgment*. It may be based on reliable statistics from the past, but that is no guarantee the situation will continue into the future.

The second claim is a special sort of claim we will call an *inference*. Whereas a claim of fact claims to describe an objective reality and is normally a product of observation, an inference is a product of our reasoning—a judgment inferred from fact. *Inference* is an exceptionally important part of almost all our intellectual processes, including argument and critical thinking.

Although the term may be unfamiliar, the process of inference is probably nothing new to you; you have been making inferences throughout your life. For example, pretend you see a close friend coming out of a classroom just after an important exam. The expression on her face is sad, angry, desperate, or all three. You may infer from the objective fact of her facial expression that she did poorly on the exam. Is the judgment you've made absolutely accurate? Of course not. The expression on her face may be caused by something entirely different—dental problems, a bad-tempered boyfriend, or car troubles—the possibilities are numerous.

Now consider two claims from the Social Trends Index.

Percentage of college freshmen who say "being well off financially" is important: 72%
Percentage of college freshmen who say "developing a philosophy of life" is important: 42%

If we accept those statistics as factual, can we infer that financial comfort is more important to college freshmen than developing a philosophy of life? Perhaps. But we will want to ask more questions before we accept such a determination as accurate. Still, the statistics and the inference we've made from them provide a place to start, an entry into the inquiry.

Collaborative Activity

- In class, divide into groups of 3-5 students.
- From the Social Trends Index, each group should write down at least six claims of *fact* that are related in some way.
- After discussion, each group should write down at least three judgments that can be inferred from the facts they selected. Preferably, each judgment can be inferred from or supported by at least two of the facts from the Index. Be sure to include the facts from the Index in the written report of the judgments.
- Each group should also write a sentence or two that explains or justifies the inferences they have made.

Collaborative Activity

- Each group should present its findings to the full class. There should be time for questions and comments from the rest of the class and the various groups must be ready to defend their reasoning.
- Each group should reconvene to produce a written evaluation of its performance.
- All that has been written by the members of the group should be assembled as a packet and copies should be made for all group members. Also, a copy should be given to the instructor, if requested.

Reading

Much of what you write in college will incorporate what you read. You may not consider yourself a bookish type, but if you think of reading in its broadest sense, that is, as interpreting the sights, sounds, and signs of your environment, then you are reading all the time. You read moods, attitudes, styles, values, and meanings in your friends and family. You carefully read the facial expressions and gestures of friends and strangers for clues to their personalities and to how you might relate to them. This kind of reading is not only fundamental to human interaction; it also involves the basic interpretive skills you bring to texts.

As a college student you need to know how to use information–how to interpret, evaluate, and make connections. All the work that follows from your reading–writing papers, taking exams, and making oral presentations–presumes your understanding of a variety of texts. To fully grasp their importance, you must not only attend to the writers' shaping of content, but you must also evaluate what you read against evidence provided by other texts and by your own ideas and experience.

Each reading in this book engages you in a dialogue with the writer. To participate in that dialogue, you must draw on your personal values and beliefs. Think of these writers not as lecturers but as partners in conversations. Of course, a good conversation requires mutual respect. You must honor the richness of these writers' ideas and expression and take the time to understand their perspectives. By giving each writer a full and thoughtful hearing, you establish a fair grounding for your critical response.

Active, critical reading of scholarly, scientific, and professional texts is a little more complex than skimming through those entertaining thrillers on the bestseller list. A quick scan of the library shelves or the World Wide Web will provide any number of techniques for quick and efficient reading. However, we suggest four approaches that might make your reading more effective: *previewing, asking questions, marking the text,* and *making margin notes.* We'll also provide a text to practice on.

Previewing

When you are faced with a text of some complexity, don't immediately start reading. First, *preview* the text. Before attempting a close, critical reading, you need to have an idea of a text's general positions and purpose. Start by looking at the title, for it often suggests the nature and scope of the topic and it may even reveal something of the writer's tone and point of view. Read the opening paragraphs, for there the writer often states or suggests key ideas. Skim the remainder of the text by noting the headings (if any) that introduce each section and by reading the opening sentence of each paragraph. Skimming will give you a sense of the flow of the text, of how it thematically develops. Read the final paragraphs, looking for a summary that recaps the main points or for concluding statements that suggest the writer's position.

Asking Questions

After you have explored the material, you may find it helpful to consider questions that you have about the topic. What do you already know about the topic? Have you any personal experience with the issues the writer has raised? What is your present attitude or feeling about the topic and the issues?

Marking the Text

Always read with a highlighter, pen, or pencil in hand to mark key terms and phrases. Mark transition sentences, for in them writers often summarize what they have presented before introducing a new focus. Noting major transitions can help you recognize and remember how a writer intends a text to work.

Identify and mark any terms, concepts, or passages you do not understand to make it easy to return to them for further reflection. Do not ignore difficult parts of a text, since they might contain ideas or information essential to your understanding the writer's argument. Perhaps you might find it useful to have a specific way to mark such parts, so that you can discuss them with your instructor or with other students.

Making Margin Notes

Make a habit of responding actively to your reading by making notes in the margins. Your comments and questions check the text against your own ideas and experience. When you engage what you read, you cease being a remote and detached observer and join the author in making discoveries.

In the annotated passage below, notice how marking the text and writing margin notes help the reader analyze and question the author's assumptions and evidence. Also, compare this reader's approach to the way you mark and annotate what you read.

¶ 1 . . .Psychology as much as science will. . .determine the planet's fate, because action depends on overcoming denial, among the most paralyzing of human responses. While it affects most of us to varying degrees, denial often runs particularly deep among those with heavy stakes in the status quo,including political and business leaders with power to shape the global agenda.

Agree?

¶s 1-2:
—*Change is needed*
—*Change is difficult (we tend to "deny" severe problems)*
—*Change is possible*

Denial among world leaders

¶ 2 This kind of denial can be as dangerous to society and the natural environment as an alcoholic's denial is to his or her own health and family. Because they fail to see their addiction as the principal threat to their well-being, alcoholics often end up destroying their lives. Rather than face the truth, denial's victims choose slow suicide. In a similar way, by pursuing life-styles and economic goals that ravage the environment, we sacrifice long-term health and well-being for immediate gratification—a trade-off that cannot yield a happy ending.

Is this a legitimate comparison?

Discuss in group.

Transition

Comparison (alcoholism)

Harmful effects of denial

Comparison with alcoholism extended:
—*experiencing denial (negative) (¶ 1-2)*
—*overcoming denial (¶ 3-4)*

Overcoming denial: Intervention

¶ 3 There is a practice in the treatment of alcoholism called intervention in which family members and friends, aided by counselor, attempt to shake the alcoholic out of denial. In a supportive but candid manner, they help the person grasp the gravity of the disease, the harm it is causing at home and at work, and the need for fundamental change if life for them all is to improve. A successful intervention results in the alcoholic finally acknowledging the problem, and deciding to embark upon the challenging path back to health.

Part of Postel's persona?

Intervention defined

¶ 4 A similar kind of "intervention" is needed to arrest the global disease of environmental degradation, and a uniquely suitable forum is already

Transition

¶s 3–4
Change is possible, despite denial

Research
Rio
Conference:
successful
intervention?

planned. For the first time in 20
years, people around the world – including heads of state, scientists,and
activists – will gather in <u>June 1992</u>
to focus on environment and development. <u>This U.N. Conference in Rio de</u>
<u>Janeiro</u> offers a historic opportunity
to shake up our senses, to admit – individually as earth citizens, and col-
lectively as a community of nations –
that dramatic course corrections are
required.

Example of
global interven-
tion: UN Rio
Conference

"Denial in the Decisive Decade" Sandra Postel,
State of the World, 1992.

Points to Consider

1. Other than underlining or highlighting what other strategies does the reader use to analyze Postel's work? List them and explain how each helps the reader to explore the text.

2. What kinds of questions did the reader ask to better understand Postel's ideas? What kinds of challenges do the reader's questions pose? Where on the page do most of these questions appear?

3. In the right-hand margins the reader makes some comments right next to the text, and others further out in the margin. Drawing on specific examples, explain the different purposes the two kinds of notes serve in the reader's analysis of the text.

To practice active and critical reading, try the four strategies—*previewing, asking questions, marking the text,* and *making margin notes* on the text below.

Stone Soup
What Does It Mean to Be a Family Anyway?
Barbara Kingsolver

IN THE CATALOG of family values, where do we rank an occasion like this? A curly-haired boy who wanted to run before he walked, age seven now, a soccer player scoring a winning goal. He turns to the bleachers with his fists in the air and a smile wide as a gap-toothed galaxy. His own cheering section of grown-ups and kids all leap to their feet and hug each other, delirious with love for this boy. He's Andy, my best friend's son. The cheering section includes his mother and her friends, his brother, his father and stepmother, a stepbrother and stepsister, and a grandparent. Lucky is the child with this many relatives on hand to hail a proud accomplishment. I'm there too, witnessing a family fortune. But in spite of myself, defensive words take shape in my head. I am thinking: I dare *anybody* to call this a broken home.

Families change, and remain the same. Why are our names for home so slow to catch up to the truth of where we live?

When I was a child, I had two parents who loved me without cease. One of them attended every excuse for attention I ever contrived, and the other made it to the ones with higher production values, like piano recitals and appendicitis. So I was a lucky child too. I played with a set of paper dolls called "The Family of Dolls," four in number, who came with the factory-assigned names of Dad, Mom, Sis, and Junior. I think you know what they looked like, at least before I loved them to death and their heads fell off.

Now I've replaced the dolls with a life. I knit my days around my daughter's survival and happiness, and am proud to say her head is still on. But we aren't the Family of Dolls. Maybe you're not, either. And if not, even though you are statistically no oddity, it's probably been suggested to you in a hundred ways that yours isn't exactly a real family, but an impostor family, a harbinger of cultural ruin, a slapdash substitute—something like counterfeit money. Here at the tail end of our century, most of us are up to our ears in the noisy business of trying to support and love a thing called family. But there's a current in the air with ferocious moral force that finds its way even into political campaigns, claiming there is only one right way to do it, the Way It Has Always Been.

In the face of a thriving, parti-colored world, this narrow view is so pickled and absurd I'm astonished that it gets airplay. And I'm astonished that it still stings.

Every parent has endured the arrogance of a child-unfriendly grump sitting in judgment, explaining what those kids of ours really need (for example, "a good licking"). If we're polite, we move our crew to another bench in the park. If we're forthright (as I am in my mind, only, for the rest of the day), we fix them with a sweet imperious stare and say, "Come back and let's talk about it after you've changed a thousand diapers."

But it's harder somehow to shrug off the Family-of-Dolls Family Values crew when they judge (from their safe distance) that divorced people, blended families, gay families and single parents are failures; that our children are at risk; and the whole arrangement is messy and embarrassing. A marriage that ends is not called "finished," it's called *failed*. The children of this family may have been born to a happy union, but now they are called the *children of divorce*. . . .

Arguing about whether nontraditional families deserve pity or tolerance is a little like the medieval debate about left-handedness as a mark of the devil. Divorce, remarriage, single parenthood, gay parents, and blended families simply are. They're facts of our time. Some of the reasons listed by sociologists for these family reconstructions are: the idea of marriage as a romantic partnership rather than a pragmatic one; a shift in women's expectations, from servility to self-respect and independence; and longevity (prior to antibiotics no marriage was expected to last many decades—in Colonial days the average couple lived to be married less than twelve years). Add to all this our growing sense of entitlement to happiness and safety from abuse. Most would agree these are all good things. Yet their result—a culture in which serial monogamy and the consequent reshaping of families are the norm—gets diagnosed as "failing."

For many of us, once we have put ourselves Humpty-Dumpty-wise back together again, the main problem with our reorganized family is that other people think we have a problem. My daughter tells me the only time she's uncomfortable about being the child of divorced parents is when her friends say they feel sorry for her. It's a bizarre sympathy, given that half the kids in her school and nation are in the same boat, pursuing childish happiness with the same energy as their married-parent peers. When anyone asks how she feels about it, she spontaneously lists the benefits: our house is in the country and we have a dog, but she can go to her dad's neighborhood for the urban thrills of a pool and sidewalks for roller-skating. What's more, she has three sets of grandparents!

Why is it surprising that a child would revel in a widened family and the right to feel at home in more than one house? Isn't it the opposite that should worry us—a child with no home at all, or too few resources to feel safe? The child at risk is the one whose parents are too immature themselves to guide wisely; too diminished by poverty to nurture; too far from opportunity to offer hope. The number of children in the U.S. living in poverty at this moment is almost unfathomably large: twenty percent. There are families among us that need help all right, and by no means are they new on the landscape. The rate at which teenage girls had babies in 1957 (ninety-six per thousand) was twice what it is now. That remarkable statistic is ignored by the religious right – probably because the teen birth rate was cut in half mainly by legalized abortion. In fact, the policy gatekeepers who coined the phrase "family values" have steadfastly ignored the desperation of too-small families, and since 1979 have steadily reduced the amount of financial support available to a single parent. But, this camp's most outspoken attacks seem aimed at the notion of families getting too complex, with add-ons and extras such as a gay parent's partner, or a remarried mother's new husband and his children.

To judge a family's value by its tidy symmetry is to purchase a book for its cover. There's no moral authority there. The famous family comprised of Dad, Mom, Sis, and Junior living as an isolated economic unit is not built on historical bedrock. In *The Way We Never Were,* Stephanie Coontz writes, "Whenever people propose that we go back to the traditional family, I always suggest that they pick a ballpark date for the family they have in mind." Colonial families were tidily disciplined, but their members (meaning everyone but infants) labored incessantly and died young.

Then the Victorian family adopted a new division of labor, in which women's role was domestic and allowed time for study and play, but this was an upper-class construct supported by myriad slaves. Coontz writes, "For every nineteenth-century middle-class family that protected its wife and child within the family circle, there was an Irish or German girl scrubbing floors . . . a Welsh boy mining coal to keep the home-baked goodies warm, a black girl doing the family laundry, a black mother and child picking cotton to be made into clothes for the family, and a Jewish or an Italian daughter in a sweatshop making 'ladies' dresses or artificial flowers for the family to purchase."

The abolition of slavery brought slightly more democratic arrangements, in which extended families were harnessed together in cottage industries; at the turn of the century came a steep rise in child labor in mines and sweatshops. Twenty percent of American children lived in orphanages at the time; their parents were not necessarily dead, but couldn't afford to keep them.

During the Depression and up to the end of World War II, many millions of U.S. households were more multigenerational than nuclear. Women my grandmother's age were likely to live with a fluid assortment of elderly relatives, in-laws, siblings, and children. In many cases they spent virtually every waking hour working in the company of other women—a companionable scenario in which it would be easier, I imagine, to tolerate an estranged or difficult spouse. I'm reluctant to idealize a life of so much hard work and so little spousal intimacy, but its advantage may have been resilience. A family so large and varied would not easily be brought down by a single blow: it could absorb a death, long illness, an abandonment here or there, and any number of irreconcilable differences.

The Family of Dolls came along midcentury as a great American experiment. A booming economy required a mobile labor force and demanded that women surrender jobs to returning soldiers. Families came to be defined by a single breadwinner. They struck out for single-family homes at an earlier age than ever before, and in unprecedented numbers they raised children in urban isolation. The nuclear family was launched to sink or swim.

More than a few sank. Social historians corroborate that the suburban family of the postwar economic boom, which we have recently selected as our definition of "traditional," was no panacea. Twenty-five percent of Americans were poor in the mid-1950s, and as yet there were no food stamps. Sixty percent of the elderly lived on less than $1,000 a year, and most had no medical insurance. In the sequestered suburbs, alcoholism and sexual abuse of children were far more widespread than anyone imagined.

Expectations soared, and the economy sagged. It's hard to depend on one other adult for everything, come what may. In the last three decades, that amorphous, adaptable structure we call "family" has been reshaped once more by economic tides. Compared with fifties families, mothers are far more likely now to be employed. We are statistically more likely to divorce, and to live in blended families or other extra-nuclear arrangements. We are also more likely to plan and space our children, and to rate our marriages as "happy." We are less likely to suffer abuse without recourse or to stare out at our lives through a glaze of prescription tranquilizers. Our aged parents are less likely to be destitute, and we're half as likely to have a teenage daughter turn up a mother herself. All in all, I would say that if "intact" in modern family-values jargon means living quietly desperate in the bell jar, then hip-hip-hooray for "broken." A neat family model constructed to service the Baby Boom economy seems to be returning gradually to a grand, lumpy shape that human families apparently have tended toward since they first took root in Olduvai Gorge. We're social animals, deeply fond of companionship, and children love best to run in packs. If there is a *normal* for humans, at all, I expect it looks like two or three Families of Dolls, connected variously by kinship and passion, shuffled like cards and strewn over several shoeboxes.

The sooner we can let go the fairy tale of families functioning perfectly in isolation, the better we might embrace the relief of community. Even the admirable parents who've stayed married through thick and thin are very likely, at present, to incorporate other adults into their families—household help and baby-sitters if they can afford them, or neighbors and grandparents if they can't. For single parents, this support is the rock-bottom definition of family. And most parents who have split apart, however painfully, still manage to maintain family continuity for their children, creating in many cases a boisterous phenomenon that Constance Ahrons in her book *The Good Divorce* calls the "binuclear family." Call it what you will—when ex-spouses beat swords into plowshares and jump up and down at a soccer game together, it makes for happy kids.

CINDERELLA, LOOK, needs her? All those evil stepsisters? That story always seemed like too much cotton-picking fuss over clothes. A childhood tale that fascinated me more was the one called "Stone Soup," and the gist of it is this: Once upon a time, a pair of beleaguered soldiers straggled home to a village empty-handed, in a land ruined by war. They were famished, but the villagers had so little they shouted evil words and slammed their doors. So the soldiers dragged out a big kettle, filled it with water, and put it on a fire to boil. They rolled a clean round stone into the pot, while the villagers peered through their curtains in amazement.

"What kind of soup is that?" they hooted.

"Stone soup," the soldiers replied. "Everybody can have some when it's done."

"Well, thanks," one matron grumbled, coming out with a shriveled carrot. "But it'd be better if you threw this in."

And so on, of course, a vegetable at a time, until the whole suspicious village managed to feed itself grandly.

Any family is a big empty pot, save for what gets thrown in. Each stew turns out different. Generosity, a resolve to turn bad luck into good, and respect for variety—these things will nourish a nation of children. Name-calling and suspicion will not. My soup contains a rock or two of hard times, and maybe yours does too. I expect it's a heck of a bouillabaisse.

Excerpt from *High Tide In Tucson*, HarperCollins. 1995.

When you become actively involved in your reading, you enter into a discussion with its author. You ask questions and make observations to which you can return. Making such notes may seem time consuming, but it will help you to find ideas for writing assignments and to prepare for exams.

Writing

While collaborative work and reading are clearly invaluable parts of the writing process, sooner or later you must actually put words on the page. In a sense, this entire book is aimed toward that goal. Here we offer two suggestions to make your efforts more effective. For one thing, you need to learn how to distinguish among the various writing situations you will encounter. You must also recognize how to respond to the goal and the context of each situation. Also, you will need to take advantage of one of the writer's primary tools—the writing journal.

Understanding the Writing Situation

Most of the writing you have done has likely been in response to assignments that were designed to have you demonstrate your grasp of a subject. However, as you progress through college and into your profession, you will increasingly create your own "assignments." Your writing will become more involved in revealing your ideas, plans, and objectives to others.

In either case, your writing will be more successful if you take time at the beginning of each project to determine its scope and purpose. What, really, do you need to do? What content and structure are demanded by the way the assignment is phrased or conceived? What kinds of reasoning should you exhibit to complete the assignment?

Some of these considerations are straightforward and completely within every student's control, yet the work is often unproductive because the student ignores them. For example:

Length:

Instructors will often indicate the range for an assignment. They specify a minimum length to indicate the amount of writing they believe that you must undertake to develop the assignment. They specify a maximum length because they want you to learn the value of precision and conciseness.

Format:

Most of the writing you will do in college and in your professional life will follow specific conventions. Academic papers, lab reports, grant proposals, or business plans have specific structures and formats. You must follow those conventions. Your work may be compelling, but if it's not in the format your audience expects, it may be discounted or ignored.

Audience:

> We will have much to say about understanding your audience. For now, just keep in mind that someone is going to read (and in some cases, evaluate) your work. This may seem obvious, but it's surprising how easy it is to get caught up in the work itself and forget that your ultimate goal is to communicate with others.

Length, format, and audience are among the concrete elements you will confront as you write. However, when you turn to considering the purpose and content of your work, the situation becomes more complex.

There are few things more discouraging than having your writing rejected or be undervalued because you didn't address the designated topic or goal. This normally means you didn't understand exactly what you were asked to do.

It will help to remember that every writing project requires an *inquiry* of some sort; that is, it implies one or more questions. If you can determine what questions are being asked, then your answers and, consequently, your response to the assignment will be better developed and more thoughtful.

Consider the following topic:

> *In "Stone Soup" (pp. 14–18), Barbara Kingsolver seems to say that much current lamentation over the alleged "collapse of the American family" is largely unwarranted and that, in fact, parents and children in non-nuclear family situations often have more rewarding lives than those in the semi-mythical "Family of Dolls" of the 1950s. Do you agree? Why or why not?*

Two issues that you must develop are obvious—because they're phrased as questions: "Do you agree?" and "Why or why not?" It would be easy to focus immediately on those two and start writing. But consider what other questions may be implied by the topic. For example:

- What is the current state of marriage in the United States? Is it really "collapsing" or is it evolving into new and often more effective forms?

- Kingsolver examines the language sometimes used to describe the characteristics of non-nuclear families. What are some of those characteristics? Are the points she makes important? How does the language we use to describe family structures shape our definition and understanding of the concept of "family"?

- What attitudes toward a traditional view of the family does Kingsolver communicate with the "Family of Dolls" metaphor? Is her use of this metaphor appropriate?

- Kingsolver mentions the lack of understanding many of us have about non-typical family structures. What problems might result from this?

- What other effects might the idealization of the "Family of Dolls" cause? Which seem positive? Negative?

- Are the situations Kingsolver explores in "Stone Soup" serious ones? Are they worth our time and energy? Why or why not?

- On what criteria is Kingsolver basing her value judgments? On what criteria do you base your value judgments about families?

- In "Stone Soup," what level of commitment does Kingsolver want from us? Does she just want us to understand her point of view? Or does she want us to adopt it? Does she want us to take some action about the situation? If so, what action?

While you might not have time to answer all these questions, just asking them clarifies the assignment and suggests approaches for responding to the topic. In this case, it is obvious you're being asked to create arguments in defense of a position. Considering such questions would help to strengthen your response.

Keeping a Journal

Keeping a journal is an essential part of the writing you are asked to undertake in this text. Almost all assignments begin as journal activities, for they provide an informal way to explore and develop your ideas. Recording ideas, questions, and insights as they arise will help you to reflect on the assignments, identify possible directions for your writing, and apply what you learn from your reading. Your journal will not only be an important resource for information, but it will also provide a safe place to deepen your understanding of issues and strengthen your confidence as a writer.

You may also want to carry a pocket-sized notebook in which to jot things down on the spot. Odd little occurrences on the street, striking images, off-the-wall notions, all may provide the starting point for a good essay.

Journal Activity

To help you explore some of the topics in this chapter, try the following approach. Divide a page of your journal down the middle. In the left-hand column, list significant or interesting entries from the Index presented earlier. In the right-hand column, respond to the entries with questions or comments. This should get you involved in some of the debates and issues you will explore as you work through the chapter.

Sample Notes

Here are some notes that student Mark Camp made in his journal in response to a similar exercise.

(1) Average duration of an American marriage (in years): 9.4

Portion of American households made up by a single person in 1955: 1/10. Today: 1/4

Percentage of increase since 1973 in three- and four-year olds attending nursery school: 77

(2) Increase, since 1980, in the median income of an American, in constant dollars: $64 Increase, since 1980, in the median cost of a new home, in constant dollars: $16,170

(3) Number of murders the average American child has seen on television by the age of 16: 18,000

Chances that the victim of a violent crime is under the age of 20: 4 in 5

Percentage increase, since 1986, in the number of boys under 13 arrested for rape in New York City: 333

(1) Most of my friends came from divorced parents . . . no supervision . . . latch key kids that went home to an empty house and a microwave oven . . . others had both parents working to keep up the bills . . . Jim's dad was home all the time because he was laid off from Weyhauser and couldn't find a job . . .

Are these increases due to Headstart programs or the push for raising super smart kids? It seems that school starts for kids as soon as parents can find a reason to go back to work . . . do families really need these two incomes . . . are kids in school so early because parents need a place to send them so they can go to work? Maybe some parents feel they're doing the right thing for their kids, but I think most are just too busy.

(2) Homes in my neighborhood are unaffordable to most of the older people who own them . . . and young people can't afford them either. Is my generation going to be the next one to go through a major depression or what? What stress does this have on two working parents and how does it affect the lives of their children?

(3) TV and violence again . . . there's so much hype about what causes what . . . can children really be that vulnerable to something that happens on television . . . I don't know . . . aren't the values and attitudes of their parents more likely to influence their behavior? Children follow the crowd anyway, not some television program . . . but cop shows are popular, somebody must be watching them . . . criminals or law abiding citizens? The interest in the law is really big today . . . L.A. Law, Cops . . . I wonder how many hours of television programming are related to law and order . . . what's the attraction? Too many incidents of kids either missing or being accused of some terrible crime that you can't believe anyone would dare to commit. . .are children just victims striking back at absent parents . . . casualties of neglect? ? ? ?

(4) Total number of hours of television watched in American households in 1983: 213,000,000,000

Rank of watching television among activities people look forward to during the day: 1

(4) Is TV taking the place of real life for some people . . . fantasy lives and false expectations instead of real life decisions . . . *every* problem gets solved by the end of the hour . . . we see every new product from running shoes to fast foods . . . but who is watching the 25 commercials an hour that tell us what we should want? What need is TV fulfilling . . . the need to escape the realities of everyday life?

Collaborative Activity

Exchanging journal entries with classmates and comparing your responses to the sample notes in the text will help stimulate fresh ideas. Comments from peers will also help you to see which of your ideas might be worth pursuing.

A Thinking Tool: Types of Questions

When you first engage in academic and professional conversations, you will face new demands. Most probably, you will have to operate on a higher level than in the past. You will be expected to exhibit more forceful insight, more careful reasoning, and clearer, more effective ways of expressing yourself. You will also be required to show that you are creative.

Creativity is the ability to bring something *new* to a subject, a talent for seeing things that are not obvious or immediately apparent. So, what makes someone creative? We all know people who always seem to come up with new and interesting ideas. How did they get that way? Is it a natural talent? Or can it be learned?

While some abilities seem to be innate, much of what people think of as creativity can be learned. At least you can learn methods and processes to enhance whatever natural ability you may have. Here, we're interested in the process of *inquiry*, which we'll define as a process that produces new ideas and insights.

While inquiry is much more than simply asking questions, the questions we ask are in some ways the most important part of the process. They initiate the inquiry. They help restrict a subject to make the inquiry manageable. They focus and direct one's efforts. And, to some degree, the questions you ask and the *way* you ask them determine the answers you get.

We suggest you start by thinking in general terms, by establishing broad types of questions, and then using your responses to help generate other questions. Here we offer four broad categories that can put your inquiry on a solid foundation:

- Questions about the nature of things

- Questions about the causes and effects of things

- Questions about the value of things
- Questions about what sort of action we should take

The order of these questions is important. For example, you can't really ask good questions about the value of something unless you have at least some idea of its nature; and it's difficult to answer questions about what action we should take regarding something if we know nothing of its value. However, you need not exhaust one category of questions before going on to the next. In fact, trying to answer questions in one of the later categories may suggest revisiting one of the earlier ones.

For the moment, try to avoid thinking of these kinds of questions as techniques for generating material for your essays. Instead, simply consider them as ways of thinking that are likely to produce interesting lines of inquiry. Later, in Chapter 2, we'll give you some specific techniques to help you in developing questions, coming up with some potential answers, and generating material for your essays.

Also, the list we offer is not exhaustive. Our goal is to give you a general idea of the types of questions you might pose to open up your thinking about a subject. In subsequent chapters, we will provide a more extensive list of questions, usually in the context of writing assignments.

Questions about the Nature of Things

The first logical step in any inquiry is to ask questions about the nature of the subject—about what something is, about what its parts are, and about what it is made of. You probably ask these sorts of questions all the time. Some are fairly simple and have simple answers.

- What is the weather like outside?
- How much memory does that computer have?

Others seem more important and are not so easily answered.

- What really is a family?
- Does it have to have kids?
- Does it require having two parents in the home?
- Do the parents have to be a man and a woman?
- Do they have to be married?

Notice the differences between the two sets of questions. For one thing, the answers to the second set may have much greater impact on people's lives. Consequently, they initiate more complex and more important inquiries. These are the sorts of questions you will want to ask.

Also, the second set of questions seems to be searching for a *definition* of "family." Often (but not always) questions about the nature of something look for a definition. Definitions are descriptions of reality or, in other words, they are claims about the actual nature of things.

Were you to open your dictionary to the word "family," you would find something like:

family: a group of persons of common ancestry

While this is hardly an adequate definition in the 21st century, the way the definition is stated reveals how you might structure questions into the nature of things. Notice that those who wrote the definition put the term "family" into a *category*—a group of persons—and, then, they differentiate it from whatever else might be placed in the category by specifying a *defining characteristic*—persons of common ancestry. Many dictionary definitions follow this convention.

This leads us to two important (and related) principles that can help us ask meaningful questions about the subjects of our inquiries:

> ***Questions*** about the nature of things ask what ***categories*** and ***characteristics*** may be associated with a subject.

> ***Claims*** about the nature of things associate a subject with its ***potential categories*** and ***characteristics.***

The first question you might ask is:

- *Into what different categories does my subject fall?*

This may seem the simplest sort of question and, consequently, the least promising for generating new and striking insights. However, if you use it, you may find otherwise. For example, we were considering the characteristics of the concept of family a little earlier. Before we can go further with that inquiry, we need to know just what we mean by the term. The dictionary definition is far too limited as a basis for developing a topic that might include the issue of divorce, same-sex marriage, and even test tube babies.

We will start by asking what categories "family" falls into. Just off the top of your head, you might say that family falls into the categories of:

- economic units
- social institutions
- legal institutions
- biological relations

Do any of these immediately suggest a line of inquiry? If so, make a note of it. But don't be in a hurry to move on. Play with the categories a little bit. Do any of the categories fall, either completely or in part, into another? For example, are social institutions also economic units? If so, what does that say about the connection between categories?

To help generate more ideas, try looking back at the earlier class discussion. Note that Liz seems to define a family as a biological unit—the traditional nuclear family—while Rebecca thinks of it more as a social unit, one that doesn't require both a mother and a father. By thinking in terms of general categories and classes, of similarities and differences, you sometimes can uncover the underlying source of disagreement, as well as the possibilities for finding common ground.

As you experiment with different ideas and approaches, remember that the goal of this beginning stage of the writing process is simply to generate as many ideas as possible. Your goal is to develop interesting and perhaps meaningful lines of inquiry, which brings us to our next question.

- *What are the characteristics of the categories that my subject possesses?*

Categories are defined by the characteristics their members share. For example, we said that "family" might fall into the category of legal institutions. What are the general characteristics of a legal institution? Again, just off the top of your head, you can probably come up with a few.

- They are governed by law.
- They are recognized and sanctioned by the state.
- They involve rights and responsibilities established by statute or legal precedent and there are consequences for violating those rights and not fulfilling those responsibilities.

The list could go on, but let's stop here and ask some questions. Do all of the social units we would include in the category of "family" have each of the characteristics we have noted? Perhaps more interesting, do they have to? In other words, can we still call a particular social unit a "family" if there are some characteristics of the category it doesn't share?

Also, are there any characteristics that seem to conflict in any way? For example, a family is both a biological relationship and a legal institution. Do you sense a possible conflict or contradiction there?

Remember, our goal here is not to provide an exhaustive list of questions about the nature of things. Rather, we want to give you the general *idea* of this way of approaching a subject and a few examples to make it clear. As you consider different subjects, you will create your own questions.

Exercise

1. Working alone or in small groups, develop some meaningful categories for the term 'family'.

2. List the general characteristics of each category.

3. List any characteristics of the categories you believe to be essential; in other words, are there characteristics a subject absolutely must have to be included in it?

4. Review your lists and observations and mark anything that seems insightful or that might offer a promising line of inquiry. Remember, your goal is to enhance your understanding of your subject and to discover what you might not have considered.

Questions about Causes and Effects

Other questions that we usually ask deal with causes and effects.

- Why do people live in families?
- What is the effect of interacting within a family on a person's everyday life?
- What has caused the current divorce rate?
- Has the growth of single parent families contributed to the increase in juvenile crime?

As you consider causes and effects of an entity, keep in mind the questions you asked about its nature. In fact, it may be impossible to answer such questions unless you have gained an understanding of its nature. For example, can you say what causes families to split up (or even determine that they have) unless you have previously determined what constitutes a family?

One basic principle you should keep in mind when considering causes and effects is the idea of agency—that something is sufficient to influence what follows. Again, this may seem so obvious that it's not worth mentioning; however, causation is seldom simple and you should remember that most effects have multiple causes. Rarely do we say that *A* is *the* cause of *B*. Rather, we may say that *A* is *one contributing* cause of *B*.

Finally, we must realize that when we name something or someone as a cause, we are also attributing responsibility for the effect that is produced. Often, when we say some person or group caused something, we may also be assigning them the moral or ethical responsibility for the results. When we do that, *our* responsibility is to be as careful as possible.

Now, we can begin asking questions about cause and effect. As before, we will provide some sample answers to help you to see where this method of inquiry might lead.

- *What agent caused my subject?*

By "agent" we mean who or what caused something to exist. For example, several factors may have acted together to reduce the number of two-parent households. Changes in the nature of work, the status of women, and the media are just a few. What are some other contributing factors?

One thing to remember is that sometimes it is useful to ask, "What agent caused my subject?" But sometimes it is not. For example, imagine that the origin of the family unit is your subject. Immediately, you might recognize that its origins are so far in the past that the question of what agent caused it to come into being is not answerable. In such cases, you may have to develop your inquiry with other questions, perhaps questions of motivation.

- *What motivation caused my subject?*

If we can identify an agent, we can examine the purpose, if any, the subject was designed to serve or consider the intended result or effect. Now we are asking why the agent acted to produce an effect.

Even if we can't identify specific agents for an event, we can sometimes find general motivations for actions. For example, we've seen that looking for agents that caused the institution of the family was not very profitable; however, we can identify or at least speculate on the human characteristics or needs that motivated the evolution of the human family.

One thing to remember when we ask about motives is that they are seldom simple.

- *What effects has my subject had in the past?*

Here, we're inquiring into the history of a phenomenon. It may seem that very recent phenomena have not had much history or much opportunity to generate many effects. However, if something has been around long enough to come to our attention, it will have created at least some effects.

For example, general recognition of families formed by same-sex marriages is relatively new. Yet there may be effects worth considering. For one thing, it has generated substantial controversy that will have social, political, and economic effects of its own. For another, the existence of these families may have already produced some effects upon their members. Do they feel more fulfilled? Are their lives more rewarding?

When we turn to subjects that have been around longer, determining effects might seem easier. Sometimes, however, that history complicates things. Phenomena that have a longer history have usually generated more effects. It may be difficult to isolate those effects, distinguish among them, and determine their significance.

For example, the effect of television on families is complex for a number of reasons. Some of them have to do with how long television has exerted its influence. Moreover, its effects are multiple and sometimes seem contradictory. People might know more about what is going on in the world than they did before the advent of television. However, family members who spend less time interacting with one another may feel a sense of isolation and alienation.

- *What effects might my subject have in the future?*

Exploring the effects a phenomenon has had in the past is largely a matter of examining its history; asking what effects it may have in the future is a matter of prediction and, in some cases, speculation. You may ask, "How can I know what effects my subject might have in the future?" The answer is, you don't have to know; just explore the possibilities.

One way to start is by looking at past effects. Can you predict what might happen based on what has happened? Can you detect a trend? Have observed effects increased or decreased in the past?

You might find it helpful to play the "what if" game. You may not know what is going to happen, but you might be able to predict that if one thing occurs, another will follow.

For example, the political climate of the United States seems related to the amount of public assistance provided to single parent families. Some conservative politicians see reduction in these programs as a means of encouraging people to create and stay in the conventional nuclear family. Some liberal politicians see the immediate needs of single-parent families as more important and resist such reductions. Consequently, you might predict that *if* the next presidential election goes to a liberal, single-parent families will receive greater assistance than if a more conservative candidate wins the White House.

When you're faced with a complex topic, don't back away from it – engage it and explore the possibilities as thoroughly as possible. Those subjects that seem initially the most challenging often contain the richest possibilities for interesting inquiries.

Exercise

1. Working alone or in small groups, list some of the agents that you think might have contributed to the decline in traditional two-parent families.

2. List the effects this decline has had in the past.

3. List possible effects this decline may have in the future.

4. Review your lists and observations and mark anything that offers a promising line of inquiry.

Questions about Value

Questions about value ask whether or not we should believe something is worthwhile. Answers to such questions constitute *value judgments*. Think about the questions of value you ask every day.

- Is Brad Pitt's new movie worth seeing?
- Would it be better to major in art or in computer programming?
- Is same-sex marriage immoral?
- Was invading Iraq the right thing to do?

Since the answers to such questions are judgments, we do not accept them as being facts and we insist on some justification for them. Very often, the justification will be found in the answers we have generated to questions about the nature of our subject and about its causes and effects. While questions about its nature and causation ask what *is*, questions of value often ask what *should be*.

Again, we'll first establish some basic principles.

Questions about value generally fall into three general categories:

- Questions of *Ethics* ask whether actions are right or wrong
- Questions of *Aesthetics* ask whether things are beautiful or not
- Questions of *Utility* ask whether something is useful or not

In considering the value of something, we will normally measure it against some criteria. There are many opinions about the *types* of criteria that are appropriate for measuring value. We normally recognize two.

One says that we should judge the worth of something on its *consequences*. If we use this theory, we would assert that an action is ethical if it produces good consequences.

The other general theory says that we should judge value on whether the action or thing conforms to a predetermined set of rules. The most familiar expressions of this sort of value system are found in the doctrines of various religions. For example, someone who adheres strictly to the Ten Commandments, as a guide to ethical behavior, has a non-consequentialist value system. Notice that those commandments do not take into account the consequences of obeying them. They don't say "Thou shalt not kill, unless the killing produces a good result;" they say just don't do it.

While there are many questions you can ask about values, we ask only two to get you started.

- ***What criteria will I use to determine the value of my subject?***

Very often, we decide value on the basis of an immediate emotional or "gut-level" response. This is not a problem when the consequences of our actions or claims are slight. However, when your actions or claims are likely to affect people's lives, you have an obligation to be careful. In such cases, you need to specify the criteria that govern your decisions.

You may also want to decide whether you will consider the value of your work on the basis of its consequences or measure it against a predetermined standard. Both types of systems have their strengths and weaknesses. As the writer, you can pick whichever system you find most acceptable, but it will be your responsibility to make sure your audience understands the basis on which you're making your judgments. In the exercise below, we'll give you some practice in deciding what types of criteria would be most appropriate for evaluating a topic like the changing family.

- ***How well does my subject meet the criteria I'm using to evaluate it?***

First, notice that "criteria" is a plural noun. You'll normally evaluate subjects on the basis of several criteria, not just one. It is rarely possible to evaluate a subject on the basis of a single criterion. Value judgments, especially when they have substantial consequences, are just not that simple.

Also, notice that the question can't really be answered with a simple yes or no; rather it's a matter of degree. We don't normally say something *absolutely* is or is not worthwhile. For example, we don't normally say a painting is completely without value just because it does not completely meet all the aesthetic criteria we might measure it against. And we normally don't reject an action as completely unethical simply because its consequences are not as positive as we might have hoped.

Finally, we'll want to consider the relative importance of the criteria. Some are likely to be more crucial to our evaluation than others. Suppose, for example, we want to evaluate the ethical behavior of scientists working on a new drug. Whether or not the drug ultimately produces good results may well be one of the criteria we consider. But is it as important to our final judgment as whether or not people were hurt in the research? Obviously, there is no simple or certain way to decide such questions. The evaluative criteria you choose will be governed by the nature of the subject, your reasoning, and your personal values.

Exercise

1. Working alone or in small groups, make a list of the criteria you might use to determine the value of the traditional, two-parent family.

2. For each criterion, state whether it involves issues of aesthetics, ethics, or utility.

3. Prioritize the criteria; that is, list them in order from the most to the least important.

4. State how you will tell whether or not your subject meets each criterion. Will you use the consequences or effects of the subject as a means of evaluating it? Or will you measure the value of the subject against some given standard, ignoring the good or bad consequences?

5. Review your lists and observations and mark anything that offers a promising line of inquiry.

Questions about Action

You probably ask questions about action all the time. If you're like most people, they range from the trivial to the momentous.

- Where should we go for lunch?

- What should I major in?

- Should I get married?

- For whom should I vote?

- What should we do about terrorism?

Notice that the common element in all these questions is the "should." In each case, the fundamental question is "What should be done?" The relationship between value and actions questions is strong.

Values often direct actions. For example, if you don't value the changes marriage will bring to your life, you probably won't get married. Whether or not you think a candidate's positions on issues are ethical will likely determine how you will vote. The value we place on revenge determines what action we take in response to terrorist attacks.

The answers to questions about action are often formed as proposals that some action be taken. Because actions can have far-reaching impacts on people's lives, they are often the most important questions we can ask. In the three previous sections, we considered questions and claims about the nature of things, causation, and value; those are matters of belief. While belief is important, it becomes something more when it leads to action. It is one thing to believe in the value of helping others; it is quite something else to join the Peace Corps and spend three years building houses in Africa or South America.

Some actions are unintentional or mindless, like running a stop sign or biting your fingernails. But most actions we might want to ask questions about are directed; that is, they are designed to serve some goal. Often as not, the place to start when considering a proposal of action is with the goal that is to be achieved.

Notice what happens when we add goals to the questions above.

- Where should we go for lunch *to save the most money*?

- Where should we go for lunch *to sit in the nicest surroundings and eat the most delicious food*?

- What should I major in *to make lots of money*?

- What should I major in *to give me interesting work to do*?

- Should I get married *if I want companionship*?

- Should I get married *if I want to have children*?

- For whom should I vote *to please my parents*?

- For whom should I vote *to provide a government that won't draft me*?

- What should we do about terrorism *to keep the most people in the world safe*?

- What should we do about terrorism *to take revenge on the terrorists*?

Obviously, the goals help make the questions more complete and, at the same time, help determine the answers.

So, our first question is:

- *What goal is the action to serve?*

Often the goal is a problem to solve. For example, one of the problems single-parent families confront is the cost of day care. Ultimately, we may ask what action we can take to solve this problem, but for right now, we're concerned only with the goal itself.

It would be easy to focus questions about action solely on problem solving, but it is important to remember that not every goal involves a problem. For example, many people recognize that having children is one of their goals. That is not, in itself, a problem, and to treat it as one will very likely distort our approach to the question of what constitutes a family or the contemporary family.

It's important to define goals carefully. If the goal is to solve a problem, this means being sure there is a genuine problem and, if so, deciding what it really is. For example, some feel the solution to problems associated with single-parent families is simply to reduce the number of them. Are single-parent families really a problem, and should our primary goal be to reduce the number of them by any means possible? Or is it the problem that most single-parent families are headed by women, and women tend to be one of the lowest paid classes in our society? If so, that would imply a completely different goal.

- *What actions could possibly achieve the goal?*

The answer to this question is simply a list of possibilities. You will find many by yourself but some you will get from others. It doesn't really matter. What is important is not to reject any possibility at this stage of the process, no matter how unlikely or unattractive it might seem as an action that will achieve the goal. As you contemplate what is on your list, some will become more attractive.

One phrase we hear quite a lot today is "thinking outside the box." It typically refers to unexpected or unconventional ideas that turn out to be worthwhile. Individuals and organizations are learning to value (and reward) this kind of thinking. The key is not to reject ideas too soon; rather, it is to discover where they might lead.

Exercise

1. Working alone or in small groups, list the goals that would support your position on the traditional, two-parent family.

2. On a scale of 1 to 10, rank the various goals. Write a brief statement of how you arrived at this ranking.

3. Make a list of conditions that stand in the way of achieving the important goals you have noted.

4. Make a list of actions that could, either completely or partially, achieve your goals. Don't be afraid to speculate.

Getting Started: A First Essay

You cannot know in advance precisely how you will develop the papers you are asked to write or the exact process you will follow to complete each assignment. The work that follows can help you achieve a deeper understanding of the issues involved in upcoming writing assignments. You have already started generating ideas about contemporary American life through your work with the Social Trends Index earlier in the chapter. As you explore these ideas further and consider what new questions to ask, you will add dimensions to your thinking and recognize what you know and what you still need to learn.

The chapter readings (Kingsolver pp. 14–18 plus the Elshtain selection below) were deliberately selected to work in tandem with data from the Social Index. The issues they explore are intended to introduce topics you may not have confronted previously, engage you in conversation, and encourage you to question both your and their authors' assumptions. As you read, note how the authors' varying perspectives can help stimulate, challenge, and broaden your understanding of what you explored through your journal activity. The readings also offer terminology that will be helpful in your exploration of a variety of subjects. By engaging in those explorations, you add your voice to discussions of significant contemporary issues.

Reading: Philosophic Reflections on the Family at Millennium's Beginning
Jean Bethke Elshtain

As an active voice on issues of democracy and family life, University of Chicago Professor Jean Elshtain is an outspoken public intellectual who chairs The Council on Families in America, The National Commission for Civic Renewal, and The Council on Civil Society. In this excerpt from her article "Philosophic Reflections on the Family at Millennium's Beginning" (2000), Professor Elshtain claims that reasserting traditional family bonds and parental roles not only affirms the moral foundations of society, but also assures the protection of children by responsible adults. She argues that the varied family units that now proliferate have denied the next generation the fundamental models for marriage and child rearing that have served the culture well for centuries. She believes that those values that define us as socialized beings and lie at the core of human community are at risk in the catastrophic collapse of the traditional two-parent family.

****

The problems of teen pregnancies, deadbeat dads, violent youth, and children in poverty are well known. But we tend to overlook a common denominator behind so many of these phenomena—the spreading collapse of marriage. With each passing year of the just-completed century, an ever smaller percentage of people in the United States was married. An even larger percentage of the nation's children lived in households absent a parent—most often the father. This figure now stands at about one-third of American children overall.

By education and training, I am a political and civil philosopher. This means that I tend to what is happening to the social and political fabric of my own society in particular and other societies in general. The evidence comes from the streets, the neighborhoods, the schools, the churches, and our homes: The eloquent and often terrifying testimony of events—violence suffered and perpetrated; children unhappy, ignored, home alone; teen mothers, isolated and hovering in drug-ridden dangerous places; teachers afraid of their students; students afraid of other students; civic leaders gazing at a precipitous decline in involvement and participation in all community activities at all levels. This is one face of America as we enter this new millennium. The evidence is overwhelming, based on hundreds of studies by reputable scholars from dozens of disciplines. Indeed, none but the individual committed to the status quo can cast his eyes over this encroaching wasteland and say, "This is good. Let's have more of it. "What do we see when we look around? We see that more and more children are growing up with little or no experience of seeing married life, hence no living examples of what it means for two people to commit themselves to one another over time. More American children every day are growing up with little or no confidence that they could be, or even want to be, in an enduring marital relationship, as the Marriage Report of the Council on Families in America argues.[1]

Mind you, I for one have no desire to marry everyone off. I recognize that many people choose not to marry and that they live rich and interesting lives and contribute to their communities in a variety of ways. No, my concern is with how difficult it has been for children to grow up in America. Because, where they are concerned, regularity in human relationships is vital, and such relations go by the names "marriage" and "family."

CULTURAL MESSAGE: ROMANCE AND SEX: YES! MARRIAGE: NO!

Over the past three or four decades, the message American children receive from the wider culture is one that is high on romance and sex but hostile or, at best, indifferent to marriage. It does not seem at all far-fetched to say that during the last century we as a society have been failing in the task of social reproduction. In other words, we have not been imparting to the next generation a set of fundamental norms and beliefs about the meaning and purposes, responsibilities and freedom, of marriage and family life.

This, in turn, has had a debilitating effect on civic life overall. Democratic civic life relies on persons who have been formed in such a way that they are capable of commitment; they understand and accept responsibility; they share a sense of stewardship about their communities; and they appreciate the fact that the creation of decent and relatively stable relationships and societies is a complex and fragile task, not an automatic outcome when human beings share a territorial space or even a bedroom.

Witness the discouraging data: In the decades 1960—1990, the percentage of out-of-wedlock births skyrocketed from 5.3 percent to 30 percent. Although as the century ended there was evidence of a small decline in the rate of out-of-wedlock births—or nonmarital births, in the terminology adopted near the end of 1996—the figures were still quite high, with about three- quarters of births to teens being nonmarital and about 25 percent of the births to women over twenty. The illegitimacy rate among blacks was about 70 percent, and that for whites about 25 percent.

If the children from such single-parent units were doing just fine, perhaps there would be no problem. But they have not been doing so: They have been at far greater risk than children from two-parent households. As well, in those same decades the divorce rate doubled or tripled, depending upon how it is calculated. As a result, the percentage of children living apart from their biological fathers rose from 17 percent to 36 percent, and it is still rising.

Juvenile violent crime also increased in the past three decades. Reports of child neglect and abuse quintupled since 1976. The teen suicide rate tripled. The New York Times and many other publications reported the facts: Children from broken homes have two to three times more behavioral and psychological problems than do children from intact homes.[2] Finally, the poverty rate of young children stood at about 25 percent at the end of the century, the highest since 1969, and family formation, or the failure to form families, has been indicted as a central causal factor in the growth of childhood poverty.[3]

Because all societies have a stake in the creation and sustaining of norms surrounding sexuality, child rearing, and other vital human activities tied to our complex social and embodied identities, all societies have attempted to regularize these activities in some way. No society has ever declared any of this to be a matter of indifference. There are many possible arrangements, of course—some more restrictive, some less. But sometimes, it seems, "less" can become "more." That is, as a general laissez-faire attitude toward social arrangements has spread, it has generated many different varieties of social troubles. Or so our recent history suggests. Ironically, the growth in "self-expression" and "individualism" appears to go hand-in-hand with a growth in fearfulness, destructive forms of dependency, and even greater social conformism as the primary reference group for the young becomes an age-specific cohort, with adults scarcely in the picture.

There are big conceptual and historical issues here. There are also simple, humble truths. The humble truth is that every child needs and deserves the love and provision of caring adults in a relationship that endures. The committed, two-married-parent family is the best environment we know anything about in which to rear children. Because it is the main teacher of the next generation—and a protector and defender of our love of, and commitment to, pluralism—it is also an irreplaceable foundation for long-term civic vitality, endurance, and flexibility.

A British observer, summarizing the data for his own society, reports that "every form of psychosocial disorder among young people—crime, suicide, depression, eating problems, vandalism, alcohol and drug abuse—can be linked to the modern-day cult of juvenile freedom, to their spending power, their moral and social independence from their parents, and their entire lifestyle of music, clothes, sex and whatever. In short, the problem is a colossal and chronic breakdown in parenting. By no means does this only apply to Britain."[4]

What we seem to have lost along the way is an earlier conceptual richness that recognized, as the Marriage in America Report argues, that marriage contained, or encompassed, at least five basic dimensions. It was viewed as, in some sense, a natural institution, flowing from basic bodily impera-tives. It was a sacramental institution, surrounded by rituals and sacral norms. It was an economic institution, an arena of both production and consumption, of human fabrication and laboring. It was a social institution, helping to create cultural forms that encouraged certain kinds of behavior and discouraged others. It was a legal entity, protected and regulated by a complex body of public and private law.

In each of these arenas, the family has sustained a series of body blows that have had the effect, over time, not so much of transforming the family with each of these five interlocked imperatives in mind but deinstitutionalizing the family by removing many previous imperatives and norms and putting nothing in their place. Let me reiterate: If what we were currently seeing were a growth in child well-being, there would be little reason to raise the alarm. But that is not what we see. . . .

INEXORABLE QUESTIONS

Children lost to society may be a growing phenomenon, but it is one we must name for what it is: a loss, a crying shame. Protecting, preserving, and strengthening family autonomy and the well-being of mothers and fathers is a way of affirming our commitment to the individual and to democratic social life. We have, it appears, lost the recognition that the rights of persons are fundamentally social. What is at stake in the family debate, and in our response to it as we enter this new millennium, is nothing less than our capacity for human sociality and community.

Here are a few concluding questions for further consideration; indeed, they are inexorable ques-tions, given my analysis:

1. What are the root causes of family disintegration? What are the effects of this deinstitutionaliza-tion?

2. Why is concern with the family a civic and ethical issue?

3. What does the family (mothers and fathers, brothers and sisters, grandparents, uncles, aunts, cousins, etc.) do that no other human institution can?

4. What is the role or responsibility of individuals, communities, business, and government in dealing with family issues?

5. How can we stem the tide of out-of-wedlock births, teenage violence, and family breakdown without enhancing states' avowedly coercive apparatuses?

These are serious issues. If we are not up to the task, this twenty-first century will be a tale of further coarsening of social life and deepening pressure on democratic society to enhance its coercive pow-ers to save us from ourselves. If we hope to forestall this unhappy prospect, we must tend to our social ecology before it is too late. The family—alas!—now belongs on the list of endangered species.

[1]Marriage Report of the Council on Families in America (New York: Institute for American Values, March 1995).

[2]Susan Chira, "Struggling to Find Stability When Divorce Is a Pattern," *New York Times*, 19 March 1995, 17.

[3]This data is summarized in the Marriage Report.

[4]Clifford Longley, "Valuing the Family," *Tablet*, 10 June 1995, 735.

Questions for Discussion and Writing

1. What do you think Jean Elshtain wants you, the reader, to understand about families and what is happening to them? Why do you think this? What is your initial response to her ideas?

2. Elshtain attributes many current social problems, at least in part, to the collapse of marriage. What is the current state of marriage in the United States? Is it really collapsing? Explain.

3. What social problems does Elshtain mention? What are the causes of these problems? Is the collapse of marriage the only cause? Is it the major cause? Explain. What other effects might the collapse of marriage produce?

4. How serious are the problems Elshtain mentions? On what criteria is Elshtain basing her value judgments? What action, if any, is Elshtain proposing?

5. What do you think are the basic strengths and weaknesses of Elshtain's essay in terms of getting you interested in the topic and convincing you of her ideas? What does she do in her essay that is worth remembering? Adopting? Avoiding?

6. If you could ask for anything in the essay to be clearer or to be more complete and definite, what would it be? Why?

Making Connections

1. Elshtain provides detailed and provoking insights into the dilemmas and challenges faced by today's families. How do her perceptions square with the Social Trends entries found earlier in the chapter?

2. While Elshtain bemoans the breakdown of the traditional two-parent household, Barbara Kingsolver (pp. 14–18) contends that much current lamentation over the alleged "collapse of the American family" is largely unwarranted. What kind of support does each author provide for her views? Can you find areas in either reading in which the supporting evidence is not specific or concrete? Explain. Which author has most influenced your thinking about families and what is happening to them? Why?

Short Essay Assignments

1. At the end of her essay, Jean Elshtain presents a list of questions we need to ask about families and what is happening to them. Among them is: "What does the family do that no other institution can?" What answers does she provide in her essay? Based on what you have learned, experienced, and observed, how would you reply? How might Barbara Kingsolver respond to Elshtain's question?

2. On the one hand, Kingsolver asserts that "if 'intact' in modern family-values jargon means living quietly desperate in the bell jar, then hip-hip-hooray for 'broken.'" On the other hand, Elshtain maintains that "protecting, preserving, and strengthening family autonomy and the well-being of mothers and fathers is a way of affirming our commitment to the individual and to democratic social life." Which argument seems more convincing? Why? Do you think there are ways to combine or reconcile the two views, rather than see them as mutually exclusive? Explain.

3. When we read something that gives us additional information about an issue, it often changes the way we understand the issue. Which text caused you to reevaluate your notions regarding the traditional nuclear family? Why?

4. The entries from the Social Trends Index (pp. 7–9) present more than just facts and figures: they also reveal values, attitudes, and practices in contemporary society. Select one entry (or perhaps several related ones) that particularly interests you, and write an essay in which you describe the issue and present your conclusions about it. Or choose a topic about contemporary life that is suggested by the chapter readings. Concerned citizens often discuss such topics in the media, in academia, and in political forums, as well as in vast numbers of private conversations. Through this paper, you will add your voice to their discussions. Because this assignment is more open-ended than the others, the following prompts can help to ensure that your paper springs from the readings and discussions.

To Help You Get Started

- As you consider various topics for your paper, recall the ways in which the issues that the topic involves have affected your own life. Your personal experience is a relevant and valuable resource.
- Spend ample time with the chapter readings to consider other voices speaking on the American experience. Then, contribute your own ideas to modify or dispute those other voices. The readings offer positions, ideas, and terminology that other writers have already used. Putting this knowledge to work can help you explore the topics that

intrigue you from a variety of perspectives. The questions at the end of each reading may also help you identify an interesting topic.

- You may also conduct additional research among such sources as newspapers, news-magazines, journals, and books that discuss aspects of contemporary life.
- As you develop a plan for your essay, ask questions about the assumptions you are making and evaluate whether or not your examples and evidence adequately support your conclusions.
- Finally, whatever topic you choose, be sure to adequately represent the views of the authors you have read. For your readers, that will deepen and enrich your authority. Also, carefully review the student essay below, especially the questions at the end of the paper.

Reviewing a Student Essay

Victoria's work shows an affinity for expanding her thinking by using ideas from a variety of sources. One source is David Elkind's "The Future of Childhood" (1992), which depicts dramatic social changes that have upset the traditional values and structure of the American family. Having also read excerpts from Juliet Shor's *The Overworked American* (1991), which describes the effects of overwork on the harried American lifestyle, Victoria was able to make connections between these readings and certain Index entries she had explored in earlier freewrites. Following the essay and discussion questions, you will find a reflective piece in which Victoria examines her writing experience.

Victoria Charles   Charles 1

EXP 101, Section 007

Professor Saint-Amand

April 5, 2000

Thoughts on the American Family

Americans are the richest people in the world. They enjoy the highest standard of living and have more disposable income than any other country on the planet. According to recent indexes from *Harper's*, Americans spend the majority of their leisure time watching television, eating and shopping in that order. In cross-country comparisons, Americans have been found to spend more time shopping than anyone else (Schor 44). Shopping has become the great American pastime. This statistic may seem disturbing, but it is only a symptom of the dysfunctional value system at play in contemporary America. This value system, which places material goods above all else, is not just harmful to the psyche of the individual, it is most destructive to the American family.

Americans generally feel that acquiring material things is a way to prove themselves as people, to show that they have "gotten somewhere" in the world. The need to have has replaced the need to become. For most of the people in my own peer group, becoming rich is their highest aspiration. In other words, money is primary and everything else is secondary. We want to have more than our parents had; we want to impress our friends and neighbors. If we were raised in a working class family, we want to rise to the middle class. People with roots in the middle class aspire to join the upper crust elite. What happens along the way is that we become fixated on status symbols. We are not after wealth itself, but the illusion of wealth. We want the things that represent wealth. New cars, big houses, cell phones, etc. According to Harvard professor Juliet B. Schor, we are living in a "consumer's paradise". Advertisers and marketing experts have made products irresistible to us. We are spending a higher percentage of what we make and with consumer debt on the rise we are spending more money that we have not yet earned. This is what Schor calls the "consumerist treadmill". We have to work to pay for what we already have, and we need to work more to afford the next irresistible product that comes along. This cycle of work and spend is a major influence in the breakdown of the family structure.

Adults and especially parents are suffering from what child psychologist David Elkind calls a "time fatigue". Because of the increasing demands on parents to provide their families with more and better things, parents are forced to work more days and longer hours. Parents have less free time to spend at home, and when they are with their children they are exhausted, stressed-out, and unwilling or unable to give their children the attention they need. Americans report that they only have sixteen and a half hours of leisure a week, after the obligations of job and household are taken care of (Schor 9). "More than fifty percent of women are in the work force and some sixty percent of these women have children under the age of six" (Elkind 39).

Parents have less of a role in their children's lives. Because of hired child-care providers and the use of television as an "electronic baby-sitter", children are more exposed to outside influences, and the parents have less say in the shaping of the child's morals and values. Elkind calls this the Permeable Family Model and maintains that "Now that children are living in Permeable Families with — thanks to television — a steady diet of overt violence, sexuality, substance abuse and environmental degradation, we can no longer assume that they are innocent"(40). Not only are children no longer innocent, they are left to decipher the message of the media on their own without parental guidance. According to a *Harper's Index* from twenty years ago, the total number of hours of television watched in American households in 1983 was 213,000,000,000 (Krieger 34). Another entry from that same *Index* noted that watching television was the number one activity that Americans look forward to. This was before the advent of the Internet, yet another way for the media to invade the home. In my household the television came on at three when we got home from school and stayed on until nine or ten at night when we went to sleep. That's about fifty hours of television a week.

Charles 3

The message children are receiving from the media is very clear: Buy, spend and consume. Along with television programs come vast amounts of advertising. A half hour show has about eighteen minutes of commercials, commercials that have been engineered to make whoever is watching believe that their lives will not be complete without a certain product. This aggravates and accelerates the consumerist treadmill. Parents take on more work in order to buy more things, and have less free time. Children spend more time watching television because their parents are too exhausted to engage them in activities or conversation. Parents attempt to ease their guilt over not being available by buying things for their children, and as a result parents become more isolated from their children and their spouses. Demonstrations of love and affection are in the form of the giving and receiving of material things. What happens is that families lose the ability to communicate with each other. They get lost in the world of the physical. They use material posses-sions to make themselves feel fulfilled and to replace the bond that is lost between the members of the family.

What results is a generation of children who are emotionally stunted. Children are more violent, more suicidal and more promiscuous than ever before. "One in four teenagers drinks to excess every two weeks" and teenage pregnancy is on the rise (Elkind 41). The children and teenag-ers of America today are the products of families that have no solid foundation. Families may be well-intentioned, but are too lost in the materialism and pop-culture of American life to function as a family system. If this trend continues, what kind of environment will our children's children be raised in? What we have to ask ourselves is how the message we want to give our children can be heard above the din of the ever-invasive media, and how true bonds can be re-established in the American family.

Works Cited

Elkind, David. "The Future of Childhood." *Psychology Today* May/June 1992:38–81. Print.

"Harper's Index." *Harper's* March 1999:12. Print.

Schor, Juliet B. *The Overworked American: The Unexpected Decline of Leisure*. NY: Harper Collins, 1991. Print.

Assessing the Quality of the Essay

1. Are the subject and purpose of Victoria's essay clearly stated? What is the main point in her essay?

2. What does she hope to accomplish with this essay? Is she only trying to inform her readers, or is she arguing a specific position on an issue? Is she trying to motivate her readers to take some action? How can you tell?

3. What audience does she seem to be addressing? Does her essay seem to be slanted toward a particular age group or socioeconomic class? Does it seem more appropriate for a college educated than for a general audience? How can you tell?

4. Although Victoria's essay is based on two readings not included in this book (Elkind's "The Future of Childhood" and Schor's The Overworked American), can you, as readers, easily follow their contributions to her discussion? Has Victoria adequately represented their pertinent points? Explain.

5. How well does this essay achieve its goal? How might it be made more effective?

Victoria's Reflections

Since early adolescence I have had a sense that something was lacking in the values of American culture. I believe that I can speak for most of my peers when I say this. Until recently I have not been able to articulate exactly what this "something" is. It became more and more obvious that our society is not accommodating to the American family or to children. It is more and more difficult for families to survive and for children to grow up mentally and emotionally stable. Although I felt and sensed these problems in my own family and in the people around me, it was still unclear exactly what the problems were and where they came from. Reading the essays of Elkind and Schor helped to crystallize the ideas that were already forming in my head. It was very helpful to read other people's theories and build on them for my own essay. Some of their thoughts I agreed with and others did not ring true, but they were all useful in guiding me toward my own conclusions. They forced me to look at issues I had never considered before. I was confronted by not only the expert's ideas, but also the facts and statistics that substantiated their ideas. Writing this essay forced me to analyze feelings I have held for a long time about my own culture. These vague feelings of something being wrong became a specific hypothesis backed up with real facts. I also was forced to ask myself what this meant for me personally and how it directly affected my own life. My hope is that these beliefs I have formed will continue to grow and adapt as I learn more and as I am exposed to new ideas.

In many ways, Victoria's reflections demonstrate the whole range of behaviors that come into play in a typical writing assignment. As her reflections indicate, she already has thoughts and feelings about the topic; she has, in the terms we have been using in this chapter, some sense of what the issue or problem is, what its causes might be, what its harms are, and how she can improve the situation.

Guidelines for Assessing Your Writing

Once you have completed a draft, get some distance from it by letting it sit for a day or two. Like most writers, you probably have become attached to what you have written, and you will need some time before you can review your draft with detachment and objectivity. To aid in the process of revision, we suggest that you use the following questions.

- Does your paper stay within the limits of the topic? Do any of your sentences or paragraphs stray from the stated purpose? Did your position remain consistent throughout the paper or did it alter as you developed the topic? If it altered, have you accounted for any change?

- Are your body paragraphs complete? Does each one introduce a topic, offer supporting evidence, and discuss the connection between that evidence and your position? Do you have sufficient evidence, or do you need more examples to provide an adequate defense for your position? Is the supporting material clearly relevant to your subject? Have you provided sufficient documentation for your sources by mentioning authors and titles?

- Would your paper benefit by a reordering of your discussion? Have you weighed the value of the various examples you present in terms of their effect upon the reader? Have you arranged your examples accordingly?

- Is the final paragraph effective? Does it give unity to your thought process, bring the main point into focus, and build on the discussion you have asked your reader to join?

2 — *Entering the World of Your Subject*

In Chapter 1, we offered some of the general tools you will need to get started on your inquiries:

- An introduction to the academic and professional community in which you will locate your principal audience. Within that community you will also find collaborators.
- Ideas on how to make your reading more effective and productive.
- Four types of questions that lead to productive lines of inquiry.

We also provided some questions for discussion, as well as short writing assignments, to help you in focusing your thoughts and to give you some practice with the first stages of the writing process. Of course, that is just the beginning. In this chapter we want you to explore questions in more detail by:

- Using specific invention concepts to probe your existing understanding of subjects;
- Refining your reading skills and finding ways to report on material that is relevant to your topic;
- Generating a draft that is suitable for sharing with an audience.

To help you get started, read through the following array of facts and statistics. The listings will prove as engaging as what you found in Chapter 1. They are sure to produce some energetic exchanges with your friends and classmates.

Social Trends Index II

[1]Number of U.S. daily newspapers in 2000: 1,415

Number of companies that control the majority of those newspapers: 6

[2]Number of people who live below the government's official poverty line ($20,650 for a family of four): 39 million

[3]Proportion of those in poverty who are children under the age of eighteen: 1 in 5

[4]Percentage of the adults in 2006 requesting emergency food aid who are working people with jobs: 37%

[5]Proportion of homeless people (in 29 cities across the nation) employed in a full-or part-time job in 2000: 1 in 5

[6]Percentage increase, between 1984–2006, in the number of full-time workers who are paid minimum wage: 50%

[7]Proportion of the U.S. population that earns less than $10 per hour: 1 in 4

[8]Difference in average family income between the top 5 percent of the earnings distribution and the bottom 20 percent:

In 1979: 10: 1; In 1989: 16: 1; In 1999: 19:1; In 2006: 22:1

[9]Difference in pay between a typical CEO and typical factory worker:

In 1980: 42:1; In 1999: 419:1; In 2007: 431:1

Ratio in Japan: 55:1

Ratio in France and Germany: 11:1

[10]Average increase in income for the top 1 percent of households: $465,700, or 42.6%, after adjusting for inflation.

Increase for the poorest fifth: $200, or 1.3 %

For the middle fifth: $2,400, or 4.3 percent.

[11]Income gap between generations (earnings among age 45-64 vs 18-24):

In 1950: +34%

In 1960: +62%

In 1999: +154%

[12]Chances that one could lose his or her health insurance coverage in 1996: 1 in 1,000

In 2004: 1 in 38

[13]Number of people who did not have health insurance in 2006: 47 million

[14]Percentage of former welfare recipients making their own way in the job market: 62%

[15]Odds against a typical welfare recipient's landing a job at an hourly wage of $8.89: 97:1

[16]Reduction from 2002 to 2003 in federal spending to implement the No Child Left Behind Act: $1,200,000,000

[17]Percentage of the $548 billion allocated by the government that went to elementary and secondary education during 2006: 8.9%

[18]Rank of the prison system among the fastest growing sectors of government employment: 1

[19]Percentage of charitable contributions going to programs that help the poor: less than 10%.

[20]Percent of philanthropy funneled to support the institutions of the already-advantaged – museums, libraries, orchestras, the arts: 90%

[21]Average amount of time that a black American waits for a kidney transplant, in months: 44

Average amount of time that an Asian American waits, in months: 48

Average amount of time that a white American waits, in months: 23

Predicted time a person will have to wait for a kidney transplant in 2010: 10 years

[22]Average number of American blacks who have moved to the South each day since 1986: 349

Average percentage of blacks in the New York City area who would have to move for the races there to be evenly distributed: 80

[23]Proportion of African-American women to Caucasian women who will die in childbirth in 2007: 4/1

[24]Number of countries that have a lower rate of infant mortality than the U.S.: 39

[25]Amount the World Health Organization estimates it would cost to reduce by half the 1.1 million annual deaths caused by malaria: $1 billion

[26]Amount the Pfizer drug company made from 2006 sales of its anti-impotence pill Viagra: $1.2 billion

[27]Percentage who say Americans treated each other with greater respect in the past: 73%

Sources:

[1] The American Society of Newspaper Editors 2007

[2] The 2007 Health and Human Services

[3] U.S. Census Bureau's 2006 Status Report on Hunger and Homelessness

[4] The U.S. Conference of Mayors' 2006 Status Report on Hunger and Homelessness

[5] The U.S. Conference of Mayors' 2006 Status Report on Hunger and Homelessness

[6] U.S. Department of Labor – Bureau of Labor Statistics 2006

[7] Associated Press 2006

[8] Eitzen, Stanley D. "The Fragmentation of Social Life," *Vital Speeches*, July 1, 2000. U.S. Census Bureau 2006.

[9] Eitzen, Stanley D. "The Fragmentation of Social Life," *Vital Speeches*, July 1, 2000. 2007 World Prout Assembly

[10] Aron-Dine, Aviva, "New Data Show Income Concentration Jumped Again in 2005," Center on Budget and Policy Priorities.

[11] Males, Mike. <http://earthlink.net/~mmales/Harpers.txt> (Also see Males, Mike. *The Scapegoat Generation*, Monroe, ME: Common Courage Press, 1996.)

[12] Landon, Larry. *Danger Ahead*, NY: John Wiley & Sons, 1997;

[13] McClatchy Washington Bureau 2006

[14] U.S. Human Services Department 2006

[15] Harper's Index, *Harper's Magazine*, 1990–2001.

[16] "Matters of Scale", *Worldwatch* (2002–2004).

[17] McClatchy Washington Bureau Newspapers 2007

[18] 2007 Federal Bureau of Prisons

[19] Monetary Herald 2006

[20] Monetary Herald 2006

[21] U.S. Medicine, June 2006

[22] Harper's Index, *Harper's Magazine* 1990–2001.

[23] *The American Prospect* 2007

[24] 2006 CIA World Factbook

[25] "Matters of Scale", *Worldwatch* (1999–2001).

[26] Viagra Official Site

[27] *Aggravating Circumstances: A Status Report on Rudeness in America.* Steve Farkas, Public Agenda, and others. Prepared for the Pew Charitable Trust. (Public Agenda, New York, New York) 2002.

Exercise

To increase your curiosity, try the approach introduced in Chapter 1 (p. 21). Divide a page of your journal down the middle. Use the left column for Index entries that you find significant or interesting. Use the right column for commentary, for responding to the material with questions or insights that will help you in following up a particular line of thought.

Now, list the same entries that you selected for this exercise and answer the following questions.

1. Does the entry ring true? Why or why not?

2. What additional evidence might convince you?

3. Does the entry bother you? Why or why not?

4. If the entry rings true, what else might happen as a result? What general effect would that have? What effect would it have on you?

5. What action should be taken about the situation described by the entry? Why? What effect would this action have on you?

Facts Don't Lie?

The word "fact" seems like such a hard, clean word—one that cuts through much of the confusion and discord our arguments involve. Either something happened or it didn't. Either something exists or it doesn't. But like every other word in our language, the word "fact" has its areas of uncertainty, its "range" of meanings. We often say, "Facts speak for themselves." Unfortunately, this is not always the case. Not only are supposed "facts" sometimes hotly contested, but also what they tell us about the world—what they mean—is often in dispute as well, even in the supposedly "objective" and "certain" realm of the sciences.

Most "reasonable" people consider a fact to be something real and true, in the sense that it actually occurred in time and space and not just in the mind of the observer, and that its occurrence is something that can be demonstrated in a logical manner to a variety of potential observers. A simplified version of this might be to say that a fact is something that "most reasonable people reasonably think happened." When put this way, it's easy to spot the areas of uncertainty: What makes a person reasonable? What makes an explanation logical? How can we know the certainty of anything apart from our measurement and perception of it?

What this means for anyone using "facts" to support any kind of argument is that care must be taken to first understand how the phenomenon or occurrence was defined; how it was measured and by whom; and what meaning(s) can be assigned to it.

Let us take, for an example, one of the "facts" reported in the Social Trends Index above:

Number of people who live below the government's official poverty line ($20,650 for a family of four): 39 million.

Our first question might be: by whom and how was it determined that below $20,650 represented "poverty"? Wouldn't the amount of money vary depending on a whole host of circumstances: whether the people owned a house or rented; what ages the children were; what climate and geographical area they lived in; whether they could grow some of their own food or not; whether they had health insurance or not and so on?

Then we might wonder how the people were counted. Wouldn't we expect the poor to be less likely to remain in one place and to be less likely to be "officially" registered anywhere? Wouldn't the category include many of those who are in the country illegally? Shouldn't we expect the number to be much greater than the one "officially" recorded?

And, of course, there's the whole matter of definition. Does poverty mean difficulty in providing adequate food and shelter? Or is it more a matter of not having the "extras" most Americans have? Is there really a dramatic difference between a family of four earning $20,650 and one earning $20,655?

As this brief discussion illustrates, whenever we seek to understand complicated economic and social issues, we need to be thoughtful and careful. We have to guard against our tendency to readily accept what we see in print, to "trust" what we're told by people in authority or with credentials, and to quickly accept "facts" that seem to support our intuitions or previous experiences. The next time somebody tells us "Facts don't lie," we might think to ourselves: "Well, they don't lie still, either."

Pursuing the Inquiry: Becoming a Native

Now that you have begun to explore certain issues, you'll want to go a little further into the "world" of your subject. You should start by realizing that you probably already know more than you think you do; you just need to make what you do know explicit.

Imagine a crew of space aliens landing on earth just in time for the Super Bowl. Knowing nothing of our culture but intent on studying it, they focus their attention on the game. Imagine further that their civilization has no concept of sport, much less any understanding of the massive and complex productions of our professional sports. What do they see, and what are they likely to make of it?

They observe the physical details of the event; but, having no understanding of the context, will they interpret those details correctly? For example, we see the elaborate padding worn by the players as having a protective function. However, our aliens could just as easily note that it magnifies many of the physical attributes of the human male—musculature, head, and shoulders. Put that together with the display of female attributes exhibited by the cheerleaders, and the aliens might well conclude the whole spectacle is a mating ritual. The egg-shaped ball so vigorously pursued by both sides would certainly support such an interpretation. Or they might just as easily interpret it as a religious ritual or military campaign.

Being aliens in our world, they do not understand what seems to us, as natives, second nature. They do not understand the significance of the actions and events taking place in the stadium. Indeed, they may not even recognize important aspects of the event itself—its history, conventions, and constraints. What is meaningful to natives is not necessarily meaningful to aliens.

When you begin your inquiry into a new subject, you are, to some extent, an alien exploring a new world. Through the process of inquiry, you will become, or at least learn to think like, a native; your observations and ideas will become more meaningful; and your assertions about the subject will be more likely to achieve the goal of understanding.

Here we offer you three tools to help you become a native—an insider—as you think and write about a subject: *clarifying, extending*, and *restructuring*. Following our explanation of each tool, you'll find several invention techniques that will help you to develop your thoughts and generate a text on whatever subject you are approaching. You should note that there is no necessary connection between the invention techniques and the specific tool under which they're placed. For example, freewriting is not used just in "clarifying" situations; it's useful in the invention stage of almost any writing situation.

Clarifying

You will never begin an inquiry in total ignorance of the subject. Like our space aliens, you at least know what you have observed about the phenomenon. But, of course, you actually know much more than that. You live in this society and have at least some understanding of the societal context in which the phenomenon occurs. Your understanding of your subject and its context may be vague, tentative, or even dead wrong; but it is a place to begin. The first thing to do is clarify that understanding. Make what you think explicit by exploring its implications in writing. Here we will offer you some techniques that will help you do just that.

❑   *Freewriting*

Have you ever begun a writing assignment and found yourself almost paralyzed? This is a common experience for many writers. It comes from worrying too much about getting it "right" or producing something good. Of course, you will ultimately want to do that, but it shouldn't be your main concern at the start of the project. Freewriting is a way to begin. You just explore possibilities by putting words on the page, without caring too much what they are at this point.

Here's the process:

Take up pencil and paper or sit down at the keyboard with a general subject in mind. Set yourself a time limit, say, five minutes. Then, without really thinking about it, just start putting down words . . . any words . . . one after the other. Don't think about sentence structure, spelling, or any of the mechanical conventions of writing. Don't even worry about making sense. Don't go back and read what you've written and, above all, don't go back to correct anything. Just keep the pencil moving or the keys clicking until the time is up. You don't have to write fast, but you do have to write steadily, without stopping for anything. If you can't think of anything to say, write, "I can't think of anything to say."

Now, stop and read what you've written. You may find that most of it is nonsense. But you may also find some little gems buried in the muck, some striking ideas or bits of insight that may surprise you. Underline and save them. Also, can you find a general theme or central idea that runs through your freewriting? It may or may not be stated explicitly. If so, write a single sentence that expresses that theme or idea.

In the freewrite that follows, note how student Sarah Lynne begins the process of exploring some questions raised by the Index entries presented at the beginning of this chapter.

```
Lots of appalling statistics — number of people living below the poverty line
(many of them kids). Number of adults who work and can't feed their families.
Number of homeless people who also work. What does this say about our soci-
ety? Other unsettling statistics — For example, more full-time workers than
ever before are paid minimum wage. I think the federal minimum wage is still
under $6 hr. That's about $20,000 a year, barely above the official poverty
line. The minimum wage in some states like Massachusetts and Maine is above
the federal minimum but it's still not enough. Then there's the 47 million
people without health insurance. It seems like every presidential candidate
is calling for health care reform. I wonder if any of their plans will make
a real difference. The statistic that really got to me was the one that said
that between 2002 and 2003 funding for "No Child Left Behind" was cut by over
a billion dollars. Where did the money go? Homeland security? The wars in
Afghanistan and Iraq? Either way, the cut is hard to justify when you con-
sider that several of the statistics from the Index show a huge income gap
between those who earn the least and those who earn the most — and the gap
keeps growing larger, much more so in the U.S. than in Japan or France or
Germany . . . .I could go on, but really, it's what's behind these statistics
that really counts. I have to figure that out before I can find something worth
writing about . . .I wonder.
```

Sarah's example demonstrates that a key element in all successful writing is keeping the writing moving. Generating a free flow of ideas helps you get started, even if your direction is not always clear.

Now, repeat the process. It's not unusual for good writers to do a dozen or more freewritings as they begin a project. It helps them move toward a focus, and it helps clarify their knowledge of the subject. One way to find that focus is to combine the freewriting process with the types of questions we introduced in Chapter 1.

For example, take a topic from Sarah's freewrite, "the extent of poverty in the U.S.," a subject of increasing concern these days. You might begin with a freewrite on the general topic. But you might also want to focus your subsequent free writings a little more tightly on questions about the nature, causes and effects, and consequences of poverty in our society, as well as on what actions we might want to take regarding the issue. This tighter focus should not be constraining, and you shouldn't worry if you find yourself wandering away from it as you freewrite. Just begin with the question in mind. It should stimulate your thoughts, not constrain them.

Journal Activity

The following exercise should take you no more than an hour. The key is to get some thoughts down on paper.

1. Using the process described above, do a five-minute freewrite with a general subject derived from the Index entries in your mind. Possible topics include the extent of poverty in the U.S., the plight of the working poor, the separation between classes at the economic extremes, and differences in opportunity.

   • Write steadily, without stopping.
   • When the time is up, take a minute or two to read through what you've written to look for interesting points. Underline them.
   • Take just a few seconds to write a single sentence that expresses some general statement about what you've written.

2. Do a five-minute freewrite with questions *about the nature of your subject* in mind.

   • Begin by taking a couple of minutes (no longer) to jot down two or three questions about the facts of your subject. Also, note terms that need defining. (You may want to review the material on "Types of Questions" in Chapter 1.) Read the questions out loud to put them in your mind, then put the paper you've written them on out of sight.
   • Freewrite for five minutes. Again, don't worry if you begin to wander away from your questions. When the time is up, read through what you've written, again underlining interesting phrases or ideas before writing a single general comment about the content.

3. Repeat the process with questions about the *causes and effects* of your subject, questions about its *value or consequences*, and questions about *what action we can or should take* regarding it.

Collaborative Activity

Working in small groups, share the freewriting you did in the previous exercise.

• Pick one of your freewrites, the one that seems to offer the most interesting ideas or striking insights.

• Read it out loud to the group. As you read, the other group members should quickly jot down ideas that are interesting.

• After each reading, the group should discuss the ideas they've written down, looking for productive lines of inquiry.

• At the end of the activity, group members should give their written comments about the freewritings to the authors.

❑ *Clustering*

Another technique that many writers, especially the visually oriented, find useful is clustering. Clustering is similar to freewriting in that it is based on free-association and on not becoming inhibited or constrained by worries about getting the "right answer." The idea is to gather or group related ideas. You'll want to work quickly and express your ideas very briefly in single words or short phrases.

Here's the process:

- Write your subject in the center of a blank sheet of paper. Draw a circle around it.

- Around the circle, write words that relate in some way to your subject. How they relate is not important. Draw circles around these subordinate words and draw lines connecting them to your main subject.

- Now, think about each subordinate word and write words that relate in some way to them. Again, draw circles around them and connect them by drawing lines to the "parent" idea.

- If you continue this process for very long, you will wind up with a page full of many circles and lots of connected ideas . . . exactly what you want.

This will be easier to see with an example. We'll follow through with the topic of "poverty" Sarah worked on in the previous section.

- First, Sarah writes "the working poor" in the middle of a blank page.

- Next, she jots down things that come to mind when she thinks about the working poor.

  - She thinks about who these people are—their gender, their age, their life situations.
  - Based on some reading, additional factors come to her mind, including affordable housing, cash and food stamp benefits, education and training programs, transportation vouchers, child care, health care, minimum wage . . .
  - Narrative and statistical data from published material also figure into her thinking.

- Next she writes down ideas related to the subordinate terms.

When she finishes, her diagram looks something like Figure 2.1.

Journal Activity

Use clustering to generate ideas about the subject you worked on in the "Freewriting" section.

  1. Write the title of your subject in the middle of a blank sheet of paper. Draw a circle around it.

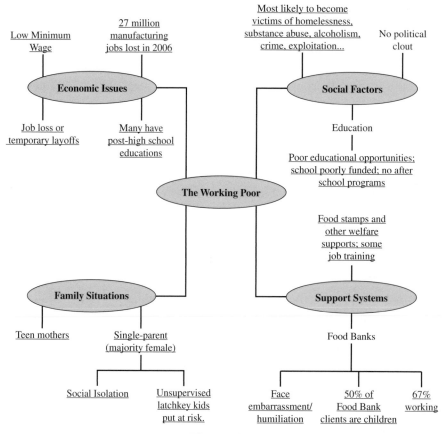

Figure 2.1

2. Working quickly and without stopping to think too much about what you are doing, write 4-6 terms, ideas, practices, phenomena, etc. that relate to your subject. Draw circles around each one and then draw connecting lines to the circle in the center.

3. Write several related ideas around each of these subordinate ideas. Again . . . circles and connecting lines.

In theory, you can continue this process until you run out of paper or patience. In practice, three or four levels of clustering are probably enough.

Collaborative Activity

Working in small groups, discuss how each idea in your diagram relates to the overall topic. Be prepared to respond to these questions.

- How are my ideas linked?
- How would I rank these ideas? Are some more important than others?

As you share your work, jot down any new ideas that come to you and consider how they might contribute to your understanding of your subject.

Extending

Once you've clarified your understanding of a subject, your next job is to extend that understanding – add new information to what you already have.

Sometimes, especially with complex or unfamiliar subjects, you don't know enough to ask meaningful questions. For example, as you worked through the journal activities in the previous section, you may have hit spots where you simply didn't know enough to proceed very effectively—specific blank spots that needed filling in. In these cases, you can use the four types of questions—nature, causation, value, and action—to focus your efforts.

Other times, you may have a better idea of just how to extend your knowledge. In either case, you'll have to go outside yourself and consult others. Here we offer two techniques for extending your understanding of a subject: the *Reporter's Formula* and *Brainstorming*.

❑ *Reporter's Formula*

The Reporter's Formula consists of six questions (mainly questions of fact) traditionally used by news reporters to generate complete accounts of events. These are sometimes thought of as "five Ws and an H."

- Who participated in the event?
- What actions did they take?
- Where did the event occur?
- When did the even occur?
- Why did it occur? Why did the participants take the actions they did?
- How did they go about it?

This technique is most useful in describing concrete examples of behaviors or phenomena related to your subject. You may find that this technique will also help show where your understanding is thin and where you need to focus your efforts to extend it.

Since this technique is strongest in identifying and exploring a specific, concrete event, let's observe how Sarah uses the Reporter's Formula to explore, in some detail, her work experience at a food pantry. Keep in mind that, by the end of her exploration, she should be able to say, "On this date, at this time, these specific things happened in this specific location, and these specific people took these real, specific actions." The result should be something like an outline for a news story. You can explore the whys and the hows later.

Here is the entry from Sarah's journal. You probably can tell from some of her inserts that she combined what she knows from her work experience with what she has learned from reading.

Who participated in the event?

- Experiencing a sudden loss of income, a neighbor's middle class family shows up for food. They have two children not yet of school age. If they were, they could be assured a healthy meal through the school lunch program.

- Lots of children accompany their families to the Food Bank. One Food Bank worker told me that at least 50% of the total number of recipients are children under twelve.

- Another volunteer said that the primary source of income for 75% of recipients is a job, retirement or disability. She added that 50% more food bank recipients have post-high school educations compared to the national average. A friend I work with said that 67% of people who request such emergency food services have jobs.

What actions did they take?

- Some arrive earlier than necessary to receive services.
- Recipients form a line around the block.
- One young mother asked for more food than I could give her.
- Most do not communicate with each other or our staff.
- Some only come in once. Others are there each week.

Where did the event occur?

- One pantry I visited is located in a mid-size coastal city, population about 358,000.
- Another was in a middle class suburb.
- The pantry where I work is housed in a church basement.

When did the event occur?

- The pantry in my town is open Monday, Wednesday, Friday from 9am to 12pm.

Why did it occur?

- Loss of income (from being laid off, being injured, getting divorced, and so forth) forces people to food banks (important here to note that 2.7 million jobs in manufacturing alone were lost between 2001 through 2003).

- Seniors and the disabled on a fixed income face high costs of medical prescriptions to keep them alive and healthy; they sometimes have to choose between filling prescriptions, buying food, or paying rent.

- A quick Internet survey of city, state, and federal government statistics show the national growing need for food banks.

  ✓ Over 150,000 people in the San Francisco area seek emergency food from their food bank. In Boston it's 400,000 a year.

  ✓ In Washington State, which reports the second worst hunger level in the nation, 630,000 people visit neighborhood food banks a year; 40% are children.

Why did the participants take the actions they did?

- A volunteer who staffs the local pantry where I work said that some eligible recipients just don't come for help. I know that some don't go because they are not part of the welfare system to know about the services. But that can't be the only explanation. In several of my classes, professors have stressed the importance of feeling useful and necessary in the world. Quite a contrast to how it must feel to have to ask for help. Could the poverty experience be one of shame and humiliation? That's an interesting aspect of this that I had not considered, although the signals were there . . . one man wouldn't look at me head on; a woman didn't call me by my name though she knew it. They just moved quickly by the fresh produce I was giving out and headed for the canned goods.

- I suspect it's much the same for the working poor. Working at low-wage jobs to survive has got to increase that feeling of shame for most people. One woman struggling to make ends meet said, "We don't go as much we need to. Who wants to stand in line outside on the street for everyone else to see?"

Like many volunteers, Sarah saw that poverty is not a mere statistic on an economic screen. Through the Reporter's Formula, she was able to extend her understanding of the realities of the problem. She discovered something not obvious or immediately apparent—a part of American society bypassed by the American Dream.

Journal Activity

Think of a moment that offered you a unique insight into the subject you worked on in the previous section. Perhaps you saw something at a local store, during a TV program, or in your local paper. Or maybe it occurred when you volunteered to help others. Once you've identified the situation, use your journal to write down responses to the Reporter's Formula questions. Make your responses as complete as possible. For example, when telling where the situation took place, don't just say Wal-Mart;

provide as detailed a description as you can. Who was involved? How did they appear? What happened? Why do you think it happened? What was the outcome? What might it lead you to consider?

Then, look for (and write down) possible relationships among the answers. For example, how did the time and place affect the participants? Were the reactions of the participants as important as the action itself?

Finally, note your response to the situation. How did it make you feel? Could you have done anything to help? If you think changes or interventions needed to occur, what are they?

Hint: The question you are most likely to have trouble answering is "Why?" If so, try a freewriting or a brainstorming session, like the one that follows, to generate some possible reasons for the behavior.

Collaborative Activity

This assignment asks you to work with a small group of your classmates to convert one of the Reporter's Formula exercises that you completed for the previous Journal Activity into a brief dramatic presentation. You are asked to collaboratively prepare the script and perform it for your class.

First, review the Reporter's Formula Journal Entries produced by each member of your group, and select one to develop into a script. The entry should, of course, include the possibility of characters; try to pick one that can be accomplished with a maximum of three characters. Also, look for an entry that involves either some sort of conflict or an interesting interaction among the characters.

Then, compose the script. It should include dialogue, of course, but also some description of the setting, situation, and action.

One member will serve as the narrator. His or her job will be to introduce the action and, if necessary, describe the characters. However, be sure that the narrator does not dominate the performance. This is a play—not a story.

The other members of the group will serve as actors.

After each group has made its presentation, the rest of the class should discuss what they have witnessed. They might take note of similarities and differences in the way the event was developed by each group. They might reveal the distortions of the event that have taken place as it is lifted from one kind of textual representation to another.

❑ *Brainstorming*

Most of the issues you will encounter in this book are complex. As you grapple with them, you will become increasingly suspicious of simple, tidy, or absolute answers. You will learn how to avoid the trap of adopting a fixed point of view that either dispenses with any inquiry or predetermines the answers you find. Instead, you will discover that important issues require open discussion and dialogue. Brainstorming is an effective technique to explore diverse viewpoints and gain insight into the complexities that underlie most subjects. The approach is presented here through a dialogue, which you can easily adopt for probing ideas on your own.

Here's the process:

- Join together with a group of your classmates.
- Find a topic that genuinely matters to you. Even if you are assigned a topic, try to relate it to your own experience.
- Enlist a timekeeper and recorder.
- Set a time limit for the full session as well as for individual speakers.
- Begin by breaking into pairs to limber up for a moment or two. Consider what you already know about the topic. Make a list of relevant first-hand experiences. Add to it some general statements of what you have learned from the reading you have done. Then, come together, say, for an additional 35-40 minutes of brainstorming.
- List ideas from the group on a chalkboard, computer laptop, or large sheets of newsprint. Make sure that everyone can easily see the list.
- Allow no more than a minute or two of silence before someone speaks. Remember your goal is to list as many ideas as possible in a short period of time.
- Drawing from the list, group similar ideas and decide which seem most striking or interesting.
- Identify areas you may want to explore further.

Some Useful Tips:

- Encourage all ideas. Don't criticize or judge them. Don't worry about being "right" and "wrong"; for now, one's mind should be free to roam at will.
- Be creative and spontaneous. This limbering up period can offer some startling insights into your subject.
- Go for quantity—Ask for ten ideas, and then ten more.
- Springboard using the ideas of others. Free associate, trying out metaphors and analogies to extend and deepen your thinking. Try to make each thought as clear and complete as possible.
- Keep the momentum going by encouraging, but not interrupting, one another's train of thought.
- Do not discount what other people offer, even if their ideas do not agree with yours.

Be assured that even when you have already thought about a subject, the process of generating more questions and ideas—either alone or in dialogue with others—can reveal more possibilities. As you add to your knowledge, the topics you consider will become broader rather than narrower, making it more likely that your thinking will change or evolve.

Collaborative Activity

Using the process for brainstorming described above, join with a group of classmates who share your interest in a particular topic for a brainstorming session. The expression of diverging opinions, strong emotions and conflicting beliefs will clarify the various options that you might pursue in the development of your topic.

Journal Activity

Go back to the notes you made while brainstorming and reflect upon the issues and themes that were generated. Look for one specific thought or theme that raises a controversial issue, one that may challenge a long-held and cherished notion. Do a short freewrite to identify and unravel some of the issues you might have to consider.

Restructuring

We can think of our understanding of a subject as a whole system of knowledge and emotions. If the issue is important and complicated—as most issues are—we probably know lots of different things and have lots of different feelings about it, and the same probably holds true for our audience. The various ways the bits of knowledge and emotion interact constitute our system of understanding. Furthermore, it's a fundamental characteristic of systems that each part interacts. As long as the parts interact smoothly and without conflict, we are comfortable. However, when we are engaged in the process of clarifying or extending our understanding, new information might disrupt or conflict with what we previously believed. When this happens, we must accommodate the new information.

Often, our first impulse may be to "block" the new information, especially when we sense that it might make us question, alter, or even reject what we believe. We know that doing so is going to require us to think, to "burn" some mental calories, if nothing else. We lead busy lives, and the more quickly we can "get on" with things, without having to slow down to measure and weigh them, the more we can get done. So, we have to fight that initial impulse to dismiss what makes us intellectually and emotionally uncomfortable. One way of doing so is just to face the conflict head on.

(1) State the Conflict or Inconsistency Clearly.
What seems to be the most fundamental area of disagreement? Does it involve a core definition; a core behavior; the quality and quantity of supporting evidence?

(2) Identify Areas of Agreement.
Are there any areas of agreement? Is there any way of acknowledging the possible truth or accuracy of both positions without having to entirely dismiss or discredit one or the other? This can often mean showing that the two sides aren't as far apart as they might initially seem.

(3) Identify the Emotional Needs that Are Met by Each Position.

What do you gain by believing X? Disbelieving Y? How does having to say "some" or "most" instead of "every" or "all" make you feel? Try to imagine how your reader might feel on encountering your argument?

(4) Which of Your Values Are in Conflict?

As clearly as you can, state and prioritize the values involved. Can you modify any of them without feeling hypocritical or defeated? Can you make concessions on the less important ones, while still preserving the commitment to the more fundamental ones? In other words, is it an all or nothing situation?

(5) Question Your Assumptions. Question Your Facts.

Given our tendency to see what we want to see and not see what we don't, go back and examine those basic assumptions and facts again. This time, look to poke holes in them, look to find insufficiency, inconsistency, and indefiniteness. Play the devil's advocate.

Resolving Conflicts and Inconsistencies

Clarification

Think of Clarification like cleaning a dirty windshield. You essentially see, as before, only now everything is brighter, sharper, and more detailed. Generally, the kinds of changes that come from clarification seem fairly easy to accommodate, to accept without feeling as if you are compromising your understanding of the subject. Still, for some, it can seem as if they were inviting criticism or dismissal. In a "super-size" world, quiet precision too often gets labeled as nit picking or uncertainty, and so we may initially resist making some kinds of clarifications.

Exercise

Usually writers have their readers foremost in their minds; however, very often writers find that, as they incorporate one or more of the three tools we're dealing with here (clarification, extension, restructuring) in their writing, they inadvertently enhance their own understanding of their subject and purpose.

Try to think of a time in the writing you've done in the past when, as you generated the prose, you found yourself inadvertently *clarifying* your own understanding. Describe the episode in your journal. Be sure to describe the rhetorical situation as completely as possible but, most especially, describe any changes you made to your original plan and explain why you made those changes.

A Collaborative Alternative

Your instructor may decide to have you work collaboratively to complete this exercise. The benefit of collaborative work is that you will have many more experiences to think about. This enhances your chances of making this journal activity more interesting.

Extension

Think of Extension like turning on the bright headlights of a car on a dark night. You not only see more clearly and sharply, you can see much further ahead. These kinds of changes are more likely to meet some intellectual or emotional resistance. Though the information is generally consistent with what was previously known, the added information can change the way one understands and feels about the situation.

Exercise

Try to think of a time when, as you wrote, you found yourself inadvertently (say through brain-storming or research) *extending* your own understanding. Describe the episode in your journal. Be sure to describe the rhetorical situation as completely as possible but, most especially, de-scribe any changes you made to your original plan and explain why you made those changes.

A Collaborative Alternative

Your instructor may decide to have you work in small groups to complete this activity. This will give you a much larger pool of experiences to draw on.

Restructuring

Think of Restructuring like someone not only cleaning the windshield and turning on the bright lights, but suddenly also realizing that the car is going in the wrong direction. There are all sorts of possible reasons for the restructuring of information we previously had come to rely on. In the first place, we may have incorrectly understood the information we collected. Or we may have relied on inaccurate or incomplete information. Or we may have too easily dismissed any contrary informa-tion. Or better methods have now made more accurate information available—information that challenges what we previously thought. The more important the previous information, the more completely we embraced it and acted upon it, the more difficult it will be to consider and act upon what conflicts with it.

You may recall our earlier discussion of restructuring when we wrote of the whole complex of facts, ideas, and values that contribute to our overall picture of a subject as a *system*. Recall that each and every component of a system is connected in some way. One consequence of such connections is that, if you add or change a component, it will have some effect on all the other components. If the added or changed component is consistent or congruent with the other aspects of the system, the effect is positive and the operation of the system is enhanced. If, however, the added or changed component is inconsistent or in-congruent, then it may become impossible for the system to do what you want it to. In physical systems, this is fairly easy to see. If, for example, you add a component to your audio or computer system, and the machine begins to exhibit bizarre behaviors, you can be pretty sure that the added component some-how doesn't "fit." When we're dealing with *systems of ideas or concepts*, we sometimes encounter the same problem, although it's often not quite so obvious. The following exercise should provide an ex-ample.

Exercise

Think of a writing project in which you encountered the following difficulty. You were well into the project. Things were going well; ideas were flowing smoothly; the overall logical structure of the piece was solid; all the subordinate assertions and supporting details were consistent and clearly in support of your tentative thesis. Then you discover a reliable study that contradicts important assertions you have been making in support of your thesis.

In your journal, describe what you did to resolve this situation.

Note: When faced with such situations, the most common impulse is probably to "forget" about the contradictory material and get on with the project. We hope you found a more creative resolution. If so, you then restructured the project.

Alternative

Perhaps you've been lucky enough that you've never encountered the situation described above. If so, there are a couple of ways to change the exercise and still achieve its overall goal; they both involve drawing on the experiences of others.

1. If after interviewing several of your friends or classmates or perhaps one of your instructors you find someone who has encountered a situation in which some restructuring was necessary, use his or her experience to complete the journal assignment.

2. Suggest to your instructor that the class complete this exercise in small groups, as a collaborative exercise. That will give you many more experiences to draw on.

Student Example

After the brainstorming session mentioned earlier, Sarah sat down to take stock of her progress so far in her writing project. A glance at her notes made it clear that she would have to reconsider some of the points she had made note of earlier to address what other students offered in the discussion. She decided to start with a simple list of the claims she had encountered in the various invention activities she had completed so far in the process.

First, she reviewed the results of the Reporter's Formula exercise on her work at a food bank. The first line of thought that grew out of that exercise was that there is a need for such programs because of the many unemployed and underemployed people in our society. The number of children involved and the effects of the situation on them seemed particularly important to her. The problem with this line of thinking was that it seemed to lack any real insight. That there are lots of poor people in this country who need help is not exactly newsworthy. She would certainly need to establish the existence of the situation in her writing, but it wouldn't really serve as a core or central point.

However, one thing that she responded to emotionally was the shame and humiliation she thought she detected in those who were served by the food bank. She realized that her response was fairly subjective and that she could not safely generalize about such feelings among those served by various agencies, but she didn't want to let go of that idea for some reason—especially after she participated in the brainstorming session.

After she made some observations in the discussion, one of the students, Cyrus, fairly aggressively maintained that many of the poor show little interest in helping themselves and *should be* humiliated and feel ashamed. His view was that there are plenty of jobs and that a majority of unemployed or underemployed could support themselves if they wanted to. Shame and humiliation were the price anyone would pay for being a charity case.

Cyrus's sentiments were not particularly well received by the group. However, in the clamor that followed his comments, Sarah realized that, while she found his point of view distasteful, there was something of his point of view in her feelings about the situation. She wondered if her observations of shame and humiliation in the people she served at the food bank were accurate, or had she "seen" those behaviors because she somehow expected to? This left her more than a little perplexed. Did she unconsciously believe that the poor should be ashamed of their situation? She found even considering the question very uncomfortable and not at all in keeping with what she had believed her values to be.

Another student responded to Cyrus by offering something he'd encountered in a sociology course, a passage from "Rewards and Opportunities: The Politics and Economics of Class in the U.S.," an essay by Gregory Mantsios. The passage was:

> *"When we look at society and try to determine what it is that keeps people down—what holds them back from realizing their potential as healthy, creative, productive individuals—we find institutionally oppressive forces that are largely beyond their individual control."*

Sarah recognized that Mantsios's point was that people don't choose to be poor but are forced into it—that is, denied opportunities to succeed—by oppressive aspects of our social system. The student who brought his work into the discussion also offered a summary of the substantial statistical data Mantsios cited to support his claims.

Sarah wondered what she could do with this. Mantsios seemed to be saying that the poor are trapped by a system that compounds their struggle to overcome poverty. How did that fit into her emotional interest in how the poor people she'd dealt with felt about themselves? At least she'd resolved one thing. If she really had been somehow subconsciously agreeing with Cyrus, she could certainly be on the lookout for those feelings and put a stop to them right now.

Then a formidable challenge seemed to strike. Another student distributed some material in which Katherine Newman, a researcher at Harvard, was quoted.

> *"[A]ccounts from nearly 300 workers and job-seekers (from Harlem's working poor) reveal . . . [that] this group of low-wage earners, even with the heavy burdens of child care, health insurance, and an increasing number of low-wage job-seekers, want to work."*

Moreover, Newman wrote "low-wage, low-status jobs often require more skill in operating equipment, planning and dealing with difficult people on a daily basis than many higher paid higher status jobs . . . ." and beyond the social stigma of a low-end fast food job, these workers value their contribution and see themselves as worthy workers who have a strong sense of self-respect.

Now what? Maybe the shame and humiliation Sarah thought she saw was an illusion. At the very least, it may not be the most common response of the poor to their condition. Now Sarah has two conflicting claims to deal with.

A bit of soul searching made her sure that she has read the people she had served with at least some degree of accuracy. Some of them *were* expressing shame and humiliation. And they weren't all unemployed, either. Some of them would be classed as working poor.

But she has no reason to doubt Newman's findings either. How can she reconcile these two apparently contradictory claims in such a way as to develop some insight about her experience?

Then, toward the end of the brainstorming session, a student handed out a quote from Rollo May's *Man's Search for Himself*:

"I do not mean to imply that there are not an infinite number of deterministic influences in anyone's life. If you wished to argue that we are determined by our bodies, by our economic situation, by the fact that we happened to be born into the twentieth century in America, and so on, I would agree with you; and I would add many more ways in which we are psychologically determined, particularly by tendencies of which we are unconscious. But no matter how much one argues for the deterministic viewpoint, the person still must grant that there is a margin in which the alive human being can be aware of what is determining him or her. And even if only in a very minute way to begin with, the person can have some say in how he or she will react to the deterministic factors. . . . Freedom is thus shown in how we relate to the deterministic realities of life."

Something about the passage set off bells for Sarah. The passage seemed to offer a key to her problem and a way to reconcile the conflicts with which she was wrestling.

May didn't contradict any of the other claims she was considering, except for Cyrus's biased ones, which she'd already discounted. May didn't contradict Mantsios—that is, he didn't claim that people weren't victims of determinism; he didn't contradict Newman; in fact, Newman's claims seemed to support his. And he didn't contradict Sarah's subjective experience. More to the point, his claims seemed to be the most important of all those she'd been considering.

She closed out her study session certain there was something in May's words that would help her restructure her thoughts and resources into a meaningful, insightful claim that could serve as a core concept for her thinking. She just had to figure out how.

Application

Overall, the discussions and activities under "Clarifying" "Extending" and "Restructuring" are meant to illustrate how you can use your initial exploration of a subject to examine your own knowledge and beliefs, so that you can have confidence in the quality and accuracy of what you understand before you offer it to others. It is critical that this exploration be done as openly and honestly as possible, given the constraints you (and all students) have to work under. If you don't make a meticulous effort to explore the subject as "objectively" and as "thoroughly" as you can, there is a good chance you will "end up" "knowing" only what you knew at the beginning.

There are many reasons why this is likely to happen:

(a) *Ego*—we like to be right, like to find out that our initial intuitions were correct;

(b) *Practicality*—once we've invested time and energy in a way of knowing, it's hard to abandon that position;

(c) *Simplicity*—with so much of the world filled with complexity and diversity and change, it's nice to think that at least some things are sure and certain.

One way to guard against the tendency to find what you're looking for, instead of what really may be there, is to play the devil's advocate or, in more modern terms, the prosecuting attorney. See if you can imagine or find "other" ways of defining or categorizing your subject; other ways of thinking about cause and effect; other ways of measuring and evaluating the consequences; other ways of acting appropriately. That old expression, "Be your own toughest critic," does have validity when it comes to questioning your ideas, judgments, and conclusions. In fact, if you begin by already "conceding" that there must be other approaches to your subject and other ways of exploring your topic, you will be more inclined to seek some of those out.

You can do this in a number of ways. One is by using a computer search engine as a tool to discover what other kinds of viewpoints are out there. Take a "loaded" topic like racial segregation, where it would seem there would be a clear understanding about its effects. Google returned a count of over 16,000,000 entries for the words "racial segregation," beginning with the following:

> ***Founded in the core belief that segregation is, was and has always been wrong, this campaign is intended to make people stop, think and perhaps get a little . . .***
> **www.remembersegregation.org/ - 4k - Cached - Similar pages**

Google surprisingly returned a count of over 1,000,000 entries for the phrase "support for racial segregation."

If you had accepted the notion that racial segregation was evil, considering how some people argue in its support doesn't mean that you have to abandon your position; nor does it mean that you need to accept each argument that you might encounter. But, making your position more forceful, more convincing, might involve "understanding" how those opposing positions were constructed. Doing activities like this can have several important benefits, beyond improving the quality and accuracy of the information you possess. For one thing, if you do this kind of questioning and exploration, you can gain a better sense of the complexity of an issue. It can also make you aware of the need to address the concerns of an audience that will very likely contain people with competing views and who have varying degrees of intensity in holding them. Thus, in a very important way, a sound argument is like participating in a relay race. You take what you already "know" about a subject (the knowledge that has been passed onto you); then you do your own interrogation of that knowledge (your own research and analysis) in order to "validate" or "refute" or "modify" that knowledge; and then, at the end of that process, you pass to your readers an "enriched" sense of the subject.

A graphic representation (see Figure 2.2 below) shows how these exploratory tools work together as an integrated system that can provide new ideas and insights. The chart is specifically designed to indicate how the knowledge that one seeks to clarify, extend, and, perhaps, restructure invariably involves some combination of understanding what something is, what caused it to be that way, what its value or effect is, and what one can do now that he or she understands the situation more accurately.

Expanding the Inquiry: Reading Actively and Critically

The readings in this book present a variety of people (and literary characters) undertaking the same process: trying to understand reality better so that they can act appropriately and help us to do the same. At every stage the process involves clarifying, extending, and restructuring their knowledge of what things are, how they came to be, what results from them, and what they should do when they reach understanding.

Reading is an activity that depends on your ability to get inside a piece of writing and search for meaning. You respond to a writer's words, attending carefully to the issues and questions you encounter. At the same time, you might fill the margins with signposts of your own thinking: you mark the writer's arguments, your own disagreements, and your mutual understandings.

Intelligent reading does not simply happen. It is a conscious, directed effort to perceive a writer's message so that you can make critical decisions about the material for use in your own thinking and writing. You will recognize that you are a strong reader when you want to—even must—read to satisfy your curiosity and interests. Your aim is to be so confident an interpreter of texts that you can easily present your interpretations of them to an audience in a persuasive fashion.

Asking Questions: Inquiring into Possibilities

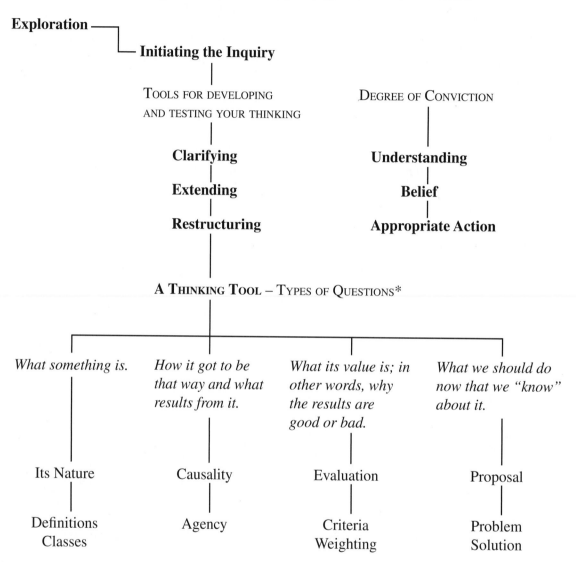

Exploration ——┐
            └—— **Initiating the Inquiry**

TOOLS FOR DEVELOPING
AND TESTING YOUR THINKING

DEGREE OF CONVICTION

Clarifying

Understanding

Extending

Belief

Restructuring

Appropriate Action

A THINKING TOOL – TYPES OF QUESTIONS*

What something is.

How it got to be that way and what results from it.

What its value is; in other words, why the results are good or bad.

What we should do now that we "know" about it.

Its Nature

Causality

Evaluation

Proposal

Definitions
Classes

Agency

Criteria
Weighting

Problem
Solution

Figure 2.2
A Process of Inquiry into Possibilities

*We wish to acknowledge Jeanne Fahnestock and Marie Secor (*A Rhetoric of Argument*, 2nd Ed., 1990) who proposed this taxonomy.

Understanding the Reading Situation

A text is given life only through the energies brought to it by readers who construct, interpret, and question its possible meanings. In a sense, then, a text serves as a catalyst for human response: its value lies not in some abstract notion of inherent truth, but in the ways meanings are negotiated between reader and text. In turn, what matters for the reader is to discover what is interesting, compelling, and insightful about the text, rather than coming up with a single "correct" response to it.

Interpretations of texts—even those by authorities—may differ widely and generate heated debate. Thus many students ask, "Whose reading is the right one?" Let us begin by moving away from the idea of right and wrong. As we have said, the intelligent reading of a text requires an investment of the reader's personal experience; since people do not have the same background and experience, the reading of a text must necessarily accommodate reasonable differences among readers. In fact any well-organized, logically developed, and clearly supported interpretation—no matter how far it may diverge from other views—merits serious consideration.

The Myth of Sisyphus
Albert Camus

The French novelist, philosopher, and playwright Albert Camus (1913–1960) was born in Algeria, the setting for his best-known novels. At the onset of the Second World War, he moved to Paris where he became a leader of the French resistance against the Nazis. In 1957, he was awarded the Nobel Prize for Literature. At the core of Camus's writing lies a perplexing question—Can one continue toward one's goals without having any hope of achieving them? He explores this question in his explication of the Ancient Greek Myth of Sisyphus. A brief synopsis of the myth follows.

> Sisyphus is a well-known character in Greek mythology. Most people think of him in connection with repetitious physical labor that has neither end nor purpose. According to legend, he lived a reckless and riotous life, one that was punctuated by acts of plunder, rape, theft, and murder. The poet Homer called him "the craftiest of men." After his death, Zeus, the ruler of Heaven and Earth, sent him to Hades where he was required perpetually to roll a large boulder up a hill. Upon reaching the crest, Sisyphus's rock would roll back down to the bottom, and he would have to begin the process all over again.

In this excerpt from *The Myth of Sisyphus* (1955, 1983) Camus invites his readers to ponder the significance of Sisyphus's perseverance. Recall that Rollo May (p. 65) suggests that people can have some degree of freedom in choosing their responses, even to the most dreadful of circumstances, and that the importance of this choice can outweigh the circumstances themselves. With May's perspective in mind, read "The Myth of Sisyphus."

****

The gods had condemned Sisyphus to ceaselessly rolling a rock to the top of a mountain, whence the stone would fall back of its own weight. They had thought with some reason that there is no more dreadful punishment than futile and hopeless labor. . . .

Nothing is told us about Sisyphus in the underworld. Myths are made for the imagination to breathe life into them. As for this myth, one sees merely the whole effort of a body straining to raise the huge stone, to roll it and push it up a slope a hundred times over; one sees the face screwed up, the cheek tight against the stone, the shoulder bracing the clay-covered mass, the foot wedging it, the fresh start with arms outstretched, the wholly human security of two earth-clotted hands. At the very end of his long effort measured by skyless space and time without depth, the purpose is achieved. Then Sisyphus watches the stone rush down in a few moments toward that lower world whence he will have to push it up again toward the summit. He goes back down to the plain.

It is during that return, that pause, that Sisyphus interests me. A face that toils so close to stones is already stone itself! I see that man going back down with a heavy yet measured step toward the torment of which he will never know the end. That hour like a breathing-space which returns as surely as his suffering, that is the hour of consciousness. At each of those moments when he leaves the heights and gradually sinks toward the lairs of the gods, he is superior to his fate. He is stronger than his rock.

If this myth is tragic, that is because its hero is conscious. Where would his torture be, indeed, if at every step the hope of succeeding upheld him? The workman of today works every day in his life at the same tasks, and this fate is no less absurd. But it is tragic only at the rare moments when it becomes conscious. Sisyphus, proletarian of the gods, powerless and rebellious, knows the whole extent of his wretched condition: it is what he thinks of during his descent. The lucidity that was to constitute his torture at the same time crowns his victory. There is no fate that cannot be surmounted by scorn. . . .

"I conclude that all is well," says OEdipus,* and that remark is sacred. It echoes in the wild and limited universe of man. It teaches that all is not, has not been, exhausted. It drives out of this world a god who had come into it with dissatisfaction and a preference for futile sufferings. It makes of fate a human matter, which must be settled among men.

All Sisyphus' silent joy is contained therein. His fate belongs to him. His rock is his thing. Likewise, the absurd man, when he contemplates his torment, silences all the idols. . . . At that subtle moment when man glances backward over his life, Sisyphus returning toward his rock, in that slight pivoting he contemplates that series of unrelated actions which becomes his fate, created by him, combined under his memory's eye and soon sealed by his death. Thus, convinced of the wholly human origin of all that is human, a blind man eager to see who knows that the night has no end, he is still on the go. The rock is still rolling.

I leave Sisyphus at the foot of the mountain! One always finds one's burden again. But Sisyphus teaches the higher fidelity that negates the gods and raises rocks. He too concludes that all is well.

This universe henceforth without a master seems to him neither sterile nor futile. Each atom of that stone, each mineral flake of that night-filled mountain, in itself forms a world. The struggle itself toward the heights is enough to fill a man's heart. One must imagine Sisyphus happy.

Editors' Note: *OEdipus Rex* by the Greek dramatist Sophocles depicts OEdipus as a victim of forces he does not understand and over which he has no control.

Questions

1. Why do you think Sisyphus continues even though he sees no hope?

2. In the preface to his book, Camus states, "Although 'The Myth of Sisyphus' poses mortal problems, it sums itself up for me as a lucid invitation to live and to create, in the very midst of the desert." What do you think Camus means by this statement? Consider Rollo May's assertion that the acceptance of "limitations need not at all be a 'giving up,' but can and should be a constructive act of freedom [that] will have more creative results for the person than if he [or she] had not had to struggle against any limitation whatever." What do their comments suggest about the limits and possibilities of human choice?

3. Camus compares the plight of Sisyphus to the struggle of the modern worker who "works everyday in his life at the same tasks." Can you justify this comparison? Why, or why not?

4. In his interpretation of the myth, Camus asks: "Where would [Sisyphus's] torture be, indeed, if at every step the hope of succeeding upheld him? . . . Sisyphus, proletarian of the gods, powerless and rebellious, knows the whole extent of his wretched condition . . . The lucidity that was to constitute his torture at the same time crowns his victory." What is the significance of this "hour of consciousness" that defines for Sisyphus both his plight and his triumph? Why do you think Camus gave Sisyphus this consciousness of his fate?

As you begin to interpret a text, let your initial reactions guide you. Do not assume they are wrong or misguided, merely because they are tentative. Reading is a probing, constructive process, so there is no harm in refining or shifting your position as you go along.

Also, remember that reading is not an entirely isolated activity: whenever possible discuss your interpretations with others. You may find affirmation from others and feel that you are on the right track, or you may find that others offer different perspectives that could broaden your own. At the very least, sharing your ideas will keep your reading from becoming too idiosyncratic or subjective. Furthermore, such discussions and debates are often lively and enjoyable.

Links Between Reading and Writing

Reading and writing are interdependent. Strong readers, as we have noted, take control of texts, finding ways to clarify complex and difficult points. When you write, you call upon critical reading skills at virtually every stage of the writing process. As with your reading, you probe and explore the subject, sample the various perspectives you might use, and struggle to articulate abstract and complex concepts. Not surprisingly, as you learn more about what good readers do, you will make more effective decisions as a writer. For example, you will learn to critically evaluate material before incorporating it in your work and you will apply critical reading skills in the analysis and revision of your writing. Effective reading and writing do not merely resemble each other but work together as reflexive processes, each one enhancing the other.

Short Essay

Write an essay in which you describe recent changes that have taken place in your patterns and habits as a reader. Using an assignment that caused pivotal struggles for you as a reader, explain why previous patterns and habits no longer suffice as strategies for close interpretative reading. Discuss what new approaches you were able to apply that were more effective.

Collaborative Activity

Exchanging drafts and talking with classmates about this assignment can help you to explore problems and struggles you have in common and discuss new approaches you have tried.

A Word on Visual Communication

We are often told that "we live in a visual age." We are bombarded with statistics claiming that the average American student watches 15 or more hours of television a week and surfs the Internet for an additional 20 hours, while spending only 5 or 6 hours reading books or magazines. Thus it seems as if engaging the world visually were a recent phenomenon that requires a new kind of theory and practice. But like all sweeping generalizations, the reality the statistics describe is much less certain and much more complex.

Except for the blind, most human beings in all ages and all cultures—including our own—have lived in a visual world, surrounded by faces and images, shapes and textures and colors—both natural and created. When we are spoken to, we are aware of the person speaking to us, of his or her appearance, manners, gestures, and movements. When we read, we respond to the shape, color, and size of the letters and words. From those who painted in caves; from those who sent smoke signals into the sky; from those who made igloos or massive cathedrals; from those who painted their lips and fingernails to those who filled their bodies with tattoos—human beings have always understood the power of the visual to convey or influence meaning. What is different about our "visual age" is the technological sophistication with which we can shape, send, and receive messages. From giant billboards to postage stamps, from massive plasma televisions to palm-sized cell phones, our world is filled with images. Using sophisticated computers and cameras, telescopes and microscopes, we can capture or create or re-arrange or fabricate almost anything we can see or sense or imagine. And yet, all those images and all that sophistication essentially serve the same communication purposes we always have had: to better understand the world in which we live and to share that understanding with others. Whether we just <u>underline</u> an important word in our text or incorporate into it a photograph, cartoon, or graph, we do so in order to help clarify, extend, or restructure our knowledge about the nature of something, or how it got to be that way, or what its value is, or what we should do about it. Once we understand this, once we understand the basic ways that visual information serves these traditional aims, we will be better able to function in this, the latest, of our "visual ages."

You will encounter a variety of images throughout the book to help you refine your skills in responding to visual information. We encourage you to go beyond the obvious information they contain and consider some of the basic elements of their design. If the image is in color, you might reflect on the effects that are created by the choices that have been made by the image's designers. Or you might reflect on the various shapes in the images. Are they triangles, circles, or rectangles? What sorts of feelings do the shapes inspire? You may want to analyze other elements of the images, such as their composition. Where do the main lines of the image lead your eye? Are the main lines horizontal, vertical, or diagonal; and what emotional response do such patterns elicit?

The book's Appendix offers some tools for exploring images. ***Consult the Appendix each time you analyze a visual text.*** At the same time, remember that these texts can tell us a great deal about our common culture: its ideals and values, its dominant views about social life, and its assumptions about who wields power and has status. They reveal what is desired or preferred in our culture; they can also reveal how class, gender, and race relate to the culture's dominant values. Your ability to approach visual texts with a discerning eye can play a significant role in developing your arguments.

3

Building on the Perspectives of Others

Since an effective paper often integrates material from many different and even divergent sources, you will have to decide how to bring such material into your writing. No doubt you will have notes or even outlines and summaries of what you have read. This chapter covers strategies to help you incorporate sources into your papers—the ideas you discovered in your reading that you want to explain, interpret, refute, confirm, or challenge. The techniques that follow provide the means for accomplishing that integration.

As you begin to use source materials in your writing, be aware of a tendency to rely excessively on the language of these sources. You may feel uncomfortable about altering the wording of an authority whose thinking and writing were good enough to be published in a journal or textbook. But you must not let your paper become a string of quotations. If you make frequent references in your paper, you will need to do some paraphrasing or summarizing, if only to keep the paper in the province of your own voice. Remember that the sources you use are meant to serve the goals and purposes of your own writing. Also, keep in mind that whether you choose to summarize, paraphrase, or quote, you enter into a kind of contract with another writer for the use of his or her ideas. You must always honor that contract by giving full credit to the writer. If you fail to do so, you are subject to a charge of plagiarism. (For more on citing sources, see Chapter 15.)

Sometimes you will find that the wording of your source gives a particular energy or flavor to your paper. Or you will decide that a passage contains wording that so clearly and specifically advances its development that it would be a mistake not to use it. In such situations direct quotations are called for. More often, however, your discussion will be better served by a paraphrase or a summary.

One final thought: effective writing is unified and interdependent; that is, the writer's meaning is made by the whole text. Because a quotation, paraphrase, or summary necessarily involves removing material from its original context, it is most important, as you incorporate borrowed material, that you not distort or misrepresent the meaning intended by the original text. When you are finished with a paper, it is a good idea to take a break and then read it through again specifically to make sure isolated quotations, paraphrases, and summaries maintain the sense and the spirit of the original text.

Quoting Directly

When you quote directly you must use the words of another writer just as they were written in the original work. You use quotation marks and you are not permitted to change the writer's words. (See below for the use of brackets and ellipses to indicate minor changes.)

Use quotations when the wording or phrasing of the source is particularly resonant and especially relevant to your own discussion. Passages that contribute solid support for your paper but do not contain noteworthy wording should be paraphrased or summarized in your own words. Be careful not to overuse the words of others, particularly in short papers, or you will risk losing ownership of your work. As a rule of thumb, avoid using more than two or three brief quotations or one long quotation on a single page.

Quotations provide support for your writing, but remember that your readers will not automatically see the connection between quoted material and your own ideas. Unless the text of your paragraph clearly suggests the significance of a quotation, you will need to provide a discussion of how the quoted passage specifically relates to your paper.

Brief Quotations. If a passage uses no more than four lines (or three lines of poetry) of your page, you can integrate the words into your sentence in an in-text quotation by placing quotation marks at the beginning and end of the passage. By and large, writers attribute such quotations to their source within the text of the paper. This attribution can fall almost anywhere within the quotation, as long as the text reads smoothly. For example, student Scott Davies attributes a quotation to Alan Murray at the beginning of a passage.

> Alan Murray writes, "The nation can afford to provide, if it wants, wide-ranging services and subsidies for the poor. What it can't afford, without much higher taxes, is to continue to expand government subsidies and services to the middle class" (A1).

The attribution of the quotation could as easily go at the end or even in the middle of the quotation, as long as it is appropriately punctuated. Two alternate possibilities follow.

> "The nation can afford to provide, if it wants, wide-ranging services and subsidies for the poor. What it can't afford, without much higher taxes, is to continue to expand government subsidies and services to the middle class," writes Alan Murray (A1).

> "The nation can afford to provide, if it wants, wide-ranging subsidies for the poor," Alan Murray writes. "What it can't afford, without much higher taxes, is to continue to expand government subsidies to the middle class" (A1).

Experiment with your own text to incorporate direct quotations as smoothly as possible.

Passages similar to the one above should be quoted in their entirety sparingly and only when absolutely necessary; overuse of full quotations can leave your readers with the impression of a choppy, patchwork paper. Experienced writers quote directly only when there is some specific reason, usually when the language of the source is particularly striking or elegant or otherwise effective. These writers frequently use a combination of quotation and paraphrase, a more sophisticated and flexible technique of embedding short quotations within their own prose, as in the following example.

```
Economist and social critic Alan Murray maintains that our country
can "afford . . . wide-ranging services and subsidies for the poor"
but can't "expand government subsidies and services to the middle
class" without increasing taxes (Al).
```

Such prose is more economical and smoother; however, to avoid distorting the author's meaning, the technique requires special care with punctuation and syntax. (See the discussion of ellipses and brackets below.)

To keep your paper from sounding static and repetitive, learn to vary your methods of quotation. You cannot change the words of your sources, but you can change the ways you incorporate those words into your paper.

One final thought: when the writer wishes to emphasize the information instead of the author, he or she names the author in the parenthetical citation. Look at the following example.

```
A conservative estimate from 2000 puts the number of slaves in the
world at 27 million. As the author of that figure puts it, "no paid
workers, no matter how efficient, can compete economically with unpaid
workers—slaves" (Bales 39).
```

Block Quotations. Longer quotations are known as *block* quotations because, in a paper, they have the visual form of a block. If you were following the style of the Modern Language Association, you would use block quotations for quotations that span four or more lines (or three or more lines of verse). Usually you will use a colon (:) at the end of the introductory phrase that precedes the quotation. You must double-space before the quotation, indent an inch or ten spaces on the left margin for each line of the passage, which itself is double-spaced, and double-space again when you return to your own text after the block quotation. You do not use quotation marks because the ten-space indentation on the left margin identifies the passage as a block quotation. If you were following the style of the American Psychological Association, you would use block quotations for quotations of forty or more words, indenting five spaces on the left margin for each line of the passage. In the example that follows, look at how Scott's essay uses MLA style for a block quotation from Michael Harrington.

Harrington writes,

> The poor get sick more than anyone else in society. That is because they live in slums, jammed together in unhygienic conditions; they have inadequate diets and cannot get decent medical care. When they become sick, they are sick longer than any other group in society. Because they are sick more often and longer than anyone else, they lose wages and work and find it difficult to hold a steady job. And because of this, they cannot pay for good housing, for a nutritious diet, for doctors. At any given point in the circle, particularly when there is a major illness, their prospect is to move to an even lower level and to begin the cycle, round and round. . . . (16)

While block quotations can be helpful and even necessary on occasion, do not overuse them. There are no absolute limits, but you should try not to use ones that are so long that they dominate an entire page of your paper. Remember that long quotations draw your reader's attention away from your own writing. The quotations you select should clearly serve the goals and purposes of your own writing; and the dominant, memorable voice in your paper should be your own.

Ellipses and Brackets. As you become more proficient at incorporating short quotations into your own text, you may want to make certain changes within the quoted material to maintain the continuity of your prose. You may want to leave out nonessential parts or change a word or two within a quotation. This is perfectly acceptable as long as you follow certain conventions that let your readers know what you've done. The tools used to change quoted material are ellipses and brackets.

An *ellipsis* indicates an omission of original material in a quotation. Ellipsis dots are a form of punctuation consisting of three spaced periods (. . .). As with most punctuation marks, there are conventions governing the proper use of ellipses in specific contexts.

When you leave words out of the middle of a sentence, you simply replace what has been left out with an ellipsis. Note how ellipses can be used to reduce the length of part of the block quotation shown above.

> When they become sick, they are sick longer than any other group in society. Because they are sick more often and longer, ... they lose wages and work and find it difficult to hold a steady job.

To delete words following an internal punctuation mark (comma, semicolon, dash, colon), retain that mark and then add the ellipsis points. If the deleted material occurs after a complete sentence, use the original period, add a space, and then add the ellipsis. Use this format if your deletion spans one or more sentences. This punctuation in the middle of a passage can indicate an omission of several paragraphs.

When an ellipsis occurs at the end of your quotation, remove any internal punctuation following the last quoted word, skip a space, insert the ellipsis points, put in a closing quotation mark with no intervening space, and place a period after the parenthetical citation. You do not need ellipsis points if the passage you quote ends with a complete sentence. Notice the ellipses in the following quotation from Scott's paper.

> Workers will overthrow a system that has failed them, for, according to Marx and Engels, "it becomes evident that the bourgeoisie is unfit any longer to be the ruling class in society, . . . because it is incompetent to assure an existence to its slave within his slavery . . ." (19).

When you delete words from the end of a block quotation, place a period at the end of the sentence and follow it with three spaced periods, as Scott did at the end of the block quotation in his paper.

> At any given point in the circle, particularly when there is a major illness, their prospect is to move to an even lower level and to begin the cycle, round and round. . . . (16)

Generally, if you omit words from the beginning of a quotation, no ellipsis points are needed. Simply lead from the opening quotation mark directly into the quoted material. If the material you are quoting contains ellipses, enclose yours within square brackets or add an explanatory note in the parentheses after the end of the quotation.

In general, omissions within quoted verse follow the prose conventions outlined above. If, however, you omit an entire line or more in a block quotation of verse, you will mark the omission with a series of spaced periods the length of a complete line of the quoted verse.

When it seems preferable to change part of a quotation rather than omit it, use *square brackets* [   ] to indicate the change. You might need to use bracketed text to maintain consistent verb tense or point of view within your paper. If, for example, the source you were quoting from were written in the present tense and your paper were in the past tense, it might be necessary to change the tense of the quotation for consistency. You would simply change the verb from present to past tense and enclose the changed material within square brackets followed by an ellipsis to show that text has been deleted. Likewise, if the source material were written in the first person point of view and you were maintaining the objective, third person throughout your paper, you might find it necessary to change *I* or *me* to *she* or *her* to make the quotation read smoothly. Again, simply make the change and enclose the new wording in square brackets followed by an ellipsis. When you make such changes, be careful to do so consistently throughout the passage.

Square brackets are also used in MLA style to change single letters within a quotation from upper- to lowercase or vice versa to make your text grammatically correct. In APA you may alter the first letter of a quotation without using brackets. APA also allows for punctuation changes without explanation.

If omitting or changing quoted text leaves you with a graphic nightmare of square brackets and ellipses, recast your paragraph to remove most of them or consider paraphrasing the quoted material. Two or three uses of brackets and ellipses in an average paragraph are about the most you can expect most readers to tolerate. Also keep in mind that when you use brackets and ellipses you must retain the writer's meaning. If your deletions or changes in words, phrases, or sentences alter the import of the author's words, you misrepresent the author—a serious error.

Journal Activity

Incorporate each italicized quotation, its author, and context into a single, well-crafted sentence. Next, construct an alternative sentence using the same material. Try to use a variety of strategies to keep your prose vibrant and clear.

1. *No people can be great who have ceased to be virtuous.*

   – Samuel Johnson, on the behavior of the British colonists in America; "An Introduction to the Political State of Great Britain."

Sample Sentence: In "An Introduction to the Political State of Great Britain," Samuel Johnson warned Britain's American colonials about their behavior, pointing out that "No people can be great who have ceased to be virtuous."

2. *I do not feel obliged to believe that the same god who has endowed us with sense, reason and intellect has intended us to forgo their use.*

   – Galileo Galilei, Astronomer and Physicist, 1564–1642

3. *The mass of men serve the State . . . not as men mainly, but as machines, with their bodies. . . . A very few, as heroes, patriots, martyrs, reformers in the great sense, and men, serve the State with their consciences also, and so necessarily resist it for the most part; and they are commonly treated by it as enemies. . . .*

   – Henry David Thoreau on the role of individual conscience in a society.

4. *I propose to take an income no greater than $50,000 per annum! Beyond this I need ever earn, make no effort to increase my fortune, but spend the surplus each year for benevolent purposes!*

   – Philanthropist Andrew Carnegie upon his retirement from business.

Collaborative Activity

Teaming up with some of your classmates, compare the sentences you just constructed and choose the best examples to share with the full class. Also discuss the strategies you used to keep your sentences from sounding static and repetitive.

Paraphrasing

When you paraphrase, you are putting someone else's ideas into your own words. Paraphrasing is usually preferable to quoting directly unless the wording of the source adds a distinctive flair or authority to your discussion. Because you are stating a writer's ideas in your own words and style, you can integrate this material more smoothly into your writing. Furthermore, by paraphrasing you demonstrate that you are able to explain and interpret your source and you can claim some mastery of the ideas it contains.

Since you are using the content of your source to further the discussion in your own paper, you still need to acknowledge its origins and accurately restate its creator's ideas, point by point, as you reshape the language. Thus the paraphrase not only provides support for your thesis, but also identifies a useful reference for your readers.

You should paraphrase if

- the wording of your source is fairly ordinary and a direct quotation would not be more effective than your own words,
- you want to express complex concepts in a way that your audience would easily understand, or
- the source is written in a special kind of jargon.

In his reading, Scott came across a compelling passage from Richard L. Rubenstein:

> Both the Nazis and the Bolsheviks under Stalin have demonstrated that a properly organized modern state can inflict total domination upon any segment of its population it chooses (91).

Choosing to paraphrase Rubenstein, Scott wrote,

```
In fact, Richard L. Rubenstein suggests that recent history shows the
opposite, namely, that the knowledge and technology of any modern gov-
ernment, led by a Hitler or a Stalin, can be directed to oppress and
enslave any social group or class (91-92).
```

Remember that when you paraphrase, you must be sure that your wording accurately represents the ideas you found in the source. Furthermore, it is not true that you may simply change a few words, or even most of the words, of the source. In fact, you must be sure that your paraphrase is a complete rewriting of the passage. It is also essential to document the source of your paraphrase. Claiming the ideas of another writer as your own, even if you change the wording, is plagiarism.

Summarizing

A summary highlights, in condensed form and in your own words, the main ideas of a source passage. In a summary you can present the main points of several paragraphs, a full article or chapter, or even a whole text—material that would be too lengthy to quote or paraphrase. Also, if you are writing a paper that requires some quantitative interpretation, you can save space by summarizing data and statistics instead of reproducing the charts and graphs from your source materials. However, if you use too many summaries your writing may sound general and vague. It is important to support your ideas with specific examples and evidence. Summaries should comprise only a part of your supporting strategies and should work together with the more specific techniques of quoting directly and paraphrasing.

In his reading Scott was very taken by the following passage from Robert Heilbroner.

> It is possible, of course, that in the future men may be so altered in their genetic characters, or nurtured in such carefully planned circumstances, that the "class" or "patriotic" attributes of political life would disappear because they no longer answered to an inner need. But at this juncture in history, our attention had better be focused on what men are likely to be, rather than on what they could eventually become. The human prospect forces us to deal with human change within an indeterminate, but not indefinite, time period, and speculations as to the degree of potential change must give way before the degree of change that is imaginable within that period. (140)

Scott did not want to quote the entire passage, but rather wished to convey the general sense of Heilbroner's words. Below is Scott's summary.

```
Finally, for those who view human culture as evolving over the millennia
in ever positive ways, and thus dismiss poverty in the present as an
eventual relic or curiosity, I suggest, as Heilbroner says, that future
utopias are only possibilities, at best, and that for now we must deal
with the present realities of class, poverty, and politics in our so-
ciety and in our times (140).
```

The author is named in the text when the student wants to emphasize the authority of the source, and in the parenthetical reference when the student wants to emphasize the information. In this next example, note that by naming the author in the parenthetical citation, the information, not the source, is emphasized.

```
The U.S. may be echoing the recent histories of Cuba and Russia, and
thereby creating the conditions for its own demise. The gap between the
wealthy and poor classes in America has grown nearly every year since
World War II (Harrington 194). Notably, the severe gap in 1935 between
the American rich and poor was strikingly similar to that of 1958 Cuba,
for in both cases the wealthiest fifth of society received more than
```

half of their respective nation's income, while the poorest fifth received less than 6% (194). However, the creation of a welfare state
under President Roosevelt and the economic boom of World War II averted
— postponed? — an American revolution. Still, by the late 1950s,
according to the U.S. Census, the rich and poor in America were again
drifting drastically apart. In 1958, only months before the Cuban revolution, nearly 40 million Americans were poor, and their collective
share of the bountiful American income was a paltry 4.7% (194).

Remember that whether you quote, paraphrase, or summarize, you enter into an unwritten con-tract with your source writers for the use of their language or ideas. You must always honor that contract by acknowledging them properly in your paper. For more on documenting sources see Chapter 15.

Extending Your Work

When you need to analyze a reading carefully, selecting just enough of the right material and pre-senting it succinctly enough to meet the needs of an audience is a relatively sophisticated process. The suggestions and techniques in this section offer some hints to make the job easier.

Tips for Paraphrasing Lengthy Passages

Here are some suggestions for restating a writer's ideas, point by point, from several paragraphs.

1. Read the whole passage carefully to be sure that you have a clear sense of its general meaning.

2. Start with the first sentence. Read the sentence carefully, phrase by phrase. Be sure you are familiar with the writer's terminology. When you are sure of the writer's meaning and can hold the idea of the sentence in your mind, cover the sentence and write your own sentence in your own language entirely.

3. Use synonyms where necessary and find words to take the place of special language or jargon. A thesaurus and a dictionary may come in handy.

4. Do not feel that you must duplicate the structure of the writer's sentence. Your sentence may be shorter and simpler in structure.

5. Go through the remaining sentences in the passage in the same way.

6. When you are finished, place the two passages side by side and check your paraphrase for originality of wording and for accuracy in representing the writer's original ideas. Remember that your sentences must be coherent and clear on their own.

In the following example, student Lee Adams paraphrased the introduction to Earl Shorris's *New American Blues: A Journey Through Poverty to Democracy.* As you compare the original passage with Lee's rephrasing of the publisher's words, note how she has taken special care to state the ideas in her own words.

Example
New American Blues
Publisher's Introduction

Original

In a narrative of unsparing detail leavened by compassion and even hope, Earl Shorris takes us inside the lives of the poor—in Oakland, rural Tennessee, El Paso, the South Bronx, and many points in between—so that we understand who they are and see through their eyes the "surround of force" that is their horizon, that prevents them from achieving a full and true citizenship. So rich is this book in the words and thoughts of the poor themselves that they are in a sense its authors.

Like any good story, this one has a beginning, a middle, and an end. We begin by listening to what the poor have to say about their lives. Once we know who they are and how much like us they are, we are ready to understand the world they live in, and *why* they are poor. Finally, and most surprisingly, we are asked to consider a revolutionary idea that has been taking quiet shape before our eyes all through the narrative: if the poor are human, and if the cultivation of their humanity benefits both society and the poor themselves, then why not teach them the humanities as the basic tools of citizenship?

In order to test his theory, Shorris started a school on the Lower East Side of New York City. He used donated books and borrowed space, and he enlisted friends to him teach logic, poetry, art, and moral philosophy to a group of young people whose collective background included prison, hard drugs, and homelessness. This experiment, which forms the triumphant climax of *New American Blues*, yielded extraordinary results: a majority of the students are now enrolled in four-year colleges, and it is no exaggeration to say that their lives have been transformed. One of the students, describing a difficult decision in his personal life, said: "I asked myself, 'What would Socrates do?'"

Paraphrase

In his book, *New American Blues*, Earl Shorris approaches a bleak subject — urban and rural poverty across America — with uncompromising realism. Drawing on the language and ideas of the poor themselves, Shorris invites readers to join him inside the world of poverty: a world of limited opportunities and marginal citizenship. Through Shorris' work, we become acquainted with the poor, recognize our common humanity, and move into an understanding of their environment and its causes.

Shorris proposes that we operate from the concept of our shared humanity and teach the poor using the branches of knowledge that are concerned with human beings and their culture. He offers this as a solution to poverty that will enhance both the poor themselves and the broader culture in which they live.

The idea was an abstract principle; to move it to a concrete application, Shorris opened a school on New York's Lower East Side. His students had experienced the grim circumstances associated with poverty: homelessness, hard drugs, prison in some cases. They came to a school where they could experience the richness of human beings caring about other human beings. Donations included books, space, and even the instruction itself. Classes included the traditional subjects covered in the term humanities: logic, fine arts, poetry, and philosophy. Shorris' account of the success of this endeavor vindicates his vision and lends a concluding note of hope to his *New American Blues*.

As this example shows, paraphrasing is the accurate recreation, in your own language, of another writer's ideas, and not a mechanical word-by-word hunt for synonyms. To paraphrase effectively, you must analyze and interpret not only the syntax at the sentence level, but also the writer's thinking and reasoning expressed in the ideas throughout the passage.

As you reconstruct passages in your own language, you establish authority over the thoughts and ideas in both the original and your own version. Bear in mind, however, that the authority you establish is not the same as that of original ownership. When you paraphrase you must fully acknowledge your source and must not claim another writer's ideas as your own. Only in certain cases, when information in a text becomes, over time, common knowledge to the general public, may you drop the reference. (For more on common knowledge, see Chapter 15.)

Journal Activity

If you find it difficult to reconstruct the language of your sources in your own words, you will find that working collaboratively in small groups can help you learn to paraphrase more effectively. Whether you work alone or in a group, this exercise will give you practice in the strategy of paraphrasing. Paraphrase the following two sample excerpts; as you work on each sentence, follow the steps for paraphrasing listed above.

Sample 1 (paraphrasing exercise)

In 1859, Charles Darwin published the first of his major works explaining the origin of the species. His theory struck a blow at one of the predominant religious views of the time: special creation; this is sometimes counted as a victory of enlightenment over ignorance. But religion took it on the chin, regrouped, and continued its domination of people's minds pretty much as it always had. Yet, Darwin's theory of speciation did have a profound effect upon the dominant ideology, but in an unexpected way.

Not long after Darwin's first major publication, Herbert Spencer incorporated Darwin's theory of speciation into his own explanation of the rise and fall of civilizations, societies, and social institutions. Darwin's general statement said that existing species arise from preexisting species and that all modern species trace their origins to a common ancestor. He also proposed a mechanism by which species arise, a mechanism called *natural selection*. However, for natural selection to change the character of species, there must exist natural (genetic) variation within species. Spencer translated Darwin's concept of natural selection into the more descriptive phrases, "survival of the fittest" and "nature is red in tooth and claw"; to this translation, he added the authoritative and unscientific dictum that civilizations, societies, and social institutions compete for survival and that the *biologically fit* ones win.

(Excerpt from Woodward, Val. *Biology as a Social Weapon*, Minneapolis, MN: Burgess, 1977.)

Sample 2 (paraphrasing exercise)

In 1994, Charles Murray of the American Enterprise Institute and Richard J. Herrnstein, a member of the faculty of Harvard University until his death, published an 845-page tract, *The Bell Curve*. With the publication of *The Bell Curve*, Murray [and Herrnstein] had at last given the underclass theory a scientific basis: Blacks were simply inferior. . . . There is no way to know what went on in the minds of legislators and university trustees in California and other states, but it seems reasonable to think that Murray's rewriting of what had been a commonly accepted view among civilized persons of the equality of all human beings had its effect.

The philosophical implications of Murray's thesis cannot be overestimated. For example, if blacks are not equal to whites, do they or should they have the same rights, according to natural law? Or if blacks have one of the highest percentages of poor people of any large defined group, is it not simply a result of their natural endowments or lack thereof, and therefore beyond remedy? Or if there are fewer blacks in universities, can it be that nature rather than society has done the discriminating and that nature cannot be overturned by legislation, including affirmative action? Or if a third of young black men have some involvement with the prison system, can it be that nature rather than society has chosen this disaster for them, and there is no remedy for it but to build more prisons and incarcerate more young black men? . . .

There would be something verging on the comic about [the Murray-Herrnstein thesis] . . . were it not that it can be used as validation for the existence of an underclass, a genetics of poverty, if you will, and an attack on the universality of natural rights. Like nothing else, Murray's [and Herrnstein's] tainted research points to an internal cause of poverty. And despite its flaws, it has, so far, been able to out shout solid evidence to the contrary.

(Excerpt from Shorris, Earl. *New American Blues*, NY: W. W. Norton, 1997.)

Alternate Journal Activity

Form groups and select passages from your readings that individual members want to incorporate into their essays. Work together to reconstruct and rephrase sentences in your own language. Comment on each other's work, providing feedback and advice. Finally, revise your paraphrases, strengthening their language and accuracy in capturing the original writer's ideas.

Tips for Summarizing Lengthy Passages

Here are some suggestions for presenting the main points of part of an article or book chapter in your own words. While you are not expected to adhere slavishly to these guidelines (note the student example below), understanding the principles involved can help you prepare a well-considered summary.

1. Read the entire passage over, identifying the main ideas by marking the text, making margin notes, and asking questions. Remember that because you are looking for main ideas, you do not have to note each specific supporting example.

2. Identify the main point, or thesis, of the passage and write it down in your own words.

3. Using your annotations, identify the main stages of thought that develop the author's thesis and restate each one in a summary statement of a sentence or two, again using your own words. Note key concepts and terms as you prepare the statements.

4. Write a first draft of your summary by combining the thesis with your summary statements. Arrange your sentences so they represent the order of the writer's main ideas. Add details from the text only if the main ideas are not clear without them. Do not simply list examples or specific supporting evidence.

5. Be concise and accurate in your wording, and do not allow the writer's language to slip into your own text.

6. Check your draft to make sure it accurately represents the progression of the writer's main points. Be sure that your sentences represent the writer's ideas precisely, but in your own words.

7. Revise your summary to strengthen the language and accuracy of your representation. Add transitional words and phrases where necessary to create a smooth progression of ideas in your writing.

Below you will find a marked passage from Earl Shorris's book followed by a set of summary statements again written by Lee Adams. As you review the marked reading, note how Lee uses her careful annotations of Shorris's text to identify his main ideas, claims, and supporting data. Also, note that Lee took great care to represent Shorris's discussion accurately, but always in her own words.

Example
Summary Statements
(STAGES OF THOUGHT)
Earl Shorris
Conclusion: Goodbye Blues

1. New American Blues

¶ 1   MANY YEARS AGO, in a third-rate night-club South Side of Chicago, where Billie Holiday was working, I heard a man say that she did not sing jazz any more. "She sings blues," he explained. "<u>Blues is when you know you can't get out of it.</u>"

Section 1
(¶ 1)
Introduces a definition of the blues

Source: From *New American Blues: A Journey Through Poverty to Democracy* by Earl Shorris. Copyright © 1997 by Earl Shorris. Used by permission of W.W. Norton & Company, Inc.

¶ 2   There is no accepted definition of the blues, nor does anyone know exactly when the blues began. The first recordings were made around 1920, but the blues had been around for a long time by then. Although the early history of the blues was vague, the <u>evolved form was purely American, southern, and black.</u> Form and content blended easily in the early versions of the blues, which were more like chants than what we think of as songs. The <u>blues came out of the music of laboring</u>, and like laboring, the first blues were repetitions: one line said to fit the form, the sad mechanics of life.

Section 2
(¶ 2)
Provides historical context

¶ 3   People of entirely European descent did not sing the blues, unless perhaps some indentured servants or prisoners sang beside slaves or the descendants of slaves. The blues belonged to one race. They were so identified with the African-American experience that James Baldwin, in an essay about "The Discovery of What It Means to Be an American," told of finding his identity in the blues. He arrived in Switzerland with nothing American but a couple of Bessie Smith records, he said, and that was all he needed. The tone and cadence of the music were his madeleine. Out of the blues he was able to recall his childhood, the meaning of color, segregation, race and race hatred, America as only a black man could see America.

Section 3
(¶ 3)
Expands historical context and introduces James Baldwin's experience

Thesis
(Shadow/Boxed)

¶ 4   <u>For James Baldwin, the blues represented race.</u> He could not recall poverty based on the blues <u>for he was not born in poverty</u>. *Go Tell It on the Mountain,* his autobiographical novel about childhood in Harlem, begins: "Everyone always said that John would be a preacher when he grew up, just like his father." Baldwin's young hero was raised in the ambiance of the church, studying the Bible, listening to the exegesis of sermons and discussions, singing the songs.

The political life that grows out of the humanities was his from birth. When he heard the blues in Switzerland, <u>James Baldwin heard two songs: the music he associated with race and the music and poetry any student of the humanities might hear.</u>

¶ 5   For over two hundred years it had been virtually impossible to separate race from poverty in America. James Baldwin was born into one of the first generations where any sizable number of blacks could draw the distinction. <u>The blues still belonged to people like him racially, but not economically or culturally or politically.</u>

Section 4
(¶ 4 &6)
As the blues evolved, its meaning and influence transcended race.

¶ 6   Baldwin was certainly right about the blues as American music, but <u>the origin of the blues was not only racial. The blues are American in another way</u> as well. They are made of many cultures: the iambic pentameter of the verse is English, as is the language; the African rhythms are abetted by those of Spain, Europe, and the Americas. <u>The blues are a syncretism of woes, all the loneliness in the world concentrated in a single voice.</u>

→ Expansion of Thesis

¶ 7   The <u>essence of the blues</u> has always been the same. It is the music of the aftermath, love lost, happiness gone, dead broke, door closed, good-bye. It is not hungry music, but <u>it is always a song about hungers.</u>

Blues are about what can't or won't be . . .

¶ 8   The blues come out of the realization that nothing will change. There is no sign of surrender in the blues, but there is no hope either. The blues are about the way it is: So you might as well. There are no blues for winners. <u>The blues belong to those who begin as equals</u> in the game of the modern world <u>and end up less than equal;</u> the blues sing of the irretrievable, irreparable, unredeemable, unlovable, lost and lonely Americans, the poor.

Section 5
(¶ 7-8)
Expands on thesis: the blues applies to everyone who has felt hopeless and unfairly treated.

¶ 9   The blues are never a result of nature. There are no desert blues, flood blues, snow blues. There are only insurmountable blues, because everybody else got dealt a better hand. The blues are based on the undeniable truth that life is a game, and the game is unfair. There are lamentation blues and supplication blues, but nobody ever wrote a blues about justice.

Section 6
(¶ 9-10)
Explains the nature of that hopelessness and applies it beyond race.

¶ 10   There are old blues, and those are best, because they are the nearly forgotten blues. And there are this morning's blues, which do not necessarily belong to one race or another, but to all those people who do not know how to get out of the isolation of life inside a surround of force. Those are the do or die blues, the new American blues.

■ Summary Statements

Once you mark the main ideas and identify key concepts and terms, you are ready to write summary statements. Note that Lee begins by restating Shorris's central idea in her own words. Next, she creates brief sentence summaries from paragraphs 1-5 in support of Shorris's thesis; she rewrites her opening paragraph and drafts her second paragraph. Finally, she creates summary statements from paragraphs 6-10 to show how Shorris expands his thesis; she rewrites her second and drafts her third paragraph. Keep in mind that once Lee rewrites the main points of each section in her own words, she can more readily incorporate those ideas into her own writing. Also, note that even though the Summary Tips listed above may seem clear-cut, the writing process rarely follows a straight line. Lee wrote, analyzed, reviewed, and rewrote at every stage in the development of her summary.

Example
Summary Statements

Step One: Identify author's thesis in Paragraph 3:

"The blues belonged to one race . . . Blues . . . recall . . . the meaning of color, segregation, race and race hatred, . . . "

Thesis

Paraphrase the claim:

"The music of the blues is linked to race and the culture of racism in America."

Identify thesis expansion in paragraph 6:

"The blues are a syncretism of woes, all the loneliness in the world concentrated in a single voice."

Paraphrase: *"The blues apply to everyone who experiences the same emotions that racism produces."*

Shorris's Part 2 (A Dangerous Corollary) provides the broader context of poverty.

Paraphrase: *"Poverty produces the same emotions that racism produces."*

Step Two:

Write the opening paragraph for the summary:

In his "Conclusion: Good-Bye Blues," author Earl Shorris uses the blues as a metonym for poverty. He describes the blues as inextricably linked to race and the culture of racism in America, yet applicable to all who experience the kind of hopelessness conveyed by the music. He uses the loss of hope characterized by the music of the blues to illustrate the same emotional condition of those who live in poverty.

Step Three:

Identify Shorris's support for his thesis from paragraphs 1-5. Paragraph 1 introduces a definition of the blues and Paragraph 2 provides historical context.

Paraphrase: *"The blues are identified as a uniquely African-American art form arising from the experience of slavery in the American South."*

Paragraph 3 expands the historical context and introduces James Baldwin's experience to illustrate Shorris's claim.

Paraphrase: *"For James Baldwin, the blues evoke both his personal experience of being black, which did not include poverty,*

*and a universal experience of appreciating a particular genre
of music and poetry."*

Step Four:

Rewrite my opening paragraph:

In his "Conclusion: Good-Bye Blues," author Earl Shorris uses
the blues as a metonym for poverty. He ~~describes~~ defines the
blues as *an art form chiefly African-American in its origin,*
inextricably linked to race and the culture of racism in America,
yet applicable to all who experience the kind of hopelessness
conveyed by the music. He uses the loss of hope characterized
by the music of the blues to illustrate the same emotional condition of those who live in poverty.

Step Five:

Write my second paragraph:

Shorris introduces the blues with an anecdote. "Blues is when
you know you can't get out of it" ( ). He explains the southern
black labor history of the music and explores its evocative
power with a reference to James Baldwin. For Baldwin, an African-American living in Switzerland, the music of the blues recalls his personal experience of what it meant to grow up black
in America. Unlike the generations that preceded him, Baldwin
cannot link his experience of race to poverty, but this does
not prevent him from identifying with the historical context of
the blues.

Step Six:

Identify support for Shorris's expansion of his thesis in paragraphs 6-10.
Paragraph 6 develops the statement in paragraph 4:

"James Baldwin heard two songs: the music he associated with race and the music
and poetry any student of the humanities might hear" by detailing the evolution of
the blues.

Paraphrase: *"Although the blues developed from the culture of
slavery, they may be appreciated by anyone. The form of the
blues demonstrates its syncretistic origin."*

Paragraph 7 describes the essence of the blues; paragraph 8 emphasizes the element of hopelessness in the blues.

Paraphrase: *"The blues reflect a recognition and an unwilling acceptance of hopelessness and inequality."*

Paragraphs 9 and 10 explain the nature of that hopelessness and apply it beyond race.

Paraphrase: *"Everyone who experiences hopelessness and inequality can relate to the blues."*

Step Seven: Rewrite my second paragraph:

Shorris introduces the blues with an anecdote *that underscores the essential element of hopelessness in the blues.* "Blues is when you know you can't get out of it" ( ). He explains the southern black labor history of the music and explores its evocative power with a reference to James Baldwin. For Baldwin, an African-American living in Switzerland, the music of the blues recalls his personal experience of what it meant to grow up black in America. Unlike the generations that preceded him, Baldwin cannot link his experience of race to poverty, but this does not prevent him from identifying with the historical context of the blues.

Step Eight: Write my third paragraph. Begin by linking Shorris's paragraph 5 with his paragraphs 6-10:

Baldwin heard more than one song in the blues: besides the music of race, he heard "the music and poetry any student of the humanities might hear" ( ). Shorris uses this duality and the syncretistic origin and evolution of the music to support his thesis that the music of the blues has moved from a primarily African-American expression of hopelessness to encompass all who "begin as equals . . . and end up less than equal" ( ). The music of the blues is for everyone who knows from bitter experience that life is unfair and that there is no prospect of change.

It is not the music of acceptance or surrender; it is the music of recognition and lament.

■ Full Summary

Here Lee compiles all her paragraphs into a full summary. Because she has produced a thorough restatement of the main stages of Shorris's thought, she doesn't need to make substantial changes to achieve a smooth flow in her work. Note how Lee takes great care to represent accurately Shorris's ideas.

Example
Full Summary

Step Nine:

In his "Conclusion: Good-Bye Blues," author Earl Shorris uses the blues as a metonym for poverty. He defines the blues as an art form chiefly African-American in its origin, inextricably linked to race and the culture of racism in America, yet applicable to all who experience the kind of hopelessness conveyed by the music. He uses the loss of hope characterized by the music of the blues to illustrate the same emotional condition of those who live in poverty.

Shorris introduces the blues with an anecdote that underscores the essential element of hopelessness in the blues. "Blues is when you know you can't get out of it" (135). He explains the southern black labor history of the music and explores its evocative power with a reference to James Baldwin. For Baldwin, an African-American living in Switzerland, the music of the blues recalls his personal experience of what it meant to grow up black in America. Unlike the generations that preceded him, Baldwin cannot link his experience of race to poverty, but this does not prevent him from identifying with the historical context of the blues.

Baldwin heard more than one song in the blues: besides the music of race, he heard "the music and poetry any student of the humanities might hear" (136). Shorris uses this duality and the syncretistic origin and evolution of the music to support his thesis that the music of the blues has moved from a primarily African-American expression of hopelessness to encompass

> all who "begin as equals — and end up less than equal" (137). The music of the blues is for everyone who knows from bitter experience that life is unfair and that there is no prospect of change. It is not the music of acceptance or surrender; it is the music of recognition and lament.

Paraphrasing and summarizing begin with careful analysis of the language of the source, but you cannot stop there. You must work with the wording, even struggle with it, to recreate the text in your own words while keeping the original meaning intact. This process will help you to absorb the ideas embedded in the material and thus to enjoy a kind of shared ownership over them. Furthermore, as you gain experience in paraphrasing and summarizing, your confidence as a writer will grow. Thinking critically about ideas and finding ways to express them in your own language are central to claiming authority as a writer.

Journal Activity

Writers who do not use a systematic approach to summarizing often find the strategy difficult. You may find working collaboratively in a small group helpful for learning how to summarize. Whether you work alone or in a group, this exercise, based on Part 2 of Shorris's conclusion, will help you to practice summarizing in a step-by-step fashion. As you proceed through the exercise, be sure to review the Summarizing Tips listed above.

Sample (summarizing exercise)
Conclusion: Goodbye Blues
2. A Dangerous Corollary

¶ 1.   The success of America has always rested on the certainty that the poor are not dangerous. If that seems an overstatement, said for shock value or merely to gain the reader's attention, . . . that was not my intention. I want only to show that poverty and the blues, the feeling that "you can't get out of it," live in the same house.

¶ 2.   They have lived there for generations, since the founding of the country in a revolution different from any other in history. In all the others, the people, mainly the poor, took power away from the rich. The lesson of those revolutions was simple and memorable: The poor can be dangerous. Watch out for the poor.

¶ 3.   In the British colonies in America, it was not the poor but the aristocracy who revolted. The poor fought and died in the war —

they always do — but they did not make the revolution. They were not dangerous. When it came time to write a constitution, it did not have to address the problems of the poor. With its Lockean origins, the Constitution had great concern about property rights, but no interest at all in distributing the wealth of the nation in some way that included the poor.

¶ 4.   The dominant view of the poor in the young nation, and still the view in many quarters, was that of Herbert Spencer, who coined the phrase "survival of the fittest." The social Darwinists, following Spencer, believed that the only reason to give charity to the poor was to improve the character of the donor. That took care of the moral question. And with no reason to fear a violent uprising, it made no sense to those in power even to consider sharing the wealth of the nation with the poor. There were dissenting voices, of course, socialists and do-gooders, but they had no power; they were not dangerous either.

¶ 5.   In the South, slaveholders worried about runaways but not about revolt, even when blacks vastly outnumbered the whites on plantations in isolated areas far from any town or military installation. On the way west, the Indians offered some resistance, but their destiny was manifest. William Graham Sumner expressed the popular view: Either the Indians became "civilized" or they became extinct.

¶ 6.   When civil war did come to the United States, it was not between the rich and poor, although the immediate cause of the war was economic. The poor did not ever gain anything in the United States by threatening to overthrow the established order.

¶ 7.   The poor are timid, conditioned by life within a surround of force; they kill each other. Even during the morally and politically tumultuous sixties, when McGeorge Bundy of Harvard and the National Security Council returned from seeing the American dead on the battlefields of Vietnam, and said to send more Americans to die, the poor shouldered their rifles and went. And died. They did not want to die. The unfairness of rich men choosing to send the poor to die enraged them, so in Watts, in Detroit, and in Chicago they burned down their own houses and killed their brothers.

¶ 8.   Americans do not like such civil disorder, even when it does not touch them, but the response to disorder has not been to close the income gap between rich and poor. It is, in fact, far greater now than it was during the riots of the sixties. The response to public disorder among the poor is not to end or even to alleviate poverty. It is more like the sentiment expressed by Lieutenant David I. Harris of the Riviera Beach, Florida, Police Department, who said, "If we don't do something about poverty in the next twenty or thirty years, my job will be to shoot people down in the street." Lieutenant Harris does not fear the overthrow of the government by the poor so much as he fears the effect of killing people on his own character. Herbert Spencer again, but in a mirror image:

¶ 9.   Poverty is a problem in America because exposure to it may coarsen the rest of the population. That is why the poor are generally kept hidden and why the homeless and the mendicants, who wander among the affluent, are both feared and detested.

¶ 10. The fear of mendicants and other visible poor has to do with the only real danger the poor have ever posed in America, which is to our sense of our own moral worth. Franklin Delano Roosevelt, for all that he is said to have wanted to save capitalism, also sought to salvage the nation's sense of itself as capable of goodness. A generation later, Lyndon Johnson and the War on Poverty, misguided and underfunded as it was, took the same path.

¶ 11. It was not until the rise to moral dominance of Ronald Reagan that the poor ceased to be a danger to our sense of our own moral worth. Reagan dismissed all moral questions in his own life and that of the nation through the deceits of charm. [Later] . . . at the end of the [20th] century, under cover of being a Democrat, Bill Clinton has turned the nation's attitude toward the poor back to the time before Roosevelt. He . . . made them morally and politically inconsequential. Only the poor are not covered by the quilt of political correctness that intends the protection of all persons who are, in truth or imagination, deprived of their natural or civil rights.

¶ 12. Since no one will help them, the poor have no alternative but to learn politics. It is the way out of poverty, and into a successful, self-governing life, based upon reflection and the ability to negotiate a safe path between the polar opposites of liberty and order. But to learn politics may also be a way for the poor in America to become dangerous at last.

¶ 13. Coming into possession of the faculty of reflection and the skills of politics leads to a choice for the poor: They may use politics to get along in a society based on the game, to escape from the surround of force into a gentler life, and nothing more. Or they may choose to oppose the game itself. If it is the latter, if the poor enter the circle of legitimate power and then oppose the cruelty of the game, they will pose a real danger to the established order.

¶ 14. No one can predict the effect of politics, although we would all like to think that wisdom goes our way. In their newfound autonomy people may turn to the left or right or choose to live smugly, disinterestedly, in the middle. That is why the poor are so often mobilized and so rarely politicized. The possibility that they will adopt a moral view other than that of their mentors can never be discounted. And no one wants to run that risk.

¶ 15.   Tens of thousands or even millions of poor people entering the public world may not endanger the established order at all. But the possibility that it could must perforce change the view of the poor held in America since the eighteenth century: The rest of the citizens would have to pay heed. Then the remaining poor might be spared some of the forces that make misery of their lives. And that, in turn, would make it easier for more of the poor to move out of the private life and into the public world, where all persons may think of themselves as having effect.

¶ 16.   If the poor who learn politics do not become dangerous, if they choose to survive modestly in peace and comfort, that is surely good enough. The goal is to end poverty, to consign the blues to history and romance, to make citizens of the poor. If that can be accomplished, the question of danger changes, for then the poor will be dangerous in the way that all citizens are dangerous in a democracy — they will be power.

¶ 17.   In one way or the other, politics will make dangerous persons of the poor. The certainty of that has worried the elites of this earth since politics was invented. But Plato was wrong about politics then and his fundamentalist followers are wrong now. The happiness of others is a goal worth pursuing, and the method for achieving it, democracy, is a risk worth taking.

Alternate Journal Activity

Join with two or three other students to select passages from your readings that you want to incorporate into your drafts. Discuss those passages and, then, working individually, create summaries in your own language. When you have finished, comment on each other's summaries, offering suggestions and constructive criticism. Finally, revise your summary for use in assignments.

Bringing Together Multiple Viewpoints: Synthesizing

As you gather, develop, and focus your ideas, you may feel that inserting the voices of others into a text provides scholarly breadth, maybe even depth, to your perspective. Nevertheless, you need to remember that other writers' voices will not help you if your reader does not see the relevance of such material to your own thinking. The quality of your writing depends on your ability to synthesize, or bring together, various viewpoints in a coherent and purposeful fashion. To accomplish this, you will need to review your reading notes, looking for patterns and relationships among your different sources that can help develop the direction and purpose of your thought. Unlike a summary that recounts an author's message, a synthesis points to connections and interpretations that will form the basis for your critical response.

Writing An Effective Synthesis

Here's the process for bringing together various viewpoints to help validate your thinking. Working through these steps, either alone or with classmates, can help you make more informed choices about what to assimilate from your reading and how to use these source materials to develop your own perspective.

1. Review your reading notes from the sources you wish to use, making sure you have gathered a wide range of perspectives.

2. Look for connections, patterns, and relationships among ideas in your sources and note them in your journal. To see these links more easily, you might group related ideas into categories or represent them in a diagram.

3. Review your purpose for writing; if necessary, revise or refine it in response to the connections you have established among ideas in your sources. A careful reading of source material followed by an analysis of the relationships among ideas will often lead you to modify your original reasons for writing. Note in your journal how sources have helped you to affirm, refine, or revise specific positions that you intend to take in your writing.

4. As you prepare to build a synthesis into your draft, be sure to interpret and present these connections in a coherent manner that clearly and logically serves your purpose.

One final thought: be aware that the very sources you draw on for substance and authority may actually work against you if you haven't fully grasped their ideas.

Sample Excerpts

Below you will find excerpts from papers students wrote on the biases used to justify the existence of an underclass. The first illustrates how the writer's attempt to enlist authoritative sources does not fully contribute to advancing her argument. By contrast, in the second, a collaborative piece, the writers successfully use some of the same sources to contextualize their assertions.

Excerpt #1

Comments
start on the
next page

        The desire to link intelligence to genetic fac-
tors is one that has been around for centuries. During
the nineteenth century, a practice known as craniometry was born. Essentially, scientists took measurements of the skull in an effort to determine the

1. Note how you allow your sources to finish your sentences with minimal input from you. By overusing the words of others, you risk losing ownership of your work and authority over the thoughts and ideas of your sources. That said, when you do quote you must establish an adequate context for all quoted material.

2. Be assured that stringing quotations together does not make adequate use of a source's authority. Unless you can offer, in your own words, a more complete account of Gould's perspective, your reader will have difficulty following your discussion and sense that you are not in control of the material.

3. When you make frequent references in your writing, the sources you use are meant to serve the goals and purposes of your own perspective. If you have a position, it is not clearly stated.

intellectual capabilities of its owner. According to Stephen Jay Gould, a professor of geology and zoology at Harvard University, another "equally irresistible" trend "swept through the human sciences around this time: the allure of numbers, the faith that rigorous
1 measurement could guarantee irrefutable precision, and might mark the transition between subjective speculation and a true science as worthy as Newtonian physics" (*569*). The forerunners of the craniometry movement "regarded themselves as servants of their
2 numbers, apostles of objectivity" (*569*). Through their studies "they confirmed all the common prejudices of comfortable white males — that blacks, women, and poor people occupy their subordinate roles by the harsh dictates of nature" (*569*).

Gould cautions that one should hesitate before
3 relying too much on such studies as evidence of proof because theories "are built on the interpretations of numbers and interpreters are often trapped by their own rhetoric" (*570*). Although these theorists trust their ability to be objective, they often "fail to discern the prejudice that leads them to one interpretation among many consistent with their numbers" (*570*). As evidence for this claim, Gould points to a physician from Virginia, Robert Bennett Bean, who performed a study in which he measured the front and back parts of the corpus collosums of the brains of both white and black Americans. Bean published his findings in 1906. As Gould states, with "a kind of neurological green thumb," Bean found "meaningful differences wherever he looked — meaningful, that is, in his favored sense of expressing black inferiority in hard numbers" (*570*). A key fault in Bean's study was the obvious lack of one measurement one might expect to find in such a study, the actual size of the whole brain. Bean's explanation for leaving this information out of his study was simply that "black and white brains did not differ in overall size" (*571*).

Such prejudicial invasions of the sciences were not limited to the early 1900's. Equally controversial research conducted by Charles Murray and Richard J. Herrnstein was published in 1994 in an 845-page book entitled, *The Bell Curve*. Their findings were later defended, albeit in a much softer voice, by the two researchers in an article entitled

4. A paraphrase would have allowed you to integrate this material more smoothly into your own writing.

5. You need to explain why the scientific community would object to this portrayal of Lynn's credentials.

"Race, Genes, and IQ. — An Apologia" which was published in the October 1994 issue of *The New Republic* and included excerpts from their book. Like Bean, Murray and Herrnstein argued that their research indicated that the I.Q. differences between blacks and whites were genetically based, claiming that, in one
4 study after another, "the idea that the black-white difference is caused by questions with cultural content has been contradicted by the facts" (*Apologia*
5 30). They further their argument by citing studies and findings of such experts as Richard Lynn, a scientist whom they refer to as "a leading scholar of racial and ethnic differences" (*The Bell Curve* 273), a contention to which many in the scientific community might object. . . .

The margin notes address the student's difficulty in synthesizing external sources: she has not consolidated the sources' ideas. To establish a meaningful context for the two readings, the student needed to give each work a more complete and thoughtful reading. Her next step might be to forge links—or recognize the conflicts—between Gould and Murray that could clarify the problems that derive from uncritically accepting certain arguments. By deepening her personal relationship with each reading, she can establish her authority more convincingly and gain control of her subject.

Now, turn to the second excerpt, a critical analysis of an article and a book purporting to offer scientific evidence for the researchers' findings. As you review the text, note the types of critiques in which the student writers engage, particularly how they move away from the sources' precise words to achieve their own authority and control over the issues. Also, pay close attention to how coherence and unity are built into the text by the way the students relate each aspect of their discussion to a critical analysis of each source. You might follow their approach, their analysis of the evidence, in your own arguments.

Excerpt #2

"Race, Genes, and I.Q.— An Apologia, "an article by Charles Murray and Richard J, Herrnstein, was published in the October 1994 issue of *The New Republic*, a magazine of political analysis and opinion. The "Apologia" incorporates sections from the authors' controversial 1994 book *The Bell Curve*, a publication that has created considerable political and scientific controversy because in it the authors assert that the differences between IQ scores of blacks and whites are directly linked to genetics. Their project is an ominous argument for biological determinism.

In the "Apologia," this finding was aggravated by their resolute claim that their conclusions are based upon "scientific" research. Since we expect science to be value-neutral and free of bias, scientific statements often go unchallenged because of the credibility afforded the scientific enterprise by "disinterested seekers of truth." Such is the case with the Herrnstein and Murray article. We tend to forget the possibility that scientists, being human, cannot wholly free themselves from their own reconceptions. As Stephen Jay Gould reminds us, "Theories are built upon the interpretation of numbers, and interpreters are often trapped by their own rhetoric. They believe in their own objectivity, and fail to discern the prejudice that leads them to one interpretation among many consistent with their numbers" (570).

Murray and Herrnstein do not appear to be as disinterested as they would have us believe. A closer investigation of their "Apologia" is called for. What bears particular scrutiny within the article is the way in which they reach their conclusions. In other words, we must carefully examine the data that they have gathered and the presumptions they bring to interpreting that data.

The way that Murray and Herrnstein present the evidence in the "Apologia" is suspect, at best. Most of their claims are either unsupported opinions or vague generalizations. For example, Murray and Herrnstein attempt to discredit the idea that the structure of intelligence tests is to blame for the disparity of scores between black and white subjects. "In study after study," the authors claim, "the idea that the black-white difference is caused by questions with cultural content has been contradicted by the facts" (30). The phrase "study after study" sounds impressive, but proves to be nothing less than a loosely worded generality. Readers are never told exactly how many studies such a phrase equates to, and this knowledge is essential to determining how much weight to give this evidence. If, for instance, only three studies were conducted, we would assign far less credence to this data than we would if one hundred studies were performed. Since we must assume that Herrnstein and Murray would give us a number if it was in their favor, we can only conclude that the omission of such a detail means that the number of studies done was probably minimal.

Such vagaries are common in their "Apologia" article. On any given page, phrases such as "among the experts"; "most scholars"; "There are, of course, many arguments"; and "many studies have shown" suggest an unwillingness to specify exactly what their data has been based upon, leading a reader to question the veracity of their research and its legitimacy.

In looking for clarification of these vague references, we turned to their book *The Bell Curve*, only to find ample fodder for criticism. The authors base the initial impetus for the direction their research has taken on studies that have unequivocally been discredited by the scientific community. Moreover, their findings are derived from statistics that have been misused and misinterpreted for the authors' own purposes.

Citing a study by Ken Owen in 1992, Murray and Herrnstein contend that "the I.Q. of 'coloured' students in South Africa — of mixed racial background — has been found to be similar to that of American blacks" (289). From the authors' perspective, this implies that mixing genes between Caucasian and blacks, both in Africa and the United States, has led to an increase in I.Q. points.

But a closer look at how these authors derived their figures reveals a major flaw in their thinking. While the source that Murray and Herrnstein cite does exist as a valid scientific study by Ken Owen, its findings have been misappropriated. Owen attempted to compare the performance of colored students (racially mixed) with that of whites, blacks, and Indians in South Africa. He conducted his research using a less culturally biased test Raven's Progressive Matrices and found differences between groups on cognitive measures of performance. However, in his concluding remarks, Owen stated emphatically that his intention was not to compare intelligence quotients, but merely performance on thinking tasks. He cautioned that his raw data could not be correlated to a mean I.Q. score, a caveat that undermines any suggestion of some kind of link between race and intelligence. One reviewer for *Scientific American,* a reputable lay source for current scientific information, reports the following about the study's inapplicability to Murray and Herrnstein's claim: "Matrice scores, unlike I.Q.s, are not symmetrical around their mean (no "bell curve" here) There is thus no way to convert an average of raw Matrice scores into an I.Q. score, and no comparison with American black I.Q.s is possible" (Kamin 100).

By assuming that an I.Q. score could be assigned to Owen's data, Murray and Herrnstein from the outset play fast and loose with previous research data to support their own assertions. Other such blatant biases permeate their book and are glossed over in *The New Republic's* "Apologia." whose point was to soften the implications of their findings.

Since this article does not mention sources by name it is difficult to pinpoint whose research Murray and Herrnstein have chosen to follow. One must go to the original work *The Bell Curve* to find a name or two that would provide some kind of insight into whose research formed the basis of Murray and Herrnstein's work. What one finds is revealing: among their "experts" are such maligned scientists as Richard Lynn, a researcher who Murray and Herrnstein have proclaimed to be "a leading scholar of racial and ethnic differences" (*The Bell Curve* 273). A cursory look at Lynn's 1991 article entitled "Race Differences in Intelligence: A Global Perspective" reveals a stunning statement of racial bias that cannot be overlooked. Richard Lynn writes that "the Caucasoids and the Mongoloids are the only two races that have made any significant contribution to civilization" (284), a confounding slur that sets the tone for much of Lynn's "scientific" work and whose notoriety has not escaped the scrutiny of the scientific community. "Lynn's distortions and misrepresentations of the data constitute a truly venomous racism, combined with scandalous disregard for scientific objectivity" writes *Scientific American* book reviewer Leon J. Kamin (100).

Having looked briefly at the obvious challenges to Murray and Herrnstein's scientific project, we now turn to the implication that these authors want us to consider about their findings. The most pronounced is their claim that blacks are intellectually inferior to whites because of genetic makeup. In their "Apologia," the authors attempt to console both liberals and Afro-Americans themselves by introducing the concept of "clannishness."

Their argument goes like this: different races and ethnic groups are genetically "better" suited for different activities, and, of course, worse at other activities. They suggest that 1.4. is but one measure of competence: after all, each group has pride in the activities it values the most, sort of a cultural equivalent of "do what you do best." The implication is that each group should contribute to society from its predetermined "best" shot at success. Would Murray and Herrnstein have black children emulate Michael Jordan rather than Toni Morrison, even though academic achievement provides far more opportunities for personal and group success than athletic prowess?

The authors make another flawed assumption in their "Apologia" — since lower I.Q. scores are genetically predetermined and influenced very little by environment, money spent on programs aimed at improving intellectual abilities is no doubt wasted. Such programs, they claim in their apologia, raise I.Q. scores "by a few points on the exit test, and even those small gains quickly fade" (34). Implicit in this position is that funding for these programs would be better spent elsewhere. It is in this final attempt at correlating "evidence" that a discerning reader begins to get the hint of a political project that lies outside the acknowledged objectivity of science. . . .

Works Cited

Gould, Stephen Jay. *The Mismeasure of Man.* New York: Norton, 1981. Print.

Herrnstein. Richard J., and Charles Murray. *The Bell Curve: Intelligence and Class Structure in American Life.* NY: Free, 1994. Print.

Judis, John B. "Taboo You." *The New Republic.* (Oct. 31, 1994): 18. Print.

Kamin, Leon J. "Behind the Curve." *Scientific American.* (Feb. 1995): 99-103. Print.

Lynn, Richard. "Race Differences in Intelligence: A Global Perspective." *Mankind Quarterly.* 31 (1991):255-296. Print.

Murray. Charles, and Richard J. Herrnstein. "Race, Genes and I.Q. — An Apologia." *The New Republic.* (Oct. 31, 1994): 27-37. Print.

Rosen. Jeffrey. and Charles Lane. "NeoNazis!" *The New Republic.* (Oct. 31, 1994): 14-15. Print.

Questions

1. What principal objections do the student writers have to the work of Herrnstein and Murray? Are they more offended by the thesis of the work, by the evidence offered to support it, or by the way Herrnstein and Murray construct their arguments. How do you know? Do you agree with them? Why, or why not?

2. You commit a logical fallacy if you reject a thesis simply because you do not like its implications. Are there any spots in their paper where the students seem to be committing or leaning toward this fallacy? What would be the best way to avoid a similar logical fallacy in your own work?

3. Clearly, the student writers strongly disagree with the findings of Herrnstein and Murray. Do you think any of the students' comments are more emotional than logical? If not, how do you think they avoided responding emotionally? If so, what steps could you take to avoid this sort of response in your own paper? Should you avoid emotional appeals when responding to or making such arguments?

Collaborative Activity

In groups of two or three, analyze and evaluate the first student excerpt. Decide what you think of both the work and the instructor's comments. How useful were the instructor's comments in helping the student resolve the problems she confronted in making her argument more effective? Next, do a thorough analysis of the second excerpt. How well does the excerpt embody the principles of writing covered thus far in this book?

Collaborative Activity

Working from the preceding analysis, join with two or three other students and select passages from the readings that you wish to incorporate into your drafts. Working together, follow the steps above for creating an effective synthesis.

Formulating a Reputable Voice

Particularly in the Information Age—the age of the Google search—two dangers confront the student writing an argument about a complicated issue. The first is that the essay will seem like an exercise in cutting and pasting quotations, with the student's own voice and understanding lost in a sea of facts, figures, and quotations from a variety of experts. The easy availability of information on the Internet and of pre-packaged essays makes this danger ever more real. The second danger is almost the polar opposite. The writer, either relying on a direct and dramatic personal experience or on one or two well-known supporting authorities, believes his or her understanding of the subject is so accurate and convincing that the issue is now settled once and for all—dissenters be damned! In the former instance, the writer's voice is too distant or timid; in the latter, the voice is too certain or condescending.

The remedy, of course, as with so much else in life, is to adopt the "middle way," to be quietly confident that the hard work you have done in inquiring into the subject makes your position worth considering and adopting. This means letting your reader know early on what information you began with, how you explored your subject and validated both the information you found and the credibility of those who supplied it, and, most importantly, why you have come to arrive at the understanding you have. Then, even though much of the information has been derived from others, instead of having to constantly say, "So and So says," or "They write," you can say, "I believe," or I think," or "It seems to me that So and So's explanation or study is the most compelling." Or you can say, "These facts and figures seem the most relevant to me"—to you as the inquirer, the analyst, and now, the presenter of the position to your reader.

It's like being the director of a chorus and not just one of the voices in the back. You inquire. *You* explore the pros and cons; *you* consider the advantages and disadvantages; *you* investigate the credibility of the supporters and the critics, and then *you* tell the reader what *you* think after all that effort. Others may have done the studies and the experiments and the measurements, but you have done the hard work of analyzing and authenticating and synthesizing that work—at least to the best of your abilities in the time available. And keep in mind that sometimes, even after all that hard work, you may only be able to say to the reader: "I can't solve this problem for you," but only offer what you believe is the best, most up-to-date information available about the topic for the reader to consider. Remember, even Socrates said, "I am wise because I know that I do not know [all there is to know]."

Readings and Essay Assignments

Immersing Yourself in the Conversation

As we suggested in Chapter 1, writing generally begins with conversation. Like those of all writers, your ideas and points of view are not somehow prior to or outside of the conversations going on in your life. Indeed, you are always being influenced by peers and teachers, by your reading, and by putting your thoughts on paper.

Concerned citizens often discuss and debate the critical issues presented throughout this text—in the media, in academia, and in political forums, as well as in vast numbers of private conversations. Through this chapter's essay assignments, you will add your own voice to these discussions.

Using the Readings

Exploring Moral, Economic, and Social Trends

The readings in this chapter address issues related to the Index entries presented in Chapter 2. Some readers find such material credible simply because it has appeared in print. This is a mistake: you need to develop the habit of critically evaluating all material before incorporating it in your work. The questions following each selection will help you to probe its implications and, at the same time, test the accuracy of the author's views.

Created Unequal
Merit and the Ones Left Behind
Dinesh D'Souza

Dinesh D'Souza (b.1961) is the Robert and Karen Rishwain Research Fellow at the Hoover Institution. He appears frequently on such programs as *This Week, Nightline, Crossfire,* and the *News-Hour with Jim Lehrer*. He also has written a number of books, including the *New York Times* bestseller, *Illiberal Education* (1991) and *The Virtue of Prosperity: Finding Values in an Age of Techno Affluence* (2000), from which this excerpt was taken. D'Souza was a senior domestic policy analyst under President Ronald Reagan. Consequently, he is interested not only in understanding the causes of economic inequality, but also in trying to determine what our government's response to that inequality should be.

* * * * * * * * *

The protection of different and unequal faculties of acquiring property . . . is the first object of government.
—*The Federalist Papers*

If you are pondering the fairness of life in America, you could do worse than to begin with Jerry Yang. Yang was a graduate student at Stanford who liked to fool around with the computer. Recognizing that Web sites were proliferating, Yang posted "Jerry's Guide to the World Wide Web," a categorized list of sites managed by a search engine. Soon Yang teamed up with another graduate student, David Filo, who helped him with programming. "You could call it a hobby," Yang said later, "you could call it a passion. Call it instinct. But it wasn't really business. We weren't making money doing it, and we were actually forsaking our schoolwork to do it." Yang said they just felt "jazzed up" about doing something on the exciting new medium of the Internet.[1]

But soon the duo realized that their directory had commercial value. So they started a new company and, in keeping with the irreverent tone of the site, called it Yet Another Hierarchical Officious Oracle!—Yahoo! for short. Today it is one of the most visited sites on the Web. And Yang, whose title remains Chief Yahoo, is now a billionaire, one of the richest men in the world. Recently he endowed the Yahoo Chair at Stanford University. It is now occupied by an extremely brilliant older man who draws a salary of around $100,000 a year. That's Christmas spending money for Yang.

Wonderful for Jerry, you say. One lucky dude. But that makes you wonder, as lots of young tech entrepreneurs wonder every day: What does Yang have that I haven't? Sure, Yang is a smart and hardworking guy, but you know lots of people like that, and they don't have a billion dollars. You're like that, and your net worth still has a way to go before you hit nine zeroes. Truth be told, it probably won't. Yang hit the jackpot, and you didn't. It's great this happens in America, but it's not fair that it doesn't happen to you. So is this what America offers its citizens, a one-in-a-million chance to hit Free Market Lotto? Or—a scary thought—is Yang's fortune based upon merit? Perhaps he didn't luck out; perhaps he "made his fortune." And if that is so, if the market has awarded Yang his just deserts, then perhaps you too are precisely where you ought to be. Yang is a winner and you are, well, a bit of an also-ran.

It's easy to feel outrage at the fortunes of those who have scored bigger than you have. Thousands of waiters and waitresses in Los Angeles cannot understand what it is that separates them from Tom Cruise and Gwyneth Paltrow. How come that jerk is riding so high? How did that bitch get where she is? There is more than a molecule of envy in such thoughts. But not just envy. These sentiments also raise the issue of justice, ennobling them and giving their bearers a conviction of justified outrage: you aren't just jealous, you have a right to feel this way.

Source: Dinesh D'Souza, "Created Unequal." Reprinted and abridged with the permission of The Free Press, a Division of Simon & Schuster Adult Publishing Group, from *The Virtue of Prosperity: Finding Value in an Age of Techno-Influence* by Dinesh D'Souza. Copyright © 2000 by Dinesh D'Souza. All rights reserved.

But has it occurred to you that there might be many people in this world who might feel exactly this way about you? You probably live in a nice house. You have lots of stuff. Yet there are many people in America, and countless more in the rest of the world, who are just as talented and determined as you, who work just as hard if not harder, and yet they don't have nearly as much as you do. Some of them have a great deal less. Do they deserve their relative misfortune? Are they too getting their just deserts? Sure, you are outraged at the fortune of the Silicon Valley tycoon. But do you feel a wee bit of guilt that there's a fellow in Dubuque, Iowa, and another in Karachi, Pakistan, and they're every bit as good as you are but they'll never live the way you do?

This [essay] . . . is an exploration of the inequalities that exist and have become very large in our society and our world. We accept these inequalities as part of life. They have been delivered to us by the god of the market. Perhaps we believe that they're necessary to make the system run better. But is that really true? Is inequality on the scale that we now see inevitable? Is it just? Do we deserve what we get? Our sense of being fairly treated by our society, and ultimately our cohesiveness as a community, depend on our answers to these questions.

The atmosphere at the American Enterprise Institute on the afternoon of February 9, 2000 is thick with anticipation. In the left corner, facing the audience largely made up of academics and policy experts, sits Edward Wolff, a New York University economist who is one of America's leading experts on wealth and income inequality. In the right corner, straightening out his tie and adjusting his notes, is John Weicher, a former Labor Department official and now a scholar at the Hudson Institute. Sitting in the middle, in a sense playing the role of umpire, is Arthur Kennickell, a senior economist at the Federal Reserve Board.

Conscious that he is in hostile territory—a free-market-oriented think tank—Wolff has come prepared with his research paper densely packed with charts and tables. Adjusting his spectacles, Wolff, a middle-aged man with curly hair and a mustache, methodically begins to outline his data, which appear on a screen behind him. His bottom line is a shocker. In 1983, his numbers show, the median net worth per household in the United States was $55,000. Today it's $54,000. During that same period, according to his data, the net worth of the richest 1 percent of Americans soared from a whopping 34 percent of the country's wealth to a staggering 40 percent. "We've had a rising stock market and a booming economy," Wolff says. "Eighty-five percent of the wealth increase went to the top one percent of wealth holders. And all the rest went to the next nine percent." The bottom 90 percent, Wolff concludes, are no better off today than they were almost two decades ago.[2]

John Weicher's numbers tell a less alarming tale. A round-faced man with a booming voice, Weicher contends that between 1983 and the present, median wealth per household climbed from $57,000 to nearly $72,000, a modest but not insignificant 25 percent increase over a 15-year period. Weicher's data also show the richest 1 percent increasing its take, from 32 percent to 35 percent, but the margin of increase isn't as steep as Wolff would have it. Weicher argues that for most of this century, with some variation depending on whether the economy is doing well or poorly, the richest 1 percent have controlled a third of the national wealth; the next 9 percent, another third; and the bottom 90 percent, the rest. In short, there is substantial inequality, but it isn't really increasing.

Weicher's real point, however, is: Who cares? Inequality per se is not a concern; the real question is whether America is a land of opportunity where people have a chance to become successful. He emphasizes that the vast majority of very rich people today didn't inherit their wealth; they made their own money. "I don't like the products that Microsoft makes and I'm not a big fan of Disneyland, but I have to say that Bill Gates and Michael Eisner have created a lot of value, both for their shareholders and for millions of Americans." So if they've earned what they have and they pay taxes on what they make, where's the problem?. . . .

During the discussion, I raise my hand and pose a question to Kennickell. "I need you to adjudicate a dispute," I say. "Mr. Weicher says that wealth inequality hasn't really increased over the past decade and a half; Mr. Wolff says it has increased greatly, and that all the gain in net worth produced by the new economy has gone to the richest ten percent of Americans. Who is right?" Kennickell now faces the dilemma of the man in the middle, but it's a position he seems to have been in before; he tweaks his mustache like Poirot preparing to reveal the identity of the malefactor. "Ah, yes," he says. "Who is right? Well, perhaps that depends on how you perceive the data." With a beaming smile, Kennickell returns to his seat, and the debate is over.

From the perspective of the Party of Nah, that's precisely the problem. The debate is indeed over—or, to put it differently, there is no real national debate about inequality. "It's mystifying," says Michael Walzer, author of Spheres of Justice, a critique of social inequality, and leading social scientist at Princeton's Institute for Advanced Studies. "The inequalities in our society continue to get worse, and the public shows no real interest in the subject. Even the people most hurt by inequality appear unwilling or unable to mobilize against it."

Walzer points to several examples of grotesque inequalities of wealth and income. According to a recent study by the Center on Budget and Policy Priorities, the average income of the top 20 percent of U.S. families is now ten times that of the bottom 20 percent of families. That's a much bigger multiple than in the late 1970s, when the richest 20 percent took in "only" seven times the income of the poorest 20 percent.[3] It seems that the most affluent Americans are living like royalty, while for the poorest people the American Dream is, well, just a dream.

These huge differences, Walzer points out, are replicated worldwide. The United Nations recently completed a study showing that the income gap between the wealthiest 20 percent of the world and the poorest 20 percent, which was thirty to one in 1960 and sixty to one just seven years ago, has now jumped to nearly seventy-five to one.

What this means is that the affluent citizens of the West can spend thousands of dollars on a shopping spree on Madison Avenue or the Champs-Élsées while their less fortunate counterparts in Third World countries must make do on a dollar or two a day.

Recently *Business Week* reported on the compensation of America's top executives, including salary and long-term benefits. Charles Wang of Computer Associates topped the list with a stratospheric $655 million. Dennis Kozlowski of Tyco was second, with $170 million. The list goes on. . . . Consider how far the wealth of America's tycoons could go toward solving the world's problems. The Census Bureau estimates that there are 13 million children in the United States living in poverty.[4] At $1,000 per child per year, it would cost $13 billion annually to provide for the nation's existing child poverty population in perpetuity. Bill Gates alone should be able to manage that, shouldn't he? On a more modest scale, Fortune estimates that if Michael Dell dipped into his portfolio he could purchase a computer for every high school student in the United States for $13.5 billion, leaving him more than $6 billion to spare.[5] If they pooled their resources, the world's richest people could easily feed the starving people of the world, with enough left over for them to live very comfortably.

But there's no reason to hold only the superrich responsible. Consider a paltry $1 million, a figure that hundreds of thousands of Americans could spare without making a dent in their lifestyle. It's interesting to speculate on alternative uses for that money. You could use it to occupy the best suite for 104 days on the cruise ship *Queen Elizabeth II*, or you could send 4,600 inner-city kids to a week at summer camp. You could rent the most expensive penthouse in New York for three months, or you could shelter 10,000 homeless children for a night. You could add a lavish wing to a mansion, or you could build several hundred dwellings in an African, South American, or Indian village.[6]

Walzer speaks in an urbane, clipped tone, but clearly he is outraged by the scale of global inequality. What gives some people the right to so much while others have so little? How can multimillionaires indulge themselves like pigs while others must endure a life that is nasty, brutish, and short? "What we are seeing is the replication of Third World conditions in the United States," Walzer says. "Black men in our inner cities have a life expectancy lower than people in Bangladesh. And the working class is living precariously from paycheck to paycheck. In many cases the family income is only sustained by more people working longer hours. And still they're weighed down by mortgage debt and credit card debt.". . .

Twirling his pasta at the trendy Il Fornaio restaurant in Palo Alto, my friend Rich Karlgaard, the publisher of *Forbes*, ponders the inequality problem with a look of dismissive amusement. With his navy blue blazer, open shirt, slacks, and tennis shoes, Karlgaard is the epitome of new-economy fashion. And as someone who's known him for a few years, let me assure you that Karlgaard isn't insensitive; he's a really nice guy. He cares as much as the next fellow, he just thinks that when professors such as Walzer get started on their pet peeve of inequality, all we are getting is envy in disguise, statistical hogwash. In short, a load of crap.

"I've heard the entire greed-sin, red-in-tooth-and-claw, orphan-empty-porridge-bowl dreary lecture," Karlgaard says, "and it bores the hell out of me. You know what is really galling these intellectuals? The fact that they have lost power. The fact that no one is listening to them. Not the poor, not the working class, no one cares what they have to say. And you know why? Because they're all at the mall, shopping. Because America's doing too damn well, that's why. People have seen their lifestyles go up with the market. Even the poor are living better, thanks to technology. Inequality is only a problem in the minds of intellectuals."

I wasn't sure I agreed with Karlgaard, and I relayed to him an experience at a recent conference sponsored by his own magazine. During a session devoted to executive salaries, CEO after CEO had stood up to complain about criticism they had received for making too much money. Finally one corporate titan said, "I don't understand the American people at all. They don't begrudge Jerry Seinfeld or Michael Jordan their millions. Why do they care about what I earn?" To this, one of his colleagues retorted,

"Because the average Joe turns on his TV, he sees Jerry Seinfeld do his comedy routine and Michael Jordan hit those baskets, and he says, 'I can't do that.' But he thinks he can do what you do."

Karlgaard laughed. "And maybe he's right. I don't begrudge him his arrogance. But he's got to go out and prove it. Don't tell me how smart you are. Go out and start a company. Stop whining about the wealth gap because, when you think about it, the wealth gap is a good thing."

A good thing? "You know who's responsible for the wealth gap?" Karlgaard adds. "I am. I'm responsible. I used to be a poor, unpublished writer. I drove a 1964 Ford Falcon with the trunk tied down by a jump rope. But at least I wasn't contributing to the wealth gap, because I was broke. Now I own a house, two cars, a retirement plan, shares in a few companies, and shoes to fill a closet. I'm a dirty rotten capitalist. I'm the cause of global inequality. You're right—it's unconscionable."

Yes, Karlgaard is on a roll. "I know how we *could* have solved the problem of inequality in America. Maybe Steve Jobs shouldn't have popularized the personal computer. If only Jeff Bezos had stayed in his hedge fund job instead of starting Amazon. Too bad Michael Dell didn't obey his parents and become a doctor. Wouldn't it be great if Ted Waitt had taken up cattle ranching instead of starting Gateway? And who can deny that David Filo and Jerry Yang would have done more for society if they had finished their Ph.D. dissertations! Unfortunately, these things didn't happen, because, if they did, America's wealth gap would be a trifle instead of a cancer."[7] So what now? Karlgaard says there's only one viable solution to inequality: a 98 percent capital gains tax. That, he says, would pretty much take care of the wealth gap.

Karlgaard's point—made in his inimitable style—is that inequality is necessary for markets to flourish efficiently; in this sense, inequality is the natural outcome of a growing economy. In one sense he is right. In 1980 the vast majority of people in the United States earned between $12,000 and $55,000. If you made more than $55,000, you were in the top 5 percent of wage earners. Today the income spread is between $12,000 and . . . what? $200,000? $500,000? You name it. So, many people who were previously in the lower ranks have ascended rapidly. As they have become well off, they have increased the gap between themselves and the rest of the population. Karlgaard's point is that an excessive focus on inequality carries the implication that this growth and its ensuing affluence are a bad thing, when in fact they are manifestly a good thing.

But is the inequality itself a positive good? Are the current levels of inequality necessary even for the economy to keep up its rapid growth? Karlgaard presumes they must be, because the market created them. The logic of this view is that without the chance of greater rewards people such as Jeff Bezos and Ted Waitt wouldn't have the incentive to do what they're doing. This is true as far as it goes, but it doesn't go very far. The reason is that we don't know how much greater those rewards would have to be to provide an adequate incentive. Would Bezos and Waitt slack off if they made 25 percent less than they do now? Would they work harder if they stood to make even more? The direct testimony of many of these Internet tycoons is that they aren't primarily motivated by money. So it's not obvious that such Himalayan reward structures are necessary to convince them to go to work every day.

For me, Karlgaard's most intriguing point is his suggestion that perhaps the people at the bottom and middle rungs of a society don't mind if inequality increases as long as they too enjoy some of the gains of the new economy. This makes a certain economic sense: Why should I care if the rich pull further ahead if I'm also moving forward? If this is true, however, it requires a revision in our conception of the problem. Traditionally, the debate about inequality has been conducted as if the acquisition of wealth were a zero-sum game. Thorstein Veblen writes, "The accumulation of wealth at the upper end of the pecuniary scale implies privation at the lower end of the scale."[8] This is the old mantra: "The rich are getting richer and the poor are getting poorer." Embedded in it is a big assumption, namely that the rich are getting richer *at the expense of* the poor.

But what if these premises turn out to be false? What if the rich are getting richer because they have created new wealth that didn't exist before? What if we live in a society where the rich are getting richer and the poor are also getting richer, but not at the same pace? If you drive a Mercedes and I have to walk, that's a radical difference of lifestyle that might warrant speculation about first- and second-class citizenship. But is it a big deal if you drive a Mercedes and I drive a Hyundai? If I have a four-bedroom house, do I have cause to be morally outraged that you have a twelve-bedroom house? These considerations suggest that in order to address the question of inequality, we must examine the significance of the differences in the way that people live today. It turns out that our old categories for examining the issue are largely obsolete. We need a new way of thinking about inequality.

In the past, inequality was largely a synonym for poverty, and moral concern about inequality was simply a different way of voicing concern about poverty. . . . But now, according to champions of the Party of Yeah, poverty in the biblical sense is no longer a problem. "The problem of poverty has been solved," writes Peter Huber, a new-economy enthusiast at the Manhattan Institute. "If history is still being written a thousand years from now, it will record that after countless generations of mortal struggle, humanity finally triumphed over material scarcity, in America, at the close of the twentieth century." This doesn't mean, Huber adds, that we've achieved some egalitarian utopia. "Oh yes, we do still have richer and poorer all about us," he writes, "but that's relative—it's poverty that has ended in our time, not inequality."[9]

Suffice it to say that Huber hasn't been spending a lot of time in Harlem, New York, Anacostia, in Washington, D.C.; or rural West Virginia, for that matter. The homeless man rummaging through a garbage dump looking for a sandwich will surely not be reassured to know that his country has achieved a historic triumph over material scarcity. The clergy and volunteers who serve long lines of people in the soup kitchens across America also have reason to question Huber's smug assertions. Yet it remains to be seen whether, as a general proposition, Huber is right.

The extravagance of everyday life in America is striking enough to support Huber's proposition that the United States has reached the age of plenty. Just go to any airport, any mall, any car dealer, any coffee shop, and you will be surprised to see ordinary people spending money in ways that until recently were considered quite extraordinary. Or open the phone book in your nearest city, and count the number of listings under "Plastic Surgeons." Once restricted to Hollywood stars and aging heiresses, plastic surgery has gone mainstream. Now virtually every pair of bouncy breasts requires a second look, not for prurience but for the purely sociological purpose of ascertaining whether they are real. A couple of years ago, an acquaintance of mine, upon receiving a big bonus, found herself in a peculiar dilemma. "I don't know whether to go in for a piano," she said, "or a nose job."

Another telling social indicator: pet surgery. At animal clinics around the country, such as the Animal Medical Center in New York, dogs, cats, hedgehogs, guinea pigs, rabbits, and even snakes arrive daily: "My snake isn't eating." "My rat has skin problems." "My dog needs a kidney transplant." "My cat needs brain surgery." For sums ranging from a few hundred to several thousand dollars, these animals receive medical treatment as if they were people. I mentioned this to a friend of mine, expecting him to find the whole concept ridiculous. But he didn't: his cat, he explained, was seeing a pet psychiatrist to deal with mood fluctuations. As in my friend's case, the customers who attend the Animal Medical Center aren't rich old ladies toting dainty little poodles with obscure ailments; they are everyday folk who prefer to pay for these treatments rather than accept nature's verdict and make another visit to the pet store.[10]

If these medical examples seem quirky, consider how ordinary Americans live today, compared with the way their parents lived a generation ago. The real story in real estate isn't the McMansions and "starter castles" of the nouveau riche; it is the fact that the average house built in the United States today is nearly double the size of its counterpart of the 1950s. In Levittown, New York, the archetypal 1950s suburban development, the average home was 1,100 square feet, today's homes average 2,150 square feet. And most of our homes are fully loaded; they have dishwashers, two-car garages, multiple color TV sets, full indoor plumbing, and central heating and air-conditioning, which relatively few homes in the 1950s had, as well as microwave ovens, personal computers, videocassette recorders, CD players, cell phones, and answering machines that nobody in earlier generations had because they didn't exist.[11] . . .

I once asked the novelist Tom Wolfe if he was awed at the levels of opulence that he observed in New York society. "What I find even more remarkable," Wolfe said, "is that at this very moment, your plumber or my electrician is vacationing with his third wife in St. Kitts. I can see him sunning himself and lazily fondling the gold chain on his chest. Soon they will take a walk along the shore, sipping glasses of designer water and getting ready to sample the local cuisine." And guess who employs servants these days? Maria America, a southern California agency that places housekeepers, nannies, and other domestic help, reports that its recent clients included a plumber, a Pizza Hut manager, and a cashier at Costco.[12] Admittedly, some of these clients are two-wage earners who need additional help at home; even so, in the past hiring help was a luxury that the lower middle class could not possibly afford. As for the servants, even they don't make out too badly: I contacted the agency and was informed that they earn around $80 for a day's work. . . .

The comforts of the ordinary American do not, of course, disprove of the existence of poverty. Indeed, the U.S. Bureau of the Census claims that more than 30 million Americans, or 12 to 13 percent of the population, are poor. But what does "poor" in this context really mean? Does it mean that millions of Americans are starving or don't have clothes to wear or a roof to sleep under? It does not. I cannot help but recall the saying of a school friend in Bombay. "I am going to move to America," he vowed, "I want to live in a country where the poor people are fat."

Today's poor people in the United States spend less than half their income on basic necessities.

Some people may be surprised to learn that 50 percent of Americans defined by the government as "poor" have air-conditioning, 60 percent have microwave ovens and VCRs, 70 percent have one or more cars, 72 percent have washing machines, 77 percent have telephones, 93 percent have at least one color television, and 98 percent have a refrigerator. Not only are poor Americans today better housed, better clothed, and better fed than average Americans were half a century ago; in many respects they live better than the average western European does today.[13]

How is this possible if poor people make so little money? One reason is that the Census Bureau does not take into account government benefits such as welfare, food stamps, unemployment provision, and rent subsidies, all of which supplement the earned income of the poor. A second reason is that poor people often grossly underreport their incomes, no doubt to maintain their eligibility for federal programs. We know this because the average poor person reports a standard of living—measured in terms of consumption—that considerably exceeds his earning capacity. Finally the census counts as poor many elderly people who are fairly well off but earn little income, as well as young people who live comfortably on parental assistance but whose incomes are small because they are just starting out in life.

The good news is that the Census Bureau is aware that its poverty numbers are inadequate. The bad news is that instead of downsizing them to correspond with a more mainstream understanding of poverty, the bureau wants to revise them upward in an apparent effort not just to maintain but to multiply the number of Americans officially classified as poor. Recently the *New York Times* reported that census bureaucrats want to raise the poverty threshold from $16,600 for a family of four to $19,500, a move that would immediately plunge more than 10 million Americans into poverty, even though their standard of living would remain unchanged. Rebecca Blank, dean of the School of Public Policy at the University of Michigan, explains that the Census Bureau's new definition would go beyond life's necessities to define poor people as those lacking "a socially acceptable standard of living."[14]

Using statistical legerdemain, the Census Bureau seeks to guarantee the biblical assertion that "the poor you will always have with you." But by any absolute or historical standard, Huber is right. Poverty, understood as the absence of food, clothing, and shelter, is no longer a significant problem in America. What remains is relative inequality and the question, does that continue to matter?

Robert Frank, a political scientist at Cornell University and author of *Luxury Fever*, thinks it does. . . . To illustrate the kind of equality that has serious social consequences, Frank cited the case of Wendy Williams, who lives in a trailer park in Dixon, Illinois. Williams has never known grinding poverty. Her father earns $9 an hour as a welder; her mother works part-time as a cook. Williams's problem is that her public school is largely made up of the sons and daughters of doctors, lawyers, and business executives. These parents think nothing of taking their children on expensive vacations or buying them designer clothes and the latest toys. "Wendy goes to school around these rich kids," her mother says, "and wonders why she can't have things like they do."

What Williams suffers is not the physical hardship of going hungry but the psychological suffering of everyday humiliation. Some of the children call her "trailer girl." She compliments another student on a stylish outfit, asking where she got it, and the girl replies, "Why would you want to know?" Williams speaks with her lips pursed because she is aware of her protruding front teeth. Her new nickname at school is "Rabbit." She hates it and is constantly begging her parents to send her to an orthodontist. Her parents ask her to be patient, but they know that they might never have enough money to pay for her to get her teeth fixed.[15]

In a rich country, where the body is secure from the depredations of extreme deprivation, the spirit is nevertheless vulnerable to a different kind of torment: the feeling of inferiority. It is hard not to sympathize with the plight of a little girl who, through no fault of her own, feels like a second-class citizen. Frank's argument is that the social gap between Wendy Williams and her classmates constitutes a kind of offense against the equality provision of the Declaration of Independence. Aren't this young girl's woes precisely what Jefferson was concerned about when he articulated the principles that Frank appeals to, principles that have shaped the American understanding of the role of government?

Actually no. . . . If Jefferson were alive today, I am quite sure he would have sympathized with young Wendy Williams's plight. But private concern for an individual does not translate into a public responsibility involving the federal government. Jefferson had a clear sense of the government's role: not to undo all harms, not to secure equal sympathy for everyone, but to secure equal rights. In Jefferson's view, what we make of these rights, what social status we obtain as a result of our efforts is not a subject of public concern; it is entirely up to us. . . .

NOTES

1. "Turn On, Type In and Drop Out," *Forbes ASAP*, December 1, 1997, p. 51.
2. Edward Wolff, "Reconciling Alternative Estimates of Wealth Inequality from the Survey of Consumer Finances," American Enterprise Institute Seminar Series on Understanding Economic Inequality, Washington, D.C., February 9, 2000.
3. Jared Bernstein, Elizabeth McNichol, Robert Zahradnik, and Lawrence Mishel, *Pulling Apart* (Washington, D.C.: Center for Budget and Policy Priorities, January 2000), p. 72.
4. U.S. Bureau of the Census, *Statistical Abstract of the United States* (Washington, D.C.: U.S. Government Printing Office: 1999), Table 761.
5. "Inside the Forty Richest," *Fortune*, September 27, 1999.
6. Rick Hampson, "What Would $1 Million Buy?" *USA Today*, December 22, 1999, pp. A1–2.
7. For his column detailing these views, see Rich Karlgaard, "Wealth Gap Follies," *Forbes*, October 11, 1999, p. 45.
8. Thorstein Veblen, *The Theory of the Leisure Class* (New York: Penguin, 1994), p. 204.
9. Peter Huber, "Wealth and Poverty," *Forbes*, December 27, 1999, p. 110.
10. Steve Fishman, "The Intensive Pet Care Unit," *New York*, January 17, 2000.
11. Michael Cox and Richard Alm, *Myths of Rich and Poor* (New York: Basic Books, 1999).
12. Jonathan Kaufman, "Even Leftists Have Servants Now," *Wall Street Journal*, June 23, 1999, p. B1.
13. Cox and Alm, *Myths of Rich and Poor*, p. 15; see also Liz Spayd, "In Excess We Trust," *Washington Post*, May 26, 1996, p. C1; Robert Rector, "Not so Poor," *National Review*, October 25, 1999, p. 28.
14. Cited in Louis Uchitelle, "Devising New Math to Define Poverty," *New York Times*, February 23, 2000.
15. Dirk Johnson, "When Money Is Everything, Except Hers," *New York Times*, October 14, 1998, p. A1.

Questions for Discussion and Writing

1. D'Souza discusses several complicated ideas in his essay, including "fairness," "inequality," and "poverty," How does he define and discuss them. Are they clear to you? If not, why not?

2. In talking about the large and growing inequalities that exist in contemporary America, D' Souza claims "we accept these inequalities as a part of life." Is he correct? Were you aware of these inequalities and do you accept them as inevitable?

3. Later, he argues thats if we think poverty means lacking the essentials for life, then poverty "is no longer a significant problem in America." How does this claim relate to the data presented here and in the Social Trends Index? Explain.

4. He quotes Princeton scientist Michael Walzer who writes that "black men in our inner cities have a life expectancy lower than people in Bangladesh." Yet, D'Souza concludes that our concern for particular individuals shouldn't automatically lead to government intervention. What logic does he use to arrive at this position, and do you agree or disagree with him? Why?

5. D'Souza speculates that Thomas Jefferson believed that the government's role was "not to undo all harms . . . but to secure equal rights." What do you think he means by this? Assuming it is a fair representation of Jefferson's thinking, how does this affect your response?

6. If you had the opportunity to ask Mr. D'Souza questions, what would they be?

Making Connections

1. D'Souza presents the voices of various leaders proclaiming that American institutions have altered the status of its people for the better. But he also presents others who say something very different about access and mobility. Who are these voices, and what do they tell us? Based on other materials in Part One of the book, give examples that either support or challenge this portrayal of America as a nation of increasing prosperity and opportunity.

2. How does the argument D'Souza makes about poverty and inequality relate to the statistics presented in Chapter 2's Social Trends Index (pp. 45–47)?

Visual Exercise

While numerical data appropriately cited and honestly interpreted are compelling evidence, they can induce a certain drowsiness in your reader. Consider the appeal of a graphic presentation over a list of statistics.

Real family income growth by quintile, 1947–2004

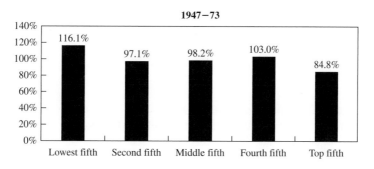

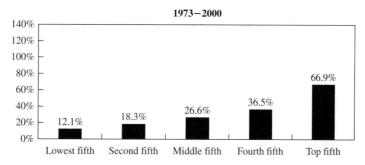

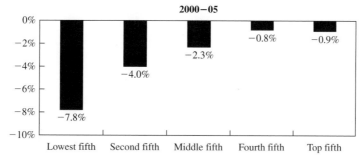

Source: Authors' analysis of U.S. Census Bureau data.

Figure 11 from: Mishel, Lawrence, Jared Bernstein, and Sylvia Allegretto, *The State of Working America 2006/2007*. An Economic Policy Institute Book. Ithaca, N.Y: ILR Press, an imprint of Cornell University Press, 2007.

Source: Economic Policy Institute, 2008. http://www.epi.org

Questions

1. What is your first impression of the visual? Thoughts? Feelings? Explain.

2. Who is generating the data and for what purposes?

3. Does the visual accurately portray the data in terms of consistency and proportion?

4. What additional information, if any, would you need to understand and/or believe the claims being made by the graphic? Explain.

5. In terms of effective design, what do you see as the strengths and weaknesses of the graphic? Explain.

6. How does this visual clarify, extend, or restructure your understanding of the state of income inequality in the U.S.? How does it square with D'Souza's portrayal of the "Party of Nah" and the "Party of Yeah"?

Class in America: Myths and Realities (2000)
Gregory Mantsios

Gregory Mantsios (b. 1950) is Director of Worker Education at Queens College of the City University of New York and writes and lectures on the nature of class in American society. In this 2000 essay, Mantsios disputes government estimates about the extent of poverty and points out the increasing separation between classes at the economic extremes. He adds that education and employment—the two main avenues for economic improvement—are not easily or equitably available to those on the lower end of the scale. Note how Mantsios uses data to support his position, and consider carefully his argument that institutions tend to reinforce myths about poverty.

* * * * * * * * *

People in the United States don't like to talk about class. Or so it would seem. We don't speak about class privileges, or class oppression, or the class nature of society. These terms are not part of our everyday vocabulary, and in most circles they are associated with the language of the rhetorical fringe. Unlike people in most other parts of the world, we shrink from using words that classify along economic lines or that point to class distinctions: phrases like "working class," "upper class," and "ruling class" are rarely uttered by Americans.

For the most part, avoidance of class-laden vocabulary crosses class boundaries. There are few among the poor who speak of themselves as lower class; instead, they refer to their race, ethnic group, or geographic location. Workers are more likely to identify with their employer, industry, or occupational group than with other workers, or with the working class.[1]

Neither are those at the other end of the economic spectrum likely to use the word 'class.' In her study of thirty-eight wealthy and socially prominent women, Susan Ostrander asked participants if they considered themselves members of the upper class. One participant responded, "I hate to use the word 'class.' We are responsible, fortunate people, old families, the people who have something."

Another said, "I hate [the term] upper class. It is so non-upper class to use it. I just call it 'all of us,' those who are wellborn."[2]

It is not that Americans, rich or poor, aren't keenly aware of class differences—those quoted above obviously are; it is that class is not in the domain of public discourse. Class is not discussed or debated in public because class identity has been stripped from popular culture. The institutions that shape mass culture and define the parameters of public debate have avoided class issues. In politics, in primary and secondary education, and in the mass media, formulating issues in terms of class is unacceptable, perhaps even un-American.

There are, however, two notable exceptions to this phenomenon. First, it is acceptable in the United States to talk about "the middle class." Interestingly enough, such references appear to be acceptable precisely because they mute class differences. References to the middle class by politicians, for example, are designed to encompass and attract the broadest possible constituency. Not only do references to the middle class gloss over differences, but these references also avoid any suggestion of conflict or exploitation.

This leads us to the second exception to the class-avoidance phenomenon. We are, on occasion, presented with glimpses of the upper class and the lower class (the language used is "the wealthy" and "the poor"). In the media, these presentations are designed to satisfy some real or imagined voyeuristic need of "the ordinary person." As curiosities, the ground-level view of street life and the inside look at the rich and the famous serve as unique models, one to avoid and one to aspire to. In either case, the two models are presented without causal relation to each other: one is not rich because the other is poor. Similarly, when social commentators or liberal politicians draw attention to the plight of the poor, they do so in a manner that obscures the class structure and denies class exploitation. Wealth and poverty are viewed as one of several natural and inevitable states of being: differences are only differences. One may even say differences are the American way, a reflection of American social diversity.

We are left with one of two possibilities: either talking about class and recognizing class distinctions are not relevant to U.S. society, or we mistakenly hold a set of beliefs that obscure the reality of class differences and their impact on people's lives.

Let us look at four common, albeit contradictory, beliefs about the United States.

Myth 1: The United States is fundamentally a classless society. Class distinctions are largely irrelevant today, and whatever differences do exist in economic standing are, for the most part, insignificant. Rich or poor, we are all equal in the eyes of the law, and such basic needs as health care and education are provided to all regardless of economic standing.

Myth 2: We are, essentially, a middle-class nation. Despite some variations in economic status, most Americans have achieved relative affluence in what is widely recognized as a consumer society.

Myth 3: We are all getting richer. The American public as a whole is steadily moving up the economic ladder, and each generation propels itself to greater economic well-being. Despite some fluctuations, the U.S. position in the global economy has brought previously unknown prosperity to most, if not all, North Americans.

   Myth 4: Everyone has an equal chance to succeed. Success in the United States requires no more than hard work, sacrifice, and perseverance: "In America, anyone can become a millionaire; it's just a matter of being in the right place at the right time."

   In trying to assess the legitimacy of these beliefs, we want to ask several important questions. Are there significant class differences among Americans? If these differences do exist, are they getting bigger or smaller, and do these differences have a significant impact on the way we live? Finally, does everyone in the United States really have an equal opportunity to succeed?

THE ECONOMIC SPECTRUM

We will begin by looking at differences. An examination of available data reveals that variations in economic well-being are in fact immense. Consider the following:

- The wealthiest 20 percent of the American population holds 85 percent of the total household wealth in the country. That is, they own nearly seven-eighths of all the consumer durables (such as houses, cars, and stereos) and financial assets (such as stocks, bonds, property, and savings accounts).[3]
- Approximately 144,000 Americans, or 0.1 percent of the adult working population, earn more than $1 million **annually**, with many of these individuals earning over $10 million and some earning over $100 million annually. It would take the average American, earning $34,000 per year, more than 65 **lifetimes** to earn $100 million.[4]

Affluence and prosperity are clearly alive and well in certain segments of the United States population. However, this abundance is in contrast to the poverty and despair that is also prevalent in the United States. At the other end of the spectrum:

- A total of 13 percent of the American population—that is, one of every eight[5]—live below the government's official poverty line (calculated in 1999 at $8,500 for an individual and $17,028 for a family of four).[6] These poor include a significant number of homeless people—approximately two million Americans.
- Approximately one out of every five children in the United States under the age of eighteen lives in poverty.[7]

The contrast between rich and poor is sharp, and with nearly one-third of the American population living at one extreme or the other, it is difficult to argue that we live in a classless society. The income gap between rich and poor in the United States (measured as the percentage of total income held by the wealthiest 20 percent of the population versus the poorest 20 percent) is approximately 11 to 1, one of the highest ratios in the industrialized world. The ratio in Japan and Germany, by contrast, is 4 to 1.[8]

   Reality 1: There are enormous differences in the economic status of American citizens. A sizable proportion of the U.S. population occupies opposite ends of the economic spectrum.

In the middle range of the economic spectrum:

- Sixty percent of the American population hold less than 4 percent of the nation's wealth.[9]
- While the real income of the top 1 percent of U.S. families skyrocketed by 89 percent during the economic growth period from 1977 to 1995, the income of the middle fifth of the population actually declined by 13 percent during that same period.[10] This led one prominent economist to describe economic growth as a "spectator sport for the majority of American families."[11]

The level of inequality is sometimes difficult to comprehend fully with dollar figures and percentages. To help his students visualize the distribution of income, the well-known economist Paul Samuelson asked them to picture an income pyramid made of children's blocks, with each layer of blocks representing $1,000. If we were to construct Samuelson's pyramid today, the peak of the pyramid would be much higher than the Eiffel Tower, yet almost all of us would be within six feet of the ground.[12] In other words, the distribution of income is heavily skewed; a small minority of families take the lion's share of national income, and the remaining income is distributed among the vast majority of middle-income and low-income families. Keep in mind that Samuelson's pyramid represents the distribution of income, not wealth. The distribution of wealth is skewed even further.

Reality 2: The middle class in the United States holds a very small share of the nation's wealth, and its income—in constant dollars—is declining.

Lottery millionaires and celebrity salaries notwithstanding, evidence suggests that the level of inequality in the United States is getting higher. Census data show the gap between the rich and the poor to be the widest since the government began collecting information in 1947. Furthermore, the percentage of households earning between $25,000 and $75,000 has been falling steadily since 1969, while the percentage of households earning less than $25,000 has actually increased between 1989 and 1997.[13] And economic polarization is expected to increase over the next several decades.[14]

Reality 3: The middle class is shrinking in size, and the gap between rich and poor is bigger than it has ever been.

AMERICAN LIFE-STYLES

At last count, nearly 35 million Americans across the nation lived in unrelenting poverty.[15] Yet, as political scientist Michael Harrington once commented, "America has the best dressed poverty the world has ever known."[16] Clothing disguises much of the poverty in the United States, and this may explain, in part, its middle-class image. With increased mass marketing of "designer" clothing and with shifts in the nation's economy from blue-collar (and often better-paying) manufacturing jobs to white-collar and pink-collar jobs in the service sector, it is becoming increasingly difficult to distinguish class differences based on appearance.[17]

Beneath the surface, there is another reality. Let us look at some "typical" and not-so-typical life-styles.

American Profile No. 1

Name:	Harold S. Browning
Father:	manufacturer, industrialist
Mother:	prominent social figure in the community
Principal child-rearer:	governess
Primary education:	an exclusive private school on Manhattan's Upper East Side
	Note: a small, well-respected primary school where teachers and administrators have a reputation for nurturing student creativity and for providing the finest educational preparation
	Ambition: "to become President"
Supplemental tutoring:	tutors in French and mathematics
Summer camp:	sleep-away camp in northern Connecticut
	Note: camp provides instruction in the creative arts, athletics, and the natural sciences
Secondary education:	a prestigious preparatory school in Westchester County
	Note: classmates included the sons of ambassadors, doctors, attorneys, television personalities, and well-known business leaders
	After-school activities: private riding lessons
	Ambition: "to take over my father's business"
	High-school graduation gift: BMW
Family activities:	theater, recitals, museums, summer vacations in Europe, occasional winter trips to the Caribbean
	Note: as members of and donors to the local art museum, the Brownings and their children attend private receptions and exhibit openings at the invitation of the museum director
Higher education:	an Ivy League liberal arts college in Massachusetts
	Major: economics and political science
	After-class activities: debating club, college newspaper, swim team
	Ambition: "to become a leader in business"
First full-time job (age 23):	assistant manager of operations, Browning Tool and Die, Inc. (family enterprise)
Subsequent employment:	3 years—executive assistant to the president, Browning Tool and Die
	Responsibilities included: purchasing (materials and equipment), personnel, and distribution networks
	4 years—advertising manager, Lackheed Manufacturing (home appliances)
	3 years—director of marketing and sales, Comerex, Inc. (business machines)
Present employment (age 38):	executive vice president, SmithBond and Co. (digital instruments)
	Typical daily activities: review financial reports and computer printouts, dictate memoranda, lunch with clients, initiate conference calls, meet with assistants, plan business trips, meet with associates
	Transportation to and from work: chauffeured company limousine
	Annual salary: $315,000
	Ambition: "to become chief executive officer of the firm, or one like it, within the next five to ten years"
Present residence:	eighteenth-floor condominium on Manhattan's Upper West Side, eleven rooms, including five spacious bedrooms and terrace overlooking river

	Interior: professionally designed and accented with elegant furnishings, valuable antiques, and expensive artwork
	Note: building management provides doorman and elevator attendant; family employs au pair for children and maid for other domestic chores
Second residence:	farm in northwestern Connecticut, used for weekend retreats and for horse breeding (investment/hobby)
	Note: to maintain the farm and cater to their needs when they are there, the Brownings employ a part-time maid, groundskeeper, and horse breeder

Harold Browning was born into a world of nurses, maids, and governesses. His world today is one of airplanes and limousines, five-star restaurants, and luxurious living accommodations. The life and life-style of Harold Browning is in sharp contrast to that of Bob Farrell.

American Profile No. 2

Name:	Bob Farrell
Father:	machinist
Mother:	retail clerk
Principal child-rearer:	mother and sitter
Primary education:	a medium-size public school in Queens, New York, characterized by large class size, outmoded physical facilities, and an educational philosophy emphasizing basic skills and student discipline
	Ambition: "to become President"
Supplemental tutoring:	none
Summer camp:	YMCA day camp
	Note: emphasis on team sports, arts and crafts
Secondary education:	large regional high school in Queens
	Note: classmates included the sons and daughters of carpenters, postal clerks, teachers, nurses, shopkeepers, mechanics, bus drivers, police officers, salespersons
	After-school activities: basketball and handball in school park
	Ambition: "to make it through college"
	High-school graduation gift: $500 savings bond
Family activities:	family gatherings around television set, bowling, an occasional trip to the movie theater, summer Sundays at the public beach
Higher education:	a two-year community college with a technical orientation
	Major: electrical technology
	After-school activities: employed as a part-time bagger in local supermarket
	Ambition: "to become an electrical engineer"
First full-time job (age 19):	service-station attendant
	Note: continued to take college classes in the evening

Subsequent employment: Present employment (age 38):	mail clerk at large insurance firm, manager trainee, large retail chain assistant sales manager, building supply firm *Typical daily activities:* demonstrate products, write up product orders, handle customer complaints, check inventory *Transportation to and from work:* city subway *Annual salary:* $39,261 *Ambition:* "to open up my own business" *Additional income:* $6,100 in commissions from evening and weekend work as salesman in local men's clothing store
Present residence:	the Farrells own their own home in a working-class neighborhood in Queens

Bob Farrell and Harold Browning live very differently: the life-style of one is privileged; that of the other is not so privileged. The differences are class differences, and these differences have a profound impact on the way they live. They are differences between playing a game of handball in the park and taking riding lessons at a private stable; watching a movie on television and going to the theater; and taking the subway to work and being driven in a limousine. More important, the difference in class determines where they live, who their friends are, how well they are educated, what they do for a living, and what they come to expect from life.

Yet, as dissimilar as their life-styles are, Harold Browning and Bob Farrell have some things in common. They live in the same city, they work long hours, and they are highly motivated. More important, they are both white males.

Let us look at someone else who works long and hard and is highly motivated. This person, however, is black and female.

American Profile No. 3

Name:	Cheryl Mitchell
Father:	janitor
Mother:	waitress
Principal child-rearer:	grandmother
Primary education:	large public school in Ocean Hill-Brownsville, Brooklyn, New York *Note:* rote teaching of basic skills and emphasis on conveying the importance of good attendance, good manners, and good work habits; school patrolled by security guards *Ambition:* "to be a teacher"
Supplemental tutoring:	none
Summer camp:	none
Secondary education:	large public school in Ocean Hill-Brownsville *Note:* classmates included sons and daughters of hairdressers, groundskeepers, painters, dressmakers, dishwashers, domestics

	After-school activities: domestic chores, part-time employment as babysitter and housekeeper
	Ambition: "to be a social worker"
	High-school graduation gift: corsage
Family activities:	church-sponsored socials
Higher education:	one semester of local community college
	Note: dropped out of school for financial reasons
First full-time job (age 17):	counter clerk, local bakery
Subsequent employment:	file clerk with temporary service agency, supermarket checker
Present employment (age 38):	nurse's aide at a municipal hospital
	Typical daily activities: make up hospital beds, clean out bedpans, weigh patients and assist them to the bathroom, take temperature readings, pass out and collect food trays, feed patients who need help, bathe patients, and change dressings
	Annual salary: $14,024
	Ambition: "to get out of the ghetto"
Present residence:	three-room apartment in the South Bronx, needs painting, has poor ventilation, is in a high-crime area
	Note: Cheryl Mitchell lives with her four-year-old son and her elderly mother

When we look at the lives of Cheryl Mitchell, Bob Farrell, and Harold Browning, we see life-styles that are very different. We are not looking, however, at economic extremes. Cheryl Mitchell's income as a nurse's aide puts her above the government's official poverty line.'[18] Below her on the income pyramid are 35 million poverty-stricken Americans. Far from being poor, Bob Farrell has an annual income as an assistant sales manager that puts him in the fifty-first percentile of the income distribution.'[19] More than 50 percent of the U.S. population earns less money than Bob Farrell. And while Harold Browning's income puts him in a high-income bracket, he stands only a fraction of the way up Samuelson's income pyramid. Well above him are the 144,000 individuals whose annual salary exceeds $1 million. Yet Harold Browning spends more money on his horses than Cheryl Mitchell earns in a year.

Reality 4: Even ignoring the extreme poles of the economic spectrum, we find enormous class differences in the life-styles among the haves, the have-nots, and the have-littles.

Class affects more than life-style and material well-being. It has a significant impact on our physical and mental well-being as well.

Researchers have found an inverse relationship between social class and health. Lower-class standing is correlated to higher rates of infant mortality, eye and ear disease, arthritis, physical disability, diabetes, nutritional deficiency, respiratory disease, mental illness, and heart disease.[20] In all areas of health, poor people do not share the same life chances as those in the social class above them. Furthermore, lower-class standing is correlated with a lower quality of treatment for illness and disease. The results of poor health and poor treatment are borne out in the life expectancy rates within each class. Researchers have found that the higher your class standing, the higher your life expectancy.

Conversely, they have also found that within each age group, the lower one's class standing, the higher the death rate; in some age groups, the figures are as much as two and three times as high.[21]

Reality 5: From cradle to grave, class standing has a significant impact on our chances for survival.

The lower one's class standing, the more difficult it is to secure appropriate housing, the more time is spent on the routine tasks of everyday life, the greater is the percentage of income that goes to pay for food and other basic necessities, and the greater is the likelihood of crime victimization.[22] Class can predict chances for both survival and success.

CLASS AND EDUCATIONAL ATTAINMENT

School performance (grades and test scores) and educational attainment (level of schooling completed) also correlate strongly with economic class. Furthermore, despite some efforts to make testing fairer and schooling more accessible, current data suggest that the level of inequity is staying the same or getting worse.

In his study for the Carnegie Council on Children fifteen years ago, Richard De Lone examined the test scores of over half a million students who took the College Board exams (SATs). His findings were consistent with earlier studies that showed a relationship between class and scores on standardized tests; his conclusion: "the higher the student's social status, the higher the probability that he or she will get higher grades."[23] Fifteen years after the release of the Carnegie report, College Board surveys reveal data that are no different: test scores still correlate strongly with family income.

Average Combined Scores by Income (400 to 1600 scale)[24]

Family Income	Median Score
More than $100,000	1130
$80,000 to $100,000	1082
$70,000 to $80,000	1058
$60,000 to $70,000	1043
$50,000 to $60,000	1030
$40,000 to $50,000	1011
$30,000 to $40,000	986
$20,000 to $30,000	954
$10,000 to $20,000	907
less than $10,000	871

These figures based on the test results of 1,302,903 SAT takers in 1999.

A little more than twenty years ago, researcher William Sewell showed a positive correlation between class and overall educational achievement. In comparing the top quartile (25%) of his sample to the bottom quartile, he found that students from upper-class families were twice as likely to obtain training beyond high school and four times as likely to attain a postgraduate degree. Sewell conclud-ed: "Socioeconomic background... operates independently of academic ability at every stage in the process of educational attainment."[25]

Today, the pattern persists. There are, however, two significant changes. On the one hand, the odds of getting into college have improved for the bottom quartile of the population, although they still remain relatively low compared to the top. On the other hand, the chances of completing a college degree have deteriorated markedly for the bottom quartile. Researchers estimate the chances of com-pleting a four-year college degree (by age 24) to be nineteen times as great for the top 25 percent of the population as it is for the bottom 25 percent. "Those from the bottom quartile of family income are faring worse than they have at any time in the 23 years of published Current Population Survey data."[26]

Reality 6: Class standing has a significant impact on chances for educational attainment.

Class standing, and consequently life chances, are largely determined at birth. Although examples of individuals who have gone from rags to riches abound in the mass media, statistics on class mobil-ity show these leaps to be extremely rare. In fact, dramatic advances in class standing are relatively few. One study showed that fewer than one in five men surpass the economic status of their fathers.[27] For those whose annual income is in six figures, economic success is due in large part to the wealth and privileges bestowed on them at birth. Over 66 percent of the consumer units with incomes of $100,000 or more have some inherited assets. Of these units, over 86 percent reported that inheri-tances constituted a substantial portion of their total assets.[28]

Economist Harold Wachtel likens inheritance to a series of Monopoly games in which the winner of the first game refuses to relinquish his or her cash and commercial property for the second game. "After all," argues the winner, "I accumulated my wealth and income by my own wits." With such an arrangement, it is not difficult to predict the outcome of subsequent games.[29]

Reality 7: All Americans do not have an equal opportunity to succeed. Inheritance laws ensure a greater likelihood of success for the offspring of the wealthy.

SPHERES OF POWER AND OPPRESSION

When we look at society and try to determine what it is that keeps most people down—what holds them back from realizing their potential as healthy, creative, productive individuals—we find institu-tionally oppressive forces that are largely beyond their individual control. Class domination is one of these forces. People do not choose to be poor or working class; instead, they are limited and confined by the opportunities afforded or denied them by a social and economic system. The class structure in the United States is a function of its economic system—capitalism, a system that is based on private rather than public ownership and control of commercial enterprises, and on the class division between those who own and control and those who do not. Under capitalism, these enterprises are governed by the need to produce a profit for the owners, rather than to fulfill collective needs.

Racial and gender domination are other such forces that hold people down. Although there are significant differences in the way capitalism, racism, and sexism affect our lives, there are also a multitude of parallels. And although race, class, and gender act independently of each other, they are at the same time very much interrelated.

On the one hand, issues of race and gender oppression cut across class lines. Women experience the effects of sexism whether they are well-paid professionals or poorly paid clerks. As women, they face discrimination and male domination, as well as catcalls and stereotyping. Similarly, a black man faces racial oppression, is subjected to racial slurs, and is denied opportunities because of his color. Regardless of their class standing, women and members of minority races are confronted with oppressive forces precisely because of their gender, color, or both.

On the other hand, class oppression permeates other spheres of power and oppression, so that the oppression experienced by women and minorities is also differentiated along class lines. Although women and minorities find themselves in subordinate positions vis-à-vis white men, the particular issues they confront may be quite different, depending on their position in the class structure. Inequalities in the class structure distinguish social functions and individual power, and these distinctions carry over to race and gender categories.

Power is incremental, and class privileges can accrue to individual women and to individual members of a racial minority. At the same time, class-oppressed men, whether they are white or black, have privileges afforded them as men in a sexist society. Similarly, class-oppressed whites, whether they are men or women, have privileges afforded them as whites in a racist society. Spheres of power and oppression divide us deeply in our society, and the schisms between us are often difficult to bridge.

Whereas power is incremental, oppression is cumulative, and those who are poor, black, and female have all of the forces of claims, racism, and sexism bearing down on them. This cumulative oppression is what is meant by the double and triple jeopardy of women and minorities.

Furthermore, oppression in one sphere is related to the likelihood of oppression in another. If you are black and female, for example, you are much more likely to be poor or working class than you would be as a white male. Census figures show that the incidence of poverty varies greatly by race and gender.

Chances of Being Poor in America[30]

White Male/ Female	White Female Head*	Hispanic Male/ Female	Hispanic Female Head*	Black Male/ Female	Black Female Head*
1 in 10	1 in 4	1 in 4	1 in 2	1 in 4	1 in 2

Persons in families with female householder, no husband present.

In other words, being female and being nonwhite are attributes in our society that increase the chances of poverty and of lower-class standing.

Reality 8: Racism and sexism compound the effects of classism in society.

NOTES

1. See Jay MacLead, *Ain't No Makin' It: Aspirations and Attainment in a LowerIncome Neighborhood,* Boulder, CO.: Westview Press, 1995; Benjamin DeMott, *The Imperial Middle,* New York: Morrow, 1990; Ira Katznelson, *City Trenches: Urban Politics and Patterning of Class in the United States,* New York: Pantheon Books, 1981; Charles W. Tucker, "A Comparative Analysis of Subjective Social Class: 1945–1963," *Social Forces,* no. 46, June 1968, pp. 508–514; Robert Nisbet, "The Decline and Fall of Social Class," *Pacific Sociological Review,* vol. 2, Spring 1959, pp. 11–17; and Oscar Glantz, "Class Consciousness and Political Solidarity," *American Sociological Review,* vol. 23, August 1958, pp. 375–382.

2. Susan Ostrander, "Upper-Class Women: Class Consciousness as Conduct and Meaning," in G. William Domhoff, *Power Structure Research,* Beverly Hills, CA, Sage Productions, 1980, pp. 78–79. Also see, Stephen Birmingham, *America's Secret Aristocracy,* Boston, Little Brown, 1987.

3. Jared Bernstein, Lawrence Hishel, and John Schmitt, *The State of Working America: 1998–99,* ILR Press, Cornell University Press, 1998, p. 262.

4. The number of individuals filing tax returns showing a gross adjusted income of $1 million or more in 1997 was 144, 459 (Internal Revenue Service, *Statistics of Income Bulletin, Summer 1999,* Washington, DC, 1999, p. 268). The total civilian employment in 1997 was 129,588,000 (U.S. Bureau of Labor Statistics, 1997).

5. Joseph Dalaker, U.S. Bureau of the Census, "Current Population Reports," series P60–207, *Poverty in the United States: 1998,* Washington, DC, U.S. Government Printing Office, 1999, p. v.

6. "Preliminary Estimates of Weighted Average Poverty Thresholds in 1999," Department of Commerce, Bureau of Census, 2000.

7. Ibid, p. v.

8. See The Center on Budget and Policy Priorities, Economic Policy Institute, "Pulling Apart: State-by-State Analysis of Income Trends," January 2000, fact sheet; U.S. Department of Commerce, "Current Population Reports: Consumer Income," Washington, DC, 1993; The World Bank, "World Development Report: 1992," Washington, DC, International Bank for Reconstruction and Development, 1992; The World Bank "World Development Report 1999/2000," pp. 238–239.

9. Jared Bernstein et al., op. cit., p. 262

10. Derived from Ibid, p. 95.

11. Alan Blinder, quoted by Paul Krugman, in "Disparity and Despair," *U.S.* News *and World Report,* March 23, 1992. p. 54.

12. Paul Samuelson, *Economics,* 10th ed., New York, McGraw-Hill, 1976, p. 84.

13. "Money Income of Households, Families, and Persons in the United States: 1992," U.S. Department of Commerce, "Current Population Reports: Consumer Income" series P60–184, Washington, DC, 1993, p. B6.   Also, Jared Bernstein et al., op. cit, p. 61.

14. Paul Blumberg, *Inequality in an Age of Decline,* New York, Oxford University Press, 1980.

15. U.S. Census Bureau, 1999, op. cit., p. v.

16. Michael Harrington, *The Other America,* New York, Macmillan, 1962, p. 12–13.

17. Stuart Ewen and Elizabeth Ewen, *Channels of Desire: Mass Images and the Shaping of American Consciousness,* New York, McGraw-Hill, 1982.

18. This is based on the *1999* poverty threshold of $13,290 for a family of three.

19. Based on a median income in 1998 of $38,885.

20. E. Pamuk, D. Makuc, K. Heck, C. Reuben, and K. Lochner, *Socioeconomic Status and Health Chartbook, Health, United States, 1998,* Hyattsville, MD, National Center for Health Statistics, 1998, pp. 145–159; Vincente Navarro "Class, Race, and Health Care in the United States," in, Bersh Berberoglu, *Critical Perspectives in Sociology,* 2nd ed., Dubuque, IA, Kendall/Hunt, 1993, pp. 148–156; Melvin Krasner, *Poverty and Health in New York City,* United Hospital Fund of New York, 1989. See also U.S. Dept. of Health and Human Services, *Health Status of Minorities and Low Income Groups,* 1985; and Dan Hughes, Kay Johnson, Sara Rosenbaum, Elizabeth Butler, and Janet Simons, *The Health of America's Children,* The Children's Defense Fund, 1988.

21. E. Pamuk et al., op. cit.; Kenneth Neubeck and Davita Glassberg, *Sociology; A Critical Approach,* New York, McGraw-Hill, 1996, pp. 436–438; Aaron Antonovsky, "Social Class, Life Expectancy, and Overall Mortality," in *The Impact of Social Class,* New York, Thomas Crowell, 1972, pp. 467–491. See also Harriet Duleep, "Measuring the Effect of Income on Adult Mortality Using Longitudinal Administrative Record Data," *Journal of Human Resources,* vol. 21, no. 2, Spring 1986.

22. E. Pamuk et al., op. cit., fig. 20; Dennis W. Roncek, "Dangerous Places: Crime and Residential Environment," *Social Forces,* vol. 60, no. 1, September 1981, pp. 74–96.

23. Richard De Lone, *Small Futures,* New York, Harcourt Brace Jovanovich, 1978, pp. 14–19.

24. Derived from The College Entrance Examination Board, "1999, A Profile of College Bound Seniors: SAT Test Takers," www.collegeboard.org/sat/cbsenior/yr1999/NAT/natbk499.html#income

25. William H. Sewell, "Inequality of Opportunity for Higher Education," *American Sociological Review,* vol. 36, no. 5, 1971, pp. 793–809.

26. The Mortenson Report on Public Policy Analysis of Opportunity *for* Postsecondary Education, "Postsecondary Education Opportunity," Iowa City, IA, September 1993, no. 16.

27. De Lone, op. cit., pp. 14–19.

28. Howard Tuchman, *Economics of the Rich,* New York, Random House, 1973, p. 15.

29. Howard Wachtel, *Labor and the Economy,* Orlando, FL, Academic Press, 1984, pp. 161–162.

30. Derived from Census, 1999, op. cit., p. vi.

Questions for Discussion and Writing

1. Mantsios begins his essay by saying, "People in the United States don't like to talk about class. Or so it would seem." Based on your experiences, do you agree with him or not? Why?

2. A little further on, Mantsios argues that one exception to this avoidance of class discussion is the media's presentation of "the wealthy" and "the poor." In terms of your own experiences with "the media," do you think Mantsios is correct? Why? Why not?

3. Mantsios lists four common beliefs (myths) about the United States. Have you heard them before? When and where?

4. Mantsios examines each myth and then declares his results as a "reality." How does Mantsios arrive at his conclusions, and are you convinced that they are more accurate than the beliefs they revise? Justify your answer.

5. Mantsios presents the profiles of three Americans. Do these profiles help us to understand the nature of the myths and realities that Mantsios presents to us? If they do, how? If they don't, why not?

6. If you were the host of a cultural affairs program and the three people profiled were guests, what questions would you ask them? Why?

Making Connections

1. Based on your understanding of D'Souza and Mantsios, how would each interpret the following statement: "Let us use the opportunities of America to create the American Dream"? Which interpretation is closer to your own? Explain.

2. How well do the profiles support or contradict the claims made by D'Souza? How well do these profiles relate to the general statistics found in the Social Trends Index (pp. 45–47)? Explain.

3. In terms of your own understanding of the complex issues presented in this chapter, have the readings and discussions clarified, extended, or restructured your perspectives? If so, how? If not, why not?

4. Often, the more we begin to understand a complex issue, the more we realize just how much we need to know in order to understand it. Given your experience with the readings in this chapter, what additional information would you need to have in order to judge the accuracy and the quality of the arguments presented? Why? Can you express this need for additional information in the form of specific questions that further research can help answer?

Visual Exercise

Some images are used as attention getters, as ways of adding interest or variety to a text. Consider whether the following image powerfully influences both emotions and logic.

BREAKING
the middle class bank

Milwaukee Journal Sentinel, Sunday March 31, 1996 by Tim Brinton.

Questions

1. What are your first impressions of the visual?

2. How do the various visual elements work to: a) attract attention b) convey information c) elicit emotion?

3. How does this visual relate to the article preceding it? Does it support or modify or refute the informational claims that Mantsios makes?

4. Was your understanding of the "myths and realities" of the class system in America clarified, extended, or restructured by the visual?

The Myth of Equal Opportunity
Adriana Hemans (Student)

Adriana Hemans, a first-year student, wrote this essay based on a text of Gregory Mantsios and some additional reading. Her analysis of the nature of class in America led her to argue that the gulf between the rich and the poor is rapidly widening and that our institutions are set up to perpetuate that gulf. As you read, evaluate the effectiveness of the evidence she uses to show how the wealthy depend upon and benefit from the poor.

* * * * * * * * *

Unless you have been living under a rock for your entire life, you have probably heard the phrase *equal opportunity*. By most people's definitions equal opportunity is the idea that every child born in America has a chance to be successful. Equal opportunity can also mean that every person is treated equally by laws and institutions. This is a very politically correct idea and something that we should certainly strive to have in our society. While many people recognize that there is a continuing struggle to create more equality, most do not realize that the oppression of disadvantaged groups in America is both intentional and systematic.

The general tendency is for people to seek their own personal gains and to favor the system that benefits them directly. The late John Rawls, a social scientist at Harvard University, has created a theoretical system of social contracts that is called Rawlsian justice. In this theory, John Rawls states that all people are self-interested by nature, and that in order to have equality in society we must have a social contract with moral restraints. The founding principle of the moral contract is the "veil of ignorance" (Saint-Amand, Lecture Notes). A person would not know his or her sex, age, class, intelligence or disabilities, if any. This person would choose principles of justice for society's institutions. The only logical way to choose would be to give priority to the least well off, or equality in general. Under this system every citizen would have equal access to medical care, and disadvantaged people would be first in line for benefits like scholarships and government aid. We are very far from this ideal in America.

Critics of this system claim that it is unfair to expect the healthy to subsidize the unhealthy. They say that catering to the lowest rung on the social ladder would bring down the entire system. However, it is not merely by chance that some people are confined to the lowest tier of society. This condition is the cause and the result of the system in place that favors the wealthy and enforces the status quo.

Rich begets rich and poor begets poor. Gregory Mantsios, Director of Worker Education at Queens College of the City University of New York, argues that class structure is deliberately built and that opportunities for economic improvement are not equitably available to those on the lower end of the scale. "Even when IQ test scores were the same," notes Mantsios, "a young person's ability to obtain a job that will pay in the top 10% of the income structure is 27 times as great if he or she comes from a wealthy background" (67). The poor are physically as well as financially disadvantaged. "'The findings clearly indicate that certain segments of the population—poor, minority, and other disadvantaged groups—are especially vulnerable and bear a disproportionate amount of preventable and therefore unnecessary deaths and diseases'" (65). Mantsios's evidence suggests that the top of the socioeconomic ladder is an exclusive club into which members are generally born.

Most people agree that government has a responsibility to care for the poor and the needy, although how much support people are willing to give to the poor is largely based on the image of the poor in question. A study of public opinion about welfare programs conducted by social scientists Fay Lomax Cook and Edith Barrett found that negative views of African-American welfare mothers generated greater opposition to welfare than comparative views of white welfare mothers. Attitudes among whites were strongly influenced by their perception of welfare as supportive of minority groups, who were commonly referred to as lazy (19–22). Many conservatives argue that the poor as a group possess negative attitudes about work and success that keep them from aspiring to higher accomplishments. Researcher Greg Duncan, in his 10-year study of the economic life of American families, found that there was no distinctive set of attitudes distinguishing the poor from the non-poor. He found that most people in poverty situations were victims of circumstance who had found themselves in poverty after events such as being laid off, being injured or getting a divorce (188–190).

Despite Duncan's findings, Americans, like many people, are prone to preconceived notions about certain populations. To be a member of a group that is associated with certain undesirable elements is to carry a lifelong stigma, while being a member of a group that holds an elite place in society opens doors and creates opportunities. In an article titled "White Privilege and Male Privilege," Wellesley College researcher Peggy McIntosh argues that many are willing to see women and blacks as disadvantaged, but are not willing to see themselves as advantaged. McIntosh emphasizes, "This is not a free country; one's life is not what one makes it; many doors open for certain people through no virtue of their own" (76). McIntosh describes what she calls the myth of meritocracy, which is the assertion by advantaged groups that their place of prominence has been earned by merits alone. McIntosh writes, "Keeping most people unaware that freedom of confident action is there for just a small number of people props up those in power and serves to keep power in the hands of the same groups that have most of it already" (81).

In America, democracy may be a thing of the past. Our government seems to follow the elite model more than any other. And the elite are the ones who have wealth. The surest way, and some say the only way, to win elections is to be willing to spend lots of money on a campaign. The two major candidates in the 2000 election each spent more than 90 million on their campaigns (Ayres 19). The most often used method of gaining access to government is by donating money to government officials. The higher one's socioeconomic status, the more likely one is to vote. All of these factors point to a system in which not every citizen has equal access to government. Rather, the people who have more power to begin with, are the ones who continue to gain political clout.

The class system in the United States is not accidental. Those who have power are invested in the current system. The rich are rich because others are poor. Industries and corporations want to see a large pool of unemployment because it keeps their work force in check, and allows them to set low wages. Capitalism is a system that places emphasis on private ownership and prosperity rather than on the collective good. The goal of a business owner is to create more profits for himself and to see his employees as a means to generate profits rather than as a person who forms a partnership with his employer. The common experience of working class Americans is one of frustrated expectations and the sense of being under appreciated and badly paid.

Clearly, there is no equal opportunity in America. People generally are confined to the class into which they were born. The means for improvement of social standing—education and employment— are not equally attainable by all people. We are all living within spheres of oppression. The wealthy are guaranteed certain privileges, while the poor, overall, are guaranteed discrimination. The great irony is that we are all affected by this system of oppression while most refuse to admit that it even exists. It may be too late to change our misconceptions about each other or to create a way for the disadvantaged to become more equal. What we must do is change our definition of success. We must stop penalizing people who cannot succeed within a structure that is dependent on their failure.

Works Cited

Ayres, Drummond B. Jr. "The 2000 Campaign: Campaign Briefing." *New York Times* 21 July, 2000: A19. Print.

Cook, Fay Lomax, and Edith J. Barrett. *Support for the American Welfare State*. New York: Columbia UP, 1992. Print.

Duncan, Greg, and Jeanne Brooks-Gunn, eds. *Consequences of Growing Up Poor*. New York: Russell Sage, 1997. Print.

Mantsios, Gregory. "Rewards and Opportunities: The Politics and Economics of Class in the US." *Dialogue and Discovery: Writing and Reading across Disciplines*. Eds. Barbara Jo Krieger, Paul G. Saint-Amand, and Robert W. Emery. New York: St. Martin's,1996. 59–74. Print.

McIntosh, Peggy. "Working Paper 189. 'White Privilege and Male Privilege: A Personal Account of Coming to See Correspondences through Work in Women's Studies.'" 1988. 76–81.TS. Wellesley College Center for Research on Women, Wellesley, Massachusetts.

Saint-Amand, Paul. Class Lecture. Writing and Critical Thinking. SUNY Potsdam, Potsdam, NY. 12 Jan. 2001.

Questions for Discussion and Writing

1. What do you think Adriana most wants us to understand? Which of her claims are the most important and how well are they presented and supported?

2. The term "equal opportunity" is used both in the title and throughout her essay. Do you think the term is clearly defined and consistently employed? If so, how? If not, why not?

3. Adriana makes a number of controversial assertions.

    (a) "In America, democracy may be a thing of the past."
    (b) "The rich are rich because others are poor."
    (c) "Capitalism is a system that places emphasis on private ownership and prosperity rather than on the collective good."

    Could Adriana's statements put off some readers? Does she account for the views of readers who might not support her perspective? As her discussion progresses, does her position gain or lose credibility, specifically for those who might not share her point of view?

4. Having now read an essay by Gregory Mantsios, a recognized "authority" on complex social issues, and an essay by an undergraduate student on one of them, what rhetorical comparisons/contrasts can you make?

5. Do you have any experience, direct or indirect, concerning "equal opportunity" that you could use to support, modify, or refute any of Adriana's claims? Explain.

6. If you could ask Adriana any questions, what would they be? Why?

Making Connections

1. Gregory Mantsios writes that "the privileged in our society require a class-structured social order in order to maintain and enhance their economic and political well-being." What specific examples does Adriana offer to show that the wealthy depend upon and benefit from the poor? Are her assertions sound or do any of them bother you? Explain.

2. How well does Adriana's argument support or contradict the claims of Dinesh D'Souza's "Party of Nah" and his "Party of Yeah"? How do her various claims reflect the statistics found in the Social Trends Index (pp. 45–47)?

Short Essay Assignments

1. Use the reading selections and any other resources to construct your own Social Trends Index. Try for an array of controversial entries on subjects such as the gap between individual aspirations and economic realities; the society's focus on self-interest and materialism; the persistence of social problems such as poverty, violence, and racism; and the desire for stronger communal bonds. After sharing your entries with classmates, select one (or perhaps several related ones) and write an essay in which you describe the issues it points to and present your judgments about them. As you develop your paper, refer to ideas you found in this book, as well as to your own experiences. Be sure to provide specific examples to support your points.

2. Choose an author from the chapter and create an essay based on the following questions. What assumptions about American society does the author make in his or her discussion of poverty, inequality, and race? What kind of support does the author provide for these assertions? What do the author's views suggest about issues such as economic opportunity and social mobility? Is the author's perspective consistent with your own experience? Explain.

3. Citing a World Bank index that measures democratic quality—democratic elements like free and fair elections, degree of tolerance toward popular dissent, and so forth—researchers found that "the more accountable a government is to its own people, the more it helps those to whom it is not accountable." Matching the World Bank index to CDI (Commitment to Development Index), the United States ranked 13th out of 21 countries—one of the six lowest providers. The high scorer, the Netherlands, scored first on democratic elements and ranked first in CDI. Do such findings square with what you have read in this chapter? Be specific.

❏ Major Essay Assignment

In this chapter, you have encountered an array of voices speaking about recent trends and attitudes in the United States. Now you are poised to write an essay that builds on your preliminary exploration of these social forces. Your first task is to find a topic that genuinely interests you, one that will hold your attention and stimulate your thinking. Instead of jumping quickly to a definite position, your job is to decide what the important questions surrounding the topic or issue really are, why these questions are important, and what is to be gained from answering them. By structuring your inquiry to help bring out a variety of viewpoints, you can generate a paper that is apt to be a lot more thoughtful than the usual thesis-support essay.

A Word on Thesis Statements

Some of you may have been taught that in developing an argument one must begin with a thesis. However, that is a rather unrealistic expectation. In fact, writers often begin the writing process with only a hazy idea, too vague or general to be termed a thesis. This starting point may be called a "writing idea" or, if reasonably thought out, a hypothesis. With it writers begin to explore and test their thinking. Of course, the idea or hypothesis will be developed during the drafting process, but even then the concept will shift and the wording will change. Bear in mind that arriving at a final thesis should be one of the last steps in the process. In fact, the whole purpose of producing an argument is to shape the thesis. By developing and testing your ideas, you discover its final wording.

Spending ample time with the readings will help you to explore and learn as much as possible about the divergent themes that emerge from them, such as materialism, inequality, racism, gender and poverty. Note that we present these readings not merely as sources of criticism and complaint, but also of hope. As you contemplate possible lines of inquiry, consider how the issues explored in this chapter have influenced your life. Your personal experience is a relevant and valuable resource for the completion of your writing projects.

Because this assignment's topic is open-ended, the guidelines in the next chapter can help to insure that your paper springs from the readings and discussions. To that end, whatever topic you choose, be sure to make use of the relevant facts, data, and ideas from your readings.

To Help You Get Started

. . . The late sociologist and activist Michael Harrington (borrowing from philosopher John Rawls) defines a just society as one you would accept when it was described to you even if you did not know your place within it. (See the student essay pp. 134–135.) Go back through the readings and develop a description of contemporary American society. Then, taking your cue from Harrington's definition of a just society, decide whether you would accept American society as you have described it. Justify your response.

5

Putting Techniques to Work in Your Writing

Charting a Direction

Chapter 5 presents a sequence of guidelines that will help open your mind to different possibilities for discovering and shaping your ideas. While you are not expected to adhere slavishly to these guidelines, understanding the principles involved can help you prepare a well-developed essay.

As you gather your thoughts, remember that the goal is to focus on a series of questions that will generate thoughtful lines of inquiry. Also keep in mind that, generally speaking, readers come to a discussion as outsiders. You must therefore recognize your audience's needs as you try to draw them into your exploration. This is an opportunity for readers to observe your mind at work, as you move between the wisdom of different sources to develop your own vision. At the same time, you need to give readers good, forceful reasons for attending to your inquiry. Nobody will want to listen unless you can get the audience to recognize the relevance and importance of your message.

As you begin to explore possible directions for your essay, be aware that writers who jump quickly to a definite position tend to write narrow papers that do not adequately consider all aspects of an issue. To help undercut this tendency, you are to frame the focus of your discussion as a question—or a series of questions—rather than a statement. Asking questions can help you confront a topic from diverse viewpoints and deepen your understanding of emerging issues and themes. Your questions can also serve as a guide for examining and clarifying your reasoning. They will also stimulate more extensive consideration of the concepts involved. Of course, you must ask the right kinds of questions. You want questions that will help you look at your subject in new and imaginative ways, not questions that will restrict your thoughts or narrow your focus too much.

Generating a Focus for Your Writing

To find a subject and develop a tentative focus for your paper, review your reading and class discussion notes. Try to recall a time when someone's point of view compelled you to speak out in class. Or try to remember some delight or discomfort provoked by one of the readings. Did the reading or discussion reinforce your thinking, or did it make you reconsider a previously held view? What new facts or perspectives were offered that you thought might be worth considering?

In your journal, jot down any ideas that surface as you try to identify a topic or problem and, in it, formulate some questions to direct your exploration. As you explore your ideas and decide what questions to ask, you will begin to sense what you know and what you still need to learn. Then you will be in a better position to concentrate on particular readings.

As we have said, there are no shortcuts, special diets, miracle drugs, or esoteric practices that will endow you overnight with a mastery of critical inquiry and the power of logical thinking. But there are specific types of questions, first introduced in Chapter 1, that can help you examine your reasoning and clarify your thinking on any issue. To help you with your current assignment, observe how we use the following exploratory probes to raise questions about the chapter readings.

Questioning the Nature of Things

When we looked at questions about the nature of things in Chapter 1, we offered as samples some "top of the head" answers. While they served our purpose at that point, they tended to be fairly simplistic and, in some cases, completely obvious—not quite up to the standard we want to see in college and professional writing. Now we want to dig a little deeper to generate answers that would be more significant, insightful, and better expressions of your individual creative intellect. Often, the best place to begin in an exploration of the nature of things is by meaningfully defining terms important and relevant to the discussion. You have no doubt been taught to look up terms in a good dictionary when you have questions about their meaning. While this is a decent start, dictionary definitions are limited in their usefulness to a good writer and a good critical thinker. They tend to leave out much more significant information about a term than they include.

Take, for example, the term "individuality." What is "individuality"? What categories and characteristics do you associate with the term? Do you believe that society deprives people of their individuality? Do you think that being an individual primarily means standing apart from the crowd? Have any of our questions led you to rethink your own assumptions about the term? Why or why not?

When you think beyond simple "dictionary definitions" and instead really inquire into the "what," into the complicated behaviors and attitudes involved, let's say, in asserting one's own individuality, you can better appreciate the fundamental importance of developing a clear and thorough understanding of a subject.

Exercise

Earlier we stressed how experimenting with other ways to express complex ideas can help to insure that you understand the material. Find a passage from the chapter readings that seems to be seeking a definition of a term. Put the author's ideas into your own words, taking special care to represent his or her thoughts accurately.

Remember that reconstructing the language of a source in your own words strengthens your grasp of the material and leads to a fuller comprehension of the writer's thinking and reasoning. For this reason, paraphrasing key passages is a useful strategy for initiating any inquiry.

Paraphrasing and clarifying specific terms can help to insure that you understand the main point of a passage. You can also enlarge and enhance your understanding of a subject by using one perspective as a frame for examining another. Consider, for example, the life-long project of Boston College Professor Alan Wolfe, a project that touches on a critical concern: how to balance individual freedom with social responsibility. Contrary to Wolfe, Colorado State Professor Emeritus D. Stanley Eitzen portrays individualism as leading to selfishness and isolation, as undermining the collective good, and as an indicator of reduced social cohesion. The contrast between these two views might lead you to ask how these contrary assumptions came to be.

Questioning Cause

When you're faced with a complex topic, inquiring into the causes of the subject can help you ask more significant questions and make better sense of the answers. But you need to remember that causation is seldom simple. Indeed, in the previous example, the deep differences between Wolfe and Eitzen reflect attitudes and values that are far more complex than our discussion indicated. To deepen your inquiry, let's turn to literary and cultural critic Raymond Williams for an historical analysis of particular "key words," fundamental terms that both convey and create our social reality. His examination of the word "individual" can help reveal the historical conflicts and struggles embodied in the term. To make good use of this reading, list any points you don't understand and bring the list to class.

Individual
Raymond Williams

Individual originally meant indivisible. That now sounds like a paradox. "Individual" stresses a distinction from others; "indivisible" a necessary connection. The development of the modern meaning from the original meaning is a record in language of an extraordinary social and political history. . . . The emergence of notions of individuality, in the modern sense, can be related to the break-up of the medieval social, economic, and religious order. In the general movement against feudalism there was a new stress on a man's personal existence over and above his place of function in a rigid hierarchical society. There was a related stress, in

---

Source: Raymond Williams "Individual" from *Keywords: A Vocabulary of Culture and Society, Revised Edition* by Raymond Williams. Reprinted by permission of Oxford University Press and HarperCollins Publishers Ltd. © 1985 Raymond Williams.

Protestantism, on a man's direct and individual relation to God, as opposed to this relation mediated by the Church. But it was not until IC17 [last third of the seventeenth century] and C18 [eighteenth century] that a new mode of analysis, in logic and mathematics, postulated the individual as the substantial entity . . . from which other categories and especially collective categories were derived. The political thought of the Enlightenment mainly followed this model. Argument began from individuals, who had an initial and primary existence, and laws and forms of society were derived from them; by submission, as in Hobbes; by contract or consent, or by the new version of natural law, in liberal thought. In classical economics, trade was described in a model which postulated separate individuals who decided, at some starting point, to enter into economic or commercial relations. In utilitarian ethics, separate individuals calculated the consequences of this or that action which they might undertake. Liberal thought based on "the individual" as starting point was criticized from conservative positions—"the individual is foolish . . . the species is wise" (Burke)[1]—but also, in C19 [nineteenth century], from socialist positions, as most thoroughly in Marx, who attacked the opposition of the abstract categories "individual" and "society" and argued that the individual is a social creation, born into relationships and determined by them.

The modern sense of *individual* is then a result of the development of a certain phase of scientific thought and of a phase of political and economic thought. But already from eC19 [early nineteenth century] a distinction began to be made within this. It can be summed up in the development of two derived words: *individual* and *individualism*. The latter corresponds to the main movement of liberal political and economic thought. But there is a distinction indicated by Simmel[2]: "the individualism of uniqueness—*Einriegheit*—as against that of singleness—*Einzelheit*."

"Singleness"—abstract individualism—is based, Simmel argued, on the quantitative thought, centered in mathematics and physics, of C18. "Uniqueness," by contrast, is a qualitative category, and is a concept of the Romantic movement. It is also a concept of evolutionary biology, in which the species is stressed and the individual related to it, but with the recognition of uniqueness within a kind. Many arguments about "the individual" now confuse the distinct senses to which *individualism* and *individuality* point. *Individuality* has the longer history, and comes out of the complex of meanings in which *individual* developed, stressing both a unique person and his (indivisible) membership of a group. *Individualism* is a C19 coinage: "a novel expression, to which a novel idea has given birth" (tr. Tocqueville, 1835): a theory not only of abstract individuals but of the primacy of individual states and interests.

Editors' Notes:

[1] Edmund Burke (1729–1797) British statesman and philosopher.

[2] George Simmel (1858–1918) sociological theorist and co-founder of the German Sociological Society.

For Discussion

1. In your own words, trace those elements of European intellectual history that help explain the conflicts and struggles embodied in the term *individual.*

2. Do you believe that individuals must strive to be distinct from others in order to express their uniqueness? What assumptions about individual expression does your response suggest? How did your assumptions get to be that way?

3. Can you conceive of a society that fosters the development of each person's unique qualities, one in which a person would not have to guard against prescribed values and norms? Justify your response.

Questioning Assumptions

To add to your deliberations, consider the contrary assumptions about American society you found in the texts of Dinesh D'Souza and Gregory Mantsios. D'Souza, you may recall, concludes his discussion by suggesting that, while all citizens should expect equal treatment under the law, one should not expect social institutions to intervene on behalf of an individual's private struggles. To the contrary, in his discussion of race and poverty, Mantsios tries to show how our institutions are set up to restrict economic opportunity and social mobility for those on the lower end of the scale, suggesting the need for dramatic changes to reverse what he views as disturbing and dangerous trends. Fortunately, complicated and controversial arguments like these can generally be unraveled—thus helping you to arrive at useful answers—if you question and thus make explicit the point of view or perspective motivating a writer's position. Also, being acutely aware of your own perspectives, and how they came to be, can help you seek out tensions and contradictions, thus contributing to a more informed response.

Questioning Effects and Consequences

Just as you can inquire into the causes of any subject, you can also try to discover some of the effects and consequences. You can explore some of these possible outcomes by asking "What if. . ." For example, you might ask if D'Souza means by his argument that society should stop trying to improve the lives of the poor and the disadvantaged? If so, what about early-childhood programs like Head Start? What about programs aimed at reducing unemployment?

At the same time, Mantsios alleges that "[w]hen we look at society and try to determine what it is that keeps most people down—what holds them back from realizing their potential as healthy, creative, productive individuals—we find institutionally oppressive forces that are largely beyond their individual control" (p. 129). In response to his point, you might consider what attitudes or values would follow if one were to hold this deterministic viewpoint. Or you could challenge this viewpoint by contemplating how acceptance of his argument could lead to a denial of responsibility for one's circumstances.

When you carry your thinking out in this way, you look at ways in which someone's ideas relate to other important issues. When someone's position advocates action on an issue, it is especially important to investigate what could happen if that action were indeed taken.

Questioning Evidence: Examples, Testimony, Statistics

Finally, you should question the accuracy and credibility of any evidence you offer in support of your assertions, as well as the relevance of the evidence to your argument. Whether or not you agree with a particular writer, you will want to be sure that the evidence shows what the writer says it shows. Here we'll examine examples, testimony and statistics as types of support that add strength and credibility to a writer's ideas.

Examples. Because the claims in arguments are often general and abstract, writers need concrete examples that illustrate and support their claims. Consider again Mantsios's assertion that there is a conscious and deliberate effort on the part of the privileged class to maintain "a class-structured social order." What are some examples of how the wealthy depend upon and benefit from the poor? Are these examples relevant to Mantsios's overall argument, and do they truly exemplify the claims he wants the data to support? Explain.

Testimony. Writers do not support their claims only by examples. They support them with testimony as well. When writers use testimony to justify claims, they ask readers to believe that a statement is true because an expert says it is. Because Mantsios recognizes that his own view is a minority opinion, he uses several outside references to persuade his audience that his position is sound. Identify a few of these references and decide whether Mantsios uses them well to convey an honest, thorough effort to set the record straight. Repeat this exercise with the D'Souza piece, bearing in mind that he presents the voices of various leaders, some of whom express contrasting views.

Statistics. Society uses statistical evidence for everything from selling soap to probing galactic history. Statistics can provide legitimate and convincing support for many types of claims if the data are accurate, if a reputable organization conducted the study, and if the findings are relevant to the writer's point. Bearing in mind these criteria, do you think Mantsios uses convincing figures when supporting controversial positions? If so, what information establishes their credibility? D'Souza also uses statistics to support controversial claims. Do you think his figures are accurate? Has he attributed his data to reputable sources? Explain.

The exploratory probes presented above (probes about the *nature of things, cause, assumptions, effects and consequences,* and *types of evidence*) can help to focus your inquiry on important aspects of a subject and to bring out a variety of viewpoints. But you shouldn't use these probes as an exhaustive or even preferred list of questions. If you think of other kinds of questions that lead you to a deeper relationship with your material, don't hesitate to use them.

Journal Activity

Look back through your initial journal and reading notes for specific thoughts or themes you would like to explore further. Try listing these items and brainstorming (either alone or with a group) to discover the kinds of questions that can take you beyond your initial reflections. Also consider how the five types of probes presented above can help to clarify complex and difficult concepts and lead to more expansive ways of seeing your subject. While you might not know precisely what you want your essay to accomplish, try sketching a preliminary plan that suggests ways of directing your exploration.

Sample Notes

Below you will find excerpts from the notes that student Keith Mantia made in his journal. Note how Keith's journal writing gave him a way to begin exploring possible directions for his essay and helped him as well to raise serious questions.

What I know: Facts and Ideas from Readings

- ✓ Fact: 35 million people live below the poverty line
- ✓ Some people seemingly do not have the chance to succeed because of background, schooling, other issues.
- ✓ Yahoo's Jerry Yang makes billion of dollars while 47 million Americans can't afford health insurance.
- ✓ The class book <u>The Cheating Culture</u>, says that "the top one-percent" of Americans have more money than the 90 percent at the bottom. . . .
- ✓ Eight American business men ("Bill Gates, Paul Allen, Steve Ballimer and 5 WalMart heirs") are worth more than the GNP of Sweden.

What I Don't Know

Questioning the Nature of Things	Questioning Cause	Questioning Assumptions	Questioning Effects, Consequences, and Values	Questioning Evidence: Examples, Testimony, Statistics
— Who are the poor? What is the "poverty line" exactly? Even if the poverty line were raised from $17,463 (for a family of four) to $19,500, how would they live today?	— What forces bring people down? Do they create their own economic instability (drugs, alcoholism, bad decisions) or is it not their fault (family dysfunction, poor schooling, no role models, job loss, medical bankruptcy, just bad luck)?	— How do I feel about the plight of the poor? As a person with opportunity, would I give up a share of my chances to help someone out?	— Could those marginally above the poverty line also be seriously at risk? Is society at large at risk in not helping those less fortunate? —Do some people who succeed turn their backs on those less fortunate left behind in their communities?	— Testimony of Edward Wolff and John Weicher (D'Souza pp. 110–111) is inconsistent. How can one ask readers to believe that a statement is true because an expert says it is when the experts report different findings on the same issue, in this case, the degree of economic inequality?

(Cont.)

Questioning the Nature of Things	Questioning Cause	Questioning Assumptions	Questioning Effects, Consequences, and Values	Questioning Evidence: Examples, Testimony, Statistics
— Because the rich don't always use their wealth to help out, is this arrogance? — Eitzen defines individualism as "an emphasis on the individual." Is it really as "excessive" in American society as he claims? — Are people, like Eitzen claims, more isolated than ever before from neighbors, family, and others?	— Are the entitlements (tax breaks, loop holes) afforded the rich in part responsible for the wealth/poverty gap? — Is inequality of opportunity the main issue or is it something else? — Does competition contribute to creating the incentive to succeed? Does being on the bottom build incentive? — How is it that 1 in 4 kids live below the poverty line? — Does the way advertising portrays American life as successful and easy negatively affect how those who don't "have it all" see their lives?	—Should the rich be more charitable? Should they be responsible for helping those less fortunate or is it the poor person's responsibility to lift him or herself out of poverty? — Is it fair for people to depend on others to help them out of poverty? Do people feel better if they "go it alone"? What do they gain/lose? — Do people in poverty really want help but can't bring themselves to ask for it for reasons of pride, or something else? — Do we expect the poor to fix their situations themselves? — Eitzen puts down individualism but a person has to take charge of his or her own welfare, right? Is there a middle ground?	— What are the consequences for us as a society if we help to bring the majority out of poverty — if that's possible? What does it do for the go-it-alone work ethic? — How would the capitalist system be affected if everyone had jobs and succeeded? — Do we want America to have an upper class that grows while lower classes struggle in poverty? — Is there something sordid about the big gap between the rich and the poor? Is it ethically or morally wrong that Yang has made billions while millions of poor lack basic necessities—shelter, food, health care, medication?	— Mantsios presents the profiles of three Americans (pp. 124–127). Professor K asked whether Mantsios has presented adequate evidence to show that these single examples demonstrate the existence of a general condition. — I understand better why professors caution us to question whether writers use examples, testimony, and statistics honestly and effectively.

Creating a Working Thesis

Freewriting is an effective technique for fashioning a working thesis. You can use the questions that have emerged from class discussions and as a result of your reading to stimulate your writing. At this stage, you are not committed to what emerges as you put your thoughts on the page. Your aim is to generate as much text as possible. Feel free to jot down ideas, play with words and concepts, and arrange and rearrange what you are creating on the page.

For most writers, the key idea that will structure their thinking does not emerge as a perfectly formed sentence or group of sentences. As they mull over the impressions that their reading and conversations have produced, as they fix those impressions tentatively on the page, they begin to see what might be presented to their readers. Sometimes, they just have the beginnings of what might be of interest to readers; often, they recognize that they have reached a dead end and must start over. So, do not be frustrated if the core idea for an essay does not immediately pop out. Just write!

Keith returned to the questions he had formulated earlier. When he considered them again, several possibilities emerged. Observe how the following "focused" freewrite gave him a way to consolidate his thoughts.

Is self interest the driving force today?

I sense that a lot of Americans feel, "You have to take care of yourself because nobody is going to be interested in you or your situation." This feeling is certainly in keeping with Eitzen's ideas about individualism. On the other hand, individualism got people to where they are on the ladder of success, not following others (like D'Souza said) but pushing themselves. . . Maybe I can look into individualism more to see where it fits into the trends we have discussed in class. . .Is individualism exclusively bad or good? The entrepreneurial spirit of "rugged individualism" is considered by most of my peers as a hallmark of American pride and progress. How to reconcile that with the excessive self interest that Eitzen claims makes us oblivious to anybody's welfare but our own . . . Is it some kind of arrogance? How about elected public officials? Should they be the voice of the people or adhere to a policy of non-interference? In other words, let the market decide? What is the government's role for creating jobs so people can break out of that cycle of poverty? In class, we discussed the difference between simply giving people handouts as opposed to helping the less fortunate to help themselves. I need to go back through the readings to sort some of this out. Another issue: does success keep people who overcome their poverty less caring about those still in it? I read about how some who leave never look back...why? Does the wealth gap reflect Social Darwinism at work, and if so, does the ethic of survival of the fittest breed even more selfishness and self-interest?. . .

Like Keith, you need to draw freely from your initial reflections and be willing to speculate on possible links that can take you beyond your preliminary journal entries. This culling, connecting, and reflecting upon emerging issues and themes can help you define a direction and purpose for your paper. While your personal observations and experiences will likely provide the origin of the question or problem you choose to explore, your close reading of the assigned texts can lead to unexpected discoveries. Try to remain open to these discoveries as you move back and forth between your own perceptions and the perspectives found in the readings, using each set of ideas critically to cross-examine the other.

Teaming up with peers, explore the ways in which the questions you raised helped you to develop insight into your own thinking. Also consider how you were informed or enlightened by the questions of your peers.

Now try using the following grid to examine even more explicitly how your questions function in your writing. In groups of two or three, see if you can identify examples of each category. Then, for each example, explain how the question helped the writer gain insight into a perplexing issue.

Questioning the Nature of Things	Questioning Cause	Questioning Assumptions	Questioning Effects, Consequences, and Values	Questioning Evidence: Examples, Testimony, Statistics

Recognize that when you are generating ideas and beginning to shape them into coherent form, your goal may be provisional—subject to change as you acquire more information and think the subject through. But at some point, you must develop and convey, either explicitly or implicitly, the purpose of your essay—to inform your audience about the existence of some phenomenon, challenge an established viewpoint, explore the diverse aspects of an issue, pose solutions to a problem, and so forth.

Each purpose requires a different approach, and consequently a different strategy for structuring and developing your essay. Moreover, as you get to know your audience, your purpose will be shaped, in part, by your understanding of their expectations. Because the issues of purpose and audience are so complex, we continue to discuss these vital elements throughout the book.

Deciding Purpose and Goals

Our daily communications include numerous rituals and routines. As you move through the day saying, "Hi. How're you doing? What's up?" and so forth, you minimize the energy expended on minor matters. However, when your purpose is more complex, you cannot rely on such cultural conventions. Your approach will be more measured.

Depending on the level of involvement you seek from your audience, your strategies will vary. At the first level, you seek *understanding* of your point of view. At the second level, *you require acceptance of your beliefs* and the exclusion of competing ideas. At the third level, you encourage *appropriate action* on shared convictions. The questions below will help you to develop strategies for situations that involve these levels.

1) *Understanding:* While focusing on developing and expressing your point of view, recognize that your audience will have connections to your issues and take them into account. As you write, ask yourself the following questions:

   - *What does my audience know and feel about my subject?*
   - *What do they need to know to gain a more complete picture or make a good decision?*
   - *What examples or data are most honest, reliable, and relevant?*

2) *Acceptance:* When your purpose is to ask for commitment, you might be asking your readers to prioritize their values. Consider, for example, those who believe that free markets are

the means for creating wealth. Asking if this principle should outweigh the effects of escalating social inequality surely puts into conflict at least two core beliefs. It could be difficult for them to respond as you desire. Therefore, before presenting such challenges, you need to probe some issues.

- *What are my readers' values? Which are most important to them?*
- *Does adopting my position require them to devalue or completely abandon any of their fundamental principles? If so, is my argument sufficient for that to take place?*

3) *Appropriate Action:* At the third level, your purpose is to have others accept your views and take appropriate action. Sometimes, what you are asking opposes what they have done before. So, you have to supply rhetorical and logical energy to get them finally to say, "Yes, I know about . . . but I didn't realize how. . . or that it's going to affect . . . and now I'm going to . . . ."

For example, imagine you were to argue that, to achieve a just and balanced approach to relieving income inequality, we need to encourage a national dialogue to address educational and employment inequities. You might ask your readers to initiate a campus forum. You might ask them to help bring community and state leaders to your campus or to promote workshops, demonstration booths, presentations, and discussions. On a broader scale, you might urge them to join in a call for a national economic summit, asking them to write letters, make phone calls, or donate money to organizations lobbying Congress for this goal. However convinced your readers might seem, recognize that their willingness to participate depends largely on the strength of their commitment. Ask yourself the following questions.

- *What can my readers do about the situation? What will they do?*
- *Have I taken into account their reluctance to act on issues that seem so distant from them?*
- *What risks am I asking them to take? What is the possible cost to them, either emotionally or materially, of the action I am advocating?*

Remember that the phases of involvement are cumulative. People usually must understand before they will believe, and they must believe before they will act. Note that the sequence dictates an escalation of the degree of engagement and risk you impose upon your readers.

You will not always want to move your readers through all the phases of involvement. Sometimes you will want them only to understand or, perhaps, to sympathize with your position even if they don't agree with you. Even if they accept your point of view, you may not have a solution to offer. You might only want others to agree that the situation demands one.

Understanding Your Audience

Significant and actual attention to audience is one of the most difficult aspects of composition. One reason may be that it often becomes a sort of "let's pretend" game for students. Unless the composition course culminates in a publication of some sort, you might feel that you have no "real" audience. One thing you can surely do is to understand who your teacher is and what he or she represents. When your instructor responds to your work, he or she is representing an intellectual and academic tradition that has been centuries in the making. Consequently, your audience is neither general nor hypothetical. Rather, your conversation is with very real minds—thinkers and writers, past and present, who have earned recognition in a specific field. When your instructor responds to your work, he or she is, in a sense, speaking for all those minds. And when you write, you are speaking to them.

Your instructor's responses can be a source of growth and challenge for you as a writer. These responses do not merely reflect personal reactions to your text; the instructor will also try to introduce you to the conventions that apply to academic writing, for instance, the type of evidence permissible in a specific field and the way it should be presented. Your instructor can play a key role in helping you earn recognition and respect from a wide range of readers. While you might assume that the instructor has final authority over your text, we want to suggest a more constructive student/instructor relationship. Your instructor's comments reflect knowledge of established patterns of writing and thinking that can offer new avenues for expressing your ideas. You will need to carefully evaluate how these conventions might help you to articulate your ideas more effectively. By participating in an ongoing dialogue with your instructor, you can uncover new ways of organizing and understanding your experience and thereby achieve greater control over your written expression.

Audience and purpose, of course, are closely linked. For example, if your purpose is to challenge an established viewpoint, you will need to imagine how those who hold this perspective might respond to your essay. You will want to anticipate how your readers—those who share your viewpoint as well as those holding an opposing viewpoint—would react to the evidence you use to advance your thinking. Would they find your thesis well considered, whether or not they agreed with it? Would your examples seem appropriate? Bear in mind that readers are more likely to respond favorably, even if they do not share your perspective, if you show that you understand how your position is situated within the range of competing viewpoints. You may also wish to consider how your peers, your fellow students, would respond to your essay. Would they consider it to be well organized, interesting, and logical? You might have the opportunity to share early drafts of your essays with fellow students. Their observations and suggestions may reveal areas where you have not accomplished the purpose of the assignment. Be prepared to make careful decisions about the suggestions they make. For example, if a peer tells you that a paragraph is unclear, you will need to reread the paragraph carefully to determine whether the criticism has merit before you make any revisions.

As you respond to suggestions and comments, keep in mind that your goal is to take charge of your own writing. Claiming control of your language and subject matter demands that your personal reactions figure prominently in your composing. After all, the writing is yours: it comes from your experiences, your thought processes, and your skill as a writer. It is important to recognize that you are an important part of your own audience. Look at your writing as objectively as you can to find out whether it is persuasive, convincing, and accurate. Remember that your writing is actually a piece of reading. As a reader, think about what compels you to become involved in someone else's writing. Ask yourself why you might begin to lose interest. As you apply such questions to your own text, make any changes that would help you fulfill your purpose more effectively.

Journal Activity

Pick one of the readings in Chapter 4 that you found particularly interesting, insightful, or well written. Read it again and, this time, look for examples of four kinds of claims—claims of the nature of things, claims of cause and effect, claims of value (benefits/harms), and claims that propose action. Try to find two of each kind of claim, and write them in your journal; be sure to label them appropriately.

Go back through the claims you've selected and, for each claim, list an audience or type of audience that would probably be receptive to the claim *before* reading the article and an audience that would be more likely to reject it. Then, in each case, speculate on *why* the audience would probably respond as you think it would, and write down your speculations.

Finally, in each case, speculate on what the author might do—what kind of decision he or she might make—to make the negative audience more receptive.

Collaborative Activity

Your goal is to form small groups and explore how various types of readers are likely to respond to your writing and what sorts of decisions you will need to make to have your audience accept your point of view. The writing you will focus on in this discussion will depend on what assignments your instructor has made from Chapter 4. If you wrote one or both of the Short Essay Assignments, pick one of them. If you didn't write a Short Essay Assignment, pick the work you completed in response to the "To Help You Get Started" Assignment at the end of Chapter 4. In your group, discuss how various audiences might respond to your work—that is, what questions and concerns might the audience have about it. Be sure to take notes on relevant comments from the group. Then try to determine what questions you'll need to answer, what decisions you'll need to make, and/or what changes in your existing work you'll need to consider to respond to the audience concerns you've discussed. Again, be sure to take notes on any of the interesting or useful comments of your classmates.

Bringing Your Reading into Your Writing

As you consider how to put the readings to work in your writing, look for ways that the authors can help to sharpen your own judgment. Experiment with some of their expressions, arguments, and insights, while carefully considering the relevance of their ideas to your own thinking. Though you may not know what material you will need to develop your discussion, your work with the readings can help you to clarify difficult concepts and put you in a strong position to chart a direction that can lead to new ways of seeing your topic. As you enlist the support of specific writers, give full consideration to how you can bring their arguments to bear on your writing. This is an opportunity to test and examine the lines of argument shaping each reading, drawing as much from the reading as you can to deepen your inquiry.

You may also find it helpful to explain your interpretations to others in your class, drawing on specific passages for the support you think you will need in your essay. You will also want to see how others make use of the same passages, considering how their interpretations either add or call into question your reading of the material. By considering classmates' perspectives, you are less likely to settle on meanings that are overly subjective or too far removed from the full context of the reading. Whether you work individually or collaboratively, you will need to reread your sources to decide how each text best serves the purpose and goals you have set for your writing.

The Working Draft: Shaping Your Thoughts

You can get ideas about how to start your paper by reviewing your journal entries, looking for links between your thinking and reading. Perhaps you had made a judgment about the prevalence of *materialism, inequality, racism* or *poverty* long before you responded to the opposing viewpoints in this part of the book and your journal work reinforced your original position. Or your systematic listing of arguments and your hard thinking on these subjects might have led you to a new point of view. One way or another, you have arrived at a tentative perspective and have gathered supporting evidence that will help you to join in with the competing voices you have encountered, each of which argues for a distinct relationship between individual and collective interests.

Journal Activity

In your journal try sketching a preliminary plan that will help develop and focus your thoughts. The following questions, derived in part from the exploratory probes presented earlier in this chapter, will help coalesce your thinking into a more defined point of view.

- What are the main ideas you want to work with?
- How do these ideas create a focus for the assignment?
- What assumptions about people or society do you bring to your understanding of the readings and to class discussions?
- Can you support your understanding with evidence from the readings and from other sources? Justify your answer.
- Why do you approach your subject from one viewpoint instead of another? What would someone who disagrees with you say? Could other interpretations of the texts be equally compelling and convincing?
- In what ways might your thinking relate to other important issues?

As you examine and clarify your reasoning, recall the classroom discussion at the beginning of the book. The students struggled with several complex issues that could not be easily resolved. As with any thoughtful discussion, a combination of curiosity and critical skepticism can help you to confront contradictory information in constructive ways. Do not hesitate to raise questions when you have doubts or to modify your position if you are offered a persuasive argument.

Collaborative Activity

Below we offer explicit suggestions for sharing your drafts with classmates. For now, compiling a list of questions that addresses your specific concerns about your essay should help you get meaningful and useful feedback from discussion of your work.

Researching the Broader Context

Your knowledge and experience, combined with the information contained in the readings, may provide you with sufficient information to proceed with your writing. However, if you feel that your knowledge of your topic is still incomplete, you might want to conduct your own research. Research is a vital tool for all kinds of writers. It can broaden and clarify your thinking and provide you with helpful support for your arguments. Research is also useful if you want to examine a very current issue or if you want to explore a topic that is beyond the bounds of your own experience and the limits of the assigned readings. And research can help you ground a topic that is very personal if you feel you need to get some distance and objectivity to do it justice.

It might help to think of research in terms of throwing that proverbial stone into a pond. If you think of the stone as representing your current knowledge of the subject, and you think of the pond itself as representing the full body of knowledge, then imagine each concentric ripple leading you further into that world of information. You can seek out the experiences and observations of others you know personally, or others you come to know through primary or secondary research. Theoretically, if you had enough time and resources, you would, in terms of those spreading ripples, be able to investigate all of the current information—reach the shoreline of the pond, as it were.

Of course, as we have seen, almost no one has the time and resources to explore all of the information available about a very complicated subject area. So we do the best we can under the circumstances. Fortunately, a college is expressly designed to bring many different people with many different areas of expertise together—some of whom may have extensive knowledge of your subject. Depending on the issue, these can be classmates, other undergraduates, graduate students, faculty and staff, and visiting speakers, etc.

Field Research

As you ponder your options for research, always include the local human resources who may provide a windfall of material and are just a short walk away. Let's say you are exploring the issue of poverty in the United States and have narrowed your focus to why poverty should exist in a nation with such wealth and resources. Since this topic clearly involves the disciplines of economics and sociology, perhaps it would make sense to make an appointment with one of the economics or sociology professors on campus—to get some advice on efficient ways to explore such a topic so that your research is as thorough and unbiased as it can be. It is likely that the professor will mention several ways, in addition to library research, to obtain useful information. These approaches can include the interview, firsthand investigation, and the survey/questionnaire. Students who have a lot of time for their projects might use all or a selection of these field research methods.

❑ *The Interview*

To begin with, the interviewer must be sure that the interviewee, or subject, has sufficient expertise to provide useful and relevant insights on the topic. Of course, the subject must also be willing to be interviewed. The first contact, whether by phone or letter or email letter, is very important.

- First, ask permission for the interview. Inquire about the subject's availability, since most often you will need the information more than the person needs to give it to you. Also describe the nature of your research and the kinds of questions you would ask.
- Second, set a time and place for the interview, which must be at the subject's convenience and choice. A reasonable amount of time to ask of a busy person is one-half hour, although some will volunteer more.
- Third, ask permission to tape the interview. If your subject feels uncomfortable about being tape recorded, you will need to take notes so that you do not misquote or misrepresent your subject. In such circumstances, as in a lecture, you must be able to listen, write, and think simultaneously, and the wording must be accurate, all of which may take some practice.
- Fourth, ask your subject to suggest additional local resources such as other scholars, conferences, or campus clubs and organizations.

In the days before the interview, draw up a list of direct, clearly worded questions, similar to those you initially presented, that could be covered in thirty minutes. You need to phrase your questions neutrally to avoid showing bias or obvious leading intentions. For subjects to respond directly and fully, it is important to avoid questions that suggest any preconceived notions. Many subjects will refuse to answer leading questions and will feel put off by them. After the interview, read through your notes carefully to select what quotations would best fit in your paper and to be sure that you have recorded them word-for-word.

❑ *Direct Observation*

Another kind of field research you might conduct is direct observation, or firsthand investigation, in which you watch behavior, looking for patterns and the underlying meanings they suggest. To get the best results from direct observation you need to do the following:

- Write down your objectives and any research questions or working hypotheses that you wish to use for your observation, but do not allow these tentative thoughts and ideas to influence either what you see or how you interpret what you see. You must watch objectively and remain open to new insights that your observation suggests.
- Build a research schedule. Determine the best time of day for your observation, and allow enough time to get meaningful data. An hour or two may not be enough to observe many behavioral patterns. Plan to spend at least several hours over several days, and remember that your full attention is required for the task.
- Use a notebook, or logbook, in which to record your observations. Record data carefully and accurately because later you will be dependent on the data for interpretation. Faulty data produce tainted results.

When you have completed your observation, use your data to write summaries, in prose paragraphs, of your data and your interpretations of the data for later use in your paper.

❏ *The Survey/Questionnaire*

Another form of field research is the survey, or questionnaire, which consists of questions that ask how a specific group reacts to an issue or concept. The group may be very broad (college students) or narrow (senior female sociology majors). Surveys are valuable if your specific research question would be informed by a sampling of group attitudes and values. A good starting place is to write down the goals and intentions of the survey. Before you begin, ask yourself the following questions.

- How will a survey provide useful information for your research question?
- Is the purpose of the survey simply to report data (numbers, percentages) for readers to interpret?
- Is the purpose to report data and provide interpretations for readers?
- To what population do you wish to direct your survey, and why would that group's response be relevant?

Next you will need to produce a set of survey questions. The questions should be brief, logical, and clearly worded. Make sure your questions focus on the topic and are unbiased. Avoid confusing statistics, jargon, abstract terms, and leading or slanted language. To make sure that your questions are free from flaws, test them on peers or an instructor familiar with survey research. Ask your readers to identify any flaws and use their responses to revise, edit, or rewrite your questions. Because details of sentence structure and language are so important in the survey, it is helpful to design and conduct this kind of research in collaboration with others. Finally, you will need to set aside sufficient time to design, administer, and tabulate the results of your survey, and to think about how to use the results in your writing.

A Word on Library Research

You could also supplement your resources by conducting library research, either in the library itself—the "bricks and mortar" approach—or the virtual approach by using an Internet "search engine" such as Google or Yahoo. At this stage, you're not trying to find specific documents to read but trying to get a sense of the contours of the subject or issue—the size and shape of the pond, to use our earlier analogy. You're looking for key terms, concepts, classifications, subject headings and subheadings—ways to focus the broad area into a more manageable and bounded "argument."

Next, with those key concepts (categories) in mind, you can begin reading newsmagazines or newspapers, academic journals and texts, recent books about the nature and quality of contemporary life, published interviews with people who are knowledgeable on your topic, novels and short stories that address your topic, web sources, and any other relevant references.

Because library research is such a broad and important topic, involving many different formal methods for obtaining information from sources, we have given it a full treatment in Chapter 9. For now, remember that when you use information from sources, you must make specific reference to the sources in your writing. If you include phrases and sentences that come directly from your sources, be sure to use quotation marks. Most important, when you use ideas from your sources but not the actual words, you must express those ideas in your own words entirely, and you still must give full credit to your references. Chapter 15 provides very important information about how to document your sources. (*Consult this chapter as you conduct research for any writing assignments in this book.*)

Follow Up: Moving Toward a Public Draft

As you draft different parts of your paper, be critical of your ideas, ask questions about the assumptions you make, and evaluate whether or not your examples and evidence adequately support your judgments. In developing your perspective, be sure to account for the strengths and weaknesses in each of the contending points of view. Re-examining some of the readings may enable you to advance your ideas further and may suggest more key passages and supporting evidence to make your judgments more persuasive. Because your discussion will likely encompass contending viewpoints, questioning yourself about your basic assumptions will help you to examine your reasoning more closely and add clarity and insight to your viewpoint.

Try to anticipate important differences between your reader's perceptions and your own to win the agreement, or at least the respect, of those who might view the issue differently. Remember that you cannot afford to be careless in composing your message or creating the effects you wish to achieve. All writers must draw their readers into their discussions and give good reasons for attending to their statements. You cannot expect people to listen unless you get them to see that your message is relevant and important.

Organizing a Drafting Workshop

Your instructor may ask you to write and bring to class a completed draft of your essay for peer critique. This small group activity can help you to analyze and revise your working draft. Though the group will consider aspects of drafts such as their structure, support, and reasoning, the main focus of the workshop should be conceptual. What ideas are the papers developing, and how might the writers explore those ideas more thoroughly and effectively? Consider the following suggestions as you prepare for and participate in the workshop.

1. Remember that the focus of the workshop is to help, not discourage, your peers.

2. Prior to attending the workshop, create a brief list of questions you would like the group's help in answering about your draft. The questions should focus on specific problems or areas of concern that you have with the draft.

3. Make enough copies of your draft and questions for all group participants.

4. Some of you may prefer not to share your responses to drafts until you have finished reviewing them, while others may choose to engage in discussion as the workshop progresses. It's probably worth experimenting with both formats to see which works best.

5. During the workshop, read the entire paper through once without marking it.

6. Read the paper through again, this time marking thesis statement, main points or stages of thought, and supporting details. You are looking here for the progression of ideas in the paper. Using highlighters of different colors for the different elements can be helpful.

7. Mark sections in the paper you think are particularly strong or effective and those that could use improvement. Such parts might include specific examples or the progression of ideas in the paper. At this stage of the process, don't worry too much about language (though if some lines seem especially good, these could be pointed out); you should especially avoid any worry about grammar, spelling, and the like. Consider instead

   - which points to trim,
   - which ones to develop further,
   - which ones to include that were omitted,
   - which ones to eliminate all together.

8. Try to write out brief answers to the specific questions each writer has asked about his or her draft.

9. If you have chosen not to share responses until the end of the workshop, now is the time. Exchange your marked drafts and written comments and, if at all possible, discuss them.

10. Evaluate and try to make use of the suggestions offered by the other workshop participants. First, make sure your thesis and main points have been clear to the participants. Then con-

sider carefully the responses to your original questions and other comments of your peers to see which are worth following up. One way you can approach this is to prioritize the suggestions, picking the two or three that seem to provide the most useful advice.

You should find it fairly simple to adapt the criteria above to a drafting workshop for any of the assignments in this book.

Reviewing a Student's Work

Earlier in the chapter you read excerpts from Keith Mantia's journal. Now you will read his first draft, the comments it received from peers, and Keith's strategy for addressing their reactions. His final draft will appear later in the chapter.

Your title effectively communicates the direction your topic will take

Fighting Income Inequality
Draft

America is at war. The recent struggle for financial security within American society is becoming increasingly important for all American citizens. While the United States stands as a super power among the rest of the world, the battle for economic equality and wealth stands, in my opinion, as one of our biggest weaknesses. In the American economy, "while the real income of the top 1 percent of the U.S. families skyrocketed by 89 percent during the economic growth period from 1977 to 1995, the income of the middle fifth of the population actually declined by 13 percent during that same time period" (Mantsios 188.) Increasing wealth gaps and income inequalities have continued to make the rich richer and the poor poorer, and while some people are willing to accept that as reality, others believe this problem can be solved. Before any solutions are possible, however, certain pieces of information surrounding the issue need to be found and understood. This information can be found by formulating provocative questions that are relevant to the issue and its solution. Questions such as what is the underlying cause of the growing income gaps? What are its effects on society? What, if anything, is being done about it? All of these questions tie into each other because each answer provides a little more information about the problem as a whole, which can help when trying to solve it.

1. My sociology professor would disagree with the idea of ONE root cause for the "widening gap." Also, you need to define what you mean by "individualism".

1

So what is the underlying problem? In most cases I believe the main issue to be individualism. Understanding the basic problem is the first step to finding a solution. People's selfishness and blatant disregard for the well-being of others is the primary cause for the wealth inequality in America. As a capitalistic economy, we are solely responsible for our own economic well being. This notion of everyone for themselves is, however, harmful to the distribution of wealth among classes. It has been determined that "the top 1 percent of households have more wealth than the entire bottom 90 percent combined" (*The Cheating Culture* 18). In most cases, the people within the top 1 percent of wealth got that way in one of three ways, either by inheritance, luck, or because their parents were wealthy enough to allow them to have more opportunity for success.

2. Is this the only way wealth is acquired? What about hard work?

2

Additionally, being in the top percent of wealth in society comes with a certain amount of power as well, not only financially, but often politically. These people will use their money and power to influence politicians and representatives to create and defend laws, rules, and regulations that protect their affluence. Some examples of this may include laws relative to taxes within certain income brackets, and while this doesn't seem like it would have a large effect on the general public, it does. Across the country, people in low-income tax brackets are paying a higher percentage of their earnings to taxes while the wealthy pay less. According to author David Callahan, "Individualism and self-reliance have morphed into selfishness and self-absorption; competitiveness has become social Darwinism; desire for the good life has turned into materialism; aspiration has become envy" (*The Cheating Culture* 19). What this means is that within American society, a theme of economic Darwinism was born where only the rich survive. This new 'monster' as I like to call it, has largely affected all of society in a severely negative way.

3. This claim about "protecting influence" needs more specific support by way of facts and examples.

3

One way that shows how it has hurt society is in the education of youths. By making the rich richer and poor poorer, the better resources and opportunities are being given primarily to those with money. For example, wealthy families are able to send their children to reputable private schools with good teachers and unlimited resources. Those without money, however, often

4. I really take exception to what you're claiming about the benefit of attending a private school vs. a public school. Can you support this? Also, how does this support your thesis?

4

have no choice other than to send their children to a public school with limited resources and under qualified teachers. Even in some really bad cases, children have to attend schools that aren't even accredited, which will then make it even harder for them to get into college. These examples will also continue to affect society when the students join the work force. A child from a wealthy family is likely to get into a better paying job because they received a better education from a private school. Therefore, it could take an average student graduating from a regular college years to get a job like the private school student was given after graduation. The bottom line seems to be that the more money you have, the better your education will be, positively impacting your chances of academic success.

5. These hypothetical examples are not convincing . . . can you give evidence of this attitude and show how it fits with "individualism"?

5   Another factor contributing to the basic issue is arrogance with regard to social class. Being in a class of wealth is like being a member at a prestigious country club. The people in this 'rich club' often believe that they are better than those who are not, and may sometimes try to prevent other people from joining. This is to ensure that their club of wealth remains exclusive. What does this have to do with income distribution? Well, an example might be a rich, successful businessman working only with rich successful businessmen he knows instead of with a company started by an average guy. This provides the already wealthy company with more money, while possibly holding back the average man's business. Additionally, the amount of money earned by the people in higher social classes is substantially more than any of its lower classes. According to the Economic Policy Institute in Washington, almost 30% of the American work force earns $8 an hour or less (*Nickel and Dimed 3,*) making it very hard to earn enough money to break into a higher social class.

6. I like your solutions - raising the minimum wage and taxing more fairly. This section could be developed further.

6   Now knowing a lot more about the causes of economic inequality, one is better able to determine suitable solutions to help stop it. One solution that could help to balance the income gap could be to raise the minimum wage. This would allow low-income families to better support themselves and their families so they can have more opportunities in life. Another possible solution could be to reevaluate the taxing one specific income brackets, making

those who earn more money pay at least the same if not a higher percentage of their earnings to taxes that would help benefit the community and its citizens. From the information given, countless solutions can be derived in many forms to help solve the growing issue of wealth inequality.

7. Good statements, but how does this tie into your thesis - how excessive individualism and self interest are the central cause of income inequality?

7

Although there are some 'Cinderella' stories where people jump from lower class status to upper class, it is, in reality, a rare thing. Most people in the upper class were born into wealth; "For those whose annual income is in the six figures, economic success is due in large part to the wealth and privileges bestowed on them at birth" (Mantsios 194.) The idea of wealth inequality is stuck in a vicious cycle where money continues to flow back to the wealthy, and until we break down all the causes of inequality, we will never fully be able to stop it from happening.

Keith made the following notes in response to his classmates' comments:

1. Ok, definite economic, political and social failings—a thin job market and other structural problems that also contribute to the income gap besides rampant individualism. Define "individualism".

2. The top 1% is too much of a generalization? Check on my claim.

3. Find more support for my "protecting influence" claims—"examples and facts". Reinforce that the rich seem to be nurturing their own kids' education to the detriment of other kids who must rely on public schooling.

4. Show how the idea of class reinforces the idea of individualism and leads to more privatized situations.

5. Extend discussion on fair wages and taxation.

6. Reinforce thesis throughout.

As he reworked his draft, Keith found that his classmates' comments gave him an opportunity to think more deeply about his topic and helped to inform his position. As important, his group served as a form of support and encouragement as he further developed his paper, leading him to make changes that appear in his final draft (pp. 164–170).

Preparing Your Final Draft

Consider what you have accomplished to this point. For this assignment you have chosen to write about a particular issue in contemporary American society. You have combed the readings in this chapter for ideas and have thought about the ways your own life experience, beliefs, and values play against the issue. You have found informative materials and written a draft in which you incorporated those source materials as evidence for your position. And you have considered options for further research, either library or field research. As part of the revising process, your instructor may schedule a revising workshop. Here you and your classmates can read each other's work and offer responses.

Organizing a Revising Workshop

Like the drafting workshop, this is a small group activity. In this workshop, however, you'll focus more on execution than on concepts, looking carefully at how each person arranges sentences and paragraphs to create a clear and coherent structure. The workshop can be organized much like the drafting workshop, with group members providing copies of their papers for other participants. Below you will find a comprehensive set of criteria to focus on as you review and comment on each other's papers. While the criteria are designed for checking your draft on your own, you should find it fairly simple to adapt them to a revising workshop.

Guidelines for Assessing Your Writing

The questions here will help you review your writing for coherence, development, and consistency. The questions also address matters of audience, authority, and purpose. Keep in mind that the questions are intended to support the careful development and expression of ideas and are not meant as a formula for writing essays.

1. Is the topic important and worth writing about? Sometimes you may have to write a draft, or part of one, to realize that the topic does not work and that you must abandon it.

2. Does the introduction clearly set up what follows? Let your readers know what the paper is about and where it is going. Early on state your topic and your position.

3. Is your purpose clear? If not, you will have to clarify the focus of your discussion. You may need to rethink some of your writing to adequately respond to the central questions of your topic.

4. Do you envision a body of readers beyond yourself? Writing is a communicative act, and you need to include in your audience everyone—peers, classmates, instructors, and the broad intellectual community of scholars you have joined—who is interested in your topic, the position you adopt, and the supporting evidence that you select.

5. Do you anticipate how your audience may react to your writing? Recall appropriate conversations, class discussions, debates, and conferences and try to anticipate the questions and concerns that will be raised by others.

6. Is there a strong voice behind your text? You should recognize a distinct voice and personality driving the language of the piece.

7. Do sentences and paragraphs build on one another? Carefully examine the logic governing sentence and paragraph arrangement and consider whether a different order would more effectively develop the purpose of your paper. You may want to outline what you have written to see if the structure is coherent.

8. Do you stick to and develop your point? Look carefully at the relationship between your introduction and your body paragraphs. Delete information that, while interesting, is off the topic. If you change your position as your paper develops, which sometimes happens, revise earlier sections.

9. Is your evidence relevant and accurate, and are your arguments convincing? As mentioned above, be critical of your ideas, ask questions about the assumptions you make, and carefully evaluate whether or not your examples and evidence adequately support your judgments. If you see weaknesses, you may need to reconsider the kind of support you need.

10. Is the wording concise and clear? Always strive for clarity. Revise your sentences and rethink your word selection wherever you have doubts that your reader will be able to follow you.

Remember that no two writers operate in exactly the same way. One writer may produce a first draft that will come quite close to the desired, finished piece and may only need some sentence editing. Another may rewrite entire sections of text, replace whole passages with new materials, or rearrange the body paragraphs to create a new sequence of ideas. Because it is hard to project how much rethinking, rewriting, and reordering the first draft of a paper will need, it is important to get an early start on a project. Allow plenty of time—at least two or three days—for revising the draft and be sure to leave time to proofread for errors in spelling, punctuation, and grammar.

Reviewing a Student Essay

Here is the final draft from the student whose work you followed throughout the chapter. You know from earlier discussions that the paper did not spring instantly into being with everything worked out so neatly. You saw how Keith's preliminary notes contributed to his final draft and how his peers helped him develop his discussion. Whether or not you agree with the essay, note how the writer strives to offer not simply an opinion but an informed viewpoint, one that incorporates several sources as support for his thinking. To establish your own interpretation of this essay, first read it without consulting the accompanying instructor's comments.

1. Keith's title signals several main ideas: that the subject will be income distribution; that by using the term "inequality" a judgment has been made that the distribution (whatever it turns out to be) is not desirable or fair; and that strong action ("fighting") needs to be taken in response.

2. In keeping with the title, the opening sentence is very strong, connecting the word fighting in the title with the idea of war - a civil war - this time economic. This is immediately followed by the word "battle."

3. Keith then uses information from one of the readings to underscore the point about disparity.

4. Here he makes a small concession that some may not be alarmed by this "gap," but given the title and opening it's not surprising that Keith then frames the situation as a problem needing resolution.

5. In order to confidently propose solutions to problems, we have seen that it is first necessary to describe and define the situation, analyze the causes and consequences, and then show how those consequences are harmful or unjust. Keith alludes to this strategy by formulating a series of questions that will take us through these steps.

6. Keith begins by listing what he believes is the central causal agent— individualism. Keith then gives a very strong extended definition of the term (some would say a "loaded" definition) using sources which

Keith Mantia   Mantia 1
EXP 101, Sec. 2
Professor Krieger
February 6, 2007

1.
2.

Fighting Income Inequality

America is at war with its own people. The constant struggle for financial security is becoming increasingly important for all Americans. While the United States looms as a super power among the rest of the world, the battle for economic equality and wealth highlights, in my opinion, one of our country's major embarrassments. In the American economy, "[W]hile the real income of the top 1 percent of the U.S. families skyrocketed by 89 percent during the economic growth period from 1977 to 1995, the income of the middle fifth of the population actually declined by 13 percent during that same time period" (cited in Mantsios 188) . Increasing wealth gaps and income inequalities have continued to make the rich more financially secure and the poor more apt to fall behind. While some people are willing to accept that as reality, others believe this problem can be resolved. Before any solutions are possible, however, certain pieces of information surrounding the issue need to be identified and understood. One can start by formulating provocative questions relevant to the issue and its solution. For instance, what is the underlying cause of the growing income gap? What are its effects on society? What, if anything, is being done about it? All of these questions intersect because each response provides a little more information about the problem as a whole, allowing those interested to address it.

So what is the underlying problem? Sociologists have found a number of causes – social, economic and political – for this widening income gap. While many argue that such causes are systemic and inherent in the capitalist economic system, I wish to highlight the issue of "individualism" – a uniquely American value that champions "the primacy of individual... interests" over the concern for others (Williams 214). Personal selfishness and blatant disregard for the well—being of others reinforce whatever other causes may create wealth inequality in America. As workers in a capitalistic economy, we are encouraged to think that we are solely responsible for our own economic well-being. However, this notion seem to equate it less with independence and self-reliance and more with selfishness and self-absorption.

of everyone for themselves severely impacts the distribution of wealth among classes.

Experts have determined that "the top 1 percent of households have more wealth than the entire bottom 90 percent combined" (Callahan 18). In most cases, the people within the top 1 percent of wealth got that way in one of three ways, either by inheritance, luck, or because their parents were wealthy enough to allow them to have more opportunity for success. This is not to discount those few determined souls who have gained a measure of economic wealth by their own sweat, or a good run in the stock market. But, generally speaking, privilege not only sets a firm foundation, but also perpetuates by having and using that wealth.

7. In a way, it is as if Keith is suggesting that this is the remote cause which then influences everything else. Once some people have wealth they will seek to keep it for themselves (and their heirs). They do this through using the political system to pass favorable tax laws. They do this by using their resources to obtain a better education. And finally they do this by developing a kind of elite class attitude which further separates the rich from the poor in both material and psychological ways.

7.

However one attains wealth, being in the top percent comes with a certain amount of power, not only financially, but also often politically. These people can use their money and power to influence politicians and representatives to create and defend laws, rules, and regulations that protect their affluence. For example, economist Paul Krugman, in a brief history of this influence, writes in *The New York Times* that

> Ronald Reagan put supply-side theory into practice with his 1981 tax cut. The tax cuts were modest for middle-class families but very large for the well-off. Between 1979 and 1983, according to Congressional Budget Office estimates, the average federal tax rate on the top 1 percent of families fell from 37 to 27.7 percent. (A5)

Later in the piece, Krugman turns to George W. Bush's 2003 tax cuts. Krugman writes "The 2003 tax act sharply cuts taxes on dividend income, another boon to the very well off. By the time the Bush tax cuts have taken full effect, people with really high incomes will face their lowest average tax rate since the Hoover administration" (A5). Other examples of this trend may include laws that affect certain income brackets. And while this may not seem like it has a large effect on the general public, it does. Across the country, people in low-income tax brackets are paying a higher percentage of their earnings to taxes while the wealthy pay less. Krugman explains that even though low income families with more than two children were supposedly the beneficiaries of tax breaks under

Mantia 3

a 2001 child tax credit plan, "at any given time only a small minority of families contains two or more children under 18 – and many of these families have incomes too low to take full advantage of the child tax credit" (A5). This disparity is especially unsettling when the very core of family life in America – supporting families with children – is put at risk.

According to author David Callahan, "Individualism and self-reliance have morphed into selfishness and self-absorption; competitiveness has become social Darwinism; desire for the good life has turned into materialism; aspiration has become envy" (19). Here Callahan is suggesting that within American society, a theme of economic Darwinism has emerged in the scramble for survival – only the rich survive. This new 'monster' as I am apt to call it, has a negative effect on all segments of society.

Take education. By favoring the wealthy over the poor, the better resources and opportunities are being given primarily to those with money. For instance, wealthy families are able to send their children to reputable preschools and private schools with good teachers and unlimited resources. Those without money, however, often have no choice but to send their children to a publicly funded school with fewer resources and generally less qualified teachers. In some really bad cases, children have to attend schools that aren't even accredited, which will then make it even harder for them to finish high school or get into college.

How can these trends not continue to affect society when the students later join the work force? Conventional wisdom suggests that a child from a wealthy family is likely to get into a better paying job because he or she received a better education from a private school. One study found that students from private schools

> have better labor market experiences than those who attended public schools, even when reasonable measures of school quality, family background, educational achievement, occupation and motivation are included. This result is consistent with the hypothesis that private schools are of a higher quality than public schools and supports the human capital theory relating educational quality to earnings. (Sandy and Duncan 311)

Consequently, it could take an average student graduating from a less prestigious college years to get a job commensurate to one that the private school student was given after graduation. The bottom line seems to be that the more money one has, the better the possibility of one's education enhancing chances for academic and professional success.

8. In the last three paragraphs, Keith suggested a series of reciprocal causes - causes that intensify each other. Wealth makes better education possible, which in turn makes it easier to obtain wealth, which in turn breeds arrogance, and so on.

8.

Another factor contributing to excessive individualism is social class arrogance. Belonging to the wealthy class is like being a member at a prestigious country club. The people in this 'rich club' often believe that they are better than those who are not, and may sometimes try to prevent other people from joining. This is to ensure that their club of wealth remains exclusive. What does this have to do with income distribution? An example might be a rich, successful businessman working only with rich successful businessmen he knows instead of with a company started by an average guy. This provides the already wealthy company with more money, while possibly holding back the average man's business.

Add to that the amount of money earned by the people in higher social classes, which is substantially more than a person from a lower class earns. According to the Economic Policy Institute in Washington, almost 30% of the American work force earns $8 an hour or less making it very hard to earn enough money to break into a higher social class through investments or entrepreneurial success (Ehrenreich 3).

9. Keith begins to consider solutions to the "problem" of income inequality. One way to add income to those on the bottom, Keith suggests, is to raise the minimum wage.

9.

Just knowing a bit more about the causes of economic inequality, one can propose suitable solutions to help curb it. One solution that could offset some of the income gap would be to raise the minimum wage. This would allow low-income families to better support themselves and their families so they could have more opportunities in life. The federal minimum wage hasn't been raised since 1997, almost ten years ago. An Economic Policy Institute briefing paper claims that

> Over 650 economists, including five Nobel Prize winners and six past presidents of the American Economics Association, recently signed a statement stating that federal and state minimum wage increases 'can significantly improve the lives of low-income workers and their families, without the adverse effects that critics have claimed.' (Fox 1)

Mantia 5

10. Since early education seems so important, Keith proposes increasing the wages of people who teach poor children, ostensibly to attract more qualified people into the field. Given the importance of education in Keith's analysis, this particular proposal seems very limited and indirect.

11. Finally, Keith returns to the issue of the tax code, indicating that some changes need to be made in order to have the wealthy pay a higher percentage of their income. Again, given that he began with a fairly extensive description of the Reagan and following tax cuts, the treatment here seems a bit too brief and general.

12. The last paragraph reminds the reader again of the "problem" situation and ends with a re-statement of what Keith sees as the main cause - excessive individualism. While this does seem to bring "closure" to the analysis promised in the beginning, it does raise this important question: if it is this basic American ethic that is the root cause of all the inequality and suffering, how will a few governmental economic policies remedy the situation?

10. Another possibility is to rethink the kinds of salaries paid in certain fields, especially to workers in those preschool programs often geared to giving poor and minority students a head start. The Carnegie Foundation reports that college graduates have no real encouragement to establish a career as a child-worker in these kinds of pre-school situations. The Foundation indicates that "According to the U.S. Department of Labor, Bureau of Labor Statistics, child-care workers earn an average of $7.42 an hour, or about the same as parking lot attendants; preschool teachers earn an average of $9.43 an hour, or about $3 an hour less than the average animal trainer" (Hinds 3).

11. A further solution might be to restructure the tax codes, making those who earn more money pay at least the same if not a higher percentage of their earnings to taxes that would help benefit the community and its citizens. These are but a couple of the potential solutions to help resolve the growing issue of wealth inequality.

Although some 'Cinderella' stories exist where people rise from lower class status to the upper class, this phenomenon is, in reality, a rare occurrence. Most people at the top were born into wealth. "For those whose annual income is in six figures, economic success is due in large **12.** part to the wealth and privileges bestowed on them at birth" (Mantsios 194). And while having wealth is not a crime, disregard for unjust policy because of individual or corporate self-interest, maybe should be. The vicious cycle of wealth inequality where money continues to flow back to the wealthy will continue until we break down a principal cause of economic, social and political inequality: an emphasis on self-serving individualism over the concern for others.

Works Cited

Callahan, David. *The Cheating Culture: Why Americans Are Doing Wrong to Get Ahead*. 2004. Rpt. Media, PA: Harvest, 2004. Print.

Ehrenreich, Barbara. *Nickel and Dimed: On (Not) Getting By in America*. 2001. Rpt. New York: Owl, 2002. Print.

Eitzen, D. Stanley. "The Fragmentation of Social Life: Some Critical Societal Concerns for the New Millennium." Krieger et al. 160-66.

Fox, Liana. *Minimum Wage Trends: Understanding Past and Contemporary Research*. EPI Briefing Paper 178. *Economic Policy Institute:*

Research and Ideas for Shared Prosperity. Economic Policy Institute.
25 October 2005. Web. 8 March 2006.

Hinds, Michael DeCourcy. "Early Childhood Education: Distance Learning for Teachers Adds a New Dimension." *Carnegie Reporter* 1.3 (Fall 2001): n. pag. Web. 3 March 2006.

Krieger, Barbara Jo, Paul G. Saint-Amand, Warren A. Neal, and Alan L. Steinberg. *Inquiry, Argument, & Change: A Rhetoric with Readings.* Dubuque, IA: Kendall Hunt, 2005. TS.

Krugman, Paul. "The Tax-Cut Con." *New York Times* 14 Sept. 2003: A5. *Academic Universe. Lexis-Nexus.* Web. 8 March 2006.

Mantsios, Gregory. "Class In America: Myths and Realities (2000)." Krieger et al. 185-97.

Sandy, Jonathan, and Kevin C. Duncan. "Does Private Education Increase Earnings?" *Eastern Economic Journal* 22.3 (Summer 1996): 303-312. *ProQuest.* Web. 6 March 2006.

Williams, Raymond. "Individual." Krieger et al. 213-14.

Establishing a Dialogue With Your Instructor

An instructor's comments often suggest corrective measures to improve your writing, but this is only part of the shaping process. While the notes can help with your essay's development, you should see them as part of an ongoing dialogue between reader and writer. By fully considering the comments, in conjunction with your own intentions, you participate in an exchange that offers opportunities for developing more consciousness as a writer. Now, review the instructor's annotations appearing in the margins of Keith's paper and note how Keith responds to these remarks.

I feel good about what I've accomplished in this paper. My group had pointed out some problems with audience that I remedied. For example, I added a definition for individualism, gave more support on some points and did reinforce my thesis in my conclusion. I handled my facts and sources much better in this final draft and I thought my argument overall was more effective. But I wish I had received a more thorough critique of my argument and its support, especially after reading your comments.

You pointed out that my proposal for raising teacher salaries and getting better teachers into low-income school districts were only part of the educational answer to the inequality gap. I needed to elaborate on educational reforms that could shift the imbalance rather than offer only one proposal.

You also pointed out that my proposal for shifting the tax codes to help the poor achieve more opportunity also needed more development. I needed to provide a far more comprehensive proposal including where and how increased revenues from the wealthy could be spent. This critique came toward the end of my paper (which was newer material that I had included in the last day or two), and I didn't give it enough attention.

However, it was your final comment about the unlikelihood of governmental economic policies impacting the American ethic of individualism that left me somewhat troubled. Then I thought, what if I could make the case statistically that the more a country spends on humane and social improvements, the more civic-minded its people seem to be (and so, less focused on excessive individualism)? I read about countries like this in my sociology class—countries whose populations are more focused on citizenship and community building, therefore less on mere consumerism and self-interest.

Collaborative Activity

Teaming up with your peers, discuss the instructor's annotations to Keith's paper using the following questions:

1. Which annotations are the most important for Keith to consider? Why? How might he address them?

2. What has Keith learned from "writing back" to his instructor?

3. How might each member of the group benefit from a similar exchange with your instructor?

4. How would the members of the group respond to Keith's comments if they were the instructor?

Journal Activity

Discuss your own experience with this chapter's writing assignment. Focus not so much on the paper itself, but on the interactions you had with your instructor, with your classmates, and with the authors you consulted as you wrote the paper. Also make note of what you wish to accomplish in your next paper. List two or three specific goals that are the result of reactions to your writing.

A Word about Form

It is tempting to think that practicing a precise pattern of organization will bring mastery to your writing. After all, for centuries teachers of writing have stressed the imitation of specific models and forms of writing as the way to perfect the task. Also, when you read an article or a book, you see before you a polished, finished product, and—knowing nothing of the author's struggles—it may seem as if the writer had a complete picture of the whole piece in mind from the first moment.

While there are undoubtedly some general concepts that describe the organization of various kinds of writing—we have treated some of them in our discussion of Keith's paper—there are no product molds through which you can simply pour ideas to produce writing. Rather, your ideas take form as they develop in your mind, in your notes, and in your drafts. You must make decisions about what position you will take, the order in which you will present ideas to best support your position, the length and flow of your sentences, and the sounds and rhythms of your words. It is through your decision-making processes that your writing begins to take form; and as you think, plan, and draft, the form evolves. Thus, form is not a tool separate from your ideas; form is your ideas, as you choose to develop them. Introducing your topic, presenting and supporting your position, reaching a conclusion, and using transitions to connect your ideas are all active elements of the writing process. They are not "out there," perfect, complete, and recyclable, waiting for you to find them; instead, you create them each time you write.

Bear in mind, then, that beyond the most general matters of organization, you will define what an introduction or body paragraph should look like in a given instance, and you will arrive at that definitive moment by working through the ideas you want to express to your audience. Do not hesitate to try a variety of approaches. It is through experimentation—trying different methods, working through them, listening to how they read aloud, shaping them, rejecting them, and recreating them—that you will discover what works best for you.

Short Essay

Write an essay in which you describe how your writing and the ways you think about writing have changed in college. As you examine yourself as a writer, take into consideration changes in the kinds of writing challenges you now face, changes in the expectations of your audience, and changes in the options that are now available to you in terms of structure, voice, and language.

To Help You Get Started

1. Think about the various kinds of instruction you have received in high school and college about how to structure and organize a paper. How do the forms and patterns you have been taught serve you as a writer? Have you found it necessary to change your thinking about form in order to capture in words what you are reading and thinking about in college?

2. Consider your emerging voice, your presence, if you will, in your writing. What struggles and challenges have you experienced as you develop a personal voice? How does your voice fit in with other voices—the authors of the readings, for example—who also appear in your writing?

Collaborative Activity

You may find it helpful to compare and contrast your growth experiences with those of another person also in the midst of discovering new territory as a writer.

PART TWO

Creating Answers: Making an Argument

The vast majority of writing you will ever do, in college or on the job, will be argument. Analyses of various phenomena in your other college classes, project proposals, even letters of application for a job may all be thought of and effectively developed as arguments. Even process analyses are, in effect, arguing that the steps described constitute an effective method for achieving the goal. In short, people write to make a point, and that point is the conclusion of an argument. This part of the book introduces the elements of argument that come into play as writers learn about and understand their subjects, develop and test their points of view, and ultimately, strive to communicate what they've discovered to their readers.

Chapter 1 elaborated on one of the principles underlying nearly every aspect of this book. It bears repeating here: argument *is* inquiry, that is, the *process* of inquiry. The public draft of an argument is merely the last step in the process. Chapter 1 also offered you four types of questions to help stimulate your innate creativity and help guide your initial inquiries:

- Questions of the Nature of Things
- Questions of the Causes and Effects of Things
- Questions of the Value of Things
- Questions of what Actions we should take towards the issue at hand

This part of the book takes you through another step in the process: the answers to at least some of those questions will become claims you will develop, support, and, ultimately present to your audience in a public draft.

As such, argument is treated first and foremost as a way of discovering, testing and sharing ideas. We introduce the ways we think argument actually works in the world. We ask you to reflect upon those principles through a series of varied activities; to observe and analyze those principles at work in a challenging set of chapter readings; and, finally, to make use of those principles in several different writing assignments, including a major essay—both as a way of discovering knowledge and then sharing and perhaps persuading others to accept and eventually act upon this same knowledge.

6

There is an old saying that goes: You can gain everything from solitude but character. When we live among and interact with other people, people who may have different ideas, values, and interests, our need to communicate becomes vital. We must make decisions about everything: how to organize our communities, our economy, our security—in short, our lives. The more freedom people have in determining the direction and shape of their lives, the more important it is to understand the ways they go about making those decisions.

The particular decisions you make about the shape of your life are often complex and difficult, involving many factors and perspectives. Fortunately, most people in our society share a basic understanding of how to think about and communicate those decisions. That way of thinking and communicating often involves argument and uses the same skills you learned and practiced in the first five chapters. Creating answers to the important questions of our lives, first for ourselves and then to present to others for their consideration, involves the same strategies you used to explore an issue, ask relevant questions about it, and fully and impartially seek answers. In a way, then, what we do is present to our audience essentially the same argument we used to come to our own understanding of the issue. We take them through the same processes we used—only now we can do it more efficiently and more confidently. We make our claims and then we explain the evidence that led us to those claims in the first place. Our claims are the answers we find to the types of questions we have already explored: *what something is, what caused it and what its effects are, what its value is,* and *what we should do now that we know all this.*

These ways of thinking work in all sorts of situations—from the most informal to the most formal. Whenever someone says to you, "We (you) should" do something, that person is really making a proposal, though we often don't think of it in such formal terms. Whenever someone claims that one thing is somehow better than another, that person is making an evaluation. When someone uses words like *because* or *consequently,* that person is often discussing causality. And when someone tries to describe, identify, or define anything, that person is making a claim about the nature of that thing. As we have seen, each distinct way of thinking about the world comes with its own special kind of logic and rhetoric and with its own special kind of proof or support.

Let's try it out. The following are the kinds of claims or statements that we've all heard or read or made ourselves. See if you can identify which type of question each claim answers.

1. A democracy is very different from a monarchy.

2. Consumption is good for the economy.

3. Television viewing causes obesity.

One very important thing to note about the four claims (*nature, causality, value, and action*) is that they are sequentially progressive, meaning that we can stop at any point if we're going from left to right. But we often can't do that moving from right to left. In other words, we can make a claim about the nature of something without having to explain what effects it will produce. For example, we can say, "A democracy is very different from a monarchy" and then give the reader the examples that led us to believe that claim. We don't have to go into why those differences exist, or how those differences can affect our lives, or whether one system is better than the other, or if there's anything we should do in response to those differences. But if we make the value claim that a democracy is a better system than a monarchy, we will probably have to give examples of those differences, as well as show the different effects that each system produces, and then explain why democracy's effects are more beneficial and desirable than a monarchy's.

In the second example, "Consumption is good for the economy," the word "good" signals that the statement or claim is about value, about the qualities of things and whether those qualities benefit or harm us, have advantages or disadvantages attached to them. But before we can fairly assess that value, we might first have to define and describe what consumption is, how consumption produces effects on the economy, what specific, measurable effects consumption has on the economy we are investigating, and why those effects can be evaluated as "good" as opposed to "bad."

In the third example, "Television viewing causes obesity," the word "causes" obviously signals a causal argument. We know we will probably have to explain why we believe spending a lot of time in front of a television makes us fat, but even before we do that, we may need to define and describe what obesity is. Once we've done this—define the term and demonstrate the connection between television viewing and getting fat—we're not obligated to go further and show why and how this is a bad thing or suggest ways to keep this from happening.

You may note that we've used the word "probably" quite often in explaining these requirements. That's because just how much of the sequence (nature, cause and effect, value, and action) you'll have to complete in your arguments depends not only on the kind of claim you're making but also on your *audience*. For example, if you're arguing the third claim, that watching too much television causes obesity and you're certain that your readers understand the meaning of "obesity," it's probably not necessary to explain the term. In fact, it may be counter-productive if your readers feel you're disparaging their knowledge or intellectual ability.

Knowing the logical and rhetorical shapes of these different kinds of claims and arguments can help us understand a situation better and can help us articulate that understanding more effectively, but it doesn't mean that our audiences will automatically accept our claims. There can be all kinds of disagreements about the accuracy and relevance of the examples we use, the nature of the causality we demonstrate, the criteria we use for judgment, and the different ways we indicate we should respond to the situation. These disagreements indicate just how difficult it can be to make our reasoning about a complex issue clear to our readers. But if you believe that argument is first and foremost a way of discovering, testing, and sharing ideas, then the effort involved can never be wasted.

The Globalization of the Economy
Thomas L. Friedman

Excerpt from Thomas L. Friedman. *The Lexus and the Olive Tree:*
Understanding Globalization (2000).

New York Times columnist Thomas Friedman provides readers with an overview of the central reorganizing force of the 21ˢᵗ Century, globalization, the theme of this chapter. From Friedman's perspective, the Cold War system that once defined our international relations has given way to a dynamic new set of relationships based on an increasingly interwoven globe. Friedman views this integration as the new path to international understanding and development. Other authors you will read present a more foreboding reality, one gripped by the denigration of cultures, traditions, environments and communal interests. In this introductory excerpt from Friedman's *The Lexus and the Olive Tree* (2000), he sketches the balancing act a globalized world must continually renegotiate so that its potential effects reinforce its promise and not its liabilities.

* * * * * * * * * * *

THE NEW SYSTEM

Globalization is not just some economic fad, and it is not just a passing trend. It is an international system—the dominant international system that replaced the Cold War system after the fall of the Berlin Wall. We need to understand it as such. If there can be a statute of limitations on crimes, then surely there must be a statute of limitations on foreign policy clichés. With that in mind, the "post-Cold War world" should be declared over. We are now in the new international system of globalization. When I say that globalization has replaced the Cold War as the defining international system, what exactly do I mean?

I mean that, as an international system, the Cold War had its own structure of power: the balance between the United States and the U.S.S.R. The Cold War had its own rules: in foreign affairs, neither superpower would encroach on the other's sphere of influence; in economics, less developed countries would focus on nurturing their own national industries, developing countries on export-led growth, communist countries on autarky and Western economies on regulated trade. The Cold War had its own dominant ideas: the clash between communism and capitalism, as well as détente, nonalignment and perestroika. The Cold War had its own demographic trends: the movement of people from east to west was largely frozen by the Iron Curtain, but the movement from south to north was a more steady flow. The

Cold War had its own perspective on the globe: the world was a space divided into the communist camp, the Western camp, and the neutral camp, and everyone's country was in one of them. The Cold War had its own defining technologies: nuclear weapons and the second Industrial Revolution were dominant, but for many people in developing countries the hammer and sickle were still relevant tools. The Cold War had its own defining measurement: the throw weight of nuclear missiles. Here and lastly, the Cold War had its own defining anxiety: nuclear annihilation. When taken all together the elements of this Cold War system influenced the domestic politics, commerce and foreign relations of virtually every country in the world. The Cold War system didn't shape everything, but it shaped many things.

Today's era of globalization is a similar international system, with its own unique attributes, which contrast sharply with those of the Cold War. To begin with the Cold War system was characterized by one overarching feature—division. The world was a divided-up, chopped-up place and both your threats and opportunities in the Cold War system tended to grow out of who you were divided from. Appropriately, this Cold War was symbolized by a single word: the *wall*—the Berlin Wall. . . .

The globalization system is a bit different. It also has one overarching feature—integration. The world has become an increasingly interwoven place, and today, whether you are a company or a country, your threats and opportunities increasingly derive from who you are connected to. This globalization system is also characterized by a single word: the *Web*. So in the broadest sense we have gone from a system built around division and walls to a system increasingly built around integration and webs. In the Cold War we reached for the "hotline," which was a symbol that we were all divided but at least two people were in charge—the United States and the Soviet Union—and in the globalization system we reach for the Internet, which is a symbol that we are all increasingly connected and nobody is quite in charge.

This leads to many other differences between the globalization system and the Cold War system. The globalization system, unlike the Cold War system, is not frozen, but a dynamic ongoing process. That's why I define globalization this way: it is the inexorable integration of markets, nation-states and technologies to a degree never witnessed before—in a way that is enabling individuals, corporations and nation-states to reach around the world farther, faster, deeper and cheaper than ever before, and in a way that is enabling the world to reach into individuals, corporations and nation-states farther, faster, deeper, cheaper than ever before. This process of globalization is also producing a powerful backlash from those brutalized or left behind by this new system.

The driving idea behind globalization is free-market capitalism—the more you let market forces rule and the more you open your economy to free trade and competition, the more efficient and flourishing your economy will be. Globalization means the spread of free-market capitalism to virtually every country in the world. Therefore, globalization also has its own set of economic rules—rules that revolve around opening, deregulating and privatizing your economy, in order to make it more competitive and attractive to foreign investment. In 1975, at the height of the Cold War, only 8 percent of countries worldwide had liberal, free-market capital regimes, and foreign direct investment at the time totaled only $23 billion, according to the World Bank. By 1997, the number of countries with liberal economic regimes constituted 28 percent, and foreign investment totaled $644 billion.

Unlike the Cold War system, globalization has its own dominant culture, which is why it tends to be homogenizing to a certain degree. In previous eras this sort of cultural homogenization happened on a regional scale—the Romanization of Western Europe and the Mediterranean world, the Islamification of Central Asia, North Africa, Europe and the Middle East by the Arabs and later the Ottomans, or the Russification of Eastern and Central Europe and parts of Eurasia under the Soviets. Culturally speaking, globalization has tended to involve the spread (for better and for worse) of Americanization—from Big Macs to iMacs to Mickey Mouse.

Globalization has its own defining technologies: computerization, miniaturization, digitization, satellite communications, fiber optics and the Internet, which reinforce its defining perspective of integration. Once a country makes the leap into the system of globalization, its elites begin to internalize this perspective of integration, and always try to locate themselves in a global context. . . .

THE LEXUS AND THE OLIVE TREE

Once you recognize that globalization is the international system that has replaced the Cold War system, is this all you need to know to explain world affairs today? Not quite. Globalization is what is new. And if the world were made of just microchips and markets, you could probably rely on globalization to explain almost everything. But, alas, the world is made of microchips and markets and men and women, with all their peculiar habits, traditions, longings and unpredictable aspirations. So world affairs today can only be explained as the interaction between what is as new as an Internet Web site and what is as old as a gnarled olive tree on the banks of the river Jordan. . . .

Olive trees are important. They represent everything that roots us, anchors us, identifies us and locates us in this world—whether it be belonging to a family, a community, a tribe, a nation, a religion or, most of all, a place called home. Olive trees are what give us the warmth of family, the joy of individuality, the intimacy of personal rituals, the depth of private relationships, as well as the confidence and security to reach out and encounter others. We fight so intensely at times over our olive trees because, at their best, they provide the feelings of self-esteem and belonging that are as essential for human survival as food in the belly. Indeed, one reason that the nation-state will never disappear, even if it does weaken, is because it is the ultimate olive tree—the ultimate expression of whom we belong to—linguistically, geographically and historically. You cannot be a complete person alone. You can be a rich person alone. You can be a smart person alone. But you cannot be a complete person alone. For that you must be part of, and rooted in, an olive grove. . . .

But while olive trees are essential to our very being, an attachment to one's olive trees, when taken to excess, can lead us into forging identities, bonds and communities based on the exclusion of others. And when these obsessions really run amok, as with the Nazis in Germany, or the murderous Aum Shinrikyo cult in Japan or the Serbs in Yugoslavia, they lead to the extermination of others.

Conflicts between Serbs and Muslims, Jews and Palestinians, Armenians and Azeris over who owns which olive tree are so venomous precisely because they are about who will be at home and anchored in a local world and who will not be. Their underlying logic is: I must control this olive tree, because if the other controls it, not only will I be economically and politically under his thumb, but my whole sense of home will be lost. I'll never be able to take my shoes off and relax. Few things are more enraging to people than to have their identity or their sense of home stripped away. They will die for it, kill for it, sing for it, write poetry for it and novelize about it. Because without a sense of home and belonging, life becomes barren and rootless. And life as a tumbleweed is no life at all.

So then what does the Lexus represent? It represents an equally fundamental, age-old human drive—the drive for sustenance, improvement, prosperity and modernization—as it is played out in today's globalization system. The Lexus represents all the burgeoning global markets, financial institutions and computer technologies with which we pursue higher living standards today.

Of course, for millions of people in developing countries, the quest for material improvement still involves walking to a well, subsisting on a dollar a day, plowing a field barefoot behind an ox or gathering wood and carrying it on their heads for five miles. These people still upload for a living, not download. But for millions of others in developed countries, this quest for material betterment and modernization is increasingly conducted in Nike shoes, shopping in integrated markets and using the new network technologies. The point is that while different people have different access to the new markets and technologies that characterize the globalization system, and derive highly unequal benefits from them, this doesn't change the fact that these markets and technologies are the defining economic tools of the day and everyone is either directly or indirectly affected by them. . . .

The challenge in this era of globalization—for countries and individuals—is to find a healthy balance between preserving a sense of identity, home and community and doing what it takes to survive within the globalization system. Any society that wants to thrive economically today must constantly be trying to build a better Lexus and driving it out into the world. But no one should have any illusions that merely participating in this global economy will make a society healthy. If that participation comes at the price of a country's identity, if individuals feel their olive tree roots crushed, or washed out, by this global system, those olive tree roots will rebel. They will rise up and strangle the process. Therefore the survival of globalization as a system will depend, in part, on how well all of us strike this balance. A country without healthy olive trees will never feel rooted or secure enough to open up fully to the world and reach out into it. But a country that is only olive trees, that is only roots, and has no Lexus, will never go, or grow, very far. Keeping the two in balance is a constant struggle. . . .

Questions

1. Does Friedman provide a clear definition of "globalization"? If so, what is it? If not, how is his definition obscure?

2. When he speaks of The Lexus and the Olive Tree what does he mean?

3. What constitutes your olive tree?

4. Do you agree with the claim, "You can be a rich person alone. You can be a smart person alone. But you cannot be a complete person alone. For that you must be part of, and rooted in, an olive grove . . ."? Justify your answer.

Exercise

To further stimulate involvement in your reading, try the following approach first introduced in Chapter 1. Divide a page of your journal down the middle. Use the left-hand column for any of Friedman's passages that you found significant or thought-provoking. Use the right column for your commentary, for responding to the material with questions or insights that will help you follow up a particular line of thought.

Collaborative Exercise

Form small groups, exchange your journal notes on the Friedman reading, and allow time to read and discuss each person's ideas. Then, in your individual journal, write down any ideas you encountered in the discussion that are different from those in your original journal. These should include what others believed were significant passages from the reading and their commentary on those passages. You should especially look for promising lines of inquiry that didn't occur to you.

By exchanging views, you enhance your ability to learn from others and to contribute as an active and valued member of a group. You also gain insight into the kinds of questions, responses, disagreements, and agreements that your points of view may elicit from others.

A Thinking Tool: Types of Claims

In Chapter 1 we explored the concept of families. Your questions about the nature of families may have included something on the order of "What are the necessary characteristics of a family? Does it have to include mother, father, and children to be considered a real family? Are there any other structures we can legitimately call families?" And you may have come up with any of a number of intuitive answers based on your understanding and experience at that time. It was probably a good start. Now, however, we need to explore topics more fully and develop more informed and more meaningful answers with which to work.

Again, we'll turn to the four categories we worked with in Chapter 1, but now, instead of questions, we'll be making claims based on the answers to our original questions:

- Claims of the Nature of Things
- Claims of the Causes and Effects of Things
- Claims of the Value of Things
- Claims of what Actions we should take on the issue at hand

Under each category you'll find related subordinate concepts and activities to help you develop claims. A *claim* (also sometimes called a statement or proposition) is an assertion about some aspect of reality that we believe to be true. It may be an *absolute* claim, using words like *always* or *never*. However, since meaningful writing often deals with complex issues, we may frequently find it more representative of our actual beliefs to *qualify* our claims with words like *often, many, most,* or *seldom*. Whatever the case, we'll see that the many ways writers categorize claims helps shape their understanding of issues and events.

We may know the more superficial aspects of the realities we intend to discuss, but we need to know, as fully as possible, the experience of those realities. We gain that experience by temporarily stepping out of and putting aside our current understanding of reality and looking at issues from new, more methodical and more objective perspectives.

Claims about the Nature of Things

When we looked at questions about the nature of things in Chapter 1, we offered as samples some "top of the head" answers. While they served our purpose at that point, they tended to be fairly simplistic and, in some cases, completely obvious—not quite up to the standard we want to see in college and professional writing. Now we want you to dig a little deeper and generate answers that are not simplistic or obvious but more significant, insightful, and better expressions of your individuality and creativity.

Often, the best place to begin in an exploration of the nature of things is by meaningfully defining terms important to the discussion. You've no doubt been taught to look up terms in a good dictionary when you have questions about their meaning. While this is a decent start, dictionary definitions are fairly limited in their usefulness to a good writer and a good critical thinker. They tend to leave out much more significant information about a term than they include.

This section will focus largely on definition. While it may seem that the "nature" of something requires more than just a definition, we can also consider a *complete* definition of something a complete statement of its nature. Of course, complete definitions stating all aspects of the nature of a thing are probably impossible. Still, a focus on definition can help structure our thoughts and help us cut through the often chaotic *appearance* of reality to get to an essential and meaningful *experience* of it.

To explore this more fully, we need to consider different varieties of meaning. We'll also want to look at different types of definitions and techniques for creating them.

❑ *Varieties of Meaning*

When you consider the vast number of purposes we try to achieve with language, it is no surprise that an expression or even just a single term can offer a substantial number of possible meanings and interpretations. And each of these different, sometimes contradictory, meanings can provide us with new and insightful ways of examining the nature of the things or actions described by the expression or term. Perhaps the simplest distinction we can make is between the *denotation* and *connotation* of terms. While linguists and logicians offer different usages of the two terms, here we'll use *denotation* to mean an objective (that is, devoid of emotion or individual associations) statement of what the term is most commonly taken to mean. One type of denotative meaning is the simple dictionary definition; dictionary definitions rarely stir much emotion.

Connotation, on the other hand, brings an emotional component into the situation and lends a subjective element and a shade of meaning not provided by denotation. Writers frequently use terms with positive or negative connotations to elicit emotional responses from their readers. Think of the difference between being described as slender rather than skinny or scrawny, creative rather than undisciplined, firm rather than stubborn.

Now consider the following line from the third paragraph of the Friedman essay above:

> *The world was a divided-up, chopped-up place. . . .*

Specifically, consider the terms "divided-up" and "chopped-up." Denotatively, the two terms are synonymous; they mean fundamentally the same thing. Yet they have different connotations. "Divided" is, for the most part, emotively neutral. We read the word and our response is intellectual; we primarily register the objective denotation of the word. "Chopped-up," in contrast, has a substantial negative connotation. It has a denotation similar to divide, but it also implies a violent rending with a bladed tool, like chopping wood with an axe. Friedman's repetition of the concept in a single line is not simple redundancy; rather, he is drawing us into the concept with the emotively neutral word and then leading us into an emotive response that suits his purpose as a writer. The new depth of meaning is especially important when you read the rest of the paragraph and put the expression in context.

Exercise

Return to the Friedman reading and, in your journal, list 10 or 12 expressions or terms he uses that have positive or negative connotations. For each one, list an emotively neutral synonym. Finally, in a sentence or two for each one, speculate on why Friedman chose the emotionally charged term or expression.

Another powerful distinction we can make regarding the varieties of meaning of terms is between the *intension* and *extension* of terms. The extension of a term refers to the list of members of the category described by the term and the intension refers to the key characteristics we use to define members of the group. For example, Friedman mentions "communist countries" in his essay. He then lists the former Soviet Union as a member of the category.

Exercise

List a half dozen other countries that at one time fell into the category "communist countries."

As mentioned above, the *intension* of a term refers to the characteristics of the members of the category described by the term. Friedman seems to associate a number of defining characteristics with the term "communist countries"—an "us and them" mentality and lack of a free market economy are two.

Exercise

List any other attributes of "communist countries" Friedman either mentions or implies in his essay. List 5 other attributes based on your understanding of history.

Some logicians find potential correspondences between the *denotation* of a term and its *extension,* as well as between the *connotation* of a term and its *intension.* For example, the list of countries that might formally have been described as "communist" may be viewed as an objective fact and, by itself, unlikely to inspire much emotion. However, the list of characteristics frequently attributed to the term "communist"—its intension—might well be subjective and full of emotionally charged connotations, depending on the context and the reader.

Exercise

Consider the term "Islamic countries." In your journal:

1. Create the *extension* of the term; that is, make a list of all the countries you can think of that are predominantly Islamic in their religious make-up.

2. Create the *intension* of the term; that is, create a list of all the attributes you can think of that characterize Islamic countries. Then:
   - Label each attribute according to its connotation: emotively positive, neutral, or negative.
   - For each term, state whether or not the attribute truly characterizes all Islamic countries.
   - In a sentence or two, generalize about your findings. Was your intension of the term completely accurate?

When you are exploring the deeper meanings of terms, *denotation, connotation, extension,* and *intension* are important tools you should bring to bear on the inquiry. When we focus on certain attributes from those that make up the *intension* of a term and not others, or when we limit the *extension* of the term by including certain members of the category and excluding others, we can fundamentally alter our perception and shape our exploration of the category named by the term.

For example, we can categorize wine as an agricultural commodity, a grape beverage, an alcoholic drink, or a religious symbol. Each of those categories has distinctive connotations.

❑ *Types of Definitions*

Logicians and linguists provide many ways to categorize types of definitions; here we'll explore the types most commonly and frequently used.

■ *Lexical or Dictionary Definitions*

Lexical Definitions provide the ways in which words are commonly used, that is, the usage that has come to be accepted over time. While these are the sorts of definitions you'll find in a dictionary, you should remember there may be common usages that don't appear in your dictionary, depending on how abridged or how old it is. It's also interesting to note how these definitions change and evolve over the years.

For example, the 1963 edition of *Webster's Seventh New Collegiate Dictionary* defines "cold war" simply as "a conflict characterized by the use of means short of sustained overt military action."

However, the current version of the *Merriam-Webster Online Dictionary* offers the following lexical definitions:

1. *a conflict over ideological differences carried on by methods short of sustained overt military action and usually without breaking off diplomatic relations; specifically often capitalized C&W: the ideological conflict between the U.S. and the U.S.S.R—compare HOT WAR*
2. *a condition of rivalry, mistrust, and often open hostility short of violence especially between power groups (as labor and management)*

Lexical definitions are technically *descriptive* rather than *prescriptive*; that is, they tell you how the word is commonly used, not how you *should* use it. However, in practice, one implies the other. Writers who persist in using words in non-standard or idiosyncratic ways will not be easily understood by average readers. That doesn't mean you can't be creative in this regard; it does mean that you should do it in such a way that your intent is clear to the reader.

Dictionary definitions can be useful, depending on the dictionary; however, they can also be maddeningly circular. For example, one dictionary defines "iconology" as "the branch of art dealing with the interpretation of icons." This is one flaw you'll want to avoid when your purpose requires you to write your own lexical definitions.

Exercise

In the Friedman reading above, the author uses forms of the following terms: *autarky*, *détente*, and *modernism*. Without consulting a dictionary, write your own lexical definitions of these terms in your journal. If you're not sure of the meanings, try to pick them out from what you've heard and read and from the context in which they are used in the Friedman reading. Then look up the three words in a good dictionary and write down the definitions in your journal. Finally, make note of the differences between your definitions and those provided by the dictionary and, in two or three sentences for each term, try to state how a reader's perception of the relevant passages in the reading might have been altered if he or she read them with your definitions in mind instead of the standard definitions.

■ *Operational or Working Definitions*

One way to avoid confusion on the part of your reader when dictionary definitions are ineffective is to offer an *operational* or *working definition*. An operational definition involves telling your reader directly "I'm going to use this word in this way" and then going ahead and doing it. We normally use operational definitions in two situations:

- When we want to coin a word or use it to mean something new. For example, very few people on the planet at this point are unfamiliar with the word "byte" as a term denoting a measure of computer memory. However, in the beginning of the "computer revolution" someone, somewhere first informed readers that he or she would be using this word in a certain way. The development of new technologies often requires a great many operative definitions.

- We also use operational definitions when we want to use a word in non-standard fashion in a specific rhetorical context. This is quite all right as long as we play fair with readers and let them know up front. For example, much of the controversy over including biblical explanations in science classes might be simplified if writers offered the operational definition of "scientific hypothesis" they intend to use in their discourse. If one stipulates that the defining characteristic of a "scientific" hypothesis is its testability using material means, divine creation would seem not to be a logically appropriate position. Likewise, if we want to use "globalization" in our argument, we might directly tell our readers at the beginning of our essay that we are defining "globalization" as "the international trading system involving all the goods and services exchanged across the borders of existing countries."

In either case, the operational definition somewhat limits the discussion but also makes it more manageable.

Exercise

Select three terms that you think might have been coined or taken on new meanings in the last ten years. In your journal, write definitions for them. For each term, write two or three sentences exploring how, if you used the terms in an essay, they might be more appropriate or more effective for one audience than for another.

Exercise

Pick three important terms in the Friedman essay and, in your journal, write an operational definition of each that would be appropriate in a *different* rhetorical context than that in which the essay was written. Describe each context in a sentence or two.

■ *Precising Definitions*

Another way to avoid confusion is to use a *precising definition*. This sort of definition limits the *intension* of the term to make it more precise and avoid ambiguity. The Friedman reading offers excellent and extended examples of precising definitions throughout the first section in its discussion of "international system," "the Cold War," and "globalization."

For example, in his definition of "globalization" as the new "international system," Friedman claims it has "one overarching feature—integration." If he left it at that, the ambiguity of the characterization would weaken his point; "integration" could mean any number of things, each with its own denotation and set of connotations. Instead, he goes on to provide a precising definition of what sort of "integration" he means:

> *"The world has become an increasingly interwoven place, and today, whether you are a company or a country, your threats and opportunities increasingly derive from who you are connected to."*

Exercise

In your journal write *different* precising definitions for "globalization" and "integration" than those Friedman uses; that is, use different aspects of the *intentions* of the terms to define them.

■ *Persuasive Definitions*

Another type of definition is the *persuasive definition*. In these sorts of definitions writers (consciously or unconsciously) sacrifice a bit of objectivity to their desire to make a persuasive point or have an emotional effect on the reader. You are likely to see a great many definitions surrounding controversial issues. While persuasive definitions certainly have their place in creative expression, it's important as a reader to recognize them when you encounter them and as a writer to know what you're doing when you use them.

For example, many states have instituted lotteries to better finance public functions. Consider the following definitions of "lottery":

> *The lottery is the greatest benefit to public education since the number two pencil.*

> *The lottery is little more than a tax on the logically bewildered.*

Both are obviously persuasive definitions, and their subjective nature seems clear.

Such definitions are certainly not without value. They can be enlightening and amusing, and they can give us new ways to think about things. However, when we create them, we must remember they are expressions of our own individual values and, as such, are judgments; readers will also want more objective support of our points of view.

For example, Friedman, in his defining remarks on globalization, provides the following:

> *Culturally speaking, globalization has tended to involve the spread (for better and for worse) of Americanization—from Big Macs to iMacs to Mickey Mouse. . . .*

His play on words, while effective, also offers a persuasive definition of sorts. Of all the symbols he might have picked to characterize American culture, why those three? What point of view do they communicate about "Americanization"?

Exercise

Go back to the Friedman reading. See if you can find several other instances of persuasive definition and copy them in your journal. In a sentence or two, state the value judgment inherent in the definition. Finally, see if Friedman has also provided more objective support for those judgments. If so, cite it in your journal.

■ *Definitions by Association: Synonyms, Metaphors, Etymologies*

A powerful way to create a definition is to relate the particular thing we are defining to something we believe is more familiar to our audience. Perhaps the easiest way is to provide a simple *synonym* for the word or term. Consider the following statement.

> *In the imagination of their worshippers, Western deities are almost invariably anthropomorphic, that is, human-like.*

The polysyllabic jawbreaker "anthropomorphic" becomes much more meaningful to an average reader when defined with the simpler synonym—"human-like."

So why provide the first term at all? Because it meets the needs of a broader range of audiences. In the context above, "anthropomorphic" means somewhat more than just "human-like." More fully, it means human-like in both physical *and* psychological characteristics. By using both terms, we provide a more exact idea of our meaning to those know the word and still give at least part of the story to those who don't.

Synonyms are useful, but we have to be careful with them. They rarely provide the exact or complete meaning of the target term, and they even more rarely provide all the emotional shades associated with the target term.

Exercise

Pick three terms from the Friedman reading that you think are somewhat complicated and might be misunderstood by an average reader. Write them down in your journal and, for each one, write a synonymous word or short phrase that you think helps clarify the meaning of the term.

Another sort of definition by association that skillful writers frequently use is a definition by *metaphor*. A metaphor is a figure of speech in which a writer tries to communicate the important aspects of a term or concept his or her readers might not know (called the *tenor* of the metaphor) by comparing the term or concept with something they are more likely to have some experience of (the *vehicle* of the metaphor).

For example, 18th century Scottish poet Robert Burns writes *"O, my luve's like a red, red rose. . . ."* Here he's trying to explain the essence of his lover, and how he feels about her, to readers that don't know her (the *tenor)* by comparing her to something they're likely to know— a rose (the *vehicle).* A metaphor often says quite a lot in very few words. In eight simple words, Burns effectively communicates her beauty, delicacy, fragility, strength, and many other characteristics, including her mortality. Since "red" often connotes heat or passion, he's also communicating the depth of his feelings for her.

Of course, metaphor is not the special property of poets. Non-fiction writers often use metaphors to communicate the essence of a concept as well as a whole host of emotional associations. For example, in the reading above, Friedman uses metaphors—the *Lexus* and the *olive tree*—to help define somewhat complex concepts for his reader. Since the connections between the Lexus and the olive tree and the concepts Friedman explores in the essay are not quite so obvious as those between a woman and a rose, he provides *precising definitions* to make sure his readers get the point:

Olive trees are important. They represent everything that roots us, anchors us, identifies us and locates us in this world—whether it be belonging to a family, a community, a tribe, a nation, a religion or, most of all, a place called home. Olive trees are what give us the warmth of family, the joy of individuality, the intimacy of personal rituals, the depth of private relationships, as well as the confidence and security to reach out and encounter others.

So then what does the Lexus represent? It represents an equally fundamental, age-old human drive—the drive for sustenance, improvement, prosperity and modernization—as it is played out in today's globalization system. The Lexus represents all the burgeoning global markets, financial institutions and computer technologies with which we pursue higher living standards today.

Since Friedman provides definitions of the metaphors, you may wonder why he bothers to use them. Actually, the metaphors help shape the entire essay, providing touchstones that he will return to again. Also, he's counting on our emotional response to the images of the Lexus and the olive tree to shape our emotional responses to main points throughout the essay. The Lexus is known as a fairly upscale machine—expensive, powerful, slick, and efficient—an effective metaphor for "burgeoning global markets." The olive tree is associated with the Mediterranean area and the Middle East, where it is a profoundly important and very ancient staple. Considering the nature of those societies and that they include some of the major trouble spots in the world, the metaphor is appropriate and effective.

You may find definition by metaphor very useful in enhancing the interest and depth of your essays and in eliciting emotional responses from your readers that help them care about your points of view.

Exercise

In your journal list three events or states of affairs currently important in areas of the world other than the United States. Then create metaphors for them that would help define their essence for your readers and create an appropriate emotional response. Finally, in two or three sentences each, state the emotional responses you want the metaphors to elicit and explain why you think they might be successful.

Another interesting technique of definition is to explore the *etymology*, or life history, of a term. All languages evolve over time; they change their structure and vocabulary to meet the needs of the people using them at any given point in history. Almost all modern languages are largely derived from one or more older languages. Tracing that history can often provide insight into how terms are currently used, enhance your credibility in dealing with complex subjects, and simply make your essays more interesting to read.

A good dictionary will provide at least a brief etymology of some terms. The standard reference in this regard is the *Oxford English Dictionary*, which is designed to be a historical dictionary of the English language. Since the hardbound edition of this work comprises 20 volumes, you'll probably need to visit your school library to use it. It's also available online or on CD-ROM, but either version is fairly expensive. Think *library*.

You might be surprised at where some of the words you use every day come from and what they originally meant. For example, Friedman uses forms of the word "global" throughout his essay. "Global" is an adjective, and the dictionary won't give you much about that; however, if we turn to the noun "globe," we find that it comes into English through Middle French from the Latin *globus*, which may, in turn, have come from the Latin *glebus* meaning "clod." Might you put that to work in an essay on the idiocy of war? Perhaps.

We might note that if you begin researching etymologies, you will find that most dictionaries use a somewhat arcane system of abbreviations for the historical sources of words. You should find a key to those abbreviations at the bottom of selected pages or in the introductory matter at the front of the dictionary.

Exercise

Pick a half dozen words from any of the readings you've done so far in this or any other course or from your local newspaper. Then research and write the etymologies of those words in your journal. Finally, add a line or two to each entry speculating on how you might use those etymologies in an essay.

■ *Best-Case Scenario: Extended Synthesis of Types*

In the invention stage of your writing projects, when you are trying to generate as many ideas and develop as much insight as you can about the nature of your subject, you will find it useful to create as many different types of definitions of that subject as your time and creativity will allow. When you get around to the drafting or composition stage, when you are generating claims and structuring them into an argument, you may find that a single type of definition serves your purpose. However, you may also find that working several different types of definition into an extended synthesis will enhance the depth, scope, and texture of your writing. As we've seen, Friedman uses just such a synthesis to good effect. In fact, many of his major points turn on the extended definitions he's created, and the purpose of his essay is largely to explore the nature of his subjects by defining them effectively. Think what the essay would be like if he had been content with lexical dictionary definitions of "cold war" and "globalization."

Exercise

Get a recent copy of your local newspaper. From the front page or the editorial page, pick two or three terms that you think are important in discussions of a current issue. The issue can be international, national, or local. In your journal, write simple definitions of the terms by class and differentiation; then follow those with a more extended definition of one of the terms using the Friedman essay as a model. In your more extended effort, try to create a synthesis of several different types of definition—operational, precising, persuasive using a variety of the techniques discussed above. The stronger your synthesis, the more fully you will explore the nature of the issue.

The Golden Arches Theory of Conflict Prevention
Thomas Friedman

Excerpt from Thomas Friedman. *The Lexus and The Olive Tree:
Understanding Globalization* (2000).

Every once in a while when I am traveling abroad, I need to indulge in a burger and a bag of McDonald's french fries. For all I know, I have eaten McDonald's burgers and fries in more countries in the world than anyone, and I can testify that *they* all really *do taste the same*. But as I Quarter-Poundered my way around the world in recent years, I began to notice something intriguing. I don't know when the insight struck me. It was a bolt out of the blue that must have hit somewhere between the McDonald's in Tiananmen Square in Beijing, the McDonald's in Tahrir Square in Cairo and the McDonald's off Zion Square in Jerusalem. And it was this:

No two countries that both had McDonald's had fought a war against each other since each got its McDonald's.

I'm not kidding. It was uncanny. Look at the Middle East: Israel had a kosher McDonald's, Saudi Arabia had McDonald's, which closed five times a day for Muslim prayer, Egypt had McDonald's and both Lebanon and Jordan had become McDonald's countries. None of them have had a war since the Golden Arches went in. Where is the big threat of war in the Middle East today? Israel-Syria, Israel-Iran and Israel-Iraq. Which three Middle East countries don't have McDonald's? Syria, Iran and Iraq.

I was intrigued enough by my own thesis to call McDonald's headquarters in Oak Brook, Illinois, and report it to them. They were intrigued enough by it to invite me to test it out on some of their international executives, at Hamburger University, McDonald's in-house research and training facility. The McDonald's folks ran my model past all their international experts and confirmed that they, too, couldn't find an exception. I feared the exception would be the Falklands war, but Argentina didn't get its first McDonald's until 1986, four years after that war with Great Britain. (Civil wars and border skirmishes don't count: McDonald's in Moscow, El Salvador and Nicaragua served burgers to both sides in their respective civil wars.)

Armed with this data, I offered up "The Golden Arches Theory of Conflict Prevention," which stipulated that when a country reached the level of economic development where it had a middle class big enough to support a McDonald's network, it became a McDonald's country. And people in McDonald's countries didn't like to fight wars anymore, they preferred to wait in line for burgers.

Others have made similar observations during previous long periods of peace and commerce—using somewhat more conventional metaphors. The French philosopher Montesquieu wrote in the eighteenth century that international trade had created an international "Grand Republic:' which was uniting all merchants and trading nations across boundaries, which would surely lock in a more peaceful world. In *The Spirit of the Laws* he wrote that "two nations who traffic with each other become reciprocally dependent; for if one has an interest in buying, the other has an interest in selling; and thus their union is founded on their mutual necessities." And in his chapter entitled "How Commerce Broke Through the Barbarism of Europe," Montesquieu argued for his own Big Mac thesis: "Happy it is for men that they are in a situation in which, though their passions prompt them to be wicked, it is, nevertheless, to their interest to be humane and virtuous."

In the pre-World War I era of globalization, the British writer Norman Angell observed in his 1910 book, *The Great Illusion*, that the major Western industrial powers, America, Britain, Germany and France, were losing their taste for war-making: "How can modern life, with its overpowering proportion of industrial activities and its infinitesimal proportion of military, keep alive the instincts associated with war as against those developed by peace?" With all the free trade and commercial links tying together major European powers in his day, Angell argued that it would be insane for them to go to war, because it would destroy both the winner and the loser.

Montesquieu and Angell were actually right. Economic integration was making the cost of war much higher for both victor and vanquished, and any nation that chose to ignore that fact would be devastated. But their hope that this truth would somehow end geopolitics was wrong. Montesquieu and Angell, one might say, forgot their Thucydides. Thucydides wrote in his history of the Peloponnesian War that nations are moved to go to war for one of three reasons—"honor, fear and interest"—and globalization, while it raises the costs of going to war for reasons of honor, fear or interest, does not and cannot make any of these instincts obsolete—not as long as the world is made of men not machines, and not as long as olive trees still matter. The struggle for power, the pursuit of material and strategic interests and the ever-present emotional tug of one's own olive tree continue even in a world of microchips, satellite phones and the Internet. [My] . . . book isn't called *The Lexus and the Olive Tree* for nothing. Despite globalization, people are still attached to their culture, their language and a place called home. And they will sing for home, cry for home, fight for home and die for home. Which is why globalization does not, and will not, end geopolitics. Let me repeat that for all the realists who read this book: *Globalization does not end geopolitics.*

But it does affect it. The simple point I was trying to make—using McDonald's as a metaphor—is that today's version of globalization significantly raises the costs of countries using war as a means to pursue honor, react to fears or advance their interests. What is new today, compared to when Montesquieu and even Angell were writing, is a difference in *degree.* Today's version of globalization—with its intensifying economic integration, digital integration, its ever-widening connectivity of individuals and nations, its spreading of capitalist values and networks to the remotest corners of the world and its growing dependence on the Golden Straitjacket [the rules of the free market] and the Electronic Herd [the often anonymous stock, bond, currency, and multi-national investors]—makes for a much stronger web of constraints on the foreign policy behavior of those nations which are plugged into the system. It both increases the incentives for not making war and it increases the costs of going to war in more ways than in any previous era in modern history.

But it can't guarantee that there will be no more wars. There will always be leaders and nations who, for good reasons and bad reasons, will resort to war, and some nations, such as North Korea, Iraq or Iran, will choose to live outside the constraints of the system. Still, the bottom line is this: If in the previous era of globalization nations in the system thought twice before trying to solve problems through warfare, in this era of globalization they will think about it three times.

Of course, no sooner did the first edition of this book come out, in April 1999, than nineteen McDonald's-laden NATO countries undertook air strikes against Yugoslavia, which also had McDonald's. Immediately, all sorts of commentators and reviewers began writing to say that this proved my McDonald's theory all wrong, and, by implication, the notion that globalization would affect geopolitics. I was both amazed and amused by how much the Golden Arches Theory had gotten around and how intensely certain people wanted to prove it wrong. They were mostly realists and out-of-work Cold Warriors who insisted that politics, and the never ending struggle between nation-states, were the immutable defining feature of international affairs, and they were both professionally and psychologically threatened by the idea that globalization and economic integration might actually influence geopolitics in some very new and fundamental ways. Many of these critics were particularly obsessed with the Balkans precisely because this old-world saga, in which politics, passion and olive trees always takes precedence over economics and the Lexus, is what they knew. They were so busy elevating the Balkans into a world historical issue, into the paradigm of what world politics is actually about, that they failed to notice just what an exception it was, and how, rather than spreading around the world, the Balkans was isolated by the world. They were so busy debating whether we were in 1917, 1929 or 1939 that they couldn't see that what was happening in 2000 might actually be something fundamentally new—something that doesn't end geopolitics but influences and reshapes it in important ways. These critics, I find, are so busy dwelling on what happened yesterday, and telling you what will happen someday, that they have nothing to say about what is happening today. They are experts at extrapolating the future from the past, while skipping over the present. It's not surprising this group would be threatened by the McDonald's argument, because, if it were even half true, they would have to adapt their worldviews or, even worse, learn to look at the world differently and to bring economics, environment, markets, technology, the Internet and the whole globalization system more into their analyses of geopolitics.

My first reaction to these critics was to defensively point out that NATO isn't a country, that the Kosovo war wasn't even a real war and to the extent that it was a real war it was an intervention by NATO into a civil war between Kosovo Serbs and Albanians. And I pointed out that when I posited my original McDonald's theory I had qualified it in several important ways: the McDonald's theory didn't apply to civil wars, because, I explained, globalization is going to sharpen civil wars within countries between localizers and globalizers—between those who eat the Big Mac and those who fear the Big Mac will eat them. Moreover, the theory was offered with a limited shelf life, because, I said, sooner or later virtually every country would have McDonald's, and sooner or later two of them would go to war.

But I quickly realized that no one was interested in my caveats, the fine print or the idea that McDonald's was simply a metaphor for a larger point about the impact of globalization on geopolitics. They just wanted to drive a stake through this Golden Arches Theory. So the more I thought about the criticism, the more I told people, "You know what, forget all the caveats and the fine print. Let's assume Kosovo is a real test. Let's see how the war ends." And when you look at how the war ended you can see just how much the basic logic of the Golden Arches Theory still applies.

Here's why: As the Pentagon will tell you, airpower alone brought the 1999 Kosovo war to a close in seventy-eight days for one reason—not because NATO made life impossible for the Serb troops in Kosovo. Indeed, the Serbian army ended up driving most of its armor out of Kosovo unscathed. No, this war ended in seventy-eight days, using airpower alone, because NATO made life miserable for the Serb civilians in Belgrade. Belgrade was a modern European city integrated with Western Europe, with a population that wanted to be part of today's main global trends, from the Internet to economic development—which the presence of McDonald's symbolized.

Once NATO turned out the lights in Belgrade, and shut down the power grids and the economy, Belgrade's citizens almost immediately demanded that President Slobodan Milosevic bring an end to the war, as did the residents of Yugoslavia's other major cities. Because the air war forced a choice on them: Do you want to be part of Europe and the broad economic trends and opportunities in the world today or do you want to keep Kosovo and become an isolated, backward tribal enclave: It's McDonald's or Kosovo—you can't have both. And the Serbian people chose McDonald's. Not only did NATO soldiers not want to die for Kosovo—neither did the Serbs of Belgrade. In the end, they wanted to be part of the world, more than they wanted to be part of Kosovo. They wanted McDonald's re-opened, much more than they wanted Kosovo reoccupied. They wanted to stand in line for burgers, much more than they wanted to stand in line for Kosovo. Airpower alone couldn't work in Vietnam because a people who were already in the Stone Age couldn't be bombed back into it. But it could work in Belgrade, because people who were integrated into Europe and the world could be bombed out of it. And when presented by NATO with the choice—your Lexus or your olive tree?—they opted for the Lexus.

So, yes, there is now one exception to the Golden Arches Theory—an exception that, in the end, only proves how powerful is the general rule. Kosovo proves just how much pressure even the most olive-tree-hugging nationalist regimes can come under when the costs of their adventures, and wars of choice, are brought home to their people in the age of globalization. Because in a world where we all increasingly know how each other lives, where governments increasingly have to promise and deliver the same things, governments can ask their people to sacrifice only so much. When governments do things that make economic integration and a better lifestyle—symbolized by the presence of McDonald's—less possible, people in developed countries simply will not tolerate it for as long as they did in the past. Which is why countries in the system will now think three times before going to war and those that don't will pay three times the price. So let me slightly amend the Golden Arches Theory in light of Kosovo and what are sure to be future Kosovos. I would restate it as follows: People in McDonald's countries don't like to fight wars anymore, they prefer to wait in line for burgers—and *those leaders or countries which ignore that fact will pay a much, much higher price than they think.*

Questions

1. What do you think Friedman wants you, the reader, to understand about the impact of globalization on geopolitics?
2. Does the "Golden Arches" metaphor seem a useful analogy to show that "globalization and economic integration might actually influence geopolitics . . ."? Explain your answer. Note that for analogies to work, there must be a clear and sensible relationship between the items being compared.
3. What might be some limitations of using analogies to support your writing?

Claims about Causality

As our knowledge of the world has increased, so has our understanding of how many powerful forces are at work in all events—big and small, distant and near. As our instruments have improved, we've been able to see more fully into the vastness of the universe and also into the microscopic smallness of it. As a result, we now know much more than we did. The question is how do we make sense of all this knowledge? Writing about cause and effect is a good start.

The reason causal arguments interest us is because we believe if we can learn the causes of what is beneficial to us we can help promote them, and if we can learn the causes of what is harmful to us we can eventually block or inhibit them. In addition, if we can predict the consequences of an action before it actually occurs, we will know whether to undertake that action or not; or if it is something beyond our control, we can at least prepare to react effectively to that event or action. Think Homeland Security or Hurricane Katrina.

In Chapter 1 we worked on asking questions about the causes and effects of things; and, as we did with our work on the nature of things, we generated some preliminary answers. Now we want to look at ways to expand our answers, deepen our understanding of the issues involved, and generate more insightful claims about causation.

❏ *Some Basic Principles*

First we need to establish some basic principles of writing and thinking about cause and effect. One of the most effective things we can do is think about the categories of our subjects into which our claims might fall. Four obvious possibilities come to mind (though you may think of others). We can make *causal* claims about:

- Things or classes of things—that is, material items like a computer or *the* computer
- Ideas or theories—like Friedman's "Golden Arches Theory of Conflict Prevention" in the earlier reading.
- Actions or events—like the U.S. invasion of Iraq
- States of affairs—like the political tension between the United States and Iran

Also, when we're making claims about causes and effects, we need to remember that the causes must be *different* from the effects and must *precede them in time*. This is not always as easy as it sounds, especially when causes and effects seem circular. For example, consider the relationship between crime and poverty. Social scientists have substantial data to suggest that poverty causes crime. The relationship seems obvious. Poverty creates extreme need; and when people's needs are extreme, they are more likely to turn to extreme measures to meet those needs. And it seems just as obvious that crime causes poverty. When criminals are locked up, their families often live in poverty. So, what's the cause and what's the effect? In this sort of cycle, determining cause and effect in any absolute sense may become impossible; however, we can, *for the purposes of the inquiry*, artificially isolate one factor in the cycle as cause or effect. When we do this, it's important to make that stipulation clear to the reader.

Finally, our claims about cause and effect may require us to consider multiple causes of a single effect and may also require us to consider a *causal chain* in which A causes B, which causes C, which causes D and so on. Whether any particular element of the chain is acting as cause or effect depends on where in the chain we look at it. This characteristic of causation gives us some other things to think about as well. For example, in the causal chain mentioned above, what causes D? Is it A, B, or C? Actually, it's all three, but C is the most immediate cause, B is a more remote cause, and A is more remote still. Our claims should make a clear distinction between *immediate* or *precipitating causes* and *remote causes*.

For example, say the reason we failed our morning Physics exam is because we were so tired we could barely focus on the questions. And the reason we were so tired is because we didn't sleep that night. And the reason we didn't sleep that night is because we stayed up all night studying. And the reason we did that is because we had to work all day. And the reason we did that is because we needed money to help Grandma pay her house payment. So, is Grandma the reason why we failed our Physics examination? In this case, what is the *precipitating cause* of the effect—failing the exam—and what are the *remote causes*?

Exercise

Return to the Friedman's "Golden Arches Theory of Conflict Prevention". Find a passage that presents a causal chain. In your journal state the effect and then state the immediate and remote causes; be sure to label them appropriately and put them in the order in which they occurred.

In Chapter 1, we provided several general questions about causation:

- What agent caused my subject?
- What motivation caused my subject?
- What effects has my subject had in the past?
- What effects might my subject have in the future?

Perhaps the most frequent comprehensive sort of claim that evolves from these questions, and the one we'll discuss here, is the claim of *agency*. Remember, however, that many of the principles we'll explore below are equally applicable to claims of motivation, past effect, and prediction of the future.

Whenever something happens, it seems to be in our nature to ask why. An uncaused event seems a logical absurdity. So, almost immediately, we begin to ask: who or what caused the event? In other words, what is the *agency*? The answers will, of course, depend on the nature of the event. Events seem to fall into two very general (and arguable) categories: natural events and events caused by human action. And the different types of events have different types of agencies.

Natural events include the biggies that make the papers such as hurricanes and earthquakes. But they also include everyday events: the rain falls, acorns grow into oak trees, puppies get born and grow into dogs that bark and chase cats. Some would attribute all these events, big and little, to a supernatural or divine agency that has some overall plan in mind. Others would argue that the world just *is* and perhaps has always been. While such ultimate issues are certainly worth thinking and writing about, it's often more productive to tackle less ambitious questions. And no matter whether or not there is some *ultimate* agency, when we look into natural events, we're compelled to look for the *natural processes* that bring them about. Very often, this is the role of science, and we can write about science.

Some natural processes are very complex and not entirely understood. For example, the meteorological processes that bring about hurricanes are aspects of a system so large and complicated that we're only now beginning to understand them. Still, we are able, to some degree, to predict hurricanes and detect tornados in time to provide at least some warning to those in their paths.

Exercise

What causes earthquakes? Google "plate tectonics." Based on what you find, write two or three paragraphs explaining the causes of earthquakes. Keep it simple and don't get involved in a lot of scientific jargon. Make the level of detail appropriate to the length, but be sure that an average reader would understand your meaning and get a clear picture of the process.

If you have trouble with the search, try starting at http://www.ucmp.berkeley.edu/geology/tectonics.html

Note that your original question of agency—What causes earthquakes?—led you to a number of claims about natural processes and their effects.

When we turn from natural processes to human agents or agencies, the situation becomes simpler and more complex at the same time. We don't have to try to understand the intricacies of natural systems, but we do have to try to understand the actions of human beings—a precarious position indeed because we have to consider human needs and desires. Still, we do seem to live in an age in which, no matter what happens, we seek to blame or praise someone for it. If the levees fail to keep the floodwaters from New Orleans, who is the person responsible? If a team fails to do well in whatever sport, fire the manager; if it does well, double the manager's salary—no matter that it is actually a number of people other than the manager all contributing to the effort that makes a team succeed or fail.

Though this matter of causation is complex, we are aided by two powerful forces: our culture's traditional way of thinking about agency, which each of us learns at home and in school, and our culture's determination to make that information available to us through a variety of media—including the Internet. Consequently, we already share with our readers certain ways of thinking about agency.

Exercise

Get a copy of your local newspaper. Find three or four stories about events, states of affairs, or ideas that interest you. Clip them from the paper and paste or tape them into your journal. Then, for each story write a sentence or two that summarizes the event, state of affairs, or idea. Finally, for each entry, list the human agent(s) or agency that caused the phenomenon.

❏ *Conditions, Influences, and Precipitating Causes*

Earlier you encountered the concept of a *causal chain* in which a series of distinct, remote causes led, one after the other, to an *immediate* or *precipitating* cause. Sometimes we can find this sort of nice, clean sequence or chain of causation. Very often, though, the situation is more complex and the causal sequence is not quite so clear. In these situations, we'll find it more accurate to speak of a set of pre-existing *conditions* and *influences* that set the background for an effect—that is, the persistent physical setting, social and historical factors, natural and artificial circumstances underlying an event.

One tragic, though instructive, example is the Columbia Space Shuttle disaster in 2003. Approximately 16 minutes before Columbia was to have landed at Florida's Kennedy Space Center something happened that caused the disintegration of the shuttle and the deaths of the seven astronauts aboard.

Immediate examination of the film revealed nothing out of the ordinary that might have caused the disaster, so NASA, in its investigation, considered the same sorts of causal factors we're introducing here.

For example, in trying to explain the causes of the explosion, we might first look into the *existing conditions* that might have contributed to the event. We might begin with an examination of the meteorological conditions that surrounded the launch and might have contributed to the disaster—prevailing wind speed and direction, atmospheric temperature, barometric pressure at the shuttle's altitude, and the like might have been relevant.

Next, we would look for any other *influences* that might have caused or contributed to the explosion, or controlled the speed at which it took place and its intensity. For example, Columbia made the first shuttle flight and was the oldest ship in the fleet. Might an aging component have failed suddenly, causing the problem? The extreme measures NASA takes to refit shuttles for subsequent flights would seem to make this unlikely; nevertheless, we must include the possibility in our examination of other potential causal influences.

Finally, we want to look for a *precipitating cause*—that last thing that happened to "set off" the event itself. In this case, NASA determined that the most likely *precipitating cause* was that a piece of the foam used to insulate the rocket boosters had come loose during the launch 16 days earlier, hitting the leading edge of the left wing, puncturing it, and allowing the superheated air the shuttled encountered during the landing to fill the wing and, ultimately cause the explosion.

Exercise

Again, using that copy of your local newspaper, see if you can find a story that describes an event and its causes in this manner. List the event itself, the prevailing *conditions*, the heightening *influences* and, finally, the *precipitating cause*.

❑ *Necessary and Sufficient Conditions*

This is a slightly different way of thinking about causation that starts with our understanding of conditions, influences, and precipitating causes but takes that understanding a little further to make it even more useful in analyzing and creating arguments.

At this point, you need to understand and consider the difference between *causes* and *conditions* more carefully. In short, a *condition* is not necessarily a *cause*. In this context, "cause" is a somewhat ambiguous term. People often say "cause" when they mean "condition." *Causes* are more properly thought of as dynamic events that initiate other events. *Conditions* are more properly thought of as static sets of existing characteristics that may make an event possible, contribute to its occurrence, or have some influence on the ultimate outcome. For example, to call a two-dimensional figure a square, we must know that the figure has four equal sides. The fact that it has four equal sides is not a cause; it is a condition (or characteristic) of the figure. More precisely, it's a definition of the term "square."

Technically, it's probably more appropriate to speak of *causes* as *sufficient* to initiate an event and *conditions* as *necessary* to permit the event to occur. However, we'll find that it's a common practice among writers to use the two terms synonymously.

We'll return to this distinction between causes and conditions a little later. First, we'll find it helpful to establish some of the vocabulary of causation a little more firmly.

In the situation described earlier—the Columbia catastrophe—we can think of the *precipitating cause*—loose foam striking the wing—*as sufficient cause*. That is, given the prevailing conditions and influences, the impact was sufficient to cause the puncture and, ultimately the explosion. Notice, however, that the foam collision was not *necessary to* create the puncture; it might have been created by a meteorite, some other part of the shuttle that had come loose, or even a piece of "space junk" put into orbit decades earlier that, in an incredibly unlikely (but not impossible) circumstance, hit the shuttle as its orbit decayed and it re-entered the earth's atmosphere.

We can identify some *necessary* conditions for the explosion, that is, those existing conditions without which it could not have occurred. They would certainly have included the superheated air through which the shuttle was traveling and the puncture that allowed the air to enter the wing.

Notice that, while the superheated atmosphere was *necessary* to create the explosion, it was not by itself, *sufficient* to cause it. Something had to happen to put a hole in the wing and initiate the explosion.

In technical terms, an event may have a number of different possible *sufficient causes* which are not, by themselves, necessary and a number of *necessary conditions* (or *causes*) which are not, by themselves, *sufficient* to initiate the event.

Exercise

In your journal, list two or three clear and distinct examples of each of the following: sufficient conditions, necessary conditions, sufficient causes, and necessary causes. You'll find examples many places. The newspaper is a good start, but you might also turn to your textbooks. College texts, especially science texts, are often loaded with causal claims and explanations.

Necessary and sufficient conditions or causes for events are often different, as in the example above. Sometimes, however, we find a cause or condition that is *both necessary* and *sufficient*. In other words, if the cause is present the effect must occur, and if it's absent the effect cannot occur.

Our definition of a square provides a simple example. It is *necessary* that a two-dimensional figure have four equal sides before we can call it a square; and having four equal sides is *sufficient* to make it a square. Definitions, especially of material things (as opposed to events) often provide *necessary* and *sufficient conditions* (or *characteristics*) of the item being defined.

When we begin to write about the causes of events, the situation is a little more complex.

For one thing, it's relatively easy to find examples of *conditions* that are both necessary and sufficient. Definitions, for example, often imply necessary and sufficient conditions as in the definition of a square above. However, representative examples of *causes* that are both necessary and sufficient are much more rare.

One of those rare examples is Down syndrome. A particular flaw in a person's 21st chromosome is both a necessary and sufficient cause of Down syndrome. This flaw (trisomy) causes every cell in the body to produce three copies of chromosome 21 instead of the usual two. Consequently, the person has 47 chromosomes instead of the normal 46. If a child has that characteristic, he or she will be born with Down syndrome; however, if the chromosome is normal, the child will not be born with the syndrome.

It's often tempting to suggest necessary and sufficient causes of an event because it seems to give us more control; that is, we might more easily prevent an undesirable event or bring about a desirable one.

For example, the human immunodeficiency virus (HIV) was, when it first appeared, often spoken of as a necessary and sufficient cause of AIDS. Since being HIV positive seemed a "death sentence," this led to a great deal of unnecessary despair and fear and no little discrimination against those with the virus. Subsequent research seems to have established that HIV is a *necessary* cause of AIDS, that is, you don't get the disease if you don't have the virus; however, it may well not be a *sufficient* cause. Many people are walking the streets today carrying HIV (some of whom don't even know it), but many of those may never manifest the disease. There seem to be other factors at work, perhaps one's general health or the strength or nature of one's immune system.

Another very important thing to remember is that *correlation in time and/or space* does not necessarily mean *causation*. In the example of the Columbia earlier, it's clear on film that a piece of foam hit the wing, but it's not absolutely necessary that the impact caused the puncture and subsequent explosion. As we've seen, something else could have served as the precipitating cause. It's hard to overstate the significance of this distinction. People often mistake correlation for causation, and this logical mistake often has unwarranted and unfortunate consequences.

Consider the example of a man found by the police at approximately the same time and place a robbery occurs. Very likely he will be questioned and perhaps arrested, even though he may have had nothing to do with the robbery. Fortunately, our legal system, though it sometimes does not function perfectly, is designed to avoid inflicting unwarranted consequences on the man due to the logical error of mistaking correlation for causation.

Again, the AIDS phenomenon provides another, potentially disastrous, example. When the disease first made its appearance in the United States, most of its victims were homosexuals. This led some to refer to it as the "gay plague" and some to think of it as a disease that afflicted only homosexuals; in other words, they saw homosexuality as a *necessary* cause of AIDS. Time has demonstrated that this was completely wrong. That the first major vector of the disease was in the homosexual community is a historical coincidence. Thus there was a *correlation* between sexual preference and the disease; but homosexuality is not a *cause*, sufficient or necessary, of AIDS. In this case, mistaking correlation for causation, coupled with discrimination, may well have led to substantial and inexcusable delays in seeking preventative measures and effective treatments for a deadly disease.

Clearly, avoiding these two mistakes—incorrectly attributing both necessary and sufficient cause to an event and mistaking correlation for causation—is extremely important in our writing, especially if people will believe or act upon our claims.

Exercise

Return to the Friedman readings earlier in this chapter. Find two or three examples where Friedman makes causal claims. In your journal, analyze these claims on the basis of the principles presented above.

- Are they claims of agency, motivation, past effect, prediction, or a combination?
- Explain how he develops the claims. What details does he provide to support them and how does he explain the logical connection between the details and the claims they support?
- Does he state any conditions or influences that bear on the effects? If so, list and explain them. If not, explain why you think he should or should not have provided them.
- Does he identify precipitating or immediate causes of the effects? If so, list and explain them. If not, explain why you think he should or should not have provided them.
- Does he offer any necessary or sufficient causes? If so, list and explain them. If not, explain why you think he should or should not have provided them.
- Does he offer any causes that are both necessary and sufficient? If so, list and explain them. If not, explain why you think he should or should not have provided them. Are any of them *unwarranted* claims of necessary and sufficient cause? If so, explain why.
- Does he ever mistake correlation for causation? If so, explain how you would revise his writing to avoid the mistake.

Claims of Value

Values seem to have been a hot topic for human beings throughout the recorded history of the species. These days the print and broadcast media, especially around election time, seem to be saturated with "these values," "those values," "our values," "their values," values of every description. Questions of value seem fundamental to human existence. We seem compelled to assign value or worth to almost everything—natural objects, constructed things, people, actions, ideas, abstractions. List of the "Ten Best" this and the "Ten Worst" that abound. Let somebody name something, and somebody else will make a value claim about it—good, bad, beautiful, ugly, right, wrong, useful, worthless . . .

However, to make our *claims of value* or *value judgments* more than arbitrary matters of personal taste, we need to provide logical reasons in support of them. In other words, we'll need to demonstrate to our readers that we have an accurate and informed sense of the subject at hand.

When we discussed questions of value in Chapter 1, we mentioned three general categories of value judgments:

- judgments of *Ethics*—whether actions are right or wrong
- judgments of *Aesthetics*—whether things are beautiful or not
- judgments of *Utility*—whether something is useful or not

We also mentioned two general theories describing the kinds of criteria against which people normally measure the value of something:

- Non-consequentialist theories—measuring things against an absolute standard
- Consequentialist theories—measuring things against the positive or negative consequences they have had or may have in the future

You will find it useful to keep these two sets of organizing principles in mind as you begin to develop claims of value in your essays. You may also find it useful at this point to review the material on questions of value as well as the material on fact and judgment, both in Chapter 1.

In our discussion of non-consequentialist and consequentialist approaches below, we'll deal with the two types of value judgments you'll most likely encounter and write about—those of *ethics* and *aesthetics*.

❑ *Non-Consequentalist Approaches*

Explaining a judgment by measuring it against standards or criteria requires us to:

- clearly define relevant standards;
- logically weight those standards, that is, explain which are most important and why and then clearly indicate how the subject of our claim meets or fails to meet the standards.

When we use a non-consequentialist approach, we can either use an existing standard produced by other minds or we can define our own standards or criteria by creating an operative definition of them. (You may want to refer to the section on operative definitions earlier in this chapter.) In either case, we must make the source of the standard and the individual criteria it comprises absolutely clear to our readers.

One common non-consequentialist type of *ethical* standard is the "divine command" theory (mentioned in Chapter 1), which maintains that a god or gods have defined an absolute and unarguable set of criteria for right and wrong behavior. We very often find such a standard in cultures which have a document which they hold as a guide to their religious beliefs and practices as well as to ethical or unethical behavior. The *Torah* and *Talmud*, the *Koran*, and the *Bible* are good examples. In each case, many practitioners of the related faith regard the document as a repository of, among other things, divine commands that define right or wrong behavior.

However, not all non-consequentialist ethical standards involve some sort of divine command. Probably the most well known secular non-consequentialist theory comes from 18th century German philosopher Immanuel Kant. In Kant's view ethical standards or moral law ultimately derive from human reason, and we should abide by those standards solely out of respect for reason. He maintains that, since we and all other human beings are rational, self-determining beings, we are morally bound by what he called the *categorical imperative*. This imperative comprises three related aspects:

- The Formula of Universal Law—We may consider our actions ethical only if we consider the behavior ethical in all human beings. (This is sometimes seen as a version of the "golden rule.")

- The Formula of Humanity—All human beings have their own individual goals or ends; consequently, we must treat human beings as ends in themselves and never merely as means to achieve our own selfish goals or ends.
- The Formula of Autonomy—We must act as if we and all other human beings are equal partners in "a union of different rational beings" working together to create a "system of common [moral] laws."

Obviously, Kant's categorical imperative is somewhat more far-reaching than most divine command theories and covers a wider range of human behaviors.

One problem with appeals to standards worth noting is that they can be relatively inflexible, which may make it difficult for them to deal with new situations. The problem is compounded if they were established long in the past, when it was impossible to foresee developments that might occur hundreds or even thousands of years in the future. For example, it has been argued that Biblical directives could not take into account many modern scientific and social developments, and thus are not an adequate guide to behavior in current times. When we turn to aesthetics, we might consider perhaps the earliest expression of a non-consequentialist aesthetic theory in Aristotle's *Poetics*. In this work, Aristotle explains criteria by which he and many of his contemporaries would define an ideal drama. Another example is Edgar Allan Poe's statements regarding criteria for the short story. Of course, while Aristotle and Poe may get credit as the first to state defining criteria for the relevant genre, very few modern writers would accept their criteria as standards against which to measure the beauty or quality of their work. Thus, as in the case with the Biblical standards, rule-based standards can have serious limitations. We can only imagine what Aristotle or Poe might have thought about the aesthetic value of a modern graphic novel like *Sin City* or a film based on a modern computer game such as *Resident Evil*.

The non-consequentialist standards mentioned above are clearly examples of pre-existing standards generated by other minds. Of course, we can create our own non-consequentialist standards if it will make our inquiries more productive or make our arguments clearer to our readers. To help make sure that your audience will accept the criteria you have established as relevant, you can do the following:

- Base them on "shared" values: Freedom is vital to any political system.
- Back them up with "authority": Aristotle called freedom "the soul of a community."

Exercise

Create your own non-consequentialist standard of ethics or aesthetics (pick only one category). Select a single, well-defined aspect of human existence relevant to the category and, in your journal, write a set of rules that would govern and help shape the value judgments you might make about that aspect of our lives. Keep it simple; limit the scope of your subject and the number of rules you create.

Exercise

In class, divide into small groups based on which of the categories (ethics or aesthetics) you picked in the exercise above and discuss your criteria. At the end of the discussion, create a document that states general rules that cover as many of your individual rules as possible.

❑ *Consequentialist Approaches*

As you saw in Chapter 1, a *consequentialist* approach bases *claims of value* or *value judgments* on the effects or consequences that the subject of the claim has produced or may produce. At first it may seem a relatively simple equation—good effects require us to infer the subject has a positive value, and bad effects require us to infer its value is negative. In practice, however, the situation is not so black or white. In our exploration of causation, we saw that any effect may have multiple causes as well as a whole host of contributing conditions or influences; we also saw that any cause may produce multiple effects, either immediately or in the long run in a causal chain. So, rather than saying any particular cause or effect is absolutely good or bad, we will more often create a system of prioritization in which causes or effects are *relatively* good or bad.

Most people will probably maintain that it's wrong to steal. We can argue this from a non-consequentialist approach by referring to the Ten Commandments—Thou shalt not steal. Or we can argue this claim from a consequentialist approach by noting that a society which does not regard theft as an unethical act may be full of ill will, insecurity, and general chaos—all undesirable consequences.

From the consequentialist point of view, however, we may find that competing values temper the absolute nature of the claim. For example, while most would claim it is unethical to steal, many would, if it were the only way to feed their children, steal a loaf of bread from the grocery store. Does this mean they regard theft as an ethical act? Probably not, but it may mean that they regard stealing as *less unethical* than letting their children go hungry.

The conquentialist approach frequently leads to *values conflicts* that require us to prioritize values in this fashion, and how we prioritize them may well depend upon the context of the action.

Consider the following passage from Friedman's "Golden Arches Theory" above:

Once NATO turned out the lights in Belgrade, and shut down the power grids and the economy, Belgrade's citizens almost immediately demanded that President Slobodan Milosevic bring an end to the war, as did the residents of Yugoslavia's other major cities. Because the air war forced a choice on them: Do you want to be part of Europe and the broad economic trends and opportunities in the world today or do you want to keep Kosovo and become an isolated, backward tribal enclave: It's McDonald's or Kosovo—you can't have both. And the

Serbian people chose McDonald's. Not only did NATO soldiers not want to die for Kosovo—neither did the Serbs of Belgrade. In the end, they wanted to be part of the world, more than they wanted to be part of Kosovo. They wanted McDonald's re-opened, much more than they wanted Kosovo reoccupied. They wanted to stand in line for burgers, much more than they wanted to stand in line for Kosovo. Airpower alone couldn't work in Vietnam because a people who were already in the Stone Age couldn't be bombed back into it. But it could work in Belgrade, because people who were integrated into Europe and the world could be bombed out of it. And when presented by NATO with the choice—your Lexus or your olive tree?—they opted for the Lexus.

As Friedman describes the context, the people of Belgrade were clearly faced with a values conflict between their "olive tree" (the value of nationalism) and the "Lexus" (the value of joining the European economic community). Since the well-being of a nation was at stake, the consequentialist ethical aspect of the choice is clear.

While most people probably operate on a consequentialist basis, such criteria are not without their own problems. One problem is determining whether consequences will actually be good or bad. It's impossible to predict the future with much accuracy, and an action motivated by the best of intentions can have disastrous results. For example, the Manhattan Project in World War II created the first nuclear weapons. Whether or not this event can be considered ethical from a consequentialist point view is certainly arguable. One aspect of the project provides an interesting specific example of the point here. Making the weapon required relatively large quantities of enriched uranium. The facilities that refined this uranium were somewhat distant from Los Alamos, New Mexico, where the weapon was created and tested. The enriched, highly radioactive uranium was carried on public transportation by Secret Service agents in cardboard suitcases. The consequences of radiation exposure to the public and the agents were not foreseen. Since that time, we have learned that such exposure can have extremely negative consequences.

And what about the question of intent? Should you take a person's intentions into account when evaluating his or her behavior? Your friend wants to create a beautiful painting but winds up with something vaguely resembling a train wreck. Does your friend's intent influence your aesthetic judgment? A local politician develops some social program out of a genuine desire to make people's lives better. Unfortunately, the program results in massive unemployment. Is the politician's desire to do good one of the criteria by which you'll make your ethical evaluation of his or her behavior? Obviously, there is no simple or certain way to decide such questions. The evaluative criteria you choose will be governed by the nature of the subject, your creative intellect, and your personal values.

Exercise

In your journal, write a page or two analyzing the positive and negative aspects of consequentialist and non-consequentialist approaches to making value judgments. Provide specific, concrete examples to support your claims and be sure to explain your reasoning.

Claims about Action

One very common type of writing involves claims that something should be done—a *proposal* that some action should be performed. Almost always, our proposals claim the action will likely achieve a *goal* designed to make things better in some way. Human beings seem to have the capacity to imagine any number of possible goals. The most important of these goals often have an impact on others and/or require the participation and contribution of others for their achievement. If this is the case, we are obligated to conduct a thorough and logical inquiry into the situation and first make sure that the goal is worthwhile and actually in the best interest of others. Then we must make sure we arrive at an action that we honestly and objectively believe is most likely to achieve the goal. Finally, we must clearly explain our reasoning and evidence to our readers in a way that gives them the best chance of making an informed and thoughtful decision about the issue. When we conduct our inquiries and make our proposals, we must make at least three things clear to our readers and ourselves:

- That our proposed action is workable, that is, something we *can* do.
- That it will ultimately produce a beneficial state of affairs or avoid a negative one.
- That the actions we're proposing are, in themselves, ethical.

At this point, you may find it worthwhile to review the other three sorts of claims you've explored in this chapter, because they all often come into play as we create arguments in support of claims of action. Before we can construct good proposals that meet the three criteria listed above, we may first need to enhance our understanding of the *nature* of the situation and the factors involved, the likely *causes and effects* of acting or not acting as we propose, and the likely positive *value* of the result if our proposals are accepted and followed.

You may frequently find the need to write good proposals in your professional lives. As a working professional in almost any area, you may be expected to suggest courses of action that will serve the goals of your company, organization, or agency.

For example, a high-tech company might ask a software engineer to recommend a company-wide purchase of a new word-processing package. Doing this well will obviously have a positive effect on the software engineer's career. However, if the proposal is deficient in some way, that is, the writer has not conducted a thorough or logical inquiry or explained it clearly to his or her readers, then the proposal may not be acceptable or, worse still, it may be accepted anyway, and hundreds of people may be stuck with an inappropriate or ineffective tool with which to do their jobs.

In the medical fields, the consequences can be even more severe. In those fields, professionals are frequently expected to develop proposals or policies that direct patient care. Here a failure can have a negative impact on the quality or even the continuation of human lives.

Obviously, writing good proposals on the job is a matter of some consequence, both to you and to those your writing will affect.

Exercise

Think about your current major or the profession for which you're preparing yourself. If you haven't decided yet, pick one that seems interesting. Then, in your journal, make a list of three or four types of proposals you mi ght be expected to write on the job. You may want to consult someone working in the field or your faculty advisor. Then, for each entry in your list, provide two or three sentences stating important aspects of the task—things you might need to keep in mind as you conduct the inquiry and write the proposal.

Of course, writing on the job is not the only sort of proposal writing one might do. As citizens, we frequently suggest beneficial changes in the policies or practices of our society.

Often we suggest proposals that describe ways we might "move forward" from our existing state of affairs. In these cases, we're not saying that anything is necessarily wrong with the current situation, just that we have a new idea that might be able to make life better somehow—more productive, more interesting, more satisfying.

Sometimes, however, we can identify genuine problems that are causing dissatisfaction, pain, or inequity in people's lives—not allowing them to achieve the rewards they could from their lives and, in some cases, not allowing them to live at all. Then our thinking and writing seem to take on an increased importance, and our obligation to do them well becomes more pressing.

We need to remember that complex issues, complex problems, don't often have simple solutions. If the nature of the reality we are exploring is complicated, we should also expect the forces at work producing it to be numerous and varied. Therefore, our attempts to modify or eliminate those forces are likely to be difficult and complicated, as well.

We can identify several questions we need to answer for ourselves and, ultimately for our readers, as we conduct our inquiries, logically consider the evidence at hand, and construct our proposal arguments.

❏ First of all, *is the situation genuinely a problem*?

We sometimes encounter situations that seem somehow wrong to us, that is, they seem to be problems; but on further exploration, we discover they are not. For example, students sometimes falter and ultimately drop out of classes or even drop out of college altogether. Teachers, who care about students' success and well-being, often worry about such students and wonder what they might do to help; and college counseling centers devise numerous "intervention" plans. On further investigation, however, we sometimes find that students make quite rational decisions to forego a college education. They don't enjoy college, don't like the type of work required, and often pursue satisfactory and rewarding careers in fields that don't require degrees. What seems a problem for the college and the teachers is not, really, for the most important person in the equation—the student.

In the case of widespread states of affairs that affect many people, we must ask ourselves for whom is the situation a problem. For example, an increase in the prime interest rate may be a problem for people trying to buy a house, but it may also avoid an increase in inflation that makes life more difficult for the larger population.

Exercise

List several issues you think you and your classmates agree are both important and problems—that is, situations in need of solutions. For each one, indicate what the important negative effects are and who will most likely suffer them. Then, try and imagine which people or groups will benefit from the situation and exactly how they will benefit—using the term "benefit" as broadly as possible.

❏   The second important question we must answer is, *what are the relative benefits and harms of acting or not acting?* In other words:

  • What benefits may be gained by acting as we propose?

  • What harms may be avoided?

  • What are the chances we might make the problem worse by taking the proposed action than by just leaving things alone?

These two considerations, phrased a bit differently as "what effects has my subject had in the past" and "what effects might my subject have in the future" were introduced in Chapter 1 and helped us guide our efforts to inquire into an issue; they also helped us shape our evaluation of the situation.

Exercise

In your journal, list several recent, well-publicized problems and the solutions that have been proposed for each. In each situation, try to list the effects the situation has had in the past and those that it might have in the future. Then provide two or three sentences analyzing the proposed solutions according to the three questions stated above. Finally, indicate whether or not you think any of the proposed solutions are completely adequate and explain your reasoning.

❏   The third important question involves the *feasibility* of the solution; in other words, *can we actually do what's required to implement the solution?*

  We need to know that our solutions are efficient and practical. It's easy to say something needs fixing; but who will actually do it, how will it be done, and who will pay for it? Technically, this is called *feasibility*—that sense that the solution is not only worth doing but that it can be done. Feasibility requires that certain conditions be met. We must have good reasons for believing that:

  • technical means are readily available to solve the problem;

  • sufficient materials are available for the technology to work on;

- sufficient labor is available to build and use whatever is required;
- the cost of implementing the solution is not prohibitive.

Take, for example, the issue of nuclear waste. Many would agree that spent nuclear fuel represents a tremendous problem: tons of it exist; it is one of the most toxic substances on earth; and its toxicity lasts for millions of years. The question remains, what can we do about it? Right now, we have no technical means to render the substance harmless. We don't even have a good inventory of the material's current location or condition. The costs of developing and using the necessary technology are unclear at this point but are likely to be astronomical. So, while most people would agree that it is vital to do something, we currently don't have many feasible ways of addressing the issue.

Exercise

In your journal, list several important problems that currently have no feasible solutions. Then indicate what is actually being done. And finally, imagine what might be done if we could ever develop the means to do it.

❑   Finally, *is the proposed solution in itself ethical?* That is, does our proposed solution require actions that we consider ethically wrong or that might be considered unethical by those the actions will affect and whose participation we need to implement the solution?

Here we must return to the values considerations mentioned in the previous section. We offer proposals because we think the states of affairs resulting from those actions will have practical value—they will produce some good for someone. However, it is possible that the actions themselves, while they may produce a good effect, are not quite so good. We must always be careful to prioritize the values involved to make sure our actions are, after all, ethical.

Note that this is true whether one adopts a consequentialist or non-consequentialist approach to ethical considerations. The non-consequentialist must be sure that the actions proposed are more in accordance with his or her absolute ethical standards than the result of those actions. The consequentialist must be sure that the actions proposed provide more overall value than the specific result, or at least as much.

Such issues can be very difficult because they are not simply a matter of numbers. For example, in 1932 the United States government funded the Tuskegee Study of Untreated Blacks with Syphilis. In this study over 400 black men were recruited with a promise of medical treatment for the disease. Instead and unknown to them, they were given placebos, though a cure was readily available, so researchers could study their long-term physical deterioration and thus gather medical data on the progress of the disease. The study continued for 40 years until a Senate investigation put an end to it. At that time 127 of the men were still alive.

The ethical issues here seem clear. The medical data gathered were valuable, but were they worth the suffering of the research subjects? Most would say the study involved a profoundly incorrect prioritization of values.

Sometimes, however, we may believe that, even if our proposed action will cause some harm, what is achieved as the result of those actions will ethically outweigh the harm. Consider, for example, the school lunch and breakfast programs, which provide daily meals for children who might otherwise not have them. These programs are largely funded by taxpayers, which takes money out of their pockets. Most would regard losing money as at least a minor harm; however, the value of those programs vastly outweighs the harm of a few dollars added to our tax bills.

Exercise

List several problems that you think have an important moral dimension to them. Try to write a relatively complete analysis of them based on the ethical principles explained above.

Exercise

Pick one important problem. Propose and explain a potential solution. Based on *all* the principles, practical and ethical, discussed in this section, try to write a complete analysis of the problem and the solution.

7 *Surveying the Rhetorical Situation*

A Word about Communication

It is not a coincidence that the same root word underlies both communication and community. Actions might speak louder than words, but our words present and explain what we think and feel.

Moreover, much of what we think and feel is influenced by language—even from the time that we are in our mother's womb, as modern science has revealed. Language, in the broadest sense of the word, is all around us—in images, in architecture, in all the natural and unnatural sounds of the world. We come into this world ready for language, ready to hear and speak; ready to engage in a great conversation with life until there is silence once more.

The good news is that the basic process is much the same for all of us—no matter who we are, where we are, or what particular language we are using. There are the thoughts and feelings we have (many of them occasioned or shaped by previous communication experiences); there are the nouns and verbs and modifiers and connectors we select to communicate our thoughts and feelings; and there is our audience—those with whom we share our thoughts and feelings. The more we know about each aspect of the process, the greater our chances of being understood. The more time and effort we take to make sure we know precisely what it is we want to tell our audience; what words and their arrangement can best convey that information; and what words and their arrangement have the best, most honest, chance of being understood and considered by the particular audience we are trying to reach—why, then, the better our chances of communicating successfully.

We will never execute the process perfectly, but we can always seek to do it better. And, as we do, perhaps we should keep in mind that old saying: "If something can go wrong, it will." In fact, when trying to communicate complex information about almost anything to anyone, including those who know us well, it is prudent to expect to be misunderstood and then to take precautions against that happening.

The Rhetorical Triangle

Here we turn to a very ancient way of looking at many of the principles noted above—the *rhetorical triangle*. One of the virtues of the triangle metaphor is its ability to compress multiple dimensions of meaning into a simple diagram.

The rhetorical triangle looks at any communicative act from three different perspectives–

- the writer (or speaker),
- the content of the communication,
- the reader (or audience).

To help make things a little easier, from now on we will confine our discussion to *writing* as the means of transmission and *argument* as the type of content.

Traditionally, we use three ancient Greek terms to express these perspectives:

- *Ethos* refers to factors related to the position of the *writer* in the process
- *Logos* refers to factors related to the *argument itself*
- *Pathos* refers to factors related to the *reader*

Though it seems unlikely Aristotle ever structured this triad into an actual triangle, over the centuries, rhetoricians have taken that approach. The following diagram is common:

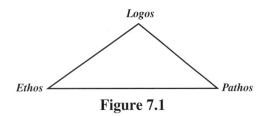

Figure 7.1

While the diagram may seem of limited value in learning this scheme (you probably don't need a diagram to help you remember three terms), there is a little more to it than that. The diagram, especially the legs of the triangle, emphasizes the *interactive* nature of the elements. It is important to remember that the three concepts—ethos, logos, and pathos—are not static points, and they are not isolated from one another. The *function* of each factor is largely dependent on the characteristics of the other two; they work dynamically together. Each is present every time we argue, every time we try to share our understanding of a subject with others.

Another issue is *control*. One challenge facing any writer is the need to control the material and *write with authority*. This is sometimes a special problem for inexperienced writers. Rather than controlling the rhetorical situation as much as possible, they can find themselves confused by it—at the mercy of processes they don't understand very well and driven into a mad scramble just to get the work done. This tends to produce tentative writing that is unlikely to achieve the effects the writer had hoped for.

One thing we will focus on in this discussion is how to enhance your ability to write with authority and control the process rather than let it control you.

Ethos

Ethos refers to the characteristics and behavior of the writer and how they function in the writing process. Think for a moment about the aspects of your being that have some impact on making and communicating an argument.

Exercise

In your journal list at least 10 "aspects of your being" that will contribute to any rhetorical situation you might face.

We'll guess that was not an awfully demanding task. Indeed, it's hard to imagine *any* aspect of your being that wouldn't contribute something to your writing—everything from your personal philosophy to whether or not you ate breakfast this morning. Of course, some aspects are more important than others and will have a greater impact on the arguments you create (logos) and on how your readers will react to those arguments (pathos).

Perhaps it will be helpful to identify a few of the more important *ethos* factors and explore how they function with the other parts of the rhetorical situation. All of these will, to some degree, control the arguments you make and how your readers will receive and respond to them and to you as a writer.

1. Knowledge of the subject

Beginning writers are often told to write about what they know. While that might seem obvious, it is sometimes not all that easy. In college or on the job, you may need to write about subjects you don't know very well or about which you haven't thought much.

From the *logos* point of view, this is clearly a problem. Your arguments will be composed of claims, and sooner or later, they will need to rest on claims of fact. No facts = no argument, or at least no effective argument. From the *pathos* or reader's point of view, the situation is worse. Readers are often very quick to detect uninformed points of view.

However, perhaps the worst aspect of the situation is the effect it will have on you. If your knowledge of a subject is slim or non-existent, you're likely very aware of that. The deficiency will make it very difficult to write with authority because you would have none. Authority is earned through the conscientious search for and use of ideas and information from those whose work in a specific field has given them extensive knowledge and expertise. Your message, and thus your authority, will become stronger as you begin a dialogue with those whose insights you have come to respect and acknowledge through your reading and thinking. You may never be able to know all there is to know about a subject, but if you can come to know more than your audience already knows, or know it in a different way, then you do have something to contribute to the conversation and you can respectfully ask your audience to listen to you.

2. *Emotions and Attitudes*

While your personal experience is certainly part of your "knowledge" of the subject, there are a couple of other factors to consider in relation to the concept of *ethos*.

For one thing, you must ask yourself if the knowledge you have gained from personal experience with a subject or phenomenon is indeed *factual* knowledge. Or does it fall more into the realm of subjective *emotion* or *attitude*? (This might be a good time to review the discussion of fact vs. judgment earlier in the book.) It may be a historical fact that you had a certain experience, but it may also be that what you took away from the experience was more emotion or attitude than an objective understanding of the situation.

Our intent is not to discount the emotions or attitudes you have picked up from your experiences; rather it is to *emphasize* them. If anything, our emotions and attitudes have more impact on our being as writers than our understanding of facts. However, we need to be aware of our emotions and attitudes, positive or negative, and know when they are coming into play in our writing.

Again, it is somewhat a matter of control. If our arguments are solely expressions of our emotions, then rationality suffers. When that occurs, the logic of the argument (*logos*) can be weakened or sometimes just collapse, and we fail in achieving our purpose. Also, readers (*pathos*) are often quick to recognize—and discount—arguments that are dominated by emotion rather than reason.

Exercise

Think of the last time you were involved in or witnessed an argument dominated by emotion rather than reason. In your journal, write a brief narrative and analysis of the event. What was the result? To what degree did either of the participants achieve his or her goal?

Again, none of this is to suggest that you should ignore your emotions or attitudes. They can provide your motivation to write and generate energy and excitement in the writing itself, all of which is extremely desirable. However, to make your emotions work for rather than against you, you must make yourself aware of them and not let them dominate the writing process.

3. *Good will*

Closely related to the concerns writers need to show for their emotions and attitudes is the need to demonstrate good will toward all sides of an issue. This is a large part of the interaction between the *ethos* and the *pathos* of the rhetorical situation. Readers appreciate and respond well to a measure of evenhandedness in argumentative discourse especially if issues are extremely sensitive. It is a sign of good critical thinking to be able to understand and respect positions with which you disagree. This matter of trying to understand and take into account different perspectives forms the heart of Rogerian or Common Ground rhetoric which we'll take up later in this chapter.

Note that this does not mean you must respect or even tolerate *every* point of view. Frankly, most people find at least a few positions on important issues detestable. However, it is important to understand those positions even if we simply can't respect them. It is also useful if we can demonstrate some understanding of the motives of those who hold positions we find intolerable.

Exercise

In the first column of a double-entry journal, make a list of five positions you find intolerable. Then, in the second column, list two or three possible motives of those who hold them. This may require some speculation on your part, but try it anyway. Finally, go back and examine the motives you've listed. How many are based on reason? How many are based on a lack of character or on deficient morality? Which motives would you mention in an essay critiquing the issue?

If, in the final part of the exercise, you selected those motives based on reason, then you're right on target. If, on the other hand, you selected mainly those motives that derived from character or morality, you should give some thought to how your readers would respond to that sort of critique.

4. *Credibility*

In the long run, many *ethos* concerns lead up to this—how can you best establish your credibility as a writer with your readers? We can identify two types of credibility:

- *Extrinsic* credibility generated by the familiarity of your readers with your past performance.
- *Intrinsic* credibility generated by the document at hand.

Well-known writers with academic credentials and/or a list of prior publications have a certain built in extrinsic credibility with their readers that has nothing to do with the document at hand. In other words, they have a track record.

As a student writer without a list of prior publications, you might think that you have little or no extrinsic credibility. Actually, that is not entirely true. Consider the educational level of most of the people in the world. Now consider how much schooling you have completed—probably a dozen years of primary and secondary education and some college. It is probable that you are one of the most educated people on the planet. Your readers—in most cases, your teachers or classmates—may or may not choose to recognize your extrinsic credibility, but you should. It will help you write with an attitude of authority.

While you can't really control the amount of extrinsic credibility your readers will grant you, you can control the intrinsic credibility you might earn with the document at hand.

Some ways of earning intrinsic credibility are fairly simple.

- Format speaks first. The first impression your reader—your teacher in this case—gets of your work will be the physical format. Make it professional. Pay attention to the format instructions in your course syllabus. If there aren't any, ask your teacher. If you don't get a specific answer, ask someone else. The college writing center might be a good place to start. Whatever the case, make the physical presence of the paper communicate professionalism, intelligence, and attention to detail.

- Learn and abide by the conventions of the discipline. Different disciplines expect different conventions. For example, we normally write about literature and about history in the past tense. Most disciplines have style guides. Get the one that's appropriate for the course subject and follow it.
- Learn and abide by the general conventions of academic and professional prose. There is no place in a college-level paper for mechanical errors. Make use of the college writing center, and whatever else you do, buy a good dictionary and use it. Don't trust the spell-checker on your word processor.

None of this really has much to do with the writing itself. But it does have to do with the practical relationship between *ethos* and *pathos*.

More importantly, review the first three sections under *Ethos* above:

- Do the work you need to do to know enough to write intelligently on the subject.
- Use whatever emotional response the subject inspires in you to generate motivation and energy, not just to rant and rave. If you want to refute a point of view, always attack the argument itself—not the character of the person making it.
- Consider alternative points of view as fully as you can and write with as much good will as possible.

Logos

The *logos* aspect of the rhetorical triangle refers to the argument itself, including the structure of your reasoning (that is, your *logic*) and the quality of the evidence you offer in support of your thesis. While we will deal with these elements in much greater detail in other chapters (for example, Chapter 11 deals extensively with logic), it will be helpful here to develop a general understanding of the principles of *logos*.

To remind you briefly of the whole "argument as inquiry" process developed throughout the book:

1. You ask meaningful questions about your subject.

2. You develop meaningful and insightful answers to those questions through introspection, reading, and research.

3. You work the answers into an appropriately focused thesis.

4. You support the thesis in a public draft that contains your own reasoning and the relevant results of your research. This is your argument.

In the language of argument, of *logos*, your thesis is the *conclusion* of your argument, and the pieces of evidence you offer in support of that conclusion are your *premises*. That intellectual step from premises to conclusion is referred to as *inference*. We say that we *infer* conclusion from premises. Another way to say the same thing is that the premises *imply* the conclusion. Of course, this is a very simplified model compared to what you will develop in your actual papers.

Still, we need to consider some important general points about the processes and structures of *logos*.

❏ *Arguable and Non-Arguable Assertions*

Perhaps the first important point to consider is whether we really have an argument or not. The word "argument" has a variety of meanings in general usage, and we need to be careful that we are using the appropriate one.

For one thing, a single statement of a point of view is not an argument. Consider the following assertion:

> *The globalization movement is simply the latest in a long line of American attempts to impose Western values on the rest of the world.*

This is not, in itself, an argument because it doesn't provide any support. It may well become the *conclusion* of an argument, but it lacks a necessary aspect—*premises*.

In contentious times, people seem disposed to offer what we might call "argument by slogan." If you want examples, check bumper stickers and billboards, or watch television commentators (often as not, these are people who should know better than shouting slogans at each other). Beware arguments by slogan. No matter how cleverly or forcefully stated, a single statement is not an argument, and we may not logically accept the point of view that is being expressed solely on the basis of that single statement.

Exercise

For the next few days be on the lookout for "arguments by slogan"—bumper stickers, billboards, etc. List any that you see in your journal. Since the appeals being made are not arguments, that is, not appeals to *logos*, see if you can identify what the appeals actually are.

Also, a simple disagreement is not necessarily an argument. Consider this exchange:

> *Bob: "Friedman's 'olive tree' metaphor is nonsense."*

> *Larry: "No, actually I think it's right on target."*

Again, this is not an argument because no support is offered for either point of view; that is, there are no *premises*.

Another important point to consider is the need to develop arguments around worthwhile and arguable conclusions. There are probably very few teachers of English composition who have not received papers arguing theses similar to the following:

- *Growing up is hard to do and presents us with many challenges.*
- *William Shakespeare is a great author and wrote many important plays.*

Could we develop premises in support of either of these conclusions? Certainly. Would it be worth our time to write or the reader's time to read the results? Probably not. Neither assertion is a news bulletin, and very few people would actually dispute the points.

Exercise

In your journal, try to revise the theses above into points that would be worth disputing. Hint: One problem is that each one is too general. You might start by trying to narrow them.

❑ *Three Rules of Good Arguments*

Once we actually have an argument with premises and conclusion, we need to take some care to make sure it is a good argument. As we said, Chapter 11 will follow this up in some detail, but here we can present three general principles of all good arguments. You can use these principles to evaluate your own arguments and to increase your *control* over your writing; they will help you to write with greater authority and confidence. *And* you can use them to evaluate both the arguments of others and the evidence encountered during your research and reading that could be useful in developing the subject of your essay.

Perhaps we can best present the principles in the nature of rules.

1. In a good argument, the premises must be *relevant* to the conclusion.

This rule very often comes into play when we are refuting the arguments of others. Consider the following argument:

> *We really shouldn't pay too much attention to Thomas L. Friedman's arguments about globalization. After all, he's a columnist for the New York Times, and that paper is known for wallowing in liberal sentimentalism. Also, he's a graduate of Oxford, and the Brits haven't been major players in foreign affairs since World War I.*

This is clearly an attempt to refute Friedman's position on globalization, but it is a very poor one because the premises are not relevant to the conclusion. Even if it were true that the *New York Times* displays a liberal bias or that Britain is not a "major player" in foreign affairs (both arguable assertions), the claims are irrelevant to Friedman's thesis. They attack the writer rather than the argument. This passage illustrates one of the more common types of bad arguments, the one in which the premises are not relevant to the conclusion.

Exercise

Get a copy of your local newspaper. Turn to the editorial section and find one argument that is unacceptable because the premises are not relevant to the conclusion. Hint: The "Letters to the

Editor" section might be a good place to start. Copy the argument in your journal and briefly explain why the premises are irrelevant.

2. In a good argument, the premises must be *warranted*.

What we mean by "warranted" is that the premises must be accurate and have some support of their own. One common type of argument that breaks this rule is the one in which the arguer mistakenly attributes a phenomenon to the wrong cause. Consider the following anecdote.

> *I had a friend one time who had incredible luck with houseplants. I mean he could even grow a Boston fern. Of course, I asked his secret. He said, "It's very simple. If one of my plants starts to go bad, I gather all the other plants around the kitchen sink and feed the bad one down the garbage disposal as a warning to the others."*

It seems clear that the attribution of learning-from-example in houseplants is a bit of a logical and factual reach. In other words, the premises of the implied argument are not really warranted.

Other arguments with unwarranted premises are substantially more consequential. For example:

The United States must attack Iraq because Saddam Hussein is stockpiling weapons of mass destruction to be used against us.

It seems the premise, that Iraq was stockpiling weapons of mass destruction, was and is unwarranted. Of course, we always want to keep in mind that things change and our knowledge grows. It is possible to imagine a future discovery that makes the premise warranted after all.

Clearly, this principle relates to the evidence you develop as you read and conduct research to pursue your original line of inquiry. You may want to review the earlier chapters in this text on evaluating and incorporating evidence. This is the challenge: You want to write with confidence; to do that, you must have confidence in the premises of your arguments. Also, consider the effect of the quality of your premises on your readers. If your evidence is sloppy or easily questioned, your authority as a writer suffers.

3. In a good argument, the relationship between premises and conclusion must not be based on vague or ambiguous language.

Language is marvelous in its flexibility, and part of that flexibility is that words often have more than one meaning or more than one *shade* of meaning. There is, of course, a price for that flexibility; we have a responsibility to try to understand the intended meaning or shade of meaning of the words used in the arguments of others and to use words appropriately in our own arguments.

This is often a matter of the linguistic and social context in which we find the language.

For example, when Robert Burns said, "my love is like a red, red rose," he probably did not mean she had long skinny green legs with stickers on them.

Sometimes arguments turn on these multiple meanings. Consider this argument.

A person should do what's right. Therefore, I have a right to do whatever I please.

Notice that the relationship claimed between premises and conclusion depends on the double meaning of the word "right." While these two examples are clearly facetious, some arguments that turn on vagueness or ambiguity are of substantially more consequence.

For example:

Jose Padilla, a United States citizen is alleged to have met with al-Qaeda leaders to plan attacks in the United States. He was arrested on May 8, 2002, and ultimately sent to a military base in South Carolina where the U.S. government is holding him as an "enemy combatant" without charges or access to an attorney, that is, without many of the rights due a U.S. citizen. Had he simply been designated a "criminal" or even "member of a criminal conspiracy," likely he would by now have been arraigned and tried like any other citizen. In any event, his civil rights would not have been ignored. *(Human Rights News Website—http://hrw.or2/english/docs/2002/06/J2/usdom4040.htm.)*

The ambiguity of Padilla's status, as well as the vagueness of the term on which the government's argument depends, has resulted in substantial negative consequences for Padilla.

Pathos

Pathos refers to the disposition of the reader and the many factors that help influence the way the reader will understand and respond to an argument. In a way, Pathos is the most "controversial" of the three terms, because it seems so directly connected to the idea of "persuasion," which itself is complex and controversial and often seems at odds with both ethics and logic. Thus, given the general, mostly negative, sense of the word "persuasion," as manipulating people to do something they initially didn't want to do, we need to be clear what we mean when we say, "Virtually all communication is persuasive, or rhetorical."

It is imperative to remember that when we speak or write our first goal is always to get our audience's attention, to get them to turn away from what they are doing and pay attention to us. When you think about it that way, you realize that nothing else can be accomplished if our audience is not willing to listen—even just hear what we're saying, never mind to actively consider it or agree with us. This, then, is at the heart of what it means to be concerned about Pathos, to be concerned about the knowledge and values and interests of the audience and to try and find ways to get that audience at least to attend to our argument. To obtain the fairest hearing we can does not mean we have to be deceptive or shocking or manipulative. It does mean that we will never get to share our ideas with someone if that person is not listening to us, and we won't get a fair hearing if the way we are communicating makes people defensive and unwilling to consider our point of view.

❏ *Resistance to Change*

Though we might think that we are curious, open-minded, and reasonable, generally we tend to be creatures of habit. We develop ways of thinking and acting with which we feel comfortable, that seem logical and reasonable, and that seem to work for us. We can change our opinions and we often do, but usually we need some "persuading" to do so. Richard Whately, an important rhetorical thinker of the 18th Century, the Age of Enlightenment, called this the "burden of proof." He argued that the burden of proof lay with the speaker or writer who was trying to convince an audience to change a traditional way of thinking or acting, and that the more ingrained the idea or action, the more "proof" the speaker would need to convince the audience to "give up the old" and "embrace the new."

In a way, it is like a default program in a computer. We are "programmed" to respond in a particular way to a particular situation. Unless we alter the program, we will respond that same way over and over and over. Along with our audience, we tend to be like that not because we are mindless robots, but because we have committed time and energy to developing those patterns and do not want to see all that we have committed go to waste. And besides, many times those traditional ways of thinking and acting have served us well.

> *In the biological realm, most mutations (changes) are harmful to the organism, and we do know that while change may be necessary not all changes are for the better.*

Exercise

Think of a situation in which you were asked to consider or act on a proposition or statement that you had trouble accepting. Describe the situation in your journal. List as many reasons as you can why you found the point of view difficult to accept. Then go back through your list and mark those reasons that would require you to make some sort of change in the way you think about the world. It doesn't have to be a big change (though it might be). Then, in a sentence or two, analyze how that change would impact other aspects of your worldview. Are those impacts on other aspects of your worldview important in your rejection of the original proposition? In each case, consider ways you might reconcile the conflicts.

To better understand Pathos, the dynamic relationship between writers and readers, we need to revisit those strategies we explored in Chapter 2: *clarifying, extending, and restructuring*. In that chapter, we presented the strategies as intellectual tools to clarify your thinking on a subject. Now we return to them as strategies to help create an audience receptive to considering your thinking.

1) *Clarifying:* If what we are trying to do is to help an audience understand a little more clearly what they already know, we would not expect much resistance. Think about the way

politicians arrange to give policy speeches to "sympathetic" audiences: a president proposing farm subsidies to a group of farmers, for instance. The basic strategy is first to present currently understood and shared information, along with the already accepted premises that support it, and then present some new, "clarifying" information, stressing how "logically consistent" it is.

Example

It is one thing to hear a corporate CEO lament that over 10 million American jobs will be lost in the future because of the attractiveness and availability of the low cost foreign products globalization offers consumers. It is quite another to read a noted economist's hard-nosed critique, detailing the depth and complexity of the problem.

NYTimes columnist Paul Krugman (Op Ed. May 14, 2007) has, in fact, "crunched the numbers" and reports that economic inequality for less-educated American workers has risen steadily since the mid-1990s. Because we now buy more imports from Mexico "where wages are only about 11 percent of the U.S. level, and China, where wages are only 3 percent of the U.S. level," Krugman remains skeptical of trade policy, and perhaps with good reason.

2) *Extending:* If what we're presenting represents adding knowledge to what an audience already knows but this "new" knowledge is consistent with the "old" knowledge, we would not expect a great deal of resistance. Again, the basic rhetorical strategy is to summarize the most important currently understood and shared information and the accepted premises, and then present the new, "extending" information, stressing how logically consistent it is. Additionally, it may be important to point out how "tested" or accurate this new knowledge is, and perhaps explain why it was not available before.

Example

People who follow current trends in India are bound to be somewhat skeptical about the effect of globalization on that developing country. Many see India as having a budding middle-class due to its democratic government and its role as a major player in textile, electronics, and other manufacturing industries. Yet for those whose knowledge includes the fact that India is still a poverty-stricken third world country, you will not have much resistance as you expand their overall view.

For instance, you might point out that, though India has opened its doors to the global economic sector, certain indigenous corrupt practices, spurred on by globalization, have made rural poverty more severe. According to activist writer Arundhati Roy, 70% of India's population lives in rural areas; these 700 million people depend upon access to natural resources. As multinational corporations enter into agreements with corrupt Indian officials to "privatize" resources like water, the poor now have to buy water or perish (Power Politics, 2001; The Hindu, 2006).

Notice that the new knowledge does not necessarily contradict the original picture; it provides a larger, more complete view. As indicated, as long as we present claims or evidence that are consistent with what our audience already understands, we should not expect serious emotional or intellectual resistance.

3) *Restructuring:* When what we are telling our audience is not only new information but something radically different from what the audience already knows or thinks it knows about a subject, then we can expect strong resistance. The more important that old knowledge is to the audience the more vigorously they will try and defend it. The burden of proof will be very great. The basic rhetorical strategy will be to summarize the previous information and their premises, and then to focus on how the new, "restructuring" information and its premises alters, dislocates or ends what came before.

Example

A good example may be found in the experience of Ralph Gomory, a former senior vice president of IBM. Mr. Gomory played an integral part in expanding IBM's high tech jobs and production initiatives across the globe. However, he is currently rethinking the "pure trade theory" that is largely driving globalization. "If free trade is a win-win proposition, Gomory asked himself, then why did America keep losing?" (William Greider, The Nation, April 30, 2007)

Gomory saw that multinational corporations worked hard to increase the flow of modern technology and products to other countries. At the same time, Gomory observes we are now "competing shovel to shovel. The people in many countries are being equipped with as good a shovel or backhoe as our people have. . . . We're making it person-to-person competition, which it never was before and which we cannot win." Gomory questions whether Americans can compensate for the one-third to one-quarter reduced wages paid to foreign workers by better educating American workers so that "they can produce four times as much in the United States."

Ardent free traders who presume that free trade and competition invariably lift the economic status of everyone may have to consider that the system is not as they have always believed it to be. And if they have even indirectly been involved in the process of globalization, they will also have to consider the possibility that they have done harm to foreign and American workers. For some readers, that would involve a thorny restructuring.

Whenever you argue complicated issues that involve fundamental attitudes and beliefs, you must proceed carefully, fully accounting for your readers' strong resistance to change. Remember that everyone in your audience will hold a distinct view and will probably have acted on that view. So while you might assume you are only clarifying or extending your readers' understanding of an issue, your message may demand a complete restructuring for some readers. If you are not aware of diverse positions when you begin writing, any point you make will likely alienate some and threaten others.

Consider how even the following casual bantering between two friends unearths surprising rhetorical consequences.

> *Andre*: "So, you want to head to Sammy's Grill tonight?"
> *Dan*: "Not again tonight. Don't you ever, uh, study?"
> *Andre*: "All the time. That's why I can really use a break."
> *Dan*: "Right. . . . You're always on break. By the way, how did you do on Herrick's essay exam?
> *Andre*: *"What's that supposed to mean? I did better than you, I'm sure of that!"*

The same emotional undertones that exist in this casual encounter can be found in formal arguments as well. Only there, the audience, the arena, the methods, and the structures are more public. If you engage in a formal argument, you must anticipate other views and other investments of energy and time. If you cannot anticipate these contending voices, either you are stating the obvious (in which case, why ask for the reader's attention?) or ignoring the fact that some readers are likely to hold opposing viewpoints.

Ultimately, the degree of authority that you claim will depend on what you can support logically, taking into account what your audience is likely to believe and how willing they are to accept your position. In most cases, you persuade by being reasonable. You will appear reasonable if you show your readers that you have thought carefully about each perspective on an issue and if you temper your conviction with a modesty that equally balances certainty and reservation.

❏ *Rogerian Rhetoric*

Carl Rogers, one of the developers of humanistic psychology, helps us to better understand Pathos, this psychological or cognitive aspect of communication. After many years of counseling patients, Rogers came to believe that most people, even those deeply disturbed and conflicted, really wanted to be helped—wanted to understand what was making them so unhappy and how they could go about changing the situation. But as long as they felt threatened, as long as they felt they were being blamed or judged, they would become defensive and unwilling to listen or consider new ways of acting. Rogers found that if he could convince his patients that he was less interested in judging them than in trying to find out what the real problems were and identify possible ways of solving those problems, the patients often would let down their defensive guards and actively cooperate in seeking solutions.

The rhetoric that developed from this, *Rogerian Rhetoric*, came to be known as seeking common ground. It is based on the idea that intelligent and sincere people can have fundamental disagreements about complex matters, and that usually much more can be accomplished by trying to understand and accommodate the other position than by ignoring it or dismissing it. The focus is on letting the other person know that she is being listened to and respected, even when being disagreed with or refuted. We try to keep our audience from becoming defensive by not dismissing their ways of knowing, believing, and acting. Instead, we attempt to demonstrate what our positions have in common and what advantages and improvements might be gained by viewing the situation our way. This effort will not guarantee acceptance of our claims, but it can help ensure that our ideas are at least being heard and considered.

Just think how many times we have said during an argument or debate, "Will you just stop for a minute and listen to what I'm saying?" It is important to understand that the other person may have a great deal invested in the point of view that you are putting into question. Perhaps he or she has made a series of decisions based on that point of view—decisions which can be reversed only with great difficulty or embarrassment. Perhaps what you are saying is translated in the other person's mind as something along the lines of "You wasted your time" or "Your money went down the drain." Unless you handle the discussion very carefully, you may be threatening the other person's self-esteem. And, in any case, you may be asking the other person to make up for actions that, according to you, were mistaken and/or harmful.

Exercise

In your journal describe several situations in which you acted on beliefs that you held at the time but which you later came to doubt. Describe your feelings about each situation. Can you remember situations in which you felt a need to make up for results of earlier actions but just could not bring yourself to do it? In a sentence or two, try to describe why.

After this exercise, maybe you can better appreciate why we often meet with such strong resistance at the level of ideas, at considering what we know and understand about some disputed aspect of the world. If we are not aware that there are other valid ways of knowing something, we do not have to spend any time trying to know them or weighing them against what we already know. And we certainly won't have to admit we were wrong and apologize and/or compensate for whatever we did when we thought that other way. If you're never wrong, you never have to say you're sorry.

❑ *The Dynamic Nature of Argument*

As we have seen, a rhetorical situation is by nature dynamic. As the situation unfolds, all the elements—writer, reader, and subject—interact with each other. As writers, we find ourselves in much the same position as a conductor of an orchestra. Though the musicians play different and constantly changing parts, on a wide variety of instruments, all must work well together if the orchestra is to achieve its effects. The conductor makes this happen by constantly interacting with the various parts of the orchestra. We, as writers, like the conductor, must coordinate all the elements of the rhetorical situation, including our understanding of the facts of the situation, our purpose in making the argument, and—the focus of this section—the disposition of the reader.

Note that reader here means the reader as he or she exists in our minds—what we believe the typical member of our expected audience already knows about the topic and how committed to that knowledge we think that reader is likely to be. Our reader will determine how we present our argument, how inclusive or limited we want our claims to be, and how much support we offer for them. Our reader will, to some degree, determine the sources we will cite in support of our argument. And often, though we are in a college class and hoping to receive a good grade, that reader is not simply the individual professor. Particularly in undergraduate subject matter and writing classes, the professor will attempt to respond to the main rhetorical features of our arguments as any well-read, skeptical, intelligent lay reader would. In more advanced classes, the professor will usually also respond to our writing from the perspective of an expert in the discipline.

❑ *What Is at Stake*

You should remember that arguments have real-world dimensions to them. They exist, that is, not only "for argument's sake," but for "people's sake" as well. In the papers and exams you create for your courses, it can seem that you are arguing about "artificial" (academic) matters only to impress your professors and so get a good grade. However, if you think of argument as a way of communicating your understanding of the important aspects of the reality that you share with your audience, then the task of constructing an argument becomes much more meaningful.

The danger, of course, is that responding to the "situational" aspects of argument and not just to the "logical" or "organizational" elements can be abused. Then, it can seem like deliberate and even deceitful manipulation. It is like that stereotype of the politician who loudly voices support for high farm subsidies when speaking to farmers in Iowa but criticizes them when addressing senior citizens living on fixed incomes in New Jersey. The ancient Greeks rightly had a fear of "demagoguery" and superficial manipulation, but they also understood the importance of a speaker or writer being aware of those factors that would contribute to an arguer getting a "fair" hearing from the audience.

Exercise

To some degree, this is an exercise in defining groups based on the characteristics and preferences people exhibit. When we do this, we are stereotyping just as surely as the politician mentioned above. While the politician's behavior is clearly unethical, we can make ethical use of our understanding of people in shaping our arguments. But we must also take care not to pander to people's existing positions on issues just to win their assent. If you will forgive the cliché, we must offer our readers "the whole truth and nothing but the truth" as we understand it. We can, however, respond to audience considerations by taking some care in how we express that truth.

First, make a list of significant characteristics by which you define a particular group on campus. If you will put your mind to it, you could turn out a lengthy list. Then, read through a couple of editions of your local newspaper and make a short list (2 or 3) of the current issues or questions it has covered. You may find it more interesting to focus on local issues instead of huge, complex national issues. Hint: The editorial page should be a good source, but do not neglect the rest of the paper.

Now, pick six of the characteristics you associated with your chosen group and predict what effect these characteristics could have on the group's response to the issues. Note any combinations of defining characteristics that might create conflicting responses in any individual member of the group. For example, if an ardent environmentalist works for a company that must built a new factory on a local wildlife preserve to stay in business, that person could be somewhat conflicted about the issue.

You don't really have to do anything else with this exercise right now. Just take note of how the characteristics of individuals in the group might affect their responses to issues.

We will discuss these matters in more detail as we go along, but it is important to keep in mind the dynamic, organic nature of real argument. Each element of the rhetorical triangle depends on the other elements. What might constitute a sophisticated argument for a first-year college class might seem basic and introductory in an upper-division seminar; what might simply be clarification for one kind of audience might be major restructuring for another. Changing our strategies to take a particular audience into account is not being manipulative or deceitful or wishy-washy. If we want to share our understanding of an issue that will have consequences both for us and for our audience, why wouldn't we want to get the fairest, most open kind of hearing we can get?

Exercise

Find an argumentative article or passage that makes you angry because of its inflammatory language or some inherent unfairness in its presentation of an issue. Copy or paste the material into your journal. Then, write a brief analysis of why it makes you angry. Finally, revise the piece to make essentially the same point without using the inflammatory language or inherent unfairness.

Collaborative Exercise

Divide into groups of 4 or 5 and discuss your responses to the previous exercise. Do all the members of your group agree that your anger with the article or passage you have chosen is justified? Do all the members of the group agree that your revision is effective? Would any of them have revised it differently? How?

❑ *An Audience and Its Expectations*

After we finish our schooling and enter careers, we will need to write for various communities. Sometimes they are very different from the ones we wrote for in college; sometimes they are not. But each will have its own profile based on the same general features. Boiled down to their essence, these features have to do with:

(a) the kinds of subjects that are appropriate to argue;

(b) the structure and language used in the argument; and

(c) what constitutes valid support and the way it is presented.

In a way, all this is a matter of common experience and common sense. Somewhere along the way, we have all been taught that certain behaviors are appropriate in certain situations. You do not wear the same clothes to bed that you wear to a wedding; you don't speak the same way to your friends as you do to your grandparents, and so on. Each audience and each occasion has its own informal and formal "rules" or conventions. The same is true for most writing occasions. Each particular audience has certain expectations about what issues it is being asked to consider, how that issue will be presented, and what kind of evidence it will accept as valid.

Exercise

Go back to the Friedman selections in Chapter 6. Find a single statement or proposition regarding some aspect of globalization that you think is arguable. Copy it in your journal.

Then, make a list of as many diverse groups as you can, each of which is bound by its own defining factors, and pick two of them. In a brief paragraph, describe the kinds of decisions you would have to make as a writer in order to argue the proposition you copied from Friedman for the two groups you picked. Are there any differences in how these groups are likely to respond to the issue that would require different language or a different approach to your argument? Explain them. If your two groups do not require a difference in approach, find a group that would require one and explain what decisions you would have to make to write an effective argument for it.

❏ *Documentation Style*

Too often, this issue is presented simply as a matter of arbitrary rules—i.e. this is the way we document our sources in the Modern Language Association style (MLA), or the American Psychological Association style (APA). Sometimes, the individual elements seem to be trivial or a matter of preference, but they standardize how we engage an audience within a particular discipline. And the reason we standardize is so that our readers focus more readily on what is being argued. In other words, by following the conventions that the audience has accepted, you minimize the number of distractions that your reader might confront.

A Review of the Basic Tools of Argument

One of the most fundamental concepts presented in this text is that to argue well we must first inquire into the subject as thoroughly and openly as the situation allows. Then, based on what that exploration yields, we can honestly and confidently offer that information to our readers for their consideration and/or approval. In this way, we begin as relative *outsiders* to the subject. Through the course of our inquiry, as we learn and consider more and more information, we become relative *insiders*. We use the term "relative" because even though we now know more than we did when we began, we realize there is always much more to know. Our task is to offer this information to our readers, who, we believe, remain as we once were: relative outsiders. In that sense, then, they as a group represent us as we were before we began our inquiry, and we must always keep that in mind when deciding how we will construct our argument.

Three Choices

In communicating to our audience what we have discovered, we will have to make three important choices—each having to do with one leg of the rhetorical triangle (Figure 7.1).

The first choice concerns our relationship with the subject matter of our argument. What is it that we know confidently, in an inside way, about the subject or issue at hand? That is, what information do we now possess that is more than mere opinion and that takes us past what is easily available to the ordinary reader (the outsider, in our terminology)? Is that information primarily about the nature of the subject? Is it about its causes? Given the time and space available to us, what do we most want to reveal about the subject or issue we have spent our time and energy exploring?

The second choice has to do mainly with our actual audience, the specific or typical reader for whom we are writing—whether that is a particular classroom instructor, our classmates, or, as in many writing course assignments, "a generally skeptical college-educated reader." We need to determine what overall understanding of the subject our reader is likely to have, and what kind of response we wish from our reader. Do we want the reader simply to consider what we have written, or do we want the reader to commit to that knowledge—to accept it and perhaps act on it? Is the information we are presenting likely to be easily accepted because it conforms closely to what the reader already knows, or is it likely to run counter to what the reader knows and therefore be more difficult for the reader to accept?

The way we decide these first two matters will greatly influence the way we make our third choice: how to structure our argument in order to get the fairest and most attentive reading we can—given all the uncertainties and complexities that most knowledge involves. This is where the Rhetorical Model represented by Figure 7.2 below comes into play. As we discussed in Chapter 2, where we used these concepts to guide our own inquiry, we believe the Model represents the basic way people in Western culture rationally act upon information that affects their lives. Here, we will use the concepts to guide us in presenting to our reader the information we have gathered and analyzed.

Shaping the Argument

Having already determined the nature of the information we are communicating, the likely mindset of our reader, and what we, as arguers, wish from our reader, we now need to focus on the various claims we will make and the form and structure of our argument in support of them.

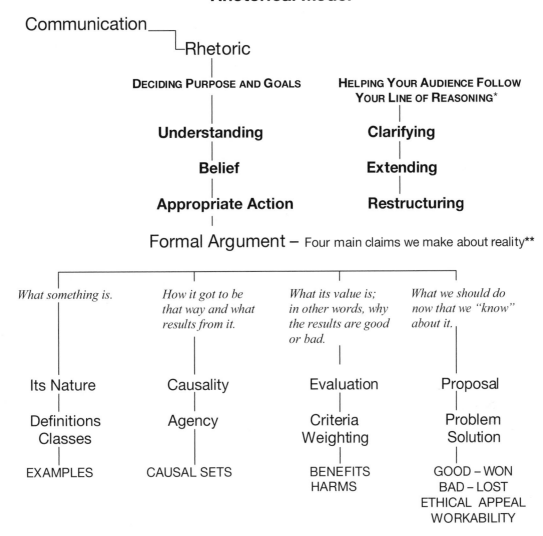

Figure 7.2
Basic Elements of Argumentative Rhetoric

*We are indebted to Young, Becker, and Pike (*Rhetoric: Discovery and Change,* 1970) whose work contributed to our treatment of these rhetorical aspects of argument.

**We wish to acknowledge Jeanne Fahnestock and Marie Secor (*A Rhetoric of Argument,* 2nd Ed., 1990) who proposed this taxonomy.

Essentially, at this stage, that means attending to the logical support each claim requires, while being aware of how receptive or resistant our audience is likely to be to our claims and the support we provide. If we are only helping to clarify what our audience already accepts, then we only have to supply a few additional examples that are verified by appropriate authority. If we are radically trying to reconstruct our audience's understanding of a significant issue, we will have to do much more than that. We will have to precisely define our subject and give a number of cogent examples that are validated by reliable and authoritative experts. Additionally, we could make explicit that we are aware of what our readers currently understand about the subject and that we have measured their commitment to that knowledge. We might note that, while we respect their knowledge, we also believe that the information we are presenting is more accurate and that we will explain why that is so.

As we have indicated throughout the text, this attempt to get a fair hearing is not at all duplicitous. It is practical, ethical, and logical. If we are presenting information that mostly clarifies or modestly adds to what our audience already knows, then we need to quickly review the knowledge we hold in common and offer our readers the new knowledge, stressing how it is consistent with what is known and how it further validates and extends that knowledge. If we suspect that our information runs counter to what is already known, we will need to go over what that common knowledge is, how it was derived, why we believe it is no longer accurate, what we think the more accurate knowledge is, how that knowledge was derived and validated, and, perhaps, how we can now integrate and make use of that new knowledge. And because we know that complicated issues are seldom black and white, either-or sorts of things, we need to acknowledge that—first to ourselves and then to our readers. Do we say "All" or "Most" or "Many"? Do we say, "The evidence is now overwhelming that . . ." or do we say, "Even though many informed people accept . . . we hold the contrary view"?

A key component in all this is working within the constraints that exist in any writing assignment. If we are limited by time and space, we need to take those limits into account. If we are given a task that restricts us to 3–5 or 6–10 pages, then we'll need to decide how much of that space to devote to background and how much to the new or "inside" information; we'll also need to determine how much of that limited space should be devoted to "opposition" views, and so on. All of these are important decisions. They depend on the particular subject, our understanding of that subject, and the understanding of the audience we are seeking to reach.

Though all this takes time and planning, it is vitally important. It is as if we have been given one chance to address an auditorium full of people willing to hear us, but only if we stick to the topic advertised on the marquee, speak loudly and clearly enough to be heard, do not go too fast or too slow, and try as best we can to keep our audience attentive and open-minded. This is the rhetorical triangle in real, dynamic human action—making particular choices because this audience, in relation to this topic, needs to be addressed in this manner. The more important the issue, the more care we need to take to ensure that we get a fair and open hearing, whether on paper or in person!

8

Audience, Purpose and Authority

When you write you lose the advantage that a speaker has, direct contact with an audience that gives you an immediate response to your message. Still, you should try to anticipate what your readers already know and what they are willing to consider. Whether we speak or write, we usually want people to agree with us because their agreement reinforces our perceptions of ourselves as smart, well informed, and generally okay. But if you make any significant assertions in your writing, as you should, you can be sure that someone, somewhere, will disagree with you. Try to anticipate those times when your audience may be skeptical and disbelieving.

If you have a strong opinion about your position, arguing with forceful conviction might work well for the believers in your audience. But what about the skeptics? Can you give them a sense that they would not be diminished by considering your position, not be deprived of their fundamental beliefs? What values or attitudes are you asking your readers to relinquish in order to accept your point of view? Will this acceptance call for a major restructuring of their beliefs? If so, will you offer them any incentives or just try to coerce them into taking your side? Remember that you can believe strongly in your position but still be sensitive to the way you state your beliefs.

Establishing a Mindset for Your Thinking and Writing

To help provoke your interest or curiosity about the upcoming assignments, consider the following claim of President John F. Kennedy: *If a free society cannot help the many who are poor, it cannot save the few who are rich.* Drawing on relevant readings from earlier chapters or on other works you may have read, identify reasons for agreeing or disagreeing with his claim. This initial inquiry is meant to spark lively discussion about the chapter's central theme: coming to terms with the dominant forces shaping our interdependent global economy.

As you turn now to the chapter readings, keep in mind the following thoughts:

- In the wake of 9/11 and the war against terror, there has been talk of a "clash of civilizations" between the Muslim and Western worlds. As you tackle the issues addressed in the readings, consider how the debate over globalization is involved in this struggle.

- A word from Benjamin R. Barber (an excerpt from a speech he delivered appears later in the book pp. 414–418) might spark some reflection. Professor Barber states that when the global market economy creates injustices that go unchecked, the climate this triggers can be used to recruit a new generation of terrorists.

Using the Readings

Confronting Global Challenges

This chapter's readings present reflections on the effects of globalization. As you read, mull over the moral issues surrounding the conflict between self-interest and the interests of others. Also consider how moral reasoning can apply to countries as well as to individuals. The questions that follow each reading suggest how you can connect what you have read to your own experience.

The Global Economy: Positive and Negative Developments
Thomas Friedman

Thomas Friedman (b. 1953) is a journalist, a contributing editor to *The New York Times,* and a three-time Pulitzer Prize winner. A graduate of Brandeis University and Oxford University, Friedman writes about foreign affairs, often focusing on the Middle East, where he served as bureau chief first in Beirut and then in Israel. His book, *The Lexus and the Olive Tree,* won the 2000 Overseas Press Club award for the best nonfiction book on foreign policy. Friedman has become one of the most important advocates of globalization, a stance that also has brought him much criticism. In this excerpt from *The Lexus and the Olive Tree,* Friedman claims that globalization, if properly negotiated, creates a more open market system, thereby creating opportunities for advancement. He warns, however, that there is a tension inherent in the system that places the human need for advancement at odds with the core values of identity and community.

* * * * * * * * *

DEMOLITION MAN

In the Cold War system, not to mention earlier periods in history, countries and cultures simply didn't meet each other quite as frequently, directly and openly as they do today. Travel to many areas was more difficult, and there were countless walls, fences, iron curtains, valleys and trenches for individual cultures to hide behind and preserve themselves in. But today cultures are offered up for global consumption and tested against one another over the Internet and through satellite television and open borders in a brutal Darwinian fashion. I go to villages in northeastern China to see what the world looks like beyond the frontiers of globalization and I find the teenage girls in go-go boots. I walk through Singapore airport and what do I see but two little old Indian ladies, in traditional robes, sitting, transfixed, in the television lounge watching American wrestling on Rupert Murdoch's Sky TV. I couldn't help wondering, as I watched them watching these hulking wrestlers in Tarzan outfits body-slamming each other, what they made of it all. Plug into globalization without the right software and operating system and it will melt down your economy with the blink of an eye. Plug into it without the right environmental surge protectors and it will pave over your forests in a flash. Open your borders to globalization's cultural onslaught, without protective filters, and you could go to sleep at night thinking you're an Indian, an Egyptian, an Israeli, a Chinese or a Brazilian and wake up the next morning to find that all your kids look like Ginger Spice and your boys all want to dress like Hulk Hogan.

A month after I was in Qatar, where I encountered Taco Bell, I went to Kuala Lumpur, Malaysia, where I stayed in the Shangri-La Hotel, one of the grand old hotels of Southeast Asia. I love that name "Shangri-La." It sounds so exotic. I arrived in Kuala Lumpur late at night and couldn't really see much when I drove into town, so the next morning, as soon as I got up, I threw open the curtains of my hotel room and the first thing I saw on the adjacent building was a two-story-high picture of Colonel Sanders from Kentucky Fried Chicken.

"Oh jeez," I said to myself, "what is *that* doing here? I came fifteen thousand miles to Kuala Lumpur to stay in the Shangri-La, and the first person I meet is Colonel Sanders!"

On another occasion I was visiting a businessman in downtown Jakarta and I asked him for directions to my next appointment. His exact instructions to me were: "Go to the building with the Armani Emporium upstairs—you know, just above the Hard Rock Cafe—and then turn right at McDonald's." I just looked at him, laughed and asked: "Where am I?"

India is a country that has actively tried to resist much of this global cultural homogenization. But even there, among India's elites, the Electronic Herd is fast at work. On a stiflingly hot afternoon in New Delhi, during the summer of 1998, I interviewed seventy-eight-year-old former Indian Prime Minister I. K. Gujral, one of India's most enlightened politicians. He began by recalling something that a Canadian representative to a UNESCO conference had said to him after the Indian statesman introduced a resolution meant to ensure that the "new information order" that was taking hold around the globe would be a two-way exchange of culture and information—not just the developed countries pouring their culture down the gullets of the developing nations. The Canadian representative had stunned Gujral by supporting his resolution. "I asked him why Canada would support this," Gujral recalled. "He said, 'Because we are already experiencing what you are fearing. There is no more Canadian music, theater, film, culture or language.' It has all been Americanized."

When I asked him why this issue was so important to him, Gujral, who was dressed in traditional Indian garb, basically said that unless you preserve at least some of your own olive trees in your own backyard, you will never feel at home in your own house. "What are my roots?" he asked aloud. "My roots are not only the fact that I live here in India. My roots are the fact that I hear someone reciting a couplet in my native language. I hear someone singing a song in my native language when I walk down the street. My roots are when I sit in my home with you in my native dress. Our traditions are a thousand years old. You cannot just let them go like that. The world will be much richer if the colorations and diversities are sustained and encouraged with different cultures."

I identify thoroughly with Gujral, maybe because I was born and raised in a relatively small community in Minnesota. Globalization can be deeply disorienting. To have your own cultural olive trees uprooted or homogenized into some global pulp is to lose your bearings in the world.

I was musing about this in Jerusalem one afternoon with my friend Yaron Ezrahi, the political theorist, when he made a trenchant observation. He said: "You know, Tom, there are two ways to make a person feel homeless—one is to destroy his home and the other is to make his home look and feel like everybody else's home."

How do we prevent this sort of homelessness? The first thing to do is to understand that Americanization-globalization is not just about push, it is also about pull. People all over the world want in on globalization, for a lot of reasons. Those Qataris who were packing into Taco Bell on the Doha corniche were not coming from some charming pub or neighborhood bistro full of polished brass and oak. Before Taco Bell was there on the corniche, there was probably a fly-infested sidewalk stand, some guy grilling on charcoals in less than sanitary conditions, no lighting and no bathroom. In its place Qataris were being offered something they had never tasted before, Mexican food, with a clean bathroom, international sanitation standards, smiling service and quality controls—all at a cheap price they could afford. No wonder it was crowded.

And there is something more they were being offered, something less visible but even more valuable to many of them. I first discovered it in Malaysia. I went to see the finance minister, and while I was waiting in his anteroom, his press aide introduced me to a Malaysian businessman also there to see the minister. He introduced him by saying: "This is Mr. Ishak Ismail, he owns all the Kentucky Fried Chicken franchises in Malaysia." I immediately took out my IBM ThinkPad and insisted on interviewing him.

"Tell me something," I asked. "What is the great appeal of Kentucky Fried Chicken to Malaysians?" Not only did they like the taste, he said, but they liked even more what it symbolized: modernity, Americanization, being hip. "Anything Western, especially American, people here love," explained Mr. Ismail. "They want to eat it and be it. I've got people in small [rural] towns around Malaysia queueing up for Kentucky Fried Chicken—they come from all over to get it. They want to be associated with America. People here like anything that is modern. It makes them feel modern when they eat it." Indeed, walking into Kentucky Fried Chicken in the rural areas of Malaysia is the cheapest trip to America many Malaysians will ever be able to take.

The Malaysians go to Kentucky Fried and the Qataris go to Taco Bell for the same reason Americans go to Universal Studios—to see the source of their fantasies. Today, for better or for worse, globalization is a means for spreading the fantasy of America around the world. In today's global village people know there is another way to live, they know about the American lifestyle, and many of them want as big a slice of it as they can get—with all the toppings. Some go to Disney World to get it, and some go to Kentucky Fried in northern Malaysia. Ivy Josiah, a young Malaysian human rights activist, once expressed to me the mixed feelings her generation has about this phenomenon. "I get emotional when I think of how our traditional restaurant stalls are going to be eaten up by Kentucky Chicken, McDonald's and Chili's," she said. "We are losing our own identity. We grew up with those stalls. But younger people did not. You go in those stalls now and they have rats and bad water. For a Malaysian kid today the big treat is going to Pizza Hut. Globalization is Americanization. Elites here say, 'You should not have McDonald's,' but for the little people, who don't get to travel to America, they have America come to them."

For all these reasons it would be naive to think that somehow we can stop the global juggernauts of McDonald's or Taco Bell from opening franchises everywhere around the world. They proliferate because they offer people something they want, and to tell people in developing countries they can't have it because it would spoil the view and experience of people visiting from developed countries would be both insufferably arrogant and futile.

Yet, culturally speaking, something will be lost—for them and for us—the more these global franchises greet us atop every hill, in the terminal of every airport and around every corner. The only hope—and it is only a hope—is that countries will also learn to develop multiple filters to prevent their cultures from being erased by the homogenizing pull and push of global capitalism. Because given the force and speed of globalization today, those cultures that are not robust enough to do so will be wiped out like any species that cannot adapt to changes in its environment.

I believe the most important filter is the ability to "glocalize." I define healthy glocalization as the ability of a culture, when it encounters other strong cultures, to absorb influences that naturally fit into and can enrich that culture, to resist those things that are truly alien and to compartmentalize those things that, while different, can nevertheless be enjoyed and celebrated as different. The whole purpose of glocalizing is to be able to assimilate aspects of globalization into your country and culture that adds to your growth and diversity, without overwhelming it. . . .

WINNERS TAKE ALL

I am a season ticket holder to the Washington Wizards NBA basketball team, and the summer of 1996 was a dark moment for all Wizards fans. The Wizards' star forward, Juwan Howard, was a free agent that summer and the cash-rich Miami Heat were trying to lure him away with an offer in the range of $120 million over seven years. The Wizards were initially offering "only" $75 million to $80 million. At the peak of Howard's contract negotiations, I happened to run into political commentator Norman Ornstein of the American Enterprise Institute, also a Wizards fan, and we were bemoaning the seemingly inevitable loss of Howard to Miami.

"You realize," Ornstein said at one point, "it's all NAFTA's [North American Free Trade Agreement's] fault."

We both laughed, knowing there was a lot of truth behind what Ornstein was saying. Put simply, globalization creates much more of an open, unified global market for many goods and services. As a result, when a country plugs into this system, those with the skills or talent to sell their goods and services into this unified global market can really cash in, because they can sell to a marketplace the size of the whole wide world. Juwan Howard's good fortune was that the improvement in his jump shot and rebounding skills coincided with the fall of the Berlin Wall, NAFTA, the European Monetary Union, GATT [General Agreement on Trade and Tarriffs], the collapse of communism and other market-merging forces that enabled the NBA to become a global sport and enabled fans from Moscow to

Mexico to Miami to help pay Howard's salary. The NBA in 1998 sold more than $500 million worth of NBA-licensed basketballs, backboards, T-shirts, uniforms and caps outside the United States, not to mention millions of dollars more in satellite and cable viewing rights.

Indeed, NBA basketball today has begun to rival soccer as the most global sport. How global is it? You know those Matrushka dolls that they sell in Russia—the wooden dolls with one doll inside a larger doll inside a larger doll. Well, when I visited Moscow in 1989 the hottest-selling Matrushka dolls were those of the different Soviet leaders and the last Czars. You could get Lenin inside Stalin inside Khrushchev inside Brezhnev inside Gorbachev. But when I visited Moscow for the Russian presidential election in 1996, I found that the hottest-selling Matrushka doll outside the Kremlin was Dennis Rodman inside Scottie Pippen inside Toni Kukoc inside Luc Longley inside Steve Kerr inside Michael Jordan! You don't like the Chicago Bulls? Hey, no problem. Street vendors in Moscow were selling every NBA team as a set of Matrushka dolls that year.

But while globalization helps to explain Howard's good fortune, it also helps to explain one of the most serious by-products of plugging into the globalization system—the fact that during the 1980s and 1990s, as globalization replaced the Cold War system, income gaps between the haves and have-nots within industrialized countries widened noticeably, after several decades in which that gap had remained relatively stable.

Economists will tell you that there are many reasons for this widening income gap. These include massive demographic shifts from rural to urban areas, rapid technological changes that increasingly reward knowledge workers over the less skilled, the decline of unions, rising immigration into developed countries which drives down certain wages and the shift in manufacturing from high- to low-wage countries, which also holds down salaries.

All these factors have to be taken into account when trying to explain the widening gap between haves and have-nots, but for the purpose [here] . . . , I want to examine the factor that may be the most important, and has certainly been the most visible in my own travels. This is the phenomenon of "winner take all"—which refers to the fact that the winners in any field today can really cash in because they can sell into this massive global marketplace, while those who are just a little less talented, or not skilled at all, are limited to selling in just their local market and therefore tend to make a lot, lot less. *USA Today* noted that the Miami Heat's first offer to Howard of $98 million over seven years would pay the average salary of an elementary school teacher ($30,000 a year) for 3,267 years.

Economists Robert H. Frank and Philip J. Cook pointed out in their classic book, *The Winner-Take-All Society*, that globalization "has played an important role in the expansion of inequality" by creating a winner-take-all market for the globe. They note that with trade barriers and tariffs being reduced or eliminated all over the earth, travel costs being slashed, internal markets being deregulated and information now being freely and cheaply disseminated across borders, a single unified global market is being created in many industries and professions. The traveling salesman who used to be confined to a five-state area can now use faxes, satellite phones and the Internet to create a national or global clientele for himself. The doctor who was limited to one hospital can now give his diagnosis and advise treatment of patients through data transmission networks that stretch the world over. The singer who used to be heard only in his or her country can now use CD technology and worldwide pay-per-view cable systems, not only to reach a global audience, as the Beatles did, but to profit from it in myriad ways. At the same time, Frank and Cook argue, the elimination of formal and informal rules that limited competitive bidding for the best in any particular industry—rules such as the reserve clause in professional sports, which restricted a player's ability to put himself out to the highest bidder, or informal rules in industry which led companies to promote executives from within rather than scour the world for the best and the brightest—have also contributed to an open, global auction market. (Consumers can also benefit from this. If you are sick with some rare disease, you will appreciate being able to consult with the best specialist anywhere in the world through the Internet; and if you are a shareholder of a slumping Fortune 500 company, you will be pleased that it can lure the best free-agent executive from as far away as Australia, and won't feel compelled to promote some dolt from within.)

You put all these factors together and you end up with a situation in which the potential market for any good or service, for any singer or songwriter, for any author or actor, for any doctor or lawyer, for any athlete or academic, now extends from one end of the world to the other. This unprecedented openness and opportunity for mobility enables, encourages and in many ways requires firms, industries and professionals to try to cover this worldwide market—otherwise somebody else will. And when one of these players emerges as the winner—as "*The* Accounting Firm," "*The* Doctor," "*The* Actor" "*The* Lawyer" "*The* Singer," "*The* Salesman" "*The* Basketball Player" "*The* Man" or "*The* Woman" in any particular field, that person can potentially win not only the United States or Europe, not only Japan or China. He or she can reap enormous profits and royalties from everywhere at once. Ford Motor's double-edged advertising slogan says it best. "Ford: Winning the World Over."

"In this global village' write Frank and Cook, "the top players—those who can deliver the best product—can earn enormous profits. Consider Acme Radials, a hypothetical tire company in Akron, Ohio. If Acme were the best in, say, northern Ohio, they were once guaranteed a decent business. But today's sophisticated consumers increasingly purchase their tires from only a handful of the best tire producers worldwide. If [Acme] is one of the best, it wins and its profits will skyrocket; otherwise, its future will likely be bleak."

As Frank and Cook point out, while the winners can do incredibly well in this global market, those with only marginally inferior skills will often do much less well, and those with few or no skills will do very poorly. Therefore, the gap between first place and second place grows larger, and the gap between first place and last place becomes staggering. Of course, in many fields there is rarely one winner, but those near the top get a disproportionate share. The more that different markets get globalized and become winner-take-all markets, the more inequality expands within countries and, for that matter, between countries.

These inequalities are becoming one of the most disturbing social byproducts of this system. . . .

This is one of the central economic dilemmas of the globalization system: the Golden Straitjacket, the Electronic Herd, free markets and free trade produce far greater incomes for a society as a whole. That is a fact. But that income is highly unequally distributed and the whole let-her-rip capitalism that comes with it is enormously socially disruptive. But to stick with a closed, regulated, bureaucratically run economy in today's world will impoverish a society as a whole, and can be even more socially disruptive—without generating any of the resources to ameliorate conditions for those left behind. Look at Fidel Castro's socialist Cuba in the 1990s. There was little in the way of income gaps there, but the society as a whole became so poor that Cuba in the mid- 1990s became the sex tourism capital of the western hemisphere, as thousands of Cuban families had to assign a wife or daughter to take up prostitution to earn hard currency to survive. I met a Canadian diplomat while in Cuba who told me her job was to "get Canadian sex tourists out of jail." Eventually, in the latter part of the 1990s, Castro opened the Cuban economy a bit and allowed a limited amount of free enterprise, and this immediately produced huge income gaps. As my Cuban tour guide told me while I was on a 1999 visit to Havana: "In the old days, I might have two pairs of shoes and you would have three. But today, because I am a guide and I have access to foreign currency, you might have three pairs of shoes, and I might have thirty." In the long run, these income gaps, if they continue to widen, could turn out to be globalization's Achilles' heels. There is something inherently unstable about a world that is being knitted together tighter and tighter by technology, markets and telecommunications, while splitting apart wider and wider socially and economically. . . .

THE BACKLASH

Let there be no doubt, globalization has fostered a flowering of both wealth and technological innovation the likes of which the world has never before seen. But this sort of rapid change, as the [earlier sections] . . . indicate, has challenged traditional business practices, social structures, cultural mores and environments and, as a result, has generated a substantial backlash—with one of its loudest and most visible manifestations coming at the World Trade Organization summit in Seattle in late 1999. This is not surprising. Markets generate both capital and chaos; the more powerful markets become as a result of globalization, the more widespread and diverse their disruptions.

Beyond this general sense of disruption and dislocation, the opponents of globalization resent it because they feel that as their countries have plugged into the globalization system, they have been forced into a Golden Straitjacket that is one-size-fits-all. Some don't like the straitjacket because they feel economically pinched by it. Some worry that they don't have the knowledge, skills or resources to enlarge the straitjacket and ever really get the gold out of it. Some don't like it because they resent the widening income gaps that the straitjacket produces or the way it squeezes jobs from higher-wage countries to lower-wage ones. Some don't like it because it opens them to all sorts of global cultural forces and influences that leave their kids feeling alienated from their own traditional olive trees. Some don't like it because it seems to put a higher priority on laws to promote free trade than it does on laws to protect turtles and dolphins, water and trees. Some don't like it because they feel they have no say in its design. And some don't like it because they feel that getting their countries up to the standards of DOS capital 6.0 is just too hard.

In other words, the backlash against globalization is a broad phenomenon that is fed by many different specific emotions and anxieties. This backlash expresses itself in different forms, through different characters in different countries. This [segment] . . . is about those different emotions, forms and characters, and how they have come together to create a whirlwind that—for the moment—is only buffeting the globalization system but one day might become strong enough to destabilize it if we don't take the serious backlashers seriously. . . .

And don't kid yourself, the backlash is not just an outburst from the most downtrodden. Like all revolutions, globalization involves a shift in power from one group to another. In most countries it involves a power shift from the state and its bureaucrats to the private sector and entrepreneurs. As this happens, all those who derived their status from positions in the bureaucracy, or from their ties to it, or from their place in a highly regulated and protected economic system, can become losers—if they can't make the transition to the Fast World. This includes industrialists and cronies who were anointed with import or export monopolies by their government, business owners who were protected by the government through high import tariffs on the products they made, big labor unions who got used to each year winning fewer work hours with more pay in constantly protected markets, workers in state-owned factories who got paid whether the factory made a profit or not, the unemployed in welfare states who enjoyed relatively generous benefits and health care no matter what, and all those who depended on the largesse of the state to protect them from the global market and free them from its most demanding aspects.

This explains why, in some countries, the strongest backlash against globalization comes not just from the poorest segments of the population and the turtles [people who feel threatened by globalization for fear of being left behind], but rather from the "used-to-bes" in the middle and lower-middle classes, who found a great deal of security in the protected communist, socialist and welfare systems. As they have seen the walls of protection around them coming down, as they have seen the rigged games in which they flourished folded up and the safety nets under them shrink, many have become mighty unhappy. And unlike the turtles, these downwardly mobile groups have the political clout to organize against globalization. The AFL-CIO labor union federation has become probably the most powerful political force against globalization in the United States. Labor unions covertly funded a lot of the advertising on behalf of the demonstrations in Seattle to encourage grass-roots opposition to free trade. . . .

If you want to see this war between the protected and the globalizers at its sharpest today, go to the Arab world. In 1996, Egypt was scheduled to host the Middle East Economic Summit, which was to bring together Western, Asian, Arab and Israeli business executives. The Egyptian bureaucracy fought bitterly against holding the summit. In part, this was politically inspired by those in Egypt who did not feel Israel had done enough vis-à-vis the Palestinians to really merit normalization. But in part it was because the Egyptian bureaucrats, who had dominated the Egyptian economy ever since Nasser nationalized all the big commercial institutions in the 1960s, intuitively understood that this summit could be the first step in their losing power to the private sector, which was already being given the chance to purchase various state-owned enterprises and could eventually get its hands on the state-controlled media. The Islamic opposition newspaper *al-Shaab* denounced the economic summit as "the Conference of Shame." For the first time, though, the Egyptian private sector got itself organized into power lobbies—the American-

Egypt Chamber of Commerce, the President's Council of Egyptian business leaders and the Egypt Businessmen's Association—and tugged President Mubarak the other way, saying that hosting a summit with hundreds of investors from around the world was essential to produce jobs for an Egyptian workforce growing by 400,000 new entrants each year. President Mubarak went back and forth, finally siding with the private sector and agreeing to host the summit, and bluntly declaring in his opening speech: "This year Egypt joined the global economy. It will live by its rules." But the Egyptian bureaucracy, which does not want to cede any power to the private sector, is still fighting that move, and every time there is a downturn in the global economy, such as the Asian collapse in 1998, the Egyptian bureaucrats go to Mubarak and say, "See, we told you so. We need to slow down, put up some new walls, otherwise what happened to Brazil will happen to us." [Environmentalists from Conservation International had put loggers out of business in villages that were not prepared for life without logging.]

For a long time, I thought that this Egyptian reluctance to really plug into the globalization system was rooted simply in the ignorance of bureaucrats, and a total lack of vision from the top. But then I had an eye-opening experience. I did an author's tour of Egypt in early 2000, meeting with students at Cairo University, journalists at Egyptian newspapers and business leaders in Cairo and Alexandria to talk about the Arabic edition of [my work]. . . .

Indeed I was struck, after a week of discussing both the costs and benefits of globalization, how most Egyptians, including many intellectuals, could see only the costs. The more I explained globalization, the more they expressed unease about it. It eventually struck me that I was encountering what anthropologists call "systematic misunderstanding." Systematic misunderstanding arises when your framework and the other person's framework are so fundamentally different that it cannot be corrected by providing more information.

The Egyptians' unease about globalization is rooted partly in a justifiable fear that they still lack the technological base to compete. But it's also rooted in something cultural—and not just the professor at Cairo University asked me: "Does globalization mean we all have to become Americans?" The unease goes deeper, and you won't understand the backlash against globalization in traditional societies unless you understand it. Many Americans can easily identify with modernization, technology and the Internet because one of the most important things these do is increase individual choices. At their best, they empower and emancipate the individual. But for traditional societies, such as Egypt's, the collective, the group, is much more important than the individual, and empowering the individual is equated with dividing the society. So "globalizing" for them not only means being forced to eat more Big Macs, it means changing the relationship of the individual to his state and community in a way that they feel is socially disintegrating.

"Does globalization mean we just leave the poor to fend for themselves?" one educated Egyptian woman asked me. "How do we privatize when we have no safety nets?" asked a professor. When the government here says it is "privatizing" an industry, the instinctive reaction of Egyptians is that something is being "stolen" from the state, said a senior Egyptian official.

After enough such conversations I realized that most Egyptians—understandably—were approaching globalization out of a combination of despair and necessity, not out of any sense of opportunity.

Globalization meant adapting to a threat coming from the outside, not increasing their own freedoms. I also realized that their previous ideologies—Arab nationalism, socialism, fascism or communism—while they may have made no economic sense, had a certain inspirational power. But globalism totally lacks this. When you tell a traditional society it has to streamline, downsize and get with the Internet, it is a challenge that is devoid of any redemptive or inspirational force. And that is why, for all of globalization's obvious power to elevate living standards, it is going to be a tough, tough sell to all those millions who still say a prayer before they ride the elevator.

This tug-of-war is now going on all over the Arab world today, from Morocco to Kuwait. As one senior Arab finance official described this globalization struggle in his country: "Sometimes I feel like I am part of the Freemasons or some secret society, because I am looking at the world so differently from many of the people around me. There is a huge chasm between the language and vocabulary I have and them. It is not that I have failed to convince them. I often can't even communicate with them, they are so far away from this global outlook. So for me, when I am pushing a policy issue related to globalization, the question always becomes how many people can I rally to this new concept and can I create a critical mass to effect a transition? If you can get enough of your people in the right places, you can push the system along. But it's hard. On so many days I feel like I have people coming to me and saying, 'We really need to repaint the room.' And I'm saying, 'No, we really need to rebuild the whole building on a new foundation.' So their whole dialogue with you is about what color paint to use, and all you can see in your head is the whole new architecture that needs to be done and the new foundations that need to be laid. We can worry about the color of paint later! Brazil, Mexico, Argentina, they now have that critical mass of people and officials who can see this world. But most developing countries are not there yet, which is why their transition is still so uncertain". . . .

THE GROUNDSWELL (OR THE BACKLASH AGAINST THE BACKLASH)

In the winter of 1995 I visited Hanoi. Every morning to get my exercise I would walk around the pagodas on Hoan Kiem Lake, in the heart of Hanoi, and every morning I would stop to visit a tiny Vietnamese woman crouched on the sidewalk with her bathroom scale. She was offering to weigh people for a small fee. And every morning I would pay her a dollar and weigh myself. It wasn't that I needed to know how much I weighed. I knew how much I weighed. (And my recollection is that her scale was not particularly accurate.) No, doing business with that lady was my contribution to the globalization of Vietnam. To me, her unspoken motto was: "Whatever you've got, no matter how big or small—sell it, trade it, barter it, leverage it, rent it, but do something with it to turn a profit, improve your standard of living and get into the game."

That lady and her scale embody a fundamental truth about globalization which too often gets lost in talk of elite money managers, hedge funds and high-speed microprocessors. And it is this: globalization emerges from below, from street level, from people's very souls and from their very deepest aspirations. Yes, globalization is the product of the democratizations of finance, technology and information, but what is driving all three of these is the basic human desire for a better life—a life with more freedom to choose how to prosper, what to eat, what to wear, where to live, where to travel, how to work, what to read, what to write and what to learn. It starts with a lady in Hanoi, crouched on the sidewalk, offering up a bathroom scale as her ticket to the Fast World. . . .

No wonder, then, that while the backlash against globalization is alive and well, this backlash is constantly being tempered by the groundswell for more globalization—more people wanting into the system. You don't need to be a political scientist to figure that out. All you have to do is walk down the street in practically any developing country:

You'll meet Chanokphat Phitakwanokoon, a forty-year-old Thai-Chinese woman, who sells cigarettes and Bao Chinese dumplings from her little stand on Wireless Road in the heart of downtown Bangkok. I was staying at a hotel near there in December 1997, the week the government closed most of the country's finance houses, and I asked the *New York Times* interpreter to accompany me on a walk to get some reactions from the street merchants. The first person I chatted with was Chanokphat. I began by asking her "How's business?"

"Off by forty or fifty percent," she said sullenly.

I asked her if she had ever heard of George Soros, the billionaire hedge-fund manager who was then being blamed for speculating on the Asian currencies and triggering their collapse.

"No," she said, shaking her head. She had never heard of Soros.

"Well, let me ask you this. Do you know what a stock market is?" I asked.

"Yes," she answered without hesitation. "I own shares in Bangkok Bank and Asia Bank."

"How in the world did you think of buying bank shares?" I asked.

"My relatives were all buying, so I bought too," she answered. "I put them away in the bank. They are not worth much now."

At that point, I looked down and noticed that she wasn't wearing any shoes. Maybe she had shoes somewhere, but they weren't on her feet. I couldn't help thinking to myself: "She has no shoes, she has a fifth-grade education, but she owns bank stocks on the Thai stock exchange." Some questions then occurred to me: What are her interests? Is she going to lead a march to burn down the IMF [International Monetary Fund] office that is imposing all these conditions on Thailand to reform its economy? Or, because she is now somehow part of the system, would she be prepared to work harder, save more and sacrifice more, even to the IMF, if it would help revive the Thai economy? Something tells me it's the latter. That's the groundswell at work. . . .

You'll meet Liliane, a thirty-two-year-old Brazilian social worker who lived in the Rocinha *favela* in Rio and works for the municipal government. She gave me a tour of a day-care center in the *favela* and along the way explained that she had saved for years to finally be able to move her family out. Now that they were out of the *favela* and into the Fast World, the last thing she wanted was for that world to fold up, even if it was a struggle to get in. She said to me: "When I was young everyone in our neighborhood in the *favela* had to watch TV in one house. I am now moving to a place that is one hour and twenty minutes from my work, instead of twenty minutes, but it is not in the *favela* and it is away from the crime. I am moving there for my children because there are no drug dealers. I make nine hundred reals a month. [Now] I can buy a telephone. Now our house is made of bricks, not wood, and at the end of the month I still have some money left. When we had inflation, no one could buy on credit because you could not afford the inflation interest rates. Today even the poor people here have a phone, they have cable television and they have electricity. I have all the basic things that rich people have. Now we can complain about the service [from the electricity or the phone company]. Before, we didn't have them, so we couldn't complain about them." That's the groundswell at work.

You'll meet Fatima Al-Abdali, a Kuwaiti environmental health scientist, who owns the most popular Internet cafe in Kuwait City, Coffee Valley, where you can sip latte and surf the Net. Educated in America, Al-Abdali wears a veil, as a sign of Islamic piety, but is a total Web-head underneath. I gave a lecture on globalization in Kuwait, and she was one of the people in the audience. Afterward, she invited me to visit her cafe and meet some students there. The cafe was located in an urban shopping mall. As I sat down at a corner table, I said to her: "Look, I'm a little confused. Do the math for me. You are wearing an Islamic head covering, you are obviously a religious person, but you were educated in an American university and now you are bringing the Internet to Kuwait. I don't quite see how it all adds up."

Her answer, in essence, was that so many times in the past the Arab Islamic world had been invaded by outsiders, with their often alien influences and technologies. Well, she said, they were being invaded again. But this time she was going to own that invasion, not let the invasion own her. She was going to put a veil around that Internet and make sure the youths who frequented her cafe used it properly. I admired the effort. Don't lash out against it—own it yourself.

"I had this idea three years ago for an Internet cafe," she told me in 1997. "I knew it was coming and that if I didn't open one, someone else would. I realized we can have some control over it, so let's teach people the good parts and make it consistent with our own culture, rather than wait to be invaded by it. I adopted it, and adapted it, and on our Web page now we are slowly introducing some [Islamic] women's rights issues."

Al-Abdali invited some students from Kuwait University to join us. One of them mentioned in passing that they had just held student elections at the university and the Islamic fundamentalist candidates got wiped out by the independent, liberal and secular parties. Student elections are very important in the Arab world, because they tend to be the most free and therefore often the most indicative of public attitudes, at least among young people. I asked Abdul Aziz al-Sabli, a twenty-one-year-old communications student, why the Islamists were so roundly defeated. "The Islamists are not that impressive anymore," he said. "The secular parties are helping the students more with the small things that students care about now—Xeroxing, E-mail problems, library books, parking. The society is less ideological now. We need to look for a job." That's the groundswell at work. . . .

If the intellectual critics of globalization would spend more time thinking about how to use the system, and less time thinking about how to tear it down, they might realize what a lot of these little folks have already realized—that globalization can create as many solutions and opportunities as it can problems. But can it create the biggest solution of all? Is there anything about globalization, and the rise of the Internet and other modern technologies, that can make a difference for those at the bottom of the barrel—the 1.3 billion people still living on one dollar a day? . . .

I already tried to explain [in parts of *The Lexus* not included in this excerpt] . . . how globalization can promote better, more accountable government and give individuals, activist groups and companies much greater power to become shapers of the new world without walls. What's noteworthy is how much the poor are beginning to understand this and exploit it. As harsh as the globalization system can be, it also gives those brutalized by it a greater ability to tell people about their pain or get organized to do something about it, and this helps explain and sustain the groundswell.

Thanks to the Internet, for instance, it is no longer just the few big media conglomerates who talk to the many. It is now the many who can talk to the many. I learned this from Chandra Muzaffar, president of a Malaysian human rights organization called International Movement for a Just World. I went to see this gentle Malaysian Muslim at his barren office in a suburb of Kuala Lumpur. I went for the express purpose of hearing him blast globalization in the name of the left-outs and leftbehinds, for whom his organization is such a strong advocate. But I got a subtler, more interesting message from him.

"I think that globalization is not just a rerun of colonialism," said Muzaffar. "People who argue that have got it wrong. It is more complex than that. Look around. As a result of globalization, there are elements of culture from the dominated peoples that are now penetrating the north. The favorite food of Brits eating out is not fish and chips today, but curry. It is no longer even exotic for them. But I am not just talking about curry. Even at the level of ideas there is a certain degree of interest in different religions now. So while you have this dominant force [Americanization], you also have a subordinate flow the other way. . . . There are opportunities now for others to state their case through the Internet. Iran is highly linked to the Internet. They see it as a tool they can use to get their point of view across. In Malaysia, Mahathir now gets some coverage [all over the world] through CNN. The campaign for banning land mines was launched through the Internet. This is what globalization does for marginalized groups. To argue that it is just a one-way street is not right and we should recognize its complexity. People operate at different levels. At one level they can be angry about injustices being done to their society from Americanization and then talk about it over McDonald's with their kids who are studying in the States?' That's the groundswell meeting the backlash. . . .

THE WAY FORWARD

If there is a common denominator that runs through this [essay] . . . it is the notion that *globalization is everything and its opposite*. It can be incredibly empowering and incredibly coercive. It can democratize opportunity and democratize panic. It makes the whales bigger and the minnows stronger. It leaves you behind faster and faster, and it catches up to you faster and faster. While it is homogenizing cultures, it is also enabling people to share their unique individuality farther and wider. It makes us want to chase after the Lexus more intensely than ever and cling to our olive trees more tightly than ever. It enables us to reach into the world as never before and it enables the world to reach into each of us as never before.

As I have tried to demonstrate, since the onset of globalization as an international system, different countries and communities have seesawed between being attracted to its benefits and repelled by its negatives. Up to now, in the ebb and flow between globalization and the backlash against it, globalization has consistently come out on top in every major country that has plugged into the system. In no major country has the backlash against globalization managed to take power and in no major country has the backlash against globalization become so popular that this country would be willing to undermine the whole system—the way the Austro-Hungarian Empire did before World War I or Germany and Japan did before World War II.

Will it always be thus? Is globalization irreversible? My sense is that it is "almost" irreversible. Why do I say "almost" irreversible and not just plain old irreversible? Globalization is very difficult to reverse because it is driven both by enormously powerful human aspirations for higher standard of living and by enormously powerful technologies which are integrating us more and more every day, whether we like it or not. Theoretically, these aspirations and these technologies can be choked off, but only at a huge price to a society's development and only by building ever higher and ever thicker walls. I don't think that is likely to happen around the world, but it's possible. It is possible if the system gets so out of whack that not only disadvantaged minorities feel abused by it but also big majorities, in big countries. . . .

In July 1998, *The New Yorker* ran a cartoon that showed two longhaired, scraggly bearded Hell's Angels types, one wearing a skull and crossbones T-shirt and the other sitting on his motorcycle. Each is obviously asking the other how his day went. One Hell's Angel finally says to the other: "How was my day? Advancing issues led declines."

And so it is with globalization. Globalization is always in the balance, always tipping this way or that. Our job as citizens of the world is to make certain that a majority of people always feel that advancing issues are leading the declines. Only then will globalization be sustainable. And no nation has a greater responsibility and opportunity to ensure this than the United States of America. . . .

Put simply: As the country that benefits most from today's global integration—as the country whose people, products, values, technologies and ideas are being most globalized—it is our job to make sure that globalization is sustainable. And the way we do that is by ensuring that the international system remains stable and that advances lead declines for as many people as possible, in as many countries as possible, on as many days as possible. In the Cold War system the fundamental political question was: Which hardware and operating system do you choose? In the globalization era, the fundamental political question is: How do you make the best of the only hardware and operating system that works—globally integrated free-market capitalism? America can be, and should be, the world's role model in answering this question.

America has had two hundred years to invent, regenerate and calibrate the balances that keep markets free without becoming monsters. We have the tools to make a difference. We have the responsibility to make a difference. And we have a huge interest in making a difference. Managing globalization is a role from which America dare not shrink. It is our overarching national interest today, and the political party that understands that first, the one that comes up with the most coherent, credible and imaginative platform for pursuing it, is the party that will own the real bridge to the future.

Questions for Discussion and Writing

1. What do you think are the most important claims that Friedman makes about globalization, and how does he support these claims?

2. Do you have any personal experience, direct or indirect, concerning globalization that you could use to support, modify or refute any of Friedman's claims? Explain.

3. Friedman writes, "Today, for better or worse, globalization is a means for spreading the fantasy of America around the world." Is this trend likely to result in favorable consequences either for individuals or societies? Explain. Note that *The Lexus* was first published in 1999. When you presently hear the word globalization, do you perceive "Americanization" as a central trend? Why or why not?

4. When Friedman speaks of "glocalization," what does he mean?

5. Are the case studies Friedman cites under "The Groundswell" likely to be about the rule or the exception? Justify your answer.

6. Who is the audience for Friedman's writing? What does he expect his readers to understand, believe, and perhaps do in relation to globalization as a result of reading his article?

7. If you had the chance to ask Friedman some questions about any of the matters contained in his article, what would they be? Explain.

8. Friedman summarizes his own essay this way: "If there is a common denominator that runs through this . . . it is the notion that *globalization is everything and its opposite*." While this may sound dramatic and clever, what do you think it actually means? How in the text is this notion developed and supported? If one of the most fundamental rules of logic states that "a thing cannot both be and not be," how, then, can globalization be "everything and its opposite"?

Making Connections

1. Friedman writes (Chapter 6, p. 178) that "the driving idea behind globalization is free-market capitalism." The assumption is that globalization only can thrive in an unfettered, deregulated free market where all can compete and make themselves economically attractive to foreign markets. The argument that globalization can succeed in increasing everyone's economic and social well-being seems based on this assumption. Do you agree that virtually every nation can benefit by accepting the fundamental principles of the free market"? Why or why not?

2. Are Friedman's metaphors—"the Golden Straightjacket", the Electronic Herd", "The Golden Arches Theory of Conflict Prevention" and "The Lexus and the Olive Tree"—useful in discussing and clarifying the complicated subject of globalization? If so, why? If not, why not?

3. In Chapter 4, Gregory Mantsios argues that what keeps most people economically, socially, and politically oppressed are institutional forces that they cannot influence; specifically, he argues that their futures are controlled by class domination. Taking his argument that being poor or working class is not a matter of choice but a question of limited opportunities, how can globalization provide the necessary elements to allow ordinary people to control their own lives rather than having someone else control their future?

Visual Exercise

In news stories accompanied by photos, usually photo editors, not the reporters, choose the images. Consider how effectively the following image arrests our attention, catches our eye.

A McDonald's restaurant worker in traditional Muslim dress takes an order in Jakarta Monday, Feb. 2, 1998. With the country's franchises facing increasingly harder economic times and a weak rupiah, Western eateries such as McDonald's are already cutting costs, striking French fries from meal combination offers because the potatoes are imported and must be bought with dollars. Firdia Lisnawati/AP Images

Questions

1. Because photographs are often first "received" in a "big picture," in an impressionistic way, what is your first, quick response to the McDonald's photo? What made you respond that way?

2. Looking more closely at just the photograph, is it clear what situation or behaviors are being portrayed? If so, what are the behaviors and the situation? If not, why are they obscure?

3. What is the relationship between the text and the photograph? Referring to the Appendix on Visual Communication, answer the following:
    a) Who is responsible for the visual?

b) Is the visual essential to understanding the text? Useful? Merely decorative? Does it support or contradict the information presented in the text?

c) Are there multiple ways of understanding the photo and its connection to the text?

d) What are the informational claims the text and visual together make?

e) Does the photo clarify, extend, or restructure your understanding of McDonald's role in globalization?

Global Citizenship: Promises and Problems
Nel Noddings

An expert in childhood education, Nel Noddings (b. 1929) has written on moral education and global citizenship. Her experiences as a classroom teacher, a school administrator, and a curriculum specialist have contributed to her research and publication in educational philosophy and theory. President of the National Academy of Education, Nel Noddings was also the Lee J. Jacks Professor of Childhood Education at Stanford University. She has written over 200 articles, and 13 books including *Educating Moral People (2002)* and *Happiness and Education* (2003). In her introduction to *Educating Citizens for Global Awareness* (2005), from which the following passage was excerpted, Nodding argues for a comprehensive curriculum to educate students for global citizenship.

✱ ✱ ✱ ✱ ✱ ✱ ✱ ✱ ✱

My country is the world; to do good is my religion.

—Thomas Paine

ON A RECENT DAY, I SENT e-mail messages to people in Japan, Argentina, the Netherlands, and England. Before I finished reading my own messages, I had an automatic response from the recipient in England, telling me that he was in Ethiopia and would respond to the substance of my message later. In a world of instant communication and swift travel, we have become keenly aware of our interdependence. Many of us are now concerned about the welfare of all human and nonhuman life, preservation of the Earth as home to that life, and the growing conflict between the appreciation of diversity and the longing for unity. We are concerned, too, that our technological capacity has run far beyond our moral competence to manage it. We dream of peace in a world perpetually on the edge of war. One response to these concerns is the promotion of global citizenship.

But what do we mean by *global citizenship?* This is not an easy question to answer, and the issues that arise as we try to answer it are difficult. However, even if we cannot answer the question entirely

---

Source: Nel Noddings "Global Citizenship: Promises and Problems." Reprinted by permission of the Publisher. From Nel Noddings, *Educating Citizens for Global Awareness*, New York: Teachers College Press, © 2005 by Teachers College, Columbia University. All rights reserved.

to our satisfaction, these issues belong in discussions of schooling practices and curriculum. In what follows, I . . . explore the basic question: What is *global citizenship?* . . . Is global citizenship primarily a matter of economics? How can we protect the Earth as our home and that of future generations? What sort of diversity should we try to preserve, and can we encourage unity while we maintain diversity? What role should peace education play in promoting global citizenship?

WHAT IS GLOBAL CITIZENSHIP?

The words *citizenship* and *citizen* usually refer to a national or regional identity. One who is recognized as a citizen of a particular nation has the special rights and duties prescribed by the government of that nation. Global citizenship cannot yet be described in this way. There is no global government to which we as individuals owe allegiance, and there are no international laws that bind us unless our national government accepts them. Thus, we can't look to the familiar, technical definition of citizenship to help us in describing global citizenship.

Sometimes *citizen* is used synonymously with *inhabitant,* as in "the deer is a citizen of the forest." Although this statement is charming, most of us think that citizenship involves more than a reference to where we live and even more than the technical description of our national (or regional) rights and responsibilities. Educators have been trying for years to describe citizenship more fully and to figure out ways to promote it. For example, some social studies educators believe that the study of American history promotes American citizenship (Thornton 2001). Does it? To answer this question, we have to say much more about what is meant by citizenship. [University professor] . . . Gloria Ladson-Billings points out that even within a nation, some of those who qualify formally for citizenship do not feel as though they share fully in that citizenship.

Perhaps we can agree that a citizen of Place X has (or should have) an interest in, or concern about, the welfare of X and its people. Such a citizen cares about and wants to protect its interests and way of life. This is a description with which Americans are familiar, and it is used often to arouse national pride and commitment. It would take us too far afield to explore all the ways in which people have described "American interests" and the "American way of life." But we know that attempts at such description exhibit complexity and conflict. It is not an easy job to say exactly what is meant by "the" American way of life. We fall easily into slogans and clichés.

Consider, then, how much harder it will be to define global citizenship. Is there, for example, a global way of life? Some think that there could be—even that there should be—a global way of life, and it usually looks suspiciously like their own way. Advocates of globalization—"the removal of barriers to free trade and the closer integration of national economies" (Stiglitz 2002, ix)—come close to defining global citizenship solely in terms of economics. A global citizen, from this perspective, is one who can live and work effectively anywhere in the world, and a global way of life would both describe and support the functioning of global citizens.

Many careful thinkers are critical of this approach, and international meetings of world financial organizations have been marked by riotous protests. What sparks the protests? What are the objections to globalization? First, there is evidence that present efforts at globalization have aggravated existing economic injustice. Good global citizens should be concerned about this, just as good national citizens are concerned about injustice within their own boundaries. This observation prompts us to think more about the idea of *interest.* It may be better for present purposes to use *concern* instead of *interest. Interest* too often conveys the notion of self-interest or concentration on the benefits to one's own group. Indeed, when citizens of one nation speak of their *interests,* people of other nations are understandably wary. When our interests are truly global, this worry should be relieved. But for now, to avoid this problem, let's speak of *concern.* When we are concerned with the welfare of X—our nation, region, or globe—we are concerned with the well-being of all its inhabitants.

Second, globalization's emphasis on economic growth has led to practices that threaten the physical environment—the life of the Earth itself. The problems in this area are so complex that even scientists are unsure about the harms and benefits resulting from certain practices. It seems clear that global warming is a reality and that the reduction of carbon emissions is imperative. However, other practices—the genetic engineering of plants, for example—need much more study. Closely related to problems concerning the global environment are those that affect people in particular locations. What may be good for people in a large region (say, a huge dam designed to provide electricity) may be a disaster for those in the particular locality. Some global citizens may be willing to live anywhere, but others want to live in a particular place that they love. Is love of place compatible with global citizenship? At the very least, we've added another factor to the concerns of global citizens—the well-being of particular physical places.

Third, critics object to construing global interest entirely in economic terms. Even if it were possible and just to establish one world economic order, other aspects of life must be considered. If global citizens appreciate cultural diversity, they will speak of *ways* of life, not one way, and they will ask how a valued diversity can be maintained. But what sorts of diversity should we appreciate? If a culture wants to maintain the inequality of women or the slavery of children, should we accept these practices as tolerable facets of cultural diversity—as simply "their way"? When cultural diversity pushes us toward moral relativism, we must back away. And so we have to think carefully about the merits of diversity and those of unity or universality and how to achieve an optimal balance between the two. We should be interested in social as well as economic justice.

Fourth, because globalization points to a global economy, we have to ask whose economic vision will be adopted. As noted earlier, the powerful nations are likely to impose their own vision. At the present time, the most powerful view is that of the huge international corporations. Even if it could be argued that their vision is benign and requires only tinkering to be just, many of the world's people harbor doubts, and while the disparity between rich and poor grows, it is predictable that groups (even nations) will protest violently. Moreover, nations of the First World often associate corporate capitalism with their own overall way of life, and this association adds a strong ideological component to the problem. Citizens of wealthy nations may feel it a patriotic duty to defend economic practices that seem inseparable from their way of life. These citizens then try to persuade or even force others to accept that way of life "for their own good."

We must ask, also, whether global citizenship—defined in part as the activation of the concerns so far identified—is compatible with national citizenship. Should we put the concerns of globe or nation first, or is this a bad question? Should our choice depend on the particular concern under consideration? Is there an inherent conflict between patriotism and global citizenship? Can patriotism be redefined in a way that removes the conflict?

It would seem that peace is a precondition of global citizenship. I cannot be a global citizen if my country is at war with others, any more than a loyal citizen of Virginia could be a U.S. citizen during the Civil War. One could argue, of course, that a progressive orientation toward global citizenship will promote world peace. This is a chicken-and-egg argument. However we arrange the priorities, peace education must play a vital role in the promotion of global citizenship. A global citizen must see war as contrary to all of the concerns we have identified—to worldwide economic and social justice, to the health of our physical world, to the preservation of well-loved places, to the balance of diversity and unity, and to the well-being of all of earth's inhabitants. Yet if war comes, the vast majority of us will stand—sadly, perhaps even angrily—with our own nation. Even our enemies, educated as badly as we are, would think less of us if we did not. This underscores our earlier claim that war cannot be reconciled with global concerns, and so peace education must play a vital role in supporting global citizenship.

References

Stigliz, J.E. (2002). *Globalization and its discontents*. New York: W.W. Norton.

Thorton, S.J. (2001). Legitimacy in the social studies curriculum. In *A Century of study in education: The centennial volume*, ed. L. Corno. Chicago: National Society for the Study of Education.

Questions for Discussion and Writing

1. How does Noddings go about supporting her argument that global citizenship must be defined and carefully considered? Do you find her argument convincing? Why or why not?

2. Noddings argues that when we become "keenly aware of our interdependence," this realization naturally would lead to a concern for establishing global citizenship. Do you agree? If so, why? If not, why not?

3. "War," Noddings claims, "cannot be reconciled with global concerns," an assertion that has led her to call for a curriculum of "peace education." What do you think such a curriculum would contain?

4. Noddings raises a troublesome question: "whether global citizenship . . . is compatible with national citizenship." Are the two closely related? Explain. Can you imagine circumstances in which national allegiance could be at odds with global needs and desires? If so, what might be the outcome?

Making Connections

1. Find a document called the Earth Charter at **<http://www.earthcharter.org/>**. The Charter expresses hope for ethical and achievable "best practices for building sustainable communities." How might the Charter help to advance Noddings's call to educate students for global citizenry? Be specific.

2. Noddings believes that our economic policies reflect the values of our culture. Can you give specific examples from her essay and from other readings in the book that show the direct relationship between American economic policies and the values the nation privileges? What are the values that lie behind our current economic policies with regard to fossil fuel consumption, for example? Are there any conflicting values involved? If so, how would you reconcile the conflict?

Globalization Since the Cold War
(Abridged)
Matthew Burkhardt (Student)

College students, even in specialized classes, are often put in the difficult position of having to explain complicated and controversial issues with only a short period of time for research and reflection. One effective way of dealing with this situation is to isolate a manageable aspect of the subject—particularly if you have some direct experience with it. College student Matthew Burkhardt tried to figure out how the global economy operated by connecting it to his experience of traveling abroad and his love of coffee. If he could understand the process that led to his encountering a Starbucks coffee shop almost everywhere he traveled, and how the coffee that steamed from his cup came to be the second most traded commodity (after oil) in the world, he hoped his understanding would be deeper and more shareable. Given the complex and controversial nature of a topic like Globalization, perhaps the best Matthew (and most undergraduate students) can hope for is to clarify and extend the reader's understanding and, eventually, to offer some appropriate ways to act in response to that understanding. Using coffee as an iterative or representative example, Matthew wrote the following essay.

* * * * * * * * *

1. Matt has decided to label each section of the essay as he "moves" through the four types of claims.

2. Matt begins the essay with a personal experience, a brief but significant anecdote that helps establish

1

2

I. The Nature of Globalization

Six weeks shy of my fifteenth birthday, my life was changed forever. That summer, I secured a job as part of the nature lodge staff at Baiting Hollow Scout Camp in Calverton, New York. Each and every day of my camp staff experience began the same way: I got out of bed, dressed and trekked, zombie-like, from my cabin atop one of the big hills in camp to his interest in and experience with an otherwise formal and abstract subject—globalization.

the dining hall on the other. Not even yet half-awake, I pulled the door open and, once inside, made as clear a beeline as a zombie might towards the coffee, knowing that no matter what the day's agenda, it was impossible without at least one cup. My camp staff experience not only introduced me to a commodity that would restructure my existence, but also it created an added sense of community among my fellow staff members. We even characterized entire weeks by the quality of the coffee. There were "good" weeks, when a staff member's father brought gourmet coffee, and there were "bad" weeks, when we were stuck with whatever the food service provided. . . .

Throughout most of my high school career, not a morning went by that I was not standing in line at my local bagel shop at seven in the morning. My camp staff experience initiated me into a broader community. I matured from an indifferent, yet coffee-aware teenager, into an eager, if novice, consumer, joining the ranks of consumers across the planet and throughout time.

3. Here, Matt quotes from an established "authority" to support his point that coffee can serve as a good model for understanding the way globalization works. Thus, he can move from the personal to the more objective, making his experience less individual and more representational or iterative.

3

As I would learn, coffee is a global phenomenon, and has been ever since its discovery. In the very opening of the preface to their 1999 book, *The Coffee Book: An Anatomy of an Industry from Crop to the Last Drop*, Gregory Dicum and Nina Luttinger place coffee into its proper historical and social context:

> Coffee is an ancient commodity that weaves together a mosaic of histories dating back over a millennium and stretching all the way around the world. . . . Much more than the mere chemicals that compose it, coffee is a bit of history itself. And we consume it zealously. The world drinks about 2.25 billion cups per day—the United States alone drinks one fifth of this. (xi)

4. Still using that same "expert" source, Matt underscores the point that the production and consumption of even a single commodity involves many complex forces.

4

A commodity with a long history, coffee can help the twenty-first century consumer to understand many of the socio-economic forces operating in the modern world. Clearly a monopoly item in the Arab-controlled market, its production and processing were a closely guarded secret. Though foreigners were forbidden access to coffee farms, the Europeans soon integrated Arab markets and by the 17th century had infiltrated coffee production and sale. Dicum and Luttinger acknowledge an Indian pilgrim, Baba Budan, who in 1600 smuggled out germinable seeds from Mecca to Mysore. And by 1616, Dutch spies smuggled out coffee plants to be cultivated in Java. "Coffee," Dicum and Luttinger note, "was now in the hands of enough different interests to make its spread around the world inevitable" (8).

5. Matt now begins to move directly into globalization by discussing its fundamental nature: the exchange of goods based on supply and demand, and reminding us again that coffee is not unique but related to many other consumer goods.

5

Here we can see the fundamental principles of supply and demand at work. One group has coffee; another wishes to have it. Thus, imperial expansion is a globalizing force often underlying the discovery and distribution of commodities long before they become industrialized. From the patterns in the example of coffee, it is possible to note similarities with other consumer goods, such as tea, sugar, and oil, as well as to draw conclusions regarding how we might expect future consumer products to develop in a globalized world. . . .

Because all consumers and producers everywhere in the twenty-first century are implicated in it, everyone should gain a concrete understanding of precisely what globalization is. In his book, *The Lexus and the Olive Tree*, Thomas L. Friedman, foreign affairs columnist for *The New York Times*, claims that globalization is the socio-economic-political "system" which immediately followed the Cold War:

6. Quoting Thomas L. Friedman, a leading proponent of globalization, Matt now gives the reader a clear, working definition of globalization as dynamic, integrative, and extensive.

6

When I speak of "the Cold War system" and "the globalization system," what do I mean? To begin with the Cold War system was characterized by one overarching feature—division. The world was a divided-up, chopped-up place and both your threats and opportunities in the Cold War system tended to grow out of who you were divided from. Appropriately, this Cold War was symbolized by a single word: the *wall*—the Berlin Wall. . . . The globalization system is a bit different. It also has one overarching feature—integration. The world has become an increasingly interwoven place, and today, whether you are a company or a country, your threats and opportunities increasingly derive from who you are connected to. (7)

Elaborating further on this distinction, Friedman writes:

The globalization system, unlike the Cold War system, is not static, but a dynamic ongoing process: globalization involves the inexorable integration of markets, nation-states, and technologies to a degree never witnessed before—in a way that is enabling individuals, corporations and nation-states to reach around the world farther, faster, deeper and cheaper than ever before, and in a way that is also producing a powerful backlash from those brutalized or left behind by this new system. The driving idea behind globalization is free market capitalism—the more you let the market forces rule and the more you open your economy to free trade and competition, the more efficient and flourishing your economy will be. (7–8)

7. Signals the movement into causality—why something happens and what results from it.

7 ## II. Causes of Globalization

The *World Trade Organization* (*WTO*) website acknowledges the complexity of relationships posed by globalization.

8. Matt begins by directly quoting what he believes are the two most important causes of modern globalization. These causes can

8

Globalization, like many huge ideas, results from two opposite, but eerily complimentary forces:

1. Early efforts by well-meaning people to build a better tomorrow (on the raw material of historical horror).

be understood as remote/
proximate causes ("early
efforts" "long-term efforts"),
which together become
both necessary and suf-
ficient to keep driving
globalization along.

2. Long-term efforts by single-minded corporations to build better profits (on the raw material of the above).

(*Globalization* ¶ 1)

The Cold War provides a strong example of the "historical horror,"
the constant threat of nuclear war between the United States and the
Soviet Union at the time. This, then, translates into people wanting their
children to live in a world drastically unlike that of the Cold War. . . . In
place of a Cold War mentality, there is now a focus on making the
world a better place. . . . Given the impact of a nation's economic
policies on all other aspects of its citizens' lives, it is possible to
understand the push towards free market capitalism and comparative
advantage (Friedman 8). Whereas the economic, social, and political
policies of the United States and the Soviet Union during the Cold War
promoted an "us vs. them" worldview, which nearly led to nuclear war,
this era of globalization attempts to contrast with the danger of the
Cold War by focusing on the cooperation of all nations of the world
towards the prosperity of all.

The monumental foreign policies that helped to shape the Cold War
Era explain part of the reason why America is the single-most fervent
proponent of globalization in the early twenty-first century. Though
certainly not the first time the United States advocated a policy that
promoted increased interaction between nations of the world, the 1947
Truman Doctrine was the initiative which addressed the entire world. . . .
The Truman Doctrine itself demonstrates Truman's feelings that America,
by necessity, should be a globalizing agent:

9. Here, Matt uses prominent historical information
to help explain the
connection between
markets and social struc-
tures—economic and
political—thus connecting
the analysis to the earlier
section on the dynamic
and integrative nature of
globalization.

9

To ensure the peaceful development of nations, free from coer-
cion, the United States has taken a leading part in establishing
the United Nations. The United Nations is designed to make
possible lasting freedom and independence for all its members.
We shall not realize our objectives, however, unless we are able
to help free peoples maintain their free institutions and their
national integrity against aggressive movements that seek to
impose upon them totalitarian regimes. This is no more than a
frank recognition that totalitarian regimes imposed upon free
peoples, by direct or indirect aggression, undermine the foundations of international peace and hence the security of the
United States (Truman ¶ 29). . . .

10. Matt now uses this
same quotation to alert
the reader to the clearly
favorable evaluation of
these economic and political forces that led to their
adoption which will be
examined more closely in
the next sections.

10

The United States, so this paragraph of the Truman Doctrine suggests, is the fittest proponent of the United Nations. This idea is largely
founded upon the ideas of *laissez-faire* capitalism and Charles Darwin's
"survival of the fittest." Inherent in this market-driven philosophy is the
belief that free market economics constitute the most civilized form of
human competition in which the "fittest" would naturally rise to the top

and be self-regulating. Accordingly, the role of the United States in the global arena is re-imagined. It is implicit that, because the United Nations is "designed to make possible lasting freedom and independence for all its members," that, if the United Nations fails in particular, the United States has failed in general. As Truman's last sentence here indicates, he was thinking on a global scale, in that the welfare of one nation or a group of nations was a reflection of the success or failure of the United States to realize its aims when helping to establish the United Nations. Failure, he claims, threatens world peace and, thus, homeland security (Truman ¶ 29). . . .

11. Matt signals the move into evaluation by putting a question mark after the contrasting evaluative terms: salvation or destruction.

11   III. Changes in a Global Era: Salvation or Destruction?

Particularly regarding the rapidity with which it is occurring, globalization in the twenty-first century has become distinct from earlier globalizing efforts. It is still inevitable and irreversible, affecting each and every one of our lives in innumerable ways. But, the question that remains is: what are its consequences?

12. In this section Matt examines the various effects of globalization and how those effects can be "judged" or evaluated. He makes direct reference to three kinds of effects or as Friedman describes them "balances" or "equilibriums."

12   Where the Cold War system was one of tension and the attempt to avoid nuclear war at all costs, the globalization system is one of openness. Friedman describes the globalization system in terms of three "balances," which he argues have common characteristics and influence each other: the equilibrium between nation-states of the world as we have come to know it, the equilibrium between nation-states and global markets, and the equilibrium between nation-states and individuals (11–12). . . .

Although Friedman's balances work together to establish a super-ordinate equilibrium, the relations between both global markets and nation-states, as well as between individuals and nation-states are more apt to accentuate the vast changes to be seen in the globalization era compared with the Cold War. Friedman explains the relations between the nation-states and the global markets:

13. Matt also critically re-considers the "positive" evaluation of that major force behind globalization—free market capitalism.

13   These global markets are made up of investors moving money around the world with the click of a mouse. I call them "the Electronic Herd," and this herd gathers in key global financial centers, such as Wall Street, Hong Kong, London and Frankfurt, which I call the "Supermarkets." The attitudes and actions of the Electronic Herd and the Supermarkets can have a huge impact on nation-states today, even to the point of triggering the downfall of governments. You will not understand the front page of newspapers today—whether it is the story of the toppling of Suharto in Indonesia, the internal collapse in Russia or the monetary policy of the United States—unless you bring the Supermarkets into your analysis. (11–12)

The workings of "the Electronic Herd," and the "Supermarkets" help to explain the implications of this new globalization system in both its evil and benign forms. . . . Like any big process on such a vast scale as globalization, many results are to be seen, neither all beneficial nor destructive. . . .

In addition to giving greater power to individuals to shape the future of the world, Friedman observes that "no two countries that both had McDonald's had fought a war against each other since each got its McDonald's" (195). He queries: "to what extent does a country, by plugging into the Electronic Herd . . . restrict the capacity for war-making by its leadership?" (196). In an age where the interconnectedness between nations, people, and businesses is ever-increasing, the cost of warfare keeps getting higher and higher. This is inherent in the difference between the globalization system and all other systems that came before it. Friedman states that in his history of the Peloponnesian War, Thucydides wrote that people are motivated towards war for one of three reasons: interest, honor, and fear. Globalization, because it is an increased interdependence among the nations of the world, makes the cost of warfare all the greater (197).

14. He examines each kind of equilibrium and how well it is working, using a variety of authorities to provide support first for the positive general aspects or effects of globalization.

14   In an article for *IslamOnline* entitled "Globalization and Religion: Some Reflections," Chandra Muzaffar argues that globalization is not a "replica of the Western colonial experience." Although many of the "centers of power" are located in the West, there is also one in Japan and, he argues, other centers are rising in Northeast and Southeast Asia as well (¶ 5).

Thus, Muzaffar argues, globalization is not only a spread of Western ideals to the "rest" of the globe, but it is also a matter of some reciprocity. Not only are McDonalds popping up around the world, but foods from other countries are spreading to the West (¶ 6). . . .

15. Matt then returns to the example of coffee to focus on the negative aspects or disadvantages, and to reinforce the original idea that coffee is a good example of globalization's complex processes and consequences.

15   As with many large-scale shifts in society, globalization certainly being one of the largest, there is another side to the coin . . . The coffee industry serves as a good indicator of the fact that we, as a global society, have not yet achieved Friedman's balances. The very market practices allowing people to obtain coffee faster and cheaper in the First World are devastating the livelihoods of coffee growers in the Third World . . . To illustrate this, Paul Jeffrey in the *National Catholic Reporter* offers the following example:

> Maria Ramos doesn't understand why she works so hard and earns so little. A single mother in the village of Tauquil, high in the rugged mountains of northern Nicaragua, Ramos works her hillside farm with her two children. She produces organic coffee, for which she earns a higher price than she would if she produced it by other methods, yet world coffee prices have fallen so low in recent years that she cannot earn enough to make ends meet . . . Ramos and millions of other coffee farmers around the world, poor in the best of times, are having an even harder time

> surviving today because the price paid for the coffee they grow has fallen to historic lows. It's not just fickle markets that are generating their suffering, however. What's wrong with coffee is what's wrong with globalization. (pars. 1, 3)

The problem with globalization, as evidenced by the example of Maria Ramos, is that the universal benefits have not yet been achieved.

Still, if, as reported by Dicum and Luttinger, the 1999 global community is consuming 2.25 billion cups of coffee daily, then this is certainly not an issue of coffee not being a strong enough commodity to survive in the global market (ix). It is obviously fit enough, in Darwinist terms, to stay afloat . . . What can be seen here are the beginnings of the failure of the globalization system in its current form to do precisely what it is designed to do. There is no widespread prosperity in the global community, at least not if the coffee industry is any indication. If consumers worldwide are drinking 2.25 billion cups of coffee per day, then it should follow that the price of coffee should rival that of gas (Dicum & Luttinger ix). The problem might be that the market is in need of regulation, until such a time as it is capable of regulating itself. Jeffrey notes the disparity in the coffee industry, possibly indicative, to varying degrees, of the current state of globalization at large:

> Coffee is the most heavily traded commodity in the world after petroleum. Seventy percent of the world's coffee is grown on farms smaller than 10 hectares (less than 25 acres), many of them small family-run operations. When prices for coffee are stable, farm families earn money to send their children to school. Steady coffee prices contribute to social stability. In war-torn Columbia, for example, mountainous areas where coffee is produced have been less perplexed by violence. Yet coffee prices have plummeted spectacularly in recent years, leaving children starving (¶ 4). . . .

16. Matt concludes the evaluation by pointing out that globalization, like any other complex system or process, has advantages and disadvantages, and he indicates that future actions should be aimed at minimizing the disadvantages and maximizing the advantages.

16   What is beginning to come to light is the fact that globalization has the potential to be a very good thing for the world's economy. However, it is not currently at a stage where it is ready to operate under *laissez-faire* according to free market principles without monitoring, as evidenced by the poverty-stricken coffee growers. Economic Darwinism, *laissez-faire*, and the free market are wonderful ideas. If a global economy founded upon these principles is to succeed, however, it should be experimented with, using trial and error and substituting different variables, such as tariffs, subsidization, both to prepare certain industries like coffee to catch up to a point where it can make a strong entrance onto the global economic stage and not need its training wheels, so to speak. This is not only true of coffee, but of all commodities. Coffee is simply a crowbar with which to break in and understand the workings of globalization. Because of the disparity between prices paid to growers and the amount consumed daily on a global

scale, coffee is a viable subject to analyze how globalization might best be set back on the track towards global prosperity, precisely because it is not an issue of simple supply and demand. The factor doing the most damage, argues Jeffrey, is this price difference between what Americans pay for roasted coffee by the cup or pound, and the amount paid to the growers. Jeffery cites a 2002 study by Oxfam International which reveals that third world farmers receive about 24 cents a pound for their coffee beans, while the largest transnational corporations—Kraft, Sara Lee, Proctor & Gamble and Nestle—sell the same beans for $3.60 per pound to western markets. "We coffee farmers are subsidizing those giant companies," complains Fermin Perez, president of a coffee growers association in Honduras" (¶ 9).

17. Matt agrees with the claim that globalization, particularly as modeled by coffee, has not achieved all of the benefits ascribed to it.

17   It is extremely difficult to follow the logical path between coffee being the second most heavily traded commodity in the world and the abject poverty of those who grow and cultivate it until this information comes to light. Jeffrey is absolutely right in claiming that "what's wrong with coffee is what's wrong with globalization" (¶ 3). The only comparative advantage currently being seen is split by the stockholders of Sara Lee, Kraft, Proctor & Gamble, Nestle and, to a lesser extent, Starbucks, Dunkin Donuts, et al . . .

Economic Darwinism is hard at work, but *currently* not in the interests of 99% of the world's citizens. What we are witnessing in the coffee and other industries is precisely what Hondurian coffee grower Fermin Perez claims: the survival of those best able to subsidize (¶ 9).

18. Matt clearly labels the appropriate action section.

18   **IV. What is to be Done?**

To be clear, globalization has the potential to produce prosperity for the entire globe, but the global markets as well as the citizens of the world need time to adjust to the new system. Globalization, as a dynamic force, was able to swoop down and perch upon the remains of the Berlin Wall. Whether or not global markets are capable of such sudden change remains to be seen; the coffee industry clearly is not ready to be integrated into the system. It also seems a safe assumption that the majority of the world's citizens are not capable of coping with such sudden change. We are not ready for the free market, economic Darwinism, and laissez-faire to take over our lives, and we are likely to be skeptical for some time yet. For this reason, globalization needs to be managed. There is a need for an institution that can reign in globalization, until such a time as the Supermarkets, the superpower, i.e., the United States, and Super-empowered individuals are ready to interact towards the mutual benefit of all (Friedman 11-12) . . . By managing globalization in the short-term, we will be removing the roadblocks so that its goals can be realized in the long term.

19. In this final section Matt attempts to suggest to his readers a set of behaviors or actions that can be undertaken—even in a modest way—to help minimize the harms of globalization. Thus, he moves from the international to the national to the local and finally to the individual level, as he began.

19   First, in the sphere of global markets, efforts should be made to prepare industries, such as coffee, for globalization. In the instance of coffee, the first thing that should be done to insure prosperity is to attempt to alleviate the disastrous effects of the "race to the bottom."

For example, my college has made the switch towards providing fair trade coffees to the students, for which its growers were paid a living wage (Arnold) . . . Not only is this an instance of a business, in this case Dining Services at SUNY Potsdam, making the choice to provide a fair trade option to its consumers, it is also an instance of a business empowering people to choose how they participate in globalization. Consuming coffee means participating in globalization. There is no choice about that. But, by making students aware that there is fair trade and non fair trade and that how they spend their dollar makes a difference in the livelihood of someone across the globe, students are being empowered to make a difference in the global economy. Thus, as Friedman suggests, the balances between nation-states, markets, and individuals, do overlap and work together. They have the potential to work either towards mutual prosperity or widespread devastation (11–12).

Another possibility for conglomerates with stakes in the coffee industry is to narrow the price gap between what is paid to the coffee grower and what is paid for a cup of coffee at Starbucks or beans or grounds in the grocery store. One way to do this, as Dining Services at SUNY Potsdam did, is to provide a balance of fair trade and non-fair trade coffees and super-empower customers to choose between them, giving individual customers a choice in how they participate in the globalization system. Using the Aristotelian notions of *ethos* and *pathos*, i.e. ethical and emotional appeals, it might be possible for advertisers to convince consumers that the extra cost for fair trade coffees and other products is worth paying because it spreads wealth around the world and enables citizens of the Third World to earn a living wage. This would enable producers to do the morally upright thing without eating into profits, if it were to work.

Once the race to the bottom is addressed, it will then be possible for a regulating body to address the issue of supply and demand in the coffee industry. They could, quite simply, pay the farmers to destroy their crop until supply and demand begin to operate as they should for a commodity consumed 2.25 billion times a day worldwide (Dicum & Luttinger xi).

Regardless, just as the United States took a leading role in the establishment of the United Nations to protect the autonomy of member nations, so too, it could take a leading role in the establishment of a global commission to oversee the progress of globalization. The worst by-product of globalization appears to result from it wanting to occur at a rate to which the national economies and individual citizens of the world are incapable of adapting. The time has come for those in support of globalization to realize that certain samples of the world population, both people and markets alike, are not ready for free market, *laissez-faire* globalization. An institution similar to the United Nations comprised of representatives who are educated in the workings of globalization should be empowered towards its management. This institution would have the ability and the capital necessary to stabilize the markets and to ready the people to transition smoothly into an age of globalization under the auspices of the free market. It would be this organization which would make sure that before an industry could go global, its supply and demand and other influential factors, come under control.

Last, but certainly not least, individual consumers need to understand that living in a global age does not mean that we are helpless to affect change. First, people need to become aware that a cup of coffee is not simply a cup of coffee. A beer is not just a beer. Consumer goods represent the livelihoods of thousands of individuals worldwide. Globalization is not a choice. What is a choice is *how* we help the system proceed along the right course. Just as industry and governments have a say in this, so do individuals. Every dollar, pound, yen, peso, lira, mark, etc. in the wallets of every citizen around the world purchases not only goods and services in the global market, but represents a voice in the world forum regarding the shape that globalization will take in years to come. Each individual can either help or hinder globalization to achieve its aims. . . .

Coffee provides a unique opportunity to those who wish to change the nature of their participation in the global system. Via the Internet, it is possible to purchase unroasted, green coffee beans to roast at home. There are many different methods for home-roasting, from the more elaborate and expensive commercially available coffee-roasters, to a simple method using a certain type of popcorn popper. This venue provides a host of benefits for everyone involved in coffee "from crop to the last drop," in Dicum & Luttinger's language. First, consumers can go online and choose beans from various coffee producing regions of the world according to their flavor profile. This avoids the homogenization process that occurs in going to the store and buying from Nestle, Sara Lee, Proctor & Gamble, or Kraft. In addition to the variety inherent in the availability of the beans, there are also different types of "roasts," varying from dark to light. At various stages in the roasting process, certain flavors will be more evident than others, and some roasts produce darker coffee than others. Roasting at home provides the ultimate control over the cup of coffee. Also, as no two roasts are exactly the same, homogenization has thus been avoided. In the process, the race to the bottom can also be avoided because the consumer has the choice to buy fair trade beans. This way, the coffee grower benefits because fair trade allows the opportunity to earn a living wage. The consumer also benefits not only from an all-around better cup of coffee, but from taking an active role in globalization, having a say, and making a difference, if even only on a very small scale, in how the world is globalized.

While not all consumer goods provide the vast opportunities that coffee does, many are nonetheless available in both fair trade and non-fair trade forms. Consumers have the opportunity to become super-empowered through the goods and services they consume. Consumers can choose to pay a little extra to support the small farmer. Rest assured, the conglomerate will subsidize the difference. Consumers who are interested might begin by purchasing a balance of fair trade and non-fair trade goods, as an all-out switch is probably not practical.

Long story short, the Cold War is out and globalization is in, and each and every citizen in the now global community is implicated in it. That means that until the economy is able to self-regulate with the foundations of *laissez-faire* and free market capitalism, people need, now more than ever, to be aware of how far their money really goes and how much a difference an extra dollar or so here and there can make in helping globalization to achieve its aims. Until such an event as a self-regulating, fully-realized, free market globalization occurs, it needs to be nurtured and guided like a young child, that it might allow the markets and world citizens to catch up with its overabundance of energy. Then, hopefully we will be able to experience globalized prosperity.

WORKS CITED*

Arnold, George. Personal interview. 27 Mar. 2006.

Dicum, Gregory and Nina Luttinger. *The Coffee Book: Anatomy of an Industry from Crop to the Last Drop*. New York: The New Press, 1999. Print.

Friedman, Thomas L. *The Lexus and the Olive Tree*. New York: Farrar, Straus, and Giroux, 1999. Print.

Gevalia.com: Gourmet Tea & Coffee Collections. 2006.Web.1 Apr. 2006.

Globalization: A Solution for Some. World Health Organization. WHO.10 February 2001 Web. 15 Apr. 2006.

Halweil, Brian. *Eat Here: Reclaiming Homegrown Pleasures in a Global Supermarket*. Washington: Worldwatch Institute, 2004. Print.

Jeffrey, Paul. "Depressed Coffee Prices Yield Suffering in Poor Countries." *National Catholic Reporter*. 7 Feb 2003: 12-15. Proquest. Web.13 Apr. 2006.

Merrill, Dennis. "The Truman Doctrine: Containing Communism and Modernity." Presidential Studies Quarterly. March 2006. 6–7. ProQuest. Web.13 Apr. 2006.

*Muzaffar, Chandra. "Globalization and Religion: Some Reflections." Islam-OnLine.IslamOnLine.net.19 June 2002.Web.15 May 2006.

Otis, John. "Left Behind . . . Globalization is Pushing Coffee Prices to Historic Lows and Brewing Poverty." *Houston Chronicle* 13 July 2006: 01. ProQuest. Web. 20 Mar. 2006.

Steger, Manfred. Globalization: *The New Market Ideology*. Lanham, MD: Roman & Littlefield, 2002. Print.

Truman, Harry S. "Address Before a Joint Session of Congress March 12, 1947." *The Avalon Project: Truman Doctrine*. Yale Law School Lillian Goldman Law Library. The Avalon Project. 3 Jan. 2006 Web. 16 Apr. 2006.

*Some of these references are not included in this abridged version of Matt's paper.

Questions for Discussion and Writing

1. What are the most important claims that Matt makes in his essay? Explain. How well has he defined and supported those claims?

2. Matt focuses on coffee as an iterative example to model all globalization. What are the advantages and disadvantages of that choice? Explain.

3. Was your knowledge of globalization clarified, extended, or restructured by your reading of Matt's paper? If so, how? If not, why not?

4. Matt's paper takes the reader through the entire sequence of claims—what something is, what causes it, what its effects are, and what, if anything, we can do about it. How well has he satisfied the rhetorical requirements of each part of the sequence?

5. If you could ask Matt a question or two, what would they be? Why?

6. Having read portions of Friedman's book on globalization, do you think Matt has accurately reflected Friedman's positions in the quotations and paraphrases he uses and in the way he frames them? Explain.

Making Connections

1. Matt Burkhardt writes that "Coffee is simply a crowbar with which to break in and understand the workings of globalization." Do you think the focus on coffee yields insight into how economic globalization works? Was Matt's choice more illuminating than say a focus on slavery, outsourcing, or the environment? If so, why? If not, why not?

2. Compare the harmful effects of globalization addressed in Matt's essay with those presented in this chapter's other readings. Which reading best illustrates the harmful effects Matt indicates? What made the illustrations effective? Repeat the comparison, but this time focus on the positive aspects or effects of globalization.

3. All the chapter readings suggest ways to minimize the harms and maximize the benefits of globalization. What do you think could be the most critical actions to alleviate problems and maximize advantages? Using a variety of authorities, explain why you chose these actions.

Short Essay Assignments

1. In *The Lexus and the Olive Tree* Thomas Friedman describes how globalization seemingly forces people and cultures to change whether they are ready to, or want to, or not. His book indicates one potential problem created by globalization, the erosion of unique cultural heritages. One of our students, Sarah Elkhayat, details how striking competitive cultural and social elements can be.

> As a young Egyptian girl, my aunt took us to the Pyramids for the day. When we got out of the car, the first thing I spotted was not the Sphinx nor was it the base of Khufu, the Great Pyramid. It was those famous Golden Arches, brazenly telling me that over 99 billion burgers were served there! Merely two blocks away from the last remaining Wonder of the World, and the greatest architectural mystery, stood a multi-colored McDonald's – the symbol of all things temporary and superficial, and above all, American.

With Sarah's experience in mind, write an essay that considers whether this trend of globalization is likely to result in good or bad consequences for individuals or for societies in general. Also consider whether aspects of this trend could be good for the individual and bad for society or vice-versa. Use the chapter readings to help frame and support your argument.

2. Travel writer Pico Iyer (*The Global Soul*, 2001) defines a global soul as "somebody who lives in the cracks between cultures, or lives in a world so international that he or she has to devise some scratch answers to the most fundamental questions: what is your home, what is your community, what tradition do you belong to, and even who are you." Unlike in the past, when people could feel a part of a tradition and were strongly defined by it, you face a very different future because of globalization. Write an essay that envisions some of the changes you might encounter during your lifetime, using the authors you have read to substantiate the changes you have imagined.

To Help You Get Started

Pick a few changes and try creating a potential chain of causation (See Chapter 6) in which a cause produces an effect that in turn becomes cause. What other changes might result as the causal chain extends into the future? Take today as the beginning of the chain and the year in which you turn 60 (an unimaginable age for some of you) as the, admittedly arbitrary, end. The final element of this assignment is for you to determine what the world will be like when you reach your 60th year.

❑ Major Essay Assignment

In a 2002 issue of *The New York Times* Sunday Magazine, Tina Rosenberg presents globalization as "a phenomenon that has remade the economy of virtually every nation, reshaped almost every industry and touched billions of lives, often in surprising and ambiguous ways." Working from this chapter's readings, you will determine the dominant forces that have shaped this global wonder. You will then write an essay to take Nel Noddings' concept of "global citizenship" a bit further. Drawing on the readings, your essay will answer the following general questions:

- how can we, both as a nation and as individuals, become *good* global citizens?
- how can we insure that globalization promotes social and economic *justice*?

Your essay will provide effective arguments in support of your responses to these questions. Obviously, the questions, as they are phrased here, are very broad. Clearly, you have to narrow the focus, refine your lines of inquiry, and determine the specific direction you will take in your essay.

Invention: Finding Promising Lines of Inquiry

The process that follows is meant to direct your preliminary exploration. Your ultimate goal is to create an integrated paper that develops thoughtful answers to a central question (or series of questions). What you discover in your exploration will help to determine that goal.

■ Defining and Refining the Subject

The key term, *globalization*, is unwieldy. Your first job will be to develop a narrow but cogent definition and a list of its characteristics.

Fortunately, the readings provide much to direct your thinking.

1. Each author states or implies one or more general definitions of the term. Find those definitions and either quote or paraphrase them in your journal. As much as you can, think of them as behaviors, actions, and activities (opening, competing, bringing down barriers. . .).

2. In your journal, note similarities and differences in the definitions and characteristics you discovered. Try to group those that seem similar.

While *globalization* is certainly the key term in this inquiry, it is linked to other concepts. Make a list of some of those and repeat steps 1 and 2 for each of them. Here are some examples:

- free markets
- privatization
- integration

Perhaps there are important terms that are not mentioned in the readings. Add them to your list. Do not be stingy with your listing and freewriting; the more text you generate, the more material you will have to draw on as you work through the rest of the process.

Your final task is to narrow the general topic by picking a few—no more than two or three concepts, questions, ideas, or behaviors that seem most interesting or promising.

■ Looking for Causes and Effects

Now, consider the causes and effects behind the concepts, questions, or ideas you just picked. Try to form your observations as questions.

Obviously, you will want to deal with the term describing the overall topic—globalization. Some of the questions you might ask would be:

- What causes globalization? Is it a natural consequence of economic forces that will happen despite the steps we might take to impede or accelerate it? Or are there human factors at work that are creating the phenomenon? If so, what motivates those who would either impede or accelerate the process?
- What are some *necessary* causes of globalization; that is, are there any causes without which globalization would not occur?
- What factors accelerate the process but are not entirely necessary for it to occur?

Also, what about the effects of globalization?

- For example, some people oppose the process because they fear that "globalization" will necessarily mean "Americanization" and the loss of their current cultural identities. Is that necessarily the case?
- Countless reports deal with the phenomenon of American workers losing their jobs to lower paid workers in other countries. Is that a significant effect? Is it a necessary consequence of globalization? Are there alternative strategies?

You should respond to as many questions as you can formulate about the causes and effects of globalization, and you should reflect on the significance of any other key terms or concepts you have discovered in your reading.

Be sure to consider the substantial changes that globalization might produce in your lifetime. These may include bringing down barriers on where people can go, what they can buy, where they can invest, and what they can see, hear, and read. They may include the income inequality that free markets can produce, the way it pulls jobs out of higher wage countries, and the pressure it puts on the environment.

■ Assigning Value

So far, you've worked to define and refine terms and imagine causes and potential effects. Probably, you have not assigned value to the concepts and phenomena you are considering. It is unlikely, however, that you have been able to work through this material without at least some consideration of the merits of globalization and its related characteristics. Now, look carefully, thoroughly, and systematically at the positives and negatives of these phenomena. Are the effects of what you have identified good or bad, or is there, in some cases, a middle ground? As you answer such questions, you are generating material that you can use to determine your stance in relation to globalization.

Some of the readings may make the picture seem fairly grim. Some writers state or imply that globalization means forcing American economic, cultural, and social practices on other nations, inevitably incurring backlash. Some stress the negative impacts on Americans—for example, the loss of jobs. Others—Friedman, for example—are just cautionary. He warns us about the difficulties that global forces pose to our society, but his warning is accompanied by some suggestions for dealing with them.

Your job is to write an essay that points out how to do things *right*, at least with regard to the specific aspects of globalization on which you have decided to focus. Sometimes, however, you have to focus on what is problematic in the current situation, before you can imagine what meaningful, effective things we can do to make things right.

First, in your journal, list the concepts and characteristics associated with globalization that you have chosen to consider. Then, drawing on your previous work and on any new ideas that occur to you, for each entry, list the effects that globalization is likely to have on you, on other Americans, and on other nations. Divide your lists into columns—one for positive effects, the other for negative. For each effect, describe what brought it about—do not be afraid to speculate. Be sure to offer explanations for your conclusions.

Finally, list all the characteristics you can think of that would make a person a *good* global citizen. Some seem obvious—knowledge, understanding, and respect for other cultures. Are there others?

■ Considering Action

Finally, you will contemplate possible actions we might take, either as individuals or as a society, to become global citizens. You will also want to consider what actions individuals and societies can take to make globalization work. How can they influence the phenomenon to provide the greatest good, while avoiding, as much as possible, potentially negative consequences?

This obviously sounds like a huge and impossible task; but, remember, you do not have to do the whole job—just offer ideas and insights regarding the characteristics of globalization you chose earlier. It can be a single subject— education, for example, or the equitable distribution of wealth, or the environment. The possibilities are certainly endless, but you have to deal with only one of them.

Before turning to the more developed tools in the next chapter, make journal entries for potential central or controlling ideas for your essay. As you ponder possible lines of inquiry, determine the assumptions they might involve, and evaluate whether or not your examples and evidence effectively support the conclusions you might present. As with previous assignments, be sure that you have adequately represented the views of the authors you have encountered in this text, as well as any others you have found useful in deepening and enriching your own understanding and authority.

Drafting: Making Claims

Way too often, the various components of an argument are treated like items on a menu. "I'll have one of these and one of those," or "I'll begin with this one here," and so on. In reality, however, what we formally argue should not be so accidental or arbitrary. We become involved with an issue because we believe it is important to us and to our audience, and we take a position because we have worked hard to come to an understanding of that issue. Thus, we make our rhetorical choices primarily on the basis of what we understand and what we want our audience to understand about a subject, and on the basis of the limits or constraints we are working under. Our arguments are always addressed to a particular audience in a particular context.

The only rhetorical element that is absolutely necessary, no matter what we argue or to whom, is the one establishing the "what," the aspect of the world we share with our readers. It seems so self-evident that we often don't pay careful attention to it, yet we have seen in the earlier chapters how essential that rhetorical element is. Though we often think that the "main" purpose of argument is to convince our audience of something or get them to do something, what must come first is asking them to consider our way of understanding the subject or issue—our way of describing or defining it. No intelligent, reasoned discussion can proceed if they and we do not share a basic understanding of the issue at hand: what it is and what it is not—the kinds of information that we get by asking the traditional journalistic questions: who, what, where, when, and how. Simply put, without a *what* there's no *why*, no *so what?* and nothing really *to do*.

Beyond establishing the "nature of" our subject, all other rhetorical choices are optional. They will depend on what we know about the subject; what we wish our audience to know; and how much time and space we have for making our argument. Do we know enough to discuss the causal aspects of our subject—why it is what it is and what results from it? Do we wish to evaluate it—judge what it is or its effects? Do we have a plan for promoting its desirable and inhibiting its undesirable aspects? Is our audience in a position to take action? Or is it enough that we ask them to consider our way of thinking about the subject? Do we have enough time, given our writing task, to take the issue all the way through to a plan of action? Is there enough information available? Too much?

It is our answers to these and similar questions that should determine what we argue and how we shape that argument. Our choices must reflect the limits of our knowledge, our goals in relation to our audience, and any practical constraints.

Charting a Direction

Since we've been working with globalization, let's continue using that as an example of how to engage with a subject in a natural and organic way. In Chapter 8, we considered globalization from two distinct, yet related, perspectives—the personal (how each of us can become a good global citizen) and the communal (how we can help make globalization work for all the peoples of the world). As we investigated how a meaningful argument works, we had to spend time exploring (inquiring into) some larger issues because, although we probably had some idea in mind of how to respond, we couldn't really know how to behave as "good global citizens" until we understood more fully the nature of the global economy and how it works and what kinds of effects it has locally, nationally, and globally. This is especially true when we present our thinking to an informed but skeptical audience. We don't do the research because it's a "research paper"; we do it to understand an issue more fully and to determine what actions are reasonable, given all the complexities and limitations involved.

Almost always, even with an "assigned" topic, you are likely to have formed an opinion or, more generally, an attitude about the issue—even if you are not fully aware of it as you begin. With globalization, for example, it may be that you like things small and local as a general preference and so are wary of a whole world so deeply inter-connected; or it may be just the opposite—you can't wait to get someplace big and full of energy and activity and so find the idea of a global economy stimulating and full of promise. Your task, as a good arguer, will be to take these preliminary ideas and attitudes and test them out, first, by reflecting on what you actually do know and then by inquiring into the subject to find out what others with more experience and knowledge think.

Collaborative Activity

This is a two-part activity designed to expand your understanding of the possibilities inherent in "globalization" as a general topic. The first part is a full class activity; in the second part, you will break into small groups. Both parts involve a "word-association" game. The goal is to find ideas or concepts about globalization that are interesting and insightful, rather than those that are overused, obvious, and/or trivial.

First part—25–30 minutes (actually, it might take longer depending on how active the class is):
Select a moderator—it could be your instructor or one of your classmates. You may also need to select a timekeeper.

The moderator will write a single word—either "globalization" or "global" on the board as a target term. When the moderator says "go," all the members of the class should jot down any concepts or even single words that seem connected *in any way* to the target term. You've already done some thinking and writing about the concept, so you shouldn't find coming up with related terms too difficult. However, try to let your mind run freely and don't feel compelled to stay too close to what you already think about the target term. Don't worry about including anything that seems weird or off-target. There are no right or wrong answers. At the end of five minutes, the timekeeper will call time, and you'll quit writing. At that point, your job will be to share your list with the whole class. The moderator will put a collective list on the board so the whole class can copy it.

Then, the class should spend another 10 or 15 minutes discussing the entries. At the end of that discussion, the class should take a vote to select the 8–10 most striking, interesting, or enigmatic terms or concepts.

Second part—this part can take as long as your instructor is willing to devote to it, so you may want to save it for the following class meeting.

Divide the class into small groups of 4–5. Each group will take one of the terms or concepts the class selected in the first part of the exercise. This time, you'll want to select a note-taker. Treat the term assigned to your group as your target term and simply repeat the free-association exercise you did in the first part of the activity. Spend 15–20 minutes generating a list of concepts or single terms related in any way to your target term. Then spend another 20–30 minutes discussing the viability—that is, the positive and negative aspects—of each term on your new list as a possible focus or direction for your paper. As always, be sure to take notes of the ideas and insights of your classmates.

If your instructor thinks it wise, a final step might be to photocopy the results of each group for distribution to the rest of the class.

Remember, the goal of this exercise, indeed, of many of the exercises that follow, is to help you reduce the enormous scope of the general topic, "globalization," and narrow the target of your efforts to a few of the most likely possibilities.

Let's say that as you do this you come to realize that you have some strong reservations about the ways globalization seems to be changing the world. You can see some potential benefits—the way globalization can bring together all the peoples of the world, for example, but you are also very uneasy about the way globalization forces people and cultures to change whether they are ready to, or want to, or not. In other words, it is the Lexus and the Olive Tree idea, only you are not as sanguine as Friedman is or seems to be. But is that because he has more knowledge than you do, and if you had that knowledge you might also think the way he does; or is it because, independent of the extent of his or your knowledge, he values certain results and behaviors differently than you do?

Journal Activity

In your journal, make a list of 10 general subjects or areas of knowledge that Friedman seems to know about that you don't. For each one, write a few lines speculating on how his enhanced knowledge *might* have shaped his ideas on globalization.

Then, for each of the 10 subjects you listed above, tell whether or not you would like to learn what Friedman knows (or even a part of it). Write a few sentences to explain your reasoning. Also speculate on how your increased understanding might either reinforce or change your existing ideas on the subject.

You know it is not possible to obtain, in the time allowed, the kind of knowledge—the breadth and depth of it—that experts have. But there are some things you can do to help compensate for that limitation. First, you can explore a range of expert opinions about the subject, not only those who agree with you but those who disagree. The various electronic search engines make finding this range much easier.

Journal Activity

This journal activity involves several Internet searches. Google is probably the best-known Internet search engine, but if there are others with which you're more comfortable, don't hesitate to use one of them instead.

You might be tempted to start with the general topic "globalization" as your search term. However, as you'll see later in this chapter, the term is too broad to be useful. You must narrow the term by adding one or more relevant qualifying terms.

For example, you might select one or more of the words you generated in the previous collaborative activity (pp. 272–273) as a qualifying term. Pick something fairly specific. You might also use additional qualifiers to make your search even more manageable. See the "Caveat" on p. 288 for more detailed instructions on how to go about this.

Be sure to copy the URLs of promising websites and a few lines describing the content of each site and evaluating its quality. Then, go back and review the sites you found most promising and, in your journal, write a few lines for each one stating whether or not any of these sources raise points and/or provide support that you hadn't thought of before or didn't feel confident enough to raise and defend.

At this point, you've begun to narrow the topic, to select certain features or behaviors to focus your attention on. Now, you need to take that "narrowing" further to make the topic and the work you'll need to do to develop it more manageable.

Consider the following examples:

- You can concentrate on the changes that a global economy can create in a particular group of people—concentrate on the effects, that is, rather than remedies.

- Or, you can select a particular product or service and, therefore, not be concerned with the way globalization affects a number of goods or services.

- Or, you can focus on a particular time period.

- Or, if you're feeling particularly ambitious, you can consider all of the above.

This further narrowing will help limit the subject enough so that you will be more confident. Maybe you can't fully know all there is to know about globalization, but you can know quite a lot about a specific aspect of it. And if you do your narrowing thoughtfully and carefully, in understanding this more focused area, you will have a more accurate understanding of your subject than by just skimming its surface.

You can also look for what is called an *iterative* example—a single example of the general subject you are exploring that is representative of the larger phenomenon. Thus, in understanding the one, you might come to better understand the many. And if you are careful (and fortunate) this focused subject might give you the opportunity to take advantage of your own direct or indirect experience.

In terms of globalization, consider coffee, the second most traded commodity (after oil) in the world. (See the student essay in Chapter 8, pp. 254–265.)

By thoroughly understanding the way coffee is grown, processed, traded, sold, and consumed, and the various impacts it has had on all the people and places involved, you can gain insight into how economic globalization in general works. Moreover, you can participate in the inquiry by exploring the way your family, campus, or community participates in the global process.

And notice, as you have been working your way through all of this, you haven't been making arbitrary or mechanical choices; instead, you have been thinking about how you can test and deepen your knowledge before you decide what to present to your audience or how to challenge it. Everyone might have a right to an opinion, but not every opinion is valid. A good, sound argument doesn't often end the debate about a complex subject, but it can serve to clarify issues and focus attention on the major points of dispute and uncertainty.

Providing Evidence

Socrates once said, "I'm wise because I know that I do not know." Yet, we do know that he knew a great deal. Unfortunately, there is always more to know about everything, including ourselves. We go to medical doctors to find out about our own bodies—to a specialist for each part, even. We go to another kind of doctor for help in interpreting our own dreams. That old piece of advice from the Oracle at Delphi, "Know Thyself," is not so easy to accomplish.

Yet, we can't wait until we know all there is to know about a subject, assuming we can ever know that much. We live in the here and now; we have to act on what we know now or in the near future—even though much of what we know will change as we respond to the rapid advances in all fields of knowledge. So, it's a real balancing act: having confidence in our ability to develop a sound understanding of a subject and, at the same time, having the humility to recognize that there is always more to know and other ways of knowing. This sense of the complex nature of knowledge, together with our awareness that audiences can have many attitudes towards that knowledge, should guide us as we create arguments. Perhaps now, we can better appreciate just how dynamic and organic "real" argument is—how much a "real" exchange of ideas, a "real" give and take, and not just a transfer of information from "us" to "them". We take what we have learned through all the difficult work of inquiry and exploration and find the most efficient and effective way to present it to our readers.

In terms of the subject matter, we will need to decide what represents the most important and useful information we have acquired, information that we believe our audience doesn't already know as well as we do, and whether this information is primarily about the nature of the subject, or the causes of it, or the value of it, etc. Then, we also will need to estimate how much "resistance" to this information we should expect from those we are delivering it to. Such assessments will determine what kind of evidence and how much of it we will need to present to support the claims we are making. We are helped in accomplishing this by the limited number of ways we have for providing support for any claim we make. Whether we are freshmen writers or Nobel laureates, whether we are writing a 500-word in-class essay or a PhD dissertation, we have only four basic ways of providing evidence or testimony in support of whatever claim or claims we are making. And, once again, as in every other aspect of argument, each comes with its advantages and disadvantages.

❑ *Direct Experience*

The first source of support is our own *direct experience*—our observation of, or participation in, that aspect of the world (our subject) that we want to communicate to our audience.

If, for example, you argue that globalization is having an effect on your hometown or on your campus, you might let your audience know that you lost a job due to a factory relocating to a third-world country. Or maybe you have seen an increasing number of older students in your classes, retraining because they've lost jobs.

Maybe you have a job in a local company that serves the international market. Perhaps your employer offers tuition assistance. Or you might have seen the content of your courses change due to an increased interest in non-American cultures.

The advantages of using this kind of direct "knowledge" about your topic are obvious. You are not only the arguer; you are the "informed" witness. You are not only the researcher; you are the subject. You are not just repeating what you have heard; you are reporting what you have experienced. Thus, your audience gets the information directly, not second– or third-hand.

Also, because you are the witness, the examples or evidence seem more dramatic, certainly more personal, and perhaps even more authentic. These are powerful advantages. Because they enhance your credibility, they have a definite impact on the *ethos* of your argument.

The disadvantages of such "evidence" are real, as well. First, we could become too involved in the experience, too certain that because it actually happened to us the claim must be clear and compelling: "I said globalization was having an impact and look at what happened to me." We sometimes use our personal, biographical experience to support our general claim, assuming that it is representational—that if it's happening in such a dramatic fashion to us it must be happening to others. But though that may sometimes be true, it is not always or invariably true. Sometimes, what happens to us is not representative at all, but exceptional. Consider the hypothetical examples of direct support stated above. Are they common occurrences in many towns throughout the country or are they rare events? If the latter, your "experience," though certainly real and authentic, would have limited relevance because it does not characterize the common experiences of others. Consequently, we should always be cautious in assuming that what we have experienced or witnessed is, in fact, representational of the general condition or claim; in other words, we should be sure that it is what we earlier called an *iterative example* and that the occurrence is not an isolated incident.

Journal

Quickly review the readings by Thomas Friedman in Chapters 6 and 8. In your journal, list several spots where Friedman provides his own direct experience to develop ideas in the piece. Then write a brief analysis, based on the principles offered above, of his experiences as support for his claims. Are they effective? Why or why not?

❏ *The Experience of Others*

In addition to our own experience, we often turn to another source of support for our claims: the *experience of others* we know personally. Sometimes we may know these people quite well, but often our knowledge is limited to an interview conducted in a specific writing context.

Again, the advantages are those associated with our own direct experience—immediacy and authenticity. Though we may not have observed the behaviors directly, we have somewhat observed the person who has. We can describe to our readers our knowledge of the person, our relationship to him or her, and how the information was reported to us. Thus, we can say to our audience concerning our claim about globalization: "Not only did I experience these things, but two people I interviewed had similar experiences." The disadvantages of this sort of support mirror those of your own personal experience. While it seems less likely that these experiences could also be uncharacteristic or unrepresentative, they still could be. What guarantee do you have that the experiences of the other people are any more representative than your own? The support for your claim may seem powerful and dramatically supported, but it still may not be statistically significant.

Journal

Quickly review the essays in Chapter 8. In your journal, list several first-person accounts from the readings of globalization's effects on the lives of American or non-American workers. How effective are these narratives? Support your answers.

❏ *Expert Testimony*

While first-person experience may be engaging and interesting, we'll normally explore our claims more fully by turning to other sorts of information about the situation. Often, especially in the academic community, we'll turn to the *experience and testimony of experts*: people who are generally recognized as having the knowledge and skills that make their opinions about a particular issue especially (though not absolutely) credible. In a sense, these are people we come to know through active research, either by direct contact or, more frequently, through reading about their experiences and conclusions in books, magazines, or professional journals.

When these "experts" or "informed authorities" provide compelling and authoritative answers to our questions, we generally will feel more confident of our own understanding. Now, it's not only our own personal experiences and the experiences of people we know that carry weight, but the experiences of other people, strangers to us until we meet through active research ("listening" to them talk about our subject, as it were). Additionally, it's not just anyone else's experience or opinion, but those of people who have credibility and authority in our subject area.

Journal

From the readings in Chapter 8 and the Friedman excerpts in Chapter 6, locate several examples of expert testimony on the effects of globalization. List them in your journal and write analyses of their effectiveness in providing information. Are the experts qualified and do their comments seem authoritative? Also, are their comments consistent, or do the experts sometimes disagree? If so, how does this affect your attitude toward their testimony?

This combination of biographical and researched support often makes for a stronger more compelling argument, particularly if the external support comes from respected authorities who have used carefully validated and controlled methods and data. But, as with each of the other sources, it has disadvantages. For one thing, complicated issues are complicated because there are many ways of understanding, evaluating, and perhaps solving them. Often, the experts will strongly disagree about each aspect.

When that happens, we may have to carefully examine their reputations and biases, and the quality and up-to-datedness of their research. Even then, we may have to acknowledge the complexity and disagreements to our audience, indicating that our best current understanding of the subject doesn't allow us to do more than present the issue and the most reasoned ways they are argued. In that sense, we can conclude, knowledgeably and confidently, that more study and analysis are needed before the issue can be fully resolved.

❑ *Statistics*

The last kind of support, the one we often give the most credence to, is what we loosely call *statistics*—the kind of supporting information that comes in the form of numbers or percentages that try to provide some objective measure of certain aspects of phenomena.

Journal

Return to the readings in Chapter 8. In your journal, list several examples of statistical data provided in support of claims. Then, in each case, comment on the reasonableness of the conclusions that were drawn from the statistical data. Do the statistical data actually provide good measures of the phenomena they claim to describe? Explain.

Statistics, though they seem solid and indisputable, have their own limitations, their own difficulties. For one thing, they may depend on how researchers define the phenomena they attempt to describe, and whether that definition is complete, unambiguous, and still accurate or relevant. In practice, researchers rarely examine phenomena in any complete sense; rather, they carefully limit the aspects of phenomena about which they gather data. Ambiguity is another common problem. As we've seen, words sometimes entail a multitude of meanings. For example, "globalization" is often defined as primarily an economic phenomenon; in these cases, researchers tend to look at statistics relevant to economic issues. However, we can also limit our definition of globalization to our understanding and value of other cultures. In this case, statistical research might explore how many Americans are bi- or multilingual compared to citizens of other countries.

Clearly, the "reality" represented by statistics can depend more on the way the events are being measured and reported than on the behaviors themselves. Given the complexity of most important issues, and given all the different sources of support and their limitations, we can see why we need to be careful in asserting our claims—in asking other people to accept our understanding of the situation, commit to it, and perhaps significantly alter their behavior. That doesn't mean we can't have a strong opinion, or be confident that our understanding is reasoned and informed, but it does mean we should be respectful of differing views and of the incompleteness of all knowledge, including our own.

Journal

Return to your response to the Journal Assignment immediately above and to the related readings. List several bits of statistical data from the readings and try finding other inferences that might be drawn from them. Can you find instances where definitions of phenomena shape what statistics have been presented? If so, state them and explain your reasoning.

The Working Draft: Shaping Your Thoughts

Here you will find detailed notes from student Stephan Demers's journal. They demonstrate how you might clarify difficult concepts and chart a direction for your writing by using your reactions to what you have read and your responses to what you are experiencing in class.

Excerpt from Earlier Freewrite

. . . globalization means many things to many people . . . you have winners and losers . . . for winners . . . prosperity; for losers—suffering . . . Friedman writes that the driving ideas behind this system are "deregulation," "privatization," and "free markets" Dr. L's lecture on deregulation was pretty heady stuff . . . deregulate means that no one sets limits on "free market" commerce . . . is that good or bad? . . . Consider countries without much, which only have labor and no products so people are a cheap source of production. . . . And what about the pressures globalization puts on the environment? (Review Hilary French reading even though I'm not sure I want to get into this area as a topic.)

Idea Breakdown . . .

I. Possible Advantages

— More competition increases freer trade and gives benefits like bringing down barriers on what people can buy and how they can invest . . .

— Friedman's Golden Arches Theory of globalization . . . guarantees (?) no war because no one wants to give up their prosperity. The trend is towards interdependence. . ."mutually beneficial economics" . . . no two countries ever fought a war if they both had McDonalds . . . too good to be true?

— As the globe becomes more "connected" will it raise developing countries out of poverty? . . .

— Will more friendly trade lead to valuing culture and traditions different than ours? Consider impact of laptops in Indonesian Muslim schools, effects of the Internet, etc. . . .

II. Possible Disadvantages

— Review Friedman's section on the Lexus and the Olive Tree. Friedman defines the olive tree as a person's values and traditions . . . culture and motivations . . . are they becoming Americanized? Is that good or bad? Afraid that globalization will take away those basic elements that make a culture and a person what they are.

— Review Adler reading—Mollie's Job . . . the loss of those jobs and how multinationals just keep moving the job to a cheaper location . . . making use of cheap labor leads to outsourcing U.S. jobs . . .

— Most people don't know that cheap goods means that someone is working for very little. Think WalMart . . . other big box stores . . . cut-rate goods . . . undermine competition . . . sweatshops . . .

— See article about Pennsylvania's rust belt and how the closing of the steel mills is just the beginning of manufacturing dissolving in the US. . . . Katy's comment . . . get a copy of the article from her economics class . . .

More Questions . . .

Using the double-entry notebook approach (first introduced in Chapter 1), Stephan creates a set of questions and responses.

What it is:

What fuels the globalization engine?

According to Friedman, products and people . . . free market, deregulation and privatization are probably the most important . . . I can't focus on all these. When it came up in class, someone in our group talked about colonialization and that globalization isn't necessarily a new idea . . . it's about market access and really cheap labor (China and WalMart, for example). Prof. L. mentioned this . . .

Who is most positively affected?
Who is the most negatively affected?
Why?

Americans get lots of products from places we've never heard of or been to . . . it's kind of exotic. That's some positives . . . Friedman's Golden Arches idea makes globalization sound pretty good for everyone. Something about codependency(?) sounds good but the word reminds me of being in somebody else's control. . . . And there's another side to this and that's the control part . . . somebody who doesn't play the game fairly can limit the benefits for someone who is powerless to do anything about it.

Is "deregulation" necessary for globalization to be successful?

That's the part I'm not sure about . . . this deregulation business being a part of globalization to succeed. Is it necessary to remove all the plugs so innocent people are abused and put at risk so I can have a cheap pair of socks?

What it does:

How do some people become victims and others winners in the globalization game?

Seba in Bale's story is a good example. Wanted a better life but got trapped. Since women have the least amount of power in some situations, children and a single mother would be the most at risk in this, it seems like. Mollie's Job shows how that happens in the US as well, sort of trapped into believing that if you do a good job, it will pay off . . .

Is Kevin Bales right about 27 million slaves, and if he is, what effect does it have on commerce?

I read in one of my sociology textbooks *The Third Side* that there was no slavery today . . . the author is wrong! And what about the 8 and 10 year old child soldiers that Prof. L told us about? It's not a "level playing field" when there are no regulations because people want to make a profit . . . and the most profitable resource is free human labor . . .

Besides supply and demand, what are the "rules of free markets"? Who decides about these rules and enforces them?

It seems that multinational corporations make up the rules . . . as they go. I haven't really studied NAFTA or CAFTA to know how these rules apply to our situations across the globe but I remember the sweat shop controversy with Nike shoes, so we're implicated obviously . . . like Bales says, unpaid workers definitely undermine the competition . . . One student said she was paid $15 an hour over the summer for a local factory job but didn't know where she was going to get her tuition money because the job had been "outsourced" to China or Vietnam.

What are the positive effects of globalization? How does it affect middle class Americans, or the middle class in other countries?

It seems like if you're upper middle class, then maybe globalization can work for you . . . We live in a land of plenty and don't really think about where this stuff we buy comes from unless somebody in the media decides they need a headline . . . I think the Nike controversy was exposed as a result of Michael Moore's movie *Bowling for Columbine*. So it's good that we do pay attention when someone points out this disparity to us . . . that's sort of a causal chain . . . we hear, we listen, we change our habits

Is there a "causal chain" to globalization?
Benefits or harms?

. . . but there's another part with an upside and a downside and that's what's happening in India where the technology industry has exploded causing a lot of people to be able to get out of poverty and join the middle class. . . . But this comes with a price to the higher-wage countries— Should I get into the outsourcing issue?

What to do:

Can we get freedom, peace and prosperity from a system that keeps some people down while raising the standards for others?

Globalization is complicated . . . some have-nots of the world are lifted out of misery and others are further victimized . . . India is becoming middle class. Americans can buy cheaper goods and so have money for other uses . . . At the same time, China actually holds our currency afloat because we have a trading deficit . . . The answer may be about the kinds of rules we are willing to abide by . . . if we could consciously think about the costs of what we buy . . . or what we take from a country's

> natural resources . . . maybe what it even costs them in terms of losing their culture. . . . again, I'm back to the regulating and the deregulating conundrum . . . Grrrr . . .

Journal Activity

Drawing on Stephan's journal work, explore some strategies to clarify what you want your essay to accomplish. Your work should culminate in a completed first draft. As you work through this "developmental stage," do not hesitate to experiment with different arrangements. Your goal is to find the one in which each idea leads smoothly to the next. During your explorations, jot down the new ideas that come to mind and decide whether you should incorporate them.

Collaborative Activity

Join with others in small groups to exchange drafts of your papers. At this early stage, do not stop to correct spelling or grammar errors and do not worry about how the drafts sound. Instead of focusing on style, center your discussion on each writer's ideas. Determine their significance and discover how well they are supported. As you comment on each other's work, remember to offer support and encouragement. Consider, also, the following:

- Look to see how effectively the writer has incorporated the types of support covered earlier in the chapter—examples, statistics, and testimony. Remember that a detailed discussion of source material is critical to the effectiveness of an essay. Do not assume that a reader will automatically follow each writer's line of thought. The writer has the responsibility for effortlessly moving the reader from point to point. Each supporting detail must have adequate discussion—at least a sentence or two—to show how it relates to the writer's position.

- Evaluate whether the supporting material will engage a reader's imagination, curiosity, and interest and determine whether it adds strength and credibility to the writer's ideas.

Below are peer critiques of excerpts from Stephan's working draft that are followed by Stephan's revisions.

Peer Critique #1: Can you make "things" and "many" more concrete and not so repetitive? Also, "consuming side" is confusing.

DRAFT

Globalization <u>means many things to many people.</u> There is no doubt that for those lucky enough to be in the northern hemisphere and be middle class or above it means <u>good things</u>. <u>There are</u> winners elsewhere as well; globalization has created a middle class in parts of the world that few Americans can find on a map. For the vast majority of the world, however, globalization has created the same suffering seen since the days of colonialism. For those not fortunate enough to be on the <u>consuming side</u> of globalization a grim reality exists.

Stephan's Response: I got rid of the wordiness and used more specific terms to make my point clearer . . . You were right; the phrase "consuming side" leaves the reader wondering how to interpret that statement.

REVISION

Globalization. Big term. Larger meaning. But what exactly does it mean to the average American? Clearly, for those lucky enough to be in the northern hemisphere, and be middle class or above, globalization means human possibility and economic prosperity. We find winners elsewhere as well; globalization has created a middle class in parts of the world that few Americans can locate on a map. For the vast majority of the world, however, globalization has created the same suffering seen since the days of colonialism. For those not fortunate enough to be able to afford to buy even the goods they make, the reality is grim.

Peer Critique #2: Because Friedman is a central source for your argument, maybe you could introduce him early in your discussion to establish his credibility.

DRAFT

When people want to point to successes of globalization, chances are that they will be quick to mention the "Golden Arches Theory of Conflict Prevention" (Friedman 249). The name, a tongue in cheek reference to the fact that no two countries which both have McDonalds have ever fought a war against each other, does raise an interesting point. Globalization has created an environment in which countries are too economically codependent not to settle peacefully. The financial benefits of global trade outweigh any benefits of winning a war in most cases.

Stephan's Response: I realize that Friedman's expert testimony helps to justify some of my claims. In fact, I use The Lexus and the Olive Tree . . . later but I don't mention Friedman's credentials. So you're right; I should show that he is a reliable source.

REVISION

When people want to point to globalization's successes, chances are that they will quickly mention the "Golden Arches Theory of Conflict Prevention," a metaphor coined by *New York Times* columnist Thomas Friedman (*The Lexus and The Olive Tree*, 2000, 249). The metaphor, a tongue in cheek reference to the fact that no two countries which both have McDonalds have ever fought a war against each other, does raise an interesting point. Globalization has created an environment in which countries are often too economically codependent not to settle disputes peacefully. The financial benefits of global trade outweigh the costs of winning a war in most cases.

Peer Critique #3: China can be a good illustration for your point, but you need examples to support your statement. Saudi Arabia has a high rate of trained people with no available work, so I wonder how buying our oil from them contributes to this abysmal situation? You also use the word "codependence" and not "interdependence." Maybe you could clarify the difference here?

DRAFT

Codependence can come with a hefty price tag though. The United States holds trading ties with countries with practices most Americans would consider medieval. The list is long, but the first to come to mind is China. America turns a blind eye to China's abysmal working conditions, totalitarian government, and human rights abuses. Cheaply priced Chinese goods have given Americans a lifestyle which they are not ready to surrender. Similarly, America not only tolerates but supports Saudi Arabia, a monarchy. America is willing to support a monarchy because in return Saudi Arabia gives America access to their oil.

Stephan's Response: I had a general idea from class discussions about the role these two countries played in negative aspects of globalization, so adding real "data" from my library web research increased the support for my point for sure. I didn't exactly focus on the cause-effect relationship you asked about or the difference between codependence and interdependence. But thanks; your comments did get me to think about something I hadn't really thought about.

REVISION

But codependence can come with a hefty price tag, if not economically, certainly ethically. The United States holds trading ties with countries whose practices by American standards would be considered medieval. The list is long, but the first to come to mind is China. America turns a blind eye to China's abysmal working conditions, totalitarian government, and human rights abuses. In the last ten years, reports have underscored the seedier problems inherent in our trading partner's treatment of people. See, for example, "Women as Chattel: In China, Slavery Rises" (Faison). Nevertheless, cheaply priced Chinese goods have given Americans a lifestyle that they are not ready to surrender. Certainly no moral or ethical questions about business partners who currently own an estimated $900 billion dollars in American debt seem forthcoming.

Similarly, America not only tolerates but also supports Saudi Arabia, a monarchy whose foreign workers, comprising about a third of their population, "face torture, forced confessions, and unfair trials when they are accused of crimes" (Human Rights Watch). America is willing to support such a monarchy because in return Saudi Arabia gives America access to their oil.

Peer Critique #4: You're emphasizing the evidence here and not the source, a strategy which features the quoted material. I think this strategy could have been effective if you had already certified Bales as an expert. Also your last sentence seems misplaced.

DRAFT

. . . A conservative estimate from 2000 puts the number of slaves in the world at 27 million. As the author of that figure puts it "No paid workers, no matter how efficient, can compete economically with unpaid workers — slaves" (Bales 344). A very widespread trend in globalization is the export of secure, well paying jobs in western nations to places where the work can be done at a significantly lower cost with less regulation.

Stephan's Response: I originally had placed Bales earlier in the essay before Friedman but I needed Friedman first to introduce the Golden Arches, so I rearranged my paragraphs. In my next draft, I will mention Bales's credentials in my introduction to his study. Also, I will put the last sentence before the Bales quote and link it to the loss of middle class jobs.

Peer Critique #5: This section seems thin without some "data" to support your claims of prosperity.

DRAFT

For some people, even in the worst parts of the world, globalization has proved that it has a positive side. It has brought technology and opportunity all over the world. India, for instance, has seen exponential growth in its middle class. Americans are getting their goods and services from places they cannot pronounce. And in return, some of those places are becoming better places to live. Middle class life is becoming a reality for people in places that a generation ago, did not have a basic infrastructure.

Stephan's Response: I could probably add more countries to this passage and show more instances of increasing growth, but for my purposes, I think giving the percentage increase in India supports my point.

REVISION

For some people, even in the most economically depressed parts of the world, globalization has demonstrated a positive side. It has brought technology and opportunity all over the world. India, for instance, has seen exponential growth in its middle class. Manufacturing in India has grown at over a 10% rate (Thakurta 1). Ironically, Americans, whose exports are often seen as one-dimensional, are getting their goods and services from places they cannot even pronounce. And in return, some of those places are becoming better places to live. Middle class life is becoming a reality for people in places that a generation ago, did not have a basic infrastructure.

Researching the Broader Context

As you consider your options for further research you may find it useful to consider human resources near at hand. (This might be a good time to review the approaches covered in Chapter 5, including the interview, first-hand investigation, and the survey/questionnaire.) There are numerous other research options that can help you take a more critical stance towards the ideas you want to use to develop your paper. For example, since all the readings in Chapter 8 have been taken from the writers' larger works, you could explore those texts. This kind of research can be rewarding if you are particularly drawn to a given author's writing and wish to see the broader context of the selected reading. This research-by-immersion is also useful if you sense some ambiguity or incompleteness in one or more readings.

Should you decide to supplement your resources by conducting library research, you will need to develop an effective search strategy.

Library Research

Libraries contain vast resources of written materials, including news and academic journals, newspapers, texts, studies, theses and dissertations, and many other pieces of writing by scholars and experts, recorded either on the printed page or on a computer file. In library research, you study the *literature* of your topic by reading what a wide variety of authors have to say about it. Through familiarizing yourself with the literature, mastering the major concepts, and evaluating the various arguments and viewpoints about your topic, you become a kind of expert, able to take and defend an informed position. Because library resources are vast, it is important to conduct your research in an efficient and systematic fashion.

The following discussion of library research traces the experience of student Stephan Demers who, after reading the selections on globalization in Chapter 8, decided to conduct his own research.

❑ *Using Key Terms*

Stephan extracted from his reading several key terms he could use to begin his library research.

globalization	outsourcing	cheap goods
deregulation	job loss	slave labor
free markets		

With key terms in hand, Stephan logged on to the college library website and entered a number of different combinations into two of the available databases (Academic Search Premier, ProQuest, Wilson OmniFile, and MasterFile Premier).

globalization/job loss
job loss/deregulation/outsourcing
outsourcing/slave labor/globalization
free markets/job loss/cheap goods

A Caveat

If you were to enter only the word *globalization*, you would begin a subject search that instructed the computer to scan the collective memory of all library systems to which the computer is tied for references to that word. You would soon be stunned by the staggering number of entries—studies, dissertations, theses, newspaper and journal articles, and entire texts, numbering in the many thousands and written in dozens of languages—generated by this single term, *globalization.* Repeating the same process with another term, *free markets*, and finding the same result, you would presumably realize that each single term was too broad to generate a list of manageable references. After consulting a librarian, you might combine some of your terms, entering combinations such as

> globalization/deregulation
> globalization/outsourcing
> globalization/free markets

Still, this approach would likely turn up hundreds of sources. Only by further combining terms as Stephan did, could you narrow the search to approximate more closely your specific interests. Using combinations of key terms to narrow the focus of a topic is an effective technique for tracking down information.

It should be noted that in one database, EBSCO, Stephan was surprised to find an alternative key phrase for *labor*. The phrase *human capital* linked *labor* to information closer to one of his research interests, globalization and slavery. Learning how databases articulate important terms is an important skill to learn. Most researchers will tell you that the best way to learn these skills is to practice doing them.

❑ *Collecting Information*

Generally, when writing a major research paper, keep in mind that your goals should be

- to get a feeling for the existing knowledge on your topic through a review of the general relevant literature and
- to select those specific references that would best serve your research.

These two goals are important to the research process. First, as a researcher you need to become generally informed about your chosen subject. Reviewing the existing literature can help you to understand how academics and other authorities are considering that subject. Such awareness prepares you to join in the conversations about the subject. Second, you need to start selecting your source materials, identifying those that contain relevant information and weeding out those that, however interesting they may be, do not seem to meet the needs of your paper.

After experimenting with various word combinations from his list of terms, Stephan eventually came up with a number of journal and newspaper references that could serve as additional sources for his paper. He had already located some books that related to his topic and because one was on reserve, he had to photocopy relevant pages, marking title, author, publisher, date, and page numbers so he wouldn't have to return to the library to get this information.

Once Stephan had decided on the best resources to extend his discussion and support his argument, he recorded brief summaries of the works and the page numbers of especially useful material.

In a major research project, library work—on the library web or in the library building itself—can take many hours over several days. When you block out time for your research, choose hours when you have no distractions and no schedule conflicts. Allow for the fact that you may need several visits. If you're doing major research, beginning well ahead of your paper's due date allows you to choose your sources wisely, even to be somewhat selective about your sources. A late starter often finds that other students have already signed out the most useful resources, particularly in the last weeks of a semester when many students are writing research papers.

❑ *Creating A Working Bibliography*

Back in his room, Stephan wrote down a list of the sources he had selected, including full bibliographical information for each. This working bibliography is a tentative list of reference sources that will be used in the research paper. A working bibliography is important for several reasons. First, it gives you a quick glance at the writers and sources you plan to use, or at least to try out. Also, when you need to check quickly the name of a writer or the title of a source, you can simply glance at the list rather than look for the volume. Most importantly, it ensures that you have a record of all on-reserve titles from which you will have to make photocopies. If, at the last moment, you discovered that you lacked bibliographical information, you would have to return to the library to track these titles down again, from computer search to shelf hunt, in order to construct your final bibliography. Whenever you cannot or do not sign out a source or sources at the library, write down, as Stephan did, the bibliographical information in your notes before you leave the library.

As your paper evolves, you may eliminate sources for a variety of reasons, including the following.

- The information in a particular source may duplicate that of a better source.
- The information in a source may not be relevant to the paper.
- During the writing process your paper may change focus, rendering some of your original sources irrelevant.

You also may discover important new sources at a later time and include them in your working bibliography. It is important to list all sources, even those that do not come from the library. Had Stephan conducted an interview or administered a survey (See Chapter 5, pp. 153–155), these would also have been included in his working bibliography. Stephan's working bibliography follows.

WORKING BIBLIOGRAPHY

Bales, Kevin. *Disposable People*. Berkeley: U of California P, 2004. Print.

Faison, Seth. "Women as Chattel: In China, Slavery Rises." *New York Times* 6 Sept. 1995: A1. Print.

Friedman, Thomas. *The Lexus and the Olive Tree*. New York: Anchor Books-A Division of Random House, Inc., 2000. Print.

Human Rights Watch. *Saudi Arabia: Foreign Workers Abused. Human Rights Watch*. Human Rights Watch. 15 July 2004. Web. 29 Oct. 2006.

Kirchhoff, Sue. "U.S. Manufacturers vs China," *USA Today*, 1 July 2003: 4b. *Academic SearchPremier*. Web. 24 Oct. 2006.

Thakurta, Paranjoy Guha. "India's Double-Digit Dream" *Asia Times On-Line*. Asia Times On-Line. 24 Oct. 2006. Web. 3 Nov. 2006.

❏ *Evaluating Your Sources*

With reference materials in hand, you must identify each writer's positions, organizational approaches, and thought processes. Furthermore, while reading, you must continually remind yourself that you are not attempting to make a thorough report or a critical analysis of each text, but rather to extract from the text only information useful to your work. To approach each source critically and analytically, ask yourself the following questions.

1. What is the main purpose of the reading?

2. Is the discussion an argument? If so, what is the main claim? What are the subordinate claims, if any? What data are offered to support the claims? Are the data relevant and timely? Are they accurate?

3. Is the reading designed solely to inform? If so, is the information timely? Does the writer show any obvious biases or ignore pertinent considerations? Are the sources of information credible?

4. Is the article merely an expression of personal opinion offered without support, that is, without data? Is the writer credible? Is he or she a recognized expert in the field? What experience or credentials does the writer have?

5. Are there words I do not understand and need to look up in the dictionary?

6. What are the specific ideas that relate to my work?

7. Where does the writer summarize the major points I want to use?

Interacting with Texts

As you read various texts and try to establish and refine your own critical voice, the volume of texts and the possible interpretations facing you may lead you to wonder how to engage in meaningful dialogue with all these voices. Remember, though, that when you read, just as when you write, you are involved in a rhetorical situation. Earlier in Chapter 7, you looked at the rhetorical triangle from the perspective of the writer. Now cast yourself in the role of the reader.

As you've seen in previous chapters, your reading of a text is, in a sense, an earnest conversation with its author. Consider how you approach a conversation with a new friend. You don't know much about the person yet; but you know enough to want to spend time in developing the relationship and engaging in conversation. You have a certain respect for your friend, based solely on your recognition of him or her as a human being, much like you, with individual experiences, perceptions, and values. But you also approach the situation with a gentle and friendly skepticism. In other words, you do not blindly accept your partner's assertions; rather, you weigh them against your own experiences and ideas. Consequently, the meanings you take away from the encounter are not the simple products of your passive reception of what your friend has said; they grow out of the interaction between your partner's thoughts and your own. You have actively engaged that person, and he or she has engaged you.

You should similarly actively engage a text as you read it. Try to discern the purpose of the text and the level of commitment it asks of you. Use the reading experience to clarify your own beliefs. Weigh the assertions, whether directly stated or implied by the writer, against your own values and perceptions. When they conflict, don't immediately reject or accept either. Rather, follow the conflict as it progresses so you can decide whether to ultimately accept or reject certain notions, yours or the writer's. Possibly you will reconcile the conflict and achieve a synthesis out of which new ideas can grow. In any case, the process of engaging the text will foster your intellectual growth and enhance your understanding of yourself and the world—but only if you participate.

Journal Activity

Select a reading from Chapter 8 or from a related source. It need not be an article that has an obvious point of view, but it should be a piece of writing you find intriguing. Often, the most rewarding readings are those that first elicit a nonspecific response; we know there is something about them that speaks to us, but we are at a loss to say exactly what it is. Reread the selection, making your second reading as interactive and collaborative as you can. As you write responses to the following questions in your journal, you may begin to see what is important to you in the reading.

- What values, beliefs, and feelings do you already have that determine your initial response to the subject of the text?

- What level of response or commitment does the text seem to want from you? Does it simply want you to understand a point of view? Is it asking you to accept that point of view to the exclusion of competing ideas? Or is it trying to get you to change your behavior or take some action?

- How much initial resistance do you have to the message communicated by the text?

- What strategies does it use to try to overcome that resistance and influence your judgment? Does it clarify vague or tentative perceptions you may have had before reading it? If so, how? Does it try to extend your understanding of the subject? If so, how? Does it try to get you to restructure any of your beliefs or attitudes? If so, how?

- What will you risk by accepting its point of view?

- What qualifies the writer of this text as an authority? What moral and intellectual credibility does he or she bring to the issue?

You will answer some of these questions easily as you read; others may be more difficult. It may help to remember that these questions are interdependent; that is, the answer to many of them depends on the answers to others. While the complex process of opening up a text may seem challenging at first, asking questions such as these is an important part of bringing that text to life and making it a catalyst for your thinking.

Collaborative Activity

Pair up with a classmate who chose a different reading than you did for the previous journal activity. Working out of class do the journal activity again, this time using your partner's reading. At the next class meeting, discuss your and your partner's responses to each of the two readings. Make note of similarities and differences in your responses.

Then, in discussion, try to discover potential reasons in your backgrounds for the differences in your responses. For example, you can pay attention to:

- The nature of your home towns: Note the potential differences in population, principle industries, principle sources of recreation, tenor of the general political consciousness, opportunities for cultural experiences (museums, concerts, plays, etc), important geographical features of the area (lakes, mountains, caves), and any other features that seem interesting or significant.

- Your secondary education: Note potential differences in the size of the schools, courses available (especially courses focused on politics, philosophy, religion, cultural awareness, etc.), cultural education and productions available, campus clubs and organizations, policies regarding student behaviors (e.g. dress codes, etc.).

- The characteristics of your families. For example, were your families conventional families, with both parents in the home; or were they single-parent families; or were they structured in some other less conventional fashion? What family members were included in the household? How many siblings were included in your household; what was your position in the birth order; what was the nature of your relationship with your siblings?

Obviously, there are many characteristics in your backgrounds that you and your partner could consider as potential reasons for the differences in your responses. Once you've considered a number, try to write a general statement that explains the most significant reasons for the difference in each response.

Finally, consider and note what changes the writers might have made in the readings to illicit a more uniform response from both you and your partner.

Questions

1. How has comparing experiences with a classmate helped you better understand pivotal patterns and habits you practice as a reader?

2. Have you discovered any new approaches you wish to apply? Be specific.

Follow Up: Moving Toward a Public Draft

The following discussion concluding with Guidelines for Assessing Your Writing reinforces how the rhetorical and logical devices in the chapter can be put to work on your essay to ensure you achieve the goals you've set. You should also check to be sure that your thesis is clear in concept and that the wording reflects that clarity of thinking.

Putting Yourself in the Reader's Mind

Earlier in Chapter 7, we noted that much of our rhetorical activity is aimed at reducing our audience's perception of threat, and at making the audience more open to alternative perspectives. Here we suggest that you can reduce your readers' resistance by showing your willingness to examine opposing lines of thought. It must be a genuine willingness and not just a technique, a face you put on for your readers.

Your openness will show your readers that you understand the complicated nature of the issues and recognize that people of good will and intelligence will feel threatened or confused, whatever your position. Earning your audience's respect entails a real commitment on your part. When you care deeply about an issue, your passions must be tempered by a thoughtful deliberation, one that acknowledges your understanding of the dynamic taking place between writer and reader.

In your professional and private life, you will undoubtedly confront ethical challenges, situations in which you feel obliged to change the understanding of an audience. You will have to convince them through the same rhetorical dynamic that operates all the time, at all levels—in the family, with your loved ones and friends, in classes, and through public forums. At all levels, it is a matter of getting the right hearing, making yourself understood, persuading people to believe what you tell them, and then, sometimes, convincing them to act accordingly.

Journal Activity

In conjunction with the following collaborative activity, this exercise can help you gain further insight into the potential responses an audience might have to your argument. Begin by writing down your argument and the characteristics of your intended audience.

Collaborative Activity

Next, present the conclusions of your argument to class members. Make clear to the group how you define your intended audience so that classmates can take on roles as diverse members of this audience. You should include readers who are actively hostile to your message, others who are skeptical of your viewpoint, and some who simply don't care about it. You will also want to consider how to address those readers who are not well enough informed to understand your argument. One group member should just observe these interactions between writer and prospective readers and make notes that can help you find ways to argue more persuasively.

Your classmates' responses can help you to gauge the impact of your message—which points might demand restructuring of your readers' beliefs and attitudes, for example. Their responses can also show you what points need to be expressed more clearly. Remember that when you write about an issue, you need to provide your readers with the same standards of organization, argument, and support that you would expect to encounter during your own reading of a text.

Strengthening the Integrity of Your Argument

When you most fervently want to get a favorable hearing from your audience, you face an enormously challenging task. Issues will get complicated because many voices will be raised for or against anything you say. But if you do your work well and remain alert and open to new ideas—which includes listening to others whose work in a specific field has given them greater knowledge and expertise—then your message, and thus your own authority, will become stronger.

Two concepts, *refutation* and *accommodation*, are fundamental to the integrity of any argument.* If you cannot imagine the possibility that your argument can be refuted, most likely you have immersed yourself too deeply in a single viewpoint. When you do this, it can be intellectually damaging in several important ways. First, and most importantly, it denies you the opportunity of testing out your ideas against the experience of others when those ideas are in a formative stage. We have a powerful human tendency to "see what we want to see." That old folk saying "There is no one so blind as he who will not see" is psychologically very accurate. We've discussed that tendency to "defend" our ways of knowing earlier. Psychologists have called the process

---

*We wish to acknowledge Jeanne Fahnestock and Marie Secor (A *Rhetoric of Argument*, 2nd ed., 1990) whose work contributed to our treatment of these rhetorical aspects of argument.

by which we do that "selective perception." By that they mean we generally focus on aspects of a situation that support our perception and ignore those aspects that do not—and we often do this without being aware we are doing it. Or, we seek out the "weakest" counter-arguments or arguers, hoping and expecting to easily dismiss their inadequacies. Ideally, we should seek out the strongest opposing views in order to test the strength and accuracy of our own. Then, if our argument still seems logical and supportable, we can have more confidence in the accuracy of our position. And if it doesn't, why, then, we have a chance to re-think and perhaps modify our claims before we must present and "defend" them. Secondly, if we examine these contrary ways of knowing and still decide our position is a strong, even a superior, one, we now have the ability to bring up these other ideas on our own terms, in our own way. Instead of waiting for our audience to "think" of them or raise them in their own way, when we can't respond, we can anticipate them ourselves by indicating "Though some have argued that . . . nevertheless I believe that my proposal. . . ."

Because you may have a skeptical, doubting audience, you will want to do everything you can to ensure a fair hearing, including accommodation. Earlier in Chapter 7, you considered the kinds of adjustments you tried to get an audience to make in order to advance your own viewpoint. At this point, you will need to think about the kinds of compromises you may have to make to enlist the good will of your audience. Some people think compromise means conceding, but others see it as the only solution in a complicated world with differing viewpoints. Compromise, in this latter view, is not a matter of acquiescing and losing; it's a matter of trying to ensure your reader's willingness to consider your viewpoint. It is a complicated but honorable endeavor.

Accommodation in argument can take several rhetorical forms. The first is related to refutation. It involves not only considering opposite viewpoints and then refuting them, but letting the audience know that these viewpoints have been fairly considered, that they, too, have their merits and supporters and could be valid in certain conditions, and that the people holding them are assumed to be both intelligent and honorable. In this sense, the accommodation is one of attitude and tone—what we sometimes hear expressed in a debate as "I respectfully disagree." After all, there may be a number of people in our audience seeking to refute our position. Wouldn't we want them to consider carefully and fairly what we are arguing rather than simply refute or dismiss it?

A second way that accommodation works in argument has to do with how qualified—how extensive or limited—we want our claims to be. If we say "Every" or "All" or "Always," do we really intend to mean that there are no exceptions, ever? Are we that certain? Does "all the evidence" past and present indicate that degree of certainty? Would saying "Most" or "Many" or "Some" harm or distort the accuracy of our position? This matter of how inclusive we want our claims about complex matters to be is itself complex. By attempting to be fair and cautious, will we seem weak or uncertain? If we are confident of our position will we seem arrogant if we say so? If we say "all" or "always" and someone comes up with a single "valid" exception, will our argument be "refuted" despite its overwhelming accuracy? These are more than games about language, about "manipulating" an audience, about "mere" rhetoric. They go to the heart of what it means to debate and discuss issues of importance to readers and writers, to members of various discourse communities, and to citizens of a democracy.

Collaborative Activity

Imagine yourself out of school and well into your career. Now imagine a specific situation in which you will have to somehow change the understanding of a hostile or threatened audience. What ethical challenges are involved? How will you go about achieving your goal?

Journal Activity

Return to the essay you've been working on in response to the Major Essay Assignment in Chapter 8. Begin by stating the tentative thesis you generated in the exploratory draft you wrote earlier in this chapter. Now you want to refine your idea of your audience and what you need to do to achieve your goal. If you're like most students, you're thinking that it's obvious your audience is your instructor. To some degree, that's true, but you should keep a couple of points in mind:

- Your instructor will be evaluating your paper as if it were written for a larger audience, perhaps a much larger audience.

- Most of the writing that you do in your graduate work or in your profession may be for that larger audience, so you need to get used to thinking in those terms.

- In this class the collaborative work will provide you with a whole room full of classmates that will serve as your audience.

In short, you need to learn to write effectively for audiences of different sizes and with different characteristics.

You've already dealt fairly extensively with audience concerns in Chapter 7; it might be worth your time to review that material, specifically pp. 221–229. However, you have the two new issues discussed above to consider—refutation and accommodation. You should be able to answer the following questions about your argument:

- How difficult (or easy) would it be to refute your argument?

- What steps can you take to make that refutation more difficult, especially if your audience is likely to be hostile to your point of view?

- To what degree do you need to accommodate an audience's point of view (even a hostile one) by qualifying your claims?

Try applying these concepts to your existing draft. In your journal, answer the questions above; and in your draft make the changes needed to account for concerns of refutation and accommodation.

Preparing Your Final Draft

While you are not expected to adhere slavishly to the following guidelines, understanding the principles involved can help you prepare a well-considered analysis.

First consider what you want to achieve with your introduction. As well as introducing your readers to the subject or problem and drawing attention to its importance, this part of your essay should provide any necessary context (history or background) for the subject and identify opposing lines of thought that need to be considered. It's also a good idea to try to establish some common ground with readers—identifying shared beliefs, attitudes, or experiences—to more easily relate your position to the readers' interests or desires.

The body of your essay should clearly state the claims you want your readers to understand and should support these assertions with expert testimony, facts, statistics, and the authority of your own personal experiences. Your readers will be more willing to consider your position if you are careful to explain your reasoning throughout, that is, if you clearly show how your position logically follows from your supporting material.

Exercise

Try to organize your claims into similar levels of generality. For example, a specific detail or fact—statistical datum, direct quote, concrete example—will be at the lowest level of generality. A broader judgment, while not as broad as your thesis, will be at a higher level of generality than a statement of fact.

Now find the claims that are most general and most directly support or develop your thesis. Try these out as main points by trying to organize them in such a way that they logically support or develop your thesis. Then, one by one, go to the lower levels of generality, making connections wherever you can. Finally, try to combine all your points into an outline that looks something like this:

Thesis

I. Subordinate supporting claim
    A. Lower level subordinate claim
        1. supporting fact or detail
        2. supporting fact or detail
    B. Lower level supporting claim
        1. supporting fact or detail
        2. supporting fact or detail
II. Subordinate supporting claim and so on

> **Important note:** This is just one of many possible structures. It just happens to be the most common. However, you shouldn't limit your own creativity by slavishly following any particular structure. Remember though, that in whatever structure you create, more general or abstract claims should invariably be supported or developed by claims that are less general and/or more concrete.

Sometimes it is not enough simply to handle your side of the case effectively. It may also be necessary to acknowledge opposing views and consider them critically. If you can identify flaws in their premises or assumptions, or weakness in their evidence, you will strengthen the credibility of your stance. This doesn't mean that you should only use opposing views to find fault. You should grant merit to the opposition when and if such merit is due, often by admitting possible exceptions to your claims. Making honest concessions tells your readers that you have thought carefully about each contending perspective and that you are trying hard to be fair.

Your conclusion should provide a graceful exit from the paper. Effective writers often use the conclusion to recapitulate the steps involved in formulating their arguments. The conclusion also offers you an opportunity to close with a strong appeal for support of your position. Such an appeal often mentions the broader implications of your argument, including the benefits that would be gained and the consequences that would be avoided by accepting your viewpoint.

Reviewing a Student Essay

Here is the final draft written by the student whose journal entries earlier in the chapter modeled the kind of developmental work students engage in as they write and think through their ideas. The annotations combined with the follow-up questions lead to a thorough analysis of important aspects of this essay.

1. The title uses the strong word "losers," and indicates a focus on the effects of globalization and perhaps an evaluation of those effects.

2. Though the opening makes direct reference to the meaning of globalization, Stephan does not supply a working definition for the reader before moving to an analysis of its effects. Perhaps he is assuming that his readers will have read the articles in the chapter beforehand.

1.

2.

Stephan Demers   Demers 1

EXP 101, Section 9

December 3, 2006

Globalization's Biggest Losers

Globalization. Big term. But what exactly does it mean to the average American? Clearly, for those lucky enough to be in the northern hemisphere, and be middle class or above, globalization means human possibility and economic prosperity. We find winners elsewhere as well; globalization has created a middle class in parts of the world that few Americans can locate on a map. However, for the vast majority of the world, globalization has created the same suffering and vulnerable

Demers 2

economic status that was once linked to colonialism. For those not fortunate enough to afford to buy even the goods they make, the reality is grim. Globalization defines poverty not as a human tragedy, but as a commodity called cheap labor. This natural resource is extorted wherever it can be found for the lowest price and used without remorse to provide cheap goods and wider profit margins.

3. Here Stephan suggests that the consequences of globalization are both vitally important and still unresolved. Perhaps this focus on importance and uncertainty could have been signaled more clearly in the title.

3. As globalization spreads, like wildfire, to the farthermost reaches of the earth, the future of billions of people hangs in the balance. In the next several decades globalization will either divide the entire world along class lines, or connect the world in unprecedented ways, giving rise to peace and global prosperity.

4. Stephan begins his discussion of the positive and negative effects of globalization with reference to Friedman's well-known metaphor in favor of globalization.

4. When people want to point to globalization's successes, chances are that they will quickly mention the "Golden Arches Theory of Conflict Prevention," a metaphor coined by *New York Times* editorialist Thomas Friedman (249). The metaphor, a tongue in cheek reference to the fact that no two countries which both have McDonalds have ever fought a war against each other, does raise an interesting point. Globalization has created an environment in which countries are often too economically codependent not to settle disputes peacefully. In most cases, the financial benefits of global trade outweigh the costs of winning a war.

5. He immediately follows this with a series of negative consequences, beginning with conditions in China.

5. But codependence can come with a hefty price tag, if not economically, certainly ethically. The United States holds trading ties with countries whose practices by American standards are considered medieval. The list is long, but the first to come to mind is China. America turns a blind eye to China's abysmal working conditions, totalitarian government, and human rights abuses. In the last ten years, reports have underscored the seedier problems inherent in our trading partner's treatment of people. See, for example, "Women as Chattel: In China, Slavery Rises" (Faison). Nevertheless, cheaply priced Chinese goods have given Americans a lifestyle that they are not ready to surrender. Certainly no moral or ethical questions seem forthcoming about business partners who currently own an estimated $900 billion dollars in American debt.

6. Stephan next uses a citation from Human Rights Watch to describe the plight of workers in Saudi Arabia.

6. Similarly, America not only tolerates but also supports Saudi Arabia, a monarchy whose foreign workers, comprising about a third of their population, "face torture, forced confessions and unfair trials when they are accused of crimes" (Human Rights Watch). America is willing to support such a monarchy because in return Saudi Arabia gives America access to their oil.

Some argue that having an open and free market will lead to freedom, peace and prosperity for the world. The people who make this claim are seldom the people on the losing end of these free markets. And yet, losers abound, even in America. The manufacturing base that birthed America's middle class is disappearing. As the jobs evaporate, so goes the ability for undereducated Americans to secure a middle class future. The export of secure, well paying jobs in Western nations to third world countries where work can be done at a significantly lower cost with less regulation is a hallmark of globalization. And yet, even the heartbreak of America's rustbelt pales when we compare conditions across the globe.

7. Take, for example, a conservative estimate by Kevin Bales, a social scientist who has studied slavery worldwide; he puts the number of slaves at 27 million. Bales writes, "No paid workers, no matter how efficient, can compete economically with unpaid workers — slaves" (344).

8. Perhaps if globalization were more of an equal playing field then more people would be willing to accept the free market concept as a beneficial one. Alas, this is not the case. For those people on the losing end, globalization much more resembles Americanization than anything else. While the flow of information and culture does go both ways to a degree, the overwhelming truth of globalization is the spread of American culture and commerce. There is a backlash to this, not by a radical fringe, but by everyday people who see their own culture threatened by imposing American standards and culture. This has been especially true in the Middle East where American culture strongly clashes with the cultural roots of a region. The result has been a backlash against the West, and a return to traditional conservative religious roots. As one Egyptian quoted in *The Lexus and the Olive Tree* expresses it, "Does globalization mean that we all have to become Americans?" (Friedman 340).

Conversely, for some people, even in the most economically depressed parts of the world, globalization has demonstrated a positive side. It has brought technology and opportunity all over the world. India, for instance, has seen exponential growth in its middle class. Manufacturing in India has grown at over a 10% rate (Thakurta). Ironically,

7. Stephan concludes the discussion of the harmful effects of globalization by referring to Kevin Bales's discussion of modern slavery.

8. Here, Stephan begins his summary and conclusion, again indicating both the uncertainty of the current situation and its importance by beginning his paragraphs with the words "Perhaps" and "Conversely."

Demers 4

Americans, whose exports are often seen as one-dimensional, are getting their goods and services from places they cannot even pronounce. And in return, some of those places are becoming better places to live. Middle class life is becoming a reality for people in places that a generation ago did not have a basic infrastructure.

Globalization is clearly a double-edged sword. To say that it is a negative force would be to condemn something that certainly has brought about some positive changes. To say that it is a fundamentally good thing at this time, however, would be naïve. Regardless, globalization is a force as powerful and universal as gravity. Barring global war, this generation will see global commerce and communication become an absolute and integral part of life.

9. Stephan then makes even more explicit these aspects by using the term "ups and downs," and suggests that he believes that with time and effort globalization can fulfill its promise.

9.

Given its ups and downs, globalization can be adjusted to insure that its imprint worldwide can benefit everyone. To do this, America and its multinational companies must figure how to give capitalism a conscience. This can start by setting global standards for the way factories are run and salaries are determined. It is in everyone's long-term interest, if not in the short-term interest, to ensure that workers all over the world are paid a livable wage. Terrorism and extremism rarely flourish in places where people feel that they have a lot to lose.

Freeing ourselves from questionable alliances and practices through energy independence is another way Western nations can ethically support globalization. If America can break free of its dependence on Middle Eastern oil, it will finally be able to let its values be reflected in its policy.

As Friedman puts it, "As the country that benefits most from today's global integration — as the country whose people, products, values, technologies and ideas are being most globalized — it is our job to make sure that globalization is sustainable" (437). Modern globalization is in many ways the child of the United States. As it spreads and flourishes, it is our responsibility to make sure that it grows into something beneficial for the world, not just for a select few.

Works Cited

Bales, Kevin. *Disposable People*. Berkeley: U of California P, 2004. Print.

Faison, Seth. "Women as Chattel: In China, Slavery Rises." *New York Times* 6 Sept. 1995: A1. Print.

Demers 5

Friedman, Thomas. *The Lexus and the Olive Tree*. New York: Anchor
Books-A Division of Random House, Inc., 2000. Print.

Human Rights Watch. *Saudi Arabia: Foreign Workers Abused. Human
Rights Watch.* Human Rights Watch. 15 July 2004. Web. 29 Oct.
2006.

Thakurta, Paranjoy Guha. "India's Double-Digit Dream." *Asia Times On-
Line*. Asia Times On-Line. 24 Oct. 2006. *Web*. 3 Nov. 2006.

Questions

1. How effective is Stephan's introduction to his topic? Explain.

2. Stephan moves into a discussion of the ethical considerations of globalization. Do you think he has prepared the reader well for this focus? Why or why not?

3. What do you think Stephan most wants the reader to understand? Which claims seem the most important and how well are they presented and supported?

4. Do you think Stephan does a good job of handling more than one side to this complicated issue? Explain.

5. Has his essay clarified, extended or restructured any of your own thinking about globalization? If so, how? If not, why not?

Guidelines for Assessing Your Writing

As you begin your final draft use the following questions to determine if your writing holds up rhetorically and logically. Remember that your position should result from a careful and open-minded consideration of all relevant issues. If you merely parrot a position that you have always held, you need to do more reading and thinking.

1. Do you consider various positions on your topic that your readers may already hold?

2. Do you actively seek a particular degree of engagement (understanding, belief or appropriate action) from your audience? What strategies (clarifying, extending, restructuring) do you use to achieve that degree of engagement?

3. If you wish to change your readers' minds, do you make some effort to reduce their possible resistance and sense of threat by presenting an open and critical examination of your position?

4. Do you provide sufficient data, or evidence, to support your claims? Are the data relevant and specific?

5. Do you include information, data, or analysis from outside sources that address your topic?

6. Do you account for positions opposed to your own and the ways in which opponents may refute your argument? Remember, as you develop your argument, it is usually not enough simply to present your position and its accompanying support. You must also understand alternative positions and present their flaws. Also remember to credit the opposition when it is due.

7. Does your reading and your analysis of your position lead you somewhat closer to the other side? If so, do you reflect this modification in your paper?

8. Carefully think again about your purpose in writing and the effects you wish your paper to have upon your readers. Should you consider reordering the elements in your argument to present a stronger case to your readers?

PART THREE

Testing Answers: Refining the Argument

The preceding chapters moved you through a credible configuration of your ideas. In those chapters, the main focus was conceptual: What ideas is the paper developing, and how might you explore those ideas more thoroughly and effectively? This part of the book merges principles of execution with those conceptual concerns. Here you will look carefully at how the structural and rhetorical aspects of your papers help develop, shape, and articulate your ideas.

Chapter 11 introduces you to the Toulmin model of argument. The claim-data-warrant structure (along with the associated elements of qualification, backing, and exception) can be a valuable tool as you shape your arguments. It is particularly useful because it forces you to consider features of argument that might be neglected by beginning writers. However, the chapter extends the uses of the model beyond improving the structure of arguments and encourages you to use it as an invention technique for enhancing the content of your papers, as a guide for audience analysis, and as a formidable aid to critical reading.

You will create an essay early on; then, as you work through each of the major sections of Chapters 11 and 12, you will revise the essay to incorporate the principles and techniques you have learned.

What Makes a Good Argument

Much of the discussion in the preceding chapters centered on what some call the psychological aspect of argument: the dynamic at work between writer and reader. We now concentrate on the logical strength of your argument: the evidence you present to support your position and the precision of your reasoning. Like other forms of writing, developing an effective argument requires you to consider your subject and its content, your audience, and your purpose. Each of these considerations is integral to voicing your position convincingly and maintaining your intellectual integrity.

Though the term "intellectual integrity" may sound idealistic and vague, it is really at the center of the academic practices and conventions you are learning. The goal of scholarship is to discover, as best we can, the truth about human beings and the worlds in which they live. Our tools may be flawed and even our best understanding variable and imperfect, but that one goal is clear and unwavering. Unfortunately, it is a problematic goal in a society that values winning, sometimes at the expense of honesty. Much, perhaps most, academic writing is adversarial; that is, we try to find the truth by pitting contradictory ideas against one another and accepting the winner as at least a contingent truth. When one commits to an idea, it is far too easy, in the flurry of arguing one's point, to lose sight of the ultimate goal. One way to help keep our arguments honest is to pay special attention to the formal aspects of our reasoning. In keeping with that, this part of the book introduces principles of logical thinking you can use to judge the validity and consistency of your arguments.

Chapter 10 aims to spark critical thinking about the information industries, the various media that, by definition, inform and conceivably empower citizens to engage as active and valued members of a community. The chapter raises questions about the media's capacity for shaping what counts as fact, the influence wielded by those to whom the media grants power and status, and, especially, the repeal of long-established regulations meant to encourage a diverse and democratic media landscape. Your thoughts about these issues will become claims you will develop, support, and ultimately present.

Establishing a Mindset for Your Thinking and Writing

Part One

Two decades of media deregulation have enabled a small handful of huge conglomerates to own the majority of films, music, television, radio, books, newspapers, magazines, and important Internet sites. Based on the following chart, what are your thoughts about the impact of this consolidation on fairness, accuracy, and diversity in the media? Justify your answer.

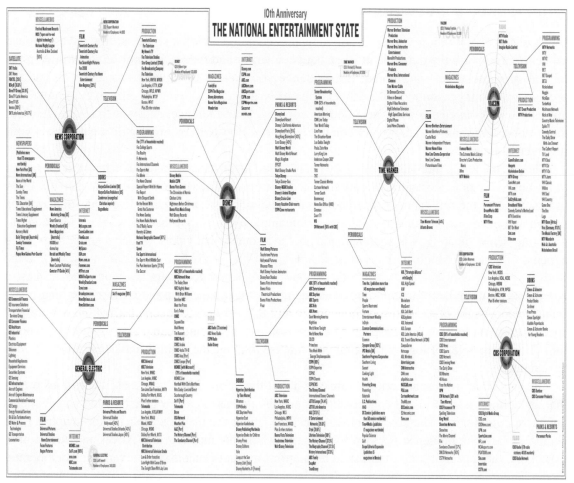

A PDF Graphic of The National Entertainment State Chart can be found at http://www.thenation.com/doc/20060703/mediachart

Part Two

Now read the following two passages. The title is derived from James Madison's cautionary note that citizens deprived of accurate information are implicated in "a tragedy or a farce" when it comes to governing themselves.

Tragedy and Farce
John Nichols and Robert W. McChesney

A popular Government without popular information or the means of acquiring it, is but a Prologue to a Farce or a Tragedy or perhaps both. Knowledge will forever govern ignorance, and a people who mean to be their own Governors, must arm themselves with the power knowledge gives.
—*James Madison*

James Madison was the most fretful founder. The crafter of the Constitution cherished the American experiment every bit as much as did the other essential men of his time, but he did not share their triumphalism. Others might be content to predict a future of easy growth and glory that would take their new nation from strength to strength, but Madison worried about the pitfalls that lay ahead. The man who served the new nation in more critical capacities than anyone save his closest comrade, Thomas Jefferson, understood the idealism of his fellows. But he also saw in the greedy and self-serving impulses of the rising political class the potential undoing of the revolutionary promise of the republic. As the co-convener (with Alexander Hamilton) of the Constitutional Convention of 1787, Madison sought to establish structures of government and to balance their powers in a way that might protect the country from the misdeeds and manipulations of men and their factions. Even after the Constitution was adopted, Madison continued to sweat the details of nation building. He became the Cassandra of the new nation, warning again and again of dangers ahead. And he did so with such insight and precision that his warnings remain in effect, and eerily appropriate, to this day.

Consider the prescience of Madison's counsel regarding presidential war-making in light of the current crisis of the nation he brought into being: "War is in fact the true nurse of executive aggrandizement. In war a physical force is to be created, and it is the executive will which is to direct it. In war the public treasures are to be unlocked, and it is the executive hand which is to dispense them. In war the honors and emoluments of office are to be multiplied; and it is the executive patronage under which they are to be enjoyed. It is in war, finally, that laurels are to be gathered, and it is the executive brow they are to encircle. The strongest passions, and the most dangerous weaknesses of the human breast; ambition, avarice, vanity, the honorable or venial love of fame, are all in conspiracy against the desire and duty of peace."

Madison understood the need for constant checks and balances against the excesses of executive power. The Congress would have its duties, as would the judiciary. But, ultimately, what in Madison's day was known as "the press" and today has become "the media" would be the most critical factor, as it alone could provide the necessary information and nurture the fundamental discourse that would maintain the democratic republic that Madison more than most of the other founders so desperately desired. It was with this understanding that Madison issued his most urgent warning: "A popular Government without popular information or the means of acquiring it, is but a Prologue to a Farce or a Tragedy or perhaps both. Knowledge will forever govern ignorance, and a people who mean to be their own Governors, must arm themselves with the power knowledge gives."

* * * * * * * *

The functionaries of every government have propensities to command at will the liberty and property of their constituents. There is no safe deposit for these but with the people themselves, nor can they be safe with them without information. Where the press is free, and every man able to read, all is safe.

—*Thomas Jefferson to Charles Yancey, 1816*

A returned Jefferson, surveying the American experiment at the dawn of its third century would be horrified at the extent to which the functionaries of our current government go unquestioned as they command at will the liberty and property not merely of their constituents but of the world. Never in the history of this country has the necessity of a free press and the free flow of information been more evident. Yet, both are under heavy assault. . . .

To understand the full extent of this crisis, it is important to remember the contribution that journalism is supposed to make to a free society. What was it that Jefferson and Madison had in mind when they battled at the founding of the country for freedom of the press? There is a good deal of consensus among democratic theorists on this issue. Democracy-sustaining journalism has three components: It must be a rigorous watchdog of those in power and those who wish to be in power; it must present a wide range of informed views on the most pressing issues of the day; and it must be able to expose deception and permit the truth to rise to the top. Each medium need not do all of the above, but the media system as a whole must assure that the whole package is delivered to the whole population.

Excerpts from Nichols, John and Robert W McChesney. *Tragedy & Farce: How the American Media Sell Wars, Spin Elections, and Destroy Democracy*. NY: The New Press, 2005.

Questions

1. Do you think the contemporary U.S. media system fulfills its responsibility to the nation? Justify your answer.

2. How do you think Jefferson or Madison would view the increasing consolidation of media ownership that concerns Nichols and McChesney? Explain.

Using the Readings

Analyzing the Role of Media in American Democracy

Whatever your first issue of concern, media had better be your second. Because without change in the media, progress in your primary area is far less likely.

Former Federal Communications Commission Member Nicholas Johnson [qtd. in Robert McChesney, "Waging the Media Battle."] http://freepress.net/action/tools/waging_battle.pdf

Remember that the chapter readings, like other readings in the text, serve two functions: they provide models of the kinds of analyses for which you should strive; and they also provide you with relevant sources to consult and use in the construction of your own essays. As you turn now to these readings, carefully evaluate each writer's purpose. Does the writer attempt to convey understanding, to win belief, or to create a behavioral change in the audience? In treating controversial issues, what kind of specific efforts does each one make to create a receptive audience? Also examine the writers' positions. Are their arguments logical and clearly developed? Are they supported by specific and relevant evidence? Can you reconcile their positions with what you have observed in your own experience? By considering how your views are validated, modified, or changed by another writer, you can gain insights into your own motives for writing.

The Actors in the Media Universe
Ben H. Bagdikian

Ben Bagdikian (b. 1920), writer, academic, and winner of the coveted Peabody Award, has been a keen media observer and analyst. Best known for his insights into how the media works, who controls it, and its influence on public opinion and affairs of state, Bagdikian has been periodically called upon to advise Congress. In the following passage from his best-selling book, *The New Media Monopoly* (2004), Bagdikian unearths not only the powerful forces usurping the news and shaping what is deemed fact, but also the purposes and audiences served by such misappropriations.

* * * * * * * * *

ONLY THE AFFLUENT NEED APPLY

Nothing in American publishing approached the profitable heresies of *The New Yorker* magazine in the 1960s. In an era when magazine editors regard covers with eye-catching headlines and striking graphics as imperative for survival, *New Yorker* covers typically were subdued watercolors of idyllic scenes. While other magazines assume that modern Americans don't read, *New Yorker* articles were incredibly long and weighted with detail. The magazine's cartoons ridicule many of its readers, the fashionably affluent who are portrayed in their Upper East Side penthouses speaking Ivy League patois. Editorial doctrine on other leading magazines calls for short, punchy sentences, but *The New Yorker* was almost the last repository of the style and tone of Henry David Thoreau and Matthew Arnold, its chaste, old-fashioned columns breathing the quietude of nineteenth-century essays.

New Yorker advertisements still are in a different world. They celebrate the ostentatious jet set. Christmas ads offer gold, diamond-encrusted wristwatches without prices, the implied message being that if you have to ask you have no business looking. A display of Jaeger-Le Goulture advised that the wristwatch "can be pivoted to reveal . . . your coat of arms." One ad for Audeman Piquet watches suggested giving three to impress a woman, while another ad did suggest a price, murmuring in fine print, "From $10,500."

There are some homely products, like a Jeep station wagon. But it was displayed with a polo field in the background and was redeemed by other ads like the one that shows a couple in evening clothes embracing in the cockpit of an executive jet. Even in advertisements for products that cost less than $5,000, the characters seem to come from adjacent ads where cuff links were offered at $675, earrings at $3,500, a bracelet at $6,000, a brooch at $14,000. A Jean Patou perfume ad has no vulgar listing of price, but said in bold letters what the spirit of all *New Yorker* ads seem to proclaim: "So rare . . . and available to so few."

Despite its violation of the most commanding conventions of what makes a magazine sell, *The New Yorker* for decades had been a leader in making money.

Over the years the magazine was the envy of the periodical industry in the standard measure of financial success—the number of advertising pages sold annually. Year after year, *The New Yorker* was first or second, so fixed in its reputation that other magazines promoting their effectiveness would tell prospective advertisers that they were first or second "after *The New Yorker*," the implication being that, like 1950s baseball and the New York Yankees, first place was unassailable.

That was true until 1967. The year before was a record one for *The New Yorker*. Most people in the industry believe that in 1966 the magazine attained the largest number of ad pages sold in a year by any magazine of general circulation in the history of publishing. In 1966 *The New Yorker* sold 6,100 pages of ads. Its circulation was at its usual level around 448,000.[1]

In 1967 a strange disease struck. *The New Yorker*'s circulation remained the same but the number of ad pages dropped disastrously. In a few years 2,500 pages of ads disappeared, a loss of 40 percent. The magazine's net profits shrank from the 1966 level of $3 million to less than $1 million. Dividends per share, $10.93 in 1966, were down to $3.69 by 1970.

The disastrous loss of advertising occurred despite a continued high level of circulation which, to lay observers, would seem the only statistic needed for a magazine's success. The popular assumption is that if enough people care enough about a publication or a television program to buy it or to turn to it, advertisers will beat a path to their doorway. That clearly was not happening at *The New Yorker*.

THE HIGH COST OF TRUTH

The onset of *The New Yorker*'s malady can be traced to July 15, 1967. That issue of the magazine carried a typically long report under the typically ambiguous title "Reporter at Large." That was the standing head for *New Yorker* articles dealing in depth with subjects as diverse as the history of oranges, the socialization of rats, and the culture of an Irish saloon. This time the subject was a report from the village of Ben Suc in Vietnam.[2]

The author was Jonathan Schell, a recent Harvard graduate who, after commencement, visited his brother, Orville, in Taiwan, where Orville was doing Chinese studies. Once in Taiwan, Jonathan decided to take a trip to Vietnam, where, according to the standard press, the American war against the Vietcong was going well. In Saigon, Schell was liked and "adopted" by the colonels, perhaps because he had proper establishment connections: He carried an expired *Harvard Crimson* press pass and his father was a successful Manhattan lawyer. The military gave him treatment ordinarily reserved for famous correspondents sympathetic to the war. In addition to attending the daily military briefing sessions in Saigon, the basis for most reports back to the United States, Schell was also taken on helicopter assaults and bombing and strafing missions and given ground transportation to battle scenes.

The assumption of his hosts was that the nice kid from Harvard would be impressed with the power and purpose of the American mission. But Schell was appalled. The war, it seemed to him, was not the neat containment of Soviet-Chinese aggression that had been advertised at home or the attempt of humane Americans to save democracy-loving natives from the barbaric Vietcong. Like all wars, this one was mutually brutal. Americans shot, bombed, and uprooted civilians in massive campaigns that resulted in the disintegration of Vietnamese social structures. And the Americans were not winning the war.

Schell returned to the United States disturbed by his findings. He visited a family friend, William Shawn, the quiet, eccentric editor of *The New Yorker*, who had known the Schell children since childhood. Shawn listened to Schell's story and asked him to try writing about his experiences. Schell produced what Shawn called "a perfect piece of *New Yorker* reporting." The story, which ran in the July 15, 1967, issue, told in clear, quiet detail what the assault on one village meant to the villagers and to the American soldiers.

Shawn said he had serious doubts about the war before Schell appeared, "but certainly I saw it differently talking to him and reading what he wrote. That was when I became convinced that we shouldn't be there and the war was a mistake."

Thereafter *The New Yorker* in issue after issue spoke simply and clearly against the war. It was not the first publication to do so, but at the time most important media followed the general line that the war was needed to stop international communism and to save the Vietnamese and that the United States was on the verge of victory. Most newspapers, including the two most influential dailies in the country, the *New York Times* and the *Washington Post*, editorially supported the war. There were growing popular protests but the mass marches were yet to come. Neither the My Lai massacre nor the Tet offensive had occurred, and the exposure of the Pentagon Papers detailing a long history of government lying about Indochina was still four years away.

The New Yorker was the voice of the elite, the repository of advertisements for the hedonistic rich, of genteel essays on the first day of spring, of temperate profiles of aesthetes, of humor so sophisticated that it seemed designed solely for intelligent graduates of the best schools. The *Wall Street Journal* once labeled it "Urbanity, Inc." When the magazine spoke clearly against the war, it was a significant event in the course of public attitude toward the American enterprise in Vietnam. If this apolitical organ of the elite said the war was morally wrong, it was saying it to the country's establishment.

THE KIDS ARE READING . . .

At the same time, the magazine was giving the message to a quite different constituency. A *New Yorker* staff member recalled that in 1967, "Our writers would come back from speaking on campuses and say that the kids are reading *The New Yorker* out loud in the dormitories."

Ordinarily this is a happy event in the life of a magazine. There is always a need for some younger readers so that when older subscribers die the magazine will not die with them. But advertisers live in the present. Throughout its crisis years after 1966, *The New Yorker* audience actually grew in numbers. But while the median age of readers in 1966 was 48.7—the age when executives would be at the peak of their spending power—by 1974 *New Yorker* subscribers' median age was 34, a number brought down by the infusion of college students in their late teens and early twenties.[3] Many college students will form the affluent elite of the future, but at the moment they are not buying $10,500 wristwatches and $14,000 brooches. They were buying the magazine because of its clear and moral stand against the war and its quiet, detailed reporting from the scene.

It was then that ad pages began their drastic disappearance. An easy explanation would be that conservative corporations withdrew their ads in political protest. Some did. But the majority of the losses came from a more impersonal process, one of profound significance to the character of contemporary American mass media. *The New Yorker* had begun to attract "the wrong kind" of reader. Circulation remained the same, but the magazine had become the victim, as it had formerly been the beneficiary, of an iron rule of advertising-supported media: It is less important that people buy your publication (or listen to your program) than that they be "the right kind" of people.

The "right kind" usually means affluent consumers eighteen to forty-nine years of age, the heavy buying years, with above-median family income. Newspapers, magazines, and radio and television operators publicly boast of their audience size, which is a significant factor. But when they sit down at conferences with big advertisers, they do not present simple numbers but reams of computer printouts that show the characteristics of their audience in income, age, sex, marital status, ethnic background, social habits, residence, family structure, occupation, and buying patterns. These are the compelling components of that crucial element in modern media—demographics, the study of characteristics of the human population.

The standard cure for "bad demographics" in newspapers, magazines, radio and television is simple: Change the content. Fill the publication or the programs with material that will attract the kind of people the advertisers want. The general manager of *Rolling Stone* expressed it when that magazine wanted to attract a higher level of advertiser: "We had to deliver a more high-quality reader. The only way to deliver a different kind of reader is to change editorial." If an editor refuses or fails to change, the editor is fired.[4]

The New Yorker faced this problem but it did not fire the editor; nor did the editor "change editorial." It is almost certain that for conventional corporate ownership the "cure would be quick and decisive. William Shawn would have "changed editorial," which would have meant dropping the insistent line on the war in Vietnam, or he would have been fired. In the place of the Vietnam reporting and commentary there would have been less controversial material that would adjust demographics back to the affluent population of buying age and assuage the anger of those corporations that disliked the magazine's position on the war.

But at the time, *The New Yorker* was not the property of a conglomerate. Later, in 1986, it would be sold to the Newhouse publishing group. The new owner altered advertising and promotion policies but left editorial content the same. After a year, however, the new owner replaced the editor, William Shawn.

Shawn, a Dickensian man, modest in manner and speech, reddens in indignation when asked whether, during the critical 1967–1974 period, the business leaders of the magazine informed him that his editorial content was attracting the wrong kind of reader.

THE UNTHINKABLE BECOMES THINKABLE

It would be unthinkable for the advertising and business people to tell me that . . . I didn't hear about it until the early 1970s. . . . It gradually sank in on me that *The New Yorker* was being read by younger people. I didn't know it in any formal way. Who the readers are I really don't want to know. I don't want to know because we edit the magazine for ourselves and hope there will be people like ourselves and people like our writers who will find it interesting and worthwhile.

Shawn's words are standard rhetoric of publishers and editors when they are asked about separation of editorial independence and advertising. The rhetoric usually has little relation to reality. Increasingly, editorial content of publications and broadcasting is dictated by the computer printouts on advertising agency desks, not the other way around. When there is a conflict between the printouts and an independent editor, the printouts win. Were it not for the incontrovertible behavior of *The New Yorker* during the Vietnam War, it would be difficult not to regard Shawn's words as the standard mythic rhetoric.

"We never talk about 'the readers,'" Shawn said. "I won't permit that—if I may put it so arrogantly. I don't want to speak about our readers as a 'market.' I don't want them to feel that they are just consumers to us. I find that obnoxious."

The full-page ads of other newspapers, magazines, and broadcast networks in the *New York Times* and the *Wall Street Journal* are often puzzling to the lay reader. They do not urge people to read and listen. They seem to be filled with statistics of little interest to potential subscribers or viewers. They are intended to show the advertising industry that the demographics of the publication or station are "correct:" that their audience is made up not of a cross-section of the population but of people in the "right" age and income brackets.

Eventually during the 1967–1974 period Shawn did hear what he called "murmurings":

There were murmurings in the background about three things: The magazine was getting too serious, the magazine was getting too much into politics, and the pieces were getting too long. My reaction was that we should do nothing about it. Whatever change took place did so gradually and spontaneously as we saw the world. . . . There's only one way to do it: Did we think it was the right thing to do? Did we take the right editorial stand?. . . . To be silent when something is going on that shouldn't be going on would be cowardly. We published information we believed the public should have and we said what we believed. If the magazine was serious it was no more serious than we were. If there was too much politics, it was because politics became more important and it was on our minds . . . I wish we could remain out of politics but we can't . . . I could enjoy life more if we could do nothing but be funny, which I love . . . but The New Yorker has gradually changed as the world changed.

Shawn noted that the Time-Life and Reader's Digest empires succeeded because they were started by men who expressed their own values regardless of the market and thereby established an identity that made for long-range success.

Now the whole idea is that you edit for a market and if possible design a magazine with that in mind. Now magazines aren't started with the desire for someone to express what he believes. I think the whole trend is so destructive and so unpromising so far as journalism is concerned that it is very worrisome. Younger editors and writers are growing up in that atmosphere. "We want to edit the magazine to give the audience what they want. What do we give them?"

There is a fallacy in that calculation . . . That fallacy is if you edit that way, to give back to the readers only what they think they want, you'll never give them something new they didn't know about. You stagnate. It's just this back-and-forth and you end up with the networks, TV and the movies. The whole thing begins to be circular. Creativity and originality and spontaneity goes out of it. The new tendency is to discourage this creative process and kill originality.

We sometimes publish a piece that I'm afraid not more than one hundred readers will want. Perhaps it's too difficult, too obscure. But it's important to have. That's how people learn and grow. This other way is bad for our entire society and we're suffering from it in almost all forms of communications.

I don't know if you tried to start up a New Yorker today if you could get anybody to back you.

****

NOTES

1. Number of ad pages, revenues, and dividends from annual reports of F-R Corporation.
2. Origins of the Schell article, its consequences, and statements of William Shawn from personal interview with Shawn, editor of *The New Yorker* 14 May 1981.
3. From periodic readership studies by *The New Yorker* and from Simmons Surveys.
4. *Wall Street Journal*, 4 June 1981, 14.

Questions for Discussion and Writing

1. Ben Bagdikian uses what happened to *The New Yorker* as an iterative, or representative, example to show how markets drive editorial decisions. Without necessarily having any specialized or expert knowledge, but relying on your own reading, observations, and experiences, do think this example adequately characterizes the news industry of the past and/or the present? Why?

2. Based on your understanding of how we argue causality, what strengths and weaknesses do you find in Bagdikian's explanation of why *The New Yorker*'s profitability declined so dramatically between 1966 and 1970?

3. William Shawn, former editor of *The New Yorker*, is quoted as saying that giving readers what they want only leads to stagnation. Do you think the media is presenting mostly popular rather than useful content? If not, why not? If so, what are the consequences?

4. If you could ask Bagdikian questions about his analysis of what happened to *The New Yorker*, what would they be? Explain.

5. Often, with "political problems," we end up pitting two 'goods' or 'positives' against each other. Is *The New Yorker* example a case in point: if we let editors publish what they choose, aren't advertisers also free to support the publications they choose? Do you agree that this is the case or not? Why? Why not? And if it is, is there any way to ensure that readers can encounter "something new they didn't know about"?

Making Connections

1. Imagine Ben Bagdikian, Thomas Jefferson and James Madison conversing about the impact of today's media on our democracy. What do you think each would find to be the most egregious aspect of media coverage? What would be the most democratically encouraging aspect?

2. Many people seem to complain or be frightened of Big Business, Big Government, and Big Media. How do you understand these terms? Do they seem real and meaningful to you? Have you had any experiences, direct or indirect, that would validate or invalidate the use of these terms?

Addresses to the National Conferences on Media Reform

Bill Moyers

Founding Director, Public Affairs Television
President, The Schumann Center for Media and Democracy

Bill Moyers (b. 1934), an award winning citizen-journalist, has produced a wide variety of public television shows over his 25 years in broadcasting, including the much celebrated *NOW* and *Bill Moyers Journal*, two in-depth investigative weekly news shows covering current events. The two addresses below position Moyers at center stage of the national media reform movement. For Moyers, this is more than a fight for media reform. Moyers warns that we are in a crisis—"a struggle for the very soul of democracy." In the first address (2003), he calls attention to the government's inordinate secrecy and lack of openness in dealing with the public, to the media's emphasis on commercial values over democratic principles, and to the close association of politically aligned media outlets with big business and the country's current leadership. The second address (2005) details Moyers's attempts to work against the grain of partisan politics by producing in-depth programs on controversial issues that take broad, non-partisan viewpoints to the public.

✱✱✱✱✱✱✱✱

I. KEYNOTE ADDRESS (ABRIDGED), NOVEMBER 8, 2003, MADISON, WI

Thank you for inviting me tonight. I'm flattered to be speaking to a gathering as high-powered as this one that's come together with an objective as compelling as "media reform." I must confess, however, to a certain discomfort, shared with other journalists, about the very term "media." Ted Gup, who teaches journalism at Case Western Reserve, articulated my concerns better than I could when he wrote in *The Chronicle of Higher Education* (November 23, 2001)

> that the very concept of media is insulting to some of us within the press who find ourselves lumped in with so many disparate elements, as if everyone with a pen, a microphone, a camera, or just a loud voice were all one and the same. . . . David Broder is not Matt Drudge. "Meet the Press" is not "Temptation Island." And I am not Jerry Springer. I do not speak for him. He does not speak for me. Yet "the media" speaks for us all.

> That's how I felt when I saw Oliver North reporting on Fox from Iraq, pressing our embattled troops to respond to his repetitive and belittling question, "Does Fox Rock? Does Fox Rock?" Oliver North and I may be in the same "media" but we are not part of the same message. Nonetheless, I accept that I work and all of us live in "medialand," and God knows we need some "media reform." I'm sure you know those two words are really an incomplete description of the job ahead. . . . Because what

we're talking about is nothing less than rescuing a democracy that is so polarized it is in danger of being paralyzed and pulverized.

Alarming words, I know. But the realities we face should trigger alarms. Free and responsible government by popular consent just can't exist without an informed public. That's a cliché, I know, but I agree with the presidential candidate who once said that truisms are true and clichés mean what they say (an observation that no doubt helped to lose him the election.) It's a reality: democracy can't exist without an informed public. Here's an example: Only 13% of eligible young people cast ballots in the last presidential election. A recent National Youth Survey revealed that only half of the fifteen hundred young people polled believe that voting is important, and only 46% think they can make a difference in solving community problems. We're talking here about one quarter of the electorate.

The Carnegie Corporation conducted a youth challenge quiz of 15–24 year-olds and asked them, "Why don't more young people vote or get involved?" Of the nearly two thousand respondents, the main answer was that they did not have enough information about issues and candidates.

Let me rewind and say it again: democracy can't exist without an informed public. So I say without qualification that it's not simply the cause of journalism that's at stake today, but the cause of American liberty itself. As Tom Paine put it, "The sun never shined on a cause of greater worth." He was talking about the cause of a revolutionary America in 1776. But that revolution ran in good part on the energies of a rambunctious, though tiny press. Freedom and freedom of communications were birth-twins in the future United States. They grew up together, and neither has fared very well in the other's absence. Boom times for the one have been boom times for the other.

Yet today, despite plenty of lip service on every ritual occasion to freedom of the press radio and TV, three powerful forces are undermining that very freedom, damming the streams of significant public interest news that irrigate and nourish the flowering of self-determination.

The first of these is the centuries-old reluctance of governments—even elected governments—to operate in the sunshine of disclosure and criticism. The second is more subtle and more recent. It's the tendency of media giants, operating on big-business principles, to exalt commercial values at the expense of democratic value. That is, to run what Edward R. Murrow forty-five years ago called broadcasting's "money-making machine" at full throttle. In so doing they are squeezing out the journalism that tries to get as close as possible to the verifiable truth; they are isolating serious coverage of public affairs into ever-dwindling "news holes" or far from prime-time; and they are gobbling up small and independent publications competing for the attention of the American people.

It's hardly a new or surprising story. But there are fresh and disturbing chapters.

In earlier times our governing bodies tried to squelch journalistic freedom with the blunt instruments of the law—padlocks for the presses and jail cells for outspoken editors and writers. Over time, with spectacular wartime exceptions, the courts and the Constitution struck those weapons out of their hands. But they've found new ones now, in the name of "national security." The classifier's Top Secret stamp, used indiscriminately, is as potent a silencer as a writ of arrest. And beyond what is officially labeled "secret" there hovers a culture of sealed official lips, opened only to favored media insiders: of government by leak and innuendo and spin, of misnamed "public information" offices that churn out blizzards of releases filled with self-justifying exaggerations and, occasionally, just plain damned lies. Censorship without officially appointed censors.

Add to that the censorship-by-omission of consolidated media empires digesting the bones of swallowed independents, and you've got a major shrinkage of the crucial information that thinking citizens can act upon. People saw that coming as long as a century ago when the rise of chain news-paper ownerships, and then of concentration in the young radio industry, became apparent. And so in the zesty progressivism of early New Deal days, the Federal Communications Act of 1934 was passed (more on this later). The aim of that cornerstone of broadcast policy, mentioned over 100 times in its pages, was to promote the "public interest, convenience and necessity." The clear intent was to prevent a monopoly of commercial values from overwhelming democratic values—to assure that the official view of reality—corporate or government—was not the only view of reality that reached the people. Regulators and regulated, media and government were to keep a wary eye on each other, preserving those checks and balances that is the bulwark of our Constitutional order.

. . . Which brings me to the third powerful force—beyond governmental secrecy and megamedia conglomerates—that is shaping what Americans see, read, and hear. I am talking now about that quasi-official partisan press ideologically linked to an authoritarian administration that in turn is the ally and agent of the most powerful interests in the world. This convergence dominates the marketplace of political ideas today in a phenomenon unique in our history.

You need not harbor the notion of a vast, right wing conspiracy to think this more collusion more than pure coincidence. Conspiracy is unnecessary when ideology hungers for power and its many adherents swarm of their own accord to the same pot of honey. Stretching from the editorial pages of the *Wall Street Journal* to the faux news of Rupert Murdoch's empire to the nattering nabobs of no-nothing radio to a legion of think tanks paid for and bought by conglomerates—the religious, partisan and corporate right have raised a mighty megaphone for sectarian, economic, and political forces that aim to transform the egalitarian and democratic ideals embodied in our founding documents. Authoritarianism.

With no strong opposition party to challenge such triumphalist hegemony, it is left to journalism to be democracy's best friend. That is why so many journalists joined with you in questioning Michael Powell's bid—blessed by the White House—to permit further concentration of media ownership. If free and independent journalism committed to telling the truth without fear or favor is suffocated, the oxygen goes out of democracy. And there is no surer way to intimidate and then silence mainstream journalism than to be the boss.

. . . So the issues bringing us here tonight are bigger and far more critical than simply "media reform." That's why, before I go on, I want to ask you to look around you. I'm serious: Look to your left and now to your right. You are looking at your allies in one of the great ongoing struggles of the American experience—the struggle for the soul of democracy, for government "of, by, and for the people."

. . . Remember, back in 1791, when the First Amendment was ratified, the idea of a free press seemed safely sheltered in law. It wasn't. Only seven years later, in the midst of a war scare with France, Congress passed and John Adams signed the infamous Sedition Act. The act made it a crime—just listen to how broad a brush the government could swing—to circulate opinions "tending to induce a belief" that lawmakers might have unconstitutional or repressive motives, or "directly or indirectly tending" to justify France or to "criminate," whatever that meant, the President or other Federal officials. No wonder that opponents called it a scheme to "excite a fervor against foreign aggression only to establish tyranny at home."

. . . Luckily, the Sedition Act had a built-in expiration date of 1801, at which time President Jefferson—who hated it from the first—pardoned those remaining under indictment. So the story has an upbeat ending, and so can ours, but it will take . . . courage. . . .

Courage is a timeless quality and surfaces when the government is tempted to hit the bottle of censorship again during national emergencies, real or manufactured. As so many of you will recall, in 1971, during the Vietnam War, the Nixon administration resurrected the doctrine of "prior restraint" from the crypt and tried to ban the publication of the Pentagon Papers by the *New York Times* and the *Washington Post*—even though the documents themselves were a classified history of events during four earlier Presidencies.

Arthur Sulzberger, the publisher of the *Times*, and Katherine Graham of the *Post* were both warned by their lawyers that they and their top managers could face criminal prosecution under espionage laws if they printed the material that Daniel Ellsberg had leaked—and, by the way, offered without success to the three major television networks. Or at the least, punitive lawsuits or whatever political reprisals a furious Nixon team could devise. But after internal debates—and the threats of some of their best-known editors to resign rather than fold under pressure—both owners gave the green light—and were vindicated by the Supreme Court. Score a round for democracy.

. . . And then there's Leslie Moonves, the chairman of CBS. In the very week that the once—Tiffany Network was celebrating its 75th anniversary—and taking kudos for its glory days when it was unafraid to broadcast "The Harvest of Shame" and "The Selling of the Pentagon"—the network's famous eye blinked. Pressured by a vociferous and relentless right wing campaign and bullied by the Republican National Committee—and at a time when its parent company has billions resting on whether the White House, Congress, and the FCC will allow it to own even more stations than currently permissible—CBS caved in and pulled the miniseries about Ronald Reagan that conservatives thought insufficiently worshipful.

. . . When that landmark Communications Act of 1934 was under consideration a vigorous public movement of educators, labor officials, and religious and institutional leaders emerged to argue for a broadcast system that would serve the interests of citizens and communities. A movement like that is coming to life again and we now have to build on this momentum.

It won't be easy, because the tide's been flowing the other way for a long time. The deregulation pressure began during the Reagan era, when then-FCC chairman Mark Fowler, who said that TV didn't need much regulation because it was just a "toaster with pictures," eliminated many public-interest rules. That opened the door for networks to cut their news staffs, scuttle their documentary units . . . and exile investigative producers and reporters to the under-funded hinterlands of independent production. It was like turning out searchlights on dark and dangerous corners.

. . . You can see the results even now in the waning of robust journalism. In the dearth of in-depth reporting as news organizations try to do more with fewer resources. In the failure of the major news organizations to cover their own corporate deals and lobbying as well as other forms of "crime in the suites" such as Enron story. And in helping people understand what their government is up to.

The report by the Roberts team[1] includes a survey in 1999 that showed a wholesale retreat in coverage of nineteen key departments and agencies in Washington. Regular reporting of the Supreme Court and State Department dropped off considerably through the decade. At the Social Security Administration, whose activities literally affect every American, only the *New York Times* was maintaining a full-time reporter and, incredibly, at the Interior Department, which controls five to six hundred million acres of public land and looks after everything from the National Park Service to the Bureau of Indian Affairs, there were no full-time reporters around.

That's in Washington, our nation's capital. Out across the country there is simultaneously a near blackout of local politics by broadcasters. The public interest group Alliance for Better Campaigns studied forty-five stations in six cities in one week in October. Out of 7,560 hours of programming analyzed, only 13 were devoted to local public affairs—less than one-half of 1% of local programming nationwide. Mayors, town councils, school boards, civic leaders get no time from broadcasters who have filled their coffers by looting the public airwaves over which they were placed as stewards.

Last year, when a movement sprang up in the House of Representatives to require these broadcasters to obey the law that says they must sell campaign advertising to candidates for office at the lowest commercial rate, the powerful broadcast lobby brought the Congress to heel. So much for the "public interest, convenience, and necessity."

So what do we do? What is our strategy for taking on what seems a hopeless fight for a media system that serves as effectively as it sells—one that holds all the institutions of society, itself included, accountable?

There's plenty we can do. Here's one journalist's list of some of the overlapping and connected goals that a vital media reform movement might pursue.

First, we have to take Tom Paine's example—and Danny Schecter's advice—and reach out to regular citizens. We have to raise an even bigger tent than you have here. Those of us in this place speak a common language about the "media." We must reach the audience that's not here—carry the fight to radio talk shows, local television, and the letters columns of our newspapers. As Danny says, we must engage the mainstream, not retreat from it. We have to get our fellow citizens to understand that what they see, hear, and read is not only the taste of programmers and producers but also a set of policy decisions made by the people we vote for.

We have to fight to keep the gates to the Internet open to all. The web has enabled many new

---

[1]Reference to Gene Roberts et al. *Leaving Readers Behind: The Age of Corporate Newspapering* published as part of the Project on the State of the American Newspaper under the auspices of the Pew Charitable Trusts.

voices in our democracy—and globally—to be heard: advocacy groups, artists, individuals, non-profit organizations. Just about anyone can speak online, and often with an impact greater than in the days when orators had to climb on soap box in a park. The media industry lobbyists point to the Internet and say it's why concerns about media concentration are ill founded in an environment where anyone can speak and where there are literally hundreds of competing channels.

What those lobbyists for big media don't tell you is that the traffic patterns of the online world are beginning to resemble those of television and radio. In one study, for example, AOL Time Warner (as it was then known) accounted for nearly a third of all user time spent online. And two others companies—Yahoo and Microsoft—bring that figure to fully 50%. As for the growing number of channels available on today's cable systems, most are owned by a small handful of companies. Of the ninety-one major networks that appear on most cable systems, 79 are part of such multiple network groups such as Time Warner, Viacom, Liberty Media, NBC, and Disney.

In order to program a channel on cable today, you must either be owned by or affiliated with one of the giants. If we're not vigilant the wide-open spaces of the Internet could be transformed into a system in which a handful of companies use their control over high-speed access to ensure they remain at the top of the digital heap in the broadband era at the expense of the democratic potential of this amazing technology.

. . . We must fight for a regulatory, market and public opinion environment that lets local and community-based content be heard rather than drowned out by nationwide commercial programming.

We must fight to limit conglomerate swallowing of media outlets by sensible limits on multiple and cross-ownership of TV and radio stations, newspapers, magazines, publishing companies and other information sources. Let the message go forth: No Berlusconis[2] in America!

We must fight to expand a noncommercial media system—something made possible in part by new digital spectrum awarded to PBS stations—and fight off attempts to privatize what's left of public broadcasting. Commercial speech must not be the only free speech in America!

We must fight to create new opportunities, through public policies and private agreements, to let historically marginalized media players into more ownership of channels and control of content.

Let us encourage traditional mainstream journalism to get tougher about keeping a critical eye on those in public and private power and keeping us all informed of what's important—not necessarily simple or entertaining or good for the bottom line. Not all news is "Entertainment Tonight." And news departments are trustees of the public, not the corporate media's stockholders.

In that last job, schools of journalism and professional news associations have their work cut out. We need journalism graduates who are not only better informed in a whole spectrum of special fields—and the schools do a competent job there—but who take from their training a strong sense of public service. And also graduates who are perhaps a little more hard-boiled and street-smart than the present crop, though that's hard to teach.

---

[2]Silva Berlusconi is former Prime Minister of Italy and also its richest citizen and its first media mogul.

. . . And as for those professional associations of editors they might remember that in union there is strength. One journalist alone can't extract from an employer a commitment to let editors and not accountants choose the appropriate subject matter for coverage. But what if news councils blew the whistle on shoddy or cowardly managements? What if foundations gave magazines such as the *Columbia Journalism Review* sufficient resources to spread their stories of journalistic bias, failure or incompetence?

What if entire editorial departments simply refused any longer to quote anonymous sources—or give Kobe Bryant's trial more than the minimal space it rates by any reasonable standard—or to run stories planted by the Defense Department and impossible, for alleged security reasons, to verify?

What if a professional association backed them to the hilt? Or required the same stance from all its members? It would take courage to confront powerful ownerships that way. But not as much courage as is asked of those brave journalists in some countries who face the dungeon, the executioner or the secret assassin for speaking out.

All this may be in the domain of fantasy. And then again, maybe not. What I know to be real is that we are in for the fight of our lives. I am not a romantic about democracy or journalism; the writer Andre Gide may have been right when he said that all things human, given time, go badly. But I know journalism and democracy are deeply linked in whatever chance we human beings have to redress our grievances, renew our politics, and reclaim our revolutionary ideals. Those are difficult tasks at any time, and they are even more difficult in a cynical age as this, when a deep and pervasive corruption has settled upon the republic. But too much is at stake for our spirits to flag.

Earlier this week the Library of Congress gave the first Kluge Lifetime Award in the Humanities to the Polish philosopher Leslie Kolakowski. In an interview Kolakowski said: "There is one freedom on which all other liberties depend—and that is freedom of expression, freedom of speech, of print. If this is taken away, no other freedom can exist, or at least it would be soon suppressed."

That's the flame of truth your movement must carry forward. I am older than almost all of you and am not likely to be around for the duration; I have said for several years now that I will retire from active journalism when I turn 70 next year. But I take heart from the presence in this room, unseen, of Peter Zenger, Thomas Paine, the muckrakers, I.F. Stone and all those heroes and heroines, celebrated or forgotten, who faced odds no less than ours and did not flinch. I take heart in your presence here. It's your fight now. Look around. You are not alone.

* * * * * * * *

II. CLOSING ADDRESS "TAKING PUBLIC BROADCASTING BACK," (ABRIDGED). MAY 15, 2005. ST. LOUIS, MO

. . . The story I've come to share with you goes to the core of our belief that the quality of democracy and the quality of journalism are deeply entwined. I can tell this story because I've been living it. It's been in the news this week, including reports of more attacks on a single journalist—yours truly—by the right-wing media and their allies at the Corporation for Public Broadcasting.

As some of you know, CPB was established almost forty years ago to set broad policy for public broadcasting and to be a firewall between political influence and program content. What some on this board are now doing today, led by its chairman, Kenneth Tomlinson, is too important, too disturbing and yes, even too dangerous for a gathering like this not to address.

We're seeing unfold a contemporary example of the age old ambition of power and ideology to squelch and punish journalists who tell the stories that make princes and priests uncomfortable.

. . . Who are they? I mean the people obsessed with control, using the government to threaten and intimidate. I mean the people who are hollowing out middle class security even as they enlist the sons and daughters of the working class in a war to make sure Ahmed Chalabi winds up controlling Iraq's oil. I mean the people who turn faith based initiatives into a slush fund and who encourage the pious to look heavenward and pray so as not to see the long arm of privilege and power picking their pockets. I mean the people who squelch free speech in an effort to obliterate dissent and consolidate their orthodoxy into the official view of reality from which any deviation becomes unpatriotic heresy.

. . . Take the example . . . of Charles J. Hanley. Hanley is a Pulitzer Prize winning reporter for the Associated Press, whose fall 2003 story on the torture of Iraqis in American prisons—before a U.S. Army report and photographs documenting the abuse surfaced—was ignored by major American newspapers. Hanley attributes this lack of interest to the fact that "It was not an officially sanctioned story that begins with a handout from an official source." Furthermore, Iraqis recounting their own personal experience of Abu Ghraib simply did not have the credibility with beltway journalists of American officials denying that such things happened. Judith Miller of *The New York Times*, among others, relied on the credibility of official but unnamed sources when she served essentially as the government stenographer for claims that Iraq possessed weapons of mass destruction.

These "rules of the game" permit Washington officials to set the agenda for journalism, leaving the press all too often simply to recount what officials say instead of subjecting their words and deeds to critical scrutiny. Instead of acting as filters for readers and viewers, sifting the truth from the propaganda, reporters and anchors attentively transcribe both sides of the spin invariably failing to provide context, background or any sense of which claims hold up and which are misleading.

I decided long ago that this wasn't healthy for democracy. I came to see that "news is what people want to keep hidden and everything else is publicity." In my documentaries—whether on the Watergate scandals thirty years ago or the Iran Contra conspiracy twenty years ago or Bill Clinton's fund raising scandals ten years ago or, five years ago, the chemical industry's long and despicable cover up of its cynical and unspeakable withholding of critical data about its toxic products from its workers, I realized that investigative journalism could not be a collaboration between the journalist and the subject.

Objectivity is not satisfied by two opposing people offering competing opinions, leaving the viewer to split the difference.

I came to believe that objective journalism means describing the object being reported on, including the little fibs and fantasies as well as the Big Lie of the people in power. In no way does this permit journalists to make accusations and allegations. It means, instead, making sure that your reporting and your conclusions can be nailed to the post with confirming evidence.

This is always hard to do, but it has never been harder than today. Without a trace of irony, the powers-that-be have appropriated the newspeak vernacular of George Orwell's "1984." They give us a program vowing "No Child Left Behind" while cutting funds for educating disadvantaged kids. They give us legislation cheerily calling for "Clear Skies" and "Healthy Forests" that give us neither. And that's just for starters.

In Orwell's *1984*, the character Syme, one of the writers of that totalitarian society's dictionary, explains to the protagonist Winston, "Don't you see that the whole aim of Newspeak is to narrow the range of thought?" "Has it ever occurred to you, Winston, that by the year 2050, at the very latest, not a single human being will be alive who could understand such a conversation as we are having now? The whole climate of thought," he said, "will be different. In fact there will be no thought, as we understand it now. Orthodoxy means not thinking—not needing to think. Orthodoxy is unconsciousness."

An unconscious people, an indoctrinated people, a people fed only on partisan information and opinion that confirm their own bias, a people made morbidly obese in mind and spirit by the junk food of propaganda, is less inclined to put up a fight, to ask questions and be skeptical. That kind of orthodoxy can kill a democracy—or worse.

I learned about this the hard way. I grew up in the South where the truth about slavery, race, and segregation had been driven from the pulpits, driven from the classrooms and driven from the newsrooms. It took a bloody Civil War to bring the truth home and then it took another hundred years for the truth to make us free.

Then I served in the Johnson administration [1964–1968]. Imbued with cold war orthodoxy and confident that "might makes right," we circled the wagons, listened only to each other, and pursued policies the evidence couldn't carry. The results were devastating for Vietnamese and Americans.

I brought all of this to the task when PBS asked me after 9/11 to start a new weekly broadcast. They wanted us to make it different from anything else on the air—commercial or public broadcasting. They asked us to tell stories no one else was reporting and to offer a venue to people who might not otherwise be heard. That wasn't a hard sell. I had been deeply impressed by studies published in leading peer-reviewed scholarly journals by a team of researchers led by Vassar College sociologist William Hoynes. Extensive research on the content of public television over a decade found that political discussions on our public affairs programs generally included a limited set of voices that offer a narrow range of perspectives on current issues and events. Instead of far-ranging discussions and debates, the kind that might engage viewers as citizens, not simply as audiences, this research found that public affairs programs on PBS stations were populated by the standard set of elite news sources. Whether government officials and Washington journalists (talking about political strategy) or corporate sources (talking about stock prices or the economy from the investor's viewpoint), Public television, unfortunately, all too often was offering the same kind of discussions, and a similar brand of insider discourse, that is featured regularly on commercial television.

Who didn't appear was also revealing. Hoynes and his team found that in contrast to the conservative mantra that public television routinely featured the voices of anti-establishment critics, "alternative perspectives were rare on public television and were effectively drowned out by the stream of government and corporate views that represented the vast majority of sources on our broadcasts." The so-called 'experts' who got most of the face time came primarily from mainstream news organizations and Washington think tanks rather than diverse interests. Economic news, for example, was almost entirely refracted through the views of business people, investors and business journalists. Voices outside the corporate/Wall Street universe—nonprofessional workers, labor representatives, consumer advocates and the general public were rarely heard. In sum, these two studies concluded, the economic coverage was so narrow that the views and the activities of most citizens became irrelevant.

All this went against the Public Broadcasting Act of 1967 that created the Corporation for Public Broadcasting. I know. I was there. As a young policy assistant to President Johnson, I attended my first meeting to discuss the future of public broadcasting in 1964 in the office of the Commissioner of Education. I know firsthand that the Public Broadcasting Act was meant to provide an alternative to commercial television and to reflect the diversity of the American people.

This, too, was on my mind when we assembled the team for NOW. It was just after the terrorist attacks of 9/11. We agreed on two priorities. First, we wanted to do our part to keep the conversation of democracy going. That meant talking to a wide range of people across the spectrum—left, right and center. It meant poets, philosophers, politicians, scientists, sages and scribblers. It meant Isabel Allende, the novelist, and Amity Shlaes, the columnist for the *Financial Times*. It meant the former nun and best-selling author Karen Armstrong, and it meant the right-wing evangelical columnist, Cal Thomas. It meant Arundhati Roy from India, Doris Lessing from London, David Suzuki from Canada, and Bernard Henry-Levi from Paris. It also meant two successive editors of the *Wall Street Journal*, Robert Bartley and Paul Gigot, the editor of *The Economist*, Bill Emmott, the *Nation's* Katrina vanden Heuvel and the *Los Angeles Weekly's* John Powers. It means liberals like Frank Wu, Ossie Davis and Gregory Nava, and conservatives like Frank Gaffney, Grover Norquist, and Richard Viguerie. It meant Archbishop Desmond Tutu and Bishop Wilton Gregory of the Catholic Bishops conference in this country. It meant the conservative Christian activist and lobbyist, Ralph Reed, and the dissident Catholic Sister Joan Chittister. We threw the conversation of democracy open to all comers. Most of those who came responded the same way that Ron Paul, Republican and Libertarian congressman from Texas, did when he wrote me after his appearance, "I have received hundreds of positive e-mails from your viewers. I appreciate the format of your program which allows time for a full discussion of ideas . . . I'm tired of political shows featuring two guests shouting over each other and offering the same arguments . . . NOW was truly refreshing."

Hold your applause because that's not the point of the story.

We had a second priority. We intended to do strong, honest and accurate reporting, telling stories we knew people in high places wouldn't like.

I told our producers and correspondents that in our field reporting our job was to get as close as possible to the verifiable truth. This was all the more imperative in the aftermath of the terrorist attacks. America could be entering a long war against an elusive and stateless enemy with no definable measure of victory and no limit to its duration, cost or foreboding fear. The rise of a homeland security state meant government could justify extraordinary measures in exchange for protecting citizens against unnamed, even unproven, threats.

Furthermore, increased spending during a national emergency can produce a spectacle of corruption behind a smokescreen of secrecy. I reminded our team of the words of the news photographer in Tom Stoppard's play who said, "People do terrible things to each other, but it's worse when everyone is kept in the dark."

I also reminded them of how the correspondent and historian, Richard Reeves, answered a student who asked him to define real news. "Real news," Reeves responded, "is the news you and I need to keep our freedoms."

For these reasons and in that spirit we went about reporting on Washington as no one else in broadcasting—except occasionally "60 Minutes"—was doing. We reported on the expansion of the Justice Department's power of surveillance. We reported on the escalating Pentagon budget and expensive weapons that didn't work. We reported on how campaign contributions influenced legislation and policy to skew resources to the comfortable and well-connected while our troops were fighting in Afghanistan and Iraq with inadequate training and armor. We reported on how the Bush administration was shredding the Freedom of Information Act. We went around the country to report on how closed door, back room deals in Washington were costing ordinary workers and tax payers their livelihood and security. We reported on offshore tax havens that enable wealthy and powerful Americans to avoid their fair share of national security and the social contract.

And always—because what people know depends on who owns the press—we kept coming back to the media business itself—to how mega media corporations were pushing journalism further and further down the hierarchy of values, how giant radio cartels were silencing critics while shutting communities off from essential information, and how the mega media companies were lobbying the FCC for the right to grow ever more powerful.

The broadcast caught on. Our ratings grew every year. There was even a spell when we were the only public affairs broadcast on PBS whose audience was going up instead of down.

Our journalistic peers took notice. *The Los Angeles Times* said, "NOW's team of reporters has regularly put the rest of the media to shame, pursuing stories few others bother to touch."

The *Philadelphia Inquirer* said our segments on the sciences, the arts, politics and the economy were "provocative public television at its best."

The *Austin American Statesman* called NOW "the perfect antidote to today's high pitched decibel level—a smart, calm, timely news program."

Frazier Moore of the Associated Press said we were "hard-edged when appropriate but never Hardball. Don't expect combat. Civility reigns."

And the *Baton Rouge Advocate* said "NOW invites viewers to consider the deeper implication of the daily headlines," drawing on "a wide range of viewpoints which transcend the typical labels of the political left or right."

Let me repeat that: NOW draws on "a wide range of viewpoints which transcend the typical labels of the political left or right."

The Public Broadcasting Act of 1967 had been prophetic. Open public television to the American people—offer diverse interests, ideas and voices . . . be fearless in your belief in democracy—and they will come.

Hold your applause—that's not the point of the story.

The point of the story is something only a handful of our team, including my wife and partner Judith Davidson Moyers, and I knew at the time—that the success of NOW's journalism was creating a backlash in Washington.

The more compelling our journalism, the angrier the radical right of the Republican party became. That's because the one thing they loathe more than liberals is the truth. And the quickest way to be damned by them as liberal is to tell the truth.

This is the point of my story: Ideologues don't want you to go beyond the typical labels of left and right. They embrace a world view that can't be proven wrong because they will admit no evidence to the contrary. They want your reporting to validate their belief system and when it doesn't, God forbid. Never mind that their own stars were getting a fair shake on NOW: Gigot, Viguerie, David Keene of the American Conservative Union, Stephen Moore of the Club for Growth, and others. No, our reporting was giving the radical right fits because it wasn't the party line. It wasn't that we were getting it wrong. Only three times in three years did we err factually, and in each case we corrected those errors as soon as we confirmed their inaccuracy. The problem was that we were getting it right, not right-wing—telling stories that partisans in power didn't want told.

. . . Strange things began to happen. Friends in Washington called to say that they had heard of muttered threats that the PBS reauthorization would be held off "unless Moyers is dealt with." The Chairman of the Corporation for Public Broadcasting, Kenneth Tomlinson, was said to be quite agitated. Apparently there was apoplexy in the right wing aerie when I closed the broadcast one Friday night by putting an American flag in my lapel and said—well, here's exactly what I said.

"I wore my flag tonight. First time. Until now I haven't thought it necessary to display a little metallic icon of patriotism for everyone to see. It was enough to vote, pay my taxes, perform my civic duties, speak my mind, and do my best to raise our kids to be good Americans.

Sometimes I would offer a small prayer of gratitude that I had been born in a country whose institutions sustained me, whose armed forces protected me, and whose ideals inspired me; I offered my heart's affections in return. It no more occurred to me to flaunt the flag on my chest than it did to pin my mother's picture on my lapel to prove her son's love. Mother knew where I stood; so does my country. I even tuck a valentine in my tax returns on April 15.

So what's this doing here? Well, I put it on to take it back. The flag's been hijacked and turned into a logo—the trademark of a monopoly on patriotism. On those Sunday morning talk shows, official chests appear adorned with the flag as if it is the good housekeeping seal of approval. During the State of the Union, did you notice Bush and Cheney wearing the flag? How come? No administration's patriotism is ever in doubt, only its policies. And the flag bestows no immunity from error. When I see flags sprouting on official lapels, I think of the time in China when I saw Mao's little red book on every official's desk, omnipresent and unread.

But more galling than anything are all those moralistic ideologues in Washington sporting the flag in their lapels while writing books and running Web sites and publishing magazines attacking dissenters as un-American. They are people whose ardor for war grows disproportionately to their distance from the fighting. They're in the same league as those swarms of corporate lobbyists wearing flags and prowling Capitol Hill for tax breaks even as they call for more spending on war.

So I put this on as a modest riposte to men with flags in their lapels who shoot missiles from the safety of Washington think tanks, or argue that sacrifice is good as long as they don't have to make it, or approve of bribing governments to join the coalition of the willing (after they first stash the cash.) I put it on to remind myself that not every patriot thinks we should do to the people of Baghdad what Bin Laden did to us. The flag belongs to the country, not to the government. And it reminds me that it's not un-American to think that war—except in self-defense—is a failure of moral imagination, political nerve, and diplomacy. Come to think of it, standing up to your government can mean standing up for your country."

. . . Someone has said recently that the great raucous mob that is democracy is rarely heard and that it's not just the fault of the current residents of the White House and the capital. There's too great a chasm between those of us in this business and those who depend on TV and radio as their window to the world. We treat them too much as an audience and not enough as citizens. They're invited to look through the window but too infrequently to come through the door and to participate, to make public broadcasting truly public.

To that end, five public interests groups including Common Cause and Consumers Union will be holding informational sessions around the country to "take public broadcasting back"—to take it back from threats, from interference, from those who would tell us we can only think what they command us to think.

It's a worthy goal.

We're big kids; we can handle controversy and diversity, whether it's political or religious points of view or two loving lesbian moms and their kids, visited by a cartoon rabbit. We are not too fragile or insecure to see America and the world entire for all their magnificent and sometimes violent confusion. There used to be a thing or a commodity we put great store by," John Steinbeck wrote. "It was called the people."

Questions for Discussion and Writing

Keynote Address

1. In your opinion, what are the most important claims that Moyers makes in his Keynote Address? Explain. How well does he define and support those claims? Explain.

2. Moyers cites a Carnegie Foundation report that maintains young people do not vote mainly because they don't "have enough information to be informed about issues or candidates." Based on your own observations and experiences, why else don't more young people vote?

3. We have learned that effective communicators are very aware of their audiences' understanding and beliefs with regard to the argument they are making. Based on your reading of this Address, what kind of audience is Moyers communicating with, and how does he go about constructing his argument with that audience in mind?

4. What kind of argument do you think Moyers is making—a causal argument, an evaluative argument, or an argument proposing action? Explain. And given that rhetorical goal, what do you think are his argument's strengths and weaknesses?

5. Since the context and/or occasion of an argument is an important rhetorical consideration, how does the fact that it is a "Keynote Address" help shape the argument?

Closing Address

6. What do you think are the most important claims that Moyers makes in his Closing Address? Explain. How well has he supported these claims?

7. Moyers references George Orwell's character Symes who explains that the purpose of "Newspeak" is to limit thinking. "Orthodoxy means not thinking—not needing to think. Orthodoxy is unconsciousness," Symes explains. Do you think Moyers is justified in connecting "Newspeak" to the way that the Bush Administration shapes the language of its policies? Why or why not?

8. Moyers discloses how he has personally been attacked for his investigative reports that often shine a light into the misconduct of government or big business. Do you believe such disclosures serve a public interest or is Moyers merely grandstanding? What does he say that convinces you one way or the other?

9. Moyers ends with a reference to writer John Steinbeck who reminds us that "the people" are this country's greatest resource. Do you agree that "the people" can be that force to create change in the media?

10. How do you think both the audience and occasion for this "Closing Address" help shape the structure and content of the argument Moyers is making?

11. Given the Internet, the proliferation of cable and satellite television and radio stations, etc., are Moyers's fears and concerns relevant? If so, why? If not, why not?

Making Connections

1. Despite their similar subject matter, Moyers's two arguments were made to different audiences in different contexts—a Keynote speech (2003) versus a Closing speech (2005). What important comparisons and contrasts can you make between them?

2. What is at the heart of Moyers's and Bagdikian's arguments? Why do you think they so passionately care about freedom and truth?

3. What is your experience of election coverage, political debates, and press conferences? Do you feel that you understand the major issues of our time well enough to voice an informed opinion? If so, provide an example or two. From your reading so far, do you think the media is effective in helping citizens to think critically about these issues? Explain.

Visual Exercise

Consider how effectively the following graph helps convey a trend whose impact could be diminished by text alone.

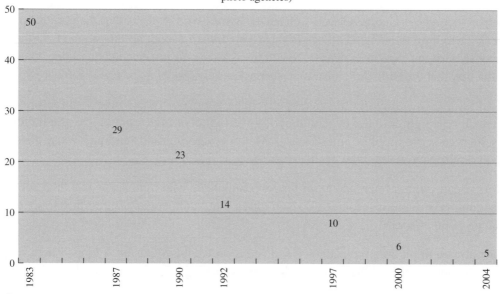

Number of corporations that control a majority of U.S. media:
(newspapers, magazines, TV and radio stations, books, music, movies, videos, wire services and photo agencies)

Source: www.corporations.org, based on the information from *The New Media Monopoly* by Ben H. Bagdikian, Beacon Press, 2004.

Questions

1. What is your first impression of the information the graph is communicating to you? Explain your response.

2. What informational claims does the graph make?

3. Explain the relationship between the visual elements and the text?

4. Is the data presented clear and are the display methods true to the data? What elements are most effective? Least effective?

5. Is the context full enough so that the data can be understood and believed? If so, why? If not, why not?

6. How does the information communicated in the visual (both the graph and its accompanying text) relate to Moyers' informational claims?

7. If you could ask questions of the person who designed the visual (both the graph and its text) what would they be? Explain.

Domination Fantasies:
Does Rupert Murdoch control the media? Does anyone?
Ben Compaine

Ben Compaine (b. 1945) is at home both in institutions of higher education and in business. He teaches entrepreneurship at Northeastern University, and he is a consultant in the area of international innovation. An author of 12 books, Compaine's interests also include mass media economics, telecommunications policy, and the social, economic, and political implications of technological change. In this article, written for the libertarian journal *Reason* (January 2004), Compaine rejects reformist claims that big business media ownership has created a monopoly that subverts the media's fundamental role and purposes in a democracy. He argues that the facts show just the opposite: since deregulation, Americans have an unprecedented amount of diversity in their mass media, and their choices are more plentiful than ever.

****

A COLLEGE PRESIDENT once told me, "I've never seen a pancake so thin it didn't have two sides." The hype and noise surrounding the Federal Communications Commission's proposed relaxation of broadcast outlet ownership rules have made the perennial debate over media concentration seem like a one-sided pancake: No right-thinking person is in favor of more media consolidation.

Yet the FCC has research, technology, and economics on its side, while its critics rely on emotion, utopian visions, and anecdotes. Unfortunately for sound policy making, the hysteria has swept along many lawmakers, who are either pandering to uninformed voters or being poorly advised by their own staffs.

Last June the FCC proposed rules easing some of its longstanding regulations. Most controversially, under prodding from several federal court decisions, it raised the maximum national audience size a single television broadcaster would be allowed to reach from 35 percent to 45 percent, while liberalizing restrictions on common ownership of newspapers and TV stations in a single local market. Sen. Byron L. Dorgan (D-N.D.) led the fight against the FCC's new rules, sponsoring a resolution to combat galloping concentration in the media.

The first problem with the anti-FCC activists is that their basic premise is false. The media industry is not, as a matter of fact, highly concentrated. Moreover, it has not become substantially more concentrated during the last decade or so, despite repeated warnings to the contrary. Most important, there is no compelling evidence that the current level of media concentration has had negative consequences for consumers, culture, or democracy.

Like blind men trying to describe an elephant by touching only a leg or a trunk, critics of media concentration are each touching different parts of a complex beast and proclaiming to know its true, malevolent nature. They tend to focus on one of three main concerns: economic power, cultural power, and political power. Each of these fears is overblown.

THE MONOPOLY THAT ISN'T

Overall, the media industry—including broadcasters, newspapers, magazines, book publishers, music labels, cable networks, film and television producers, Internet-based information providers, and so on—is not substantially more concentrated than it was 10 or 15 years ago. Even after a period of mild deregulation and high-profile mergers, the top 10 U.S. media companies own only a slightly bigger piece of the overall media pie than the top 10 of two decades ago. In my book *Who Owns the Media?,* I compiled data showing that the top 10 media companies accounted for 38 percent of total revenue in the mid-1980s, and 41 percent in the late 1990s. As important, the lists are not filled with the same companies. Meanwhile, the rest of the media universe has continued to expand and diversify: There are more magazine and book publishers than ever, and new categories of vibrant media that were inconceivable just a decade or two ago.

The general assumption is that fewer and larger companies are controlling more and more of what we see, hear, and read. Certainly a casual scanning of the headlines lends evidence: Time merges with Warner, buys CNN, and then combines with America Online. But the incremental growth of smaller companies from the bottom up does not attract the same attention. Break-ups and divestitures do not generally get front-page treatment, nor does the arrival of new players or the shrinkage of old ones.

Right now, the 50 largest media companies account for little more of total U.S. media revenue than they did in 1986. Back then, for example, CBS was the largest media company in the country, with sizable interests in broadcasting, magazines, and book publishing. In the following decade it sold off its magazines, divested its book publishing, and was not even among the 10 largest American media companies by the time it agreed to be acquired by Viacom in 1999. Conversely, Bertelsmann, though a major player in Germany in 1986, was barely visible in the United States. Ten years later, it was the third-largest media company in America. Upstarts such as Amazon.com, Books-A-Million, Comcast, and C-Net were nowhere to be found on a list of the largest media companies in 1986.

Others, such as Allied Artists, Macmillan, and Playboy Enterprises, either folded or grew so slowly they fell out of the top ranks. It is a dynamic industry.

In 1986, I employed a widely-used measure of economic concentration called the Herfindahl-Hirschmann Index (HHI), to assess the 50 largest American media industry players. In the HHI a score of 10,000 means a total monopoly. Anything above 1,800 indicates a highly concentrated market; 1,000 represents the bottom range of oligopolistic tendencies (meaning the major companies have some capability to limit price competition and perhaps indirectly constrain the range of content diversity), while any score under 1,000 reveals a competitive market. In 1997, the index for media companies stood at 268. This was up some from 206 in 1986, but hardly what you'd expect given fears of concentration. Skeptics would point out that 1997 was before AOL and Time Warner or CBS and Viacom merged, but it was also before magazine publisher Ziff-Davis broke itself up or Thomson, once the owner of more newspapers than any other company in North America, sold off most of its holdings to several established as well as newer players. Competitiveness in media compares favorably to other industries: The 1997 HHI for American motor vehicles was 2,506; for semiconductors, 1,080; and for pharmaceuticals, 446.

Much of the best-known merger activity has been more like rearranging the industry furniture: In the last 15 years, the American owners of MCA and its Universal Pictures subsidiary sold out to the Japanese firm Matsushita, who then sold Universal to Seagram's (Canada), who sold it to Vivendi (France), which is selling parts of it to General Electric's NBC. But at the same time Vivendi sold textbook publisher Houghton-Mifflin to a private investment group, and it did not include its Universal Music Group in the NBC sale. There is an ebb as well as flow, even among the largest media companies.

With all this fluidity, it is strange to read in the 1992 edition of Ben Bagdikian's influential book *The Media Monopoly* that our primary concern should be about "concentrated control" by "fifty corporations." Monopoly means exclusive control by one company. An oligopoly could involve two or three or four. In a 2001 online debate with me, academic critic and anti-consolidation activist Robert McChesney wrote that a top tier of seven "transnational giants—AOL Time Warner, Disney, Bertelsmann, Vivendi Universal, Sony, Viacom and News Corporation— . . . together own all the major film studios and music companies, most of the cable and satellite TV systems and stations, the U.S. television networks, much of global book publishing and much, much, more." Of course, he wrote this in 2001, before Comcast became the largest cable company. So now it's the top eight? McChesney continues that the media cabal "is rounded out by a second tier of 60-80 firms," including many based in Asia and Latin America.

It is hard to contend that such a large and diverse group of companies has anything like "monopoly power" certainly in the economic sense. Indeed, any industry with 60 or more major players (who frequently change positions, appear out of nowhere, and disappear altogether) seems the very definition of a strong, competitive market.

HOW DEREGULATION SAVED TELEVISION

If the charge of media monopoly is patently false, there is a set of seemingly more plausible, yet vaguer anxieties about the control of content. The basic argument here is that consolidation of the media into fewer hands results in less diversity of substance, both in terms of political views and cultural richness. Media moguls, goes this line of thinking, can and do exert substantial political clout on issues affecting their own economic interests. Like any other interest group, they push for policies that secure or improve their positions and make it more difficult for new players to enter their field. Vertically integrated media companies will favor their own in-house production over "independent" producers. The result in each case is a supposedly diminished marketplace of ideas and cultural offerings. As Bagdikian puts it, "The American audience, having been exposed to a narrowing range of ideas over the decades, often assumes that what it sees and hears in the major media is all there is. It is no way to maintain a lively marketplace of ideas, which is to say that it is no way to maintain a democracy."

There is little doubt that major players in any given industry will try to create or influence legislation to shore up their positions. Just as steel makers and the unions representing steelworkers lobby for tariffs and bailouts, we can expect media companies to push for policies they think will benefit them. This is certainly the case with recent changes in copyright, which have been strongly pushed by some media companies. But deregulation, when done properly, typically unleashes market forces that make it increasingly difficult for any one company to dominate an industry. And firms that grow under deregulation typically do so by expanding the range of their offerings. (As we'll see, this is the case with Fox, the bête noire of many media concentration activists.)

When it comes to the proposed FCC changes or questions about the effects of supposed media concentration, there's little indication that the public is exposed to a narrower range of ideas, perspectives, or culture. Indeed, the current flowering of offerings is in large part due to some small deregulatory steps taken by the FCC in the 1980s.

Television, the medium that arouses the most emotion in this debate, illustrates how this process has worked out during the last couple of decades. Consider the following points:

- As even a casual watcher would attest, television has become exponentially more competitive in the last two decades, populated by many new players and distribution channels. Often ignored is the fact that it took two deregulatory moves by the FCC to encourage the formation of the newer networks. When Newton Minow, chairman of the FCC under President Kennedy, made a speech in 1961 calling TV a "vast wasteland," television was synonymous with the three television broadcast networks that existed then and for another quarter of a century there after. Today, there are seven national broadcast networks, five of which—ABC, CBS, Fox, NBC, and the WB—have distinct ownerships. (UPN is owned by Viacom, which owns CBS; NBC has a minority interest in the VAX broadcast network.)

  Breaking the logjam was News Corp.'s Fox network, which made its debut in 1986, not coincidentally the same year that the FCC increased the number of stations a single entity could own from seven to 12. This change gave News Corp. the leverage to use a core of stations it owned to launch a network. The FCC also granted a waiver from rules that prohibited the older networks from owning their programming. News Corp. had previously bought 20th Century Fox and its television production unit, providing the company a base from which to make the costly start-up of a national network more feasible. Fox showed the way for similar ventures by station-owning and content-controlling media companies to start the WB and UPN. New, competitive networks had long been the holy grail of those who criticized television programming as dull and uninventive; they were created by deregulation and market forces, which many critics (then and now) view as the enemy.

- The universal access of households to the vast channel capacity of cable and satellite or digital broadcast satellite (DBS) services has eroded the notion that "television" is synonymous with the technology of "broadcasting." (The growth of cable and, later, DBS only became possible after deregulatory moves of the late '70s and early '80s—moves that were staunchly opposed by the broadcast networks. Mainstays of today's content universe, such as CNN, ESPN, and HBO, among scores of others, do not rely on the UHF and VHF spectrum licenses of old-time broadcasters.) Cable is available to 97 percent of American households, and DBS is available to nearly 100 percent of the country. Today, about 90 percent of households with television sets subscribe to a multichannel service, primarily cable and DBS, which is up from about 23 percent in 1980. At the same time, the number of channels available to subscribers has grown about fivefold—from a typical system with six to 12 channels in 1981 to an average of 58 in 2001. The result has been a diversity of programming niches on cable/DBS so vast as to be unimaginable 30 years ago. Among other things, channels ranging from The History Channel to National Geographic to Biography to BBC America to Bravo have meant that the Public Broadcasting Service, originally created in 1969 as an outlet for supposedly non-commercial and culturally serious programming, has had to reinvent itself. Into the 1970s, 90 percent of the prime-time television audience was tuned in to one of the three networks. Today, the new expanded line-up of broadcast networks struggles to get 50 percent, with the rest split among the many unique cable offerings. In fact, cable programs recently have surpassed broadcast programs in prime-time ratings.

- Although a very minor portion of television content can be classified as news and information at either the network or local level, worries over diversity in this form of programming are a regular theme for the opponents of regulatory relaxation. Yet there are, by several orders of magnitude, more news and information available today than 25 years ago. Then, there were just three evening network newscasts, each lasting 30 minutes. Besides CBS' 60 Minutes, there were only a handful of prime-time network specials. Local news, weather, and sports were, much as they are today, a quick and shallow gloss available in most television markets. Today there are three 24-hour news channels (CNN, Fox News, and MSNBC), plus the financial news channels CNBC and CNNfn. There are regional all-news channels like New England Cable News. Channels such as the History Channel and Biography Channel provide daily programming similar to the documentaries that used to be "specials" on the broadcast networks and PBS. The programming on these channels comes from many sources, including independent and freelance producers.

- There is nothing inherently better or more "diverse" about a media company buying its content from outside sources rather than from its vertically integrated production operation. The trend in recent mergers has been for distributors, i.e., broadcast networks, to align with production companies, i.e., film studios. Their decision to do so is a classic "make vs. buy" case. No one has criticized newspapers for running their own content-creation businesses, even though they could rely on freelancers and independent contractors. Some do more than others. Magazines do some of both. TV networks and local stations have long had their own in-house news operations. But a combination of business model and (for two decades) regulation kept most entertainment production out-of-house at the three older networks. Over time the combined studios/ TV networks are likely to find that they were better off being able to pick and choose programming from what outsiders offered them rather than being stuck with whatever their limited in-house operations offer. The economics offer powerful incentives: To cite one of many examples, Warner Brothers Television, part of AOL Time Warner, owner of the WB and HBO television networks, produces the top-rated television show, ER. It could run that show on either of those in-house networks, but instead sells it to NBC, based on a cold calculation that this is the better financial decision.

- Nor should anyone assume that smaller media entities are somehow "better" in the quality or quantity of news and public affairs programming. Or even that a commonly owned newspaper and television station in the same market create a single "voice." Studies by the FCC's Media Ownership Policy Working Group found that the local television stations owned by the large broadcast networks receive awards for news excellence at three times the rate of stations owned by smaller groups, and produce nearly 25 percent more news and public affairs programming than non-network-owned affiliates. Television stations owned by enterprises that also own newspapers have higher news ratings, win more news awards, and offer more news shows than non-newspaper affiliates. And in 10 cities where the newspaper and a TV station had common ownership, half of the combinations had a similar editorial slant in the 2000 presidential election, while the other half had divergent slants.

There are other points to consider when reflecting on the variety of material and viewpoints available in what Stanford law professor and FCC critic Lawrence Lessig decries as an era "when fewer and fewer control access to media." Movie studios now derive more revenue from video cassettes and DVDs than they do from ticket sales. The relatively new formats allow smaller and specialty producers to get distribution for their exercise tapes, music videos, documentaries, foreign language works, and other types of content that could not get theatrical or network distribution in the good old days. With the proliferation of rental stores, chain merchants such as Best Buy and Wal-Mart, and untold thousands of e-commerce sites, audiences have far greater access than at any time in history to programming from sources other than the traditional mass audience producers.

Similarly, the Internet has proved a boon for news, information, and entertainment, whether global, national, or local. While not a direct substitute for TV (yet), the Internet boasts a historically fast adoption rate. In less than 10 years since its widespread commercial availability, about 60 percent of Americans have access to the Internet and nearly 30 percent of Internet households now have broadband connections, according to figures derived from the FCC and the National Telecommunications and Information Administration. The rapid adoption of wireless networks in homes promises further portability of Internet-based content, bringing small but serviceable video and high-quality audio to computer monitors. Studies have found that households with the highest Internet usage are shifting their time away from television viewing.

There is one last paradox regarding concerns about programming "diversity." News Corp.'s Fox Network and its cable Fox News Channel are commonly trotted out by critics as icons of what is bad about the media. For example, McChesney dismisses Fox News with the assertion that it "does virtually no journalism at all. Its profitability is based on eliminating core journalism operations as much as possible, and broadcasting far less expensive commentators like Bill O'Reilly who merely pontificate ad nauseam." Yet both Fox operations are exactly what media critics have been calling for over the decades: a clear and decisive alternative to what had been considered the bland middle ground of the traditional TV networks.

HONORING PROFITS

Animus against the profit motive runs deep among FCC critics and activist groups. Consider this complaint in the mission statement of the Free Press, a lobbying group founded by McChesney: "The main problem is that the structure of the media system makes socially dubious behavior . . . the rational outcome." One proposed scenario? "If the government gave all the publicly owned radio and TV frequencies to nonprofit groups, rather than a relative handful of huge corporations, the content of our broadcasting system would probably be radically different from what exists today."

They are almost certainly half right. Content might well be different. But it wouldn't necessarily be better. Would nonprofits be able to pay their employees well? Would they have the capital to reinvest in equipment and technologies? Who would determine the content of their programming, and on what basis? This might work only in a Harrison Bergeron world of enforced equality, where no democracy of content was allowed, where the voice of the audience was not heard. The experience with the Public Broadcasting Service is instructive in this regard. At its best, PBS could rarely get the attention of more than 2 percent of the total TV audience. And that was when it had only three rivals. Who exactly would benefit from a model of only PBS-like programming?

Few Americans are aware that in the 1980s VCRs were bought in Western Europe at a far more rapid clip than in the U.S. The reason was that almost all of these societies at the time had the choice of only a handful of "public service" television stations, owned or controlled by the government. The VCR gave the audience the freedom to go to the new rental stores and spend some of their TV time watching entertainment they wanted, not what some elites thought would be good for them. In the U.S. we not only had more choice with the commercial networks, but with the added options provided by cable, VCRS eventually became pervasive, but with less urgency than elsewhere.

A.J. Liebling, the outspoken press critic of half a century ago, had a pragmatic insight into why the ownership structure of the media—primarily newspapers then—was a positive influence on content. In his 1947 book *The Wayward Pressman* he wrote, "The profit system, while it insures the predominant conservative coloration of our press, also guarantees that there will always be a certain amount of dissidence. The American press has never been monolithic, like that of an authoritarian state. One reason is that there is always money to be made in journalism by standing up for the underdog. . . . [The underdog's] wife buys girdles and baking powder and Literary Guild selections, and the advertiser has to reach her."

At the time Liebling wrote this, the Hearst newspaper chain controlled more local circulation than any newspaper company does today. But his insights are actually more relevant today than in 1947. Profit, not ideology, means that whether one wants to focus on the 10 largest conglomerates or the 50 largest players or whatever other number, the content of the media is determined not by what the chief executive officer wants, but by what thousands of editors, producers, publishers, and local operating managers determine is right for the audience they are trying to reach.

This is one reason why big business and business executives are regularly made the villains (see *The China Syndrome*, *Broadcast News*, and *Erin Brockovich*, among many) in film and television features produced by major media companies. In many instances, the profit motive means localism prevails over centralization. It is not likely to matter much (and indeed experience shows it does not) whether a local TV station is owned by a company headquartered in another city. The decisions for much news and information need to be made locally if the owner wants to attract its share of the audience. In short, both locally and nationally owned media outlets are driven by the profit motive.

In fact, the notion that local owners of newspapers or TV and radio stations are inherently "better"—usually taken to mean more "objective"—than a large corporation has no standing in the real world. Some of the most biased newspapers in 20th-century history—McCormick's *Chicago Tribune*, Annenberg's *Philadelphia Inquirer*, Loeb's *Manchester Union-Leader*—were the creations of local ownership. Local owners are more likely than remote corporate owners to have ties to the local political and business establishment. Local owners may not have the economic resources to withstand a boycott by real estate or banking or similar interests should they risk some criticism of the local industry. Large chains, on the other hand, are far less affected economically by a short-term downturn in any one community. And it is less likely that the publisher is a prep school buddy of the mayor.

On the other extreme from local ownership, Clear Channel Communications has become the poster child for all that has gone wrong with media regulation. The Web magazine *Salon* headlines it as "Dirty Tricks and Crappy Programming." The chain owns nearly 1,200 radio stations nationally and is the dominant owner in many local markets. I am not about to defend Clear Channel's acquisitions or its policies, but the other side of the pancake has received little attention.

First, some context. Clear Channel's 1,200 stations exist in a universe of more than 10,500 commercial radio stations in the U.S. (compared to less than 8,000 in 1980). On a national basis, it owns less than 12 percent of all commercial stations. Its growth, as well as that of smaller chains, has been dramatic. But, again, there is context: Until 1985, a single owner could own a maximum of just 14 stations. By 1992 this limit had been raised to 36. Still, regulation kept size artificially low. Only in 1996, when the Telecommunications Act became law, were national limits eliminated, other than existing antitrust laws.

Salon's Eric Boehlert writes that after the "domination" by Clear Channel and second-place Infinity Broadcasting, "The result, many longtime radio industry observers feel, has been the degradation of commercial radio as a creative, independent medium." Yet anyone who remembers the radio of the 1950s and the '60s can recall a bland mix of Top 40 stations, sports, talk, and pop. There were, as now, a handful of jazz and classical stations. The late 1960s and '70s saw the unleashing of the FM band and its superior fidelity. There was a brief Golden Age of freeform stations that mixed psychedelic rock with more outer forms of music. But such "innovation" had fizzled out long before Clear Channel.

The Top 40 list in Philadelphia was rarely much different than the playlist in Denver. Precious little radio programming has truly been local other than the sports scores, traffic, weather, and perhaps some early Sunday morning interview. No matter who owns the local stations, it's unlikely that Clear Channel's Boston stations will be giving the Miami traffic report.

Like television, the radio business is changing rapidly. Here, it is satellite and the Internet that are driving progress. Satellite radio services, such as XM and Sirius, are providing new options, with dozens of commercial-free "stations" for those who are willing to pay $120 annually. And the Internet is a very robust option for anyone unsatisfied with what they get on the AM and FM dials. Services such as Real One Radio and Live365 offer thousands of radio options. Some are transmissions of over-the-air stations from around the world. In a 2001 study I co-authored, we found more than 2,500 stations listed at RealOneRadio.com. The most listened-to stations were those that were Web based only.

Services such as Live365 provide the capability for anyone to put themselves "on the air" over the Internet for as little as $10 a month. And *The Boston Globe* recently reported that 100,000 listeners a day are using this nascent service. The consumer research firm Arbitron says that in August 2003, 50 million Americans viewed a video or listened to an audio stream on the Internet. "The idea that Rupert Murdoch's Fox media empire or Arthur Sulzberger's at *The New York Times* can overwhelm the voice of the people seems a little more absurd with each new broadband Internet subscription" concluded *Globe* technology columnist Hiawatha Bray.

PUBLIC CONSIDERATIONS

Publicly owned companies are frequently criticized for being too driven by quarterly earnings needs. It is a fair criticism. So it is again ironic that the poster child for the evils of media conglomerates, News Corp., is probably the least driven by short-term profits and quarterly earnings. Though the company is publicly owned, working control and ownership have been retained by its chairman, Rupert Murdoch, and his family. The company has invested hundreds of millions of dollars into its groundbreaking efforts in creating the Fox Network, then a viable second all-news cable network, then creating direct broadcast satellite service covering parts of the Third World as well as developed countries that did not have the advantage of a multi-channel cable infrastructure. While in no way endorsing his apparent political ideology, one might even point to his bankrolling of the conservative *Weekly Standard* as another contribution Murdoch has made to the marketplace of ideas and cultural offerings.

Advocates for small, local, nonprofit media companies routinely ignore or discount the benefits of profit-driven public ownership. The stocks of these companies are widely held—by teachers' pension funds, by mutual funds, by individuals, and by 401(k) plans. The boards of these companies have a fiduciary responsibility to their stockholders. Most of them, most of the time, take that seriously. Restricting their coverage, their range of films or magazine titles or news shows, is not what the big companies are about. They simultaneously seek to reach the mass market when they can and niche markets when they spot them. Given the vast diversity of interests in a nation the size of the United States, there is potential profit in reaching the right wing as well as the left wing, in programming for Spanish speakers as well as English, in publishing books for escapism and for self-help, in investigative reporting that is critical of government as well as editorials that are supportive. And if the big guys don't provide it, some small publisher or producer will.

Having said that, it remains likely that, as in many fields, a relatively small number of companies will capture a large chunk of market share. This needs to be understood properly. If large segments of the public choose to watch, read, or listen to content from a relatively small number of media companies, that should not distract policy makers from the key word there: choose. At a time when such a fragmented audience is dividing itself among niche cable channels, tens of thousands of book titles published annually, and hyper-individualized Web surfing, it may even be socially positive that there are some mass audience shows, movies, and books that, like the *Harry Potter* series, give us something common to talk about. It may indeed be that at any given moment 80 percent of the audience is viewing or reading or listening to something from the 10 largest media players. But that does not mean it is the same 80 percent all the time, or that it is cause for concern.

Walter Lippmann once wrote, "The theory of a free press is that truth will emerge from free discussion, not that it will be presented perfectly and instantly in any one account." I have never heard a convincing argument that any individual in the United States in 2003 cannot easily and inexpensively have access to a huge variety of news, information, opinion, culture, and entertainment, whether from 10, 50, or 3,000 sources. If that is what passes for media concentration, we should consider ourselves pretty lucky.

Questions for Discussion and Writing

1. At the outset of his article Compaine states, "No right-thinking person is in favor of more media consolidation." Is this strategy an effective way to reach a skeptical reader? Why or why not?

2. Media critics "rely on emotion, utopian visions, and anecdotes," argues Compaine. Throughout his article, he brings detailed factual support to his position. How effective is his statement as a rhetorical device to shape his argument? Explain.

3. Compaine maintains that deregulation unleashes market forces, thereby creating more competition and diversity. Does his argument hold up? Explain.

4. What are the most important claims in this article, and how effectively does Compaine develop and support them? Explain.

5. In terms of the way we have been discussing argument, what are Compaine's rhetorical goals? How well does he satisfy the rhetorical requirements of those goals? Explain.

6. If you could ask Compaine any questions, what would they be? Why? And how do you think he would respond?

7. Overall, what do you think are the strengths and weakness of Compaine's argument?

Making Connections

1. Whereas Compaine contends that the big players operate in a competitive market that ultimately is good for the public at large, Moyers maintains that after deregulation, newsrooms not only placed commercial values over in-depth investigative journalism, but newsrooms were also forced to cut staff. Which view do you think more insightfully explains the impact of media ownership concentration? Why?

2. Again, in each of these arguments, is there a fundamental clash between two "rights" or "goods"? If we give people the freedom to choose what to read, watch, and listen to, how can we make sure people get the kinds of information that will also make them informed citizens?

3. Throughout this book, you have observed how asking questions can help initiate meaningful inquiry. What questions or issues about the media that most concern or interest you have not been answered or addressed by the essays in this chapter?

Poverty Slighted by the Media
Melissa Manchester (Student)

In the following essay, college student Melissa Manchester investigates how American poverty is represented in the media, and how its presentation influences people's perceptions of the poor. Note, in particular, that Melissa's questions generate the kind of answers that lead to provocative lines of inquiry.

* * * * * * * *

1   The word "poverty" may conjure an immediate image of a begrimed child clothed in rags while begging on a street corner. While it certainly epitomizes poverty, could this image blind us to the face of poverty that sits next to us in our English class or passes us in the supermarket? Poverty is presented to us through various media, yet it is rarely discussed as being directly relevant to our lives. Rather than a universal problem prevalent in the United States, it is often perceived as a problem of Third World countries. Perhaps we need to ask if the media presents poverty in such a way that we tend to overlook the issue.

2   Though some, like Dinesh D'Souza, author of *The Virtue of Prosperity: Finding Value in an Age of Techno-Affluence,* argue that an income gap is the natural result of a prosperous market economy, the real question is whether or not an income gap as large as that of the United States is necessary. To a certain degree, poverty may be inevitable, but the numbers are daunting. According to Gregory Mantsios, author of *Class in America: Myths and Realities,* approximately thirteen percent of Americans live below the government's poverty line, defined as $8,500 for an individual and $17,028 for a family of four. Of these poor, nearly two million are homeless. While one third of the population lives in poverty, another third lives in extreme wealth (187). If this is the reality of our society, how is it reflected in television and news?

3   Recent television programming deals with poverty in various degrees of severity. The 90's sitcom *Roseanne* depicts a blue-collar, two-parent family dealing with the stresses of modern life. The father works in carpentry while the wife co-owns a diner. The family does not lack for food, clothing or education. While they may not enjoy the very best money can buy, they are not struggling for survival. More recently, the WB program *Dawson's Creek,* chronicles the lives of several teenagers. The characters exhibit a fair amount of wealth with the exception of Joey Potter, who is distinguished as coming from a lower economic standing. Despite this, she is always well dressed and articulate. While her family's income forces her to work to pay for college, her financial problems are conveniently lessened by a substantial scholarship to a highly prestigious university.

4   Perhaps one of the best portrayals of poverty is seen in the program *Boston Public.* Set in an urban school, children from lower income families struggle to overcome personal, social and scholarly obstacles. An attempt is made to fully explore the causes and the effects of poverty, as well as the impact it has on an individual's life. *Boston Public,* however, seems to be the exception to the majority of programs that deal with poverty as a token issue. Though these shows attempt to depict the spectrum of poverty, the argument can be made that they do not accurately represent poverty since they are primarily a source of entertainment.

5   Many turn to news programs as a source of reliable information; however, it is important to remember that they are presented through a televised medium. Consequently, they must adhere to certain entertainment tactics to ensure popularity. Issues are discussed in short segments dotted with video clips and pictures. Wealthy celebrities often warrant extensive coverage, as seen in the murder trial of O. J. Simpson. Though certainly a noteworthy trial, the media coverage was unusually extensive as opposed to an unknown person's trial. Poverty is not a glamorous or exciting issue. We are presented with short clips of the homeless and the shelters

they occupy before moving on to the next piece of news. It often seems more of a warning of what not to become than a plea for awareness. Do we even see their plight as having any direct relevance to our lives? If we have never been in their position, does television news coverage force us to relate to those stricken with poverty? Perhaps a communication medium less beholden to the rules of entertainment can offer more insight.

6   Newspapers escape some of the entertainment ploys inherent in television. Headlines draw readers to an article. In a period of six months, *The New York Times* has printed numerous articles that deal with the issue of poverty either indirectly or directly. The myriad approaches used to navigate the topic are fascinating in their content and focus. The articles dealt with poverty in a variety of ways. The majority of articles with the word "poverty" in the headline dealt solely with poverty in foreign countries like China, Lima, India and Afghanistan.

7   Many of these were actually letters to the editor in response to articles that dealt with poverty in a more peripheral manner. One particular letter related poverty to the military situation abroad by voicing the opinion that the true reason for Afghanistan's current aggression is poverty (McGovern). Thus, the issue of poverty is deflected to other countries rather than our own.

8   Very few articles directly addressed poverty in the United States. Again, several were letters to the editor written by representatives of organizations like Planned Parenthood. One such letter was written in response to Mayor Mike Bloomberg's attempt to reach out to advocates of the homeless (Hafetz). Though it dealt with poverty, it was approached within a political sphere.

9   Only one piece spoke directly and solely with poverty. It told the story of a single mother and her children dealing with sudden eviction from their apartment. A few missed paychecks had forced the mother to forego paying the rent until she was finally evicted. Her son had just received a scholarship to a better school as part of a program that tries to help students at risk financially and otherwise. Careful to portray the mother's dedication to her children, the article was compelling and thorough as the author strove to illuminate the myriad problems the poor must deal with (Donovan).

10   Often, the issue of poverty is not obvious at first glance. Recent controversy has arisen over a women's health bill that would provide health care for fetuses as well as coverage for contraceptives and screenings for conditions such as osteoporosis and cervical cancer. This proposal attempts to provide more women with adequate health care, targeting low-income women who may not be able to afford care without financial help. Though this is the core of the issue, headlines about the plan stress the political maneuverings surrounding it. Pro-choice advocates fear that the proposal is a back door attempt to stifle a woman's choice to have an abortion. The Catholic Church is not comfortable with providing its employees with contraceptives while the Republican and Democratic parties have squared off on the bills. Headlines like *Cardinal Lobbies Against Contraceptive Coverage* (Dewan) and *Party Battles Looming Over Costly Old Issue: Health Care Coverage* (Toner) draw attention to the political debates concerning the bills. While the bills will have a direct effect on poverty-stricken women, readers are not given constant reminders of the correlation.

11   Prolonged discussion of poverty is rare in today's society. The issue becomes so highly politicized that the root of the problem becomes enmeshed in the controversy surrounding it. We are kept at a distance, aided by television and news coverage that rarely gives a face to the problem. Without a sympathetic face to relate to, it becomes far easier to make judgments or ignore the problem. Civic-minded organizations are created to address the problem, but involvement is limited. These groups can only reach so many.

12   What would happen were the media to personalize poverty? The results could be staggering. Faced with real people living in poverty, perhaps more people would be instilled with a community consciousness and a sense of moral and social obligation to the poor. Seeing the stark reality of poverty daily in our papers and on our television, we would no longer be able to sidestep the issue. We might even feel compelled to search for the root of the problem and begin to make real advances toward a greater understanding of the problem. It is something worth considering, for we can no longer brush aside the plight of such a large portion of our society. To quote the late Michael Harrington, a social activist, "If in your mind you could not accept a society in which we do unto you as we do unto them, then isn't it time for us to change the way we are acting towards them who are a part of us?" (qtd in Eitzen 166).

WORKS CONSULTED*

Bingaman, Jeff, and Jon S. Corzine. "Health of the Mother." Editorial. *New York Times* 7 Feb. 2002, final ed.: A29. Print.

Boston Public. FOX. 23 Oct. 2000–1 Mar. 2005. Television.

Dawson's Creek. WB. 20 Jan. 1998–14 May 2003. Television.

Dewan, Shaila K. "Cardinal Lobbies in Albany Against Bill for Contraception Coverage." *New York Times* 13 March 2002, final ed.: B5. Print.

Donovan, Aaron. "The Neediest Cases; For Many, Sliding Into Poverty Takes Only a Few Missed Paychecks." *New York Times* 18 Nov. 2001, final ed.: A36. Print.

D'Souza, Dinesh. *The Virtue of Prosperity: Finding Values in an Age of Techno-Affluence*. New York: Touchstone, 2000. Print.

Eitzen, D. Stanley. "The Fragmentation of Social Life: Some Critical Societal Concerns for the New Millennium." Krieger et al. 160-66.

"Ending Chronic Homelessness." Editorial. *New York Times* 13 March 2002, final ed.: A24. Print.

Glick, Deborah and Sheldon Silver. Letter. "Why a Women's Health Bill is Mired in Albany."*New York Times* 11 Feb. 2002, final ed.: A26. Print.

Hafetz, Jonathan L. Letter. "Causes of Homelessness." *New York Times* 27 Jan. 2002, final ed., sec. 4:12. Print.

Works Consulted indicates Melissa has listed sources she has reviewed but not cited in her paper.

Krieger, Barbara Jo, Paul G. Saint-Amand, Warren A. Neal, and Alan L. Steinberg. *Inquiry, Argument, & Change: A Rhetoric with Readings*. Dubuque, IA: Kendall Hunt, 2005. TS.

Mantsios, Gregory. "Class in America: Myths and Realities." Krieger et al. 185-97.

McGovern, George. "The Healing in Helping the World's Poor." Op Ed. *New York Times* 1 Jan. 2002, final ed.: A21. Print.

Perez-Pena, Richard. "Bills to Widen Health Care for Women Pass Assembly." *New York Times* 29 Jan. 2002, final ed.: B6. Print.

———. "The Health Card." *New York Times* 13 Jan. 2002, final ed.: A32. Print.

Purnick, Joyce. "After Election, Health Bill Loses Allure." *New York Times*. 28 Feb. 2002, final ed.: B1.Print.

Roseanne. ABC. 18 Oct. 1988–20 May 1997. Television.

Toner, Robin. "Administration Plans Care of Fetuses in a Health Plan." *New York Times* 1 Feb. 2002, final ed.: A23. Print.

———. "Bush's Proposal on Welfare Draws Fire From Democrats." *New York Times* 13 March 2002, final ed.: A20. Print.

———. "Party Battles Looming Over Costly Old Issue: Health Care Coverage." *New York Times* 11 Jan. 2002, final ed.: A16. Print.

Questions for Discussion and Writing

1. Note how, by reasoning from a variety of viewpoints, Melissa raises numerous questions throughout her essay. How would you characterize the types of questions Melissa uses to frame her inquiry? Is her overall approach effective? If not, why not? If so, how does it help Melissa bring both substance and authority to a controversial issue?

2. Notice how, in her second paragraph, Melissa presents the views of Dinesh D'Souza and Gregory Mantsios (Chapter 4). Does she offer a sufficient account of each author's position in the development of her thesis? Justify your answer.

3. Trace the progression of Melissa's argument. How does she use transitions? How does the form of her argument compare with the work of student writers that you encountered earlier in the book?

Making Connections

1. Melissa's essay was written before Katrina ripped apart the Gulf Coast and exposed the nation to the plight of African-American communities in that region. What insights on poverty do you think Melissa's essay offers that are related to the aftermath of the devastation from that event? Be specific.

2. Critics claim that the mainstream media's coverage of poverty in America is shaped in two distinct directions. Either its focus is sentimental; that is, the poor person, usually a mother, finds herself in desperate straits not of her own making. Or, the story is sensationalist: that is, it alludes to moral or ethical impropriety or to criminal activity by the underclass. What stereotypes, if any, are represented in Melissa's portrayal of poverty in America; do you feel that either Melissa or the critics are over-generalizing? Justify your response.

3. What is your experience with newspaper coverage of poverty? With Internet coverage? With radio coverage? Be specific. Given your reading, do you think the media has betrayed those in poverty?

Short Essay Assignments

1. We began this chapter with a selection from Nichols and McChesney's *Tragedy & Farce: How the American Media Sell Wars, Spin Elections, and Destroy Democracy*. The authors cite three historically significant components necessary to sustain a democracy.

   a) The media must serve as "a rigorous watchdog of those in power and those who wish to be in power;

   b) it must present a wide range of informed views on the most pressing issues of the day;

   c) and it must be able to expose deception and permit the truth to rise to the top."

   Drawing on these principles and your reading, answer the following question:

   Does the media provide Americans with information that is accurate and diverse enough to sustain a democracy? Explain your reasoning.

   As with earlier assignments, your answer to this question will become a claim you develop, support, and perhaps qualify. Again, remember to write as though your audience has not participated in any of your class discussions and, as a way of deepening and enriching your own authority, be sure you adequately represent the authors you have read.

2. Taking *NYT*'s editors Dean Baquet and Bill Keller at their word that their "best judgments" are tempered by national security concerns, this assignment asks you to:

   • locate a news item that has been withheld from publication by major media outlets.
   • make a judgment *either* that the withholding from publication was justified *or* that major media outlets should have distributed the item.
   • write a short essay to support your judgment with a solid argument.

   To identify a withheld news item, go to *Project Censored: The News That Didn't Make the News* at the following URL: [http://www.projectcensored.org]

Project Censored describes itself as a

> *media research group out of Sonoma State University which tracks the news published in independent journals and newsletters. From these, Project Censored compiles an annual list of 25 news stories of social significance that have been overlooked, under-reported or self-censored by the country's major national news media.*
>
> *Between 700 and 1000 stories are submitted to Project Censored each year from journalists, scholars, librarians, and concerned citizens around the world. With the help of more than 200 Sonoma State University faculty, students, and community members, Project Censored reviews the story submissions for coverage, content, reliability of sources and national significance. The university community selects 25 stories to submit to the Project Censored panel of judges who then rank them in order of importance. Current or previous national judges include: Noam Chomsky, Susan Faludi, George Gerbner, Sut Jhally, Frances Moore Lappe, Norman Solomon, Michael Parenti, Herbert I. Schiller, Barbara Seaman, Erna Smith, Mike Wallace and Howard Zinn. All 25 stories are featured in the yearbook, Censored: The News That Didn't Make the News.*

On the *Project Censored* website, you will find a list of the "Top 25 Censored Stories" that have been withheld from publication by mainstream outlets. The subjects range from national security concerns, to the health risks of nanotechnology, to the future of the Internet. Select a story. Then, drawing on the following questions, evaluate whether it should have been withheld or should have been published in the major news outlets.

- Were the decisions not to disclose based on unconfirmed facts in the story, the item's threat to national security, its lack of newsworthiness, or some other reason?

- Did the decision result in good or bad consequences, either for individuals or for society? Justify your answer.

Support your judgment with sound reasoning and solid evidence.

Tips for Structuring Your Essay

Keep in mind that these guidelines are intended to support the careful development and expression of your judgments and are not meant as a formula for structuring your paper.

- You may want to introduce your readers to the Project Censored website and provide some context (history or background) prior to identifying the story you want to examine. Your introduction should also draw attention to the importance of the story.

- Early on, you should provide a thorough enough account of the story so that your readers will be able to follow your judgment of whether the information should have been disclosed. You may also want to identify the criteria upon which you are basing this evaluation. These will likely include the above bulleted questions. In the past, some of our students have combined these questions with the three tests for "Democracy-Sustaining Journalism" found on p. 310 and re-stated on p. 348.

- The body of your essay should clearly show how your position logically follows from the standards or criteria you choose to apply.

- Your conclusion, as noted in earlier chapters, should provide a graceful exit from your paper. The conclusion offers you an opportunity to close with a strong appeal for support of your position. Such an appeal often mentions the broader implications of your argument, including the benefits that would be gained and the consequences that would be avoided by accepting your viewpoint.

3. So far, you have encountered a wide array of voices speaking about pressing media issues including the media's capacity for shaping what counts as fact, the influence of those who hold power and status, and especially the repeal of long-established regulations meant to encourage a diverse and democratic media landscape. Write an essay that builds on your exploration of these trends. Show how and why you support or refute an argument of one or more of the authors you have encountered in this text, or how you would modify or qualify one or more of their views. Whatever you decide, you will need to provide a thoughtful analysis, pro or con, of the arguments, pointing out specific strong points or flaws. As you consider various topics for your paper, think about the ways in which the issues taken up by these writers have influenced your own life. While your discussion should not rely solely on your subjective experience, your personal experience can be a relevant and valuable resource here.

Below are several questions to help you find a subject and develop a focus for your writing.

I   Democracy and the Media

a) What does a democratic media actually require? Does it mean every citizen is entitled to be heard in the media? Or does it mean the media are obligated to present all views? Or are there other principles that make the media democratic? Explain.

b) How important is it that the media be guided by democratic principles? Explain. Do you think average citizens really take note of how democratic the various media are? Why or why not? Do you think they really care? Why or why not? Finally, how do you think the presence or absence of democratic principles in governing media practices might shape the ability of citizens to think critically about important issues? Explain your reasoning.

c) Do you think it is clear to the general public exactly how media outlets make the following decisions:

√ which stories to cover and which to ignore
√ the extent and nature of the coverage

√ whether or not to provide significant discussion of the outcomes or meanings of events? In each case, explain your reasoning.

II Concentration of Media Ownership

a) Provide your thoughts on the following statement: Media empires attempt to control as many different outlets as possible; in doing so, they influence nearly every aspect of American life from music to public policy.

b) The consequences of media ownership raise serious questions about the relationship between diversity and quality. First, has consolidation of ownership substantially reduced the number of individual, independent media outlets available to consumers? Second, has the diversity of media outlets been reduced; that is, are fewer distinct voices being heard? Finally, has the quality of the various media been reduced? In each case, explain your answer.

Now consider your claims carefully. Do you detect a relationship among the three phenomena you described in response to the questions above? Explain your reasoning.

c) Several authors you've read maintain that control of a great many individual media outlets by a few large corporations poses serious risks to a democratic society. Do you agree? Support your answer with verifiable facts and explain your reasoning.

d) The same authors contend that we must take steps to limit the consolidation of media ownership. Assume, for a moment, that their judgments are accurate. What would you propose as a solution for the seeming inevitability of media concentration?

e) The foregoing notwithstanding, some have observed that the big players operate in a competitive market that, by necessity, creates more diversity, not less. What are your thoughts? And what of the average citizen? Does he or she ultimately benefit by market forces that must serve and please so that the owners of the various media stay in business?

III Media and the Public Interest

a) Do you think the average citizen believes the news and broadcast media are fair and accurate? What leads you to your opinion?

b) Two terms often mentioned in this context are "public service" and "public trust." Provide working definitions of the two terms. Then explain why you do or do not believe that the current practices of media professionals exemplify the concepts you have just defined. Are they behaving in ways that should make us inclined to trust them or not? Support your answer.

c) The media constitute a commercial, profit-driven enterprise; theoretically, it should also provide open, vibrant, and diverse coverage. However, can the media meaningfully engage in "public service" and nurture the "public trust" and still make the sort of money they currently do? Or will the desire to make bigger profits actually drive media owners to provide popular rather than significant content? Explain your reasoning.

As you gather your thoughts, remember that the goal is to focus on an issue or problem that is important to you. At the same time, you will want your readers to have a stake in the outcome. Write as though your audience has not read any of the authors presented in your work.

❑ Major Essay Assignment

This chapter's readings explore the premise that access to diverse viewpoints is crucial for an engaged and educated citizenry. In a democracy, both citizens and media must share the responsibility for scrutinizing who is communicating and for what purpose. And yet, some critics maintain that the media has usurped our thinking by manipulating what we know of events and imposing an interpretation on them. No one likes to imagine being so influenced. Fortunately, we can become more than passive receivers of what the media offers. We can even learn to recognize what is not being said—perhaps deliberately so. Our challenge is to become more and more attentive to what we see, hear, or read. These ideas shape the following assignment.

Your assignment is to write an essay in which you support a significant claim about a single media outlet. The support will include a detailed analysis of a specific text. Your analysis will demonstrate how that work exemplifies the policies, biases, or ideology of the outlet.

I Invention: Finding Promising Lines of Inquiry

It might be wise to start by clarifying some of the key terms in the assignment.

Media is a hugely broad and complex term. Here, however, you want to focus on those media that attempt to communicate to large numbers of people—in other words, the *mass media*. These days, the mass media tend to take three forms—print, broadcast, or Internet.

The term *text* is likewise ambiguous. People often use it to refer to something in print. Here, however, you'll use it to denote any individually identifiable, specific production that travels over one of the mass media. For example, a single episode of your favorite television show or a single story in a magazine may be thought of as a *text*.

At this point, you should note there are two ways to proceed into the invention stage of your essay.

- In the top-down approach, you'll begin by working with the entire category of mass media and methodically narrowing the subject to a specific type of media, a specific medium, a specific media outlet, and, ultimately, to the specific text that will provide the subject for your analysis. This approach is probably most useful when you are without a definite idea going into the assignment, although it may overwhelm you if you are not constantly on the lookout for a more focused subject.

- Sometimes the bottom-up approach can be effective. In this case, you already have a specific text in mind and some idea of the claim you intend to support in your essay. You start with the text, place it in the appropriate media outlet, and then in the appropriate medium. Your work is a matter of making the connections between the specific text and the main claim you intend it to support.

While the bottom-up approach may seem easier, it embodies some dangers. It might not take you anywhere you haven't already been or provide you with an opportunity to develop new insights; that is, it may merely provide you with a means of expressing preconceived notions. Moreover, papers written with this approach can lack depth and creativity, and can lead you merely to describe the text and not analyze and evaluate it. Thus, in what follows, we'll work from the top down and encourage you to do the same as you work through the project.

■ Defining and Refining the Subject

Your goal is to focus on specific aspects of the general phenomenon—media; ultimately, you'll focus on a specific text. As you proceed, keep in mind what you've read in the chapter and do not ignore the discoveries you have made in journals exercises, responses to the readings, and in the short essays you wrote. Make notes as ideas and connections occur to you; they will help when you begin to generate the claim you'll support in your essay.

Start by listing the general types of media. We offered three above—print, broadcast, and Internet. If you think of others, add them to the list. For each type, list specific examples. Print media will include newspapers, books, magazines, etc. Continue this "listing and selecting" process down through the various levels of generality until you get to a specific text. This will give you a chain of related phenomena or a line of thought you'll find useful as you construct your essay.

For example, one line might run as follows:

Broadcast Media → Television → Cable Television → Cable News Channels → MSNBC → "Countdown with Keith Olbermann" → February 13, 2007 Show → Olbermann Interview with Jonathon Alter (Senior Editor, *Newsweek*)

One positive aspect of this sort of "refining" is that, if at any time you get "stuck," you can go back up the line and take a slightly different direction. In the line above, perhaps the Alter interview gives you a beginning or a hint of what could turn into a really good idea for your essay, but the interview itself doesn't get you where you want to be. If so, you can go back up the line to the Olbermann show and look at some of the other interviews he's conducted. Or you can go further back up the line to MSNBC and look at other programs.

With this sort of a structure, you're never without a direction; you always have someplace useful to go if you need to.

By the way, one very nice thing about the websites published by news programs is that many of them make full transcripts available online.

Once you settle on a tentative "target text," you'll want to explore it more fully. Try the following questions:

1. What is being said? That is, what is the overall message offered by the text?

2. Does the text you've chosen attempt to create, support, or alter social values? How does that text try to create, support, or alter them?

3. Does the text try to shape your understanding of issues and events? How?

4. Is the text packaged and presented to elicit a preferred response, one that reinforces a belief system? If so, explain the ways in which it tries to achieve this.

5. Is anyone left out of the target audience; that is, have any groups been written out of the text? If so, answer the following questions:
   • How might those missing groups interpret the text?
   • Does excluding them make it easier to circulate certain perceptions and assumptions? If so, how?

6. Is anything of importance not being said; is it deliberately left out? If so, determine whether or not this omission minimizes social problems. If downplaying does occur, explain its likely effects on the intended audiences.

7. How well does the text exemplify the general attitudes and practices of the outlet that produced it?

Remember that any answers you generate in this, the "invention" phase of your writing project, are tentative. You are exploring possibilities—the more the better. So don't be afraid to speculate, and don't reject any ideas because they seem far-fetched or unlikely. It's amazing how the "far-fetched" can evolve into the "creative and insightful" as you work through the process of creating your draft.

■ Looking for Causes and Effects

You will need to question the causes and effects at work in the text you've chosen. You might begin exploring the *causes* by asking who initiated and directed the work. In many cases, it may have been an individual; however, in many more cases, works are directed and shaped by companies, networks, advertisers, and the like. Who are they and what might be their motivations? Was the work motivated by a desire for self- expression? To comment on a social phenomenon? What phenomenon? To encourage individual or social action? What action? To sell a candidate or idea? What candidate? What idea? Most texts have multiple purposes, and you should try to consider each of the relevant ones. Also, determine *why* the producers of your text would *want* to comment on a phenomenon, encourage action, etc. Do they have larger goals? What are those goals and how might this text help achieve them?

One thing you shouldn't forget when considering motivation is that all media involves business. If making money is not the main motivation of those involved in all media, it's certainly in the top three or four. The decisions made about content and presentation are largely controlled by what audiences want to see and will pay for. This brings in elements of *pathos* or the nature of the audience. You would be wise not to neglect this motivation in your analysis.

You should then consider the *effects* of the presentation—both those intended by the producers of a text along with those it actually had or might have on its audience. What will readers, viewers, or listeners understand from it? What sorts of feelings might it evoke? What sorts of actions might it motivate?

What effect will these messages have on one's ability to think critically and perform effectively as an engaged, citizen? And what are the consequences when a large number of people hold informed views on important issues? Will they be willing to accept the risks of the policies they advocate? Will they be more engaged in the processes of shaping society? And what happens if their views are ill informed or if they have been misled or duped by the media?

These are complex and seemingly difficult tasks. However, undertaking them will lead to original and interesting conclusions that you can present to your readers.

■ Assigning Value

When you begin to consider values in relation to the text you have chosen, you will want to examine two somewhat distinct aspects.

First, what values are communicated by the text? In some cases, these values may be clearly stated. Indeed, very often texts are obviously shaped or determined by specific values. Consider what Marc Fisher wrote in the *American Journalism Review* (Oct/Nov. 2005):

> Without electricity, those who lived in the path of Hurricane Katrina depended on old battery-powered radios and whatever newspaper they could borrow for a few minutes from the guy in the next cot.
>
> Katrina, however briefly, took us back to a simpler time. Audiences for the cable news channels tripled and more, but their combined numbers couldn't come close to those of any one of the old broadcast networks. The Internet would come to play an essential and innovative role in bringing people together, but only in the second phase of the coverage. Those first days were a time for intrepid TV cameramen to take us into the stench and the sweat, the anger and the not knowing, the fear of those who seemed abandoned by their own country. Those first days were a time for newspapers to put aside jitters about their declining importance and worries about layoffs and cutbacks. *The old papers instead reasserted the comfort and utility of news you could hold in your hand. . . .*

At every step along the way, *when the bosses let reporters do their jobs*, the results were revelatory . . . (emphasis added)

Clearly, Fisher values the traditional role of the press—to communicate news objectively and with respect for the public's need to be informed—that "comfort and utility" he mentions. Those values drive his entire essay.

Sometimes, however, a producer's values (and goals), while they may again shape the text, are not so clearly communicated. Peter Hart, Director of Fairness and Accuracy in Reporting (FAIR) tackles this issue.* Here are some questions he raises that can reveal values that are not entirely obvious:

- Is there missing context that might undermine the premise of a given article or television segment?
- Which experts are quoted – and in turn, who isn't allowed space to weigh in? Is there a political significance to these patterns?
- When TV news shows feature a point/counterpoint debate, what political spectrum is offered?
- Are media simply reinforcing the establishment line on a given topic, even though there may be no reason to believe that it is correct?

Applying these questions (and creating others) can help you get inside a text and probe your subject more deeply.

Another question you'll want to consider about the values communicated by your text, either overtly or covertly, is whether or not the messages motivated by these values are good ones; that is, are they likely to have a positive effect on individuals and on society? Or might some of the effects be negative? Could they create a large number of poorly informed people? How? Are the effects you predicted in the previous stages of the project positive? Or are they negative or destructive? Why?

■ Considering Action

Once you've generated an enhanced understanding (and *lots* of notes) about the nature, causes and effects, and the values present in the text you've chosen, you'll want to consider what actions you can or should take. If your response is positive, how might you encourage those who produced it to continue their good practices and other media producers to adopt similar approaches and attitudes? If your response is generally negative, how might you encourage its producers to develop

---

*Source: Hart, Peter. "Media Bias: How to Spot it – And How to Fight it." *The Future of Media*. Eds. Robert W. McChesney, Russell Newman, and Ben Scott. New York: Seven Stories Press, 2005. 51-61.

better practices and higher standards? The main question is what *might* you do about the situation? What action *might* be effective?

As before, try to explore the possibilities fully and don't reject any ideas simply because they might initially seem inadequate or impossible. Even a lame idea can evolve into a good one.

Finally, you will explore possible actions one might take to promote the positive effects of the media presentation and avoid the negatives. As you think through possible actions, you will want to make sure they are workable, genuinely beneficial, and ethical.

II Drafting: Making Claims and Charting a Direction

As noted earlier, the project will culminate in an essay in which you make and support some significant assertion by showing that a specific presentation—your target text—exemplifies the nature, causes and effects, and/or values of the organization that produced it. You might also suggest appropriate actions in response to your findings in those first three categories.

In the previous section, you tentatively centered your work on a single text and examined that text from a variety of perspectives. Your primary goal was to ask as many questions as possible and generate some tentative responses. Your next task is to make things less tentative and more concrete by:

- Marking everything that seems even remotely insightful, creative, or intelligent.
- Deciding on the main point(s) you want to assert and support in your essay, that is, your tentative thesis.
- Developing and structuring your argument in a draft essay that includes:
  - ✓ a clear statement of the main points that support your thesis (You may find them in the "stuff" you wrote during the invention stage)
  - ✓ concrete details from the target text and the assigned readings (and perhaps other sources) that develop and support your main points
  - ✓ a clear explanation of your reasoning.

A Note on Research

You can draw most, or perhaps all, of your supporting detail from your target text and from the readings provided in this chapter. However, if you want to develop a more authoritative stance, you might also go beyond your target text and the chapter readings. You might, for example, collect additional information to judge the accuracy and quality of the arguments you've encountered. Or you could learn more about issues that most concern or interest you that have not been settled or addressed by the readings.

Developing Your Essay

Once you've gathered notes on your thesis, main points, and concrete details, you can begin the draft. While some writers simply sit down and start putting words on the page, you might be able to produce a better essay if you begin by establishing the structure of your argument. This is probably most easily accomplished with a simple outline of your thesis statement and your main points.

Early in your essay, clarify that you will analyze a specific text and that your analysis will demonstrate how it is typical of the organization that produced it. You could include this information in your introduction, perhaps as part of your thesis statement, or you may want to include it in a transitional paragraph between the introduction and body of your essay. But whatever your analysis and claim, you should make clear to your readers that you will clarify, extend, or restructure their understanding of something significant in their lives that this text embodies. Where that significance lies—in the nature or the causes or the value of the text—is up to you to decide, but decide you must. You should claim what you believe, but keep in mind that some situations may yield both positive and negative results. And, of course, make sure that your target text exemplifies your claim and that you can demonstrate it to your readers.

Finally, you might want argue that action should be taken on what you have discovered during your inquiry—in other words, you might want to offer a proposal. Considering that you are dealing with a mass media outlet, this may seem a little tricky. If you've discovered a problem, what can you suggest to solve it or at least make things better? Two characteristics of a good proposal are that the proposed action is possible and that it will have some impact on the situation. To be honest, one essay is unlikely to cause an organization to change directions. So what can you advocate? At the very least, you can propose that people should become critical viewers or readers. Not a bad suggestion. Another possibility might be to research organizations that are already encouraging (and in some cases lobbying legislators) to mandate more responsible media practices. If you can find some, which is likely, you might encourage your readers to explore and perhaps participate in one or more of those organizations. The point here is that, while the judgments of one person (that is, you) may seem of little account in the greater scheme of things, you can still find avenues to make your work count.

We've mentioned a few possibilities. You might be more creative and have more.

If you wrote the essay as you structured it, you're mostly done for now—except for the conclusion. If you worked the outline first, you still need to support your subordinate claims or main points with *specific*, *concrete*, and *appropriate* details from your target text—and, of course, explain your reasoning in some detail. The general rule here is *don't ask your reader to make big leaps from your main points to the details that support them*. Fill in the blanks—make the connections clear.

Finally, there is the conclusion, one of the most important parts of the essay. It is the last thing your readers sees—his or her final encounter with your paper. To remind your readers of what the essay was all about in the first place, you might have been taught to revisit your thesis in your conclusion. This is not a bad idea if you remember the word is *revisit*, not repeat. Under no circumstances should you repeat your thesis verbatim, because the last thing you want to do is leave your reader with the impression that your essay was boring. *Revisit* is another matter altogether. Perhaps "remind" is a better word. As mentioned earlier, a good conclusion gives unity to the writer's thought process, brings the main points into focus, and reinforces the effect you want to have on your reader. Also, a little passion is not completely out of place at your essay's conclusion. If you feel passionate about the issue, express it here, but do it gracefully. Moreover, recognize that a little purple prose goes a long way.

Note: Your readers have every right to expect an explicit and logical justification for any assertions you make in the course of your essay. You must also make sure that your arguments are correctly reasoned and are strong enough to justify the demands made on the reader's beliefs. As you work through Chapters 11 and 12 you will, in revision, build into your draft the analytical skills that are presented.

11

In previous chapters you studied the Rhetorical Triangle and saw how it can provide a solid foundation for all argumentative writing and speaking. You studied *ethos*—the position of the writer (in this case, you) in the process—your credibility, competence, and good will. You saw how you might enhance those aspects of your writing and communicate them more effectively to your reader. You also studied aspects of *pathos*—the role of your readers in the process. You learned to take into account the nature and needs of your readers and to exhibit concern for the level of commitment you ask of them in your arguments—understanding, belief, and action—as well as the level of risk each of those behaviors entails for the reader.

You also learned the third aspect of the triangle, *logos*, which involves the argument itself—the quality of the evidence you offer in support of your claims, and the way those claims are structured. You have already dealt with many aspects of evidence—how to find and use it effectively. Now we want to look in greater detail at the other element of *logos*—the *structure* of your arguments.

Good reasoning is largely a matter of how we structure our thoughts, and the more effectively you structure your arguments, the more likely you will be to achieve your goals. Also, the more certain you are that your arguments are correctly structured, the more secure you will be in your ability as a writer and the more likely you will be to write with authority. A greater understanding of the structure of your arguments puts you in greater *control* of your writing.

For this aspect of *logos*, we turn to *logic*. The aspects of *ethos* and *pathos* you've studied are generally considered *rhetorical* concerns. The structure of arguments is a *logical* concern. While the two disciplines—logic and rhetoric—are different in many respects, they are complementary. Indeed, taken together, they might be thought of as constituting a comprehensive "science" of argument.

The Basics of Logic: A Reminder

You have already dealt with the fundamental structure of arguments in Chapter 7 as well as simple ways to tell arguments from non-arguments and good arguments from bad. (This might be a good time to review that material.) Here we will remind you briefly of the basics.

In logic, an argument is a set of claims that includes a main claim, called the *conclusion* of the argument, supported by subordinate claims called *premises*. Another way to describe the relationship is to say that we *infer* the conclusion from the premises or that the premises *imply* the conclusion.

In the context of your essays, the main conclusion of your argument will be your thesis statement, and the premises from which you infer that thesis will be the subordinate claims that constitute the main points of your middle paragraphs. Taken together, these claims create the structure of your argument. Of course, you will provide evidence and argumentation within the middle paragraphs in support of those subordinate claims, but we will deal with argument on that smaller scale later. Right now we want to look at the larger structure of the essay. To give you an idea of how this works, let's take a look at Melissa Manchester's essay "Poverty Slighted by the Media" from the previous chapter. (You may want to review it now.)

Melissa's thesis or main claim is expressed in the last sentence of her introduction (¶ 1):

> *"Perhaps we need to ask if the media presents poverty in such a way as to overlook the issue."*

While her thesis is presented more or less as a question, it is a rhetorical question, and the real sense of it, given how she's set it up earlier in her introduction, is this:

> *It is likely that the media overlook the issue of poverty in the United States.*

If you look about halfway down in her first body paragraph (¶ 2), you'll see her first subordinate claim:

> *"To a certain degree, poverty may be inevitable, but numbers [in the U.S.] are daunting."*

Notice that point is made in the last clause, so for our purposes we'll paraphrase:

> *The amount of poverty in the United States is daunting.*

(Note: In this kind of analysis, paraphrasing is quite all right as long as we do not distort the meaning.)

In her fourth paragraph (¶ 4), she makes the subordinate claim in the last sentence:

> *". . . [television programs] do not accurately represent poverty since they are primarily a source of entertainment."*

In her next paragraph (¶ 5) she again opens with her subordinate claim:

> *"Many turn to news programs as a source of reliable information; however, it is important to remember that they are presented through a televised medium. Consequently, they must adhere to certain entertainment tactics to ensure popularity."*

Again, her intent will be easier to see if we paraphrase:

> *Like other television programming, televised news programs must adhere to "certain enter-*
> *tainment tactics to ensure popularity," and for that reason, do not offer much "insight" into*
> *poverty in America.*

The next four paragraphs (¶ 6–9) deal with her next main point—how poverty is presented in newspapers. Again paraphrasing, her subordinate claim is:

> *While newspapers are better at dealing with the issue of poverty than the electronic media,*
> *they deal mostly with poverty in foreign countries and very little with poverty in the United*
> *States.*

Her next subordinate claim is found by combining the first and last sentences in paragraph ten (¶10):

> *"Often the issue of poverty [in the United States] is not obvious at first glance . . . . readers*
> *[need] constant reminders . . ."*

Paragraphs eleven and twelve constitute her concluding remarks.

Now, let's put all this together in standard form and take a look at the structure of her argument.

> Premise: *The amount of poverty in the United States is daunting.*
>
> Premise: *. . . [television programs] do not accurately represent poverty since they are*
> *primarily a source of entertainment."*
>
> Premise: *Like other television programming, televised news programs must adhere to "cer-*
> *tain entertainment tactics to ensure popularity," and for that reason, do not offer*
> *much "insight" into poverty in America.*
>
> Premise: *While newspapers are better at dealing with the issue of poverty than the*
> *electronic media, they deal mostly with poverty in foreign countries and very*
> *little with poverty in the United States.*
>
> Premise: *"Often the issue of poverty [in the United States] is not obvious at first*
> *glance . . . . readers [need] constant reminders . . . "*
>
> Conclusion: *The media overlook the issue of poverty in the United States.*

Journal:

In your journal, write an evaluation of Melissa's argument based on the three general characteristics of a good argument presented in Chapter 7 (pp. 219–221).

- Are the premises relevant to the conclusion?
- Are the premises warranted? (That is, does she provide good detailed support for the subordinate points within the middle paragraphs?)
- Are the premises or the conclusion vague or ambiguous? Does the argument turn on double meaning of any terms?

Journal:

Pick two or three argumentative essays that you've written in the past, either for this class or for others; and in your journal, construct the same sort of analysis that we just performed on Melissa's argument. Also, using the three general characteristics of good arguments presented in Chapter 7, evaluate your own arguments.

If you find that your arguments seem weak, consider how you might rewrite the thesis statement or subordinate points to make them stronger. If you do make changes, consider what sorts of other changes you might have to make in the supporting details within the middle paragraphs to provide adequate support for your new subordinate claims.

It will be helpful at this point to make a distinction between two major categories of argument or types of reasoning—*deductive* arguments and *inductive* arguments. The main difference is that a deductive argument claims that the premises provide absolute proof of the truth of the conclusion, while inductive arguments always involve an element of probability.

Deduction

The primary characteristic of a deductive argument is that it claims a *necessary* inference. We need to discuss that term "necessary" a bit. As is so often the case in academic disciplines, in logic we use the term "necessary" in a different sense than you probably use it in your everyday conversations.

What we mean by "necessary" is probably more easily seen by looking at single claims (statements) rather than complete arguments. (Hint: This material may also be useful to you as you begin to present your detailed evidence in your middle paragraphs.)

The Nature of Claims

You may remember from previous chapters that a *claim* (also sometimes called a statement or proposition) is an assertion that something is true. As you have seen, writers categorize claims in many ways. For example, you have already dealt, in Chapter 1, with the difference between claims of fact and claims of judgment. Now we will offer a different scheme of categorization, one in which we base the categories on how we may know the truth or falsity of claims.

❑ *Logically Necessary Claims*

The truth or falsity of these sorts of claims are matters of necessity because they are based on the logical relationship that is claimed. They are sometimes called *analytical* claims.

Necessarily True Claims tend to be redundant or definitional. They can normally be reduced to the form of the logical Principle of Identity: A=A. That may seem something of a no-brainer, but it is one of the foundational principles of Western logic; and it becomes a little more interesting when we look at how it is manifested in language and in mathematics.

Sometimes the redundancy is obvious: "Every human female is a woman." Since "human female" and "woman" are synonymous, there is no way the claim can be false. Still, synonyms are often exceptionally useful to a writer and, as we'll see later, sometimes an effective way to define terms. Consequently, it is probably worthwhile to be aware of the logic on which they are based.

Mathematical equations are also examples of necessarily true claims. You may remember this one from your Basic Algebra course: $(a + b)^2 = a^2 + 2ab + b^2$. What may not have been obvious in Algebra is that a mathematical equation is actually a claim that the two expressions on either side of the equal sign will *always* have the same value, no matter what values we give to the two variables a and b.

One interesting thing about necessarily true statements is that they don't really provide us with any new information about the world; they just claim to provide alternate ways to state what is already given.

Necessarily False Claims must be false because they include a fundamental contradiction. Consider the following: " He fired three shots into the dead body, mortally wounding it." The contradiction is obvious; one can't "mortally" wound a corpse. The contradiction ensures the falsity of the claim.

One convenience of logically necessary claims is that, while they do have meaning and are frequently useful, determining their truth or falsity requires no experience or observation, just an understanding of the meanings of the words and the logical relationships claimed.

Note that logically necessary claims, whether they are true or false, are always claims of fact. Being able to recognize them and determine their truth or falsity is of some value in analyzing the reliability of our own arguments as well as the arguments of others.

❑ *Contingent Claims*

Contingent claims, on the other hand, require some experience or observation if we are to determine their truth or falsity. It is not simply a matter of logical relationships. We regard contingent claims as true when the reality they describe corresponds to the reality we observe. For example:

- "Water freezes at 32° Fahrenheit."
- "Newton was born in England."
- "Barack Hussein Obama is President of the United States."

The truth or falsity of none of these is a matter of logical necessity. Depending on the accuracy of the reality they describe, they could be true or false. And some contingent claims can be a little slippery. Consider:

The first statement, which would seem to be an undeniable and verifiable physical fact regarding one of the attributes of water, implies no *logical* necessity. It is possible to imagine a universe in which water freezes at 30° or 34° or 212° F. Even in this universe, the statement is not complete enough to provide absolute certainty. The purity of the water will come into play; for example, cold weather campers sometimes put Kool-Aid in their drinking water to keep it from freezing.

The place of Newton's birth is a matter of historical record. The experience by which we would determine its truth is reading a history book or biography. In such cases, we tend to accept the reliability of the author. However, historians are constantly researching the past, and historical "facts" sometimes change as new documents come to light.

As this is being written, Barack Hussein Obama is currently President of the United States. Now imagine he is in his second term, which will end in 2016 when a new President takes the oath of office. At that point, the claim will become false. We might also consider that the claim in the two immediately preceding sentences presents us with a different sort of "slipperiness." The claim states that President Obama will be replaced in 2016, which would be the normal state of affairs. However, when we consider the possibility that he could leave the office sooner than that, the claim becomes a predication and, therefore, a judgment.

We should remember that the reality described by contingent claims is often subject to interpretation and change when we try to determine their truth or falsity.

Also, in considering the different sorts of claims we might make, it may be useful to remember that *logically necessary* claims are invariably claims of fact while *contingent* claims may include claims of fact and judgments.

Now, back to arguments . . .

A deductive argument does not make a logically necessary *claim*; rather, it claims to make a *logically necessary inference*. The idea of necessity works exactly the same way; it is just presented a little differently.

Consider the following deductive argument:

Premise: *Socrates is a man*
Premise: *All men are mortal.*
Conclusion: *Therefore: Socrates is mortal.*

Notice that none of the claims is logically necessary. It is not necessary that Socrates be a man. The arguer may be talking about his Golden Retriever. And, while it is true that all men are mortal, that is a *material fact*, not a *logical necessity*.

However, when we look at the argument in its entirety, especially the relationship between the premises, we have a somewhat different situation. *If* (and this is an important *if*) it is true that Socrates is a man and that all men are mortal, then there is no way the conclusion can be false. That is a necessary inference.

Notice that the inference is product of the *relationship* between the premises. In this case, we need both premises to make the inference. Just knowing that "Socrates is a man" is not enough to allow us to infer, at least *in the context of the argument,* that he is "mortal." Likewise, just knowing that "all men are mortal" is not enough to allow us to infer that Socrates is mortal.

Also, the absolute nature of the overall claim in a deductive argument is something of a problem for writers. Even if the argument is well structured, we can't say we know for sure that the conclusion is absolutely true unless we know that the premises are. Given the complexities of our world, knowing that a statement is absolutely true is quite difficult. If we make such a claim, we are in danger of overstating our case and actually weakening our argument in the eyes of our readers.

You'll probably find that most argumentative writing is structured *inductively.*

Induction

One important difference between deductive and inductive reasoning is the degree of certainty claimed in the argument. An inductive argument does not claim that the conclusion is absolutely true; rather, it claims that the premises support the conclusion to a certain degree. There is always an element of *probability* inherent in an inductive argument.

For example, take another look at our analysis of Melissa's essay. Consider her original thesis statement:

> *"Perhaps we need to ask if the media presents poverty in such a way that we tend to overlook the issue."*

She has phrased it in such way as to avoid an absolute claim and to make the element of probability clear. Also, consider our paraphrase:

> *It is likely that the media overlook the issue of poverty in the United States.*

Had we left out "It is likely that . . ." we would have made the claim absolute and distorted her meaning.

Melissa's argument throughout is inductive. She is claiming that the premises support the probability that the media overlook poverty in the United States, not the certainty.

This element of probability might seem a weakness of inductive arguments. But it is, in fact, often a strength. You may remember from our earlier discussion of *ethos* that one of your goals is to demonstrate to your audience that you are reasonable and open-minded. That is more easily achieved with an inductive argument for it admits up front that you might be wrong or that there may be exceptions to your claims.

Another strength of an inductive argument is that it allows you more flexibility. You have seen how losing one premise can make a deductive inference impossible. That is normally not the case with an inductive argument. Recall that Melissa's essay offers several subordinate claims and note that her essay is organized around the different types of media. Her overall argument is that there are reasons to believe that each type tends to overlook poverty in the United States. If, in doing the research to answer her original question, she had discovered that the print media were quite thorough in discussing poverty in the United States, she might have cut that point. It might have weakened her argument, and she might have rewritten her thesis statement, limiting her claim to the electronic media. However, it would not make any inference at all impossible.

Another strategy she might have considered if she did find the print media much better in their treatment of poverty would be to rewrite her thesis statement and restructure her paper to make just that point: The electronic media overlook poverty; print media do not. The message in that case might be, "Turn off your television and pick up a newspaper." Unfortunately, that is not what she discovered.

Writers use many types of inductive arguments in their work. Here are three of the more common types.

❏ *Inductive Generalization*

In a way, this is an argument based on examples. Perhaps the most obvious version of this sort of reasoning occurs in some scientific research.

If, for example, I want to test the effectiveness of drug X in the treatment of disease Y, then I will conduct a research study. My research question is, "How effective is drug X in treating disease Y?" In my research I will administer the drug to a number of people with the disease to see how many are helped. (It's actually a little more complicated than that, but the principle is the same.) As a researcher with some experience in how people normally react to medication, I don't expect the drug to help all my subjects. However, I am hoping it will help a certain percentage. Suppose that, out of all my research subjects, 82% show improvement. The reaction of each of the subjects is essentially a *premise* in my argument, and my *conclusion* is that the drug is approximately 82% effective in treating the disease.

This is not actually all that different than the process you might follow in trying to answer the questions that shape your essays. You look for examples to provide answers to your questions. If you find enough examples, and the answers they tend to provide represent an accurate picture of the general situation, then you have a tentative answer to your question and a tentative thesis for your paper. Very often, you'll find statistical data to help answer your questions. The statistics are arrived at by inductive generalization.

Look again at Melissa's paper. In a number of spots she provides examples and statistics to support her subordinate claims.

Also, look at Bill Moyers's "Keynote Address to the National Conference on Media Reform" in Chapter 10. You don't have go very far, just to the second body paragraph, to find an argument by inductive generalization:

> *"It's a reality: democracy can't exist without an informed public. Here's an example: Only 13% of eligible young people cast ballots in the last presidential election. A recent National Youth Survey revealed that only half of the fifteen hundred young people polled believe that voting is important, and only 45% think they can make a difference in solving community problems. We're talking about one quarter of the electorate.*
>
> *The Carnegie Corporation conducted a youth challenge quiz of 15–24 year-olds and asked them, 'Why don't more young people vote or get involved?' Of the nearly two thousand respondents, the main answer was that they did not have enough information about issues and candidates."*

The conclusion is that young people are, to some degree, ill informed and, consequently, our democracy is not functioning as it should. The inductive support seems compelling.

Exercise

Take another look at your essays, the ones you gathered for the previous exercise (p. 363) in this chapter. Find arguments that are developed by inductive generalization. (Hint: look for statistics and examples.) In your journal, write the arguments out in standard form, premises first and conclusion last. Now, write a brief evaluation of each argument. How solid are your inferences? Do your premises support your conclusions to the degree you claimed? If not, consider how you might make your arguments stronger.

❑ *Argument from Authority*

You will often support your claims with premises that consist of the comments of others. These arguments are always inductive. You may trust authorities if they are informed and accurate. However, you can't be *absolutely certain* any authority is correct in any particular instance. In other words, the authority you've cited to support a claim could be wrong. And so, the argument is inductive.

Look at the second paragraph in Melissa's paper. She cites Gregory Mantsios as an authority in support of her first subordinate claim. To some degree, the quality of the inference rests on the statistical data Mantsios offers, but the quality and reliability of that data depend on his intellectual integrity.

Also, look at Bill Moyers's "Take Public Broadcasting Back" in Chapter 10. Go to the fifth paragraph:

> *". . . Take the example of Charles J. Hanley. Hanley is a Pulitzer Prize reporter for the Associated Press, whose fall 2003 story of the torture of Iraqis in American prisons—before a U.S. Army report and photographs documenting the abuse surfaced—was ignored by major*

American newspapers. Hanley attribute this lack of interest to the fact that 'It was not an of-ficially sanctioned story that begins with a handout from an official source.'"

This is a premise. The conclusion to Moyers's argument (look at the third and fourth paragraphs) is that the media sometimes tend to discount or are pressured to ignore stories that do not originate with the government's "official" version of things.

Moyers is citing Hanley as an authority whose version of events is accurate, both that the original story was accurate and that Hanley's view of the reason it was ignored is accurate.

Now consider the two examples of argument from authority: those of Melissa and Moyers. Which seems more authoritative? Note that all we know about Mantsios is that he wrote a book. Moyers is careful to mention that Hanley is a "Pulitzer Prize winning reporter for the Associated Press." Which one seems to have more credibility as a source? Most would say Hanley. Why? Lots of people write books, not all of which are reliable; however, the Associated Press is not a crew of amateurs, and winning a Pulitzer Prize is no small achievement.

Mantsios may be well qualified, but we don't know that from Melissa's paper. Her argument from authority would be stronger if she provided more information about his qualifications.

You should think of some meaningful statements of your sources' qualifications as premises in your arguments from authority. They will be significant parts of your arguments. To some degree, this is an *ethos* concern. Clearly establishing the qualifications of your authorities will enhance your credibility with your readers.

Exercise

Return to the analyses of the papers you wrote earlier. Look for arguments from authority. Then write a brief evaluation of your arguments. Are the qualifications of your authorities obvious to your audience? If not, did you provide qualifying premises that established their credibility? If neither is the case, consider how you might have improved your argument with a sentence or two.

❏ *Prediction*

Many of your arguments will involve predictions that future events will or will not occur, especially arguments that answer questions about what effects a cause may produce. Such arguments are essentially inductive, because the world is such that we never *really* know what the future will bring.

Look at Melissa's conclusion:

"What would happen were the media to personalize poverty? The results could be staggering. Faced with real people living in poverty, perhaps more people would be instilled with a community consciousness and a sense of moral and social obligation to the poor. Seeing the stark reality of poverty daily in our papers and on our television, we would no longer be able to sidestep the issue. We might even feel compelled to search for the root of the problem and begin to make real advances toward a greater understanding of the problem."

Actually, this is not, in the context of Melissa's paper, intended as an argument. Rather, it is a bit of energetic prose designed to motivate her readers and provide an interesting and entirely appropriate conclusion to her essay. However, if it were offered as the conclusion of an argument, it would require premises to support it. The resulting argument would be inductive. No matter how compelling the evidence is to indicate that people would behave in the way she suggests, we can never be absolutely certain. Her phrasing makes it clear she recognizes this:

"The results *could be* staggering."

". . . *perhaps* more people would be instilled . . ."

"We *might* even feel compelled . . ."

There is a more complete predictive argument in Bill Moyers's "Take Public Broadcasting Back" in Chapter 10.

> *An unconscious people, an indoctrinated people, a people fed only on partisan information and opinion that confirm their own bias, a people made morbidly obese in mind and spirit by the junk food of propaganda, is less inclined to put up a fight, to ask questions and be skeptical. That kind of orthodoxy can kill a democracy—or worse.*
>
> *I learned about this the hard way. I grew up in the South where the truth about slavery, race, and segregation had been driven from the pulpits, driven from the classrooms and driven from the newsrooms. It took a bloody Civil War to bring the truth home and then it took another hundred years for the truth to make us free.*
>
> *Then I served in the Johnson administration. Imbued with cold war orthodoxy and confident that "might makes right," we circled the wagons, listened only to each other, and pursued policies the evidence couldn't carry. The results were devastating for Vietnamese and Americans.*

Notice that his conclusion is the first paragraph and his premises are provided in the second and third. The basic argument is that what has happened in the past, given certain conditions, might well happen in the future if we don't mend our ways. He offers only two premises; however, what they lack in number they make up for in scope, historical significance, and emotional impact. These are desirable qualities in a predictive argument based on past events.

Another predictive argument that does not necessarily involve history is a cause-effect argument. It essentially claims that a certain current state of affairs is likely to lead to some desirable or undesirable effect. Moyers provides a good example in his "Keynote Address to the National Conference on Media Reform":

> *What those lobbyists for big media don't tell you is that the traffic patterns of the online world are beginning to resemble those of television and radio. In one study, for example, AOL Time Warner (as it was then known) accounted for nearly a third of all user time spent online. And two*

other companies—Yahoo and Microsoft—bring that figure to fully 50%. As for the growing number of channels available on today's cable systems, most are owned by a small handful of companies. Of the ninety-one major networks that appear on most cable systems, 79 are part of such multiple network groups such as Time Warner, Viacom, Liberty Media, NBC, and Disney.

In order to program a channel on cable today, you must either be owned by or affiliated with one of the giants. If we're not vigilant the wide-open spaces of the Internet could be transformed into a system in which a handful of companies use their control over high-speed access to ensure they remain at the top of the digital heap in the broadband era at the expense of the democratic potential of this amazing technology.

Moyers's conclusion is in the last sentence. Do you find his premises, stated earlier in the passage, compelling support for it?

Exercise

Get a recent copy of your local newspaper or favorite newsmagazine. Turn to the editorial pages and look for two or three arguments that make predictions. Analyze them as we have before. In your journal write the arguments out in standard form—premises first, conclusion last. Then write brief evaluations. First, are the conclusions and/or premises appropriately qualified; that is, has the writer made it clear that he or she recognizes the inductive nature of the argument? If the argument predicts future events based on what has happened in the past, do the premises provide compelling evidence that the past may indeed repeat itself? If an argument presents a cause-effect prediction, is the causal chain clear and feasible?

Evaluating Support: The Middle Paragraphs

You have seen how the framework or "skeleton" of your essay, that is, the thesis statement and main points or subordinate claims, should, taken together, clearly constitute the conclusion and premises of an argument. Now we'll turn to the interior of your essay, the body or middle paragraphs. The techniques for making effective arguments in support of your main points are similar to those we discussed for the larger structure, but there is an additional technique that you may find useful in evaluating those "smaller" arguments in your essays—the Toulmin model of argument.

The Toulmin Model

British philosopher Stephen Toulmin (b. 1922) developed one of the most usable models for argument. Toulmin draws an interesting and useful analogy between arguments and organisms. Like organisms, arguments are structured at several different levels. Both have their "gross anatomy," or larger structures, and their "physiology," or smaller structures and processes. As we have seen, the larger structure of an argumentative essay is probably best represented by a simple outline of thesis statement and main points or subordinate claims. The argument should be constructed so that if the subordinate claims are true, then the thesis statement will be true or at least adequately defended.

Toulmin has little to say about such larger structures of argumentative essays. He does, however, have a great deal to say about the smaller structures, which operate at the sentence level, and it is at this level you'll find the Toulmin model most helpful in strengthening your arguments. In constructing his model, Toulmin organizes the basic structural elements of arguments into six categories.

Claims, Data, Warrants

Given your previous work on the distinction between judgment and fact, you should have little trouble learning to express those features of argument as *claim* and *data*. Thus, our main focus will be the function of the *warrant*—the need to bridge the gap between claim and data by making the logical relationship between assertion and supporting detail explicit for yourself and your readers.

❏ *Claims*

The *claim* is the main point or assertion that you hope to establish and is the first category in the Toulmin model. When you make a claim, you do more than simply make an assertion that something is true. In a sense, you lay claim to your readers' minds by trying to direct their thoughts and sometimes their actions. Generally your readers will manifest a healthy skepticism, wanting to know why you believe as you do and what support you can offer for your claims.

Consider how this claim made by English writer George Bernard Shaw demands supporting evidence.

> . . . *all progress depends on the unreasonable man.*

❏ *Data*

Since society puts a high value on reason and on being reasonable, it is likely readers will demand some support for the claim; that is, data or factual evidence that will provide some basis for the claim and allow readers either to accept it as true or at least consider it more seriously.

Data constitutes the second category in the Toulmin model. Of course Shaw provides it:

> *The reasonable man adapts himself to the world; the unreasonable one persists in trying to adapt the world to himself.*

When Shaw's data and claim are put together, readers have his full argument.

> *The reasonable man adapts himself to the world; the unreasonable one persists in trying to adapt the world to himself. Therefore, all progress depends on the unreasonable man.*

The data here are definitions of reasonable and unreasonable men. Data in the form of definitions may seem strange if you're used to thinking of data only as experimental or statistical data. In the Toulmin model, definitions are only one of many different sorts of data that can be used to support a claim.

❑ *Warrants*

Is Shaw's argument complete? Or do you sense something is missing? There is in fact a middle step in his argument that Shaw has not stated explicitly. If you think about it for a minute, you'll probably see that the argument stands or falls on whether or not you accept one other assertion:

All progress involves people adapting the world to suit themselves.

Shaw did not leave out part of his argument because he is a less than skillful writer. Rather, he knew that he could count on his audience to provide that missing assertion for themselves. Part of the joy readers take in reading well-written prose is that it challenges them and forces them to actively engage the writer's ideas. By giving them the opportunity to provide the missing part of his argument, Shaw helped create that engagement, that active relationship between each reader and writer.

That missing part or middle step of the argument, the *warrant*, is the third category in the Toulmin model. In general, a warrant is formal permission to do something. The word probably appears most commonly in television crime dramas where investigators must get a warrant, or legal permission from a judge, to search a car, house, or office. In the context of argument, you might think of the warrant as giving you logical permission to make that leap from data to claim. In a very important way, the warrant connects the data with the claim.

We can represent the logical structure of the argument as shown in Figure 11.1

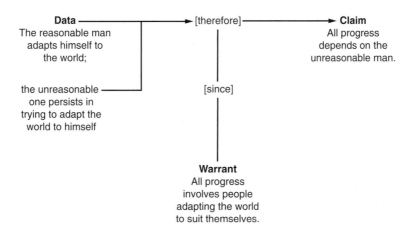

Figure 11.1

Basic Framework of the Toulmin Model: Data, Claim, and Warrant

Exercise Set 1

Analyze the following arguments from Congressman Bernie Sanders' "Why Americans Should Take Back the Media." For each argument, write out the claim, the data, and the warrant. Remember that a single claim may be supported by several data, each with its own warrant. If the warrant is unstated, write out what you think Sanders intends it to be.

1. "From a broad perspective, we can divide our major media outlets into at least two general areas. First, we have media outlets like Rupert Murdoch's Fox TV and *The New York Post,* the Reverend Moon's *Washington Times,* the editorial page of *The Wall Street Journal,* and the radical voices of talk radio like Rush Limbaugh. These right-wing outlets should simply be seen as an extension of the Republican National Committee. They are, pure and simple, the propaganda arm for rightwing Republicans and, as often as not, work closely with them."

2. "On the question of the second category of mainstream media, I believe that an examination of their record on the question of "fairness" would show that, while clearly not as extreme as the right-wing media, they also lean to the right. Let me cite a few examples. Contrast the mainstream media coverage of President Bill Clinton, a moderate Democrat, with that of George Bush, a right-wing Republican. One was attacked mercilessly from before he took office until after he left. The other has, for the most part, been given a rather free ride even as he hacks away at our civil liberties, undermines our economy, and goes to war on flimsy pretexts. Another example is the presidential campaign of Gore versus Bush, where one candidate was berated constantly for items as small as the color of his shirts, while the other was never challenged about his corrupt business dealings, his dubious military record, and his oxymoronic policies of "compassionate conservatism." Further, and very importantly, there was the coverage of the mainstream media that took place leading up to and including the war in Iraq. The situation became so bad, so completely dominated by whatever point of view and spin the Bush administration wanted to push on the American people, that large numbers of Americans literally abandoned the national media's coverage of the war and turned to the BBC, the CBC, and the international media—now accessible over the Internet—for objective coverage."

3. "Another issue. We hear from our current political leadership about the importance of religion and morality. Well, the United States now has the greatest gap between rich and poor of any major nation, and that gap is growing. While the richest 1 percent own more wealth than the bottom 95 percent, the CEOs of large corporations earn 500 times the salaries of their employees. In the United States, today, there are children who go hungry, and many of our fellow Americans sleep out on the street. Is it fair, is it just, is it moral that a tiny handful of people enjoy incredible wealth while millions of their fellow citizens struggle to keep their heads above water and many, in fact, are simply not making it economically? Why has the media determined that gross disparity in wealth and income is not a moral or religious issue?"

Qualifiers, Backing, Exceptions

Here you will find the second "triumvirate" of features in the Toulmin model. You will learn the importance of appropriate qualification of claims to insure that data support claims to the degree indicated by the qualifier. Following that, you will explore means by which proficient arguers provide backing for warrants. Finally, you will learn the importance of imagining possible exceptions to claims and appropriately adjusting arguments to allow for them.

❑ *Qualifiers*

Take a moment to review the structure of Shaw's argument. Note that there is no element of probability or likelihood in Shaw's claim; it is absolute in its assertion that "all progress depends on the unreasonable person." Consider whether or not you are comfortable with such an absolute claim. Is it at all possible that some progress might depend on *reasonable* individuals? If so, then it is unlikely you will be able to accept Shaw's claim as stated. Might you be happier with the argument if he recognized the immense variability of human experience and qualified the claim by saying that *some* or *most* progress depends on unreasonable people? *Qualifiers*, limitations on the strength of your claim, are the fourth category in the Toulmin model.

Rather than tamper with the words of George Bernard Shaw, consider a less absolute argument based on a study you might well have found in a textbook.

> *We really shouldn't pay too much attention to what Bill says about current events. He gets all his information from those television news shows, and, since one can't count on television media for serious, in-depth discussion of complex issues, Bill is probably pretty uninformed.*

Notice that this argument displays an element of likelihood or probability that you don't find in Shaw's argument. You are not, after all, claiming that Bill is definitely uninformed. The probability inherent in the warrant will not justify a claim to certainty. Rather, based on your understanding of the logical relationship between claim and warrant, you are saying it is likely that Bill is uninformed. You acknowledge a certain limitation on the force or strength of your claim by adding the qualifier *probably*.

Simplifying this argument and plugging it into the Toulmin model shows the structure clearly.

> *Claim:* Bill is uninformed about current events.
> *Qualifier:* probably
> *Data:* Bill gets all his information about current events from television news shows.
> *Warrant:* one can't count on television media for serious, in-depth discussion of complex issues

❑ *Backing*

You are justified in asserting a qualified claim based on your data and warrant. But what allows you to assert the data and warrant? This question becomes particularly acute if someone challenges your data or warrant. In the above case, it might be easy to call Bill and verify the data, but verifying the warrant is another matter. The warrant, that one can't count on television media for serious, in-depth discussion of complex issues, may be part of the popular wisdom about which you don't give a second thought. But how do you respond if you are challenged? Because the effect of television on our lives is a topic that interests many researchers, it might be a simple task to hunt up an academic study to provide some backing, or factual support, for your warrant. Indeed, ten years of existing studies strongly suggest that viewers learn very little, if anything, about public affairs from television news (Becker and Whitney 1980; Patterson and McClure 1976; Robinson and Levy 1986). Moreover, a recent study by Cornell University researchers (See Figure 11.2) shows that newspaper readers score considerably better in terms of public affairs knowledge than television viewers, except under the circumstances noted below.

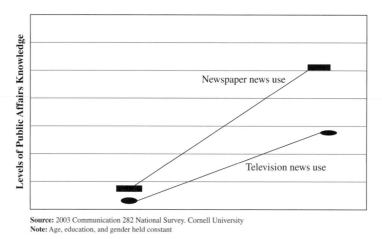

Source: 2003 Communication 282 National Survey. Cornell University
Note: Age, education, and gender held constant

Figure 11.2

We found only two special categories of viewers whose knowledge or understanding of public affairs was enhanced by television news programs. One is composed of individuals who watch public affairs programming, for example, *C-Span* or *The NewsHour* with Jim Lehrer. The other contains those who talk to others frequently about factual or current events. These conditions notwithstanding, the Cornell Study would seem to provide adequate backing for the warrant. Backing is the fifth category of the Toulmin model.

❏ *Exceptions*

Suppose, however, that your hypothetical challenger objects to your claim on the grounds that Bill may be one of those people who watches public affairs programming and/or becomes engaged in conversations. Your best course then is simply to acknowledge special conditions or exceptions, the sixth category in the Toulmin model.

When you add these two additional features, backing and exceptions, to your original argument, you will find that the passage is somewhat longer and more complicated, but your claim will be more credible.

> *You really shouldn't pay too much attention to what Bill says about current events. He gets all his information from those television news shows, and a recent study indicates that television news viewing has little effect on public affairs knowledge. So, unless Bill just happens to be one of those people who watch public affairs programming and/or frequently talks with others about current events, he is probably pretty uninformed.*

Or, set to the Toulmin model:

Claim: Bill is uninformed about current events.
Qualifier: probably
Data: Bill gets all his information about current events from television news shows.
Warrant: One can't count on television media for serious, in-depth discussion of complex issues
Backing: A recent study indicates that television news viewing has little effect on public affairs knowledge.
Exceptions: Bill just happens to be one of those people who watches public affairs programming and/or frequently talks with others about current events.

The graphic representation in Figure 11.3 clearly shows the logical structure of the argument.

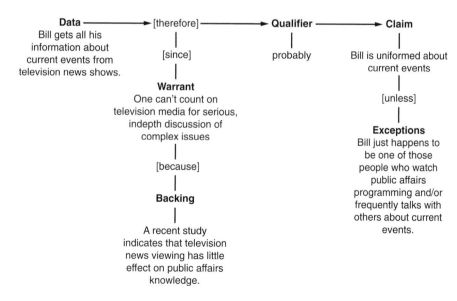

Figure 11.3
Complete Toulmin Model

Now that you have a complete outline of the Toulmin model, you can review the categories and their definitions.

Categories in the Toulmin Model of Argument

Claim:	The main point of the argument; the assertion the argument is designed to demonstrate.
Qualifier:	Any limitations on the strength of the claim. Is the claim definitely true? Probably true? Is there a special environment or set of conditions under which it is true?
Data:	The factual evidence offered to justify the claim.
Warrant:	The logical connection between the claim and data; a middle step that allows readers to proceed logically from data to claim.
Backing:	Factual support for the warrant.
Exceptions:	Special conditions under which the claim may not be adequately supported by data and warrant.

Data ⟶ [therefore] ⟶ *Qualifier* ⟶ *Claim*

[since]   [unless]

Warrant

[because]

Backing   *Exceptions*

Exercise Set 2

Analyze the following excerpts from Michael J. Copps's "Where is the Public Interest in Media Consolidation." For each passage, identify the individual argument (there could be more than one argument in each passage), and eliminate any statements that are not essential to it. Then, write out the claims, data, and warrants for each argument. If the warrant is unstated, write what you think Copps intends it to be. Remember that a single claim may be supported by several different data, each with its own warrant. Finally, for each argument, answer the following questions.

- Is the claim qualified? If so, is the qualifier stated or implied? What is the qualifier? Does the warrant justify the degree of qualification claimed?

- Does the writer offer any backing for his warrants? Is it needed? What sort of backing would make the argument more effective?

• Does the writer offer any exceptions to the claims? Can you think of possible exceptions? Do they need to be made explicit? Why?

1. "Radio deregulation gives us powerful lessons. The loosening of ownership caps and limits eight years ago created real problems in radio, most experts agree. Now, arguably, consolidation also created some economies and efficiencies that allowed broadcast media companies to operate more profitably and may even have kept some stations from going dark and depriving communities of service. And that's fine. That's why many congressmen and senators voted as they did. But the consolidation that ensued went far beyond what anyone expected, leading to outrageous concentrations of social, cultural and political influence. Conglomerates now own dozens, even hundreds—in one case, more than a thousand—stations all across the country. Nearly every market is an oligopoly at best. Competition in many towns has become nonexistent as a few companies—in some cases, a single company—bought up virtually every station in the market. More and more programming seems to originate hundreds of miles removed from listeners and their communities. And we know there are one-third fewer radio station owners than there were before these protections were eliminated."

2. "The good news is that we have an opportunity to start over and come up with a set of rules that encourages localism, diversity, and competition in the media. But this is not a complete victory. It is merely a second chance to protect the people's interest in the people's airwaves, if we decide to do so.

   So now is demonstrably not the time to slowdown. This is the best opportunity this country will have, perhaps for years, to do something about media concentration and to make sure the public's airwaves serve the public's interest. This problem needs to be fixed now. . . .

   What might be the effects of further concentration on America's minorities in terms of providing Hispanic Americans and African Americans and Asian-Pacific Americans and Native Americans and other groups the kinds of programs and access and viewpoint diversity and career opportunities and even advertising information about products and services that they need? America's strength is, after all, its diversity. Diversity is not a problem to be overcome. It is our greatest strength. Our media need to reflect this diversity and to nourish it. Yet, the number of minority owners of licensed television stations has dropped to a shocking, and nationally embarrassing, 1.9 percent. And there has been an even greater drop in minority station managers and newsroom employees."

3. "We should also have considered to a greater extent the relationship between concentration and children's programming. A recent study analyzed the market in Los Angeles and found that the number of broadcast TV programs for children dropped sharply after independent local stations were swallowed up in media mergers. The study found a 47-percent drop in children's programming, with duopolies accounting for the largest decreases. Another recent survey found that 80 percent of parents think the FCC is doing only a poor to fair job of protecting families and children. That's a sad indictment."

4. "Another area that merits attention in our effort to increase localism, competition, and diversity is low-power FM stations. These community-based stations are licensed to local organizations and can help meet the needs of underrepresented communities. They can benefit recording artists by providing more outlets for airplay, especially on a local or regional level. We need to get serious about licensing more low-power FM stations."

Using the Toulmin Model

As you progress through your college courses, you will be bombarded with arguments in various academic and intellectual arenas. At the same time, you will find yourself becoming more skeptical and more interested in testing those arguments. Certainly, as you research sources for your papers, you will want some standard for judging the findings of various authorities. The Toulmin model can be useful in evaluating the strength and credibility of the arguments you encounter. And, if you apply the same model to your own writing, you will find it a powerful tool as you revise and strengthen your arguments.

Improving Your Arguments

When you are faced with an actual argument, instead of the tidy examples in a textbook, you may find it difficult to distinguish the data from the claim, or the warrant from the backing. All the sentences in an argument are assertions; they all claim that something is true. But you can distinguish among the six categories by looking at how the sentences function in the immediate context of the argument. Consider one of our earlier examples.

> *Claim:* Bill is uninformed about current events.
> *Qualifier:* probably
> *Data:* Bill gets all his information about current events from television news shows.
> *Warrant:* One can't count on television media for serious, in-depth discussion of complex issues.
> *Backing:* A recent study indicates that television news viewing has little effect on public affairs knowledge.
> *Exceptions:* Bill just happens to be one of those people who watch public affairs programming and/or frequently talks with others about current events.

Rereading this example, you might realize that the logical relationships between data and claim, and between backing and warrant, are very similar; just as the data support the claim, the backing supports the warrant. Remember that you need the warrant to make the connection between claim and data. But what about the connection between backing and warrant? When you consider that question, you shift your focus to another argument that, in some ways, is related to the first one but, in some ways, is completely separate.

> ***Claim:*** One can't count on television media for serious, in-depth discussion of complex issues.
> ***Qualifier:*** usually
> ***Data:*** A recent study indicates that television news viewing has little effect on public affairs knowledge.

The warrant in the original argument has become the claim in the new one. As you shift your focus, the category of the assertion changes, along with its function in the argument. Now, what warrant allows you to connect claim and data? What assumption needs to be made explicit? If you make the claim based on the data given, you are, at the very least, assuming that the research study was conducted appropriately and is reasonably accurate. Does this new warrant need backing? Perhaps. The findings of scientific studies are frequently questioned and are sometimes discredited.

As you can see, arguments often exist not in isolation but as links in a chain of argumentation. But where does it end? This chain of claims and data and warrants could go on forever. If you question and demand backing for every warrant, it becomes impossible ever to finish writing an argument. Obviously, you have to expect your readers simply to accept some warrants. But which ones? What fundamental assumptions do your readers share with you? Do they believe that protecting the environment is more important than creating jobs? Will they accept a scientific study that finds that secondhand smoke causes cancer? To decide which warrants require backing and which do not, you must determine if they are explicit or not and clarify how your readers will react to them.

Besides considering which warrants need explicit backing, you will also need to consider which ones need to be stated explicitly for readers. Experienced writers frequently do not state all their warrants because they know that doing so would lead to cumbersome prose. But how do you know which ones to state? Once again, it depends on your audience. What do they already know and what do you need to tell them? One of the most common errors made by inexperienced writers is omitting warrants that need to be stated. It leaves readers either confused or with a low opinion of the writer's reasoning ability; either condition damages the writer's credibility and results in an ineffective essay. But continually flogging your readers with warrants that are obvious or already known to them will leave them bored and irritated.

Another successful strategy is to substitute backing for warrants. Consider the two versions of the earlier argument.

> *You really shouldn't pay too much attention to what Bill says about current events. He gets all his information from those television news shows, and, since one can't count on television media for serious, in-depth discussion of complex issues, Bill is probably pretty uninformed.*

> *You really shouldn't pay too much attention to what Bill says about current events. He gets all his information from those television news shows, and a recent study indicates that of the viewing public, only people who view public affairs programming and/or engage in frequent*

discussion end up well-informed. So, unless Bill just happens to be one of those people, he is probably pretty uninformed.

Note that in the second version, where backing is included for the warrant, the warrant itself is omitted. When you include backing, you don't need the warrant unless it is absolutely necessary to make the argument clear. Including the warrant in the second version would create an unwieldy piece of prose. Let careful consideration of your audience's needs be your guide.

Finally, briefly consider qualifiers and exceptions. Because both reduce the strength of a claim, you might think that they make an argument weaker or somehow less credible. Actually, the reverse is true. Qualifiers are important because they create a more reasonable claim. Good readers are often suspicious of all-inclusive claims; they are more comfortable with and are willing to consider arguments in support of a qualified claim, even if they don't generally agree with it. Acknowledging exceptions to your claim demonstrates that you have given an issue more than just superficial thought. Besides, a reader opposed to your point of view will come up with many exceptions anyway, so there's no point in trying to ignore them. Furthermore, if you explicitly mention possible exceptions and successfully refute them, you will forestall at least some objections from your opposition. Perhaps most importantly, qualifying your claims, by acknowledging justified exceptions, demonstrates an intellectual honesty that will be appreciated and respected by your readers.

At first, you will probably find the Toulmin model most useful in revising your essays. You can use it to evaluate arguments you have written in your rough draft to see what elements of the model are missing and then determine whether or not you need to provide them to make your arguments more credible and effective. With enough practice, you may find that the process of using the model becomes internalized; that is, it will shape your ways of thinking and become an unconscious pattern of thought.

The Toulmin Model at Work: A Student Conference

Armed with the principles and practice provided in the previous section, you are now poised to put the Toulmin model to work on your own arguments. But first imagine yourself in the following conference between a student and her instructor. Rebecca, a composition student, has recently read Robert W. McChesney's "The Emerging Struggle for a Free Press." This essay argues that the "press system is failing in the United States" and that media reform is essential if we hope to overcome a "severe crisis of viable self-government in this country." Responding to an essay assignment, Rebecca chose to investigate the incongruity between the media as they now perform and the needs of a democratic society. The following conference with her instructor shows how Rebecca began to shape her argument. She hoped to convince her readers that media do indeed need reform.

Rebecca: As I told you during class, I want to write about how the media are destroying our democracy.

Instructor: They are? How?

Rebecca: Well . . . have you read "The Emerging Struggle for a Free Press"? by Robert McChesney.

Instructor: The McChesney essay? Sure. Anti-democratic practices in modern American media, right?

Rebecca: Yeah. We read it in my sociology class, and it got me thinking.

Instructor: So, do you really want to say that the media are destroying democracy?

Rebecca: Well, that might be a little strong, but I do want to make the point that they're not helping it any because the big corporations are in control. And they couldn't care less about democracy.

Instructor: Considering that a democratic form of government would seem to be required for a free enterprise system, I'll have to say I find the irony of that appealing. But what evidence do you have that you're right? I mean, don't the corporations want people to be free to buy their products?

Rebecca: No. I mean you're half right. They want us to buy the products, but they don't want freedom, especially not freedom of expression. What they want are people who are susceptible to suggestion.

Instructor: Nice line. Now, tell me exactly what you mean.

Rebecca: What I mean is that the media are routinely denying us information that they should be providing. It's a means of controlling us and keeping us consistent with the government's party line.

Instructor: Wait a minute. How did the government get into it?

Rebecca: Oh, it's all the same. Government, media, control. The government lets Big Media control the industry, and media return the favor by not presenting anything the government wants to keep hidden.

Instructor: Interesting assertion.

Rebecca: Well, it's true.

Instructor: Is it? Where's your evidence?

Rebecca: What kind of evidence?

Instructor: How about an example of some sort, the more concrete the better.

Rebecca: Well, sure I have some examples. I've been collecting articles for a week. Look at this one—"Why Americans Should Take Back the Media." And it's by a congressman no less, Bernie Sanders from Vermont. He says that a very few media conglomerates control all the information we get.

Instructor: So what?

Rebecca: So what? So you can't have an effective democracy in that situation.

Instructor: You're still not getting down to what's wrong with it. Give it to me in words of one syllable.

Rebecca: Wasn't it Jefferson who insisted that democracy required an educated electorate? Media hype isn't education.

Instructor:	Good. I think you may be working up to a decent argument. Now, what about more evidence? Is this the only article that supports your point?
Rebecca:	No. I have lots of them. I can hardly read a newspaper or watch television anymore without getting mad. They're all filled with pathetically shallow nonsense that passes for news and commentary.
Instructor:	All of them? Is that what you really mean to say?
Rebecca:	Maybe not *all* of them. But there are so many, it may as well be "all."
Instructor:	No, that's not accurate. Do you remember what I said in class about appropriately qualifying your claims?
Rebecca:	I remember what you said, but to be honest, I'm not very clear on the details.
Instructor:	Let's think about what you want to do with this argument. You've taken a number of relevant facts or data, in this case the specific articles you're using as examples; and you're using these data to support a claim. Think about what that claim has to be like if this is going to be a credible argument.
Rebecca:	I don't understand what you mean.
Instructor:	Then let me ask you this. If I pick up a newspaper and turn to some article at random, are you prepared to say with absolute certainty that I'll be reading some sort of government propaganda?
Rebecca:	Of course not. It might be something on a movie star or something that doesn't have anything to do with current affairs. But there is so much shallow, government provided news that you'd probably hit one of those stories before you found the one on the movie star.
Instructor:	The key word there is "probably." What you're telling me is that the data here don't justify an absolute claim. There's an element of probability that should be acknowledged with a qualifier of some sort.
Rebecca:	So can you ever make a conclusive argument?
Instructor:	Sure. If I knew for certain that all articles in newspapers or news shows on television are shallow and come only from government sources, and there is a news show at 5:30 on Channel 6, what would I know for sure about that broadcast?
Rebecca:	You'd know that it was shallow and came from a government press release.
Instructor:	Right. That's what an absolute claim implies. There isn't any element of probability in the claim, so the argument is conclusive.
Rebecca:	But how could you know that about all articles and news shows? You'd have to look at every article ever published, watch every show, and even then you wouldn't know what would come around tomorrow. It could wreck your whole argument.
Instructor:	Now you're beginning to see one of the problems with absolute claims. Claims should always be justified by the data. In other words, the strength of the data determines the strength of the claim.

	In this case, it's not practical to make a completely exhaustive search of the relevant evidence, so it would seem an absolute claim is out.
Rebecca:	So do I need to look for a new idea for my essay?
Instructor:	Not at all. Who says your claim has to be absolute? In fact, I think you may be able to offer a very good argument here. But you need to be in control of your material. To do that, you should keep in mind that you couldn't claim your conclusion is absolutely true. Your argument is based on a selection of facts but not on all the possibly relevant facts. And you'll have to appropriately qualify the main assertion of your essay.
Rebecca:	You mean I have to waffle around about it and just say that most articles and shows might be bad? That's not very satisfying.
Instructor:	But it is more honest.
Rebecca:	Okay. So now all I have to do is start writing. Right?
Instructor:	Hold on a minute. Let's think this through a little more. What about the warrants in your argument?
Rebecca:	I was afraid you were going to ask about that. You said in class a warrant was a kind of permission, but it didn't make much sense. Since when do I need permission to think something?
Instructor:	Well, in a legal sense, you don't, of course. You have a perfect right to run around spouting any sort of unsubstantiated nonsense. People do it all the time. But do you really want to?
Rebecca:	I suppose not. Okay. So how is a warrant permission to think something?
Instructor:	Think of it in relation to your claim and data. As I understand it, you have some data, some essays that support your main claim about the media. Right?
Rebecca:	That's it.
Instructor:	Not quite. Why is the situation the essays describe destructive?
Rebecca:	Like I said, because they give incomplete or slanted information.
Instructor:	So what does that have to do with democracy?
Rebecca:	Isn't it obvious?
Instructor:	Is it?
Rebecca:	Well, it is to me.
Instructor:	And so you're writing this essay for yourself?
Rebecca:	No, no. I know I have to keep my audience in mind.

Instructor:	Then let's get back to my original question. Are you saying that giving the people only incomplete or slanted information damages democracy?
Rebecca:	Yeah. Didn't I say that?
Instructor:	No. Not exactly. And you need to, at least to yourself, because that's your warrant. It's the middle step in your argument. The information we get is incomplete or slanted. We can't make good decisions without complete and objective information. Democracy requires the electorate to make good decisions. So the bad information we get damages our democracy. See how those middle steps bridge a logical gap between the data and the claim?
Rebecca:	Yeah, I guess I do. You said I need to say it to myself. Why? I already know it.
Instructor:	Do you? Or do you just think you know it? Isn't it really just an assumption on your part?
Rebecca:	I guess. But what's wrong with assumptions?
Instructor:	Not a thing. We operate on all sorts of assumptions. Couldn't get along very well without them. But when we make arguments based on assumptions, we have to examine them thoroughly. And we can't do that until we make them explicit. That's where the warrant comes in. Many warrants are exactly like the one you've given me here—assumptions that are deeply ingrained in our values and systems of belief. Which is why they need to be questioned. It's a part of thinking these things through.
Rebecca:	Well, is it okay or not?
Instructor:	You tell me. Do we really need complete and objective information to make good decisions?
Rebecca:	Yeah. Seems like it.
Instructor:	So, what about the assumption in your warrant? Is it possible we could make some good decisions without knowing everything?
Rebecca:	Yeah . . . I guess I'm wrong. And I thought I had a good idea for this essay.
Instructor:	Actually, it's better now than it was before you began to think it through.
Rebecca:	But, if my warrant's no good . . .
Instructor:	I didn't say it was not good. In fact, it's just fine. It's just that now we've thought of the possibility there might be an exception to your claim. You can still make the whole scheme work if you'll just explain it more thoroughly to your readers. In other words, you might want to think of providing some backing for the warrant.
Rebecca:	You mean I have to put all this stuff in my essay?
Instructor:	You don't have to do anything except be in control of your writing. Do your readers need to know all this? Will it enhance your credibility and get them to consider your point of view more seriously?

Rebecca: I don't know. It might.

Instructor: It's something you'll have to decide before you finish that final draft. In fact, you have a lot of decisions to make.

Rebecca: Just what I need. What now?

Instructor: You need to look at the other side of the issue. These essays seem to have made you mad, which is good because it helped you generate some energy. But now you need to focus that energy and control it. Consider the opposite point of view.

Rebecca: It doesn't seem to me that there is much of another side to this issue.

Instructor: Don't be too sure. What do you suppose the newspaper publishers and broadcasters think they're doing?

Rebecca: I don't care what they think.

Instructor: You should, if you want to write an honest essay. Don't you suppose the advertisers have positions on this issue that should be recognized and examined in your essay?

Rebecca: Why? I've got enough to do to make my own case.

Instructor: Offhand, I can think of at least two reasons why you should consider other perspectives. For one thing, it's more honest. At this stage of the game, you should be more involved in exploration than in direct argument. And in your exploration, if you find some information that causes you to rethink or modify your hypothesis, then your essay should reflect that. Don't let the hypothesis control your thinking. That will produce a paper every bit as wrong as the situation that made you mad in the first place.

Rebecca: I see what you mean. Don't write like some fool that won't look at other points of view.

Instructor: Right. And not only do you need to think carefully about as many sides of this issue as you can, you also need to make clear to your readers that you have thought things through and are trying to be open and thorough.

Rebecca: That sounds pretty risky to me. Won't it weaken my argument?

Instructor: Not really. Don't sell your readers short. You have to assume that they're as thoughtful as you are, and if you build an argument that honestly convinces you, they're more likely to seriously consider your position.

Rebecca: Credibility, right?

Instructor: Exactly. Remember, many of your readers may be suspicious of an argument that seems one-sided. They're not only going to look at the facts you present, they'll also consider your whole approach. If you ignore obvious counter arguments, they'll feel as if you're trying to manipulate them. If that happens, you've lost them.

Rebecca: So, do I get extra credit for being so fair-minded?

Instructor: No. What you get is a handout to help you remember all this wisdom. Also, you get to start on your first draft.

Journal Activity

Working either individually or in small groups, respond in your journal to the following questions about Rebecca's conference with her instructor. If you work individually, proceed as you have in previous journal exercises, thinking carefully about the questions and responding in enough detail to develop insights that will be useful in your writing.

If you work in a group, the group should be large enough to provide a variety of viewpoints, yet not so large that any individual voice gets lost in the discussion; five or six students per group is probably ideal. Your group might reach easy consensus on some questions, while your responses may have to accommodate different points of view on others. Try to discuss the questions at enough length to take full advantage of the special energy of group processes. You should elect a recorder to produce a legible copy of the group's responses. Your instructor might ask each of you to present your responses orally to the class. Whatever the case, be sure to record the ideas generated by the discussion in your journal.

1. How strong is the claim of Rebecca's argument that the media are destructive to democracy? That is, do the data she offers justify the strength of her claim? Does she need to qualify the claim further? Can you think how she might strengthen her position?

2. What warrants does Rebecca use to justify the relationship she is trying to establish between her data and claim? Do these warrants need to be made explicit in her essay? Why or why not?

3. The articles Rebecca has read seem to have made her angry. Is that good or bad? How might she best channel that anger to make it work for her? Are there things about the media that make you angry? Are there ways in which you might use that emotion in your writing?

4. What sort of audience would be most receptive to Rebecca's argument? What sort of audience would be most resistant to it? Could Rebecca make the same essay work for both audiences, or would a change in audience require substantial revision? If so, what sorts of revisions would she need to make?

5. What is Rebecca's purpose in writing this essay? Does she want to inform her readers, ask them to commit to her position, or get them to take some action? How do you know?

6. Would accepting her position require you to take any emotional or material risks? If so, what are they? Do you think her argument would make you willing to take those risks? What about other people you know?

Journal Activity

Here you will turn to the argument you created for Chapter 10's essay assignment and examine how well your reasoning holds up. Write out the main claim of your essay, your thesis statement. Does it clearly state the whole purpose of the essay? Underneath it, write out the subordinate claims developed in the middle paragraphs. Do they all provide reasons for believing the thesis? Are any of the subordinate claims inconsistent with each other or with the thesis? Are any of them irrelevant to the thesis?

Now examine the smaller structures of your argument using the Toulmin model. Is each claim supported by data? Are the data truly relevant to the claims? Do they support the claims to the degree indicated by the qualifiers? Do the warrants (stated or implied) justify the supporting connection between claims and data? Are there possible exceptions to the claim that have not been considered? What backing exists for the warrants?

If you find providing written analysis of all your arguments too time-consuming, then work through a few selected arguments. Remember that much of the thinking and writing you do here will never find its way into your essay. Rather, your work will provide an intellectual x-ray of your thought, help you to internalize the Toulmin model, and make concern for adequate support an integral part of your composing.

Speaking to Your Audience

Here we turn to one of the great, though often overlooked, values of the Toulmin model: its ability to take audience into account in writing effective arguments. Let us consider the following excerpt from Bárbara Renaud González's essay "Resisting the *Conquista* of Words."

> *Univision, though Spanish-speaking, is not any better than the English-language stations, with its fixation on telenovelas and copycat programming. . . .*
>
> *Univision now controls 70 percent of the Spanish-language market, including television, cable, music, and radio. For singers and musicians already signed to Univision, this situation can be a blessing, but it is disastrous for independent labels and artists. Cultural commentators point out that the homogenized music promoted by radio stations has marginalized the most original musicians and their passionate audiences.*

Remember that this argument is just a small part of a larger, more complex one that is the purpose of the whole article. In this excerpt, the claim and data are clearly stated.

> ***Claim:*** Univision, though Spanish-speaking, is not any better than the English-language stations [at meeting the needs of Hispanic populations].

González offers two data statements in support of her claim:

> **Data:** [Univision is fixed] on telenovelas and copycat programming.
>
> *and*
>
> **Data:** [That] Univision now controls 70 percent of the Spanish-language market, including television, cable, music, and radio. . . . is disastrous for independent labels and artists.

To analyze this argument using to the Toulmin model, we need to look for qualifiers, warrants, backing, and exceptions.

There is no explicit *qualifier* associated with the first data statement. Does González really mean that *all* Univision programming is composed solely of 'telenovelas and copycat programming"? Probably not. "Fixed on" doesn't necessarily mean "all" and could easily be interpreted to provide some qualification of the claim. But will her audience interpret it in that way? Such a *pathos* consideration is exactly the kind you will need to make as you tailor the language of your arguments to clarify your intention for your readers.

Moreover, the passage contains no *warrant* justifying an inferential relationship between the claim and the first data statement. Of course, with no warrant, there can be no *backing* either.

Would the argument be more credible if she had provided an explicit qualifier, warrant, and backing? A charitable reader would accept the claim as stated, finding the qualification and warrant implied. But did González have charitable readers for this essay? To find out, you'll have to do a little audience analysis. The essay appeared in a book of essays titled *The Future of Media: Resistance and Reform in the 21st Century*. The title should give you a clue. It seems likely that the book's audience is generally dissatisfied with the current condition and practices of the media and would think reform a good idea. We can guess that some of the readers would tend to have a liberal or even radical political agenda. Because her readers are, in general, already strongly predisposed to agree with her point of view, González has a lot of latitude in stating her arguments. In fact, her readers are likely to give her the benefit of the doubt regarding qualification and warrants.

Also, *Booklist*, the review journal of the American Library Association, tells us this about the collection of essays:

> *The book was inspired by the first National Conference for Media Reform in November 2003, which was itself inspired by the Federal Communication Commission attempt to loosen rules on broadcast ownership, threatening further media consolidation. Contributors, primarily policy experts, lament restrictions on coverage of corporations owned by media outlets, the focus on sensationalism instead of government actions, unquestioned media support for the war in Iraq, clandestine government subsidies to "commentators" pushing government policies, and other troubling trends that don't bode well for the role of a free press in a strong democracy.*

This information would seem to support our earlier assumptions about her audience.

Let us examine the second data statement: "[That] Univision now controls 70 percent of the Spanish-language market, including television, cable, music, and radio. . . . is disastrous for independent labels and artists." Again, we will look for a warrant that connects the data statement with her original claim. This time González provides it:

> *Cultural commentators point out that the homogenized music promoted by radio stations has marginalized the most original musicians and their passionate audiences.*

Again, the qualifier is implied and backing for the warrant is absent. Of course, given her audience, she may not need it.

Journal Activity

It would seem that González has created a fairly effective argument for her audience. But you may have a different point of view on the issue than her readers. Consider carefully how the argument works for you. In your journal, respond to the following questions.

1. Would you be more comfortable with explicit and appropriate qualification of the claim? Why? What qualifications would be appropriate for you? Why those?

2. Would you like to see the warrants stated and perhaps backed? What sort of backing would be most effective?

3. Can you think of possible exceptions to the claim? What are they? Would the argument be more effective for you if she had stated them? Why?

4. What changes would you make if you were going to rewrite the essay for publication in a conservative magazine such as *National Review*?

Collaborative Activity

Form small groups, exchange your journal notes, and comment on each other's responses. Now, working in pairs, turn to your own essays and decide which structures in the Toulmin Model should be explicitly stated and which could be left unstated.

Earlier in the chapter, you made explicit all possible structures in the Toulmin Model appearing in your essay. Now you need to determine the nature of your intended audience and the degree of involvement you want from it. When do qualifiers need to be made explicit, and when may you expect your audiences to perceive the difference between "some" and "most" without being told? When are warrants likely to be obvious for a particular audience, and when must they be provided?

Does your audience share your values and worldview to the degree that a specific warrant may go unsaid, or should it be made explicit? When will a clear statement of obvious exceptions to a claim strengthen an argument, and when is it unnecessary clutter? Finally, what effect does the degree of involvement expected of the audience have on answers to the foregoing questions? Must more be said to win acceptance of a conclusion or to motivate action on an issue than simply to secure understanding of a position?

Guidelines for Appraising an Argument

The following guidelines can help you to evaluate the rhetorical and logical strategies in any argument by analyzing the dynamic at work between writer and reader. They can also help you to examine the structures writers use to justify their claims. By becoming attuned to the persuasive effects of different rhetorical devices, you not only become a better reader, but also a more astute writer of arguments.

The Rhetorical Dimension

1. Review the introductory and concluding paragraphs, as well as other places where the writer addresses the reader directly. Ask yourself what the writer wants from the reader. Does the writer seek understanding, acceptance, or some form of action based on a shared belief?

2. Look for an appeal in the introductory paragraph and evaluate the poignancy and relevance of the examples used in the body paragraphs. What strategies does the writer use to spark curiosity and maintain the reader's interest?

3. Review the examples and discussions in the body paragraphs and note the order in which this information is presented. Does the writer provide enough information and direction to help the reader understand the larger context of the piece?

4. Consider the writer's choices regarding style, language, and persona. Does the writer acknowledge opposing viewpoints? Ask yourself how the writer reduces the threat for a reader who might be resistant to the message. Do you find these strategies effective? If so, why? If not, why not?

The Logical Dimension

1. Identify the subject or problem, along with the specific claims, the writer wants the audience to understand and accept. Why has the writer chosen to develop the argument along these lines? What underlying assumptions does the writer bring to this issue? What special authority does the writer bring to the debate? Does the writer seem open to presenting opposing views? Does the writer admit possible exceptions to his or her claims?

2. Locate the specific data, warrants, and backing that substantiate the claims. These may be in the form of testimony, facts, statistics, or personal experiences. Ask yourself whether the writer's reasoning is accurate. Does the writer provide enough relevant information? Could there be reasons to doubt this evidence? Is the basis for the evidence fact or opinion?

3. Determine whether the conclusion captures the broader implications of the argument and provokes the reader to think more critically about the topic. What would be the implication of agreeing or disagreeing with the writer's position? Is there an alternative view that must be considered? Has the writer adequately presented both the pros and the cons of the argument?

12

Recognizing Informal Fallacies

Classifying Fallacies

You may remember that we established three general rules for good arguments in Chapter 7. To remind you, in a good argument:

- The premises must be relevant to the conclusion.
- The premises must be warranted. That is, in the context of writing an essay, your subordinate claims in the middle paragraphs must have some support.
- The language of the argument must not be vague or ambiguous.

A bad argument is also sometimes called a fallacy, which means an error in the reasoning. Some fallacies are formal; that is, they include a logical error in the *form* or structure of the argument. You will normally find this sort of error in deductive arguments.

Another kind of error has to do with the content of the argument, not necessarily the form. We call these errors *informal fallacies*. Some informal fallacies are so common that they have their own names. It is important for you to be able to recognize these fallacies in the arguments of others and, perhaps more importantly, in your own writing.

Most informal fallacies break one of the three rules listed above, which provides a convenient way to organize them.

Fallacies of Irrelevance

A fallacy of irrelevance breaks the first rule; the premises are logically irrelevant to the conclusion. There are several types.

❑ *Ad hominem*

You may recognize this fallacy because we've already mentioned it in Chapter 7, though not by name. "Ad hominem" is Latin for "to the man." You typically encounter this fallacy in situations in which someone is trying to refute or discredit the argument of another person. It involves an attack on the character, intellect, or special circumstances of the *person* rather than a logical refutation of the *argument*. For example:

Clearly George Bush's arguments in favor of invading Iraq must be flawed. After all, while others were serving in Vietnam, he spent his illustrious military career in Florida, in a reserve commission his father bought for him, carousing and working on political campaigns.

Even if this attack on Bush's character were true, the claims are irrelevant to the arguments he made in favor of invading Iraq. This is called an *abusive ad hominem* attack because it attacks the character or intellect of the person rather than the argument itself. Another example:

. . . it matters very little now what the King of England says or does; he hath wickedly broken through every moral and human obligation, trampled nature and conscience beneath his feet, and by a steady and constitutional spirit of insolence and cruelty procured for himself a universal hatred.

— Thomas Paine, *Common Sense*

It seems Paine probably had good reason for his attack on the character of the King of England; however, the king's defective character is not a logical reason for discounting his arguments without first considering them.

See if you can detect a difference between the previous examples and this one:

Of course Bush has argued for tax cuts. He's a Republican, and they're always in favor of tax cuts. We would expect him to make that argument. I think we can safely ignore it.

Notice that this fallacy does not attack the character of the person; it attacks his special circumstances (being a Republican) instead of the argument itself. That we might expect Republicans to be in favor of tax cuts is irrelevant to whatever arguments they might make to support the idea.

Another type of *ad hominem* is committed when one offers an inconsistency between a person's behavior and his stated point of view as a reason for discounting his or her argument. This is called a *tu quoque* argument (*tu quoque* is Latin for "You, also" or "You're another").

Child to parent: How can you insist that I not smoke cigarettes? You've been smoking for 30 years.

The parent's behavior is irrelevant to the very good arguments he or she may make against taking up the habit.

Here is perhaps a more significant example from an interview with Osama bin Laden:

Reporter: Now, the United States government says that you are still funding military training camps here in Afghanistan for militant, Islamic fighters and that you're a sponsor of international terrorism; but others describe you as the new hero of the Arab-Islamic world. Are these accusations true? How do you describe yourself?

Bin Laden: At the time that they condemn any Muslim who calls for his right, they receive the highest top official of the Irish Republican Army (Gerry Adams) at the White House as a political leader, while woe, all woe is the Muslims if they cry out for their rights. Wherever we look, we find the US as the leader of terrorism and crime in the world. The US does not consider it a terrorist act to throw atomic bombs at nations thousands of miles away, when it would not be possible for those bombs to hit military troops only. These bombs were rather thrown at entire nations, including women, children and elderly people and up to this day the traces of those bombs remain in Japan. The US does not consider it terrorism when hundreds of thousands of our sons and brothers in Iraq died for lack of food or medicine. So, there is no base for what the US says and this saying does not affect us. . . .

— Osama bin Laden, CNN Interview, 1997

Notice that bin Laden completely dodges the original question by launching an attack on the behaviors of the United States. His defense against the implied claim that he is a terrorist is that the United States has engaged in terrorism. That may be another argument, but his assertions are irrelevant to the original question.

❑   ***Appeal to Force or Fear***

If one argues that we should accept a conclusion, not on the basis of relevant premises and a well-structured argument, but simply because we will suffer negative consequences if we don't, the arguer has committed an *appeal to force or fear*—an informal fallacy. That the arguer might inflict negative consequences on us if we don't accept his or her conclusion is logically irrelevant to whether or not we *should*.

The most basic expression of this fallacy is the schoolyard bully: "Agree with me or I'll beat you up." The ultimate expression is, of course, the threat of war. This sort of appeal is nothing new. Here is an example from Classical Greece:

Socrates, I think that you are too ready to speak evil of men: and, if you will take my advice, I would recommend you to be careful. Perhaps there is no city in which it is not easier to do men harm than to do them good, and this is certainly the case at Athens. . . .

—Plato, *Meno*

Another example:

So Moses and Aaron went to Pharaoh, and said to him, "Thus says the Lord, the God of the Hebrews, '. . . Let my people go, that they may serve me. For if you refuse to let my people go, behold, tomorrow I will bring locusts into your country, and they shall cover the face of the land, so that no one can see the land; and they shall eat what is left to you after the hail, and they shall eat every tree of yours which grows in the field, and they shall fill your houses. . . .'"

— Bible, *Exodus 10:3-6*

This sort of an appeal is often subtler and doesn't necessarily involve physical force.

> *Professor McNear, I hear that you've been complaining about the new assessment program I established last summer while you were on vacation. As your immediate supervisor, I need to remind you that evaluation time is just around the corner and you might consider adjusting your attitude.*

It is important to make a distinction between an appeal to force or fear and an honest warning. For example, consider the following passage from Thomas Friedman's essay in Chapter 6:

> *So let me slightly amend the Golden Arches Theory in light of Kosovo and what are sure to be future Kosovos. I would restate it as follows: People in McDonald's countries don't like to fight wars anymore, they prefer to wait in line for burgers—and those leaders or countries which ignore that fact will pay a much, much higher price than they think.*

There is certainly a threat implied in the last line, but Friedman is not doing the threatening. He is simply warning that a certain situation will have negative consequences.

❏ *Appeal to the People*

This fallacy can take a number of forms, but they all depend on our common humanity. We are a gregarious species; most of our needs are met within a social system; most of us have a *need* to be accepted by our fellow human beings. We want to be part of the group. This makes us susceptible to appeals that tell us we will be accepted, or even admired, if we adopt a conclusion and rejected if we don't. Even if that is true, it is usually irrelevant to the conclusion and, consequently, fallacious.

> *"Any real American will support the war in Iraq. And anyone who doesn't should just move to France."*

For many people, their citizenship is an important part of their identity. To imply that they have somehow betrayed their country if they refuse to accept a certain point of view may be emotionally effective, but it is logically fallacious. One can be a "real" American without accepting all of the government's policies and actions.

One form of the appeal to the people is sometimes known as the "bandwagon appeal" or the "appeal to common practice." The parents of teenagers are intimately, sometimes painfully, familiar with this appeal.

> *"Gee, Mom. Everybody else is going. Why can't I?"*

And we must, of course, consider advertising in this context.

> *"Join the people who've joined the Army."*
>
> *"The Gizmo 2000 is the most popular car on the road. You should get yours today!"*

Another form is "snob appeal," also called the "appeal to vanity." Not only do we want to be accepted by other people, we want, if at all possible, to be just a little bit better than everyone else.

> *"Choosy mothers choose Gif."*
>
> *"The few, the proud, the Marines."*

Bill Moyers, in his "Keynote Address to the National Conference on Media Reform," (Chapter 10) opens with an *appeal to the people.*

> *Thanks for inviting me tonight. I'm flattered to be speaking to a gathering as high-powered as this one that's come together with an objective as compelling as "media reform." I must confess, however, to a certain discomfort, with other journalists, about the very term "media."*

The audience at such conferences is largely composed of journalists. In his opening, Moyers is both appealing to their vanity and making his identification with the group clear. While he is not exactly using the opening as a premise in his arguments, he is favorably disposing the audience to the arguments that follow.

❑ *Straw Man*

The straw man argument occurs when one tries to refute a position by exaggerating it out of all proportion to create an easy target, a straw man.

> *"We can't re-elect Senator Brown. He's for increasing government assistance to the poor, and we don't want a left-wing radical representing our state."*

Advocating assistance to the poor is a far cry from left-wing radicalism. Another example:

> *I just don't see how anyone can support Bush's "guest worker" notions. How stupid is it to leave our borders wide open to any terrorist that decides to waltz in and blow something up.*

Again, the arguer has distorted the original position in an attempt to discredit it. A guest worker program does not necessarily leave our borders wide open.

Sometimes there is a fine line between powerful prose and a straw man. Consider this passage from Bill Moyers's "Take Public Broadcasting Back" (Chapter 10):

"We're seeing unfold a contemporary example of the age old ambition of power and ideology to squelch and punish journalists who tell the stories that make princes and priests uncomfortable.

. . . Who are they? I mean the people obsessed with control, using the government to threaten and intimidate. I mean the people who are hollowing out middle class security even as they enlist the sons and daughters of the working class in a war to make sure Ahmed Chalabi winds up controlling Iraq's oil. I mean the people who turn faith based initiatives into a slush fund and who encourage the pious to look heavenward and pray so as not to see the long arm of privilege and power picking their pockets. I mean the people who squelch free speech in an effort to obliterate dissent and consolidate their orthodoxy into the official view of reality from which any deviation becomes unpatriotic heresy."

This is powerful prose, to be sure, but does it contain a straw man fallacy? Or perhaps an ad hominem? Both?

Exercise

Working in small groups, analyze the Moyers passage in the context of the entire reading (pp. 324–330). Try to decide whether the passage is fallacious or not. If you find that Moyers has provided sufficient support for his claims, list the support. But if you find that he has exaggerated the nature of the classes of people he mentions, in an attempt to discredit their points of view, or that he has maligned their character, explain why such reasoning should not be respected.

❑   *Red Herring*

This fallacy is said to get its name from a traditional trick used by trainers of hunting dogs. They would draw a smoked herring across a scent trail to see if the strong scent of the fish would lead the dogs off the trail. The idea was to train the dogs to ignore the scent of the herring and stay on the original trail. Like the dog trainer, an arguer who commits a *red herring* fallacy offers an emotionally compelling but irrelevant detail in an attempt to lead the reader or listener away from the actual point of the argument.

Boss: Walker, I want to speak about the number of sick days you've taken off work this month.

Walker: Well, I'm quite sure I haven't taken half as many sick days this month as you did when you had your gall bladder surgery.

In this rhetorical situation, the number of days the boss missed work is irrelevant; Walker is simply trying to turn attention away from his own performance, which is the real issue.

Consider the following:

> *I have no patience at all with all these animal rights wackos wailing about using animals in medical research. Somewhere right now some Birkenstock-shod pseudo-hippie is breaking into a research lab, snatching the lid off a petri dish, and crying soulfully, "Go, little paramecium. Be free!"*

In addition to the *ad-hominem* name calling here, we have a *red herring*. The fictional scenario offered by the arguer is irrelevant to arguments against using animals in medical research. Likewise:

> *How can you argue against using animals in medical research? You appear to be in good health. You should be thanking those scientists instead of criticizing them.*

The state of the listener's health and how he or she maintains it is irrelevant to the apparent main point of the discussion—using animals in medical research. It is a *red herring* designed to lead the listener astray.

(Note: You may want to take another look at the excerpt from the ABC interview with Osama bin Laden under the earlier section on the *tu quoque* fallacy. Osama's comments are also something of a *red herring*.)

❑ ***Appeal to Ignorance***

This fallacy occurs when one offers the premise that we *don't* know something in support of a claim. A statement of our ignorance is normally not a relevant premise. This type of argument usually takes one of two forms:

> Premise: We don't know that X is true.
> Conclusion: Therefore, X must be false

> Or

> Premise: We don't know that X is false.
> Conclusion: Therefore, X must be true.

Here are a couple of common examples:

> *Of course God exists. No one has ever been able to prove that He doesn't.*

> *Scientists have conducted many experiments in an attempt to demonstrate the existence of extra-sensory perception. None have been successful. Clearly, ESP is a myth.*

Though logically fallacious, these arguments may seem harmless enough. However, consider the following classic example from Richard H. Rovere's *Senator Joe McCarthy*, a 1960 biography of the senator. It describes an episode from the Communist witch hunts of the 1950's more or less led by McCarthy.

> *In 1950, McCarthy claimed that he had discovered 81 cases of Communist connection in the State Department. In presenting one case, he defended it with, "I do not have much information on this except the general statement of the agency . . . that there is nothing in the files to disprove his Communist connections."*

Considering that many lives were ruined during this period by such baseless accusations, we should remember that fallacious arguments can have substantial consequences.

Exercise

Collect the editorial pages from several issues of any newspaper. Find a half dozen examples of **Fallacies of Irrelevance**. Clip and paste the editorials into your journal; then write analyses in which you note the fallacies they commit and explain how the reasoning in each one is fallacious.

Exercise

Working in small groups, share and discuss your responses to the previous exercise. Try to determine how the arguer in each case might have rewritten the argument to avoid the fallacy.

Fallacies of Unwarranted Assumption

This category of informal fallacies includes those arguments that break the second general rule of good arguments listed above—in a sound argument the premises must be *warranted*; that is, there must be a good reason for believing them to be accurate.

❑ *Begging the Question*

This is a somewhat complex fallacy with several different forms. In the simplest, the arguer offers as a premise the very conclusion he or she is trying to support. In other words, the arguer wrongfully assumes the truth of the conclusion and offers it up, usually in different words, as a premise in support of itself.

> *Stealing is wrong because it's a moral lapse to take from someone else something that doesn't rightfully belong to you.*

More often, this sort of argument is more complicated with multiple premises. But the premises lead the reader in circles to a conclusion that is identical to one of the premises. Here is a common example of *circular reasoning*:

> *Of course I know that God exists. How? Because the Bible tells me He does and the Bible is the word of God. And God wouldn't lie to me.*

And another:

> *Einstein was the greatest scientist of the 20th century. This is indisputable. All the best modern scientists say so. And we can easily determine who the best modern scientists are by asking whether or not they follow Einstein's example.*

Here's a classic example. (It seems even Aristotle wasn't immune to fallacious reasoning.)

> *Every art and every inquiry, and similarly every action and pursuit, is thought to aim at some good; and for this reason the good has rightly been declared to be that at which all things aim.*
> —Aristotle, *Nicomachean Ethics*

Another common example of begging the question is *invincible ignorance*. This is basically a refusal to look at the evidence that might contradict one's existing position on an issue—the "I've got my mind made up; don't confuse me with evidence" approach. The unwarranted assumption is that one's existing position is correct, and any other need not be considered.

You may have seen this bumper sticker:

> *God said it, I believe it, that settles it.*

Here's a somewhat more complex example:

> *I wish, my dear Kepler, that we could have a good laugh together at the extraordinary stupidity of the mob. What do you think of the foremost philosophers of this University? In spite of my oft-repeated efforts and invitations, they have refused, with the obstinacy of a glutted adder, to look at the planets or Moon or my telescope.* [Through which the satellites of Jupiter were visible—seen first in January 1610]
> — Galileo, *Opera*

❏ *False Alternatives*

This fallacy occurs when the arguer assumes that a situation involves two possible choices or has only two possible outcomes. It is sometimes called the *False Dilemma* fallacy, *Either-Or* fallacy, or *Black and White* fallacy. It normally takes the following form:

Premise: Either claim-A or claim-B is true (but not both, and there are no other alternatives).
Premise: We can't accept claim-A.
Conclusion: We must accept claim-B.

The unwarranted assumption is that A or B is our only choice. The argument ignores other possibilities. For example:

We must either fight the terrorists here or fight them where they live, in the Middle East. We can't fight them here; we don't want any more airliners crashing into buildings. So, we must keep American troops in Iraq until the terrorist threat is dealt with.

As frequently as this argument has been made and as compelling as it might seem, it is based on a *false alternatives* fallacy. There are other conceivable solutions to the problem.

Here's another common example:

The illegal immigrant problem is becoming intolerable. We must either deport all illegal immigrants or open our borders wide and let anybody and everybody in. Obviously, it would be a disaster to open our borders, so we must deport all illegal immigrants.

Again, the arguer has ignored obvious alternative solutions.

And another:

George Bush justified the attack on Iraq on the basis of Saddam's alleged possession of weapons of mass destruction. Now it seems there were none. Clearly, Bush either lied about the situation or was ignorant of a truth that any competent president should have known. So, Bush is either a liar or incompetent. Either way, he should be impeached.

The arguer assumes only two alternatives: Bush is a liar or Bush is incompetent. There are other possibilities that this arguer has missed.

❏ *Unreliable Authority*

There's nothing wrong with an argument from authority. In the academic and professional communities, it is common practice to cite the comments of authorities to explain or support our points of view. However, we must make certain that those we cite are indeed reliable authorities that we can logically assume know what they are talking about.

You may be familiar with the classic commercial that begins with a man in a white coat saying, "Hello. I'm not a doctor but I play one on television . . ." and continues with an attempt to get us to buy an over-the-counter medicine. We are tempted to ask how anyone could be susceptible to such an obvious appeal to unreliable authority. Yet, we must conclude that the Madison Avenue advertising companies that create such commercials are in business because they know what sells products. Clearly the appeal is, at least in some cases, effective. Modern advertising has given us the phenomenon of the "spokesperson." This is normally a celebrity of some sort who encourages us to buy some product or service. The idea behind such commercials is that the person's celebrity status somehow lends credibility to the claims of the advertiser.

Advertising is not the only place you see this sort of appeal. Name any social issue and you will likely find a celebrity supporting one point of view or another. Celebrities have weighed in on the ethical treatment of animals, the war in Iraq, race and gender issues, just to name a few. Note that this is not necessarily bad or unethical. One well-known actress has leant her voice to public appeals for assisting sick or hungry children in third-world countries. It is difficult to fault that. However, we need to realize that, though the cause may be worthy, the appeal is not *necessarily* logical. We stress necessarily here because being a celebrity does not prevent one from becoming something of an expert on other issues. But we need to know that before we accept their testimony as reliable.

We often find appeals to unreliable authority in everyday conversation:

> *Don't believe the reports you see in the newspapers. My biology teacher says only homosexuals and junkies get AIDS.*

Given the amount of research on the subject to the contrary, we must assume that the biology teacher is too poorly informed to be considered a reliable authority.

Here's an example from early modern science:

> *But how can you doubt the air has weight when you have the clear testimony of Aristotle affirming that all elements have weight including air, and excepting only fire.*
> —Galileo Galilei, *Dialogues Concerning Two New Sciences*

Our current understanding of the nature of the material world is considerably contrary to the theories of Aristotle. Consequently, at this point in history, he cannot be considered a reliable authority on the subject. However, we must note that for Galileo, writing in the 17th century, and the scientific community in general, Aristotle was not just an authority. He was, on some subjects, *the* authority.

❏ *False Cause*

This fallacy occurs when one bases an argument on the unwarranted attribution of an effect to a certain cause. (We've already mentioned this fallacy when we first presented the three general rules of a good argument in Chapter 7 under Logos. You may want to review that material.)

Sometimes superstitions are based on *false cause* reasoning:

> *Every time I wear my blue shirt, I have a good day at work. I think I'll run and buy three or four more blue shirts. I can use the good luck.*

Here's a trickier example:

> *Thinking is a function of man's immortal soul. God has given an immortal soul to every man and woman, but not to any other animal or to machines. Hence no animal or machine can think.*
>
> — Alan M. Turing, "Computing Machinery and
> Intelligence," *Mind, 1950*

Turing attributes the cause of human intelligence to an "immortal soul." He is not necessarily wrong, but he has offered no support for the claim, at least not in this passage. So, we must regard the premise as unwarranted and the argument as a *false cause* fallacy.

We must remember that correlation does not mean causation. Just because two events are related in time or place does *not* mean that one necessarily caused the other. For example:

> *How can these liberals argue for gun control? Look at Montana, which has practically no gun control laws; it also has one of the lowest rates of violent crimes committed with hand-guns. In contrast, New York has one of the strictest gun control laws in the nation and the highest rate of gun-related violence. Clearly, if we want to stop violence committed with guns, we should do away with gun-control laws altogether.*

What this arguer has missed is that there are many other differences between the two states that may account for the differences in their crime rates.

Now, take note of the "Adam Dreamhealer" story.

> *Can a 19-year-old Canadian college student heal normally fatal diseases with just his hand? Adam Dreamhealer, who out-earns most doctors, would have us believe so, claiming to channel his personal power into "healing cancers and infections."*
>
> *And his claim is not entirely without support… until one looks a little closer at the evidence.*
>
> *For example, Linda Peterson, took time from her fourth-grade Minnesota class to try the "healing benefits of Adam's hands."*
>
> *Facing a normally fatal diagnosis of "inoperable pancreatic cancer," she took a chance on one of Adam's sessions in 2004. Two weeks later, her doctors discovered that the tumor had disappeared. Peterson, amazed by the apparent miracle, said, "There was nothing there. Gone." At least for a time….*
>
> *In two years, her cancer returned, as did she, to Vancouver, to try for a second miraculous healing from Adam's hands.*
>
> —*Adapted from ABC News, July 13, 2006*

Exercise

Working in small groups, consider the following quotation from Aristotle:

> *All human actions have one or more of these seven causes: chance, nature, compulsions, habit, reason, passion, desire.*

Decide whether or not you think Aristotle is correct in his claim. Can you think of other causes of human actions?

❑ **Slippery Slope**

The Slippery Slope, sometimes thought of as a form of false cause, is a fairly common fallacy. The unwarranted assumption in the slippery slope is that a cause-effect sequence or causal chain will necessarily follow a specific path to an undesirable end. Some are quite easily spotted. For example:

> *We most certainly cannot require registration of handguns. From there, it's a very short step to forcing people to register hunting rifles, and before you know it, we won't even be able to carry a pocket knife without having undergone a background check.*

Another way to think of the slippery slope is that it makes an unwarranted assumption that, once having caused a certain effect, we cannot make a moral, ethical, or practical distinction between that effect and a *potential* next step. Here's another common argument:

> *We should never legalize marijuana even for medical use. Once the stuff is out there, then everyone will have access to it. The next step is legal and available cocaine, and before you know it, people will be able to buy heroin in their local pharmacies.*

Again, the unwarranted assumption is fairly easy to spot. However, the slippery slope is sometimes more subtle and not so easily identified, especially if the writer is skilled. Note the following passage:

> *Why should Pennsylvania, founded by the English, become a Colony of Aliens, who will shortly be so numerous as to Germanize us instead of our Anglifying them, and will never adopt our Languages or Customs, any more than they can acquire our Complexion.*
>
> *Benjamin Franklin, 1751*

Franklin is predicting a cause/effect sequence that is both simplistic and untested. The slippery slope fallacy often presents a striking, even an alarming, prediction. To identify such a fallacy you must question whether the prediction seems reasonable or relevant. Would future events likely bear out the prediction, or does it merely reflect particular biases and prejudices that are not relevant to the first step in a valid causal chain?

Exercise

Collect the editorial pages from several issues of any newspaper. Try to find a half dozen examples of **Fallacies of Unwarranted Assumption**. You should also look at the ads for examples of *Unreliable Authority*. Clip and paste the articles and ads into your journal; then write analyses of the examples. State what fallacy they commit and explain why the reasoning is fallacious.

Exercise

Working in small groups, share and discuss your responses to the previous exercise. Try to determine how the arguer in each case might have rewritten the argument to avoid the fallacy.

Fallacies of Vagueness and Ambiguity

These fallacies break the third general rule for good arguments. They include an inference that depends on vague or ambiguous language. We will deal with three common fallacies: equivocation, composition, and division.

❏ *Equivocation*

Actually, you've already met this fallacy in Chapter 7 when we first mentioned the general rules for a good argument. When we use a word in an argument, we should make sure it means the same thing every time we use it in the course of the argument. Equivocation occurs when an argument depends on the double meaning of a word. For example:

> *"You couldn't have it if you **did** want it," the Queen said. "The rule is jam tomorrow and jam yesterday—but never Jam today." "It must come sometimes to Jam today," Alice objected. "No, it can't," said the Queen. "It's jam **every other day**: today isn't **every other day**, you know".*
>
> —Lewis Carroll, *Through the Looking Glass*

The Queen is basing her argument on the ambiguity of the phrase "every other day."

    Equivocation has sometimes been made into a fine art. For example, in the late 16th century, the new Anglican controlled government of England banned the travel of Catholic priests into England, Ireland, or Scotland. Of course, this didn't stop some priests from entering the countries. The Jesuits in particular made provisions for those smuggling priests in to defend themselves, if caught, by creating a *Treatise on Equivocation*. One technique mentioned was to tell the authorities that "a priest lyeth not in my house." The defense turned on the double meaning of the word "lie." The could mean "there is no priest in my house" or "no priest is telling lies in my house" (Dave Koppel, "Virtue in Equivocation" in *National Review Online*, November 5, 2001).

In some arguments, the significant word need not be mentioned twice. The implication creates the equivocation.

> *Avoid all needle drugs—the only dope worth shooting is Richard Nixon.*
>
> —Abbie Hoffman

❑ *Composition and Division*

Composition and Division are complementary fallacies having to do with making a distinction between the parts of something and the whole thing or between the group and its members.

Composition wrongly assumes that the attributes of the parts (or of the members of a group) apply to the whole (or the whole group) as well. For example:

> *Each individual part of your stereo receiver (resistors, transistors, wires, etc.) was probably relatively inexpensive, so you must have a really cheap system.*

Or

> *Should we not assume that just as the eye, hand, the foot, and in general each part of the body clearly has its own proper function, so man too has some function over and above the function of his parts?*
>
> —Aristotle, *Nicomachean Ethics*

Division wrongly assumes that the characteristics of the whole will be found in all the parts as well. For example:

> *I understand you're a Republican. The official position of the Republican Party is to support the war in Iraq, so I guess you're in favor of that war.*

There may well be some Republicans and Democrats who disagree with their party's official position on any number of issues. Another example:

> *Harvard is a very wealthy university with many lucrative endowments and research grants. Susan will attend Harvard in the fall, so I guess her family must have come into a substantial inheritance.*

Not everyone who attends Harvard is wealthy. Some are on financial aid just as students are at almost any other college.

Exercise

Collect the editorial pages from several issues of any newspaper. Try to find three or four examples of **Fallacies of Vagueness and Ambiguity**. Clip and paste the articles into your journal; then write analyses of the examples. State what fallacy they commit and explain why the reasoning is fallacious.

Exercise

Working in small groups, share and discuss your responses to the previous exercise. Try to determine how the arguer in each case might have rewritten the argument to avoid the fallacy.

Exercise

Make this final exercise something of a contest. First, each member of the class shall write a short argumentative paper filled with as many fallacies as possible. Then, divide the class into two groups; the group will exchange papers. Next, spend some time analyzing the other group's papers to see how many fallacies can be identified. This contest will have two winners. The group that finds the greatest percentage of the fallacies created by the other group will be one winner. The other winner will be the group that is able to slip the most fallacies by their opponents.

PART FOUR

Presenting Conclusions: Writing a Public Draft

Students sometimes believe that there is a difference between what is to be said and the way in which it is said. This is a mistake. From the reader's point of view, there is no difference. The reader experiences only the language on the page, not what is in the writer's mind.

This part of the book focuses mainly on "fine tuning" the language of your essays. Our purpose is twofold. First, we want to show you why precision and vigor in your use of language will enhance a reader's perception of your work and, consequently, its effect. Second, we wish to show you how to diagnose and repair language problems that can lead to dull, cumbersome prose or worse, a lack of clarity.

You will create an essay early on; then, as you finish each of the major sections in the next chapter, you will revise the essay to incorporate the principles and techniques you will have learned.

The last chapter of the book presents the system used by the Modern Language Association for citing and naming sources. Documentation is an exact process. Pay close attention to each kind of citation and bibliographic entry and follow precisely the examples and models in the chapter when attributing "borrowed" material to its original source.

13

A Word About Language and Voice

As you prepare to submit a public draft, you will need to determine an appropriate tone. For example, if you intend to establish an understanding of a concept, object, or process, a moderate, impersonal tone can be the most effective. Highly emotive or colorful language could distract or lead your readers to develop a response that you did not have in mind.

To win assent from an audience, you usually must choose words that will defuse resistance by establishing a reassuring tone. However, if you have determined that you can affect your readers in an emotional way, you can deploy an emotive language that reflects the passion of your and their beliefs.

To stimulate appropriate action—a more demanding goal than understanding—you can use language that is urgent or provocative, especially in the introduction and conclusion of your essay. Or, you may gradually build such a tone into the language of the essay so as to reach a compelling conclusion.

The word for such considerations is *style*. Style gives writing personality; it conveys a writer's attitudes toward the subject and the reader. Style reveals the rhythms and patterns of your thought. Just as there is no easy way to define style, there is no easy way to develop one either. It comes from experience and experimentation, trying out different arrangements of words and sentences and seeing how they work—on you and on your audience. Your work in Chapter 14 will help you better understand the concept of style. But first you will draft an essay that develops from the readings you will encounter in this chapter.

Establishing a Mindset for Your Thinking and Writing

Part One:

The late anthropologist Margaret Mead stated, "Never doubt that a small group of thoughtful, committed citizens can change the world; it's the only thing that ever does." Drawing on relevant readings from earlier chapters or on other works you may have read, identify reasons for agreeing or disagreeing with Mead's viewpoint.

In a speech university professor Benjamin R. Barber delivered on September 24, 2001, he notes, "There's a wonderful moment in a play by Bertolt Brecht about Galileo in which one character says to the other, 'Pity the country that has no heroes.' And the other says, 'No, no, pity the country that needs heroes.' America at its best, democracy at its best, is a system that doesn't need heroes because its ordinary people do the job right." In this speech, Barber defines democracy as "government without heroes, government where ordinary men and women. . . take responsibility in some small way for their lives, . . . It's the putting aside of heroes." If you don't agree with Barber, how would you argue against his views? If you do agree with his viewpoint, why do you think that, generally speaking, ordinary men and women tend not to believe they can actually make a difference, tend not to engage in activities that could have a profound effect for themselves and others?

Part Two:

Now read the following excerpt from Professor Barber's speech and consider how Barber's talk serves to clarify, extend, or refine any of the thinking you expressed in Part One. As a student, also evaluate Barber's assertion that colleges across the country should be "civicist" campuses.

The Concept of Citizenship
Benjamin R. Barber

Benjamin R. Barber (b. 1939) is a Distinguished Senior Fellow, Demos; President, CivWorld at Demos; Walt Whitman Professor of Political Science Emeritus at Rutgers University and the author of many books including the classic *Strong Democracy* (1984), international bestseller *Jihad vs. McWorld* (Times Books, 1995), and most recently, *Consumed: How Markets Corrupt Children, Infantilize Adults, and Swallow Citizens Whole* (W.W. Norton, 2007).

. . . In this dread hour[1] we know our public safety, our national security, are ambitions we can only pursue together, but there are many other more positive and beneficial things that we can also only pursue together. Education is one of them. We can't educate the children of this nation one by one by one, different school by different school, different race by different race, different class by different class. We do it together or we don't educate at all. As a consequence recently we have not been doing very much real education, which is why there is so much cynicism, pessimism, and apathy among so many young Americans. And why those same cynical, apathetic Americans who cared nothing about politics were so desperate after 9/11 to call someone, anyone who could help explain to them what happened. "I thought we lived in a safe playground of the world where my career was the only thing I had to think about and suddenly there's a larger, desperate dangerous world. Explain it to me. What's it about? This isn't the world you promised me. This isn't the world you told me about. This isn't the world in which only private things count." And so we educators are called back to our own mission.

---

[1]Editors' Note. This speech was originally delivered on September 24, 2001, The Inaugural 2001 Civil Society Lecture, College Park, MD.

Our own mission is to educate the young, not just to go to law school or get an MBA or wage a career or even to appreciate a poem or paint a picture or listen to some music. But rather that other mission of American education that rang so clearly in the 18th and 19th century. The mission that both Jefferson and John Adams on different sides of the political aisle both appreciated.

Each said in his own way, "You can't have a democracy unless you have citizens. You can't have citizens without civic responsibility. You can't have citizens and civic responsibility without public education."

And the first aim and mission of any institution of education has to be to forge responsible, thoughtful, critical, competent citizens. That was the founding educational mission. . . .

Even within the narrows of that early democracy—those white, propertied men who could vote—they would not be decent citizens without education. We've largely forgotten that in our modern universities, our public and private institutions. We've become specialists, we professors. We're trained in the liberal arts, most of us, but we've forgotten what the liberal arts mean.

The liberal arts are the arts of liberty. The liberal arts are those arts that free men and women require to achieve and secure their freedom and then stay free. The Declaration of Independence pretends we are born free, but anybody who knows anything about babies knows that babies aren't born free. They're born seven pound weaklings and they stay that way for a long, long, time. When do young men and women become free? Eight years old? 12 years old? 19 years old when you come to college? 23 years old when you go back home to live with your parents because you can't find a job? It takes a long time. Freedom as an ideal; freedom as a right. Yes, we are born with the right to freedom, to be sure. But to actually achieve and secure that liberty takes education, training, experience, competence in the world. And if our colleges and universities, our public high schools and middle schools, don't participate in that training, . . . how on earth are we going to create citizens? How are we going to create people who can engage in turning America into a global partner of other peoples and take on the challenges of terrorism, not by being special forces and going out and engaging in the bloody work that is immediately ahead, but rather by taking responsibility for their schoolrooms, their classrooms, their communities, their churches and synagogues and mosques, their neighborhoods and work places in which they eventually take up jobs and think of themselves as active and engaged in having a responsibility for what happens there? . . .

If the university won't take on its mission to engage itself in the real world the way the young men and women who live in the civicist dorm[2] are doing right now, . . . [sic] But it is not enough to have a civicist dorm and think that you're serving the interests of democracy.

Can you imagine saying, "Oh, Dayton, Ohio, that's where American citizens, where people entering citizenship, live. Elsewhere people interested in entertainment or finance live. But if you're interested in citizentry go live in Dayton. That's where all the citizens gather." We'll have one house where the people who really care about others and are going to serve. But it shouldn't be just the civicist house;

---

[2]Editors' Note. Here Barber is referring to a civic community assembled at the University of Maryland, College Park.

it should be the whole social science college. And it shouldn't just be the social science college; it should be the whole university. And it shouldn't just be the university; it should be every school in Maryland. And it shouldn't just be Maryland; it should be throughout these United States.

That should be part of what we do as students and as teachers working together. Not all that we do. There are many other things that we need too, but it has to be part, and an important part, of what we do because if we don't do it, who will? And if we don't do it, after the Special Forces guys go home and after this generation of Bin Ladens has been eliminated, who will deal with the conditions already out there in which new Bin Ladens, maybe 8, 9, 10 years old are looking at the world and saying, "This is no world for me. There's no hope, there's no opportunity, there's no wife, there's no family, there's no job. And when I grow up I know what I'm going to do. I'm going to strap a bomb to my back and walk through Times Square or College Park or Disneyland or London and blow them all up, the ones who have done this to me."

And the Special Forces can't do anything about that; that's not their job. Only we as educators, as students, as administrators working together as citizens of this country can do something about that. In insisting on a government that is a partner to the world and insisting on a world where not just the stark claims of America's retributive justice rain from the sky from B52s, but the much more complex and difficult claims of distributive justice, where we create a world with sufficient equity, with sufficient opportunity, a world in which terrorists become isolated.

There will always be some lunatics. There will always be some people who want to murder and kill for a variety of reasons, but if they're isolated from the environment, if they have no even quasi-legitimacy, if there's nobody to help them, if every ordinary mortal is going to turn them in, they'll get nowhere. They can't do it by themselves. These 18 or 20 desperate young men who did this vile act on 9/11 had hundreds who worked with them and thousands in banks and financial institutions elsewhere who looked the other way and millions around the world who thought probably it was too bad but maybe America deserved it.

And how do we deal with them because they will be the ones who make the long-term future? The only way I know to deal with them is no, not through air strikes, land forces, counter terror or intelligence. The only way I know to do it is through a more democratic world. Not democracy imposed by force of arms from the outside. Not democracy top down. But democracy from the inside, bottom up, from citizens. That may sound foolish and utopian and silly. But, in fact, it's the heart and imperative of national security policy today. . . .

And if we can't find the way to do that then we will be the losers. It is always, I think, our first impulse at times like this to ask where are the heroes; or to find heroes in our midst. There have been, we all know, if you follow the news or, as I do, live in New York, there have been some remarkable heroes. The men who conspired on that plane over Pittsburgh making a turn back towards Washington to create enough chaos on board that the plane could not finish its mission. To sacrifice themselves and their fellows in order to spare some unknown-to-us target building in Washington, maybe the Capitol, maybe the White House, maybe some other building. What heroes. The firemen and policemen who rushed up the stairs of the World Trade Center as so many frightened occupants rushed down.

The looks on their faces telling the people on the way down that the people on the way up knew they were going to meet their death even as they went. These were the people schooled and proficient in emergencies, and they knew that there was little chance that they would come down again but up they went, extraordinary heroes. And some of our political leaders, the mayor of New York who became an emblem of the spirit of New York, and the many, many emergency workers and firemen and policemen who to this day are still going through the rubble and still engaging in the horrendous business of removing bodies so that loved ones will at least have the certainty of knowing that someone has been found and can be buried. Extraordinary heroes.

But I want to say despite this yearning for heroes, we have to resist it because the yearning for heroes at a moment like this is to ask someone else to solve our problems, ask someone else to do it for us, ask Mayor Giuliani to carry the weight, the firemen and the policemen to carry the weight, the heroes on board Flight 93 to carry the weight for us. And when I think about a definition of democracy, the definition that I always think of is democracy as government without heroes. Democracy is government where ordinary men and women, not very heroic, anxious, frightened, uncertain, nonetheless take responsibility in some small way for their lives, this part of their job, this part of their community. It's the putting aside of heroes.

There's a wonderful moment in a play by Bertolt Brecht about Galileo in which one character says to the other, "Pity the country that has no heroes." And the other says, "No, no, pity the country that needs heroes." America at its best, democracy at its best, is a system that doesn't need heroes because its ordinary people do the job right.

Just as a university doesn't need celebrated professors if ordinary teachers do their job right. Just as we in America don't have to turn Colin Powell or George Bush or Mayor Giulliani into heroes (not that they want to be) but we don't need to turn them into that if we do our work well. . . .

And so we say we will do it for ourselves. We will train ourselves. We will acquire the knowledge and strength to do it for ourselves and then we will have an America that needs no heroes and a world that needs no heroes because all of us take responsibility for ourselves and our own destinies.

Right now, we Americans and many of our friends around the world are sitting and waiting and watching. And the best we can do is to wait and watch. What will the heroes do next? What will the American Air Force do next? What will Special Forces do next? What will intelligence come up with?

We sit and we watch and we wait and that of course makes us more anxious. But what are we waiting for? Because in a democracy it's us that have to become engaged in ways that initially may seem not particularly relevant to the larger struggle against terrorism, to the larger struggle for global justice.

But democracy starts with each individual taking responsibility for his family, for her community, for the environment in which we find ourselves, whether at work or in a religious or an educational or even a social environment. . . .

In the words of a remarkable old American gospel song, "We are the ones that we've been waiting for." And our engagement, our energy, our caring, our work, mimicking the energy of and work of those rescue workers at the World Trade Center in New York, can make a difference. As engaged citizens working to make democracy real at home and abroad, we are in fact the terrorists' worst nightmare because we can rob them of their martyrdom. We don't have to destroy them. We can, by creating a democratic world, make them irrelevant.

For Discussion

1.   Barber calls upon students and teachers to engage in democratic governance, to devote "this part of their lives, this part of their job, this part of their community" to insuring a democratic environment. Do you find that your educational experience is encouraging you, in Barber's words, to become "responsible, thoughtful, critical, competent citizens"? Explain.

2.   One of our students argued that our elected representatives, "schooled and proficient" in governance, should "carry the weight" of our representative democracy. Therefore, we do not need to know what they know, do what they do, or challenge their decisions. Do you agree with this position?

This initial inquiry is meant to spark lively discussion as you begin talking, reading and writing about this chapter's central theme: the merits of calling for an increasing degree of involvement from individuals and communities in the process of constructive change. To help shape and inform your inquiries, you will encounter readings suggesting engagements to bring about that change.

Using the Readings

Calling for Community Action and Social Change

The chapter readings will help you develop thoughtful definitions for an array of concepts reflecting civic ideals including *personal and civic responsibility, freedom and human dignity, equal rights, the rule of law, social and economic justice, and tolerance of diversity.* Each selection presents people actively challenging something crucial in their personal lives or challenging specific social norms. Note that your instructor might ask you to apply the Toulmin model (Chapter 11) to some of the arguments you will encounter.

Soul of a Citizen:
Living With Conviction in a Cynical Time
Paul Rogat Loeb

Paul Rogat Loeb (b. 1952) has spent over thirty years writing about the role of the citizen in the modern world. From his college days at Stanford, where he opposed the Vietnam War, until the present time, Loeb has written and lectured about citizen involvement in resolving problems—from local poverty to the threat of nuclear war. He has tried to identify the factors that make some people commit themselves to a life of social involvement and others to turn away. The following excerpt from *Soul of a Citizen* focuses on that issue.

* * * * * * * * * * *

If I am not for myself, who will be for me?
And if I am only for myself, what am I?

—*RABBI HILLEL*

A MORE HOPEFUL WAY TO LIVE

In the personal realm, most Americans are thoughtful, caring, generous. We try to do our best by family and friends. At times we'll even stop to help another driver stranded with a roadside breakdown, or give some spare change to a stranger. But increasingly, a wall now separates each of us from the world outside, and from others who've likewise taken refuge in their own private sanctuaries. We've all but forgotten that public participation is the very soul of democratic citizenship, and how much it can enrich our lives.

However, the reason for our wholesale retreat from social involvement is not, I believe, that most of us feel all is well with the world. I live in Seattle, a city with a seemingly unstoppable economy. Yet every time I go downtown I see men and women with signs saying "I'll work for food," or "Homeless vet. Please help." Their suffering diminishes me as a human being. I also travel extensively, doing research and giving lectures throughout the country. Except in the wealthiest of enclaves, people everywhere say, "Things are hard here." America's economic boom has passed many of us by. We struggle to live on meager paychecks. We worry about layoffs, random violence, the rising cost of health care, and the miseducation of our kids. Too stretched to save, uncertain about Social Security, many of us wonder just how we'll survive when we get old. We feel overwhelmed, we say, and helpless to change things.

Even those of us who are economically comfortable seem stressed. We spend hours commuting on crowded freeways, and hours more at jobs whose demands never end. We complain that we don't have enough time left for families and friends. We worry about the kind of world we'll pass on to our grandchildren. Then we also shrug and say there's nothing we can do.

To be sure, the issues we now face are complex—perhaps more so than in the past. How can we comprehend the moral implications of a world in which Nike pays Michael Jordan more to appear in its ads than it pays all the workers at its Indonesian shoe factories combined? Today the five hundred richest people on the planet control more wealth than the bottom three billion, half of the human population. Is it possible even to grasp the process that led to this most extraordinary imbalance? More important, how do we even begin to redress it?

Yet what leaves too many of us sitting on the sidelines is not only a lack of understanding of the complexities of our world. It's not only an absence of readily apparent ways to begin or resume public involvement. Certainly we need to decide for ourselves whether particular causes are wise or foolish—be they the politics of campaign finance reform, attempts to address the growing gap between rich and poor, or efforts to safeguard water, air, and wilderness. We need to identify and connect with worthy groups that take on these issues, whether locally or globally. But first we need to believe that our individual involvement is worthwhile, that what we might do in the public sphere will not be in vain.

LEARNED HELPLESSNESS

America's prevailing culture of cynicism insists that nothing we do can matter. It teaches us not to get involved in shaping the world we'll pass on to our children. It encourages us to leave such important decisions to others—whether they be corporate and government leaders, or social activists whose lifestyles seem impossibly selfless or foreign. Sadly, and ironically, in a country born of a democratic political revolution, to be American today is to be apolitical. Civic withdrawal has become our norm. To challenge this requires courage. It also requires creating a renewed definition of ourselves as citizens—something closer to the nation of active stakeholders that leaders like Thomas Jefferson had in mind.

The importance of citizens' direct participation in a democracy was expressed thousands of years ago, by the ancient Greeks. In fact, they used the word "idiot" for people incapable of involving themselves in civic life. Now, the very word "political" has become so debased in our culture that we use it to describe either trivial office power plays or the inherently corrupt world of elected leaders. We've lost sight of its original roots in the Greek notion of the polis: the democratic sphere in which citizens, acting in concert, determine the character and direction of their society. "All persons alike," wrote Aristotle, should share "in the government to the utmost."

Reclaiming this political voice requires more than just identifying problems, which itself can feed our sense of overload. I think of an Arthur Miller play, *Broken Glass,* whose heroine obsesses over Hitler. From the untroubled environs of Brooklyn, she reads newspaper articles about *Kristalnacht:* synagogues smashed and looted; old men forced to scrub streets with toothbrushes while storm troopers laugh at them; and finally, children shipped off to the camps in cattle cars. Her concern contrasts with the approach of her family and friends, who insist, despite the mounting evidence, that such horrors are exaggerated. Yet she does nothing to address the situation publicly, except to grow more anxious. Eventually she becomes psychosomatically paralyzed.

The approach Miller's protagonist takes toward the horrors of Nazism resembles the condition psychologist Martin Seligman calls learned helplessness. People who suffer from severe depression, he found, do so less as a result of particular unpleasant experiences than because of their "explanatory style"—the story they tell themselves about how the world works. Depressed people have become convinced that the causes of their difficulties are permanent and pervasive, inextricably linked to their personal failings. There's nothing to be done because nothing can be done. This master narrative of their lives excuses inaction; it provides a rationale for remaining helpless. In contrast, individuals who function with high effectiveness tend to believe that the problems they face result from factors that are specific and temporary, and therefore changeable. The story they live by empowers them.

This is not to say that change is easy, nor that everyone is in an equal position to bring it about. Some individuals and groups in America possess far more material and organizational resources than others. This reflects our deep social and economic inequities. But as social theorist and *Tikkun* magazine founder Michael Lerner has observed, we often fail to use the resources we do have, which may be of a different kind. "Most of us," Lerner says, "have been subjected to a set of experiences in our childhood and adult lives that makes us feel that we do not deserve to have power." Consequently, we can't imagine changing the direction of our society. We decide that things are worse than they actually are—a condition Lerner refers to as "surplus powerlessness.". . .

The illusion of powerlessness can just as easily afflict the fortunate among us. I know many people who are confident and successful in their work and have loving personal relationships, yet can hardly conceive of trying to work toward a more humane society. Materially comfortable and professionally accomplished, they could make important social contributions. Instead they restrict their search for meaning and integrity to their personal lives. Their sense of shared fate extends only to their immediate families and friends. Despite their many advantages, they, too, have been taught an "explanatory style" that precludes participation in public life, except to promote the most narrow self-interest.

Whatever our situations, we all face a choice. We can ignore the problems that lie just beyond our front doors; we can allow decisions to be made in our name that lead to a meaner and more desperate world. We can yell at the TV newscasters and complain about how bad things are, using our bitterness as a hedge against involvement. Or we can work, as well as we can, to shape a more generous common future. . . .

I ENJOYED THAT DAY

. . . [S]atisfaction can be found even amid the most testing of situations. Muhammad Ali recalls how good it felt to decide finally to resist the Vietnam-era draft. He lost his boxing championship title, was publicly reviled, and was sentenced to five years in prison (though the sentence was finally overturned on a technicality). If he quietly submitted, Ali was assured, he'd never face combat. But he could not live with supporting a war he felt was morally wrong and "leading more boys to death."

"That day in Houston in '67 when I went to the induction center, I felt happy," he says, "because people didn't think I had the nerve to buck the draft board of the government. And I almost ran there, hurried. . . . The world was watching, the blacks mainly, looking to see if I had the nerve to buck Uncle Sam, and I just couldn't wait for the man to call my name, so I wouldn't step forward. I enjoyed that day."

In *Revolution from Within*, Gloria Steinem describes a test of her own spirit. Steinem grew up in East Toledo, Ohio, the poor side of town. At a Toledo women's conference where she was speaking years later, she met contemporaries from her working-class high school; gutsy, highly vocal women who'd brought sex discrimination suits in their factory jobs, organized battered women's programs, and defeated an antiabortion ordinance in their heavily Catholic communities.

As always, Steinem was a political lightning rod. During a local TV interview, she described some of the women's stories that she'd heard. A man called in to denounce the conference as "antifamily" and Steinem in particular as "a slut from East Toledo." When she was growing up, the label would have devastated her. Instead, Steinem and the other women laughed. They turned an apparent insult into a tribute to their hard-won independence, their willingness to challenge prescribed roles and rules, and the sense of solidarity they'd built. "As we toasted each other as 'the sluts from East Toledo' with coffee and beer after the interview, I thought: Not a bad thing to be. Maybe I'll put it on my tombstone.". . .

BEFORE WATER TURNS TO ICE

Virtually all of America's most effective historical movements met with repeated frustration and failure before making significant progress toward their goals. At few points prior to victory could participants have proved that their individual efforts mattered. On the contrary, the reverse often seemed true. As the U.S. Supreme Court justice Louis Brandeis once wrote, "Most of the things worth doing in the world had been declared impossible before they were done." Only in retrospect does the link between small beginnings and profound social change become fully evident. Only then is the true value of persistence in the face of difficulty revealed.

Think of the apartheid-era campaign for South African divestment. American economic interests supported the apartheid government almost from its foundation. After the 1960 Sharpeville massacre, for instance, a consortium of U.S. banks (led by Chase Manhattan) invested heavily to shore up the Pretoria regime, which seemed on the verge of collapse. In response, one of the first Students for a Democratic Society (SDS) protests was held on Wall Street. Challenges to American economic support of apartheid surged and receded for the next twenty-five years. Then, after the U.S. Senate failed to pass a sanctions bill in 1984, a stream of people staged acts of civil disobedience at the main South African embassy in Washington, D.C., and at local consulates nationwide.

These protests in turn rekindled large-scale social activism on America's campuses. Even as their generation was being maligned as apathetic and uncaring, students organized rallies, petition drives, and marches, built protest shantytowns, staged sit-ins, and set up blockades—all aimed at persuading colleges and universities to divest themselves of stock in companies doing business in South Africa. Their movement caught fire as global television showed the South African government beating, gassing, and shooting peaceful demonstrators who challenged worsening economic conditions, substandard education, and a new constitution that would permanently disenfranchise black South African citizens.

At Columbia University, the divestment campaign was led by the Black Student Association (BSA). Participants used speakers, public forums, referendums, and door-to-door canvassing of the dorms to win support for their cause. They even secured an endorsement from the faculty senate. When university trustees refused to meet with the campaigners, a dozen students launched a hunger strike, and then a sit-in that they expected would last a few hours. Instead, several hundred people joined in, and the sit-in lasted three weeks. Not only did Columbia divest the following fall (while administrators insisted their action had "nothing to do with the protests") but its students inspired similar efforts across the country, prompting some 150 institutions to withdraw more than $4 billion in investment funds. The student movement proved to be the key factor in the U.S. congressional vote that finally approved sanctions against South Africa over Ronald Reagan's veto. By ending U.S. moral and economic support, this historic decision placed enormous pressure on the South African government and its white population to finally move toward democracy.

Movement participants acted mostly because they felt they had to do something, even if it had little impact on university policy. "Going into it, I wasn't at all sure the university would respond," said Winston Willis, who later headed Columbia's BSA. "I doubted the trustees would give in. Columbia's an immensely powerful institution. But a number of us felt so strongly about the issues that we were willing to risk arrest, suspension, or expulsion, and to sleep outside night after night in the sleet and the rain—in case maybe, just maybe, they would."

The sit-in was particularly hard for African American students on scholarships, many of whom were the first in their families to go to college and had no safety net of money and personal contacts. But letters and phone calls of support came from across the country. The students persisted, and their efforts bore fruit they had scarcely imagined. When Nelson Mandela was freed and came to speak in Harlem, Winston attended. He went, he says, "with a sense that I'd played a part, no matter how infinitesimal, in helping to get him out. Friends gave me a copy of that first ballot where blacks got to vote, which I still keep in our study. Recently another friend from those days, whose wife's father is now an official in the new South African government, went to visit. Desmond Tutu shook his hand and said, 'You don't know how important it was what you American students did.' We had no idea our actions would have such an impact."

None of us can predict when the causes we support will capture the public imagination, and our once-lonely quests become popular crusades. "Before water turns to ice," writes the psychologist Joanna Macy, "it looks just the same as before. Then a few crystals form, and suddenly the whole system undergoes cataclysmic change." The paleontologist Stephen Jay Gould has developed a theory he calls "punctuated equilibrium." Rather than occurring at a steady pace, evolution proceeds in fits and starts, Gould argues. Long stretches of relative stasis are followed by brief periods of intense transformation, when many new species appear and others die out. Although attempts to improve social and economic conditions usually proceed incrementally, it is impossible to foretell precisely when any of our endeavors will reach critical mass, suddenly creating change.

Nor can we predict when a single seemingly insignificant effort will produce powerful results. Shortly before the 1994 Congressional elections, a Wesleyan University student named Tess Rondeau was inspired by an environmental conference. With a few friends, Tess registered nearly three hundred fellow students concerned about environmental threats and cuts in government financial aid programs. Nearly all ended up supporting Congressman Sam Gejdenson, a Democrat of more-than-usual courage and vision. Gejdenson squeaked in to win re-election by just twenty-one votes, then recaptured his seat in 1996, and won by a landslide in 1998. Before they began, Tess and her friends feared that their modest registration campaign would be irrelevant, and worried that they'd come off "like politicians spouting a line." But they decided to go ahead anyway and do the best they could. Which to their surprise turned out to be very good indeed. Had they done nothing, Gejdenson would have lost. . . .

THE ONLY FAILURE IS QUITTING

We never know how the impact of our actions may ripple out. We never know who may be touched. That's one more reason why, although the fruits of our labors can't always be seen, they matter immensely.

[Consider black professor, scholar, and author] . . . Derrick Bell's April 1990 decision to take an unpaid leave to protest Harvard Law School's refusal to hire a single female Latino, Asian, or Native American professor. There were a few white women, a few African American men, and that was it. Although administrators made vague promises of change, they kept hiring more white men. Bell took a second year of unpaid leave, then requested a third, for which he had to obtain a routinely granted waiver of the standard rules. In his case, though, the university refused, saying that Bell must either return to his teaching duties or lose his tenured position. Bell chose to forfeit his lifetime position on the most prestigious law faculty in the nation.

This was a courageous moral stand, which drew national attention. It brought major pressure to bear on Harvard Law School, and called attention to the hiring practices of other law schools nationwide. Seven years later, Harvard Law finally relented, hiring an African American woman, Lani Guinier, away from the University of Pennsylvania. African American colleagues throughout the country have told Bell that they owed their tenure-track hirings in part to his protest. "The fact is," Bell writes, "that most of us in law teaching—whatever our qualifications and potential—are the beneficiaries of pressures, past or present, on campus or beyond." Note that the victories sparked by Bell's action came without his foreknowledge and after he'd already paid a personal price.

Bell himself says he would not have been able to make such a sacrifice if not for another difficult moral decision earlier in his career; a decision that, in turn, had been sparked by another example of commitment. In *1957*, Bell was a young lawyer for the U.S. Justice Department. He'd joined the NAACP a while before, and his bosses called his two-dollar annual membership a conflict of interest. Most of Bell's friends urged him to quit the NAACP and to work from within the system to change this policy and others. But Judge William Hastie, the first black federal judge in the country, urged Bell to follow his conscience. During World War II, Hastie had resigned as a top civilian aide to the secretary of war when the military refused to integrate its forces; his departure helped bring the issue to public attention, and Truman abolished military segregation a few years later. Bell decided not to give up his membership. When his superiors at the Justice Department transferred him to a meaningless backbench assignment, he resigned to head the Pittsburgh branch of the NAACP. There he started working with people like Thurgood Marshall on some of the most critical civil rights fights of the time.

As Bell said, what separates individuals who act to challenge injustice from those who stand aside is the sense of personal urgency they develop, "and the recognition that, in the real world, we cannot expect—and certainly should not wait for—the perfect solution." Had he not taken that first stand, Bell recalls, "I might have toiled on, unhappily, at the Justice Department for years at work less risky but certainly no less frustrating than my job with the Pittsburgh NAACP. More important, had I remained at the Justice Department, I would have missed the chance to work with the NAACP Legal Defense

Fund during some of the most exciting years of the civil rights movement." And that was precisely the experience that prepared him for the stand he took at Harvard.

As Bell's experience suggests, a key ingredient of effective social action is faith that our efforts count for something. Sometimes we don't even recognize powerful victories when they occur, because their impact is hidden. In 1969, Henry Kissinger told the North Vietnamese that Nixon was threatening a massive escalation of the war, including potential nuclear strikes, unless they capitulated and forced the National Liberation Front in the South to do the same. Nixon was serious. He'd had military advisers prepare detailed plans, including mission folders with photographs of possible nuclear targets. But two weeks before the president's November 1 deadline for surrender, there was a nationwide daylong "moratorium," during which millions of people took part in local demonstrations, vigils, church services, petition drives, and other forms of protest. A month later came a major march in Washington, D.C. Nixon's public response was to watch the Washington Redskins football game during the D.C. march, and to declare that the marchers weren't affecting his policies in the slightest. His contempt fed the frustration and demoralization of far too many in the peace movement. But privately, Nixon decided the movement had, in his words, so "polarized" American opinion that he couldn't carry out his threat. Participants in the moratorium had no idea that their efforts may have helped stop a nuclear attack.

Nowhere is the need for a long view of social change more evident than in the case of campaigns that span generations. Think of the women's suffrage movement. When Susan B. Anthony began fighting for women's right to vote, her cause seemed a long shot. She worked for it her entire adult life, then died at the age of eighty-six, fourteen years before suffrage was ratified. In retrospect, Anthony played as pivotal a role as any single individual. Yet during her lifetime, success seemed far from assured. Only by trusting that sooner or later their actions would matter could she and others keep on until they prevailed. . . .

SPECIFIC LIVES

New information—the number of America's children in poverty, the record percentage of wealth controlled by the rich, the thousands of acres of old-growth forests and fertile topsoil that have been destroyed—can give us a sense of the magnitude of our problems and help us develop appropriate responses. But it can't provide the organic connection that binds one person to another. By contrast, powerful individual stories create community, writes Scott Russell Sanders in *Utne Reader*. "They link teller to listeners, and listeners to one another." They let us glimpse the lives of those older or younger, richer or poorer, of different races, from places we'll never even see. Showing us the links between choices and consequences, they train our sight, "give us images for what is truly worth seeking, worth having, worth doing."

In a time when we're taught that our actions don't matter, stories carry greater weight than ever. They teach us, Sanders suggests, how "every gesture, every act, every choice we make sends ripples of influence into the future." Indeed, it's no exaggeration to say that the stories that gain prominence in public dialogue will significantly shape public policy.

This means that we are more likely to challenge homelessness if we hear the testimonies of people living on the street. We will work to overcome illiteracy after gaining a sense of what it's like to be unable to read. COPS [Communities Organized for Public Service] derived its political agenda from stories like the one Virginia [Ramirez] told about her neighbor [who died of pneumonia because her house was so dilapidated that it couldn't retain heat and she couldn't afford to repair it]. Ginny Nicarthy's battered women [Nicarthy organized some of the country's early battered women's groups] first shared their anguish and rage, then, with support began to change their situation. Psychological studies of those who rescued Jews during the Holocaust found they differed from their peers in their ability to be moved by pain, sadness, and helplessness. "If one woman ever told the whole honest truth about her life," writes poet Muriel Rukeyser, "the world would split open." I'd say the same would be true for any man.

As you may recall, there are dangers inherent in trying to grasp too much at one time, in wallowing in the bad news. As Joanna Macy reminds us, "Information *by itself* can increase resistance [to engagement], deepening the sense of apathy and powerlessness." Stories about particular individuals and specific situations usually have the opposite effect. By giving unwieldy problems a human face, they also bring them down to a human—and thus manageable—scale. That's why learning what it's like for a single child to grow up with inadequate food, education, and medical care, with hopes damped and broken, can help us understand the moral ramifications of allowing this to happen to millions of children every day. Similarly, feeling the loss of a specific place that's been environmentally desecrated, or adopting and reclaiming it, can give us the strength to face the larger truth—that destroying the living forms that Thomas Berry calls "modes of divine presence" has become our culture's routine way of doing business.

Concrete, particularized stories help us feel the emotional weight of the world's troubles without so burdening us that we despair of ever being able to change things. As the philosopher Richard Rorty reminds us, the best way to promote compassion and solidarity is not by appealing to some general notion of goodness, but by encouraging people to respond to specific human lives. Responsibility in this view is not an abstract principle but a way of being. It exists only in the doing.

Questions for Discussion and Writing

1. What are the major claims (assertions) about citizen involvement that Loeb makes in this excerpt? What support does Loeb provide for those claims? How adequate do you find the support?

2. Activists like Loeb have a lifetime of experiences and skills to bring to bear on civic action. Based on your own experience, do you think his claims justify his call to action?

3. If you had the opportunity to ask Loeb several questions, what would they be? Why?

4. Which of the rhetorical descriptions—nature, causality, evaluation, or proposal—best defines Loeb's essay? Why? Given your response, how well does the essay "satisfy" the rhetorical requirements of that aim? Explain.

Making Connections

1. Loeb and Benjamin Barber focus on the role students have played in various social movements. Do you feel involved in these discussions? If so, does this sense draw you into working for change or keep you at a distance? Do you identify with the students who are presented as examples? If so, why? If not, why not?

2. Are there any issues at your college that lend themselves to the kind of citizen involvement Loeb proposes? What are they? How are they being addressed currently? What about in your home community?

3. Loeb offers examples of several prominent, and not so prominent, workers for social justice who have paid tremendous personal and professional costs for their efforts. What kind of risks could be involved for you or others in "taking one's conscience to work" (Ralph Nader) on an important campus or community issue? Would the risks outweigh the benefits that could be gained? If so, why? If not, why not?

4. Loeb describes how divestment and sanctions eventually ended apartheid in South Africa. Could the kind of activism Loeb describes offer globalizers (See Chapter 8) strategies for alleviating the inequities that an unfettered free market produces? If so, how? If not, why not?

Visual Exercise

Consider how the images below bring to life a scene that conceivably could not be expressed by printed text alone. Reflect on how your grasp of the situation is enhanced by the visual.

© Angela Rowlings/*Boston Herald*

© Angela Rowlings/*Boston Herald*

**Veterans Day, November 21, 2007. Members of Veterans For Peace stand
in a silent protest at Boston City Hall. Eighteen of the veterans were arrested.**

Questions

1. What are your first impressions of the visual? Take note of its structure and its compositional elements.

2. How do the various visual elements work to: a) attract attention b) convey information c) elicit emotion?

3. What is the relationship between the images and the text—both the text *in* the photographs and the text *accompanying* the photograph?

4. Is the context full enough so that the "information" can be understood and believed? If so, why? If not, why not?

5. What questions would you ask of the veterans in the photograph? The police? The photographer?

6. How do the two images relate to the theme of the chapter—calling for community action and social change? How do they relate to Loeb's article, "Soul of a Citizen?"

The New Face of Philanthropy
Silja Talvi, J.A.

Silja J.A. Talvi (b. 1970), a prolific investigative journalist, is also a senior editor at *In These Times*, a magazine devoted to analyzing and informing the general public about social, economic, and environmental movements. Her essays and articles have appeared in several anthologies and in national magazines, including *The Nation*, *Salon*, and the *Utne Reader*. In this article, written for the *Christian Science Monitor* (2005), Talvi discusses the growing philanthropic movement among young, wealthy, and socially conscious Americans.

✳ ✳ ✳ ✳ ✳ ✳ ✳ ✳ ✳ ✳ ✳

When Karen Pittelman took the lion's share of her $3 million-plus inheritance and started The Chahara Foundation, the 25-year-old self-described activist and poet took some heat from friends and family members.

"Most everyone thought I was some combination of crazy, communist, or naive," she says. "When I was younger, I wanted to wash my hands of all the money, pretend I had never even known it existed. That was guilt. But guilt is just inertia, just indulgence. It accomplishes nothing."

Her Boston-based foundation, now in its first granting cycle, will award renewable grants of up to $20,000 per year to Boston-based organizations working with, and run by, lower-income women.

Ms. Pittelman's decision to give away much of her inheritance was rooted in her desire to use that money toward a "radical redistribution of wealth."

"Turning my inheritance into this foundation was the way I claimed my responsibility [to this community]."

Pittelman is one of a small but growing number of young, cause-oriented Americans who have dedicated themselves and their substantial financial resources to supporting each other—and to challenging each other to act in accordance with their values.

Much of the effort of the emerging "cool rich kids" movement has revolved around donating significant portions of income and overall assets to smaller, grass-roots organizations and activist groups often overlooked by large foundations.

"For anybody who is both wealthy and socially concerned, there is some contradiction in our lives," says Tracy Hewat, director of the North Cambridge, Mass.-based Resource Generation, the nation's first and only nonprofit organization specifically devoted to working with and building an alliance of young "progressives" with wealth.

Questions surrounding the relationship between a global "wealth gap" and the financial circumstances of younger people with access to substantial wealth led Ms. Hewat to co-edit a resource manual, "Money Talks. So Can We." About 2,000 copies of the manual, designed for those under the age of 30, have been distributed worldwide.

Most of those who turn to Resource Generation for advice are, in fact, multimillionaires, says Hewat. But the organization turns no one away: Hewat recalls counseling a young person who felt overwhelmed by a $40,000 inheritance and wanted to give it away, and another person with $40 million in assets who wanted to make a positive impact with a portion of the money.

"People [initially] feel like they're making decisions in isolation," she says.

Hewat emphasizes that young philanthropists and social activists with wealth are by no means a *new* phenomenon, and that some of the nation's most respected progressive foundations were, in fact, started by young philanthropists in the 1960s and '70s.

"But today, because of the intergenerational transfer of wealth and because of the growth of the computer industry—and the age of the people who are typically [employed] in that industry—we are in an unusual moment," says Hewat.

How young people with wealth learn to relate to their inheritance or big paychecks is of paramount importance, agree those involved in the movement.

Billy Wimsatt, who first used the "cool rich kids" term in his book, *No More Prisons,* explains that guilt and denial are often overriding and even paralyzing emotions among many young people with access to wealth. Mr. Wimsatt is co-director of Reciprocity, an organization focused on connecting young people across social and economic divides and making *philanthropy* "cool."

"Some of the best candidates for the cool-rich-kids movement have spent their entire lives pretending they're not [rich]," says Wimsatt, who gave away a third of his annual income last year to social-change *philanthropy*.

Young people who suddenly inherit wealth—or who cash in on stock options—are often at a particular loss to understand or cope with the influx of money, says Allen Hancock, publisher of a quarterly journal on wealth-related issues (See story below). He adds that young people like himself who have come into wealth are often concerned about how their peers will view them.

"The running stereotype is that we're spoiled, petulant, greedy, unmotivated," says Hewat. "But that doesn't represent who we're talking to, and who's talking to us."

The complex relationship that young people with progressive values have with their wealth is one of several issues addressed at an annual "Making Money Make Change" conference for people 35 and under. Now in its third year, the conference will be held from Oct. 27–29 in Briarcliff, N.Y. Vivien Labaton, director of the New York-based organization, Third Wave, is helping to organize the conference.

"Young people who have a lot of money tend to be quiet about it because it sets them apart from other people," says Ms. Labaton. "It's easy to feel like you're just a part of the problem in the growing divide between the rich and poor. But when there's an opportunity to think about these things in a more productive way, it's a welcome relief."

Increasing the amount of dollars aimed at small, community-based nonprofits and toward addressing the root causes of poverty is to be a big emphasis of the conference.

According to a 1998 study by the National Network of Grantmakers, only 2.4 percent of foundation grants—or $336 million—went to "progressive," social-change *philanthropy*.

In contrast, a study last November by the *Chronicle of Philanthropy* found many leading charities, including the Salvation Army, YMCA, and the American Cancer Society, are bringing in billions, raising 16 percent more in contributions in 1998 than they did in 1997. The desire of the cool-rich-kids movement to change the distribution of some of these dollars is strong.

Hewat, too, was the benefactor of a large inheritance. Now in her early 30s, she gives away a larger percentage of her income every year, but remains realistic about the impact.

"Even if I gave all of my money away, it would not cure all the ills of the world," she says. "But my hope is . . . that I can convince enough people to join me that [we] can have a significant impact, way beyond the money I can give—way beyond my own assets."

Where Help Is Felt Most

When Mikala Berbery went from earning $21,000 a year to losing her job, her life suddenly plunged into a dangerous abyss of homelessness.

She spent 2 1/2 years homeless, struggling to find shelter for herself and her young son. The seemingly insurmountable challenges she faced in trying to get out of that "hole," explains Ms. Berbery, fuels her dedication today to the Boston group Roofless Women.

The small organization will receive a $20,000 renewable grant later this year from The Chahara Foundation, started when 20-something activist Karen Pittelman decided that her inherited millions could better benefit her community if it were doing more than just sitting in her bank account.

Roofless Women, dedicated to training low-income and homeless women to become advocates for themselves and to educate women about housing and welfare-related state legislation, has scraped by for three years.

This year's budget is a paltry $52,000, and the organization nearly fell apart in 1998 when funding resources were too scarce.

"People aren't exactly throwing money at us," says Berbery, who is the coordinator of Roofless Women. "The Chahara Foundation grant is the biggest one we've ever received in one lump sum. We've never had that kind of show of faith before."

Organizations benefiting from this kind of social-change-oriented *philanthropy* represent an eclectic mix.

The Philadelphia-based Self Education Foundation, of which Billy Wimsatt is a part has awarded grants to groups as diverse as United Parents Against Lead (confronting the lead poisoning of low-income city children) and Books Through Bars (getting literature to prisoners).

Ms. Pittelman's Chahara Foundation will be awarding grants this year to many small, Boston-area groups including Kitchen Table Conversations (a low-income women's support group with an operating budget of $5,000) and the Welfare Education Training Access Coalition.

"I think it's wonderful," says Berbery about the increasing interest that some young philanthropists are taking in small, grass-roots groups like hers. "It does my heart good, because it gives me faith for the future."

Benefactor Becomes a Messenger for Change

Dateline: EUGENE, ORE.

Allen Hancock was a 22-year-old grad student when a substantial amount of money fell in his lap. He quickly realized it could allow him to coast for the rest of his life.

Mr. Hancock could have easily opted for a life of leisure, churning through his late grandfather's bequest. Instead, he says he was consumed with the idea that he had to do something important with his wealth.

"[It] made me ask some big questions," he says. "What do I really want to do with my life?"

Today, Hancock is the publisher of *More than Money,* a quarterly journal published in Eugene, Ore. that emphasizes the exploration of the personal, political, and spiritual impact of wealth.

In the past year he's pledged some $100,000 to the magazine. He also donates to several small environmental and "social-change" projects.

Questions for Discussion and Writing

1. What do you think Talvi most wants her readers to understand?

2. Talvi uses a number of terms like "cool rich kids," "social-change philanthropy," and "radical distribution of wealth." How well are these terms defined and supported?

3. Since the overwhelming majority of the readers of the *Christian Science Monitor* will not be "cool rich kids," what kind of response should she expect from them? Explain.

Making Connections

1. If you were a young philanthropist, what kind of help would you have offered nurse's aid Cheryl Mitchell (Chapter 4, pp. 126–127)? Explain.

2. Whereas the young philanthropists in Talvi's article emphasize interventions that involve substantial gifts of money, what alternative commitments to helping others occur to you?

Short Essay Assignments

1. Using yourself and your class as a typical modern audience, discuss which of the chapter selections (Barber, Loeb, or Talvi) you would give an award "for making the average citizen aware of specific responsibilities individuals and societies owe to themselves and others." Be sure to provide a thorough enough account of the piece so that readers will be able to follow your reasoning, most particularly the standards or criteria you apply to your judgment.

2. Writing letters to the editor is one way to circulate opinions within your community. Community action groups, individual citizens, and elected officials often write about issues to inform and to educate the public.

   Write a letter to your hometown newspaper about a local issue that you think needs attention. If you can, choose a topic suggested by the readings in the book but ground it in a concrete, local circumstance. In other words, slavery per se may not be an issue in your town, but the purchase of slave products, like certain imported chocolate, may be. The town may not be logging the rain forests, but perhaps its fast-food restaurants support imported beef from countries that have leveled forests to make grazing pastures. Whatever your topic, you might not have a ready solution to offer and only want others to agree that the situation demands one. Remember that your reader's willingness to act depends on the strength of their commitment.

3. A leading black scholar on philanthropy Dr. Emmett Carson writes,

   The word *philanthropy* brings to mind the large foundations and wealthy individuals that have not emerged in the black community. When one expands the concept to include giving money, goods, and time, blacks emerge as having a strong, substantial philanthropic tradition. Such a tradition [within any community] has an impact on the welfare of all Americans, not just on the community in which it operates.

   Often labeled "community philanthropy," this type of philanthropy is usually personally or religiously motivated. Its goals are similar to most philanthropic endeavors: to provide services and goods as well as money to promote the wellbeing of others and to better the community in which one lives and works. This service may be informal and spontaneous—a need is observed and people respond or they act to prevent a crisis. At other times, local community members form an organization and network with other already functioning groups to meet an economic, moral, or social challenge to the community. The nature and the cornerstone of this activity build on the idea that individuals can have a greater impact by working in groups.

This essay assignment asks you to identify and analyze either the actual or potential value of a service project or the activity of a campus or community organization. To find a project, you can consult your college's volunteer coordinator or its community service office for a list of community philanthropy projects or organizations. You might also find a project by reading news accounts or talking with students who are already participating in a campus project. Once you have identified a project, you can learn more about it by reading your campus and local newspaper and by collecting the group's newsletters, brochures, and flyers. You can also interview the project's leaders, survey local citizens to get their responses to the group's activities and accomplishments, or make an on-site visit to see what the project is achieving.

The following questions can help you to analyze the group's value to the community. You can use these question as well to help shape your essay.

- How is the group or project likely to benefit individuals or the community?
- How might it help people, even in some way, to live more productive, more fulfilling, and happier lives?
- How might it help the community to run more smoothly, be more peaceful, and witness less injustice?

❏ Major Essay Assignment

This assignment takes its cue from Margaret Mead's statement: "Never doubt that a small group of thoughtful, committed citizens can change the world; it's the only thing that ever does." Drawing on the readings and on your own experience and reflection, propose a significant social intervention that you, or others like you, could undertake. The following process will direct you toward a well-integrated paper that posits thoughtful answers to a central question (or series of questions) about the intervention you propose.

Most of the time, we become interested in an issue—interested at least in understanding it—because something around us doesn't seem quite "right," "normal," "satisfactory," or "sufficient." Whether that "something" is very close (a neighbor who suddenly loses her home, for example) or further away (a child starving a continent away), we become aware that what is or seems to be happening needs to be attended to and, if possible, changed. Beginning this way, with a personal observation or concern, will help you to avoid that sense of just having to pick an issue for the sake of having something to write about—or because it's a hot-button issue. Tackling a meaningful community issue often calls for lots of hard work, with little glamour and financial reward. It is often easier to write about "big things" that are far away, like hunger, than it is to find a way to actually feed your neighbors. The trick, then, is to try to find some way to connect the two: that "think globally act locally" motto.

Some examples might help you to recognize the effect that an assignment of this kind can have. Sheryl, a single parent attending a four-year college, discovered that day care costs were offset by the state only if a parent attended a two-year institution. Sheryl set out to understand why, and then proposed a policy change to institute state-supported childcare at four-year colleges in New York. As part of the work she did for this assignment, she created a brochure to catch the attention of legislators, who eventually funded a similar project.

Another example involves a group of students who discovered that their fellow students had no idea that some popular American companies abused foreign workers. And they found that many students, through their buying habits, were contributing to the success of these companies. Each of the four students took one aspect of the situation (Its nature; How it got that way; Its consequences; What action to take.) and used these tools on the topic. They submitted a collaborative essay. Acting on what they had discovered, they distributed a color brochure, "Ignorance is Bliss: What You Don't Know About the Companies You Love." at the student union to inform students of the problem and to bring the issue to the attention of the college store's management.

As you work through this project, keep two important things in mind:

- Your ultimate goal is a proposal. Some of the sections below may seem to draw you from this goal, but each one will enable and enhance your work on the final stage.
- Don't neglect the readings you encountered earlier in this chapter. You will find them an invaluable source of information as you work through the tasks that follow. For example, when you are asked to make a list, don't hesitate to review the readings for ideas.

I Invention: Finding Promising Lines of Inquiry

Since your assignment is to write an effective proposal, you might begin by reviewing the section in Chapter 1 on Questions and the section in Chapter 6 on Claims about Action. Your review will remind you that, as writing projects go, a call for action is as demanding as it gets. It asks of readers a greater commitment to your ideas than other sorts of writing; and it involves greater emotional, intellectual, and, in some cases, material risk for them. Consequently, your responsibility is to make your case as complete and as reasonable as you can.

Sometimes problems jump out at us when we least expect it. For example, consider Mindy, a second-semester freshman at a large state university. She is involved in her studies and seems to spend more time in the library than in the student union. However, one morning, in search of a Starbucks fix, she wanders into the union and goes toward the snack bar. As she ambles down the hall, she notices a number of tables on either side. Many of them obviously represent student organizations, but there are others whose purpose is not quite clear. Suddenly, a young man jumps out from behind one of the tables, fixes himself in front of her, and begins haranguing her, all the while shoving fliers and a clip-boarded petition in her face. "Sign, sign, sign" seems to be his main message. To the degree she can determine what his cause is, she is uninterested and says so. But he blocks her path and even, grabs her arm, insisting that she sign the petition. She is able to get free, though she is embarrassed, angry, and, actually, a little bit frightened by the encounter. As she moves on, she glances over her shoulder and sees that he has cornered another victim.

Mindy recognizes she has discovered a problem that may go beyond just her brief discomfort. Even if the man's "cause" is a good one, even one she believes in, people should not have to endure annoying, constraining, or threatening behavior. The question is, what should one do about it? Many would simply forget about it, but Mindy is the type that doesn't ignore problems; she wants to fix them. She's also a good writer. It is time for us to move on, but remember Mindy. We'll see her again.

❏ Defining and Refining the Subject

Start by dealing with some key terms. Since your overall subject is *community action*, the term "community" can provide a meaningful entry into the project. At this point, you should probably review the material on Definition in Chapter 6.

What is a community? We often define it *as* a group of people who can be defined *by* the specific things that bind the group.

Traditionally, simple geography has defined communities. For example, people living in a certain neighborhood may be thought of as a community. But is it really that simple? Does the mere fact of inhabiting the same area bind people together, or does their geographical nearness entail other factors that actually create the bond? If so, what other factors? Try making a list of the aspects of people's lives, in addition to the location of their homes, that might bind geographical neighbors into a genuine community.

Consider, also, that a community can extend beyond the geographical bounds of a single neighborhood to a city, a state, a nation, or even the entire world. Make lists of the "binding factors" for each of these locations. Then, compare and contrast what is on the lists. Are there any factors that appear on more than one? On all of your lists? Speculate on why or why not.

Of course, community may have nothing to do with where people live. We often think of communities of individuals in certain professions. You have surely heard the term "academic community" or "business community" or "medical community." List other "communities" that are bound by common professional interests. Then, for each entry on your list, create a second list of binding factors. Again, compare and contrast your lists.

Also, students at the same school, workers at the same factory, or members of the same organization of any kind constitute communities. Again, make lists of similar communities and note the factors that connect individuals to such communities. Again, compare and contrast your lists.

Finally, write down three or four questions that occur as you examine the connections among the items on your various lists. (If you are having trouble with this, try freewriting on any of the specific list items. Or you might set up a discussion with others in your class.) Would the answers to any of your questions provide claims to support a proposal for any kind of action? If so, make a note of the questions. You do not have to try to answer them yet; just keep them in mind as you move on.

For example, Mindy, who has finally secured her coffee and moved on to class, is still troubled by the incident in the student union. Her professor is a little late, so she uses the time to try to make sense out of the experience by making notes about it. As you might guess, Mindy helps to order and improve her life by writing about it in a journal. Clearly, the incident is a problem, but her first question is whom does it affect? Is it a problem for a community of people? If so what community? It does not take long to decide that the community most affected is students at the university. But can she identify a more specific group?

Over the next few days, after casually questioning her friends and classmates, she discovers that many have been confronted by the same young man or by others staffing his table in the union. She concludes that the entire university community is in danger of an unpleasant and threatening encounter with this small group. She next speculates about the reasons for the behavior of this group. You will read her conclusions a little later.

❑ Looking for Causes and Effects

Why do people form communities of varied kinds? In a sense, you have already begun to answer this question in the previous section. Those factors by which we define communities may also be thought of as reasons for their existence—that is, their *causes*.

Now, let us work on the same material from another point of view. Go back to the beginning and reconsider all the different communities you dealt with in the last few paragraphs. In each case, list factors that might *inhibit* the development of communities. These factors are also causal. Sometimes they are more important than those that bring things about. Compare and contrast your lists and try to note possible connections.

At this point, you can begin to think of what brings communities into being. (You should probably review the material on Causation in Chapter 6.) Clearly, some conditions, some *causes* motivate the formation of a community; for example, those "binding factors" you explored in the previous section may be *sufficient* causes.

However, are they so important that the communities they define could not exist without each of them? Can you think of any factors that are *essential causes* of communities?

Finally, what are the general effects of communities on our lives? What are the effects of the specific communities you have dealt with so far? What are the personal and social effects of the bonds and shared values that define these communities and cause them to exist? You might find freewriting or group discussion useful techniques in exploring the effects you have listed.

The material you have generated so far should reveal much about the *nature* and the *causes and effects* of communities. Do not forget, however, that your ultimate goal is to shape this material and your perceptions into a *proposal*—a call for action. We will get a little closer to that goal in the next section, when we begin to consider the *values* related to the phenomena you have been exploring.

First, let us check in on Mindy. You might remember that she is at the point in her inquiry where she is wondering what causes a few obnoxious students to threaten the peace and security of other students. She also begins to wonder if it is really a problem. Are the effects severe enough to merit going any further with it? A little research answers her questions.

She finds out that the group pestering people in the union has been recruited, organized, and actually trained by an off-campus political organization. One question answered—the group is motivated by a political agenda. But are their effects on the community serious enough to worry about? A little informal research convinces her that the group is having a substantial effect on the tenor of life at the university. Many students have been verbally assailed while walking through the union or across the campus. Many find it troubling. The group's members have resorted to haranguing and threats to goad students into signing petitions, and members of the group have also begun to tear down flyers not supportive of their views. They yell, shove flyers into student hands, and loudly berate those who dare to express an opposing view. Students who argue for a different perspective are dismissed and chastised. Mindy discovers that the group has not escaped the notice of university officials, and, in response, they have actually toned down their belligerent approach. Still, they continue to harass students. Mindy suspects that the abrasive exchanges might have a chilling effect on free and open discussion on the campus. Even students who were open to discussing diverse viewpoints have begun to limit what they are willing to discuss.

Mindy's next step, in conducting a thorough inquiry, is to assign some value to these effects. Personally, she loathes the whole group; but, to be objective, she also has to consider whether some of the effects are positive.

❑ Assigning Value

Here's a question for you: What is the value of values? Though this question is so circular as to provoke an almost instant headache, it is still meaningful. Earlier you considered general definitions of communities and gave some thought to what causes them and what effects they, in turn, produce in our lives. Now, we want to assign value to those effects. Your previous work should make that much easier.

You can start by reviewing the sections on Questions and Claims of Value in Chapters 1 and 6. Then go back to the list of effects you generated for the last part of this assignment. As a preliminary exercise, label each item on the list as having a positive or negative effect and explain your reasoning.

Did you find it difficult to identify the "bad" effects of communities? If so, you might put additional items on your list. Can a value we might consider good have a negative effect? For example, consider "human freedom" as a community value. This is certainly a principal value of our society, but is unlimited freedom conducive to good effects? What about the person who feels free to express herself in any way she sees fit? Are there situations in which society's concern for the wellbeing of individuals or groups outweighs an individual's right to unbounded expression? As is so often the case with complicated human behavior, we are forced to choose between two competing "goods"— two strong values: the "freedom" of speech versus the "freedom" to be left alone.

Also, consider the effects of *not* holding or acting on specific values. For example, what might be the effects of *not* valuing human freedom or diversity? It is easy to see that such attitudes or actions may have dire effects. All we need to do is glance at a newspaper to discover cases of repression or discrimination, to discover flagrant examples of the denial of human freedom or the right to be "different". However, can you imagine situations in which the effects might be advantageous or at least be worth the cost?

Try to explore the values questions mentioned above, as well as any you discover through listing, freewriting, group discussions, or any other invention techniques you find useful. Whatever technique you choose to employ, try to generate as much exploratory text as possible. You will find it useful as you move further into your proposal

In Mindy's exploration of the values related to her situation, she examines the materials put out by the aggressive group mentioned earlier. While she disagrees with most of the positions they advocate, she concludes that an honest and open discussion of them is completely in keeping with the values of her university community—especially the values of diversity and civic responsibility. However, she also concludes that the tactics of the group are inexcusable and, in fact, violate many of the same values. Their aggressiveness, belligerence, and refusal to let other points of view be heard negates the values a college community holds as sacred: freedom (including free speech), justice, civility, and diversity. She concludes that their tactics so violate the values of the community that there would be no benefit in attempting a serious discussion of their positions. She believes that their actions have made such a discussion impossible. Now, she wonders if she should try to do anything about it and, if so, what?

❑ Considering Action

Proposals or calls to action normally advocate some sort of change. Change is frequently difficult and sometimes threatening, and people rarely undertake it unless they see a need. We most often call for change when an existing situation continually produces undesirable effects; consequently, the relationship between questions regarding what action we should take and questions of values is clear.

At this point, you might review the sections on Questions and Claims of Action in Chapters 1 and 6. Of course, the most general question you can ask when considering change is, "What's wrong with the way things are now?" If today's news is any indication, the answer is, "Plenty." Your real challenge is not finding a problem to tackle; it is disentangling one problem from all the others that surround it and coming up with an idea that meets the general guidelines for proposals that we discussed in Chapter 6:

- Your focus must be on a genuine problem, one that is relevant to your audience
- Your proposed action must be workable, that is, something that *can* be accomplished.
- Your proposed action is likely to produce a beneficial state of affairs or avoid a negative one.
- The actions you are proposing must, in themselves, be ethical.

Earlier, you generated several lists of communities, ranging in scope from your neighborhood to the nations of the world, as well as accompanying text. Return to that text and find two or three sections that seem to offer the most interesting or promising lines of inquiry (in some cases, you should have already marked them). A second context you have considered at some length is values, more specifically, community values. Again, return to the text you generated around those discussions and find a few comments that seem to hint at promising lines of inquiry. Then generate a number of questions that evolve from the relationship between communities and values. Here are a few to get you started:

- What problems exist in the communities you have chosen?
- What specific people in what specific ways are involved/impacted?
- What causes and effects seem to be operating?
- What values do those communities hold to be most important?
- How have they prioritized those values?
- Are some problems related in any way to the values that define the communities? If so, how are they related?
- How do they reveal the values they hold?
- Are there value conflicts within the communities that are causing friction? If so, what are they, and how are the effects of those conflicts negative?

You will, of course, find many other questions worth asking about the specific communities and specific values you have chosen. As you develop your questions, be sure to consult the text you generated in all the earlier sections—Nature, Causation, and Values.

As Mindy considers what she should or could do about the problem on her campus, it occurs to her that she can act as an individual; however, it seems clear that would limit her to writing letters to university officials and the student newspaper. She also recognizes that those actions would not fix the problem. So she decides to involve others in the solution. She contacts the leaders of the campus organizations that might have a stake in the issue, including the Coalition for Student Activism, the College Democrats, the College Republicans, Amnesty International, the Black Student Union, Students for Life, and the Environmental Coalition, She states the problem and suggests a meeting of the officers of the organizations to discuss the problem. A number express an interest in working together.

After they discuss the problem, they adopt Mindy's point of view on the nature of the aggressive group's tactics, the negative effects those tactics are creating for the campus community, and the degree to which they violate the values of the community. They reach a consensus that the university needs a "code of civility" to establish parameters for campus activities. The code would be added to university policies regarding student behavior and become part of the university orientation program for incoming students. They decide the best way to accomplish the goal is to present a written proposal to the university community. Mindy is asked to draft the proposal.

II Drafting: Making Claims and Charting a Direction

By this time, you should have a good idea of what constitutes a "line of inquiry." If you look back over the text you generated in the Invention section, you probably will discover that it suggests some specific actions to address the problem you have been exploring.

Now, your job is to decide which of the many possible lines you will follow as you begin to shape the draft of your paper. Obviously, some "pruning" is in order, and quite a lot of it at that. Where to start? First, you will want to read through the material you have generated. Sometimes a question or an idea will jump off the page. It becomes the intellectual "center" of your paper and stirs up the interest and energy that make the work worthwhile. You can delete anything that is not related to it.

If you do not find an interesting issue, you can start by eliminating unworkable ones. This is where the tasks you undertook in the invention stage—as cumbersome and time consuming as they could have seemed—will pay off. Go back to one of the levels (defining, cause and effect, values, or action) and eradicate anything you find completely unattractive. We suggest that you start at the definition level. That will let you eliminate unpromising lines more quickly.

As you review your reduced list of types of communities and the actual harms, inadequacies, or deprivations that seem to need attention, do you see:

- any ideas or issues that seem especially promising? If so, pull them out and write them down in a separate document.
- any ideas or issues that grow unappealing as you look at them more closely? If so, strike those lines of inquiry.

The final stage in this review process is to look at the material to see if there are any places—direct or indirect—where the word "should" is lurking. All claims for "corrective" action are really "should" claims—they imply that some behavior in the future is needed in response to a currently "inadequate" situation. Very often these claims will take the form of "comparative value" statements—that one thing *should* be valued over another; that a list of values *should* be prioritized in a certain way; that a certain value not currently held *should* be adopted. Again, try to find a definite "winner" and eliminate all others. Since your final goal is a proposal, you will find it more productive to look for a claim of value indicating that something should or should not be done. Ultimately, this call for action will become your thesis statement—the central point of your essay.

So far you have:

- Defined and refined your general subject; in other words, you have taken a close look at and answered questions about aspects of its *nature*.
- Examined *causes* and *effects* associated with your general subjects. Again, you have answered questions about what causes your subject, or at least certain aspects of it, and about the effects those factors might produce.
- Explored the *values* associated with those causes and/or effects and made related claims of values.

Throughout the process, you have continuously narrowed the focus of your inquiry. You now confront the final stage of narrowing that leads you to finding the single claim of action your proposal will support. This would be a good time to review the general guidelines for proposals first discussed in Chapter 6:

- We must focus on a genuine problem, one relevant to our audience.
- Our proposed action must be workable; that is, it is something we *can* do.
- Our proposed action has a chance of ultimately producing a beneficial state of affairs or avoiding a negative one.
- The actions we are proposing must, in themselves, be ethical.

In her proposal, Mindy is careful to consider all the aspects of a good proposal. She defines the problem clearly and establishes its significance by showing the effects on the community of the behavior of those who confront students who are walking through the union. She also goes beyond discussion of that group to make the point that, without guidance, any contentious group could, in the future, resort to the same abusive tactics. She provides documentary evidence of the values shared by the university community. Some of her sources for this are university publications and the comments of current and former students. She then demonstrates how the group's aggressive behavior violates the community's values by presenting the experiences of students with members of that group. Finally, she argues for the adoption of a "code of civility," and demonstrates that it stands a good chance of easing the current problem and preventing similar ones in the future. She proves that it is easily accomplished, since it has the support of many student leaders, and that the code, in itself, presents no ethical problems, since it would be universally applied and is in keeping with the values she discussed earlier in the proposal. The group of student leaders approves the proposal, with minor revisions, distributes it to students and faculty, and, ultimately, submits it to the administration. The code is approved and will become university policy in the next academic year.

And what about Mindy? What does she get out of it? She doesn't get an award. She doesn't get thank you letters from the student organizations she involved in the project. She isn't credited with drafting the proposal mentioned in the student newspaper story about the event. All she gets is the satisfaction of knowing that her efforts have resulted in helping end a bad situation and making the future a bit better. That, and an unimpeded path through the union to the Starbucks booth, is a sufficient reward.

Note: As you finish your work on the essay assignment for this chapter, keep in mind that it is a draft. You will be working with it as you move through Chapters 14 and 15. In Chapter 14, you will work on polishing its language. Your goal will be to create a second draft in which the language is clear, precise, fluent, and even artful. In Chapter 15, you will work on making sure your essay conforms to the conventions of academic prose. These will include some of the stylistic conventions of academic writing, as well as appropriately attributing any "borrowed" material to its original source—adhering, that is, to the conventions of documentation.

14   *Fine-tuning the Language: A Brief Style Manual*

Writing to Engage the Reader

One of your obligations as a writer is to use words carefully and precisely. In academic and professional contexts, readers will consider what you submit, either because it is their responsibility or because they have engaged you to produce the document. However, they will be more willing to endorse your work if they enjoy what you have written. In this chapter, we will explore some of the basic principles that can help you to create prose that grabs their imagination, stimulates their aesthetic sense, or, at the very least, is easy to read.

Language That Makes the Structure Explicit

Many people find narration and description easier to write and read than exposition. This is largely because the movements in those forms parallels the way we experience reality. Narration normally moves in *time*, from one event to the next. Description moves *spatially*, from one part or aspect of what is being described to another.

Exposition is more difficult because the motion is from one *idea* to the next. At any point, the possibilities of what might come next are numerous. Argument is the most difficult form of exposition because we do not just connect ideas; we *infer* claims from other claims. Explaining the process behind our inferences involves making the relationships among our claims clear. Language provides a number of tools to help us with this; among the most fundamental are *coordination* and *subordination* in our sentences. But before considering them, let's review some of the grammatical concepts you encountered in your early schooling.

❑ *Clauses*

We normally put clauses into two categories: *independent* or *dependent*. An *independent* clause can stand by itself as a sentence. For example:

> *She found the entire fence whitewashed, and not only whitewashed but elaborately coated and recoated, and even a streak added to the ground.*

A *dependent clause* does not offer a "complete thought". Most often, a clause is dependent because it has a word or phrase that makes it incomplete. Note what happens if we add a word to the clause mentioned above:

When she found the entire fence whitewashed, and not only whitewashed but elaborately coated and recoated, and even a streak added to the ground

The "when" requires a connection to something, that explains what happened "when" she found the fence. The complete sentence reads like this:

When she found the entire fence whitewashed, and not only whitewashed but elaborately coated and recoated, and even a streak added to the ground, *her astonishment was almost unspeakable. **

❏ *Phrases*

A phrase lacks a subject or verb and, thus, does not constitute a clause. The most common are:

- *prepositional:* These begin with a preposition and end with a noun or pronoun.

   "Tom felt happy *in his success,* for he knew it was the boat's last trip for the night. "

- *infinitive:* These are made up of the infinitive form of a verb. For example:

   "He well knew the futility of trying *to contend* against witches, so he gave up discouraged."

- *participle:* These include a participial form of the verb. For example:

   "The schoolmaster, always severe, grew severer and *more exacting* than ever." *

There are other types that we will look at later.

❏ *Conjunctions*

Conjunctions are short words that link words, phrases, and clauses. However, and this is most important, conjunctions often indicate *logical relationships* between what they connect. Few errors will distract a reader as much as one indicating an inappropriate relationship. Consider the following:

Leonardo was left-handed, but he could bend horseshoes.

Of course, being left-handed has nothing to do with bending horseshoes.
   We will discuss conjunctions in more detail as we explore *coordination* and *subordination.*

❏ *Coordination*

When we want to indicate that two ideas have equal "weight", we can present them as *independent clauses* and connect them with a *coordinating conjunction.* For example:

*Tom did play hooky, **and** he had a very good time.* *

---

*These examples are from Mark Twain, *The Adventures of Tom Sawyer.*

The conjunction also shows a logical relationship, specifically that both claims are true.

Some other common coordinating conjunctions are *or, but, so*, and *for*. Consider the following examples:

> *Here, right by my side, was the actual ogre who, in fights and brawls and various ways, had taken the lives of twenty-six human beings,* **or** *all men lied about him!**

While the *or* possesses the same cognitive weight as *and*, it communicates a different logical relationship—in this case, one of *exclusion*. The entire sentence asserts that the truth of one claim excludes the truth of the other.

In the next example, *or* provides a slightly different shade of meaning.

> *[S]he had to have things handy to throw at them when she was alone,* **or** *they wouldn't give her no peace.**

Here the conjunction indicates a dependent relationship. The sentence claims that, for the second independent clause to be true, the first must be.

While the conjunction *but* indicates equality of weight and that both clauses are true, it can have other shades of meaning. For example, it can mean "on the contrary" as in:

> *Sagebrush is very fair fuel,* **but** *as a vegetable it is a distinguished failure.**

It can also mean "contrary to what one might expect" as in:

> *In place of a window there was a square hole about large enough for a man to crawl through,* **but** *this had no glass in it.**

The conjunction *so* is another small word with many possible meanings, among which are:

"with the result that" as in:

> *They took a swim about every hour,* **so** *it was close upon the middle of the afternoon when they got back to camp.**

"in order that" as in:

> *I found Jim had been trying to get him to talk French,* **so** *he could hear what it was like. . .**

---

*Mark Twain, *Roughing It*.
**Mark Twain, The Adventures of Huckleberry Finn* (Note the non-standard double negative ". . . wouldn't give her no peace." Twain writes in the 19th century vernacular from the point of view of a young boy. While such usage may create realistic and engaging characters, it is frowned on in more formal writing contexts.)
*Mark Twain, *Roughing It*
*Mark Twain, *Roughing It*
*Mark Twain, *The Adventures of Tom Sawyer*
*Mark Twain, *The Adventures of Huckleberry Finn*

"for that reason" as in:

*He was boat and captain and engine-bells combined, **so** he had to imagine himself standing on his own hurricane-deck giving the orders and executing them. . .*.*

The conjunction *for* is normally used to mean "because" as in this example:

*Tom's younger brother (or rather half-brother) Sid was already through with his part of the work (picking up chips), **for** he was a quiet boy, and had no adventurous, troublesome ways.**

Finally, the semicolon is an all-purpose way to indicate coordination. For example, when we replace the comma and conjunction in one of the previous examples with a semicolon—

Sagebrush is very fair fuel; as a vegetable it is a distinguished failure.

—we still indicate the equal weight of the clauses; however, we risk losing a shade of meaning, the expected opposition of the two ideas. While you can normally replace a coordinating conjunction with a semicolon and still have a grammatically correct sentence, you need to determine if a semicolon better serves your purpose.

Another way to indicate *coordination* is with a semicolon followed by a *conjunctive adverb*. There are many conjunctive adverbs that create coordination. Some of the more common are:

• consequently • furthermore • however • likewise • nevertheless • otherwise • then • therefore

Consider the following examples:

*Twain tends to write dialogue in the vernacular of the story's time and place; **however**, the language of Poe's characters is often more formal.*

or

*Twain became an extremely popular writer and speaker in his lifetime; **nevertheless**, his later years were plagued by personal tragedy and financial difficulty.*

There are several points worth remembering about this kind of construction. As you can see from our partial list, conjunctive adverbs tend to be multisyllabic and somewhat "fancy" words. You will most often find them in academic writing. Professional writers often prefer simpler conjunctions. Nevertheless, while they communicate many of the same logical relationships as coordinating conjunctions, conjunctive adverbs offer different shades of meaning. For example, *moreover* communicates a slightly different meaning and tone than the simpler *and*. If the difference is significant in a specific rhetorical context, you will choose the more complex word.

---

*Mark Twain, *The Adventures of Tom Sawyer.*
*Mark Twain, *The Adventures of Tom Sawyer.*

Another point to remember is that the adverb does not always have to begin the second independent clause to create the coordination. For example, we can recast one of our earlier sentences like this:

> *Twain tends to write dialogue in the vernacular of the story's time and place; the language of Poe's characters, **however**, is often more formal.*

Another option is to break the construction into two separate sentences:

> *Twain became an extremely popular writer and speaker in his lifetime. **Nevertheless**, his later years were plagued by personal tragedy and financial difficulty.*

As long as the sentence is grammatical, any *single* decision you make in this regard will likely have a minor effect on your readers. However, *all* the various decisions of this kind that you make will help to establish the voice they will encounter.

You should also follow the conventions of punctuation. If you use a coordinating conjunction to connect two independent clauses, put a comma after the first clause. If you use a conjunctive adverb at the beginning of the second clause, you will normally put a semicolon after the first one and a comma after the adverb. If the adverb appears in the middle of the second clause, set it off with commas.

A general note on punctuation: The conventions of punctuation may seem trivial, but they will guide readers through your text.

Exercise

Combine the following sentences into single grammatically correct and clearly punctuated sentences:

1. The U.S. ambassador to China began his tour of Shanghai with a televised interview.
   a. The next day he took part in a radio phone-in program.
   b. By the end of the week, he flew back to Beijing to assume his official duties.

2. The city of London maintains a very successful recycling program because of street sweeping machines.
   a. The machines sort larger items and recycle bottles and cans.
   b. Even dirt and grit gets recycled as road aggregate which means that over 50% of all street refuse is recycled.

3. An entrepreneur typically has a distinct set of values.
   a. He or she is passionate about the work.
   b. The entrepreneur is always looking for new opportunities.
   c. He or she thinks, "Hey, I can do that better!"

4. Beginning writers often find themselves looking for ideas.
    a. Observing and describing are necessary skills to learn.
    b. Having the time to think and write is crucial.

❑ *Subordination*

Earlier we mentioned sentences that combine independent and dependent clauses in a relationship of subordination. Such sentences tell us that the idea in the independent clause is the more important one. Here is an example:

> *Although he was more than twice as old as the eldest of us, he never gave himself any airs, privileges, or exemptions on that account.* *

While the first clause, regarding the man's age, is certainly relevant to its meaning, the structure of the sentence reveals that the man's behavior is the more significant point.

We create subordination with *subordinating conjunctions*. These function like coordinating conjunctions for they join clauses. However, they also identify one clause as being dependent on the other. While subordinating conjunctions create a number of logical relationships, the most common ones are *contrast* and *cause and effect*.

Some words frequently used as subordinating conjunctions to express contrast are:

- although • though or even though • whereas • while

Notice the contrast indicated in the following examples. Notice also that the subordinate clause can be either the first or second clause in the sentence.

> **Although** *well armed, she is not, I think, a ship of war.* *

> **Though** *mesmeric power may not save you, it may help you; try it at all events.* * (Note the combination of subordination and coordination here.)

> *They made him understand that his poor rags would do to begin with,* **though** *it was customary for wealthy pirates to start with a proper wardrobe.* *

> *Again, I always go to sea as a sailor, because they make a point of paying me for my trouble,* **whereas** *they never pay passengers a single penny that I ever heard of.* *

---

*Mark Twain, *Roughing It*
*Edgar Allen Poe, "Ms. Found in a Bottle"
*Mark Twain, *Roughing It*
*Mark Twain, *The Adventures of Tom Sawyer*
*Herman Melville, *Moby Dick*

While their masters, the mates, seemed afraid of the sound of the hinges of their own jaws, the harpooneers chewed their food with such a relish that there was a report to it.*

While Hester stood in that magic circle of ignominy, where the cunning cruelty of her sentence seemed to have fixed her for ever, the admirable preacher was looking down from the sacred pulpit upon an audience whose very inmost spirits had yielded to his control.*

(Note that *while* can indicate a relationship in time as well as a contrast. While we can hardly guess Hawthorne's intent, this passage may be designed to achieve both. If so, it is an artful ambiguity.)

Words most often used as subordinating conjunctions to express *cause and effect* include:

• because • since

Consider the following examples:

Tom bent all his energies to the memorizing of five verses, and he chose part of the Sermon on the Mount, because he could find no verses that were shorter.*

Since Fortune has thought fit to bestow it upon me, I have only to use it properly and I shall arrive at the gold of which it is the index.*

I'll try a pagan friend, thought I, since Christian kindness has proved but hollow courtesy.*

Exercise

Combine the following into grammatically correct sentences that maintain the meaning of each pair:

1. (a) Though we have plenty of food to feed the world, the poor cannot afford to buy it.
   (b) Malnourishment leads to illness and the inability to work which makes those in poverty poorer and less able to feed themselves.

2. (a) He maximized his musical talent by writing charts, doing back up vocals and teaching music skills to kids.
   (b) His efforts led him to a successful musical career at age 20.

---

*Herman Melville, *Moby Dick*
*Nathaniel Hawthorne, *The Scarlet Letter*
*Mark Twain, *The Adventures of Tom Sawyer*
*Edgar Allan Poe, *"The Gold Bug"*
*Herman Melville, *Moby Dick*

3. (a) Each television program has one or two seconds to catch John's attention before he clicks to another.
   (b) No one much likes watching television with John.

4. (a) The chemical defoliant Dioxin was banned in the United States.
   (b) Dioxin is highly toxic to plants and humans.

5. (a) On November 11th we celebrate Armistice Day which marks the end of World War I.
   (b) Some countries commemorate the 11 am cessation of hostilities with a moment of silence on "the eleventh hour of the eleventh day of the eleventh month."

❏ *Transitions*

Any construction that helps to orient your readers or that moves them efficiently through your text can be thought of as a transition. Any construction that clarifies the logical relationships among the parts of your text can also be thought of as a transition. Coordinating and subordinating conjunctions obviously serve this goal. However, many other types of constructions—single words, phrases, even complete sentences—can also work this way.

The more important transitional devices are constructions that signal readers when you're moving, either at the paragraph level or within individual paragraphs, from one major point to another.

Sometimes this device can be as obvious as a simple numerical ordering:

"First, ...
"Second, ...
"Third, ..."

Of course, you can use any other words or phrases that make the order explicit to the reader:

"In the first place, ...
"Moreover, ...
"In addition, ...
"Finally, ..."

Here is a complicated example from Bill Moyers's "Keynote Address to the National Conference on Media Reform." You will find it useful to explore the context of these passages in the essay in Chapter 10. This excerpt begins in the sixth paragraph.

*Yet **today**, despite plenty of lip service on every ritual occasion to freedom of the press radio and TV, **three powerful forces** are undermining that very freedom, damming the streams of significant public interest news that irrigate and nourish the flowering of self-determination.*

Moyers sets the reader up to expect three points.

> ***The first of these is*** *the centuries-old reluctance of governments—even elected governments— to operate in the sunshine of disclosure and criticism.* ***The second is*** *more subtle and more recent. It's the tendency of media giants, operating on big-business principles, to exalt commercial values at the expense of democratic value.*

He states the first two in quick succession and follows with two paragraphs developing those points. It is a fairly complicated structure, but he orients the reader throughout the passage.

> *It's hardly a new or surprising story. But **there are fresh and disturbing chapters.***

> ***In earlier times*** *our governing bodies tried to squelch journalistic freedom with the blunt instruments of the law. . . . But they've found **new ones now**, in the name of "national security."*

> ***Add to that*** *the censorship-by-omission of consolidated media empires digesting the bones of swallowed independents, and you've got a major shrinkage of the crucial information that thinking citizens can act upon.*

Then he begins the third point. Since readers have been through several paragraphs, he uses a transition to orient them and make sure they are still following his line of reasoning.

> *. . . **Which brings me to the third powerful force**—beyond governmental secrecy and megamedia conglomerates—that is shaping what Americans see, read, and hear. I am talking now about that quasi-official partisan press ideologically linked to an authoritarian administration that in turn is the ally and agent of the most powerful interests in the world. **This convergence** dominates the marketplace of political ideas today in a phenomenon unique in our history.*

Notice how he ties the three points together in the last line.

Try to keep in mind the general logic behind providing transitions. If, in reading through your drafts, you detect spots where readers might lose your line of thought or experience a gap in the flow of your prose, provide a transition.

Exercise

1. Identify the transitions in the following excerpt:

   Fourth, because globalization points to a global economy, we have to ask whose economic vision will be adopted. As noted earlier, the powerful nations are likely to impose their own vision. At the present time, the most powerful view is that of the huge international corporations. Even if it could be argued that their vision is benign and requires only tinkering to be just, many of the world's people harbor doubts, and while the disparity between rich and poor grows, it is predictable that groups (even nations) will protest violently. Moreover, nations of the First World often associate corporate capitalism with their own overall way of life, and this association adds a strong ideological component to the problem. Citizens of wealthy nations may feel it a patriotic duty to defend economic practices that seem inseparable from their way of life. These citizens then try to persuade or even force others to accept that way of life "for their own good." (Noddings p. 252)

2.   Provide transitions in the following passage:

Sex is rarely discussed in Chinese society. Homosexuality is discussed even less. Recent media coverage of the AIDS epidemic focuses on prostitution and drug use. Little time is devoted to the particular threat posed to gay men. No one is certain how many AIDS cases can be attributed to homosexual activity. A Western researcher reported that of the two hospitals in Beijing that treat venereal diseases, one-third of their AIDS patients are gay men. Officials seem to be aware that gays are a high-risk group. Most remain silent on the subject. The China Society for the Prevention of AIDS and Sexually Transmitted Diseases remains relatively close-mouthed. Tolerance for alternated lifestyles is low in China. Homosexuality was just recently removed from the country's official list of psychiatric disorders (Gill). Progress toward greater acceptance is slowly being made. Law enforcement has lessened the frequent raids on gay bars and clubs in larger cities. The stigma is still present.

(Melissa, a student)

Language That Reveals Your Attitude

In Chapter 7, when we discussed the Rhetorical Triangle, we explored the concept of *ethos*. Ethos comprises, among other things, your attitude toward the subject, toward your audience, and toward those who might offer contrary positions. Moreover, a good writer is expected to demonstrate knowledge of the subject, intelligence, and an ability to think critically. A critical thinker exhibits a number of important qualities too, including good will, fair-mindedness, and respect for other reasonable points of view and those who hold them.

Since your arguments must reflect these qualities, it is imperative that you consider the phrasing that conveys your thoughts and feelings. Even if you find some points of view distasteful, you should express your objections objectively, rationally, and without emotionally "loaded" language. If you resort to tactics that violate these principles, you risk communicating a lack of seriousness or honesty that may damage your credibility and lose your reader's respect.

This is not to suggest that humor and irony are inappropriate, but you must be careful. Some readers will appreciate wry, or even dark, humor; but others will find it abrasive. Also, the line between irony and sarcasm is exceedingly fine. In every case, it is wise to take into account the nature of the writing task you have undertaken and the sensibilities of your audience.

❏ *Objective and Subjective Voice*

Because it determines many other decisions, some critics say that "voice" or "point-of-view" is the most important initial decision a writer makes.

In a piece written in a *subjective voice*, the persona of the writer is present throughout. Use of first-person pronouns is common, and the writer makes his or her attitudes, emotions, and, sometimes, personal history explicit to the reader.

Barbara Kingsolver's "Stone Soup" in Chapter 1 wonderfully illustrates this technique. Note how Kingsolver effectively weaves her own life and experiences into this passage:

> *For many of us, once we have put ourselves Humpty-Dumpty-wise back together again, the main problem with our reorganized family is that other people think we have a problem. My daughter tells me the only time she's uncomfortable about being the child of divorced parents is when her friends say they feel sorry for her.*

In strict *objective voice* the persona of the writer is nowhere present. Third-person pronouns are used almost exclusively throughout (except in the case of direct quotes), and the author is completely distant.

The following excerpt from the student essay in Chapter 10, "Poverty Slighted by the Media," provides a good example of *objective voice*.

> *Though some, like Dinesh D'Souza, author of The Virtue of Prosperity: Finding Value in an Age of Techno-Affluence, argue that an income gap is the natural result of a prosperous market economy, the real question is whether or not an income gap as large as that of the United States is necessary. To a certain degree, poverty may be inevitable, but the numbers are daunting. According to Gregory Mantsios, author of "Class in America: Myths and Realities," approximately thirteen percent of Americans live below the government's poverty line, defined as $8,500 for an individual and $17,028 for a family of four. Of these poor, nearly two million are homeless. While one third of the population lives in poverty, another third lives in extreme wealth. If this is the reality of our society, how is it reflected in television and news?*

You may notice that the last line of the passage includes a first-person pronoun. This is a common practice. Known as the "editorial 'we'" it does not disrupt the objective voice. The one restriction on its use is that the first person pronoun must be plural—*we, us, our*, etc. In a way, you, as a writer, are also speaking for the people—at least some of them. Since other options in phrasing can be awkward, the usage is a way to smooth the prose. Since this construction is easily overused, you should employ it only when necessary.

The objective voice is used most frequently in hard news stories (not editorials or features) and in academic writing, especially in the scientific disciplines. In these situations, writers often want to assume a neutral stance to enhance their credibility. In some contexts, the objective voice has become normative; thus, writing a science lab report filled with first-person pronouns is probably a ticket to a low grade.

Many of the readings in this book switch from the subjective to the objective and vice versa. This is another common practice in less formal contexts. The switching might seem to be distracting; but readers actually seem not to notice it much, and it can be quite effective. To understand how, we will need to examine the psychological effects of the objective and subjective voices on the reader. Both have effects that can serve the writer's purpose.

One effect of the subjective voice is that it brings the writer and reader closer together. A negative effect is that it is sometimes difficult to extend the writer's experience and his or her feelings about it to larger issues. In other words, it is difficult to generalize about the experiences and feelings of a single individual. "Me" talking only about "myself" and "my" experience could make readers wonder what that has to do with the rest of the world, with them.

One effect of the objective voice is that it seems to generate credibility, and it might even lead readers to unconsciously adopt the assumptions of the writer. Whether this effect is positive or negative depends on how honestly it is used and how critically audiences read. Trying to shore up a weak argument or questionable facts merely by stating them in an objective voice is bad writing; and assuming comments are factual merely because they are stated in objective voice is bad reading.

Exercise

Go back through Barbara Kingsolver's "Stone Soup" in Chapter 1 and the excerpts from Thomas L. Friedman's "The Globalization of the Economy" in Chapters 6 and 8. In each case, note where the author switches voice. Note the nature of the switch—from subjective to objective or vice versa. In your journal, write a line or two about each switch, speculating on why the author made the decision. What effect might the switch have on the audience? (Remember, use of the "editorial 'we'" doesn't constitute a change in voice.)

❑ *Connotation*

In Chapter 6 we established that the connotations of words involve an emotional component that can be negative, neutral, or positive. (You might find it useful to review that material now.) Unless highly charged language is warranted by the facts you have stated in support of your claims, it is, in most cases, better to avoid extremely negative or positive connotations when more neutral terms are available to you. Good readers are very quick to recognize any sort of emotional inflation and may come to doubt your good will and objectivity—and perhaps rightly so.

Exercise

Collect the editorial pages from several issues of any newspaper and make note of any instances of highly positive or negative connotations. Then, in your journal, speculate on the columnist's reasons for choosing the term or phrase and explain the effect it had on you.

❑ *Jargon*

The specialized vocabulary of different jobs, technologies, sports, or activities is often considered *jargon* by those not involved in the job or activity. If your audience knows what they mean, they are a fast and efficient way of communicating concepts. If your readers would be unfamiliar with the terms, you should scrupulously avoid them. However, when a technical term is exactly the way to communicate meaning, use but explain it. Also, some words that start out as jargon make their way into general use. For example, how many Americans these days would not recognize "mouse" as a computer accessory?

The lesson here is one you have heard before—know your audience.

Language That Sets the Rhythm and Pace

We often hear about *content* and *form* or *substance* and *style* as if they were completely separate. In reality, each choice we make about any aspect of our prose affects, to some degree, every other aspect. In this sense, then, form is an aspect of content, style a way of making substance felt. The words we use to define issues or to describe behaviors; the transitions we use to move from idea to idea; the way we make use of denotation or connotation—all contribute to the clarity, coherence, and artfulness of our prose and to the effectiveness of our arguments.

A related aspect of good writing involves attention to rhythm and pace. These qualities are equivalent to what we call "delivery" in speech: the tone or pitch, the loudness or softness, the fastness or slowness that a speaker uses to make meaning clear. In a sense, readers are hearing the essay as they read it. Different rhythms and paces produce different effects, just as they do in music.

❑ *Sentence Rhythms*

We often classify sentences as cumulative or periodic. To make the best use of this distinction, you need to understand the *independent clause* discussed earlier in this chapter. (At this point you may find it useful to review that material.)

Independent clauses can stand by themselves as simple sentences; or they can be combined with other elements—modifying words, phrases, and clauses—to create more complicated ones. We often need such sentences to express complex ideas and relationships. Also, your writing will be more interesting and pleasing if your repertoire (your writing tool kit) consists of more than simple sentences.

The difference between *cumulative* (sometimes called loose) and *periodic* sentences is in the placement of the independent clause. With very few exceptions, the independent clause will express the main or dominant point of the sentence. If you place the independent clause at or very near the *beginning* of the sentence and follow it with other sentence elements, you will create a *cumulative* sentence. If you place the independent clause at or very near the *end* of the sentence, you will have a *periodic* sentence.

Here are two examples of cumulative sentences.

> *Kennickell now faces the dilemma of the man in the middle, but it's a position he seems to have been in before; he tweaks his mustache like Poirot preparing to reveal the identity of the malefactor. (D'Souza p. 111)*

> *The author was Jonathan Schell, a recent Harvard graduate who, after commencement, visited his brother, Orville, in Taiwan, where Orville was doing Chinese studies. (Bagdikian p. 313)*

Here are two periodic sentences.

> *With a beaming smile, Kennickell returns to his seat, and the debate is over. (D'Souza p. 111)*

> *The standard cure for "bad demographics" in newspapers, magazines, radio and television is simple: change the content. (Bagdikian p. 314)*

While the distinction is subtle, it involves an important decision writers make as they construct or, more often, revise their work. It is often necessary to connect "new" to "old" information. It is especially important in arguments, where the relationship may be one of *inference*, that is, when we infer the likely truth of "new" from "old" information. In such cases, you have to decide *where* you will place those elements in your sentence. A general rule is to present the old first, as this would connect what is new to points previously established in your essay. You must also determine the sort of sentence that will work best in context.*

Of course, there are other reasons to write periodic or cumulative sentences. One has to do with how people seem to read. As good readers move through a text, they are constantly evaluating what has gone before and making predictions about what might follow. This process is fast, continuous, and largely unconscious. However, an understanding of this process helps you make decisions about sentences.

The cumulative sentence establishes the independent clause as an anchor to which the reader can attach the information in the other sentence elements that follow. If the writing is fluid and the logical relationships between the sentence elements are clear, the reader will have a sense of security.

The periodic sentence leaves the reader hanging for a bit before getting to the main point in the independent clause. This creates expectation or tension early in the sentence. If the independent

---

*The ideas regarding placement of old and new information are from *Style: Ten Lessons in Clarity and Grace* by Joseph M. Williams.

clause at the end adequately resolves the tension and satisfies the expectation, the reader could feel gratified. Such a sentence is largely like a miniature murder mystery; the clues are offered throughout, and the suspense is resolved at the end.

You should remember that all this is happening subconsciously and very quickly. Few readers can tell you exactly why they enjoyed the writing in a book or article. Sometimes, it is partly due to the rhythm and pace created by the ebb and flow of security and suspense within the sentence structure.

This discussion about the placing of the independent clause may make it sound as if you have only two choices. If fact, it is just the beginning. As a writer, you have enormous latitude in where you place sentence elements.

For example, you can embed additional information within the independent clause.

> *Sitting in the middle, in a sense playing the role of umpire, is Arthur Kennickell, a senior economist at the Federal Reserve Board (p. 110).*

For even greater complexity, you can combine periodic and cumulative sentences in any number of ways.

> *But do you feel a wee bit of guilt that there's a fellow in Dubuque, Iowa, and another in Karachi, Pakistan, and they're every bit as good as you are but they'll never live the way you do? (p. 110).*

Or you can expand the subject, verb, or object of the sentence by adding modifying words or phrases. Periodic sentences typically expand the subject or verb, while cumulative sentences typically expand the verb or object.

> *These sentiments also raise the issue of justice, ennobling them and giving their bearers a conviction of justified outrage: you aren't just jealous, you have a right to feel this way (p. 109).*

Clearly, the possibilities are nearly infinite.

To worry about such considerations as you create your rough draft will simply distract and slow you down. However, you should make decisions about rhythm, pace, and sentence structure as you *revise* your text. The key to success is your willingness to experiment. One tip: as you experiment with various structures, read your sentences out loud. You will often know the best choice when you hear your own words.

Exercise

While preserving their essential meaning, add rhythm, pace, and intensity to the sentences of the paragraphs that follow.

1) My friend and I were very competitive. We would compete over trivial things and important things. We would argue over who was the faster runner or who was the better student. We would also fight over who had the best sneakers or the best cell phone deal. It didn't seem to matter what. I even remember having a big argument over whose bottled water tasted better.

2) It rained steadily all throughout the day, beginning early in the morning and lasting till well after midnight. Sometimes the rain fell straight down in great big drops, and sometimes the rain seemed to fall in sheets, as if somehow the drops had all been compressed into a single layer. Once in a while, the wind would blow the rain in waves, like you sometimes see at the ocean.

❑ *Sentence and Paragraph Length*

When you are revising your drafts, check the paragraphs and sentences to make sure they are varied in length and structure. You should avoid what might be called "tombstoning" the reader.

You have no doubt seen cemeteries in which the tombstones are identical in design and placement. You can often find a similar regularity in songs of mourning. In both cases the repetition, whether visual or auditory, evokes the appropriate mood. However, a similar regularity in your prose will rarely serve your goals. Readers need variety. Consider the way that the writer of the following passage has provided it.

> *The comforts of the ordinary American do not, of course, disprove of the existence of poverty. Indeed, the U.S. Bureau of the Census claims that more than 30 million Americans, or 12 to 13 percent of the population, are poor. But what does "poor" in this context really mean? Does it mean that millions of Americans are starving or don't have clothes to wear or a roof to sleep under? It does not. I cannot help but recall the saying of a school friend in Bombay. "I am going to move to America," he vowed. "I want to live in a country where the poor people are fat" (D'Souza p. 115).*

Keep in mind that varying the length of both sentences and paragraphs can provide needed signals to your readers of important information coming up or of a shift in topic.

> *But what if these premises turn out to be false? What if the rich are getting richer because they have created new wealth that didn't exist before? What if we live in a society where the rich are getting richer and the poor are also getting richer, but not at the same pace? If you drive a Mercedes and I have to walk, that's a radical difference of lifestyle that might warrant speculation about first- and second-class citizenship. But is it a big deal if you drive a Mercedes and I drive a Hyundai? If I have a four-bedroom house, do I have cause to be morally outraged that you have a twelve-bedroom house? (D'Souza p. 114)*

Exercise

Try varying the length of the sentences in the following paragraphs to alert your reader of "important information" or "of a shift in topic."

The American empire is at a crossroads, one that many other previous empires reached when they saw their power challenged by an elusive outside force. The real threat comes from American citizens themselves because they seem no longer to trust their government's abdication to corporate greed. Americans can taste the bad aftertaste corporate exploitation has left in their mouths. They see it in the closed steel mills in Pittsburgh, the sweatshops in Honduras that have taken American jobs, and the stunning contrast between the golden parachutes of American CEOs and their underpaid, often minimum wage, employees.

Doug, (a student)

While I share a concern that grand, abstract concepts will not bring about significant change, global thinking and local action are not mutually exclusive because each individual can exert pressure towards a greater change. Consider that movements like women's suffrage and civil rights came about not from a grand scheme alone, but from actions of individuals thinking on a variety of different levels, including individual, local, national and global.

Melissa, (a student)

❏ *Multi-Syllabic Words*

Linguists often distinguish between words that have Latin and those that have Anglo-Saxon origins. Many Latinate words contain several syllables, like *domicile*. Anglo-Saxon words tend to be simpler, many having a single syllable, like *house*.

Heavily Latinate language makes sentences and paragraphs longer, more complex, and probably inflated or stuffy. For example, while the following sentences have essentially the same meaning, the effect is noticeably different.

> *The amelioration of her condition was her primary preoccupation.*

> *Getting well was her first concern.*

Often the sort of writing in the first sentence is a product of affectation or an attempt to make a message sound more important than it really is. You will frequently find this sort of prose issuing from various bureaucracies—governmental, academic, and corporate—where inflating one's importance and status is sometimes, unfortunately, the order of the day.

As a general rule, you should prefer the shorter Anglo-Saxon word to the multi-syllabic Latinate word. However, the more complicated words are often demanded by the conventions in some academic and professional fields.

❏ *Rhythm and Cadence*

If you recall that rhythm is the regular or recurring alternation of any kind of event or action, then you will realize that rhythms are everywhere in our lives—in, for example, the changing of the seasons or the beating of our hearts. And they are in the way we speak and write. When we speak, we alternate between loud and soft, long and short, high and low. Otherwise we would just be whispering or shouting, shrieking or bellowing, and so on all the time. In fact, when people don't alternate, don't make use of the natural rhythms of our language, it seems so odd that we often become uneasy, wondering what is wrong. The same is true of what we read and write. The choice of individual words, the building of larger units such as phrases and clauses, together with the punctuation we use, sets up for the reader a rhythm or cadence. Poets have learned to shape these natural rhythms into more formal patterns called meter. Prose writers often do something similar, though generally less formally and strictly. The sentence

I go to sleep when I'm feeling blue and dream about tomorrow

has a kind of gentle, wistful rhythm to it, perhaps echoing its sentiment. Compare it to

I hate getting up early.

Long vowels, short vowels, consonants, the numbers of syllables, and the length of sentences—all contribute to giving a text a rhythm or a cadence. We can use that rhythm to underscore our meaning, or, sometimes, for dramatic effect, to oppose it.

He drifted into unconsciousness as the automobile slid silently off the narrow mountain road.

Charge! the King said to his men, and so began the long slaughter of the Hundred Year War.

We can practice such effects by taking several different "situations" and creating a variety of "moods". Let us take a "rainy day," for an example. We can make it seem a hard and disruptive event.

1) The raindrops banged on the garbage cans and splattered on the pavement.

Or we can make it seem soft and sustaining.

2) The raindrops spilled from the clouds and seeped into the parched earth.

Exercise

Try creating different moods about the following "events" by varying the sentence rhythms:

a) physical work (such as chopping wood or washing a car)
b) studying
c) being alert
d) thinking

Language That Speaks to the Poet in Us

Part of the pleasure readers find in good writing is the discovery of effective figurative language—phrasing used in a non-literal or metaphoric sense. At their heart, figures of speech are more than decorative. They represent a serious attempt, both logical and imaginative, to make sense. They can help us to grasp new experiences by connecting them to aspects of the world we already understand. They ask us to see differences in things that seem wholly similar, and similarities in things that seem wholly different. Composing images and metaphors makes demands on our intelligence and imagination, and the apt image or metaphor can crystallize an issue for your reader.

❏ *Metaphor*

The term "metaphor" is used in several different senses. It is often used in a broad sense to refer to any figure of speech or play on words. Other times it is used to refer to a specific figure of speech we might call "metaphor proper." We discussed metaphor in Chapter 6 as a method of defining terms or concepts. (You might want to review that material now.) Here, we remind you of the basics.

Generally, metaphors claim relationships. The goal of metaphor is normally to communicate information readers do not know or have not experienced by relating it, in some way, to what they are likely to know or have experienced. Probably the two most common metaphors, or figures of speech, are *metaphor* (in the specific sense) and *simile*.

A *metaphor* (in the specific sense) claims an identity between the *known* and the *unknown*. Shakespeare put metaphor to good use in *As You Like It*:

All the world's a stage
And all the men and women merely players

As you can see, Shakespeare does not stop with a single metaphor. The relationship between the two metaphors is obvious and artful. This sort of extension can be effective if you do not take it too far. While we expect a great deal of figurative language in a play by Shakespeare, a small amount of figurative language will go a long way in the work you will write for your classes and in your professional life.

A *simile* is a little different than a metaphor; in a *simile*, rather than claiming identity between two things, the writer *compares* the two, using words such as *like* or *as*. The intent is still the same—to attribute the qualities of one to the other. William Faulkner provides a good example in a clear and striking image of butterflies:

Yellow butterflies flickered along the shade like flecks of sun

Exercise

Try making metaphors (either "metaphor proper" or simile) out of the following:

a) a friend
b) life
c) darkness
d) poverty
e) globalization
f) a good sentence
g) a bad sentence

❑ *Image*

The word image will forever be associated with the visual representation of reality. Yet, when used in its specialized critical sense, as here, it has come to mean any representation of sensory experience, including smell or taste or texture, in addition to sight. Images, thus, attempt to focus our attention more on the concrete, physical aspects of experience and less on the abstract and general. We could write, for example, that "his face was rough to the touch" and most people would have a general sense of what we were describing—perhaps somebody with unshaved or with weathered skin. But if we wrote instead, "His sandpaper whiskers scraped my cheek," it is much more likely that our readers would have a richer, fuller sense of the reality being communicated.

Often, in addition to giving the reader a more vivid and a more memorable way of understanding us, our images tend to be more concise expressions as well. We could write, "Sin is a constant and threatening presence in all aspects of our lives," or we could write, as in Genesis, "Sin is lurking at the door."

In college, I had to read a number of big, thick books, one right after the other.

or

I ate my way through college, one fat book at a time.

Exercise

Keeping in mind that in writing, an "image" refers to any sensory information and not just something visual, try creating some images about the following:

a) a room

b) a hot day

c) guilt

d) fear

e) relief

f) laughter

❑ *Allusion*

An allusion, a brief reference to a text or to an historical figure, works because what we already know will influence what we read. In each culture, certain texts are widely read, highly valued, and generally remembered. Writers often make use of that shared experience by relating what they create to those texts. In our culture, the Bible, the plays of Shakespeare, the work of well-known poets and novelists can supply us with characters, actions, and figures of speech which we can "import" into our own texts—along with their associated meanings and emotions. For example, one of the more famous exchanges in the history of modern political debates involved one of the debaters telling the other that he was "No Jack Kennedy." The name of the hotel that is linked to the crisis that overtook the Nixon Administration, Watergate, is frequently used to describe potential debacles. For example, during the Reagan Administration there was Irangate.

Exercise

Try to provide allusions for the following terms to make them more meaningful:

a) a very intelligent person
b) a very deceitful person
c) a hard test
d) a steep hill
e) a hot day
f) a devastating event

Troubleshooting the Language of your Essay

Throughout this book we have made a case for a clear and honest expression of your views on urgent issues, while keeping in mind the complexity of most issues and the diversity within most audiences. This section of the book asks you to pay close attention to the words you use to achieve your ends. As with almost every other activity, your success depends on doing a number of small things well. It would be a shame to gather information and organize it into a coherent form, only to have the force of your argument undercut by damaging word choices.

In our presentation of ways to avoid some common pitfalls, we use the metaphor of troubleshooting to communicate the "find it and fix it" structure of this section. Too often, students are told to avoid such things as passive voice but are not offered effective ways to find the offending passages or fix them once they do. In each of the following subsections, we give you specific ways to locate spots that might confuse or distract a reader (usually this can be done with the search function of a word processor). Next, we provide explicit advice for recasting the construction. In each case, you will complete exercises that require you to spot and fix problems; finally, you will apply that skill to the essay you have been developing as you moved through this text.

A number of these principles also address the directness of your prose. Our basic advice is that you will make your writing lively and engaging if you are economical in your use of words.

❏ *Active and Passive Voice*

In active voice constructions, the agent performing the action is the subject of the sentence. Consider the following:

Hitch bit the plumber.

We can, however, write the sentence in another form and maintain exactly the same meaning:

The plumber was bitten by Hitch.

In this case, the subject is not the agent performing the action. Sentences with this characteristic are written in *passive voice*.

In general, unless there is a very good reason for using passive voice, you should avoid it. On occasion, however, you might have good reasons to use the passive voice. For example:

1. When the conventions of the rhetorical context require it, as in scientific lab reports.

2. When you want to (or need to) focus on the action or the consequences of the action rather than the agent:

    The full report, with all the sordid details, will be sent (by us) tomorrow.

3. When you do not know the agent:

    My bike was stolen. (By whom? You may not know, and it may not be important unless you're speaking to the police.)

Bear in mind that not knowing the agent is one thing, but not stating one to avoid questions about responsibility is another.

Mr. Baxter, this is notice of termination of your employment. **It has been decided** *that your performance is not adequate.*

Indeed? Who, exactly did the deciding?

All applicants for state aid **will be counseled** *before any funds* **are paid out***.*

Who will do the counseling? Who will pay the money?

Exercise

Try converting the following passive sentences into active ones:

a) The Devil was created by God.
b) Mistakes were made.
c) The door was slammed in his face by the girl.
d) It has been decided that the war will end.
e) Your interview was successfully completed.
f) Fun was had.
g) The passive voice was used to show the results of his exploration of style.
h) A phone call will be made to the one selected for this assignment.

There is. . . . There are . . .

Your sentences will often be more direct and concise if you avoid beginning sentences with "There is . . . ." or "There are. . . ." Since the phrase simply claims the existence of something, you can often make the point succinctly.

> *There are people in this country who do not vote in important elections.*
>
> *Some citizens **fail** to vote in important elections.*

Also notice that revising the sentence has led us to a more expressive verb—*fail*. Other examples:

> *There is a distinct flavor of nutmeg in these cookies.*
>
> *These cookies **taste** of nutmeg.*

> *There are helpful ways to avoid West Nile Virus.*
>
> ***Certain precautions** can help you avoid West Nile Virus.*

Exercise

Try eliminating the "There is" or "There are" from the following sentences in order to make them more active and concise:

a) There are more women than men alive on the planet today.
b) There is nothing more awkward than an unshaken hand.
c) There are ways for us to lose weight safely.
d) There is nothing you can do.

The "be" verb trick

A surprisingly effective technique for finding and revising passive voice, beginning sentences with "There is . . ." or "There are . . . ," and many other problems in clarity, directness, and conciseness is the "be" verb trick:

- As you revise, go through your draft and mark every instance where you use a form of the verb "to be"—*am, is, are, was, were, be, being, been*. While this is easier and faster to do with a word processor, using the "global search and replace" function, you can also do it manually, working on a hard copy.
- Then go back through the draft and, if you can get rid of these forms gracefully (stress on gracefully)—do it.

Exercise

Replace the following passive verbs "to be" with active verbs.

a) There are several different methods of self-management that can change your life if you follow them.

b) Silas found that his lack of ambition was due to confusion about his career direction.

c) Finding the wallet, and being very diligent, she counted the money before she brought it to the manager.

d) The excessive fees being charged were the result of fraudulent bookkeeping.

❑ *Nominalizations*

Nominalizations are verbs that have been turned into nouns—usually by adding *–tion* or *–ment* to the verb. For example: *govern* becomes *government*, *investigate* becomes *investigation*, *justify* becomes *justification*

Because we can turn verbs into nouns so easily, it can become habit forming. Before we know it, we may string a whole series of these words together, often losing the intensity that comes from having strong verbs lead to definite consequences.

Additionally, once a word is transformed from a verb connected to a definite noun and into a noun itself, there is a tendency to use that word in so many contexts that it becomes abstract and general.

> *Globalization may be in danger of becoming such a generalization that it will become a conceptualization with no justification.*

This does not mean that you must avoid such words. Sometimes a nominalization is apt. For example, we can turn a verb like *discuss* into a very useful noun:

> *The **discussion** went well. She raised my grade.*

In this context, the emphasis is less on the raw physical activity of conversing and more on the notion of the behavior being an event, an occurrence with an outcome—hence, the noun. In this context, too, the agents are identified and so there is a connection between the action and the agent.

Nominalizations have their efficient uses but, like the passive voice, they often lead to cumbersome, lockjaw prose.

> *I see children as an **inspiration** in my life.*
> *Children inspire me.*

> ***Cultivation** of organic food must be maximized.*
> *Grow more organic food!*

A nominalization moves us away from expression that is concrete and active to expression that is wordy and indirect.

The committee investigated the charges and declared them accurate.

The committee's investigation of the charges resulted in a declaration of their accuracy.

The easy way to find most nominalizations is to go through your draft and mark the letter sequences "ment" and "tion." Then look at each word to make sure it is a nominalization. (Many words that end in "ment" or "tion" are *not*.) Once you've identified actual nominalizations, look at them in the context of the constructions in which you find them. If the construction seems cumbersome or if you have no specific reason to use the nominalization, rewrite and use the verb instead. Be sure that your revision does what you intend.

❏   *Stacking*

The world is full of wonder and complexity, and our language provides a great storehouse of words and expressions to reflect the richness. In our desire to "get it right," we constantly seek to modify—to qualify—our agents and actions, our nouns and verbs. It is not just a "man" sitting there but an "old man, a very old man." It is not just a "home run," but a "game-winning, bases-loaded, series-ending home run."

We often write this way because, in our jam-packed and complex world, the nouns, the subjects or objects of our thoughts, need this clarification, this qualification.

Moreover, because our *primary goal* is to be understood, we want to be as clear as we can be. But we can overdo it and bring about the opposite effect. *Stacking* is the term we use for the tendency to add qualifiers to our sentences.

We can do this with adjectives:

*The **infinite, empty, frigid, silent, blackness of space** overwhelms the fragile human mind.*

We can do this with prepositional phrases:

*The woman, **in** the white dress, **with** the white lace **on** the borders **of** the sleeves, laughed.*

We can do this with nouns:

*The **Senate election committee chair** issued the following report.*

There is no easy way to find where we have fallen victim to this tendency. But you can train yourself to "hear" them as you revise. Unless the multiple modifiers are necessary and effective, eliminate them.

```
Back home, I have been stopped, frisked, and followed by white policemen
for years. (Student)
```

```
Back home, I have been detained and frisked by white policemen for years.
```

You can often fix such problems with a more effective word choice. For example, pick a single adjective that will do the work of several. You might use a descriptive noun that will do the work of an adjective-noun pair, or you can replace an adverb-verb pair with a more descriptive verb.

> *She took ponderously slow, halting, measured steps.*
> *She plodded ahead.*

> *The 1,000 lb. enormous bovine awkwardly pushed itself through the small gate.*
> *The massive cow squeezed through the small gate.*

❑ *Determiners: "That" and "This"*

"That" is a perfectly good and useful *determiner*, a class of words used to signal the number and location of nouns, as in "That topic is perfect for this assignment." In fact, when used correctly, not only can "that" or "this" make reference to the noun, they can also substitute for it, as in, "That is perfect for this." The key, of course, is that the reader must know what "that" or "this" stands for. If the reference is not clear, the reader will either have to spend time re-reading the previous sentence or sentences, or remain confused. For example:

> *She put down the book and walked out of the room without saying anything. **That** was the problem.*

What was the problem? Putting down the book? Walking out? Not saying anything?

Exercise

Determine whether a clear referent exists for each underlined determiner. If so, justify your answer. If not, revise accordingly.

1. Highly exaggerated talk is not real communication. That does nothing for me and neither does this conversation.

2. Finally, this is a sensible indication that somebody was listening.

3. Could everyone please sit down. This is how we will begin the program.

4. India's future looks grim because government programs have been abandoned. This leaves a third-world country at risk for greater poverty.

❑ *Relative Clauses*

Relative clauses function as adjectives, but contain both the subject and a predicate required of a clause. They add considerable detail to what we know about the main noun.

My friend, **who is an only child,** *wanted to have a big family.*

The senator, **who didn't care about the issue but wanted only to make a good impression,** *was the first one to second the motion.*

In each case, we are given information about the agent that helps us to understand or evaluate the action. This is the kind of information we get when the clause is introduced by a relative pronoun—*that, who,* or *which.*

We can also add information about time and place and reasons. We then use relative adverbs to introduce the clause—*where, when,* and *why.*

New Orleans was a city **where joy and sorrow both thrived.**

We're all waiting until November, **when the next election takes place.**

Because relative clauses are themselves sometimes complex and lengthy, it's easy to see how their use—and overuse—can lead to difficulty, both in terms of precision and concision and in punctuating them correctly.

The committee voted to name the dorm after the president, **which was highly unusual.**

What, exactly, was unusual—the dorm or the vote?

The book was short but complex, **which made it hard to read.**

What made the book hard to read—its brevity or its complexity?

❏ *Danglers*

Danglers include a variety of sentence elements—clauses, phrases, and single words—that are placed or punctuated so that they modify something they cannot. For example:

Flying over the jungle at 5,000 feet, elephants could be seen.

Grammatically, the phrase "flying over the jungle at 5,000 feet" is placed so that it modifies (or describes) "elephants." *Logically,* it can't. Except in Disney movies, elephants do not fly.

In many cases, the error will completely confuse the reader. In many other cases, readers will puzzle-out your meaning. However, the phrasing will distract them, especially if it creates ludicrous sentences.

Sometimes, as in the examples below, the dangler logically modifies something or someone that doesn't appear anywhere in the sentence.

When choosing a college, *climate should be a major consideration.*

Driving through the neighborhood, *poverty was visible everywhere.*

In each sentence, the missing element is what the opening phrase should modify. In the first sentence, the dangler modifies "climate." What the writer really means is:

When choosing a college, students should make climate a major consideration.

or

When a student chooses a college, climate should be a major consideration.

In the second sentence, the dangler modifies "poverty." What the writer means is unclear because we have no idea who is "driving through the neighborhood."

Here are some other examples:

Hiding in the bushes, *it was difficult to see the thief.*

Who was hiding in the bushes—the thief or some unidentified person watching the thief?

When still a child, *my father joined the army.*

Was the father still a child when he joined the army or was it the writer of the sentence? This one clearly falls into the "ludicrous" category.

The revision of either of these examples depends on the writer's intent, which, thanks to the dangler, is a complete mystery in both cases. However, in the context of a full paragraph, we *might* be able to guess the intent. In the first sentence, we might conclude:

While we were hiding in the bushes, it was difficult to see the thief.

or

It was difficult for us to see the thief hiding in the bushes.

In the second we might guess:

When I was still a child, my father joined the army.

or

My father joined the army while still a child.

But do you really want to make a guessing game of your work? The best way to guard against dangling modifiers, especially when the modifier lacks its own subject, is to go back and make sure there is a legitimate subject close by—one the words can logically modify. If it is missing, supply it and clearly connect the modifier to it.

Exercise

Correct the following sentences by inserting the "something" or "someone" the dangler actually modifies.

1. With our noses stuck in notebooks, the speeding cars whizzed past us on the open high-way.

2. Flat-footing it across the trestle bridge, the steam from the locomotive sent a shrill blast against our ears.

3. Walking across the yard, the distant roll of thunder could be heard.

4. Holding our breaths, the sailboat capsized almost completely before righting itself.

5. Turning the corner, the Statue of Liberty looms tall and majestic.

6. Laughing loudly, our jokes were a great hit at the party.

A Final Note about Nouns and Verbs

As you explain what something is, what it does, what its value is, and what can be done about it, remember that nouns and verbs lie at the center of each of those activities. The more precise your words are, the more likely readers will understand you. The more general your language, the more they will have to draw on their own understanding of issues, even though that understanding may be different from yours. You might write, for example, "The new economic system has negatively impacted a rather large number of inadequately trained people." But what, actually, have you told readers? What system? How impacted? Badly trained in terms of doing what? If, instead, you were to write that "Globalization depresses the wages of millions of computer-illiterate workers," you not only would provide more useful information, you would use fewer words. This is the ideal formula for writing (as it is for most enterprises): to get the most output (in this case meaning) from the least input (in this case language).

Concision and precision are especially important when you are writing about complex ideas and complicated behaviors. Words like democracy, racism, capitalism, or even globalization have been used to explain such a range of behaviors that readers may not understand such terms in the way you wish. Often, then, you will need to add adjectives and adverbs to "qualify" the nature or extent of your terms. You might write "Laissez-faire" capitalism to indicate the original, more unregulated, market-driven form of the economic theory; or you might need to indicate that you are focusing on "industrial" globalization as opposed to "agricultural" global-ization.

Finally, we want to underscore a statement we made at the outset of this chapter: So much depends on clearly defining and describing the nature of the reality you are exploring. One of the most powerful means to help you to accomplish that goal is to use words as precisely as you can, without sacrificing the beauty and emotional power that words can convey.

15

Documenting Sources

Why You Need to Document

Documenting the origin of "borrowed material" is a long-standing academic tradition that is crucial to the process and progress of scholarship. You must clearly identify all information taken from others, cite its origin, and attribute specific information to the appropriate source. There are many good reasons why documentation is vital; generally, they fall into three main categories: ethical, practical, and rhetorical.

The ethical reasons for documentation were touched on earlier. Passing someone else's work off as your own, even inadvertently, is plagiarism. Conscious plagiarism is theft and is, consequently, an unethical and immoral act. Our society recognizes written works—words and ideas—as the intellectual property of their creator. The academic community is one of the few arenas in which you may freely use another's property, as long as you abide by certain conventions. These conventions include acknowledging those who have contributed to your work and presenting their ideas accurately.

Aside from meeting ethical responsibilities, there are good practical reasons for meticulous documentation. Documentation enables your readers to go into a library (or to a website) and find the exact page or pages from which you drew any specific bit of information. Your documentation allows readers interested in your subject to verify your research and to more effectively conduct their own. If ethical and practical concerns are not enough, documentation also serves important rhetorical functions.

As you have seen, an important part of writing well is showing your readers that they are justified in taking you seriously. Appropriate documentation enhances your authority as a writer and, consequently, the credibility of your work. It tells your readers that you have approached the challenge of a writing project with respect, have informed yourself on the subject, and, before taking up their time with your ideas, you have carefully considered the available evidence.

Scholarship is largely a communal activity. As they develop their analyses and interpretations, scholars draw on each other's work. A sign of your professionalism and intellectual maturity, a sign that you belong in the community of scholars, is the effective and formal incorporation of the ideas and discoveries of others into your work. No one is expected to do the job alone.

Various guides to documentation, including the one that follows, provide help in constructing individual citations and bibliographies, though no guide is complete. Sooner or later, you will

We are indebted to Carrie Bates who wrote Chapter 15.

encounter situations that are not mentioned in the guide or that require some latitude in how you will document. Taken together, the three functions of documentation—ethical, practical, rhetorical—constitute a sort of logic that can help you make decisions. Remember three rules: be honest, help your fellow researchers as much as possible, and let your readers know that you have done your best to inform them of the debts you have to other writers.

Common Knowledge and Specialized Knowledge

The term *common knowledge* refers to general information that most educated people already have. This kind of information does not need to be documented. For example, when Scott Davies (Chapter 3) writes in his paper,

```
The nuclear armament buildup, the "space race," and a decade of warfare
on a distant Asian front were expensive ventures,
```

his information comes as no surprise to his readers. It is obvious that nuclear weapons are costly. People are also aware of the high cost of the U.S. effort to compete with the former USSR in space travel and of the huge military effort that went into waging the war in Vietnam. The sentence contains common knowledge and does not require documentation. Scott felt, correctly, that he could use these comments in his paper without having to supply any supporting evidence. The sentence proceeds from a common fund of general knowledge and not from his research.

On the other hand, when Scott writes

```
Harrington's theory centers on a "cycle of poverty" (16) in which in-
equality in one area of society inevitably leads to inequalities in
other areas,
```

he introduces theoretical information that cannot be considered common knowledge. Readers expect to see a reference to Scott's reading. Because Scott's research helped him to discover these new concepts, or specialized knowledge, he must acknowledge his source, Harrington (16), in the paper.

As you write papers, you will need to determine how familiar an educated audience will be with the information you are using. The more you write, the more confidence you will have in your ability to discriminate between what is common and what is specialized knowledge. When you are in doubt about your reader's familiarity with your material, it is best to provide documentation.

Methods of Documentation

The rationale for documentation holds true for every discipline, but the details of documentation vary from discipline to discipline, producing many methods of documentation—far too many to cover in this text. This chapter presents the system of documentation set forth by the Modern

Language Association (MLA). Papers written for English courses, and often for other areas of the humanities, customarily require this documentation format.

The MLA system uses in-text citations rather than footnotes or endnotes. In an in-text citation, you usually both identify its author as you present the material you have found useful in the development of your argument and, in parentheses following the material, you provide the page number of the text in which you found what you are using. This widely used combination provides readers with enough information to locate the reference work on the list of works cited at the end of your paper.

The following lists will help you quickly to find specific entries for MLA in-text and works cited formats. The items we have provided include the most common kinds of sources you are likely to use. If, however, you have a source and can find no corresponding entry for how to cite it (either in-text or in the works cited list), refer to either the hard copy or the online version of the *MLA Handbook for Writers of Research Papers*. The online version will have the most recent information and examples. If the *Handbook* does not address your specific case, you will have to improvise—to find something close to your particular kind of source to use as a model. Be consistent with your improvisations throughout your work.

Web-based research presents special challenges for documentation, as many sites do not have all of the information you are accustomed to supplying. In such cases, provide what information you can, and improvise where necessary, using existing models to guide you. Some websites disappear or move, making later verification of your source difficult, so you may want to download or print your web-based research for easy future reference. Many articles available on the Web have links to citation information. You may find these helpful, but remember that your particular focus may require you to slightly alter the entry.

MLA In-Text Citations

1. **Work by One Author**
2. **Two or More Works by the Same Author**
3. **Work by Two or Three Authors**
4. **Work by Four or More Authors**
5. **Work with an Editor in Place of Author**
6. **Work by a Corporate Author**
7. **Work by an Unknown or Anonymous Author**
8. **Novel, Play, Poem, or Classical Work**
9. **Entry in an Encyclopedia or Dictionary**
10. **Work in an Anthology**
11. **Indirect Source/Secondary Source**
12. **Entire Work**
13. **Journal Article**
14. **Article in a Monthly or Weekly Magazine**

15. **Article in a Newspaper**
16. **Electronic Sources, Computer-Accessed Databases, and Internet**
17. **Film**
18. **Television Program**
19. **Personal Interview**
20. **Sound Recording: (Tape, Record, CD)**

MLA Works Cited Entries

1.1 **Work by One Author**
1.2 **Two or More Works by the Same Author**
1.3 **Work by Two or Three Authors**
1.4 **Work by Four or More Authors**
1.5 **Work with an Editor in Place of Author**
1.6 **Work by a Corporate Author**
1.7 **Work by an Unknown or Anonymous Author**
1.8 **Novel, Play, Poem, or Classical Work**
1.9 **Entry in an Encyclopedia or a Dictionary**
1.10 **Work in an Anthology**
1.11 **Indirect Source**
1.12 **Entire Source**
1.13 **Journal Article**
1.14 **Article in a Monthly or Weekly Magazine**
1.15 **Article in a Newspaper**
1.16 **Electronic Sources, Computer-Accessed Databases, and Internet**
1.17 **Film**
1.18 **Television Program or Radio Broadcast**
1.19 **Public or Personal Interview**
1.20 **Sound Recording (Tape, Record, CD)**
1.21 **Graphic Novel**
1.22 **Manuscript or Typescript**

In-Text Citations

Below you will find examples and discussion of the most frequently used kinds of MLA in-text citations. Each example illustrates the proper format for a specific kind of source. You must key your in-text citations to your works cited entries, so be sure that your in-text reference and the works cited entry begin with the same word (usually the author's last name). If you use the author's full name in your signal phrase, key the last name of the author to your works cited. Include the page number or numbers if your source provides these, whether you are quoting directly, paraphrasing, or summarizing, unless you are citing a complete work. In that case, you do not need to provide page numbers. If your source does not include page numbers, see the guidelines for your specific non-paginated source. If you need more information, consult the *MLA Handbook for Writers of Research Papers*, seventh edition, (NY: MLA, 2009), or visit the official website at mla.org.

1. A Work by One Author

Whenever possible, mention the author's name as you introduce your source. When you first mention an author in your paper, give the full name just as it appears in your source. Thereafter, you may use only the last name unless you refer to other writers who have the same last name. Do not use the titles *Mr.* or *Mrs.*

> Johnson-Weiner states, "Today the diversity of Old Order life challenges any attempt to describe Amish or Mennonite church-communities so simply or so monolithically" (230).

"Johnson-Weiner" identifies the author. This introduction is followed by a brief quotation from Johnson-Weiner. Note that the quotation is followed by the closing quotation marks, but not by any punctuation. Next, provide the page number, in parentheses, and end the entire sentence with a period, outside the parentheses.

If you do not name the author in your sentence, be sure to mention the author's last name before the page number in parentheses at the end.

> We must realize that the diversity of Old Order life prevents us from describing Amish or Mennonite communities in monolithic terms (Johnson-Weiner 230).

Note that there is no punctuation between the last name and the page number.

2. Two or More Works by the Same Author

When your paper includes references to more than one work by an author, mention the title of the work in your introductory words.

> In *Ancestors: The Loving Family in Old Europe*, historian Steven Ozment asks, "If women were so vital and prominent a part of the productive life of the fourteenth and fifteenth centuries, might they not reasonably be expected also to have found creative outlets for their talents in the changed labor markets of later centuries?" (43).

Or you may put the title in an abbreviated form in the parentheses before the page number.

> Ozment asks, "If women were so vital and prominent a part of the productive life of the fourteenth and fifteenth centuries, might they not reasonably be expected also to have found creative outlets for their talents in the changed labor markets of later centuries?" (*Ancestors* 43).

If you introduce neither the title nor the author, then they must appear, separated by a comma, in the parentheses.

> One historian asks, "If women were so vital and prominent a part of the productive life of the four-teenth and fifteenth centuries, might they not reasonably be expected also to have found creative outlets for their talents in the changed labor markets of later centuries?" (Ozment, *Ancestors* 43).

Notice that the quotation is a question and requires its own punctuation, a question mark, directly after the last word, followed by the closing quotation marks, then the parenthetical information.

3. A Work by Two or Three Authors

Mention all the authors in your introductory words or include them in the parentheses.

> Clark, Lints, and Smith explain that their work is primarily philosophical, and readers who want a more complete theological reference volume should consult a theological dictionary (viii).

> While there is much overlap between philosophical and theological terms, this collection in-cludes only those theological terms that have a direct relationship to philosophy, and vice versa (Clark, Lints, and Smith viii).

Name the authors in the order in which they appear on the title page of their work.

4. A Work by Four or More Authors

In your introductory words, or in the parenthetical citation, give the last name of the first author followed by the Latin term et al., which means "and others" in English, without any intervening punctuation. Do not italicize et al., but do use the abbreviation's period. If you wish, give the last names of all the authors in your introductory words or in the parenthetical citation.

> Boyer et al. explain that France briefly lost Canada to England between 1629 and 1632, after which France resumed and extended its colonization in that part of the New World (95).

> France's colonization of North America was briefly interrupted between 1629 and 1632, when they lost Canada to England (Boyer et al. 95).

5. A Work with an Editor in the Place of Author

If you are referring to the entire work, treat the editor as you would an author.

> Lorrie Moore has chosen both well-known authors and talented newcomers as contributors to the 2004 edition of *The Best American Short Stories*.

If you cite a part of the work written by the editor, include the editor's name and the page num-ber, just as you would in a reference to a work by a single author.

The difficulty lies in defining a theory of the short story: "it is technically a genre, not a form . . . " (Moore x).

Note that the page reference is a roman numeral and not an arabic number, because it is part of an introduction.

6. A Work by a Corporate Author

The term *corporate author* refers to organizations and agencies, often in federal, state, and local governments. The Internal Revenue Service and the U.S. Postal Service are corporate authors that produce many documents each year. You can either name the corporate author in your introductory words or include it, in shortened form, in the parentheses.

> Trout Unlimited advises directors of youth programs not to make conservation education harder than it ought to be (2).

> Youth directors need to remember to keep their conservation programs simple (Trout Unlimited 2).

7. A Work by an Unknown or Anonymous Author

If you refer to a work whose author is unknown, provide the title of the work in your introductory words or include it, in shortened form if necessary, in the parentheses. If you shorten a title, begin with the first word so that readers can locate the source in the works cited. If you cite two or more anonymous sources that have the same title, use a distinguishing publication fact to identify each reference.

> The *World Almanac* lists sixty-six counties in South Dakota, the majority of which experienced population decline in the last decade of the twentieth century (427–28).

> In the last decade of the twentieth century, the majority of South Dakota's sixty-six counties experienced population decline (*World* 427–28).

> The 2001 edition of the *World Almanac* lists sixty-six counties in South Dakota, the majority of which experienced population decline in the last decade of the twentieth century (427–28).

8. A Novel, Play, Poem, or Classical Work

For a work of literature, try to give enough information so that your readers will know the specific edition of the work you used. When you refer to a novel, put the page number in the parentheses, and, if possible, the chapter or part (ch. or pt.) number after a semicolon (;).

> In *The Plague*, Camus underscores the inability of organized conventional religion to cope with the vital issues of life (95–100; pt. 2).

For a verse play, place inside the parentheses the act, scene, and line numbers, separated by periods. Use arabic numerals unless your instructor requires roman numerals.

> Shakespeare's Dumain, one of the lords attending the Princess of France, observes in *Love's Labor Lost*, that when an entire company is in love, no one criticizes his fellow for being too fulsome in his praise of his beloved, "for none offend where all alike do dote" (4.3.126).

For a poem, put in the parentheses the number of the part (if there are parts) and, after a period, the line numbers. In the following example, there is only a line number.

> In Lovelace's "Lucasta," war replaces Lucasta and becomes the "new mistress now I chase" (5).

For a classical work, place inside the parentheses the book, section, and the line, if provided, separated by periods.

> In *Confessions*, Augustine compares the teachings of the Manicheans with fantasy food: "dream substances, mock realities, far less true than the real things which we see with the sight of our eyes in the sky or on the earth" (3.6).

When referring to a sacred text, you do not need to italicize the general term (Bible, Talmud, Koran), but you should italicize and include the particular version/edition you cite, either in your text itself or in your parenthetical citation. Use the names of the books and the divisions within the books as they appear in the scripture. Use standard abbreviations.

> The Galatian Christ-communities envisioned by the Apostle Paul were places where prevailing societal status markers had been rendered irrelevant: "There is no longer Jew or Greek, there is no longer slave or free, there is no longer male and female; for all of you are one in Christ Jesus" (*New Revised Standard Version*, Gal. 3. 28).

9. An Entry in an Encyclopedia or Dictionary

If the entry you are citing has an author, include his or her name somewhere in your reference (either in your text or in your parenthetical reference), because you will use that author's name in your works cited entry. Also include the title of the entry you are citing.

> Various authors, such as Shakespeare, Coleridge, and Melville use Ishmael to evoke an atmosphere of alienation, while others, including Vaughan and Blake, use the name to convey a sense of promise and protection (Westenbroek, "Ishmael").

If you wish to cite a specific definition from a dictionary, include the appropriate number and letter. The title of the entry will serve as the key word in your works cited entry.

> Rationalism is "a theory that reason is in itself a source of knowledge superior to and independent of sense perception" ("Rationalism," def. 2a).

10. A Work in an Anthology

Put the author's (not the editor's) name in the introductory phrase or inside the parentheses before the page number. The editor's name will appear in the full publication data on the works cited page.

> Pope's poem, "Sound and Sense," both extols and demonstrates the virtues and vices of ono-matopoeic and echoic words (195–96).

> We hear both pleasant and unpleasant consonantal sounds in every line, none more so than these: "Soft is the strain when Zephyr gently blows/ And the smooth stream in smoother num-bers flows/ But when loud surges lash the sounding shore/ The hoarse, rough verse should like the torrent roar" (Pope, "Sound and Sense" 195–96).

11. An Indirect Source/Secondary Source

When you refer to a writer whose words appear in the work of another author, put the abbreviation qtd. in ("quoted in") inside the parentheses before the page number. If your author paraphrases or summarizes another author's work, use cited in.

> Herodotus favored Athens over Sparta as having done more to defeat the Persians in the Greco-Persians War. "I cannot myself see what possible use it would have been [for the Spartans] to fortify the Isthmus as long as the Persian navy had mastery of the sea. So if anyone were to say that it was the Athenians who were the saviours of Greece, that would not be very wide of the mark" (qtd. in Cartledge 164).

12. An Entire Work

When you allude to an entire work, mention the author's name in your introductory words rather than in a parenthetical citation. In a summary comment on the whole work, page numbers are not necessary.

> Backman offers convincing evidence that we must consider three distinct medieval worlds—the Latin West, the Islamic, and the Byzantine—in any attempt to understand the Middle Ages and its impact on the development of western civilization.

13. A Journal Article

Provide the author's name and the page number, just as you would for a book, unless you are citing the entire article, in which case, it is best to include the reference in the text, rather than in a paren-thetical reference. If you are citing the entire article and prefer to use the parenthetical reference, you do not include the page numbers. The first example below cites an entire article; the second, a specific part of the article.

Davidson, too, argues for the importance of placing texts in their historical context. Throughout his article, "The Four Faces of Self-Love in the Theology of Jonathan Edwards," Davidson contends that we will fail to understand Jonathan Edwards' position on self-love if we read that term from a twenty-first century perspective.

Davidson points out that while modern thought posits self-love as a human virtue, eighteenth-century thinkers, including Edwards, did not. Yet Edwards did not view self-love as inherently evil, either (Davidson, 88-89).

14. An Article in a Monthly or Weekly Magazine

Follow the format for a journal article (see 13 above). The first example below cites an entire article; the second, a specific part of the article.

Dixit explains how word choices reveal values and how those values are likely to translate into political policy.

Dixit notes that Obama's word choices are "typically masculine," while Hilary Clinton's are "low-profile" and "middle-of-the-road" (74-75).

15. An Article in a Newspaper

Follow the format for a journal article (see 13 above). The first example below cites an entire article; the second, a specific part of the article.

Landler raises the question of the place of religion in the judicial system.

Other indications of the growing cultural tension between Western values and Muslim sensitivities include a cancelled performance of a Mozart opera with a scene that depicts the severed head of the Prophet Muhammad (Landler A10).

16. Electronic Sources, Computer Accessed Databases, and Internet

For articles in online versions of journals, magazines, and newspapers, follow the conventions listed above (13, 14, and 15). For other online sources, such as a database, a website, or a blog, it is best to include the reference in the text (the author and/or the title of the source), rather than in a parenthetical reference. If you prefer to use the parenthetical reference, be aware that some sources have no page numbers. In these cases, you cannot cite a page number.

A one-page work does not require a page number in a parenthetical reference, but you may want to supply one to indicate where your citation ends and where your original work recommences.

Some electronic publications include paragraph numbers or other section markers: if your source uses these indicators, you should use them in your parenthetical reference. Indicate paragraphs by using the abbreviation *par.* or *pars.*, separated from the author's name (if used) by a comma. Indicate sections by using the abbreviation *sec.*, preceded by the author's name and a comma; other abbreviations follow standard usage.

If your source does not include explicit markers, do not use them (do not count unnumbered paragraphs and assign a number to them). If you have to cite a work in its entirety, but your reference is more specific (a quotation, a paraphrase, or a summary of part of the source), you may want to indicate the approximate location in your text. See below for specific examples.

> **BLOG**: MLA has no guidelines for citing a blog. This is one of those instances where you will need to improvise. We recommend that you italicize the title of the blog, in keeping with the MLA practice of italicizing the names of websites. Include the author's name, either in the text or in the parenthetical reference.
>
> > **In text**: Ayers' contentment as a young, stay-at-home mother and the positive responses generated by her blog, *Child of Grace*, offer another view of empowerment: that of a serene spirit.
> >
> > **Parenthetical reference**: The positive responses generated by a young mother's musings on the value of contentment indicate that not all young women feel pressured to build careers outside the home (Ayers).
>
> **DATABASE**: Italicize the name of the database.
>
> > **A database cited in its entirety**: Charles Laughton appeared in more than sixty films over the course of forty years (*IMBd*).
> >
> > **Specific citation with no section or paragraph number**: A glance at *IMBd*'s filmography and biography pages for Clive Owen justifies his status as one of the most versatile actors in theater, television, and film.
>
> **WEBSITE**: Italicize the name of a website. Include the name of the author, if it is available. Often the author's name, if included, appears at the end of the source or on another page of the site, such as the home page.
>
> > **Website with an author, and no page numbers**: In the *Internet Encyclopedia of Philosophy*, Keith Seddon draws our attention to six metaphors that the Stoic philosopher Epictetus used to describe the proper attitude toward life.
> >
> > **Website with no named author, and stable page numbers (PDF)**: According to their Code of Ethics, dental hygienists believe that the combination of societal and professional ethics compels them to "engage in health promotion/disease prevention activities" (*The American Dental Hygienists' Association* 30).
> >
> > **One page Web source with no named author**: *Time for Change* states that the production of 1 kg of meat causes about the same quantity of carbon emissions as does the

burning of 6 liters of gasoline. Clearly, we need to think about our eating habits as well as our driving habits if we want to be responsible global citizens.

Same source, with a discretionary page number provided to mark the end of the citation: *Time for Change* states that the production of 1 kg of meat causes about the same quantity of carbon emissions as does the burning of 6 liters of gasoline (1). Clearly, we need to think about our eating habits as well as our driving habits if we want to be responsible global citizens.

Source with no page numbers, and a quotation with approximate location given in text: About a third of the way into her text, Nussbaum notes that "child pageant contestants are not considered to be 'working' children although they receive money and prizes for their performances and practice four hours per week to achieve those goals."

17. Films

It is preferable to refer to the title of the film in your text rather than in a parenthetical reference.

The film *300* provides viewers with both accurate and "Hollywoodized" versions of Spartan life, but the average moviegoer has no way of knowing which version is which.

18. A Television Program

Include the name of the person (actor or director), or the title of the program, or the title of the particular segment, or all three, depending on your focus.

George Clooney, appearing on "Leading American Actors" on *Charlie Rose*, explains his role in the movie *The Good German*, an adaptation of Joseph Kanon's novel about murder, NASA, and Nazi technology following the Second World War.

19. A Personal Interview

The citation usually begins with the name of the person interviewed. The interviewer, if mentioned, comes second.

In an email conversation, George advised caution when presenting alternative understandings of long-standing interpretations.

20. Sound Recording (Tape, Record, or CD)

Include the name of the composer, the work, and if pertinent, the artist. Italicize the title of the work.

Although many artists, including The Beatles, Elvis, and Frank Sinatra, have recorded Consuelo Velazquez's lovely Mexican song, *Besame Mucho*, no one sings it with as much feeling as does the Italian tenor Andrea Bocelli.

Works Cited Format

At the end of your paper, you will need a separate page to list the works that you have cited. The entries in the list must include full publication information about each work. If you want to direct your readers' attention to works that you consulted, but did not cite, use the heading *Works Consulted* and follow the same procedure as you would for a works cited list. You should have complete publication information for each source on the note cards you compiled during your research. Or you might prefer to construct a working bibliography using your word processor to record the publication data for your sources. Below are general guidelines, followed by examples of specific kinds of sources.

- Begin your list on a new page, continuously numbered from your main text. If the last page of your text is numbered 8, the works cited page will be 9. This page number appears in the upper right-hand corner, after your last name, one-half inch from the top and is flush with the right margin (in the same manner as the pages numbers in your text).

- The title of the page, Works Cited, is centered an inch from the top of the page.

- Bottom and side margins are one inch.

- Double space between the title and the first entry.

- Single space after all punctuation.

- Alphabetize your entries by author's last name, or, if a work has no author, by the first word in the title other than *a*, *an*, or *the*. If your title begins with a number, spell out the number.

- Each entry should be flush with the left margin; if the entry requires additional lines, these lines are indented ½ inch from the left margin. The hanging indent feature of your format function in your word processing program will do this for you.

- Double-space the entire list, both between and within entries.

- Italicize titles of books, plays, poems published as books, pamphlets, periodicals, websites, online databases, films, television and radio broadcasts, compacts discs, audiocassettes, record albums, dance performances, and operas and other long musical compositions.

- Use quotation marks for titles of articles, essays, stories and poems published as part of larger works, chapters of books, individual pages in a website, individual episodes of television or radio programs, and short songs. If a work is unpublished, such as a lecture or a speech, use quotation marks.

- Indicate non-continuous page numbers with a plus sign after the first number: 1+.

- When some publication data is missing, indicate it with n. p. for no publisher or place of publication, n. d. for no date, and n. pag. for no pages.

- At the end of the entry, include the medium of publication: print, television, film, etc. If you have a web source, the last element in the entry will be the date you accessed the source.

- End the entry with a period.

- The general format for a source with many elements is as follows: Author. "Title of Article." *Title of Book*. Editor. Edition. Volume. Place of Publication: Publisher name, Date. Pages. Medium of Publication. Date Accessed DD/M/YYYY (if electronic publication).

1.1 A Work by One Author

The following entry is typical for most of the books that you will use. Begin with the author's last name, a comma, and then the first name followed by a period. Give the author's name as it appears on the title page; do not use initials, unless the title page uses them. Next, put the full book title (use a colon between a main title and a subtitle, unless the main title includes its own punctuation), italicized, followed by a period. Finally, enter the city of publication (followed by a colon), the publisher (followed by a comma), and the most recent date of publication (followed by a period). Finish the entry with the medium of publication.

Johnson-Weiner, Karen. *Train Up a Child: Old Order Amish & Mennonite Schools*. Baltimore: Johns Hopkins UP, 2007. Print.

If the publisher has offices in more than one city, use the first city listed. For cities outside the U.S., add the abbreviated form of the country's name if the city alone would be unfamiliar to your readers.

The full name of the publisher, in our example, is The Johns Hopkins University Press. However, on your works cited list, you need only include the key word of the publisher's name, in this case Johns Hopkins, and the abbreviation UP for University Press. If the publisher has two or more names in the title, you only need to provide the first one (for example, Little, Brown may be entered as Little). If the title page lists more than one publisher (as opposed to one publisher with multiple names), include all the names, in the order given, and separate them with semicolons.

Lamont, William P. *Marginal Prynne 1600-1699*. Toronto: U of Toronto P; London: Routledge & Keegan Paul, 1963. Print.

Some publishers group their books under imprints. If the title page of your source includes an imprint, use the imprint and follow it with a hyphen and the name of the publisher. In the following entry, the publisher's name is St. Martin's Press. The imprint is "A Wyatt Book".

Steinberg, Alan. *The Cry of the Leopard*. New York, NY: A Wyatt Book-St. Martin's Press, 1997. Print.

1.2 Two or More Works by the Same Author

When you enter two or more works by the same author, list the author's name for the first entry only; for additional entries, in place of the name, use three em dashes (———) followed by a period. The dashes stand for the name of the previous listing. The titles should appear in alphabetical order, using the first word of the titles other than *a*, *an*, or *the*. Finish the entry with the medium of publication.

Ozment, Steven. *Ancestors*: *The Loving Family in Old Europe*. Cambridge: Harvard UP, 2001. Print.

———. *When Fathers Ruled: Family Life in Reformation Europe*. Cambridge: Harvard UP, 1983. Print.

For university presses, use the abbreviation *UP* as it appears in the name of the university.

1.3 A Work by Two or Three Authors

Name the authors just as they appear on the title page. Reverse the order only of the first author's name. Separate each name from the others by a comma. Finish the entry with the medium of publication.

Clark, Kelly James, Richard Lints, and James K. A. Smith. *101 Key Terms in Philosophy and Their Importance for Theology*. Louisville: Westminster John Knox, 2004. Print.

1.4 A Work by Four or More Authors

Provide the first author's name followed by a comma, then the Latin term et al., for "and others," or list all the names to recognize the contribution of all authors. Finish the entry with the medium of publication.

Boyer, Paul S., et al. *The Enduring Vision: A History of the American People*. Vol. 1: To 1877. Boston: Houghton, 2005. Print.

Boyer, Paul S., Clifford E. Clark, Jr., Joseph F. Kett, Neal Salisbury, Harvard Sitkoff, and Nancy Woloch. *The Enduring Vision: A History of the American People. Vol. 1: To 1877*. Boston: Houghton, 2005. Print.

1.5 A Work with an Editor in the Place of an Author

The format is similar to that of a book with an author, except that you must add a comma after the name and the abbreviation *ed.*, for "editor," or *eds.* for more than one editor. Follow the abbreviation with a period to separate the entry elements. Finish the entry with the medium of publication.

Moore, Lorrie, ed. *The Best American Short Stories 2004*. Boston: Houghton, 2004. Print.

1.6 A Work by a Corporate Author

Give the name of the organization or agency that produced the work. Finish the entry with the medium of publication.

Trout Unlimited Youth. *Youth Education Handbook*. N.p.: Trout Unlimited Youth, n.d. Print.

Note that the corporate author in this example is also the publisher and therefore must be named twice in the entry. Note also that when no place of publication is provided, you indicate the missing information with the abbreviation n.p. (no place). When the date of publication is missing, use n.d. (no date).

1.7 A Work by an Unknown or Anonymous Author

Start with the title. Follow with the rest of the publication data. Finish the entry with the medium of publication.

World Almanac. New York: World Almanac Books, 2001. Print.

Remember that this entry, like all others without authors, must be listed alphabetically according to the first word in the title other than *a*, *an*, or *the*. Thus, the first word is considered *World*.

1.8 A Novel, Play, Poem, or Classical Work

Start with the author's name, followed by the title of the work, the location of the work if part of a larger work, the editor or translator if there is one, the city and publisher of the edition you referenced, and the publication date. Finish the entry with the medium of publication.

Camus, Albert. *The Plague*. Trans. Stuart Gilbert. New York: Vintage-Random, 1991. Print.

Shakespeare, William. *Love's Labor Lost*. In *The Complete Works of William Shakespeare*. Vol. 1. Eds. W. G. Clark, and W. Aldis Wright. Garden City: Nelson, n.d. Print.

Lovelace, Richard. "Song: To Lucasta, Going to the Wars." *The Norton Introduction to Poetry*. Eds. J. Paul Hunter, Alison Booth, and Kelly J. Mays. New York: Norton, 2002.18. Print.

Augustine. *Confessions*. Ed. Betty Radice. Trans. R. S. Pine-Coffin. New York: Penguin, 1961. Print.

New Revised Standard Version. The New Oxford Annotated Bible. Eds. Bruce M. Metzger and Roland E. Murphy. New York: Oxford UP. 1991. Print.

1.9 An Entry in an Encyclopedia or Dictionary

If your source is a widely used reference book, you do not need to give full publication information. Begin the entry with the title of the dictionary or encyclopedia entry, enclosed in quotation marks. Follow with the specific definition you cited, and then title of the reference book, italicized. Include the edition consulted (number and year) and the medium of publication.

> "Rationalism." Def. 2a. *Merriam-Webster's Collegiate Dictionary*. 11th ed. 2004. Print.

If your source is not a widely-used reference book, provide the name of the author of the entry (if known), followed by the title of the entry, enclosed in quotation marks. Follow this with the title of the work, italicized. Give full publication data. You may omit inclusive page numbers if the reference book is arranged alphabetically.

> Westenbroek, Anthony. "Ishmael." *A Dictionary of Biblical Tradition in English Literature*. Ed. David Lyle Jeffery. Grand Rapids: Eerdmans, 1992. Print.

1.10 A Work in an Anthology

Give the author's name, the title of the work, the title of the anthology, and the editor's name preceded by *Ed.* or *Eds.*, with each item followed by a period. Then give the city, publisher, and date. Put the page numbers for the entire piece, not just the material you quoted, at the end of the entry. Finish the entry with the medium of publication.

> Pope, Alexander. "Sound and Sense." *The Norton Introduction to Poetry*. Eds. J. Paul Hunter, Alison Booth, and Kelly J. Mays. New York: Norton, 2002. 195–96. Print.

1.11 An Indirect Source

Start with the name of the author who has done the quoting. Follow with the title of the work in which the quotation appeared. Finish the entry with the medium of publication.

> Cartledge, Paul. *Thermopylae: The Battle That Changed the World*. New York: Overlook, 2006. Print.

1.12 An Entire Work

Provide the author's name, the title of the book, and the other pertinent data.

> Backman, Clifford R. *The Worlds of Medieval Europe*. New York: Oxford UP, 2003. Print.

1.13 A Journal Article

Begin the entry with the author's name, followed by the article title, in quotation marks. The next element is the journal title, italicized (and abbreviated, if the abbreviation is well known). Omit the little words *a*, *an*, and *the* in journal titles. If your source is a journal that has been published in more than one series, write the series number with its ordinal suffix (arabic, even if it appears in roman on the journal [4ᵗʰ]) followed by the abbreviation *ser.* (for series). If your journal is divided into an old series and a new series, indicate the series by using the abbreviation *ns* (new series) or *os* (old series). Then add the volume number (not italicized). Do not use the word *volume* or its abbreviation. Follow the volume number with a period.

Next, provide the issue number (do not use the word *issue* or its abbreviation). If you use a journal that has no volume numbers, just use the issue number. Follow the volume and issue numbers by parentheses that enclose the year of publication. Some journals include a month or season before the year; MLA does not require you to include these, but you may do so if you think that the information will help readers find your source more easily. Include this information within the parentheses, before the year.

Follow the parentheses with a colon. Then, provide the inclusive page numbers for the entire article, not just the page or pages you cited in your in-text reference. If the inclusive numbers are between 1 and 99, give the second number if full (4-16, or 87-98). If the inclusive numbers are larger, use only the last two digits of the last number (125-56). An exception would be if your last number includes one more placeholder than your first number does (956- 1,001). If the article is not printed on consecutive pages (if it skips some pages), write only the first page number and add a plus sign (7+). There is no space between the number and the sign. Finish the element with the medium of publication.

Use this format whether your journal is paginated continuously throughout the year or if each issue begins with page 1.

> Davidson, Bruce W. "The Four Faces of Self-Love in the Theology of Jonathan Edwards." *Journal of Evangelical Theological Society* 51.1 (2008): 87-100. Print.

1.14 An Article in a Monthly or Weekly Magazine

For articles from monthly magazines, list the author, the title of the article, the name of the periodical, the abbreviated month and year of publication, and the page numbers of the article. Do not provide the volume or issue numbers, even if they are listed on the magazine. Finish with the medium of publication.

> Dixit, Jay. "The Candidates Between the Lines." *Psychology Today* (July/Aug. 2007): 74–79. Print.

Note that a colon must be placed after the year and before the page numbers. For articles from weekly periodicals, also provide the complete date of the periodical.

> O'Beirne, Kate. "Animosity and Amnesty." *National Review* (9 July 2007): 18–20. Print.

You can abbreviate all months except for May, June, and July. Omit introductory articles (*A*, *An*, *The*) when you cite the magazine title.

1.15 An Article in a Newspaper

Include the name of the author (if one is given), the title of the article in quotation marks (followed by a period), the name of the newspaper, italicized, followed by the date, without any interrupting punctuation, followed by a colon, followed by the section letter or number (if there is one), and the page number. Finish with the medium of publication.

Landler, Mark. "German Judge Cites Koran, Stirring Up Cultural Storm." *New York Times* 23 Mar. 2007: A10. Print.10.

If no author is given, then begin with the title of the article. Alphabetize the article in the list of works cited according to the first word in the title (other than a, an, or the). Even if the name of the newspaper begins with the word The, do not include it in the newspaper title.

If you are citing a special edition or separately titled section, indicate this between the date and the colon. 2007, late ed., sec. 5:1. Print.

1.16 Electronic Sources, Computer-Accessed Databases, and Internet

The documentation of web-based sources poses several challenges absent from documentation of print sources.

- Electronic texts are updated frequently and irregularly, thus making each viewing potentially different from past and future viewings. This is why MLA requires you to include the date of your access as part of the works cited entry, but does not require the URL. In general, do not include the URL of your source. The exception would be if you think your readers will be unable to locate your source without the URL.

- Many websites are part of larger projects or are sponsored by a parent organization. MLA guidelines show how to record the relation of works on the Web to the information hierarchies surrounding them.

- Many sources do not have the information you are accustomed to supply. MLA style is flexible, allowing for improvisation based on similar print works when necessary. Be sure to be consistent in your improvisation throughout your work.

Below, we have compiled a summary of pertinent citation data for web-based sources, such as books, journals, magazines, newspapers, databases, websites, and blogs. Sample entries for each kind of source follow the summary. For more complete information, consult the seventh edition of the *MLA Handbook for Writers of Research Papers* (2009) or visit the website at www.mla.org.

Pertinent Citation Data:

1. Cite the author, editor, compiler, director, narrator, performer, or translator (if given) of the work you have cited, just as you would for a print source.

2. Follow the author's name with the title of the piece (article, poem, short story, or similar short work) enclosed in quotation marks. If your source is a posting to a discussion list or forum, take the title from the subject line, put it in quotation marks, and follow it with the name of the list or forum.

You may add the descriptor *Online posting*. If your source is an independent work, such as a book, place the title in italics.

3. Optional: You may wish to (but are not required to) include bibliographic information for print or other non-print versions of your source.

4. Include the title of the Internet site (e.g. scholarly project, database, online periodical, or professional or personal site), italicized, or for a professional or personal site with no title, a description such as *Home page*, neither italicized nor enclosed within quotation marks.

5. For online journals, magazines, or newspapers, include the same information you would for a print version of the same source (volume and issue numbers, etc., but drop the medium of original publication).

6. For other online sources, include the date of electronic publication, of the latest update, or of the posting.

7. Include the name of any institution or organization sponsoring the site (if not cited earlier).

8. Indicate the medium of publication consulted (Web).

9. Also include the date when you accessed the source (day, month, year).

Sample Entries:

1. Scholarly project

    Martin, Alphonse, and Robert F. Grady. *The Life of Alphonse Martin, French Canadian, Woodsman: American Life Histories: Manuscripts from the Federal Writers Project, 1936–1940*. Eds. John Lomax, Benjamin A. Botkin, and Martin Royce. 19 Oct 1998. Library of Congress. Web. 14 Aug. 2007.

2. Information Database
    MLA has no specific guidelines for providing a works cited entry for an information database such as *IMBd*. The closest thing to this kind of source is a non-periodical web publication, so you will have to improvise, using that as a guideline. The important thing to remember is to keep this entry keyed to the word used in your in-text citation. Our sample entry below is keyed to our in-text example in section 19, "Database." We have included both the name of the site, italicized (*IMBd*) and the name of publisher or sponsor, not italicized (The Internet Movie Database), following the MLA guidelines for a non-periodical web publication. We added the copyright date found at the bottom of the website, included the medium of publication, and finished the entry with the date we accessed the source.

    IMBd. The Internet Movie Database. 1990-2010. Web. 25 Jan. 2010.

* Note that we used the name of the database as our key word in both the in-text citation and the works cited entry. If, in our text, we had referred to a source within *IMBd* with a specific writer, we would have used that writer's name to begin our works cited entry. Our in-text parenthetical reference would then look like this: (Brumburgh). The corresponding works cited entry is below.

*Brumburgh, Gary. "Biography for Clive Owen." *IMBd*. The Internet Movie Database. 1990-2010. Web. 25 Jan. 2010.

(Note: MLA does provide guidelines for how to cite a periodical publication in a database such as *Project Muse, JSTOR*, or others. See sample entry 8 below.)

3. Personal Site, Blog, or Website
   This is another instance where MLA has no specific guidelines. The most important thing is to use the key word in your in-text reference as the key word for your works cited entry.

Personal Site

Suppose, in your text, you had referred to the 1993 Nobel Chemistry winner, Dr. Kary Banks Mullis, citing a quotation from the home page of his personal website. Your parenthetical reference consisted of just his last name (Mullis). The works cited entry is as follows:

Mullis, Kary Banks. Home Page. 2009. Web. 15 Feb. 2010.

Do not italicize the genre label or enclose it within quotations.

Blog

We have keyed this works cited entry to the example for citing a blog in Section 19 of our in-text citations. We begin the entry with the author's name, followed by the title of particular blog entry consulted. This title is enclosed by quotation marks because it is a small work within a larger work. The title of the blog site itself comes next, in italics, followed by the date the blog entry was created. We indicated the medium of publication (Web) and then added the date we consulted the site. Lastly, we provided the URL, because the site would be difficult to locate without it. Note that the URL is enclosed with angle brackets and followed by a period and begins on a new line to avoid dividing the address. We copied and pasted the URL from the blog site itself to ensure accuracy.

Ayers, Louise. "Heartfelt. " *Child of Grace*. 25 Jan. 2010. Web. 15 Feb. 2010. <http://graciouschild.blogspot./2010.01/heartfelt.html>

Website

These samples are keyed to their counterparts in Section 19.

- Website with an author, no page numbers.

> Seddon, Keith H. "Epictetus (55-135 CE)." *Internet Encyclopedia of Philosophy*. IEP. Eds. James Fieser and Bradley Dowden. 11 July 2005. Web. 25 Jan. 2010.

Note that this entry has an author's name, an article title, the title of larger work in which the article appears, the name of the sponsoring organization of the website, the names of the editors of the larger work, the date of the most recent update, the medium of publication, and the date accessed.

- Website with no named author and stable page numbers (a PDF).

> American Dental Hygienists' Association. "Code of Ethics." *American Dental Hygienists' Association* 22 June 2009: 1-35. ADHA. Web. 25 Jan. 2010.

Note that this entry has an organization as author, followed by the title of the work cited, followed by the name of the website and a date. This date is the date provided by the website, indicating when the ADHA adopted the Code of Ethics. It serves as a date of publication, followed by the inclusive page numbers (in the same manner as an article in a journal, magazine, or newspaper). Next we included the name of the sponsoring organization of the website (in the same manner as an online database such as *Project Muse*, see below, but without italicizing it, in keeping with the guidelines for using roman print for the names of sponsoring organizations). We followed the sponsor's name with the medium of publication and the date we accessed the source.

- One page web source with no named author.

> Time for Change. "Eat Less Meat." *Time for Change*. Time for Change. Web. 25 Jan. 2010.

This entry also has an organization as author. That same organization is the name of both the website and the sponsoring organization. The website did not include any dates, so the only date included in the works cited entry is our date of access.

4. Book

> Austen, Jane. *Sense and Sensibility*. (Gutenberg text) 1811. Online Books by Jane Austen: TheOnline Books Page. Ed. John Mark Ockerbloom. 2007. U Penn. Web. 20 Aug. 2007.

5. Poem

> Lovelace, Richard. "To Lucasta, Going to the Wars." *The Oxford Book of English Verse; 1250–1900*. Ed. Arthur Quiller-Couch. 1919. Bartleby.com. Great Books Online. 2006. Web.14 Aug. 2007.

6. Article in a Journal

> Lathby, Roger. "The Avaricious and the Intransigent: A Match Made in London." *English Matters* 8 (2004) Web. 14 Aug. 2007.

7. Article in a Magazine

> Thomas, Evan, and John Barry. "Can IEDs Be Defeated?" *Newsweek Daily Edition*. 14 Aug. 2007. Web. 14 Aug. 2007.

8. Work from a Library Subscription Service or an Online Database

> Romano, Carlin. "God before Food: Philosophy, Russian Style." *Chronicle of Higher Education* (14 Aug. 2007). Lincoln Trail College Online Subscription Service. Robinson, IL. Web. 14 Aug. 2007.

> Pewewardy, Cornel. "From Subhuman to Superhuman: Images of First Nations Peoples in Comic Books." *Simile 2.2* (May 2002): n. pag. *Academic Search Complete*. Web. 2 Nov. 2009.

9. Work from a Personal Subscription Service

> Cunningham, David. "Answering the Question: What is to be Done? (education)." *Radical Philosophy* 141 (Jan./Feb. 2007) link2subscriptions.co.uk.2007. Web. 14 Aug. 2007.

10. Posting to a Discussion List

> Hebblethwaite, Antony. "The Good . . . . in the Good, the Evil and the Indifferent." *The International Stoic Forum*. Online posting. 12 Aug. 2007. The International Stoic Forum. Web. 14 Aug. 2007.

11. Material from a CD-ROM

If you have accessed material published on CD-ROM, use the following format with material from a periodically published database. Include the author's name (if available), publication information (title and date), database title (italicized), the word "CD-ROM," name of vendor, and the date of electronic publication.

> United States. Dept. of State. "Introduction to the Country Reports on Human Rights Practices for the Year 2002." *Country Reports on Human Rights Practices 2002*. CD-ROM Bureau of Democracy, Human Rights and Labor. Mar. 2002.

For a non-periodically published database, cite the material as you would for any non-periodical, but add the publication medium. As with any printed citation, you need to italicize or use quotations when necessary.

Merriam-Webster's Collegiate Dictionary. 11th ed. v.3.1. Springfield, MA: Merriam-Webster. 2004. CD-ROM.

When you cite a part of a work, always indicate which part.

"Nonessential." *Merriam-Webster's Collegiate Dictionary* 11th ed. v.3.1. Springfield, MA: Merriam-Webster. 2004. CD-ROM.

1.17 Films

In general, state the title first, followed by *Dir.* (for "directed by") and the director's name, the distributor, and the year. End the entry with the medium of publication. This reference should appear, neither underlined nor enclosed in quotation marks, at the end of the entry.

300. Dir. Zack Synder. Warner Brothers Pictures, 2007. Film.

Alphabetize as though the number is spelled. You may provide other information, such as the names of leading actors, after the director. Indicate their function with appropriate descriptors.

Cite a DVD, videocassette, laser disc, slide program, or filmstrip in the same manner. Include the original release date. Be sure to indicate the medium of publication.

Harvey. Dir. Henry Koster. Perf. James Stewart, Josephine Hull, and Jesse White. Universal Studios, 1950. DVD.

1.18 A Television Program

Enter the name of the particular segment or episode (in quotation marks), the title of the program (italicized), the network, the local station, the city, and the broadcast date. Include the medium of reception.

"Leading American Actors." *Charlie Rose.* PBS/13WNET. WNPE/WNPI, Watertown/Norwood. 21 Dec. 2006. Television.

Alphabetize the program in the works cited list according to the first word (other than *a*, *an*, or *the*) of the title. In this case, the first word is *Leading*.

1.19 Public or Personal Interview

For a public interview (either published or broadcast), start with the name of the person interviewed. Follow that with title of the interview, enclosed with quotation marks, if the interview was part of a larger publication or broadcast. If the interview was published or broadcast independently, place the title in italics. If the interview has no title, use the descriptor, *Interview*, neither italicized nor enclosed within quotation marks. Add the interviewer's name if known and if pertinent to your paper. Conclude the entry with the appropriate bibliographic material and the medium of publication.

Clooney, George. "Leading American Actors." *Charlie Rose.* PBS/13WNET. WNPE/WNPI, Watertown/ Norwood. 21 Dec. 2006. Television.

White, Shaun. Interview by Pat Bridges. "Revived Shaun White Interview." *Snowboarder Magazine.* 2009. Web. 16 Feb. 2010.

Patterson, David. Interview by Bethany Baxter. "Chestnut Memories: Oral History Transcript." University of Tennessee at Chattanooga. 22 July 2008. Print.

For a private interview, one that you conducted, give the name of the person interviewed, the kind of interview (personal interview), the medium of the interview (telephone interview, letter interview, etc.), and the date.

George, Gary. Personal interview by email. 4 Aug. 2007.

1.20 Sound Recording (Tape, Record, or CD)

The name of the composer, conductor, ensemble, or performer will be first. Be sure that the name matches the one in your in-text citation. Next, list the song title, enclosed in quotation marks, followed by the title (italicized) of the recording. If you are citing the entire album or body of work, just include the title, italicized. Follow this with the name of the artist or artists if different from the first element in your entry, the manufacturer, and the year of issue. If you do not know the year of issue, write n.d. (no date). Indicate the medium.

Velazquez, Consuelo. "Besame Mucho." Perf. Andrea Bocelli. *Amore.* Universal Music Classics Group, 2006. CD.

1.21 Graphic Novel

If the graphic novel is the work of one person who is both author and illustrator, format the entry as you would for a single author book.

Tooks, Lance. *Narcissa.* New York: Doubleday Graphic Novels-Random House, 2002. Print.

Many graphic novels are the result of collaboration. Begin the works cited entry with the name of the person whose work is most salient to your research, making sure that this name also is the one included in your in-text citation. Indicate what function this person serves: writer, illustrator, etc. List the other collaborators and indicate their roles after you list the italicized title of the work. Include the place of publication, the name of the publisher, the date of publication, and finish the entry with the medium of publication.

Mariotte, Jeff, writer. *Desperadoes: Buffalo Dreams.* 10th ed. Art and Cover by Alberto Dose. San Diego: IDW, 2007. Print.

1.22 Manuscript or Typescript

On occasion, you may cite from unpublished print material, such as a manuscript (handwritten) or a type-script (produced by a typewriter or a word processor). To cite such a work, state the author, the title, or, if the work is untitled, a description of the material (e.g., *Notebook, Handout, Lecture Notes,* etc.), the date of composition (or as much as is known or N.d. for no date if you have no information), and the form of the material—MS for manuscript, TS for typescript. You may also include the source that housed the material, such as the library, research institution, or personal collection, if that information is relevant.

> Krieger, Barbara Jo, Paul G. Saint-Amand, Warren A. Neal, and Alan L. Steinberg. *Inquiry, Argument, & Change: A Rhetoric with Readings.* Pre-print edition. Dubuque, IA: Kendall Hunt, 2005. TS.

Sample Works Cited Page

Below is a sample Works Cited list that would come at the end of a research paper. We have used the references discussed in the preceding two sections. Carefully examine the format for each entry. Pay close attention to particulars such as spacing and punctuation. On the Works Cited page, it is essential to attend to details. Many instructors will penalize you for errors—even in seemingly minor areas such as indenting, spacing, and punctuation—just as they would for sentence errors in your text. Be sure that your name and a page number appear in the upper right hand corner.

Name 16

Works Cited

Augustine. *Confessions.* Ed. Betty Radice. Trans. R. S. Pine-Coffin. New York: Penguin, 1961. Print.

Austen, Jane. *Sense and Sensibility.* (Gutenberg text) 1811. Online Books by Jane Austen: The Online Books Page. Ed. John Mark Ockerbloom. 2007. U Penn. Web. 20 Aug. 2007.

Ayers, Louise. "Heartfelt." *Child of Grace.* 25 Jan. 2010. Web. 15 Feb. 2010. <http://graciouschild.blogspot.com/ 2010/01/heartfelt.html>.

Backman, Clifford R. *The Worlds of Medieval Europe.* New York: Oxford UP, 2003. Print.

Boyer, Paul S., et al. *The Enduring Vision: A History of the American People. Vol. 1: To 1877.* Boston: Houghton, 2005. Print.

Cartledge, Paul. *Thermopylae: The Battle That Changed the World.* New York: Overlook, 2006. Print.

Clark, Kelly James, Richard Lints, and James K. A. Smith. *101 Key Terms in Philosophy and Their Importance for Theology.* Louisville: Westminster John Knox, 2004. Print.

Cunningham, David. "Answering the Question: What is to be Done? (education)." *Radical Philosophy* 141 (Jan./Feb. 2007) link2subscriptions.co.uk.2007. Web. 14 Aug. 2007.

Dixit, Jay. "The Candidates Between the Lines." *Psychology Today* (July/Aug. 2007): 74–79. Print.

George, Gary. Personal interview by email. 4 Aug. 2007.

Hebblethwaite, Antony. "The Good . . . . in the Good, the Evil and the Indifferent." *The International Stoic Forum*. Online posting. 12 Aug. 2007. The International Stoic Forum. Web. 14 Aug. 2007.

IMBd. The Internet Movie Database. 1990-2010. Web. 25 Jan. 2010.

Johnson-Weiner, Karen. *Train Up a Child: Old Order Amish & Mennonite Schools*. Baltimore: Johns Hopkins UP, 2007. Print.

Landler, Mark. "German Judge Cites Koran, Stirring Up Cultural Storm." *New York Times* 23 Mar. 2007: A10. Print.

Lathby, Roger. "The Avaricious and the Intransigent: A Match Made in London." *English Matters* 8 (2004) Web.14 Aug. 2007.

"Leading American Actors." *Charlie Rose*. PBS/13WNET. WNPE/WNPI. Watertown/Norwood. 21 Dec. 2006. Television.

Lovelace, Richard. "Song: To Lucasta, Going to the Wars." *The Norton Introduction to Poetry*. Eds. J. Paul Hunter, Alison Booth, and Kelly J. Mays. New York: Norton, 2002.18. Print.

———."To Lucasta, Going to the Wars." *The Oxford Book of English Verse*; 1250–1900. Ed. Arthur Quiller-Couch. 1919. Bartleby.com. Great Books Online. 2006. Web. 14 Aug. 2007.

Martin, Alphonse, and Robert F. Grady. *The Life of Alphonse Martin, French Canadian, Woodsman. American Life Histories: Manuscripts from the Federal Writers Project, 1936–1940*. Eds. John Lomax, Benjamin A. Botkin, and Martin Royce. 19 Oct. 1998. Library of Congress. Web.14 Aug. 2007.

Moore, Lorrie, ed. *The Best American Short Stories 2004*. Boston: Houghton, 2004. Print.

Mullis, Kary Banks. Home page. 2009. Web. 15 Feb. 2010.

New Revised Standard Version. The New Oxford Annotated Bible. Eds. Bruce M. Metzger and Roland E. Murphy. New York: Oxford UP, 1991. Print.

"Nonessential.". *Merriam-Webster's Collegiate Dictionary* 11th ed. v.3.1. Springfield, MA: Merriam-Webster, 2004. CD-ROM.

O' Beirne, Kate. "Animosity and Amnesty." *National Review* (9 July 2007): 18–20. Print.

Ozment, Steven. Ancestors: *The Loving Family in Old Europe*. Cambridge: Harvard UP, 2001. Print.

———. *When Fathers Ruled: Family Life in Reformation Europe*. Cambridge: Harvard UP, 1983. Print.

Pope, Alexander. "Sound and Sense." *The Norton Introduction to Poetry*. Eds. J. Paul Hunter, Alison Booth, and Kelly J. Mays. New York: Norton, 2002. 195–96. Print.

Romano, Carlin. "God before Food: Philosophy, Russian Style." *Chronicle of Higher Education* (14 Aug. 2007). Lincoln Trail College Online Subscription Service. Robinson, IL. Web. 14 Aug. 2007.

Shakespeare, William. *Love's Labor Lost*. In *The Complete Works of William Shakespeare*. Vol. 1. Eds. W. G. Clark, and W. Aldis Wright. Garden City: Nelson, n.d. Print.

Thomas, Evan, and John Barry. "Can IEDs Be Defeated?" *Newsweek Daily Edition*. 14 Aug. 2007. Web.14 Aug. 2007. <http://www.msnbc.msn.com/id/ 3032542/ site/newsweek/>.

300. Dir. Zack Synder. Warner Brothers Pictures, 2007. Film.

Trout Unlimited Youth. *Youth Education Handbook*. N.p.: Trout Unlimited Youth, n.d. Print.

United States. Dept. of State. "Introduction to the Country Reports on Human Rights Practices for the Year 2002." *Country Reports on Human Rights Practices 2002*. Bureau of Democracy, Human Rights and Labor. March 2002. CD-ROM.

Velazquez, Consuelo."Besame Mucho." Perf. Andrea Bocelli, *Amore*. Universal Music Classics Group. 2006. CD.

World Almanac. New York: World Almanac Books, 2001. Print.

Sample Research Paper

Chapter 15 closes with a sample research paper that employs the MLA System of documentation. The paper by Tierney Jayne examines the phenomenon of sexual abuse, specifically the popularization of incest as a thematic concern in contemporary American fiction. Using the results of research in the social sciences in her critical reading of several authors, Tierney argues that neither our growing awareness of the extent of sexual abuse in our society nor our insights into its perpetrators and victims will easily overcome the pervasive silence surrounding the problem. Tierney suggests that writers must continue to explore such material, not as a response to public tastes, but to help us break free from misinformation about the damage that incest causes. Her work is a good example of a research-based argument.

The paper is annotated to highlight both the way in which the writer used source materials and the methods she used for documentation. Tierney wrote this paper while she was a student at SUNY Potsdam. The paper has been updated to show the latest version of the MLA style of documentation.

RESEARCH PAPER USING MLA DOCUMENTATION

Cover Page

1. Here Tierney centers her title approximately one-third down the cover page. She skips four lines and centers the preposition "by," skips two more lines and centers her name.

1.

Writing on the Wounds:
Incest in Contemporary American Fiction
(Abridged)

by

Tierney Jayne

2. Tierney skips ten lines and centers the course title and section. She follows with her instructor's name and the submission date.

2.

Directed Writing, Section 001
Professor Saint-Amand
28 November 2007

First Page without Cover Page

3. Here Tierney places her last name and the page number flush with right margin, one-half inch from the top. Next she places her full name, instructor's name, course title and section, and submission date one inch from the top and flush with the left margin. She then double spaces and centers her title, and again double spaces and begins her introduction.

4. Author and page reference, both in parentheses, follow the paraphrase; then comes the period.

5. Author's name and page reference, both in parentheses, follow the quotation; then comes the period. As with the preceding citation, naming the author in the parenthetical emphasizes the information instead of the author. Note throughout the paper that Tierney incorporates the author's name into her sentence when she wants to accentuate the authority of her source.

3.

1"

½"

Jayne 1

Tierney Jayne

Professor Saint-Amand

Directed Writing. Section 001

28 November 2007

Writing on the Wounds:

Incest in Contemporary American Fiction

(Abridged)

In 1985, while interviewing an adult survivor of sexual abuse, talk show host Oprah Winfrey found herself admitting that the same thing had happened to her (Darnton 72). The subsequent flurry of personal narratives, self-help books, television dramas, and movies were certainly not a result of Winfrey's confession, but they seemed to explode into American consciousness at about the same time. This public exposure has ushered in a popular set of conceptions and misconceptions about the enigma called incest.

4.

1"

1"

The ensuing twenty years or so have seen a dramatic increase in public awareness about the occurrence of incest in American society. Researchers are conducting more comprehensive studies on the complexities of "the family secret." Psychologists are educating themselves on the specialized needs of sexual abuse victims. Survivors not only are talking openly about their experiences, but also are seeking legal action against the perpetrators. These victims are demanding changes in a judicial system that, until recently, ignored them entirely. No longer a dreadful secret, "breaking the ancient taboo against incest is now recognized as a fact of life across America" (Darnton 70).

5.

The silence surrounding incest has been lifted. Nowhere is this more apparent than on today's bestseller list. Incest has

1"

become, for better or worse, a marketable tragedy; people may still shun it, but they clearly are not opposed to reading about it. From Alice Walker to Stephen King, American writers are exploring the last formidable taboo, and, undoubtedly, also making a profit from this incursion. One critic writes the following about this obsession:

> In just a few years, a ghastly trauma of childhood has been turned into an all-purpose literary ingredient, the Cool Whip of serious fiction. Editors and agents who track new fiction are encountering incest everywhere they look. "I cannot deal with it anymore," says a magazine book-review editor. "I'm not shocked by it. I'm bored. It's not a riveting plot device. There's something opportunistic about it."(Shapiro 66)

If editors and reviewers have had their fill, can the public be far behind? What effect will the waning interest in the crime have for its survivors when the public has moved on to another social enigma? Will these survivors be forced back into their silences?

Because incest involves secrets, exposing these concealed abuses in print may do more harm than good. Why would anyone choose to write about such a deplorable topic, one might ask? Before judging an author's motivations, we must have a clear understanding of what can be called "incest fiction," and explore how this genre treats its subject. Toni Morrison's *The Bluest Eye*, Stephen King's *Gerald's Game*, Dorothy Allison's *Bastard Out of Carolina*, and Jane Smiley's *A Thousand Acres* represent some of the best examples of this type of fiction. Looking closely at each of these works may give insight into their appeal for readers and could help determine both the merits and hazards.

Toni Morrison published *The Bluest Eye* in 1970, long before the current interest in incest fiction began. Psychologists

6. Note that block quotations are indented ten spaces or one-inch from the left margin in MLA style.

7. Though quotation marks are not used for the block quotation, they are inserted for any quoted material within the quotation.

8. Author and page reference, both in parentheses, appear outside the end punctuation mark.

6.

7.

8.

Jayne 3

were only just beginning to understand the implications of childhood sexual abuse. However, Morrison's work deserves examination, primarily because her work reveals several dangerous myths about incest.

The Bluest Eye is the story of eleven-year-old African-American Pecola Breedlove, who lives in poverty with her neglectful mother, an alcoholic father, and a brother, Sammy. Pecola's world is horrific, but she firmly believes that all would be different if she had blue eyes like the little white girls everyone admires. If she had blue eyes, she thinks, her family would love her.

The only person who shows her any affection at all is her father, who rapes her. He transforms the tenderness he feels for her into a brutal act of violence, the only kind of act he knows. Cholly's sexual violence is a mixture of love for his child and hatred of his own inability to rise above his social deprivation. His self-deprecation prevents him from displaying any kindness toward Pecola, yet he feels a strange empathy for her, an empathy that can only transform itself into a vengeful mixture of confusion and caring, passion and anger, a violation against his own flesh and blood. Morrison writes:

> The confused mixture of his memories of Pauline [his wife] and the doing of a wild and forbidden thing excited him, . . . Surrounding all this desire was a border of politeness. He wanted to fuck her – tenderly. But the tenderness would not hold. . . . (128)

Morrison's social themes are always played against the personal, the individual's experience. As one critic writes, "Never is history faceless, never are individuals absolved from responsibility for their own actions" (Gates, Jr. ix). While Pecola's history is one of growing abuse and loss of her own identity, Morrison's *The Bluest Eye* is intended to explore larger social conflicts, specifically, racial prejudice in America. Incest is only

9. Author is named in the introduction to block quotation.

9.

10. No quotation marks for block quotation. Note that Tierney uses an ellipsis to show deleted words directly following an internal punctuation mark, in this case, a comma, which she retains.

10.

11. Tierney places a period at the end of the block quotation followed by an ellipsis to show that words have been deleted; then comes the page reference, in parentheses.

11.

12. Author's name and page reference, both in parentheses, follow the quotation; then comes the period. As with earlier

12.

citations, naming the author in the parenthetical citation emphasizes the information instead of the author. If Tierney had wanted to emphasize the author, she would have identified him in the introduction to her quotation.

13. Author is named in the introduction to establish the credibility of the quotation. The ellipsis of four periods in the middle of the quotation indicates that the deletion spans at least one sentence. Page reference follows the quotation; then comes the period.

13.

14. Author's name and page reference follow the paraphrase.

14.

a small part of *The Bluest Eye*: still, it figures prominently in the life of her character and cannot be treated lightly. Morrison's characterization perpetuates, perhaps inadvertently, several myths about incest survivors that demand closer scrutiny.

First, the work reinforces the myth that incest is more common to the lower socio-economic classes such as Pecola's family, a fallacious notion. As early as 1983, David Finkelhor and his fellow researchers "consistently failed to find any black-white differences in rates of sexual abuse. . . . Among reported cases, sexual abuse has consistently been the type of abuse in which blacks have the lowest representation" (69-70).

Of course, readers cannot fault a black author for dealing with black issues. Pecola is black and she does get raped by her father, but these facts are not assuredly related. Even so, a cursory look at other fiction writers—Barbara Kingsolver's *The Bean Trees* (1988) and Alice Walker's *The Color Purple* (1982)—reveal that their stories invariably involve members of minority or lower socio-economic classes. And yet, available research suggests that incest does not discriminate; it is not dependent on ethnicity or social status. Sexual abuse occurs across the social stratum (Meiselman 15).

Another myth promoted in *The Bluest Eye* (1970) suggests that incest only occurs between fathers and daughters. In most stories involving incest on the current market, father-daughter (or stepfather-stepdaughter) incest predominates. While the Finkelhor study indicates that this is the most common form of abuse, it is by no means the only form. Brother-sister abuse is sometimes fictionalized, although usually depicted humorously or sentimentally, as in John Irving's *The Hotel New Hampshire* (1981). Few books depict mother-son, uncle-niece or -nephew, or grandparent-grandchild incest. Though these types of incest do occur, they are rarely depicted in our contemporary fiction.

The final myth—that incest must always be depicted as an act of brutality—understandably goes unexamined in contemporary fiction and is not substantiated by current studies. Diana

E. H. Russell, a leading incest researcher, conducted a study of 930 women in San Francisco and found that 68 percent of the incest cases did not involve physical force. Other researchers found that only 1 percent of incest cases documented the use of severe force (Christiansen and Blake 88). . . .

15. Source authors and page reference, both in parentheses, follow the paraphrase.

The nature of sexual abuse is rooted in betrayal. Children who are victimized by adults learn quickly not to trust anyone. This concept is evident in *Bastard Out of Carolina*, by Dorothy Allison. Allison is a survivor herself; that makes her book unique. Few survivors are willing to write about their experiences in a form riddled with the possibility of misinterpretation or undeserved judgments. Allison is a refreshing and welcomed voice. Yet, even she cannot avoid the mythic pitfall as Randall Kenan comments:

16. Author appears within the text introducing the block quotation.

17. No quotation marks for block quotation. Note the ellipsis showing that words have been deleted from the middle of the quotation. Also note that brackets have been used to insert a clarifying reference followed by an ellipsis to indicate a deletion. As with other block quotations, page reference, in parentheses, appears outside the end punctuation mark.

> The stereotype of poor white trash: liquored-up, malevolent, unemployed, undereducated, country-music-listening, oversexed, foul-tempered men; and long-suffering, quickly aging, overly fertile, too-young-marrying, hard-headed women. Of course, all stereotypes derive from some root of truth. . .but [Allison]. . .seems to trust too often that we will see the charm, the hard faith, and rationale with which these folks operate and which operates them. (815)

The myths in Allison's *Bastard*, however, dissipate in the face of the lyrical beauty of her protagonist's story. Bone is truly a survivor: she denies, she weeps, she blames herself, she gets angry at her rapist. She ultimately goes on. Surviving "is a remarkable achievement" (14), explains researcher Ellen Russell, for survivors successfully avoid either institutionalization or premature death.

18. The direct quotation is followed by a parenthetical page reference. Tierney has attributed the quotation to its author within the text of her paper.

In an interview with Carolyn Megan, Allison revealed her creative process and, perhaps inadvertently, how close her protagonist's situation was to her own. Then asked about the role

19. Author is named within the text introducing the brief quotation. Tierney begins with square brackets to indicate change in letter from upper- to lowercase.   **19.**

20. Since the paper includes two works by the same author, Tierney lists the source and page number, both in parentheses, followed by a period.   **20.**
21.

21. Author is named within the text introducing the block quotation.   **22.**

22. No quotation marks for block quotation. The ellipsis of four periods in the middle of the quotation indicates that the deletion spans at least one sentence. Square brackets are used to add a clarifying reference.

23. As always with a block quotation, the parenthetical citation appears outside the end punctuation mark.   **23.**

24. Though quotation marks are not used for block quotation, they are inserted for any dialogue appearing within the block. Note the first ellipsis indicating deleted words directly following an internal punctuation mark, which is retained. Then note the second ellipsis of four periods indicating a deletion spanning at least one sentence.   **24.**

---

of story-telling in Bone's life, especially when Bone envisions a scene in which she forgives her father before she suddenly dies, Allison comments that "[i]t becomes a technique whereby she retains a sense of power in a situation where she has none. And comfort, just sheer physical comfort of retelling herself the story in which she is not the victim" (Interview 72). Asked if Allison's own writing has saved her as well, the author replies,

> Oh, absolutely. It became the way out of an enormous amount of guilt. It became the way I figured things out. . . .Bone is moving towards a kind of truth, and that's real important. She's caught in a network of lies and misrepresentation. All those things she is being told about herself by Daddy Glen [her father] are horrible. And she takes those things, and we watch it have an impact on her. The only thing that saves her are the stories, the ones that she needs to make for herself. (Interview 73)

Allison seems to understand first-hand the escape techniques of a sexual abuse victim. Retaining the illusion of control allows a victim to maintain sanity in a confusing, unstable set of relationships whose driving forces children cannot fully comprehend. Bone's sexual encounters with her father explicitly detail these terrifying confusions, mixing love and hate.

> If I went home when he was there and Mama wasn't, he was always finding something I'd done, something I had to be told, something he had to do because he loved me. And he did love me. He told me so over and over again, holding my body tight to his, . . ."you're just like your mama." he'd say, and press his stubbly cheek to mine. . . . I would stand rigid unable to pull away, afraid of making him angry, afraid of what he might tell Mama, and at the same time, afraid of hurting his

feelings. "Daddy," I would start to whisper, and he would whisper back, "Don't you know how much I love you?" And I would recoil. No, I did not know. (Allison, *Bastard* 108)

Allison's work sharply contrasts with Jane Bailey's Pulitzer-Prize winning novel *A Thousand Acres*. The major myths and stereotypes are not to be found in Bailey's book. The perpetrator is a well-respected Iowa farmer, not "the type." (Experts dispel the myth that any one, single "type" exists.) The story's narrator, Ginny, an adult survivor, only realizes the history of her abuse half way through telling the story. Fleetingly, her memories of her father's abuse surface in the simple acts of everyday living. Ginny tells of pulling down bedsheets in her father's farmhouse and as she lay down, ordinary details of this room – the position of the bedtable, the peeling yellow paint on a chest of drawers, brown-stained reflections in the mirror – all converge in a sudden appalling revelation:

> Lying here, I know that he had been in there to me, that my father had lain with me on that bed, that I had looked at the top of his head, at his balding spot in the brown grizzled hair, while feeling him suck my breasts. That was the only memory I could endure before I jumped out of bed with a cry. (Smiley 228)

Recently, psychologists have begun to dispute the kind of repressed memory incidents Smiley describes. Some, like Sigmund Freud, have long claimed that these memories are merely fantasies (Meiselman 9) or that therapists may lead clients to remember things that never really took place. "False Memory Syndrome," as it's popularly labeled, has sparked controversy in the therapeutic and legal communities over the last few years. However, evidence indicates that some survivors do not recollect their abuse for years after it has occurred (Bass, *Beginning* 5). To deflect their emotional pain, survivors will

---

25. Citing a second work by the same author, Tierney lists the author, an abbreviated title, and the page reference, all in parentheses, outside the end punctuation mark.

25.

26. Note how the parentheses let the writer interrupt the central discussion to add information.

26.

27. No quotation marks for block quotation.

27.

28. Author and page reference, both in parentheses, appear outside the end punctuation mark.

28.

29. Author's name and page reference follow the paraphrase.

29.

30. Since the paper includes two works by this author, author's name, abbreviated title, and page reference all appear in parentheses, followed by a period.

30.

psychologically block the memory from intruding into their present lives. But eventually, the images surface, and when they do, the survivor often has to confront those repressed emotions alone with a raw, uncontrollable fear shaking their mental stability. Ginny, Smiley's narrator, describes her own emotional upheaval and loss of control. Smiley writes,

> Behind that one image bulked others, mysterious bulging items in a dark sack, unseen as yet, but felt. I feared them. I feared how I would have to store them in my brain, plastic explosives on radioactive wastes that would mutate or even wipe out every-thing else in there. . . .So I screamed. I screamed in a way that I had never screamed before, full out, throat-wrenching, unafraid-of-making-a-fuss-and-drawing-attention-to myself sorts of screams that I made myself concentrate on, becoming all mouth, all tongue, all vibration. (229)

Ginny's memories are real, but are dismissed by relatives and friends who cannot fathom that a pillar of this Iowa farm community would violate basic moral codes. The community accuses Ginny and her younger sister Rose of slander against a perpetrator who is suddenly cast in the role of victim himself. Together, Ginny and Rose must weather these admonitions, and draw strength from their own truth, Ginny narrates their struggle:

> "I didn't even get Daddy to know what he'd done, or what it meant. People around town talk about how I wrecked it all. Three generations on the same farm, great land. Daddy's a marvelous farmer, a saint to boot," [Rose]. . .used my hand to pull herself up in the bed. "So all I have is the knowledge that I saw! That I saw without being afraid and without turning away, and that I didn't forgive the unforgivable. Forgiveness is a reflex for

31. Author is named in the introduction to block quotation.

32. No quotation marks for block quotation. Note the ellipsis of four periods in the middle of the quote indicating a deletion spanning at least one sentence.

33. The page number, in parentheses, appears outside the end punctua-tion mark.

34. Though quotation marks are not used for a block quotation, they are inserted for direct speech appearing within the block. Note that square brackets are used to add a clarifying reference followed by an ellipsis to indicate a deletion.

31.

32.

33.

34.

Jayne 9

when you can't stand what you know, I resisted
that reflex. That's my sole, solitary, lonely accomplishment." (Smiley 355-56)

35. Author's name and page reference, both in parentheses, appear outside the end punctuation mark.

35.

The incest victims in *A Thousand Acres* are not stereotyped
as "poor trash," poverty-stricken, or impoverished members
of a minority group: they are typical, middle-class girls. They
dutifully care for their father even after realizing what he has
done to them. In creating these strong women, Smiley has accomplished what other incest fiction has failed to do: she has
given the reader a sense of realism; she has molded characters
who can face the pain of incest without being subsumed by its
horror.

While all the stories discussed could easily teeter toward
sensationalism, none treat incest as a riveting plot device, a
way to keep a reader's interest. Each author treats the act of
incest as the tragedy it indeed is. Unfortunately, these books
are exceptions. Most sexual abuse accounts use incest as an
additive to increase marketability. Using incest to inflame such
tiresome and often paltry plots trivializes the acute suffering
most survivors endure.

When writing about incest, authors must struggle to avoid
perpetuation of damaging myths and stereotypes. Sexual abuse
does not lend itself to fiction; it is a complex and virtually
unsolvable problem. Incest survivors carry the burden of their
secrets around with them for a lifetime, and authors must realize this *before* putting pen to paper. Some social issues seem
almost made for literature—homelessness, drug abuse, and
racism—but a realistic resolution of a conflict involving incest is
often impossible to depict. While therapy can help resolve the
trauma, actual therapy sessions are not, in themselves, fast-
paced or capable of sustaining a reader's attention.

Until the late 1970s, incest had been shrouded in silence.
While breaking this silence through fiction is vital, writers have
an obligation to treat their subject matter with intelligence and

dignity. If they use this trauma simply to increase sales, they are selling someone else's pain and writing on wounds that will never heal.

Works Consulted

Heading centered one inch from the top of page. Title *Works Consulted* indicates the writer has listed sources not cited in her paper. Entries are double space, and alphabetized according to the last name of first author.

1, 9, 12, 14, 15, 16, 17, 19, 23, 24: format for work by one author (p. 485).

2, 21, 23 format for two works by same author (p. 486) 2: also format for interview in quarterly journal.

3: format for book review in an electronic version of a scholarly journal.

4: format for an electronic version of an abstract of a printed journal article.

5: format for introduction written by one editor of an edited book.

6: format for work by two or three authors (p. 486).

7: format for work in an anthology (p. 488).

8, 10, 20, 21: format for an online version of a printed weekly magazine (p. 494).

1. Allison, Dorothy. *Bastard Out of Carolina*. New York: NAL/ Dutton, 1992. Print.

2. ———. Interview with Carolyn Megan. "Moving Toward Truth." *Kenyon Review* Fall 1994: 71-83. Print.

3. Armstrong, Louise. Rev. of *The Secret Trauma: Incest in the Lives of Girls and Women* (Revised edition) by Diana Russell. *Women's Studies* 30.3 (June 2001): 399-402. *Academic Search Premier*. Web. 21 Oct. 2007.

4. Atwood, Joan D. "When Love Hurts: Preadolescent Girls' Reports of Incest." *Journal of Family Therapy* 35.4 (July 2007), Abstract, *Academic Search Premier*. Web. 21 Oct. 2007.

5. Bass, Ellen. Introduction. *I Never Told Anyone: Writing by Women Survivors of Child Abuse*. Eds. Ellen Bass and Louise Thornton. New York: Harper Collins, 1991. 30-38. Print.

6. ——— and Laura Davis. *Beginning to Heal: A First Book for Survivors of Child Sexual Abuse*. New York: HarperCollins, 1993. Print.

7. Christiansen, John R. and Reed H. Blake. "The Grooming Process in Father-Daughter Incest." *The Incest Perpetrator*. Ed. Anne L. Norton et al. Newbury Park: Sage, 1990. 88-98. Print.

8. Darnton, Nina. "The Pain of the Last Taboo." *Newsweek*. Newsweek, 7 Oct. 1991: 70-72. Web. 23 Aug. 2007.

9. Finkelhor, David. *Sourcebook on Child Sexual Abuse*. Beverly Hills: Sage, 1986. Print.

Jayne 11

10.   Gates, David. "Our Number One Fan Strikes Again." *Newsweek*. Newsweek, 6 July 1992. Web. 23 Aug. 2007.

11.   Gates, Henry Louis, Jr. Preface. *Toni Morrison: Critical Perspectives Past and Present*. Eds. Henry Louis Gates, Jr., and K. A. Appiah. New York: Amistad, 1993. ix-xiii. Print.

12.   Irving, John. *The Hotel New Hampshire*. New York: Dutton, 1981. Print.

13.   Kenan, Randall. "Bastard Out of Carolina." *The Nation* (28 December 1992): 815-16. Print.

14.   King, Stephen. *Gerald's Game*. New York: NAL/Dutton, 1992. Print.

15.   Kingsolver, Barbara. *The Bean Trees*. New York: Harper Perennial, 1988. Print.

16.   Meiselman, Karin C. *Resolving the Trauma of Incest*. San Francisco: Jossey-Bass, 1990. Print.

17.   Morrison, Toni. *The Bluest Eye*. New York: Pocket, 1970. Print.

18.   Otten, Terry. "Horrific Love in Toni Morrison's Fiction." *Modern Fiction Studies* 39 (1993): 651-67. Print.

19.   Russell, Diana E. H. *The Secret Trauma: Incest in the Lives of Girls and Women*. New York: Basic, 1986. Print.

20.   Shapiro, Laura. "They're Daddy's Little Girls." *Newsweek*. Newsweek, 24 Jan. 1994. Web. 23 Aug. 2007.

21.   ———. "Reports from the Heartland: A Thousand Acres." *Newsweek*. Newsweek, 18 Nov. 1991. Web. 23 Aug. 2007.

22.   Smiley, Jane. Interview. *Publishers Weekly* (1 April 1988): 65-66. Print.

23.   ———. A *Thousand Acres*. Thorndike, ME: Thorndike, 1992. Print.

24.   Walker, Alice. *The Color Purple*. New York: Washington Square Press, 1982. Print.

11: format for preface written by one editor of edited book.

18: format for journal paginated consecutively through annual volume (pp. 488–489).

22: format for untitled interview in a weekly magazine.

Checklist

Consider the recommendations below before you submit your final draft.

1. The manuscript should be neat and clean.

2. Many instructors require the first page of a research paper to be the title or cover page. If no format is prescribed, center the title one third of the way down from the top of the page. Capitalize the first letters of proper and common nouns, pronouns, verbs, adjectives, and adverbs. Do not capitalize the first letters of conjunctions (such as and, or, but) or prepositions (such as to, on, from) unless those words come at the beginning of the title or subtitle. Do not underline, or italicize, your title. If your title contains the name of a work (such as a book, a magazine, a journal, a newspaper, a film, or a play) that requires underlining, or italicizing, underline, or italicize, that title. As you think about a title for your paper, consider the following criteria.

   - It should be brief—no more than a dozen words.

   - It should suggest the topic. Go back to your introduction and find the sentences in which you introduce your topic. Form your title from the information in these sentences.

   - It should be a phrase, not a sentence.

   - Its tone should reflect the tone of your discussion. If your paper has a serious tone, a witty title will mislead your readers.

   - It should be imaginative, not just a dry statement of your topic.

3. On the cover page, unless your instructor tells you otherwise, center your name, course title, and date six or so lines below the title. Sometimes your instructor will want you to include his or her name as well. If a cover page is not required, simply place this information on the first page of your paper. See the sample MLA documented paper for examples of both formats.

4. Remember to paginate your paper. If you include a title page, it is not considered page 1. The first page of your text is page 1.

5. Make sure to include a complete list of Works Cited.

6. Your instructor may ask you to submit an outline or abstract (brief synopsis) of your paper. This should come after your title page and before your text.

APPENDIX

Using and Interpreting Visual Information

Basic Principles and Assumptions

Our lives are saturated with visual information. We watch television shows, turn the pages of glossy magazines and graphic novels, visit video sharing websites, pass highway billboards, and go to the movies. The textbooks that you use in most of your college courses will have many full-color, high quality photographs, charts, and diagrams to clarify the concepts that you are invited to learn. To amplify the issues that editors and reporters wish us to engage, the newspapers that we read will have the revealing photograph, the carefully drawn map, and even the clever drawing.

In our media-saturated and media-dominated world, the ability to interpret, use, and produce images is increasingly important. During your college years, you will have many opportunities to develop and to demonstrate this ability. Some of you will take courses in art and design; others will take courses in journalism and advertising; still others will study the media in sociology and psychology courses. Many of you already have a background in web page design, in the use of presentation programs like PowerPoint, and in image manipulation through a graphic editor like Photoshop. In your professional career, you probably will be called upon to deploy the skills and the insights you have accumulated.

At some point, you might determine that the proposals or reports that you will be asked to prepare for your college professors or for your employers might only be fully effective if they include photographs, charts, diagrams, or even video material. When you are called upon to analyze or to comment on such kinds of work, you will make use of the critical and interpretative skills you have acquired during the tasks you have undertaken in this book.

The Appendix was written by Anthony J. Boyle

We have some suggestions to offer so that you will neither abuse nor be abused by visual information. While a number of these will be immediately applicable, dealing with the projects you will submit to your professors, others will be more abstract, dealing with some of the ways of responding to visual communication. Many of the skills required to make meaning from images are different from the skills we use to make sense out of verbal texts. Obviously, there is no dictionary of images that we can consult to guide us in our efforts, as there is with the printed word. Moreover, though there are also rules that govern the way that words are put together, there is nothing similar to control those who craft some kinds of visual information, as your visits to art museums or exhibitions might have revealed.

In addition to prizing the economy of expression, one usually looks for clarity, precision, accuracy, and vitality in the verbal texts—the essays—that we have been discussing in this book.

These characteristics are to be found in various kinds of visual communication, in the maps, charts, and diagrams, for example, that accompany many kinds of verbal texts. However, though most of us are impatient with tangled prose, we might find a blurred photograph to be revealing. When we confront images, we tend to value what immediately arrests our eye and engages our imagination. We are enlightened and often are emotionally affected by the way the content of an image is arranged, by the way it displays the play between light and shadow, by the harmonies achieved through color, line, and texture. Images inform us, just as words do. Though they inform us in different ways, intelligence, good taste, and sound judgment are as essential to the construction of effective visuals as they are to effective writing. They are equally important to the interpretation of both forms of communication. As you move through your college years, you will certainly expand and deepen those attributes.

Preparing Your Work for Submission to Your Readers

A. Typeface

You should not ignore the visual impact of the work you will create during your college years and in your professional life. Even the plain text documents that you compose will involve elements of visual communication. A major aim is to make your work as easy on the eye as is possible. Thus, as you prepare your paper or project for submission to your instructors, your peers, your clients, or your employers, you are immediately involved in design and formatting decisions. Perhaps the first decision you will make is the selection of a typeface from the font selection menu of your word processing program.

The two categories of typefaces for most plain text documents are serif and sans serif. Because letters created in the serif form are easier to read, these fonts are usually chosen for most documents. Times, Century Schoolbook, and Times New Roman are among the popular serif fonts, and your instructor or your client might specify which one to use. Serif fonts have a small stroke added to the end or within a segment of each letter (**See Figure A.1**). Sans serif fonts, while they are sharply formed, lack the small lines that are found within the letter of the serif format (**See Figure A.2**). These small lines help the eye to move more quickly, with less effort, through the words of a document. Sans serif fonts, which include fonts that are named Helvetica, Gothic, and Spartan, are useful in those places of your text where you do not require continuous reading. There is some dispute over which typeface works best on documents that will be read on a computer. You might have noticed that most of the words you will read in web-formatted documents have been formed in a sans serif font. If you are going to circulate your work through a computer network, you might safely use a sans serif font. However, in the printed versions of your papers, it is best to reserve the sans serif fonts for titles and, if you find it useful to have them, for the headings of the major sections of your work.

AaBbCc   AaBbCc

Figure A.1   **Figure A.2**

As you no doubt know, your computer's word processing program makes available a large number of fonts and new ones can be easily downloaded from the web. However, it is best to avoid decorative fonts in your papers. You should also limit the use of italics and boldface, as such stylistic elements can also reduce the readability of your work. Reserve such elements for those parts of your text that need to be highlighted. You must have a reason for using bold or italic type in your text. Since you do not want to distract your reader with unnecessary or gimmicky graphical elements, you should aim for a clean, basic, and unadorned look in the papers and reports that you create.

If your instructor or the client for whom you are working does not specify a type size, choose one that is legible. Ironically, large type sizes are as difficult to read as small ones. One of the factors to consider is that size is not consistent across the various fonts. You probably confront something similar when you buy an item of clothing; one manufacturer's medium is another's small. Since your aim is not to challenge your reader's eye, you will have to take into consideration the nature of your audience. Generally, ten point type is easy on the eye of young readers; but if your project is going to be read and evaluated by an older audience, you might use twelve point type.

You can vary the size of your font when you insert headings into your paper, but do not do this often. Consistency is a good principle to follow. In a short paper, one that is under ten pages, headings are usually unnecessary. If your paper breaks into discrete parts, as papers in the natural or social sciences often do, as papers written for business courses or for commercial purposes also do, you might have to deploy headings for each of its section and even for its subsections. If you have subheadings, you probably will want to diminish the size of the type a bit.

The purpose of creating heading and subheadings is to make visually clear to your readers the way you have organized the information that you have collected. If you are required to follow the APA formatting rules, your headings will be centered on the page; if you follow those of the MLA, they will be placed flush with the left margin. Headings and subheadings are visual signals to your reader of what can be found in the various sections of your paper.

B. Layout

The way you arrange or place material on the page is particularly important when your work contains various forms of graphics. Again, since your aim is to have something pleasing to the eye, you do not want to create pages that might be seen as chaotic. To avoid clutter, do not over-burden any of your pages with both text and graphics. One of the surest techniques to accomplish this goal is to make intelligent use of white space. Work within the margins that have been established by your instructor or by your client. If the margin space has not been specified, leave at least an inch around your text. It is also wise not to have more than one graphical element on each page.

When you include graphics, make sure that they are functional and not merely decorative. They should complement your text, and your text should not repeat what the graphic is designed to convey to your readers. You do not want to make use of clip art in the kind of papers that we have been discussing in this text. Cute clip art is also not usually appropriate for the work you will be doing in your professional life. Reserve it for less formal work. You probably would not, for example, put clip art into a report you would submit to assess the work of those who work under you. You might, though, find it useful in many of the PowerPoint presentations that you will create for your courses and during your professional life. We cannot stress enough the importance of taking into account the reaction that your audience will have to such images.

To place graphics in your text, use the appropriate item from the Insert Menu of the word processing program you are using. Of course, you will want to visually check to see that the graphical elements pleasantly combine with your text.

The margins of your text should not be fully justified; that is, both the right and left margins should not be flush. A fully justified text has a block-like, forbidding look. Your text is more readable when the left side is aligned and the right side remains jagged (**See Figure A.3**). A fully justified text has variable spacing between words that slows down the reader's movement from word to word and from line to line (**See Figure A.4**). Since the brain must accommodate these variations, the processing of such a text is slower and, as a result, the reader might become irritated.

The margins of your text should not be fully justified; that is, both the right and left margins should not be flush. Your text is more readable when the left side is aligned and the right side remains jagged

Figure A.3

A fully justified text has a block-like, forbidding look. A fully justified text has variable spacing between words. Since the brain must accommodate these variations, the processing of such a text is slower and, as a result, the reader might become irritated.

Figure A.4

Usually, the papers you submit in your college courses will be double-spaced. Again, the aim is to avoid challenging your reader with a dense looking text. You can single-space resumes, and few of your correspondents will be dismayed if you single-space your letters and email messages.

Since most academic writing requires you to deal with complex ideas, be sure that your paragraphs fully develop an aspect of the issue you wish your reader to consider. However, to reduce the challenge that is created by a dense text, shorten your paragraphs as much as you can. Though the content of your paragraphs will determine their length, you can often diminish the effect of very long paragraphs by using graphics in your papers.

C. Using Graphics Within Your Text

Though they could be unnecessary or even unwelcome in the papers you would write for a literature course, graphical elements, including bullets and text boxes, are useful in conveying information to those who will read the papers you would submit in other disciplines and, certainly, they would be welcomed in most of the work you would prepare during your professional career. Bullets are used to list essential information; text boxes can be used to isolate important materials from the rest of your text.

Charts, diagrams, and graphs can add a visual element that immediately makes available what we wish to convey. They also can have an immediacy that words alone might not have. The flowchart you were once shown in elementary or secondary school that reveals how a bill becomes a law probably lingers in your memory. You probably have a good sense of weather trends from the charts that are printed in newspapers. Graphs are useful to display the relationship between two sets of data or two phenomena and, aside from your familiarity with them from math and statistics classes, you might have frequently studied them in history or economics courses. Certainly, you would be aware of the usefulness of diagrams when you are asked to put together a swing set for your younger siblings or for the child who lives nearby. During political campaigns, we frequently encounter maps that divide the nation into red and blue regions; and, at the end of elections, such maps are again used to suggest who will wield power.

Word processing programs have tools to help you in the creation of some of the more common graphics, and many computers are equipped with Fathom or programs like it to help you to construct tables and graphs. Often, you will find the graphic that you wish to use in another source. When you incorporate it into your text, you will want to label it, place it close to the text to which it relates, make sure that you have referred to it in your text, and, of course, make sure that it is legible. You would also reveal to your reader its source and, if you interpret or use it differently from its creator, you would note that in your text.

Photographs are another kind of visual that you might wish to incorporate into your work (**See Figure A.5**). You can use a digital camera to create one of your own or you can search for relevant photographs by using the image search function of a web browser. It is possible that your institution subscribes to Corbis, an immense collection of photographs that range from historically important images to images of the work of painters, architects, and sculptors. Using such images can add a dimension to the papers and reports you are preparing for many kinds of classes, particularly classes in history or art appreciation. The reference librarian of your institution will be able to assist you in finding the appropriate images for your paper or project.

Interpreting Visual Information

1) Visual Communication takes place whether you are aware of it or not

Images are not neutral. They not only serve the purpose of conveying information, but, as all those involved in or who have studied advertising know, they can also affect us in ways that we do not immediately recognize. As persuasive devices, images, even the charts and graphs that appear to be objective, seek to influence and modify our beliefs and actions. While some images will reinforce already existing opinions and behaviors, other images can challenge our deeply held beliefs. Because they are the result of an individual or a group's activity, they reflect the values, the ideas, and the interests of that individual or group. They are not, therefore, to be accepted at face value. We have to judge them and to do so we have to become more aware of the way we receive and react to them.

2) Visual Communication involves both emotion and logic

We can increase our awareness by asking questions about the rhetorical aspects of the images we encounter. It seems obvious that we accept all kinds of communication because of the credibility exhibited by those who have created and circulated them and because we have determined that what is being conveyed is useful, reasonable, and ethical. Of course, we must be in a situation or be put into one where we are willing to be receptive to what is being communicated. That

'Nine miles to Crawford' may as well say a million

My View

Paul Saint-Amand

When the two Secret Service boys hopped out of their air-conditioned white Suburban, no doubt Gold Star mother Cindy Sheehan felt a sudden chill pierce the 100-plus degree heat in Crawford, Texas. Saturday afternoon's unrelenting sun washed over the roadway and spilled into the ditch where Cindy and an estimated 125 veterans and activists, including myself, waited for President Bush to acknowledge this anguished mother's right to ask why her son, Casey, was killed for a lie.

I stood behind Cindy with my cell phone on speaker mode so that my wife in Massachusetts could hear her conversation with the agents. After a brief warning about Cindy's intent to camp overnight on this lonely stretch of country road, the young agent hedged his concern for her safety with a final comment. "Well, ma'am ... You have my condolences on the loss of your son." Cindy, near heatstroke, looked into his deadpan face and said quietly, "I didn't lose my son. He was killed in Iraq. If I had lost him, I would go to Iraq and find him. He's dead. Do you understand what that means? Do you understand?"

We live in a time when our language betrays us. And that's certainly true for Cindy and the other Gold Star mothers who know the agony of burying a military son or daughter without having those deaths justified by facts. For Cindy, the deception never warranted sending her son to kill and be killed.

But on this weekend afternoon in Crawford, Texas, even the blazing sun and veiled threats by officials didn't stop Cindy and others from publicly seeking an audience with President Bush. Members of Veterans For Peace, Gold Star Families for Peace, Iraq Veterans Against the War, Military Families Speak Out, Code Pink, Crawford Peace House and other Texas peace groups led chants. "No Justice, No Peace" rolled across the expansive Texas landscape. On one side of the road we yelled "Had Enough" to the counter "No More War." We wanted to know why the president has put those most vulnerable into harm's way — military men and women who depend on us only to go to war as a last resort.

Sheriff's deputies had stopped us four or so miles short of the Bush Ranch, herding the group along a half-mile long overgrown ditch. The deputies told us that we could continue the march only if we kept off the tarmac. Evidently, traffic safety on the largely deserted road overshadowed the concern for potential snakebites or the disruption of fire ant nests that dotted the ditch. Angered that the authorities would not let us continue beyond the second roadblock, we mustered in front of sheriff's deputies and Secret Service men. Sensing the need for

calm, fellow Veterans For Peace member Tony Flaherty, a retired Navy officer, led us in a recitation of the Lord's Prayer. Some two hours later, on the verge of dehydration because sheriff's deputies would not allow us to bring fresh water forward once we returned to the first roadblock, most of the group had gone back to Crawford. Cindy Sheehan and her remaining few supporters returned to the first roadblock to set up camp.

In her address the night before to the Veterans For Peace National Convention in Dallas, Cindy was determined to put herself on the line. "I have the whole month of August off, just like him [Bush] ... So, I have a lot of free time on my hands, and I'm gonna stay until he comes out and talks to me. And if he quits his vacation and goes to D.C., I'll pull my tent up, follow him to D.C., and put it on the White House lawn, and I'll be waiting for you guys when you get there on Sept. 24." On that date, activists are calling for an anti-war rally on the Washington Mall.

She continued her address, directing her comments to President Bush: "You tell me the truth. You tell me that my son died for oil. You tell me that my son died to make your friends rich. You tell me my son died to spread the cancer of Pax Americana, imperialism in the Middle East. You tell me that. You don't tell me my son died for freedom and democracy."

Associated Press

Cindy Sheehan, of Vacaville, Calif, looks at a cross bearing the name of her son, Casey, that was placed in front of her tent at a makeshift campsite along the road that leads to President Bush's Crawford, Texas, ranch. The protest by the grieving mother who lost her son in the Iraq war is gaining momentum.

Cindy had come to Crawford in the red, white and blue Veterans For Peace "Impeachment Tour" bus. I rode in a private car to Crawford with two whistleblowers — for whom telling the truth is a sacred oath. Ann Wright is a retired U.S. Army colonel, former diplomat, and peace activist who resigned her State Department position to protest the Iraq War. Jesslyn Radack is the Justice Department ethics lawyer who revealed that the FBI deliberately violated Taliban prisoner John Walker Lindh's civil rights during his interrogation. Jesslyn lost her job because she honored truth over lies. Both these women, intelligent, articulate and steadfast in their belief in honor and duty, exemplify the oath taken by veterans and elected officials who have served the country "to defend the Constitution of the United States against all enemies both foreign and domestic." Both women know firsthand that moral courage has a price, and that costs more than those who meekly follow the status quo will ever understand.

"The opposite of good is not evil; it's apathy," Cindy cautioned us that evening. "And we have to get this country off their butts, and we have to get the choir singing. We need to say, bring our troops home now. We can't depend on the people in charge to bring our troops home. Because you don't plan on bringing the troops home when you drop so

Now they are telling Cindy that if she continues her peaceful vigil, she could be considered a security risk and may be arrested. Like many others who have stepped up to be counted, the fact that this Gold Star mother could find herself vulnerable against an administration and a president more interested in dogma than people, leaves me sad and, frankly, terrified.

much of the reconstruction money into building permanent bases.

"I was hoping to come to the VFP banquet tomorrow night, but unless George comes out and talks to me, I'll be camping at Crawford."

Sharon, a single mom, and I put up Cindy's tent while we had our photographs surreptitiously taken by the two Secret Service men. Sheriff's deputies had us move the tent twice away from the large, flat, open piece of ground between the intersection of the two country roads where camping made sense. And once again, a weed-infested ditch was to be a "safer" area to house the mother of a fallen soldier. "But look out fer rattlers," a friendly sheriff's deputy called out to us as he pointed to the open ditch.

We left Cindy and several others — like Amy Branham, another Gold Star mother that day — at Cindy's "Camp Casey" on that darkening roadside in Crawford. She seemed vulnerable and, yet fully committed to being heard. The Secret Service SUVs zoomed back and forth all afternoon.

Now they are telling Cindy that if she continues her peaceful vigil, she could be considered a security risk and may be arrested. Like many others who have stepped up to be counted, the fact that this Gold Star mother could find herself vulnerable against an administration and a president more interested in dogma than people, leaves me sad and, frankly, terrified.

On the drive down, the first road sign we came upon read "nine miles to Crawford." For Cindy Sheehan, it might as well be a million miles away from a real conversation with the president.

God bless you, Cindy.

Paul Saint-Amand of Rockport teaches at the State University of New York, Potsdam, is a member of Veterans For Peace, Chapter 45, Ipswich, and chapter president of North Country Veterans For Peace, Chapter 121, Potsdam, N.Y.

Source: Gloucester Daily Times, Saturday, August 13, 2005.

Figure A.5

receptivity is not a problem for those who transmit images as we watch our favorite television show or while we are reading the magazines and newspapers that we turn to for information and entertainment. Yes, there are those who will never accept what is shown in certain media, whether it is in the *New York Times* or on *Fox News*. Most of us, however, will accept what the established media show, though we might be made aware that sometimes we are betrayed by those we trust (**See Figure A.6**). Our confidence is based on the belief that the media tends to be self-policing and self-critical. Moreover, the established media has become subject to even more scrutiny with the advent of blogging. For example, in August 2006, Reuters withdrew a photograph showing massive columns of smoke rising over the Lebanese capital of Beirut following an attack by Israeli jets. American bloggers discovered that the photographer had manipulated and altered the photo, using Photoshop to suggest much more damage than had actually occurred. Reuters promptly removed the photograph, apologized to its affiliates, and posted a full explanation of what had occurred on its website.

Figure A.6

For more on this story, see Johnson, Miki. "Reuters Pulls Doctored Photo," <http://popphoto.com/photographynewswire /2772/reuters-pulls-doctored-photo.html>

When deceptive or even just misleading images are put in circulation, we believe that those who have attempted to abuse us will be discovered and held accountable. When mistakes are made, they will be acknowledged and corrected, as the Reuters case makes clear. Though advances in digital photography have made it somewhat easier to deceive and much more difficult to identify what is deceptive, we cannot just ignore photographs that attempt to bring aspects of reality to our attention.

When interrogating an image, the first question, then, might be about the reliability of what is being shown. In other words, is the source of the image dependable? Is it published or circulated as a result of being reviewed and evaluated by a credible agent? Is there any reason to doubt the integrity of those who have produced or circulated the image? Because it is difficult for us to recognize altered or doctored photographs, we place our confidence in those who have earned the public's trust over time.

Images are generally accompanied by text, sometimes just a caption, and we need to make sure that the image is related to it. In other words, we must contextualize the image. Does the image, in fact, offer support for what is being argued? Consider, for example, a newspaper story about the current condition of those who are poor that is accompanied by a photograph of the burdened faces of Oklahoma farmers during the Great Depression. As you contextualize the image, you might acknowledge a connection between the words of the story and the image. You might say that the image captures the despair that the poor always experience or, in other words, that it conveys essential aspects of the unchanging human condition that is at the core of the story to which it has been connected. But you might instead conclude that the image makes clear weakness in the argument the story is advancing. You might conclude, that is, that the condition of the poor in our time cannot be conveyed by images of the past. As you respond to the images that fill our public media, you might ask yourself what the images ask you to recall, what they ask you to recognize, or what they ask you to experience. You need to be fully aware of the relationships that are suggested by the images you encounter.

3) Visual Communication is highly subjective, interpretive, and interactive

Many of us know the power that imagery can have over us from the print and televised advertisements that lure us to buy products that we really do not want. Photographs and many other kinds of visuals have an emotional effect, and we need to be aware of how they might be affecting us. The stark black and white photograph that presents us with the faces of the economically disadvantaged plays on our sympathy. We are shocked by photographs of the human suffering in those regions torn by conflict. When we see photographs of murder victims, we are appalled. Because images can be used to move us to action, as advertising images do, we need to be aware of what the image is presenting and what it is asking of us.

A list of the questions that could be raised about images, particularly photographs and videos, might include:

Questions about the origin of the image.

- Who made the image?

- What assurance is there that the image is an accurate and honest depiction of what it seems to represent?

- Are there images that conflict with what a particular image represents?

Questions about the purpose of the image.

- What is being depicted in the image?

- Why has the image been chosen? What does it purport to reveal?

- What point of view is conveyed by the image?

- Who is the intended audience for the image?

- What response might be expected from that audience?

Questions about the format of the image.

- How is the material in the image arranged?

- What camera angle has been used to create the image?

- Does the image use lighting or special effects to create specific responses? Or is it neutral, realistic?

- Have particular colors and shapes been isolated by those who made the image?

Our list of questions is not intended to be complete. We are sure that you can think of many others that would be useful in explorations of images. However, since many of the tasks you will confront in your college and professional life will involve the visual display of other kinds of information, we want to close this section of the book by returning to issues related to the use of charts and graphs.

4) A cautionary reminder on how we interpret and use statistics

Primarily because of the use of, and improvement of, computers over the past 40 years, we find ourselves awash in data. Data are often represented as numbers. For the most part, our brains have not evolved to easily comprehend long lists of numbers, but the field of statistics provides a body of techniques that allows us to "make sense" out of numbers. One very common technique is to describe some characteristic of the list of numbers. For example, rather than present a long list of numbers, a writer might describe the center of the list (an average), or a measure of the variability of the numbers in the list, or show how the numbers are distributed along the number line. These descriptors are themselves numbers, of course, and many readers tend to skip over *any* numbers in a text, especially a table full of averages and standard deviations. People tend to prefer their numbers to be presented as pictures: bar graphs, line graphs, pie charts, etc. Graphic depiction of descriptors is probably the least tedious, most quickly understood, way in which they may be presented.

Here is an example of a well-designed pie chart showing the major causes of death in the United States in 2004.

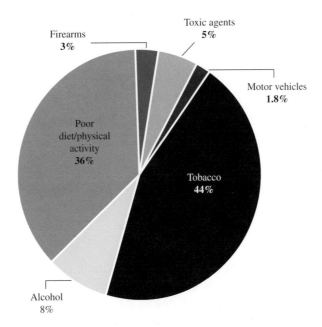

Source: *Journal of the American Medical Association (JAMA)*, March 10, 2004

Figure A.7

The impact of the following bar graph, which shows the relative importance that developed economies place on providing support to working women after childbirth, is the result of its elegant simplicity.

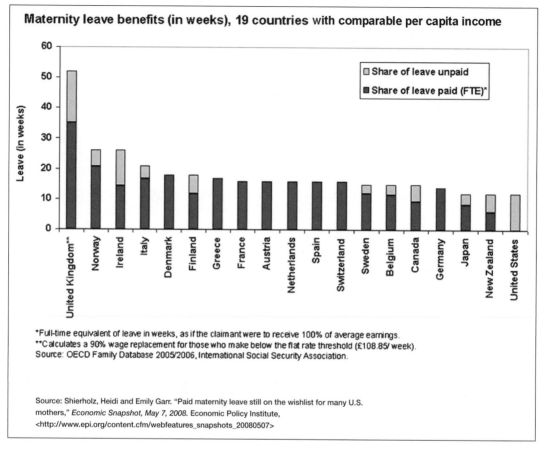

Figure A.8

Unfortunately, it is easy to present any statistical measure or result in misleading ways and the writer has an obligation to try not to do this. For example, suppose you wonder if the mean IQ for one group of people (Group 1) is different from the mean IQ of another group (Group 2). You give IQ tests to the people in each group and find that the mean for Group 1 is 100.01 and the mean for Group 2 is exactly 100.00. Below are two graphic presentations of these means. A quick glance at the first bar graph (**Figure A.9**) suggests that there is, indeed, a difference in mean IQ. A more careful examination reveals that the suggestion of a difference is the result of a highly magnified scale of means. The entire range of the ordinate on the graph is 0.025 IQ points (the scale originates at 99.99 and terminates at 100.015). If the origin of the scale is the usual 0.0, as it is in the second graph (**Figure A.10**), the apparent difference in mean IQ becomes imperceptible. Notice that nothing is "wrong" about either presentation—there is, in fact, a .01 IQ point difference, but if the writer should choose to use the first graph, she or he has an obligation to point out that the scale has been magnified.

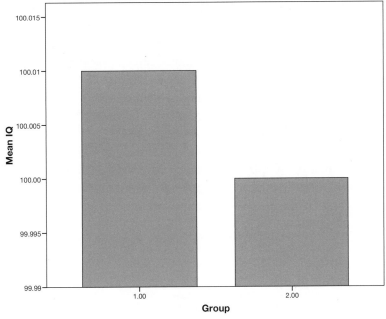

Figure A.9

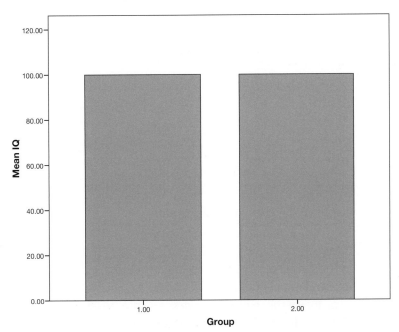

Figure A.10

Edward Tufte's well-known book *The Visual Display of Qualitative Information,* 2nd ed. (Graphics Press, LLC. 2001), discusses the important differences between accurate and inaccurate or misleading uses of visual data. Tufte explains that "the representation of numbers, as physically measured on the surface of the graphic itself, should be directly proportional to the quantities represented." Tufte calls discrepancies in this ratio "the Lie Factor." Accurate graphics have a Lie Factor of 1—meaning that there is an accurate, undistorted relationship between the numbers and their visual representation. In other words, what you "see" is what is "really" there. A badly scaled graphic can have a "Lie Factor" of 12:1 or even 14:1.

Below is a graph presenting oil consumption in the U.S. and Japan (**See Figure A.11**). *The Washington Post* article that the graph accompanied asserted that Japan's oil consumption "has remained steady since 1975, while U.S. consumption has risen steadily." The graph seeks to underscore this assertion, using one line to show the steady rise of U.S. and another to show the relative stability of Japanese consumption.

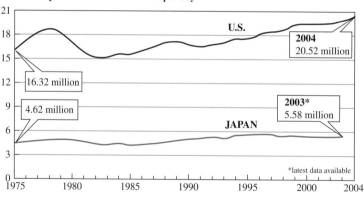

Oil Consumption

Japan has no domestic sources of fossil fuel and facing rising oil prices, has turned energy efficiency into an art form. Japan's oil consumption has remained steady since 1975, while U.S. consumption has risen steadily.

Oil consumption in millions of barrels per day

Figure A.11

Almost immediately, Russell Roberts posted a critique on his web site (http://cafehayek.typepad.com). He noted a lack of correlation between the chart and the data on which it was based. Roberts points out that the line in the graphic that indicates Japan's oil consumption appears basically horizontal, while the one indicating U.S. consumption steadily climbs. The data, he holds, conflicts with such a representation. The numbers reveal no striking contrast between oil consumption in the two countries and, in fact, show that the U.S., given the size and the growth rate of its economy, might have used this resource more efficiently than Japan. As it is drawn, the graphic will deceive those who do not recognize the data actually shows a rise in Japan's oil consumption of 21% during the time period that the chart reflects. (U.S. consumption rose by 26% in the same span.) Roberts also believes that the designer of the graphic is to be faulted for the way that the "thickness" of the contrasting lines masks the increase of oil consumption by Japan.

As the examples we have presented illustrate, there are numerous ways in which data—descriptive and inferential statistics—can be presented to lead a reader to unintentional associations or inaccurate conclusions. The Cafe Hayek website has dedicated a section to critiques of misleading or inaccurate charts, pictures, and diagrams. You might look at the site for some other illustrations. Take note, though, of the political bias of the editors of the site and of the criticism that some have made of Roberts's observations. Should you wish to explore the issue of misleading graphics further, you can consult the work of Tufte or any of the numerous books and articles with variations on the title *How Statistics* (or Graphs, or Charts, or Pictures, or Facts) *Lie*. Such explorations will show you that, when using graphics to support an argument, a writer should always ask, "Am I being as clear and straightforward as possible in my presentation of data?" Such explorations will reveal why it is wise to be sure that your data is accurately reflected by its visual representation.

5) Two examples of the profound impact that the visual display of information can have

1) Florence Nightingale (1820–1910) chose a career that was not typical for women of her social class. Nursing had, in her time, little status and the education of nurses was a haphazard affair. Nightingale changed that. The work she did among the poor and with wounded soldiers brought attention to the value of the work of nurses. Moreover, she was instrumental in creating schools of nursing and wrote the first textbook for the field.

Before Nightingale's efforts began to have a general effect, too little attention was paid to the care of those who were hospitalized. The consequences of that indifference are not hard to imagine. Many of those who could have survived their injuries and illnesses died from the neglect they experienced. Had they been given the professional, attentive, and humane care that we expect if we are hospitalized, more might have survived. In Nightingale's time, for most of the ill and infirm, hygiene, wound care, and nutrition were ignored. Only the wealthy, perhaps, had some semblance of proper care. She not only understood the need for change, but she also had the intelligence and the endurance to effect it.

The problem of patient care came sharply into focus during the Crimean War, a bloody mid-nineteenth century conflict between Russia and Turkey that also involved the British and French. The British Secretary of War, alarmed by the number of soldiers who were dying from their wounds, asked Nightingale to go to Istanbul to supervise their care. Though initially resisted by the doctors in charge of the hospital that she took charge of, Nightingale and her nurses quickly reduced the mortality rate among the wounded, primarily by introducing sound sanitary practices and paying attention to the nutrition of the patients. It was during her time in Turkey that another aspect of this complex woman came into focus.

Nightingale had a scientific approach to the problems that she wished to confront. She was one of the earliest proponents of the idea that social problems, including issues of public health, could be resolved through the collection and study of data. Thus, during her time in Turkey she collected a large amount of data and subjected it to rigorous analysis. She used the results of her inquiry to

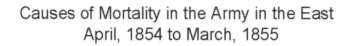

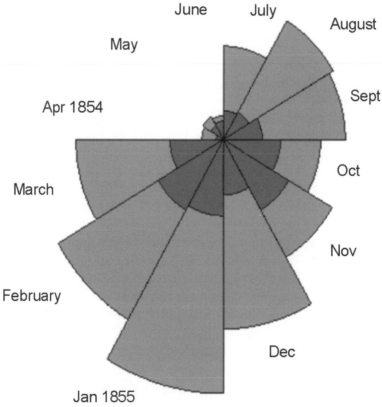

Source: F. Nightingale, "Notes on Matters Affecting the Health, Efficiency and Hospital Administration of the British Army", 1858

Figure A.12

promote radical change in hospital care. To make the case with the British government that proper nursing and hospital care would significantly reduce the number of deaths among those recovering from illness and injuries, she developed the polar area diagram, a form of the pie chart. This chart made instantly clear the implication of the vast amount of data she had collected: more deaths were taking place in hospitals than on the battlefield. The result of her study not only brought about changes in military hospitals, but it had a profound affect on all forms of patient care.

As the diagram shows, Nightingale made use of techniques that have become commonplace: shaded or colored sections, wedges, and circles. In fact, she was one of the first social reformers to use graphics to convey the significance of data to legislators and to the general public. In recognition of her innovative approach to statistics, she received many honors, including membership in the Royal Statistical Society and the American Statistical Association. For her work in reforming hospital care, she has been called "The Lady with the Lamp."

2) We still are contending with the revolutionary insights of Charles Darwin (1809–1882). Though there are many who resist the implications of his work, his theories not only laid the foundation for modern biology, but they also changed the form and direction of fields as diverse as politics and art. Originally destined for the ministry, Darwin became intrigued by natural history while a student at Cambridge University. Thereafter, he devoted his energies to the study of the origins of life. Shortly after completing his studies, he joined an expedition to chart the coastline of South America. During the many years that he spent on this expedition, he collected huge variety of fossils, including those of extinct mammals. He also explored the geology of the many regions he visited. On his return to England, he published *The Voyage of the Beagle,* a book that brought him immediate fame. It also helped to secure his place among the most significant scientists of the age.

The data and the specimens that he had collected also served as the basis of the thought that found its expression in one of the most influential books of all time, *Origin of the Species.* One of the main ideas that Darwin challenged was the notion of the immutability of species. From the data he had accumulated and from his observations of the results of the breeding of farm animals, he postulated instead that a number of factors lead to the evolution of new species. Among those, he determined, was the inheritance of characteristics that enabled an individual member of a species to survive and reproduce in a changing environment. You might recall, from your biology classes, discussions of the theory of natural selection and you might have explored, perhaps in history classes, the implications that some drew from Darwin's concept of the survival of the fittest. Our intentions here are not to join those discussions or debates. We want to note, instead, that there was but one graphic in the several hundred pages of Darwin's world-shattering book. Darwin's branching diagram was to show, in an immediate way, the concepts that he was presenting to his readers. You might immediately note the metaphor that lies behind the diagram, the tree of life. Moreover, it served, as had other graphics that he created throughout his career, as a device to assist him in developing his thought. Perhaps it is related to what you might do during freewriting activities, as you cluster your ideas before fixing them in the form of sentences and paragraphs.

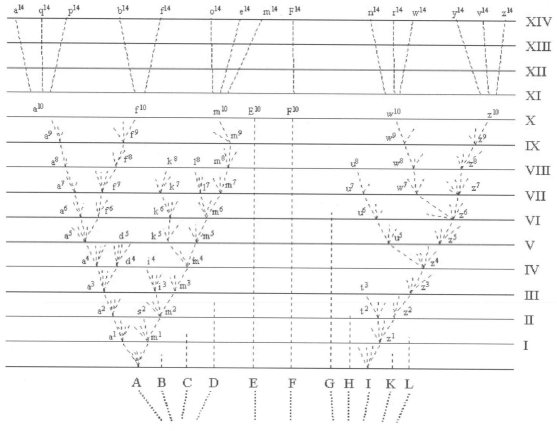

Figure A.13

Darwin devoted many pages to the exploration of this diagram. In a very concrete way, it assisted in the exposition of his argument. The capital letters represented, for example, ancestral forms; the lower case letters represented their descendents through following generations. The continuous series of dots suggested the connection and relationship of all species to common ancestors. Among the major ideas that the diagram displays is that most species become extinct when they no longer can survive in a given environment. Our intention is not to provide you with a discussion of this representation of part of the tree of life. You can explore in great detail what each aspect of the graph means by visiting any of a host of web sites. Our intention is to have you take note of the way that such graphic devices can be used to organize and clarify what you will put into words.

Ben Bagdikian, From *The New Media Monopoly* by Ben H. Bagdikian. Copyright © 2004 by Ben Bagdikian. Reprinted by permission of Beacon Press, Boston.

Benjamin R. Barber, From Speech delivered by Dr. Benjamin R. Barber on Sept. 24, 2001, The Inaugural 2001 Civil Society Lecture, College Park MD. Reprinted by permission.

Tim Brinton, "Breaking the Middle Class Bank," as appeared in *Milwaukee Journal Sentinel,* Sunday March 31, 1996. Reprinted by permission of Tim Brinton.

Albert Camus, "The Myth of Sisyphus," translated by Justin O'Brien, from *The Myth of Sisyphus* by Albert Camus, translated by Justin O'Brien, copyright © 1955, copyright renewed 1983 by Alfred A. Knopf, a division of Random House, Inc. Used by permission of Alfred A. Knopf, a division of Random House.

Ben Compaine, "Domination Fantasies," *Reason,* January 2004, Vol. 35, # 8. Reprinted by permission of Reason magazine. © Reason, www.reason.com.

Dinesh D'Souza, "Created Unequal." Reprinted and abridged with the permission of The Free Press, a Division of Simon & Schuster Adult Publishing Group, from *The Virtue of Prosperity: Finding Value in an Age of Techno-Influence* by Dinesh D'Souza. Copyright © 2000 by Dinesh D'Souza. All rights reserved.

Jean Bethke Elshtain, "Reflections on the Family at Millennium's Beginning," *The World and I*, 15:3, March 2000, p. 312. Reprinted by permission of The World & I, www. WorldandIJournal.com.

Thomas L. Friedman, excerpts from *The Lexus And The Olive Tree: Understanding Globalization* by Thomas L. Friedman. Copyright © 1999, 2000 by Thomas L. Friedman. Reprinted by permission of Farrar, Straus and Giroux, LLC.

© Tony Gutierrez/AP Images. Photo credit in "Nine Miles to Crawford."

Barbara Kingsolver, Pages 135–137, and 140–145 from "Stone Soup" from *High Tide in Tucson: Essays From Now or Never* by Barbara Kingsolver. Copyright © 1995 by Barbara Kingsolver. Reprinted by permission of HarperCollins Publishers.

© Firdia Lisnawati/AP Images. Photo of a McDonalds employee in traditional Muslim dress takes an order in Jakarta.

Paul Rogat Loeb, From *Soul of a Citizen* by Paul Rogat Loeb, Copyright © 1999 by the author and reprinted by permission of St. Martin's Press, LLC.

Gregory Mantsios, "Class in America: Myths and Realities" from *Race, Class and Gender in the United States 6e* edited by Paula Rothenberg, Worth Publishers, 2004. Reprinted by permission of Gregory Mantsios.

Bill Moyers, "Keynote Address to the National Conference on Media Reform" by Bill Moyers, November 8, 2003, from CommonDreams .org. Reprinted by permission of Common Dreams.

Bill Moyers, Speech "Taking Public Broadcasting Back," May 15, 2005, St. Louis Missouri, from CommonDreams.org. Reprinted by permission of Common Dreams.

John Nichols and Robert W. McChesney, "Tragedy and Farce" from *Tragedy and Farce: How the American Media Sell Wars, Spin Elections, and Destroy Democracy* by John Nichols and Robert W. McChesney, 2005. Reprinted with permission of The New Press.

Nel Noddings, "Global Citizenship: Promises and Problems." Reprinted by permission of the Publisher. From Nel Noddings, *Educating Citizens for Global Awareness,* New York: Teachers College Press, © 2005 by Teachers College, Columbia University. All rights reserved.

"Oil Consumption," from *The Washington Post,* February 16, 2006 issue, page A18. Used by permission of *The Washington Post.*

© Angela Rowlings/Boston Herald. Photo of Veterans Day, November 21, 2007 arrest.

Paul Saint Amand, "Nine Miles to Crawford May as Well Say a Million," Associated Press, August 20, 2005. Reprinted by permission of The YGS Group on behalf of Associated Press.

Earl Shorris, From *New American Blues: A Journey Through Poverty to Democracy* by Earl Shorris. Copyright © 1997 by Earl Shorris. Used by permission of W.W. Norton & Company, Inc.

Silja J.A. Talvi, "The New Face of Philanthropy," as appeared in *Christian Science Monitor,* July 31, 2000, Vol. 92, Issue 174. Reprinted by permission of Silja J.A. Talvi.

Raymond Williams, "Individual" from *Keywords: A Vocabulary of Culture and Society Revised Edition* by Raymond Williams. Reprinted by permission of Oxford University Press and HarperCollins Publishers Ltd. © 1985 Raymond Williams.

TOPIC

AUTHOR-TITLE